Naples, Italy

Instanbul, Turkey

Musha, Egypt

Wodabe

Nuer, Dinka

Mbuti

Hutu, Tutsi

Maasai, Kikuyu

Yarahmadzai

Hijra

Bejing, China

Shanghai, China

Na

Lua

Agata

Arapesh, Mundugamor, and Tchambuli

Trobriand Islanders

Aborigines

Maori

Europe-Asia Boundary

1. SLOVENIA
2. CROATIA
3. BOSNIA AND HERZEGOVINA
4. ALBANIA
5. MACEDONIA

# Cultural Anthropology 10e

**Serena Nanda**

*John Jay College of Criminal Justice,
City University of New York*

**Richard L. Warms**

*Texas State University–San Marcos*

WADSWORTH
CENGAGE Learning™

Australia • Brazil • Japan • Korea • Mexico • Singapore • Spain • United Kingdom • United States

## WADSWORTH
### CENGAGE Learning™

**Cultural Anthropology, Tenth Edition**
Serena Nanda and Richard L. Warms

Anthropology Editor: Erin Mitchell

Developmental Editor: Lin Marshall Gaylord

Editorial Assistant: Pamela Simon

Media Editor: Melanie Cregger

Marketing Manager: Andrew Keay

Marketing Coordinator: Dimitri Hagnéré

Marketing Communications Manager: Tami Strang

Content Project Manager: Jerilyn Emori

Creative Director: Rob Hugel

Art Director: Caryl Gorska

Print Buyer: Karen Hunt

Rights Acquisitions Account Manager, Text: Roberta Broyer

Rights Acquisitions Account Manager, Image: Leitha Etheridge-Sims

Production Service: Dan Fitzgerald, Graphic World Inc.

Text and Cover Designer: Jeanne Calabrese

Photo Researcher: Billie Porter

Cover Image: Shannon Ledford of MilleFeuille Photography, www.mfotography.com

Compositor: Graphic World Inc.

For product information and technology assistance, contact us at
**Cengage Learning Customer & Sales Support, 1-800-354-9706**
For permission to use material from this text or product,
submit all requests online at **www.cengage.com/permissions**
Further permissions questions can be e-mailed to
**permissionrequest@cengage.com**

Library of Congress Control Number: 2009936454

Student Edition:

ISBN-13: 978-0-495-81083-4

ISBN-10: 0-495-81083-5

Loose-leaf Edition:

ISBN-13: 978-0-495-81364-4

ISBN-10: 0-495-81364-8

**Wadsworth**
20 Davis Drive
Belmont, CA 94002-3098
USA

Cengage Learning is a leading provider of customized learning solutions with office locations around the globe, including Singapore, the United Kingdom, Australia, Mexico, Brazil, and Japan. Locate your local office at **www.cengage.com/global**

Cengage Learning products are represented in Canada by Nelson Education, Ltd.

To learn more about Wadsworth, visit **www.cengage.com/wadsworth**

Purchase any of our products at your local college store or at our preferred online store **www.ichapters.com**

Printed in the United States of America
1 2 3 4 5 6 7 13 12 11 10 09

# Brief Contents

# Features Contents

# Contents

### Part Two
### Families in Society

**Part Three
Equalities and Inequalities**

## 10 Gender 215

## 11 Political Organization 237

## Part Five
## Culture Change

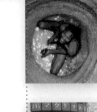

# Preface

Anthropology is the study of all people, in all places and at all times. We are drawn to anthropology as part of the realization that our lives and experiences are limited, but human possibilities are virtually endless. We are drawn by the almost incredible variability of human society and our desire to experience and understand it. We are drawn by the beauty of other lives, but sometimes by the horror as well. We write *Cultural Anthropology* to transmit some of our sense of wonder at the endless variety of the world and to show how anthropologists have come to understand and analyze human culture and society. *Cultural Anthropology,* Tenth Edition, is designed to increase students' understanding of the globally interconnected world in which they live, the human past and present, and the unity and diversity that characterize the human species. *Cultural Anthropology* enables students to "make sense" of the behavior and cultures of peoples unlike themselves, as well as gain insight into their own behavior and society. It shows them how anthropology has been applied to think about and sometimes solve critical problems facing different societies.

*Cultural Anthropology* introduces fundamental concepts, theories, methods, data, and references in ways that are exciting and informative. It is sophisticated enough to provide a firm foundation for students who intend to major in anthropology but also broad enough for those who may take only one or two courses in the subject. The topics included in the text cover the full range of cultural anthropology and are presented in an order most frequently taught in anthropology classrooms. However, the book is designed so that instructors may skip chapters or rearrange them to reflect their own interests and the emphases of their courses.

The main perspective of this book is ethnographic. Ethnography is the fundamental source of the data of anthropology, and the desire to hear about and read ethnography is one of the principal reasons students take anthropology courses. Knowledge of a broad range of ethnographic examples with enough depth for students to understand the context of cultural phenomena is essential. It engages them and encourages them to analyze and question their own culture. Ethnographic examples are used extensively in every chapter of *Cultural Anthropology.* In addition, each chapter contains one or more multipage ethnographies that provide additional detail on specific cultures. The subjects of these ethnographic features have been chosen to illuminate cultures, situations, and histories, both past and present, that students will find fascinating and relevant to the challenges they face today.

Additionally, we feel that issues of gender, power, stratification, the expansion of global capitalism, and culture change are central to understanding current-day cultures. These topics are given chapters of their own, but in addition they are integrated in appropriate places throughout the text.

Students often want to know what they can do with anthropology, in what ways the discipline can be applied. We believe that anthropological thinking is a critical component in understanding and solving the dilemmas that face people in many cultures. We further believe that there are applications for all areas of anthropology. Anthropology helps us in understanding people in other cultures but also helps us understand and respond to challenges in family life, ecology, and economics; indeed, it can illumine almost any aspect of human endeavor. Therefore, rather than presenting a chapter on applied anthropology, each chapter includes one or more illustrations of the application of anthropological thinking. These can be found both in the text and in the boxed features called "Anthropology Makes a Difference." The combined length of these features is at least as great as most chapters on applied anthropology in other textbooks.

*Cultural Anthropology* describes the major issues and theoretical approaches in anthropology in a balanced manner, drawing analysis, information, and insight from many different perspectives. It takes a broad, optimistic, and enthusiastic approach to the discipline of anthropology.

This Tenth Edition of *Cultural Anthropology* continues the collaboration between Serena Nanda and Richard Warms. Warms's specialties in West Africa, anthropological theory, and social anthropology complement Nanda's in India, gender, law, and cultural anthropology. The results have been synergistic. Our experiences, readings, discussions, and debates, as well as feedback from reviewers and professors who have adopted previous editions, have led to the production of a textbook that reflects the energy and passion of anthropology. We have revised extensively, rewritten, added hundreds of new references, and emphasized what we believe to be the best of current thinking in our field. Writing this book continues to be an exciting intellectual adventure for us, and we believe that working with it will promote students' growth as well.

In addition to its ethnographic focus, the Tenth Edition continues and expands upon many of the successful innovations of earlier editions. We have increased the use of full-color photographs and illustrations to catch the eye and engage the mind. We find that our students are intensely visual. Well-chosen photographs make them think about the text's critical points. All photographs have explanatory captions identifying their source and linking them with the text.

We continue to feature a chapter on evolution covering Darwin's theory of natural selection, distinctive characteristics of primates and their social lives, basic descriptive information about the major species of human ancestors, and material on human variation. It is written in a clear, jargon-free, accessible style. It is not necessary to read this chapter to understand the rest of the book, so instructors who do not normally cover evolution need not assign it.

Also continued is our treatment of theory as a critical component of anthropological thought, in both Chapter 4, "The Idea of Culture," and the Appendix, "A Brief Historical Guide to Anthropological Theory," which offers concise descriptions of major schools of thought in anthropology from the 19th century to the present.

# New in This Edition

We have made a number of significant changes and additions to the Tenth Edition, based partly on recent developments in the field of anthropology and partly on the valuable feedback we have received from our adopters and reviewers. Our changes include some significant reorganizations of our text. We have placed the chapter on kinship prior to the chapter on marriage and family to emphasize that forms of marriage, family, and household are set in the context of kinship systems. We have also reorganized our chapters on social stratification, race, and ethnicity to draw attention to the connections between these subjects. Although we have preserved boxed features including "Ethnography" and "Anthropology Makes a Difference," we have tried to reduce the total number of boxed features, integrating material into the main flow of the text where possible. We have also added material on globalization and culture change throughout the text, and introduced a new feature, "The Global and the Local," at the end of each chapter to emphasize the importance of the global context for contemporary anthropology. In addition, our chapter summaries are now organized as a series of questions and responses. This will help students engage with the material and promote critical thinking skills.

We list some of the most important changes to each of our chapters.

- In Chapter 1 we have added a new section focusing students' attention on the ways in which communications and the expansion of the global economy affects both anthropology and the societies anthropologists most frequently study. A second new section discusses the benefits of studying anthropology. Discussions of medical anthropology and of uncontacted peoples have been substantially rewritten. Our "Global/Local" feature in this chapter concerns uncontacted peoples.
- Chapter 2 includes more on cultural adaptation as well as information on recent fossil finds, including the controversy over *Homo floresiensis,* the "Hobbit" find. The "Global/Local" feature is "Vanishing Primates."
- Chapter 3 has been substantially rewritten. It now includes a more thorough discussion of the history of fieldwork in anthropology as well as a new ethnography on fieldwork in dangerous places. There is new information about anthropology and ethics, particularly a discussion of the use of anthropologists by the U.S. military. Our "Global/Local" feature for this chapter focuses on anthropologists and human rights and considers the case of female genital operations.
- Chapter 4 now includes a discussion of culture and autism. It has again been streamlined to provide new examples and to clarify the connections between critical questions in anthropology and particular anthropological perspectives. The "Global/Local" feature presents ideas about the analysis of the events of 9/11.
- Chapter 5 has been reorganized to provide greater emphasis on the performance of speech. The section on language change has expanded coverage of the dynamics of power as they relate to the history of language. There is a new ethnography about the use of cell phones in Jamaica and our new "Global/Local" feature discusses the English Only movement in the United States.
- Chapter 6 has been rewritten to provide more complete coverage of different subsistence technologies and greater balance of description among them. In addition, attention is paid to factors such as technology and the global market that are transforming traditional subsistence methods. There is a new ethnography focusing on climate change and how this affects the subsistence economy of foraging groups in the Arctic and a new "Global/Local" feature on the globalization of food.
- Chapter 7 has been streamlined to eliminate some redundancies with other chapters and expand coverage of political economy with particular attention to market economies and the naturalization of capitalism. There is a new ethnography on West African merchants in New York City. Our new "Global/Local" feature focuses on product anthropology and our "Anthropology Makes a Difference" box about business anthropology has been expanded to include information from an interview with Eleanor Wynn, an anthropologist working for Intel.

- Chapter 8, "Kinship," now precedes the material on marriage and family and includes the ethnography on the Minangkabau of Sumatra and emphasizes matrilineality as a significant form of contemporary kinship structure. The subject of transmigration is expanded to show its very close contemporary links to kinship relations. The "Global/Local" feature for this chapter discusses transmigration and kinship.

- Chapter 9 is now "Marriage, Family, and Domestic Groups." It shows how kinship is the matrix of social relationships within which marriage and family takes place. A new ethnography on the Na of China, a society that raises interesting questions about whether marriage can truly be considered a human universal, is now included. Our "Global/Local" feature presents a cross-cultural perspective on aging.

- Chapter 10, "Gender," includes an important new "Global/Local" feature illustrating the diverse cultural variations contained within the Islamic principle of female modesty and its relationship to female dress.

- Chapter 11, "Political Organization," has been substantially altered to incorporate material that expands the discussion of the impact of the nation-state on ethnicity, indigenous peoples, and refugees. "Crossing National Borders," the "Global/Local" feature for this chapter, explores critical issues along the "Green Line" (the 1949 armistice line between Israel and its neighbors) and the United States–Mexico border in Arizona.

- Chapter 12 has been reorganized using materials from former Chapters 11 and 12. It focuses on the interrelationships and inequalities of class, race, and ethnicity in the United States, India, and China in the context of globalization. A new ethnography focuses on the connections between health, pollution, and social stratification in the U.S. The new "Anthropology Makes a Difference" section highlights the American Anthropological Association's Race Project. The "Global/Local" feature explores the changing class system of China.

- Chapter 13, "Religion," expands our coverage of ritual, particularly liminal states, rites of passage, and rites of intensification. There is great emphasis placed on varieties of religious practitioners. The "Global/Local" feature for this chapter examines increasing religious diversity in the United States.

- Chapter 14, "Creative Expression: Anthropology and the Arts," now includes an "Anthropology Makes a Difference" feature on the impact of anthropology on museum exhibits of art and culture. The new "Global/Local" feature expands and updates the subject of world music from the previous edition.

- Chapter 15 is a new chapter that focuses on the European expansion that began in the 15th century and describes the ways in which relatively independent societies were drawn or forced into a global economy. This chapter substantially expands our coverage of colonialism and the process of decolonization. The "Global/Local" box, titled "Who Owns History?" examines controversies over the ownership of historical objects. The "Anthropology Makes a Difference" box called "Recovering Hidden Histories" describes how anthropologists attempt to tell the stories of those who have often been neglected or silenced.

- Chapter 16 focuses on the problems and prospects of globalization. It includes a brief history of attempts at economic development and then explores challenges facing the world's societies. A new ethnography describes the conditions of child labor in Olinda, Brazil. A new "Global/Local" box discusses whether or not the world is truly becoming "flat."

# Chapter Overview

Each chapter in the text begins with a short "Thinking Point" to engage students in critical thinking with provocative anthropological topics. The chapters are organized so that the main ideas, secondary ideas, important terms and definitions, and ethnographic material stand out clearly. The entire text has been thoroughly updated reflecting important recent anthropological work.

- Chapter 1, "Anthropology and Human Diversity," focuses on anthropology as a discipline whose subject is human diversity. This chapter introduces the major perspectives of anthropology and the subfields of the discipline. It highlights race as a social construction and the many ways anthropology contributes to a sensitive understanding of human differences. There is a discussion of the ways in which globalization has affected both anthropologists and the people whom anthropologists frequently study. The chapter explains the importance of anthropology as a university discipline and the reasons that understanding anthropology is critical in the world today. The classic ethnography "The Nacirema" as well as special sections on medical anthropology and contact with "stone-age" tribes are among the features of the chapter.

- Chapter 2, "Human Evolution," is designed to give introductory students a background in the theory of evolution by natural selection, the physical and social characteristics of primates, and the major groups of fossil human ancestors. The chapter concludes with a section on human variation that highlights the biology of human traits commonly used in racial classification.

- Chapter 3, "Doing Cultural Anthropology," provides a basic history of fieldwork in anthropology, focusing on the contributions of Boas and Malinowski. It describes the process of doing fieldwork and analysis including site selection, data collection, and analysis. It considers important issues in anthropological fieldwork, particularly ethical concerns, the positioning of anthropologists and informants, and the role of collaborative and engaged anthropologies. There is coverage of issues surrounding the use of anthropology in war and there is a new ethnography about doing fieldwork in dangerous places.

- Chapter 4, "The Idea of Culture," exposes students to a range of theoretical positions in anthropology by examining the ways different anthropologists have understood the idea of culture. In addition to introducing students to the history of theory in anthropology, it demonstrates that different theoretical positions lead anthropologists to ask different sorts of questions and do different sorts of research. We present anthropology as an exciting arena in which different understandings and interpretations jostle for position. The chapter concludes with a discussion of the cultural change mechanisms of innovation and diffusion. (A full discussion of culture change and the expansion of capitalism is found in Chapter 16.)

- Chapter 5, "Communication," provides a solid background for anthropological linguistics. Phonology, morphology, and other elements of linguistics are discussed. There are special highlights on language acquisition and language experiments with apes. A section on sociolinguistics focuses on speech as performance and addresses issues including linguistic minorities and cross-cultural communication. Another section explores nonverbal communication. A new ethnography explores the impact of cell phones on communication in Jamaica.

- Chapter 6, "Making a Living," brings cultural adaptation into focus. It examines the major human food-getting strategies through five extended ethnographies describing the effect of climate change on Inuit foraging in the Arctic, as well as other global factors as they affect pastoralism among the Maasai of East Africa, horticulture among the Lua' of Thailand, peasant agriculture in an Egyptian village, and industrialism through a description of the meatpacking industry in the American Midwest. Throughout there is emphasis on the roles played by technological change and expanding ties that enmesh us in a global economy.

- Chapter 7, "Economics," explores the nature of economic behavior and economic systems in cross-cultural perspective. Special attention is paid to issues of access to resources, the organization of labor, systems of distribution and exchange (including classic examples such as the potlatch and the Kula ring). There is extended coverage of market systems, including coverage of capitalism and resistance to capitalism. Our "Anthropology Makes a Difference" and "Global/Local" features focus on the use of anthropology in business and in marketing. A rewritten ethnography focuses on West African traders in New York City.

- Chapter 8, "Kinship," introduces the major kinship ideologies and the kinds of social groups formed by kinship. The chapter features an extended discussion of the Nuer as well as a comparison of kinship in the United States and North India based on Serena Nanda's experiences in both cultures. The ethnography focuses on the matrilineal Minangkabou of Sumatra, and the Anthropology Makes a Difference feature examines a dispute over inheritance in a South Korean village. The chapter concludes with a "Global/Local" feature about transmigration: international migrants who maintain close relations with their home countries.

- Chapter 9, "Marriage, Family, and Domestic Groups," focuses on types of family systems, emphasizing the diversity of forms and functions of families, highlighted by a new ethnographic section on the Na of China, who raise the question of whether marriage is universal. In addition to sections on marriage rules, marriage exchanges, and different types of families, the "Anthropology Makes a Difference" feature, on domestic violence, highlights the family as a context of uneven power and its consequences within families. We have retained the material on a cross-cultural view of aging as the "Global/Local" feature of this chapter.

- Chapter 10, "Gender," brings together a historical perspective on the examination of gender in cultural anthropology with current research on the role of women in foraging societies, the relationship between women and power, changes in women's roles as a result of European contact, and an examination of the effects of "development," globalization, and multinational corporations on women, highlighting the role of an anthropologist who advocates for female factory workers in China. This chapter emphasizes the construction of gender, using ethnographic data on masculinity in Spain and the construction of the hijra role, an alternative gender role in India. A new "Global/Local" feature addresses variation in concepts of female modesty in Islam in different national and political contexts.

- Chapter 11, "Political Organization," begins with a description of social differentiation in egalitarian, rank, and stratified societies. It goes on to explore the issue of power and social control before turning to a systematic discussion of leadership, social control, and conflict resolution in bands, tribes, chiefdoms, and states. The ethnography on the precolonial Asante highlights the interactions among power, wealth, and the development of the state. Our expanded treatment of the nation-state now incorporates contemporary issues such as ethnicity, indigenous peoples, and includes detailed descriptions of the Saami reindeer herders of Norway, ethnic conflict, and the issue of national boundaries in relation to immigration.

- Chapter 12, now "Stratification," focuses on the connections between race, class, and ethnicity. It expands the emphasis on race as a cultural construction, highlighting the Race Project of the American Anthropological Association and comparing racial constructions and racial stratification in Brazil and the United States. There is a new section on Muslim immigrants to the United States and also on the connections between race, class, and health in the U.S. The chapter retains a cross-cultural context of stratification by looking at the dynamics of caste in contemporary India and the ways in which globalization has affected the class system in China.

- Chapter 13, "Religion," moves from a brief consideration of the functions of religion to a definition of religion that includes stories and myths, symbolism, supernatural beings and powers, rituals, practitioners, and change. It then looks at each of these aspects of religion using examples from different cultures. It includes material on the globalization of religion in the United States, religion and ecology, religion and population growth, cargo cults, colonialism and ritual, and fundamentalism. An ethnography on the Rastafarians and extensive information on the Ghost Dance religion and Native American Church show the roles of religion in social change and resistance.

- Chapter 14, "Creative Expression: Anthropology and the Arts," highlights a cross-cultural perspective on the forms and functions of art. The theme of the relationship between cultural identity and art is carried through by ethnographic sections on Japanese manga and anime, and a section on Frida Kahlo. Our section on "deep play," includes material on Spanish bullfighting, American football, and Balinese cockfighting. We examine the symbolism of henna painting as it relates to women's roles in the Middle East, and orientalism as one aspect of the relationship between art and power. Our ethnography on the Toraja of Indonesia emphasizes how the art in small-scale societies has become part of the global art market, changing local cultural identities in the process. Globalization also is the underlying theme in our expanded discussion of world music.

- Chapter 15, "Power, Conquest, and a World System," is a new chapter that explores the historical processes that, beginning in the 15th century, transformed the world from relatively independent societies to a world system. We examine the methods and motives for European expansion, the roles of forced labor and joint stock companies, the processes of colonization, and the ways in which Europeans attempted to make colonialism pay. A section focuses on the role of anthropology in colonialism and another describes the process of decolonization. Our ethnography focuses on the experiences of African soldiers drafted to serve France in the 20th century. The "Global/Local" box examines controversies over the ownership of historical objects and our "Anthropology Makes a Difference" feature describes how anthropologists attempt to tell the stories of those who have often been neglected.

- Chapter 16, "Culture, Change, and the Modern World," continues the story begun in Chapter 15 by examining the attempts by wealthy nations to engage poor nations through economic development. It then turns to a discussion of critical problems facing the world's societies, including the actions of multinational corporations, urbanization, population pressure, environmental challenges, political instability, and migration. Extended examples include the 1990s campaign against Nike, China's one-child policy, environmental problems in West Africa, and political instability in Rwanda and East Africa. Features include an ethnography on child labor in Olinda, Brazil, a feature describing the roles anthropologists play in development projects, and a "Global/Local" feature asking readers to consider the degree to which technological processes mean that economic and social opportunities are available to all people.

- The Appendix, "A Brief Historical Guide to Anthropological Theory," provides a concise, historically based introduction to the major schools of anthropological theorizing beginning with 19th-century evolutionism. The critical concepts of each theory are briefly summarized and the major thinkers in each school identified. In addition to evolutionism, the Appendix covers early sociological theory, American historical particularism, British functionalism, culture and personality, cultural ecology and neo-evolutionism, neomaterialism, structuralism, cognitive anthropology, sociobiology, anthropology and gender, symbolic and interpretive anthropology, and postmodernism and its critics.

# Teaching Features and Study Aids

Each chapter of *Cultural Anthropology* includes outstanding pedagogical features to help students identify, learn, and remember key concepts and data. As befits a text in which ethnographic material holds so central a role, the major features within each chapter are the 20 boxed **ethnographies**. The ethnographies provide interesting and insightful information designed to engage students and provide a context for thinking about more abstract concepts. **Locator maps** accompany the ethnographies. **Critical-thinking questions** at the end of each "Ethnography" box tie the section firmly to the material presented in the chapter and open opportunities for discussion of anthropology's role in the modern world. New topics in the Tenth Edition of *Cultural Anthropology* include the use of cell phones in Jamaica (Chapter 5); climate change and how this affects the subsistence economy of foraging groups in the Arctic (Chapter 6); West African merchants in New York City (Chapter 7); and the conditions of child labor in Olinda, Brazil (Chapter 16).

The "Ethnography" boxes are now supplemented by only one additional boxed feature in each chapter, with material presented previously in other boxes now seamlessly integrated with the body of the text, where appropriate:

- **"Anthropology Makes a Difference"** boxes highlight the work of anthropologists who are "making a difference" in the world. This feature helps students see how anthropology relates to their own lives and provides examples of careers and the type of work in which anthropologists engage. Examples include discussions of medical anthropology in Chapter 1 and forensic anthropology in Chapter 2, as well as a new "Anthropology Makes a Difference" box on the American Anthropological Association's Race Project in Chapter 12, and one on "Recovering Hidden Histories" in Chapter 15.
- A new chapter-ending feature called **"The Global and the Local"** emphasizes the importance of the global context for contemporary anthropology. Topics covered include: uncontacted peoples (Chapter 1); vanishing primates (Chapter 2); anthropologists and human rights, including the case of female genital operations (Chapter 3); understanding 9/11 (Chapter 4); the English Only movement in the United States (new for Chapter 5); the globalization of food (Chapter 6); product anthropology (Chapter 7); cross-cultural perspective on aging (Chapter 8); transmigration and kinship (Chapter 9); the Islamic principle of female modesty and its relationship to female dress (new for Chapter 10); critical issues along the "Green Line" and the United States–Mexico border (Chapter 11); the changing class system of China (Chapter 12); increasing religious diversity in the United States (Chapter 13); an expanded and updated discussion of world music (Chapter 14); controversies over the ownership of historical objects (Chapter 15); and a discussion of whether or not the world is truly becoming "flat" (Chapter 16).

Each chapter also has several learning aids to help students understand and retain the chapter's information:

- Full-color **opening photos** are placed at the beginning of each chapter.
- An **outline** at the beginning of each chapter clearly shows the organization of the chapter and the major topics covered.
- A **running glossary** of key terms is found at the bottom of the pages.
- **Summaries,** arranged as numbered points at the end of each chapter, are now phrased as key questions followed by answers to better help students critically review and study chapter ideas.
- **Key terms** are listed alphabetically at the end of each chapter, for quick review.
- **Suggested readings** that are interesting and accessible to the introductory student are listed at the end of each chapter.
- A **glossary** at the end of the book defines the major terms and concepts, in alphabetical order for quick access.

- **References** for every source cited within the text are listed alphabetically at the end of the book.

# Supplements for Instructors

## Online Instructor's Manual with Test Bank, by Richard Warms and Marjorie Snipes

Prepare for class more quickly and effectively with such resources as learning objectives, detailed chapter outlines, suggested assignments, and film suggestions. A test bank with more than 50 questions per chapter, prepared by Richard L. Warms and validated by expert reviewers, saves you time creating tests. (0-495-90281-0, 978-0-495-90281-2)

## PowerLecture with ExamView

PowerLecture instructor resources are a collection of book-specific lecture and class tools on either CD or DVD. The fastest and easiest way to build powerful, customized, media-rich lectures, PowerLecture assets include chapter-specific PowerPoint presentations, images, animations and video, instructor manuals, test banks, useful web links and more. PowerLecture media-teaching tools are an effective way to enhance the educational experience. (0-495-90282-9, 978-0495-90282-9)

## Wadsworth Anthropology Video Library

Qualified adopters may select full-length videos from an extensive library of offerings drawn from such excellent educational video sources as *Films for the Humanities and Sciences.*

## ABC Video: *Anthropology, Volume 1*

Launch your lectures with exciting video clips from the award-winning news coverage of ABC. Addressing topics covered in a typical course, these videos are divided into short segments, perfect for introducing key concepts in contexts relevant to students' lives. (0-534-63011-1, 978-0-534-63011-9)

## AIDS in Africa DVD

Expand your students' global perspective of HIV/AIDS with this award-winning documentary series focused on controlling HIV/AIDS in southern Africa. Films focus on caregivers in the faith community; how young people share messages of hope through song and dance; the relationship of HIV/AIDS to gender, poverty, stigma, education, and justice; and the story of two HIV-positive women helping others. (0-495-17183-2, 978-0-495-17183-6)

# Online Resources for Instructors and Students

## Companion Website

The book's companion website features a rich array of teaching and learning resources that you won't find anywhere else. This outstanding site features the following resources for each chapter of the text: tutorial quizzes, InfoTrac® College Edition exercises, web links, flash cards, and crossword puzzles. And for instructors, preassembled Microsoft PowerPoint lecture slides and the Instructor's Manual are also available. (0-495-90280-2, 978-0-495-90280-5)

## Instant Access Code for Cengage Learning eBook and the Anthropology Resource Center

This online center offers a wealth of information and useful tools for both instructors and students. Students will find interactive maps, learning modules, video exercises, Cross-Cultural Miscues, Meet the Scientists, and more. For instructors, the Anthropology Resource Center includes a gateway to time-saving teaching tools, such as image banks and sample syllabi. (0-8400-3570-5, 978-0-8400-3570-7)

## WebTutor™ Toolbox for WebCT and Blackboard

This web-based software for students and instructors takes a course beyond the classroom to an anywhere, anytime environment. Students gain access to an array of study tools, including chapter outlines and chapter-specific quizzing material, while instructors can provide virtual office hours, post syllabi, track student progress with the quizzing material, and even customize the content to suit their needs. Please contact your Cengage Learning sales representative for ordering details.

# Readings and Case Studies

## Neither Man nor Woman: The Hijras of India, Second Edition, by Serena Nanda

This ethnography is a cultural study conducted by text author Serena Nanda of the hijras of India, a religious community of men who dress and act like women. It focuses on how hijras can be used in the study of gender categories and sexual variation. (0-534-50903-7, 978-0-534-50903-3)

## Globalization and Change in Fifteen Cultures: Born in One World, Living in Another, edited by George Spindler and Janice E. Stockard

In this volume, 15 case study authors write about culture change in today's diverse settings around the world. Each original article provides insight into the dynamics and meanings of change, as well as the effects of globalization at the local level. (0-534-63648-9, 978-0-534-63648-7)

## Classic Readings in Cultural Anthropology, Second Edition, edited by Gary Ferraro

Brief and accessible, this reader edited by Gary Ferraro features articles and excerpts from works that have proved pivotal in the field of cultural anthropology. Topics include culture, language and communication, ecology and economics, issues of culture change, and many more. (0-495-50736-9, 978-0-495-50736-9)

## Case Studies in Cultural Anthropology, edited by George Spindler and Janice E. Stockard

Select from more than 60 classic and contemporary ethnographies representing geographic and topical diversity. Newer case studies focus on culture change and culture continuity, reflecting the globalization of the world, and include *New Cures, Old Medicines: Women and the Commercialization of Traditional Medicine in Bolivia,* by Lynn Sikkink.

## Case Studies on Contemporary Social Issues, edited by John A. Young

Framed around social issues, these new contemporary case studies are globally comparative and represent the cutting-edge work of anthropologists today. Recent publications include *Fetal Fatal Knowledge: New Reproductive Technologies and Family-Building Strategies in India,* by Sunil Khanna.

# Acknowledgments

It gives us great pleasure to thank the many people who have been associated with this book. We are most appreciative of the helpful comments made by reviewers of the Tenth Edition:

Augustine Agwuele (Texas State University–San Marcos)

Kira Blaisdell-Sloan (University of California, Berkeley)

Patricia L. Jolly (University of Northern Colorado)

Brett J. Millán (South Texas College)

Mark Miller (East Texas Baptist University)

Aimee Preziosi (West Los Angeles College)

Jess White (Western Illinois University)

For their support and assistance we would like to thank Mrs. Raksha Chopra, Kojo Dei, Stanley Freed, Joan Gregg, and Michael Newman. For the use of photographs we would like to thank Soo Choi, Ronald Coley, Tom Curtin, Kojo Dei, Chander Dembla, Joan Gregg, James Hamilton, Jane Hoffer, Ray Kennedy, Judith Pearson, Chandler Prude, and Jean Zorn.

We gratefully acknowledge the support of our universities and the help of the staffs of our departments at John Jay College of Criminal Justice and Texas State University–San Marcos. In addition, many of our students have contributed ideas, reflections, and labor to this project.

Our families continue to form an important cheering section for our work, and we thank them for their patience, endurance, and just plain putting up with us.

We are deeply grateful to the people at Wadsworth, particularly our editor, Erin Mitchell, and our developmental editor, Lin (Marshall) Gaylord, for their support, their encouragement, and their insights. In addition, we wish to thank Media Editor Melanie Creegan, Editorial Assistant Pamela Simon, Content Project Manager Jerilyn Emori, as well as Andrew Keay and Dimitri Hagnéré. Finally, we would like to thank Dan Fitzgerald, who shepherded us through the production process, and Billie Porter, who did the photo research. The knowledge, editing skills, and superb suggestions made by the many people involved in the production of this book have greatly contributed to it.

# About the Authors

**SERENA NANDA** is professor emeritus of anthropology at John Jay College of Criminal Justice, City University of New York. Her most recent book is *The Gift of a Bride: A Tale of Anthropology, Matrimony and Murder,* a novel set in an Indian immigrant community in New York City. Her other published works include *Neither Man nor Woman: The Hijras of India,* winner of the 1990 Ruth Benedict Prize; *American Cultural Pluralism and Law; Gender Diversity: Cross-Cultural Variations;* and a New York City guidebook, *New York More Than Ever: 40 Perfect Days in and Around the City.* She has always been captivated by the stories people tell and by the tapestry of human diversity. Anthropology was the perfect way for her to immerse herself in these passions, and through teaching, to spread the word about the importance of understanding both human differences and human similarities.

**RICHARD L. WARMS** is professor of anthropology at Texas State University–San Marcos. His published works include *Anthropological Theory: An Introductory History* and *Sacred Realms: Essays in Religion, Belief, and Society,* as well as journal articles on commerce, religion, and ethnic identity in West Africa; African exploration and romanticism; and African veterans of French colonial armed forces. Warms's interests in anthropology were kindled by college courses and by his experiences as a Peace Corps Volunteer in West Africa. He has traveled extensively in Africa, Europe, and most recently, Japan. He continues to teach Introduction to Cultural Anthropology every year but also teaches classes in anthropological theory, the anthropology of religion, economic anthropology, and film at both the undergraduate and graduate level. Students and faculty are invited to contact him with their comments, suggestions, and questions at r.warms@txstate.edu.

Anthropologists study cultural practices all over the world in their attempt to understand the similarities and differences among human beings. Today, like these Maasai tribesmen, members of cultures throughout the world are deeply affected by the global market and by technological change. Anthropologists are particularly interested in the ways in which cultures respond to such changes.

**THINKING POINT:** Though the practice has fallen out of favor in recent years, in traditional times Nacireman women participated in weekly masochistic rituals during which they would bake their heads in small ovens for about an hour.

—[See pages 4–5 for details.]

{chapter 1}

# Anthropology and Human Diversity

As long as human beings have existed they have lived in groups and have had to answer certain critical questions. They have had to figure out how to feed, clothe, and house themselves, how to determine rights and responsibilities, how to lend meaning to their lives, how to live with each other, and how to deal with those who live differently. Cultures are human responses to these basic questions. The goal of **anthropology**—the comparative study of human societies and cultures—is to describe, analyze, and explain different cultures, to show how groups have adapted to their environments and given significance to their lives.

Anthropology is comparative in that it attempts to understand similarities and differences among human cultures. Only through the study of humanity in its total variety can we understand who we are as human beings, our potentials and our perils. In an era when people from different cultures are increasingly in contact with each other, and when most people in the world live in multicultural and multiethnic nations, these are important goals.

Anthropologists attempt to comprehend the entire human experience. We study our species from its ancestral beginnings several million years ago up to the present. We study human beings as they live in every corner of the earth, in all kinds of physical, political, and social environments. We reach beyond humans to understand primates, those animals most closely related to us. Some anthropologists even try to project how human beings will live in the future, exploring the possibilities of space stations and communities on other planets. This interest in humankind and our closest relations throughout time and in all parts of the world distinguishes anthropology as a scientific and humanistic discipline.

In other academic disciplines, human behavior is usually studied primarily from the point of view of Western society. Scholars in these disciplines often consider the behavior of people in the modern industrial nations of Europe and North ≫

1

America to be representative of all humanity. Anthropologists insist that to understand humanity we must study people living in many different cultures, times, and places.

Human beings everywhere consider their own behavior not only right, but natural. Our ideas about economics, religion, morality, and other areas of social life seem logical and inevitable to us, but others have found different answers. For example, should you give your infant bottled formula or should you breast-feed not only your own child but, like the Efe of Zaire, those of your friends and neighbors as well (Peacock 1991:352)? Is it right that emotional love should precede sexual relations? Or should sexual relations precede love, as is normal for the Mangaian of the Pacific (D. Marshall 1971)? What should we have for lunch: hamburgers and fries, or termites, grasshoppers, and hot maguey worms, all of which are commonly eaten in certain regions of Mexico (Bates 1967:58–59)? In anthropology, concepts of human nature and theories of human behavior are based on studies of human groups whose goals, values, views of reality, and environmental adaptations are very different from those of industrial Western societies.

Anthropologists bring a holistic approach to understanding and explaining. To say anthropology is **holistic** means that it combines the study of human biology, history, and the learned and shared patterns of human behavior and thought we call culture in order to analyze human groups.

Holism also separates anthropology from other academic disciplines, which generally focus on one factor—biology, psychology, physiology, or society—to explain human behavior. Anthropology seeks to understand human beings as organisms who adapt to their environments through a complex interaction of biology and culture.

Because anthropologists take a holistic approach, they are interested in the total range of human activity. Most anthropologists specialize in a single field and a single problem, but together they study the small dramas of daily living as well as spectacular social events. They study the ways in which mothers hold their babies or sons address their fathers. They want to know not only how a group gets its food but also the rules for eating it. Anthropologists are interested in how human societies think about time and space and how they see colors and name them. They are interested in health and illness and the significance of physical variation. Anthropologists are interested in social rules and practices concerning sex and marriage. They are interested in folklore and fairy tales, political speeches, and everyday conversation. For the anthropologist, great ceremonies and the ordinary rituals of greeting a friend are all worth investigating. Anthropologists believe that every aspect of human behavior can help us understand human life and society. <<

---

**anthropology** The comparative study of human societies and cultures.

**holistic/holism** In anthropology an approach that considers culture, history, language, and biology essential to a complete understanding of human society.

**society** A group of people who depend on one another for survival or well-being as well as the relationships among such people, including their status and roles.

**culture** The learned behaviors and symbols that allow people to live in groups. The primary means by which humans adapt to their environments. The way of life characteristic of a particular human society.

**ethnography** A description of society or culture.

**emic** (perspective) Examining society using concepts, categories, and distinctions that are meaningful to members of that culture.

---

# Specialization in Anthropology

The broad range of anthropological interest has led to specialization of research and teaching. The major divisions of anthropology are cultural anthropology, linguistic anthropology, archaeology, physical or biological anthropology, and applied anthropology.

## Cultural Anthropology

The study of human society and culture is known as cultural anthropology. Anthropologists define **society** as a group of people persisting through time and the social relationships among these people: their statuses and roles. Traditionally, societies are thought of as occupying a specific geographic location, but modern transportation and electronic communication have made specific locales less important. Societies are increasingly global rather than local phenomena.

As Chapter 4 will show, culture is an extremely complex phenomenon. **Culture** is the major way in which human beings adapt to their environments and give meaning to their lives. It includes human behavior and ideas that are learned rather than genetically transmitted, as well as the material objects produced by a group of people.

Cultural anthropologists attempt to understand culture through the study of its origins, development, and diversity as it changes through time and among people. They bring many research strategies to this task. They may focus on the search for general principles that underlie all cultures or examine the dynamics of a particular culture. They may explore the ways in which different societies adapt to their environments or how members of other cultures understand the world and their place in it.

Ethnography and ethnology are two important aspects of cultural anthropology. **Ethnography** is the description of society or culture. An ethnographer attempts to describe an entire society or a particular set of cultural institutions or practices. Ethnographies may be either emic, or etic, or may combine the two. An **emic** ethnography attempts to capture what ideas and practices mean to members of a culture. It attempts to give the reader a sense of what it feels like to be a member of the culture

Cultural anthropologists describe and analyze current day cultures. Many current studies focus on culture change and the movement of objects and ideas between cultures. Here a Moroccan tribesman gives water to his camel with a disposable plastic bottle.

© Olivier Asselin/Acclaim Images

it describes. An **etic** ethnography describes and analyzes culture according to principles and theories drawn from Western scientific traditions such as ecology, economy, or psychology. For example, the Nacirema ethnography in this chapter is an etic analysis drawn from a psychological perspective. **Ethnology** is the attempt to find general principles or laws that govern cultural phenomena. Ethnologists compare and contrast practices in different cultures to find regularities.

**Cultural anthropology** is a complex field with many different subfields. One index of this complexity is the more than 50 different sections and interest groups of the American Anthropological Association; the vast majority of these are concerned with cultural anthropology. Some examples include political and legal anthropology, which is concerned with issues of nationalism, citizenship, the state, colonialism, and globalism; humanistic anthropology, which is focused on the personal, ethical, and political choices facing humans; and visual anthropology, which is the study of visual representation and the media.

Cultural anthropologists are often particularly interested in documenting and understanding the ways in which cultures change. They examine the roles that power and coercion play in change, as well as humans' ability to invent new technologies and social forms and modify old ones. Because understanding the ways in which societies change requires knowledge of their past, many cultural anthropologists are drawn to **ethnohistory:**

description of the cultural past based on written records, interviews, and archaeology.

Studies of culture change are important because rapid shifts in society, economy, and technology are basic characteristics of the contemporary world. Understanding the dynamics of change is critical for individuals, governments, and corporations. One goal of cultural anthropology is to be able to contribute productively to public debate about promotion of and reaction to change.

## Linguistic Anthropology

Language is the primary means by which people communicate with one another. Although most creatures communicate, human speech is more complex, creative, and used more extensively than the communication systems of other animals. Language is an essential part of what it means to be human and a basic part of all cultures. **Linguistic anthropology** is concerned with understanding language and its relation to culture.

Language is an amazing thing we take for granted. When we speak, we use our bodies—our lungs, vocal cords, mouth, tongue, and lips—to produce noise of varying tone and pitch. And, somehow, when we do this, if we speak the same language, we are able to communicate with each other. Linguistic anthropologists want to understand how language is structured, how it is learned, and how this communication takes place.

Language is a complex symbolic system that people use to communicate and to transmit culture. Thus, language provides critical clues for understanding culture. For example, people generally talk about the people, places, and objects that are important to them. Therefore, the vocabularies of spoken language may give us clues to important aspects of culture. Knowing the words that people use for things may help us to glimpse how they understand the world.

Language involves much more than words. When we speak we perform. If we tell a story, we don't simply recite the words. We emphasize some things. We add in-

**etic** (perspective) Examining society using concepts, categories, and rules derived from science; an outsider's perspective, which produces analyses that members of the society being studied may not find meaningful.

**ethnology** The attempt to find general principles or laws that govern cultural phenomena.

**cultural anthropology** The study of human thought, meaning, and behavior that is learned rather than genetically transmitted, and that is typical of groups of people.

**ethnohistory** Description of the cultural past based on written records, interviews, and archaeology.

**linguistic anthropology** A branch of linguistics concerned with understanding language and its relation to culture.

## The Nacirema

Anthropologists have become so familiar with the diversity of ways different peoples behave that they are not apt to be surprised by even the most exotic customs. The magical beliefs and practices of the Nacirema present such unusual aspects that it seems desirable to describe them as an example of the extremes to which human behavior can go. The Nacirema are a North American group living in the territory between the Canadian Cree, the Yaqui and Tarahumare of Mexico, and the Carib and Arawak of the Antilles. Little is known of their origin, although tradition states that they came from the east.

Nacirema culture is characterized by a highly developed market economy that has evolved in a rich natural habitat. Although much of the people's time is devoted to economic pursuits, a large part of the fruits of these labors and a considerable portion of the day are spent in ritual activity. The focus of this activity is the human body, the appearance and health of which loom as a dominant concern in the ethos of the people. Such a concern is certainly not unusual, but its ceremonial aspects and associated philosophy are unique.

The fundamental belief underlying the whole system is that the human body is ugly and has a natural tendency to debility and disease. Man's only hope is to avert these characteristics through the use of the powerful influences of ritual and ceremony and every household has one or more shrines devoted to this purpose. The rituals associated with the shrine are private and secret. The rites are normally discussed only with children, and then only during the period when they are being initiated into these mysteries. I was able, however, to establish sufficient rapport with the natives to examine these shrines and to have the rituals described to me.

The focal point of the shrine is a box or chest that is built into the wall. In this chest are kept the many charms and magical potions without which no native believes he could live. These preparations are secured from a variety of specialized practitioners. The most powerful of these are the medicine men, whose assistance must be rewarded with substantial gifts.

Beneath the charm box is a small font. Each day every member of the family, in succession, enters the shrine room, bows his head before the charm box, mingles different sorts of holy water in the font, and proceeds with a brief rite of ablution. The holy waters are secured from the Water Temple of the community, where priests conduct elaborate ceremonies to make the liquid ritually pure.

Below the medicine men in prestige are specialists whose designation is best translated "holy mouth men." The Nacirema have an almost pathological horror of and fascination with the mouth, the condition of which is believed to have a supernatural influence on all social relationships. Were it not for the rituals of the mouth, they believe that their teeth would fall out, their gums bleed, their jaws shrink, their friends desert them, and their lovers reject them.

The daily body ritual performed by everyone includes a mouth rite, but in addition the people seek out a holy mouth man once or twice a year. These practitioners have an impressive set of paraphernalia, consisting of a variety of augers, awls, probes, and prods. The use of these objects in the exorcism of the evils of the mouth involves almost unbelievable ritual torture of the client. The holy mouth man opens the client's mouth and, using the above mentioned tools, enlarges any holes that decay may have created in the teeth. Magical materials are put into those holes. In the client's view, the purpose of these ministrations is to arrest decay and to draw friends. The extremely sacred and traditional character of the rite is evident in the fact that the natives return to the holy mouth men year after year, despite the fact that their teeth continue to decay.

It is to be hoped that, when a thorough study of the Nacirema is made, there will be careful inquiry into the personality structure of these people. One has but to watch the gleam in the eye of a holy mouth man, as he jabs an awl into an exposed nerve, to suspect that a certain amount of sadism is involved. If this can be established, a very interesting pattern emerges, for most of the population shows definite masochistic tendencies. For example, a portion of the daily body ritual performed only by men involves scraping and lacerating the surface of the face with a sharp instrument. Special women's rites are performed only four times during each lunar month, but what they lack in frequency is made up in barbarity. As part of this ceremony, women bake their heads in small ovens for about an hour.

flection that can turn a serious phrase comic or a comic phrase serious. We give our own special tilt to a story, even if we are just reading a book out loud. Linguistic anthropologists are interested in the ways in which people perform language—in the ways they change and modify the meanings of their words.

All languages change. **Historical linguists** work to discover the ways in which languages have changed and the ways in which languages are related to each other. Understanding linguistic change and the relationships between languages helps us to work out the past of the people who speak them. Knowing, for example, the linguistic relationships among various Native American languages

**historical linguists** Study relationships among languages to better understand the histories and migrations of those who speak them.

The medicine men have an imposing temple, or latipsoh, in every community of any size. The more elaborate ceremonies required to treat very sick patients can be performed only at this temple. These ceremonies involve not only the priests, but a permanent group of vestal maidens who move sedately about the temple chambers in distinctive costume.

The latipsoh ceremonies are so harsh that it is phenomenal that a fair proportion of the really sick natives who enter the temple ever recover. Despite this fact, sick adults are not only willing but eager to undergo the protracted ritual purification, if they can afford to do so. No matter how ill the supplicant or how grave the emergency, the guardians of many temples will not admit a client if he cannot give a rich gift to the custodian. Even after one has gained admission and survived the ceremonies, the guardians will not permit the neophyte to leave until he makes still another gift.

The supplicant entering the temple is first stripped of all his or her clothes. Psychological shock results from the fact that body secrecy is suddenly lost upon entry into the latipsoh. A man whose own wife has never seen him in an excretory act suddenly finds himself naked and assisted by a vestal maiden while he performs his natural functions into a sacred vessel. This sort of ceremonial treatment is necessitated by the fact that the excreta are used by a diviner to ascertain the course and nature of the client's sickness. Female clients, on the other hand, find their naked bodies are subjected to the scrutiny, manipulation, and prodding of the medicine men. The fact that these temple ceremonies may not cure, and may even kill the neophyte, in no way decreases the people's faith in the medicine men.

In conclusion, mention must be made of certain practices that have their base in native esthetics but that depend on the pervasive aversion to the natural body and its functions. There are ritual fasts to make fat people thin and ceremonial feasts to make thin people fat. Still other rites are used to make women's breasts larger if they are small, and smaller if they are large. General dissatisfaction with breast shape is symbolized in the fact that the ideal form is virtually outside the range of human variation. A few women afflicted with almost inhuman hypermammary development are so idolized that they make a handsome living by simply going from village to village and permitting the natives to stare at them for a fee.

Our review of the ritual life of the Nacirema has certainly shown them to be a magic-ridden people. It is hard to understand how they have managed to exist so long under the burdens that they have imposed upon themselves. But even such exotic customs as these take on real meaning when they are viewed with the insight provided by Malinowski when he wrote: "Looking from far and above, from our high places of safety in the developed civilization, it is easy to see all the crudity and irrelevance of magic. But without its power and guidance early man could not have mastered his practical difficulties as he has done, nor could man have advanced to the higher stages of civilization."

## CRITICAL THINKING QUESTIONS

1. It's not at all clear that the Nacirema see themselves as Horace Miner, the author of this essay, sees them. But an interpretation that makes no sense to members of the culture being described is not necessarily wrong. Outsiders may be able to perceive essential truths invisible to members of a culture. Given this, how do anthropologists know if their descriptions and analyses are accurate?

2. The Nacirema raise many critical issues for anthropologists. Miner presents a vivid picture of a culture that will probably strike you as strange and different. Do you feel that he is giving a balanced account, or is he biased? If you think he is biased, what elements of the essay make you feel that way?

3. Many essays in anthropology have political and social implications. By drawing our attention to aspects of other cultures, anthropologists implicitly ask us to examine our own. What do you think the social and political goals of this essay are?

Source: Horace Miner, "Body Ritual among the Nacirema." From *The American Anthropologist*, 1956, 58:503–507.

gives us insight into the histories and migrations of those who speak them.

The technological changes of the past two decades have opened a new world of communications. The widespread use of cell phones, e-mail, texting, and social networking sites such as Facebook create entirely new ways of communicating, changing both the occasions on which people communicate and the language they use. For example, 20 years ago, people who live at great distance from each other communicated relatively rarely. The mail was often slow and phone calls expensive. Now, such people may communicate many times daily, speaking on the phone and visiting each other's websites. Cell phones in particular have become extremely important in poorer nations. For example, in 1998 there were no cell phones in Botswana. But by 2006 there were more than 800,000, enough for half the total population and more than six times the number of land lines (OSISA n.d.). Cell phone usage is explored in more detail in

Archaeologists attempt to reconstruct past cultures by studying their material remains, as in this dig at an early settler cabin in Texas.

Courtesy of Ronald Coley

ing systems have been deciphered. However, even when an extensive written record is available, as in the case of Ancient Greece or Colonial America, archaeology can help increase our understanding of the cultures and lifeways of those who came before us.

The archaeologist does not observe human behavior and culture directly but reconstructs them from material remains or artifacts. An **artifact** is any object that has been made, used, or altered by human beings. Artifacts include pottery, tools, garbage, and whatever else a society has left behind.

In the popular media, archaeology is mainly identified with spectacular discoveries of artifacts from prehistoric and ancient cultures, such as the tomb of the Egyptian king Tutankhamen. As a result, people often think of archaeologists as collectors of ancient artifacts. But contemporary archaeologists are much more interested in understanding and explaining their finds in terms of what they say about the behavior that produced them than in creating collections. Their principal task is to infer the nature of past cultures based on the patterns of the artifacts left behind. Archaeologists work like detectives, slowly sifting and interpreting evidence. The context in which things are found, the location of an archaeological site, and the precise position of an artifact within that site are critical to interpretation. In fact, these may be more important than the artifact itself.

There are many different specialties within archaeology. **Urban archaeology** is a good example. Urban archaeologists delve into the recent and distant past of current-day cities. In doing so, they uncover knowledge of the people often left out of the history books, making our understanding of the past far richer than it was. For example, Elizabeth Scott's work at Nina Plantation in Louisiana (2001) adds to our understanding of the lives of slaves and free laborers from the 1820s to the 1890s, and the discovery of an African burial ground in New York City in 1991 provides us with insight into the lives of free and enslaved Africans in the 17th and 18th centuries.

Another important archeology subfield is **cultural resource management,** or **CRM.** Archaeologists working in CRM are concerned with the protection and management of archaeological, archival, and architectural resources. They are often employed by federal, state, and local agencies to develop and implement plans for the protection and management of such cultural resources.

the "Ethnography" section in Chapter 5. Studying these changes in communication is an exciting new challenge for linguistic anthropologists.

Understanding language is a critical task for people interested in developing new technology as well. We live in a world where computers talk to us and listen to us. We will only be able to build machines that use language effectively if we understand how language is structured and used by humans.

## Archaeology

Archaeologists add a vital time dimension to our understanding of cultures and how they change. **Archaeology** is the study of past cultures through their material remains.

Many archaeologists study **prehistoric** societies—those for which no written records have been found or no writ-

**archaeology** The subdiscipline of anthropology that focuses on the reconstruction of past cultures based on their material remains.

**prehistoric** Societies for which we have no usable written records.

**artifact** Any object made or modified by human beings. Generally used to refer to objects made by past cultures.

**urban archaeology** The archeological investigation of towns and cities as well as the process of urbanization.

**cultural resource management (CRM)** The protection and management of archaeological, archival, and architectural resources.

## Physical or Biological Anthropology

The human ability to survive under a broad range of conditions is based primarily on the enormous flexibility of cultural behavior. The capacity for culture, however, is grounded in our biological history and physical makeup. Human adaptation is thus biocultural; that is, it involves both biological and cultural dimensions. Therefore, to understand fully what it is to be human, we need a sense of how the biological aspects of this adaptation came about and how they influence human cultural behavior.

**Biological** (or **physical**) **anthropology** is the study of humankind from a biological perspective. It focuses primarily on those aspects of humanity that are genetically inherited. Biological anthropology includes numerous subfields, such as skeletal analysis, or osteology; the study of human nutrition; demography, or the statistical study of human populations; epidemiology, or the study of patterns of disease; and primatology.

Biological anthropology is probably best known for the study of human evolution and the biological processes involved in human adaptation. Paleoanthropologists search for the origins of humanity, using the fossil record to trace the history of human evolution. They study the remains of the earliest human forms, as well as those ancestral to humans and related to humans. We explore some of the findings of **paleoanthropology** in Chapter 2.

Another subspecialty of biological anthropology, called **human variation,** is concerned with physiological differences among humans. Anthropologists who study human variation map physiological differences among modern human groups and attempt to explain the sources of this diversity.

Because the human species evolved through a complex feedback system involving both biological and cultural factors, biological anthropologists are also interested in the evolution of culture. Our unique evolutionary history resulted in the development of a biological structure, the human brain, capable of inventing, learning, and using cultural adaptations. Cultural adaptation, in turn, has freed humans from the slow process of biological adaptation: populations can invent new ways of dealing with problems almost immediately, or adopt solutions from other societies. The study of the complex relationship between biological and cultural evolution links biological anthropology, cultural anthropology, and archaeology.

In addition to studying living human groups, biological anthropologists study living nonhuman **primates,** members of the order that includes monkeys, apes, and humans. Primates are studied for the clues that their chemistry, physiology, morphology (physical structure), and behavior provide about our own species. At one time primates were studied mainly in the artificial settings of laboratories and zoos, but now much of the work of bio-

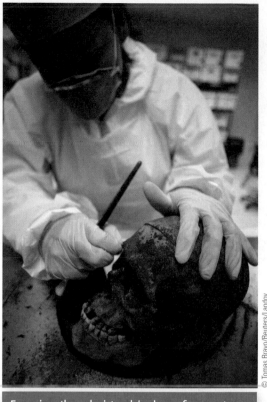

Forensic anthropologists advise law enforcement agencies and other organizations about the identity of victims of crime, political violence, and natural disaster. Here a forensic anthropologist cleans a skull exhumed from a mass grave near Juarez, Mexico.

logical anthropologists involves studying these animals in the wild. Jane Goodall and Dian Fossey are two well-known anthropologists who studied primates in the wild. Fossey, who died in 1985, worked with gorillas in Rwanda. Goodall works with chimpanzees in Tanzania.

## Applied Anthropology

Although anthropology is mainly concerned with basic research—that is, asking the big questions about the origins of our species, the development of culture and civi-

**biological (or physical) anthropology** The subdiscipline of anthropology that studies people from a biological perspective, focusing primarily on aspects of humankind that are genetically inherited. It includes osteology, nutrition, demography, epidemiology, and primatology.

**paleoanthropology** The subdiscipline of anthropology concerned with tracing the evolution of humankind in the fossil record.

**human variation** The subdiscipline of anthropology concerned with mapping and explaining physical differences among modern human groups.

**primate** A member of a biological order of mammals that includes human beings, apes, and monkeys as well as prosimians (lemurs, tarsiers, and others).

## Medical Anthropology

Over the past century important advances in preventing disease and improving health care have been made. Yet the modern medical model has serious limitations in dealing with health issues in different cultures and among different ethnic, racial, and class populations in the United States (Helman 1998/1991). **Medical anthropology** draws upon social, cultural, biological, and linguistic anthropology to better understand those factors that influence health and well-being. It is concerned with the experience of disease as well as its distribution, prevention, and treatment.

Medical anthropologists adapt the holistic and ethnographic approaches of anthropology to the study of health and disease in diverse societies. Modern biomedicine tends to regard diseases as universal entities, regardless of their contexts. However, medical anthropologists have found that disease and medicine never exist independently of particular cultural and historical contexts. Health and disease are not just biological notions, but fundamentally socio-cultural and political-economic concepts.

One result of the rethinking of the ideas of sickness and health has been to make medical anthropology more critical and more politically engaged. For example, Baer, Singer, and Sussman (1997) note that it is unproductive to think of health apart from wealth. The degree to which people in different societies have the ability to gain access to resources such as food and water as well as the goods and social positions their society values is a critical determinant of health. Medical anthropologist and psychiatrist Arthur Kleinman (1995) notes that the body connects individual and group experience. Trauma caused by violence and depression caused by chronic pain are best understood as personal experiences of broader social concerns rather than simply individual medical problems. The implication is that medical ills are closely related to social problems. Effectively treating the first sometimes requires addressing the second. Kleinman and other medical anthropologists are particularly interested in examining the culture of suffering or "the manner in which an ill person manifests his or her disease or distress" (Scheper-Hughes and Lock 1990).

Medical anthropologists do much more than provide broad social, cultural, and political perspectives on health and health-care institutions. They help to bridge the gap between medical service providers and their clientele (Schensul 1997). Their ethnographic methodology often emphasizes the patient's experience of disease and treat-

lization, and the functions of human social institutions—anthropologists also put their knowledge to work to solve human problems.

**Applied anthropologists** are generally trained in one of the four subdisciplines we have already mentioned. However, they work with governments, corporations, and other organizations to use anthropological research techniques to solve social, political, and economic problems. In this book, we highlight some of the work of applied anthropologists. Each chapter includes a feature titled "Anthropology Makes a Difference." There, you will read about some of the ways anthropologists are involved in the practical worlds of business, medicine, public policy, law enforcement, and communication.

Specialists in each of the subfields of anthropology make contributions to applied work. For example, in cultural anthropology, experts in the anthropology of agriculture use their knowledge to help people with reforestation, water management, and agricultural productivity. Cultural anthropologists have been instrumental in many organizations that promote the welfare of tribal and **indigenous peoples** throughout the world. Such organizations include Cultural Survival, founded by anthropologist David Maybury-Lewis; The Center for World Indigenous Studies; Survival International; and the Avenir des Peuples des Forets Tropicales/The Future of Tropical Rainforest Peoples, an organization devoted to the welfare of indigenous peoples living in the tropical rainforest.

Anthropologists who study legal and criminal justice systems address such problems as drug abuse or racial and ethnic conflict. Alternative forms of conflict resolution, such as mediation, which grew out of anthropological studies of non-Western societies, are now being used in American courts, as adversarial litigation proves itself unequal to the task of efficiently resolving civil disputes. Psychological and educational anthropologists contribute to the more effective development and implementation of educational and mental-health policies, and medical anthropologists apply their cross-cultural knowledge to improve health care, sanitation, diet, and disease control in a variety of cultural contexts.

**medical anthropology** A subfield of cultural anthropology concerned with the ways in which disease is understood and treated in different cultures.

**applied anthropology** The application of anthropology to the solution of human problems.

**indigenous peoples** Societies that have occupied a region for a long time and are recognized by other groups as its original (or very ancient) inhabitants.

ment. Results of their studies can be used to increase a community's ability to make positive changes in its health programs.

In addition to studying the way ill people understand disease and its cure, anthropologists are increasingly interested in analyzing the medical profession itself and the way it both influences and is influenced by larger cultural patterns. For example, Sharon R. Kaufman (2000) examined the special facilities for the terminally comatose. Her study explored how technology and the medical specialists associated with keeping alive persons in a vegetative state are transforming the concept of the person in American culture.

Anthropology has long had an interest in the cultural aspects of emotional disturbance. Well-known anthropological works on this subject include Jules Henry's (1973) analysis of families with autistic children and Ruth and Stanley Freed's (1985) study of ghost possession. In keeping with this interest, the socialization and training of psychiatric practitioners has been the subject of anthropological scrutiny. In *Of Two Minds: The Growing Disorder in American Psychiatry*, anthropologist Tanya Luhrmann (2000) examines the socialization of doctors who specialize in psychiatry in the United States. The major question that shapes psychiatric training is whether mental illnesses are a matter of biological dysfunction best treated pharmacologically, or whether they are the product of psychosocial factors such as family dynamics and thus best treated by psychotherapy. Lurhmann found that psychiatric training takes an either/or approach to this question. Psychiatric residents must decide which camp they are in by the second year of residency. Once that decision is made, it has enormous implications for their perception and treatment of emotional disturbance. However, Luhrmann notes that doctors do not make this decision in a vacuum. Antipsychotic drugs heavily promoted by pharmaceutical companies, the efforts of insurers to control their costs, and political pressure to limit the cost of health care all militate against a psychosocial understanding of disease and treatment through psychotherapy.

The work of medical anthropologists emphasizes the complex relationship of biology and culture and the ways in which cultural, political, and economic context shapes both disease and medical practice. Medical anthropologists offer insights that help improve the organization and practice of health care in the United States and around the world.

Archaeology has numerous applications. Establishing the archaeological record has often enabled native peoples to gain access to land and resources that historically belonged to them. Work in archaeology is often basic to understanding the history of groups that left little record. Excavations such as that done at the African-American burial ground in New York City (Harrington 1993) give us insight into the living conditions of groups not well represented in the written record. Such knowledge is frequently fundamental to cultural identity. Beyond this, archaeology has often produced technical applications. For example, in Israel's Negev Desert, in Peru, and in other locations, archaeological study of ancient peoples has yielded information about irrigation design and raised-field systems that allowed modern people to make more effective use of the environment and raise agricultural yields (Downum and Price 1999).

Biological anthropologists shed light on some of the major diseases of the modern industrial world. They compare our diet and lifestyle with those of prehistoric and contemporary foraging peoples who suffer less from heart disease, high blood pressure, and diabetes (Eaton and Konner 1989). **Forensic anthropologists** use their knowledge of human skeletal biology to discover information about the victims of crimes, aiding in law enforcement and judicial proceedings.

Private industry has become a major consumer of anthropological talent. More than two dozen anthropologists work for the technology consulting firm Sapient. Anthropologists can also be found working at Microsoft, Intel, Kodak, Whirlpool, AT&T, Hallmark, General Motors, and many other large corporations. They have been instrumental in developing many consumer products. For example, you might not think anthropology when you eat Go-Gurt (a popular brand of yogurt packaged in a tube), but this product was developed as a result of ethnographic research by Susan Squires, an anthropologist working for General Mills.

Although it is true that there are many careers in anthropology, it is our conviction that applied anthropology is more than just people earning their living with the skills they gained through training in anthropology. Perhaps the most important aspect of anthropology (and the primary justification for its existence) is the way an anthropological perspective demands that we open our eyes and experience the world in new ways. In a sense, anthropology is like teaching fish the meaning of water. How could a fish understand water? Water is all a fish knows; and it knows

**forensic anthropology** The application of biological anthropology to the identification of skeletalized or badly decomposed human remains.

it so well it cannot distinguish it from the nature of life and reality itself. Similarly, all humans live in cultures and our experiences are normally bounded by our cultures. We often mistake the realities and truths of our culture for reality and truth itself, thinking that the ways we understand and do things are the only appropriate ways of understanding and doing.

The fish only understands the meaning of water when it's removed from the water (usually with fatal consequences). If anthropology is not exactly about removing people from their culture, it is, in a sense, the conscious attempt to allow people to see beyond its bounds. Through learning about other cultures, we become increasingly aware of the variety of different understandings present in the world and of the social dynamics that underlie culture. This promotes an awareness of the meanings and dynamics of our own culture and, if we're fortunate, allows us to look at the problems that confront us with a fresh vision.

Applied anthropology doesn't just mean that you get paid to use your anthropological training. All of us do applied anthropology when we bring anthropological understandings and insight to bear on problems of poverty, education, war, and peace. We don't apply anthropology only when we write a report. We apply anthropology when we go to the voting booth and to the grocery store, when we discuss issues with our friends and, if we're religious, when we pray. Anthropology provides no simple answers. There is no correct anthropological way to vote, shop, or pray. However, anthropology does inform our decisions about these things. Our attempt to understand other cultures and our own lets us look on these things with new eyes.

In the "Anthropology Makes a Difference" boxes featured in each chapter of this book, you'll find interesting ways that people have made careers of anthropology and used it to help others: However, you'll also find examples of the ways in which anthropology contributes to our understanding of the world. Ultimately, our lives are more about the ways in which we exemplify the meanings and values that we hold than about how we make our living. For some, anthropology is a career, but it informs the lives of all who study it seriously.

# Some Critical Issues in Anthropology

A major contribution of anthropology is to demonstrate the importance and variability of culture in human societies. The remainder of this book describes various human societies and examines their differences and similarities in detail. However, there are several issues to consider before we begin this investigation. These include the nature of ethnocentrism, the meaning and importance of cultural relativism in anthropology, the ways in which anthropologists understand race, and the importance of the development of a global economic system. These are issues that cultural anthropologists must always address, regardless of their subject of study or their perspective. Anthropological understandings of these issues inform much of the discussion and description in this book.

## Ethnocentrism

When we look at those who are different from ourselves, we are often in the position of a deaf man who sees a bunch of people with fiddles and drums, jumping around every which way, and thinks they are crazy. He cannot hear the music, so he doesn't see that they are dancing (Myerhoff 1978). Similarly, a person who does not hear the music of another culture cannot make sense of its dance. In other words, if we assume that the understandings, patternings, and rules of other cultures are the same as our own, then the actions of other people may seem incomprehensible. One of the most important contributions of anthropology is its ability to open our ears to the music and meaning in other cultures. It challenges and corrects our ethnocentrism.

**Ethnocentrism** is the notion that one's own culture is superior to any other. It is the idea that other cultures should be measured by the degree to which they live up to our cultural standards. We are ethnocentric when we view other cultures through the narrow lens of our own culture or social position.

The American tourist who, presented with a handful of Mexican pesos, asks "How much is this in real money?" is being ethnocentric—but there is nothing uniquely American about ethnocentrism. People all over the world tend to see things from their own culturally patterned point of view, through their own cultural filters. They tend to value what they have been taught to value and to see the meaning of life in terms of their own culturally defined purposes. For example, people in Highland New Guinea understood the world of conscious beings to be composed of themselves, their allies, their enemies, and spirits, including ancestors, gods, and other figures. When they first encountered European outsiders in the 1930s, they rapidly classified them as spirits and believed that the carriers who accompanied them were their dead relatives. It was the only way that these people could initially make sense of what they were seeing (Connolly and Anderson 1987:36-37).

Although most peoples are ethnocentric, the ethnocentrism of Western societies has had greater consequences than that of smaller, less technologically advanced, and more geographically isolated peoples. The

**ethnocentrism** Judging other cultures from the perspective of one's own culture. The notion that one's own culture is more beautiful, rational, and nearer to perfection than any other.

WORLD'S HIGHEST STANDARD OF LIVING

There's no way like the American Way

© Margaret Bourke-White/Stringer/Time Life Pictures/Getty Images

Ethnocentrism is the notion that one's own culture is superior to any other. This famous photograph, taken in 1937 by Margaret Bourke-White, illustrates the ethnocentric idea that American culture is superior to others. However, it also shows us how ethnocentrism may blind us to the problems of our own society, in this case, racism. Note that the passengers in the car are white but the people in the bread line below are black.

racism—beliefs, actions, and patterns of social organization that exclude individuals and groups from the equal exercise of human rights and fundamental freedoms.

The transformation from ethnocentrism to racism underlies much of the structural inequality that characterizes modern history.

## Anthropology and Cultural Relativism

Anthropology helps us understand peoples whose ways of life are different from our own but with whom we share a common human destiny. However, we can never understand a people's behavior if we insist on judging it first. **Cultural relativism** is the notion that a people's values and customs must be understood in terms of the culture of which they are a part. Cultural relativists maintain that, for the sake of scientific accuracy, anthropologists must suspend judgment in order to understand the logic and dynamics of other cultures. Researchers who view the actions of other people simply in terms of the degree to which they correspond to the observers' notions of right and wrong systematically distort the cultures they study.

Cultural relativism is a fundamental research tool of anthropology. It is distinct from moral relativism—the notion that because no universal standard of behavior exists, people should not judge behaviors as good or evil. Anthropological methods may require researchers to suspend judgment but not to dispense with it entirely. Anthropologists are not required to approve of all cultural practices. However, it is possible to understand other cultures without approving of them. Anthropologists insist that every culture has a logic that makes sense to its own members. It is our job to understand that logic, even if we do not approve of it or wish that culture for ourselves.

Using the anthropological technique of cultural relativism helps us to see that our own culture is only one design for living among the many in the history of humankind. We can see that our culture came into being

historical circumstances that led to the spread of Western culture have given its members a strong belief in its rightness and superiority. Westerners have been in a position to impose their beliefs and practices on other peoples because of their wealth and their superior military technology. It may matter little, for example, to the average Frenchman if the Dogon (an ethnic group in Mali) believe that their way of life and beliefs are superior. The Dogon have little ability to affect events in France. However, it mattered a great deal to the Dogon that the French believed that their way of life and beliefs were superior. The French colonized Mali and imposed their beliefs and institutions on its people.

Although ethnocentrism gets in the way of understanding, some ethnocentrism seems necessary as a kind of glue to hold a society together. A group's belief in the superiority of its own way of life binds its members together and helps them to perpetuate their values. When a culture loses value for its people, they may experience **anomie,** a condition where social and moral norms are absent or confused. This results in great emotional stress and culture members may even lose interest in living. Such people may be rapidly absorbed by other groups and their culture lost.

To the extent that ethnocentrism prevents building bridges between cultures, however, it is maladaptive. When one culture is motivated by ethnocentrism to trespass on another, the harm done can be enormous. It is but a short step from this kind of ethnocentrism to

**anomie** A situation where social or moral norms are confused or entirely absent; often caused by rapid social change.

**racism** The belief that some human populations are superior to others because of inherited, genetically transmitted characteristics.

**cultural relativism** The notion that cultures should be analyzed with reference to their own histories and values, in terms of the cultural whole, rather than according to the values of another culture.

Race is a cultural construction that draws upon biologically based criteria to divide people into social groups. Race emerges in specific historical contexts. The understandings of race in the United States reflect the American slavery. Since a clear distinction between slaves and masters was essential, historically most people in the United States were assigned to either "black" or "white" racial categories. Brazil and other parts of Latin America had different historical experiences resulting in more numerous racial categories.

man groups, one of the important outcomes of human evolution is the wide variation in human form. Some people are short, others are tall; skin color covers a spectrum from very dark to very light; some people have slight builds, others are husky. The degree to which humans vary is even more startling when less obvious differences, such as blood type and other biochemical traits, are taken into account. Moreover, this biological diversity follows geographic patterns, with people from the same region tending to share more traits with each other than they do with people from distant lands. Some of these variations are discussed in greater detail in Chapter 2.

A particularly salient aspect of culture in the United States, and throughout much of the world today, is the assumption that the range of human diversity is best understood as a small number of biologically separate races. Over the past two centuries, scientists have struggled to create a consistent system to identify and classify these races. It may come as a surprise to learn that despite hundreds of years of labor by enormously creative and intelligent researchers, no agreed upon, consistent system of racial classification has ever been developed. Furthermore, other cultures construct racial categories differently than Americans (see Chapter 12).

Anthropology in the United States has always been concerned with questions of race. At the turn of the century, Franz Boas, one of the founders of modern American anthropology, argued passionately for **biopsychological equality**—the notion that although individuals differ, all

under a particular set of historical circumstances. It is not the inevitable end result of human social evolution. Understanding this provides a much needed corrective for ethnocentrism.

From its beginnings, anthropology held out a dual promise: contributing to the understanding of human diversity, and providing a cultural critique of our own society (Marcus and Fischer 1986). By becoming aware of cultural alternatives, we are better able to see ourselves as others see us and to use that knowledge to make constructive changes in our own society. Through looking at the "other," we come to understand ourselves.

## Human Biological Diversity and Race

Anthropology shows us that there are important and often dramatic differences between cultures. However, it also shows us that, despite all of these differences, from a biological perspective, people are overwhelmingly similar. In fact, compared with other closely related species, the human species shows extremely low levels of morphological (skeletal) and serological (blood type) diversity.

Despite the compelling biological similarity of all hu-

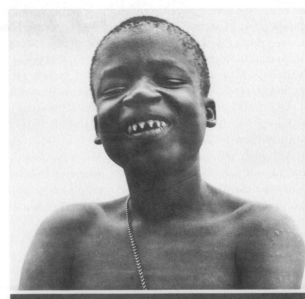

Ota Benga, a pygmy, was brought to the United States for the Africa exhibit at the St. Louis World's Fair in 1904. He was briefly exhibited at the monkey house in the Bronx Zoo in New York. The implication of the exhibit was that people such as Ota Benga were more similar to chimpanzees than to white Americans. Such exhibitions reinforced the mistaken notion that Africans were biologically inferior to Europeans.

**biopsychological equality** The notion that all human groups have the same biological and mental capabilities.

human beings have equal capacity for culture. Before World War II, however, many physical anthropologists attempted to create systems to divide humanity into races and rank them. Today most anthropologists agree that there is no way of doing this and that race, as a biological characteristic of humans, does not exist (American Anthropological Association 1998; Shanklin 1994). Human beings are truly all members of a single race.

In biological terms, no group of humans has ever been isolated for long enough to make it very different from others and, as a result, our similarities are far more compelling than our differences. Thus, anthropologists understand systems of racial classification as reflecting history and social hierarchy rather than biology. Prejudice and racism are certainly realities, but they are not rooted in biological differences between people (Kilker 1993; L. Reynolds 1992).

The notion that races are not biological categories might seem unusual and counterintuitive. Thus, it is worth a brief detour to point out the problems with the notion of biological race. These problems are many, but three are especially important: the arbitrary selection of traits used to define races; the inability to adequately describe within-species variation through the use of racial categories; and the repeated independent evolution of so-called racial characteristics in populations with no genetic relationship.

Each human being is a collection of thousands of characteristics such as skin color, blood type, tolerance to lactose (milk sugar), tooth shape, and so on. Variations in these traits result from both genetic and environmental factors as well as interactions between the two. There is no way to weight the importance of any trait in determining racial classification—no reason, for example, why blood type should be intrinsically more or less important than lactose tolerance, skin color, or hair shape. However, schemes of racial classification select a very small number of traits and ignore others. Such systems typically assume that the traits they have selected have a very strong genetic basis and that these traits are more significant than others, which they ignore. The problem with such schemes is that they identify races that are simply the result of the particular traits the researchers have chosen. In other words, if different traits were chosen, different races would result. Jared Diamond (1994) notes that identifying a race on the basis of lactose tolerance is as valid as basing a racial group on any other trait. However, if we did so, we would group Norwegians, Arabs, North Indians, and some Africans into one race, while excluding other peoples. There is no reason at all to believe that lactose tolerance correlates with features of personality such as entrepreneurial drive, intelligence, or sexuality. However, there is no reason to believe that eye shape or hair texture correlate with these either.

It is no accident that the characteristics the members of many cultural groups, including Americans, choose as racial markers are traits such as skin color, eye shape, nose shape, and hair texture. These traits are not chosen for their biological importance but because they are easily visible. Thus, they make it relatively easy to immediately assign individuals to races. Using blood types, lactose intolerance, or dry versus wet earwax to determine race would be as logical as other means of defining racial groups, but because such traits are not easily seen, they would be socially useless.

Variation within socially constructed races also presents enormous problems. Obvious and obscure physical differences between members of the same so-called race are enormous, typically exceeding differences between average members of racial groups. In fact, studies using biological measures make it clear that individual differences between people are much greater than racial differences. In other words, measured genetically, you are about as different from another person of your race as you are from another person of a different race.

To illustrate the importance of variation within races, imagine lining up all the students on your campus according to the color of their skin. Assuming the student population is large enough, all skin tones, from the very light people at one end of the line to the very dark people at the other, would be represented. The vast majority of people would fall in between the extremes. At what point would white become black? Are people who stand close to each other in the line necessarily more closely related than those who stand farther apart? In fact, there is no way to tell who is related to whom by looking at the line.

Finally, the traits that are typically used to define races have arisen repeatedly and independently throughout the world and are the result of common forms of evolution. Most theories of race assume that people who share similar racial characteristics share similar origins. The fact that traits arise recurrently, however, means that this assumption is faulty: people who share similar traits are not necessarily more closely related to each other than to people of other races.

It is often imagined, for example, that all black people are descendants of a group of central Africans and all white people are descendants of a group who lived in the Caucasus Mountains. In fact, this is biological nonsense. To illustrate this point, consider people from the Central African Republic, Papua New Guinea, and France. People from the Central African Republic and Papua New Guinea (off the coast of Australia in Melanesia) are likely to have dark skin, similar hair texture, and share other features. Most people from France are likely to have light skin and have hair texture and other features that look quite different from Africans and Papua New Guineans. From this, one might conclude that Central Africans and Papua New Guineans are more closely related to each other than either is to the French. This is incorrect. Molecular genetic data tell us that Africans and Melanesians show a great deal of genetic divergence. Europeans are more closely related to both Africans and Papua New Guineans than either is to the other (Templeton 1998:640).

The notion that perceived differences between social groups are caused by racial inheritance has no biological validity and must be dismissed. People who wish to argue that racial groups have differing biologically based abilities must first show that such groups are biologically distinct. This has not been done and is probably impossible to do.

One of the most important things we can learn by studying anthropology is that although racism is an important social fact, the big differences among human groups are the result of culture, not biological inheritance or race. All human beings belong to the same species, and the biological features essential to human life are common to us all. A human being from any part of the world will learn the cultural and behavioral patterns of the group in which he or she is raised. Adaptation through culture and the potential for cultural richness and creativity are part of a universal human heritage and override any physical variation among human groups. Issues of race and racism are treated in numerous places in this book. (See pages 40–44 in Chapter 2 for additional information about race, and pages 271–278 in Chapter 12 for a more detailed analysis of racism.)

## Anthropology in a Changing World

From the late 19th through the mid-20th century, when anthropology was developing as a field of study, much of the world was colonized by powerful nations. These nations often held ethnic minorities and traditional societies as subjugated populations within their own borders. It was frequently among these colonized and oppressed peoples that anthropologists worked. For example, British and French anthropologists worked among colonized people in Africa. American anthropologists often worked with Native American populations or Pacific Islanders in areas under U.S. control.

Doing anthropological research under such conditions had several implications. First, communities had little control over whether or not to accept an anthropologist. If the government assigned anthropologists to a village, the residents had to accept them. Second, anthropologists did not have to be responsive to the political or economic needs of the people among whom they worked. Finally, very few of the people among whom anthropologists worked either knew how to read European languages or had access to the libraries and bookstores where anthropological works were available. Thus anthropologists had little fear their work could be contradicted by those about whom they wrote. Although anthropologists during these times frequently did outstanding research, the conditions under which they worked inevitably affected their descriptions of society.

After World War II, international conditions began to change. Most colonies held by Western powers gained their independence in the 1960s. Political liberties were longer in coming in areas held by the Soviet Union, but by the close of the 20th century the vast majority of people lived in independent nations. Furthermore, education in Western languages became increasingly available, and communication by radio, television, telephone, and the Internet has become ubiquitous.

These changes have profoundly affected anthropology. In order to work, anthropologists must now negotiate with independent governments. Community members have much more say in deciding whether to accept anthropologists. Anthropologists can often be certain that at least some of the people they work with will hear about or read about the results of their research. Additionally, anthropologists now come from many of the communities that anthropologists have traditionally studied. These individuals, as well as many others, raise hard questions about the nature of the discipline (Clifford and Marcus 1986; di Leonardo 1991; Hooks 1989; Marcus 1992; Rosaldo 1993; Said 1993; Yanagisako and Delaney 1994). They challenge the accuracy of past anthropological reporting and raise doubts about the ability of anthropologists to accurately describe cultures. They urge us to consider exactly whose story gets told and why.

Issues such as these present interesting theoretical challenges to anthropology. But they are also very important because anthropological research often has political implications. As contemporary social groups, whether nations or smaller units within nations, search for identity and autonomy, cultural representations become important resources, and traditions once taken for granted become the subject of heightened political consciousness. People want their cultures to be represented to the outside world in ways acceptable to them and are holding anthropologists responsible for the political impact of their work.

Anthropologists have responded to these challenges in a variety of ways. For example, anthropologists have become much more explicit about the exact conditions under which their data were collected. They increasingly present their work using multiple viewpoints, trying to tell the story of a culture from the perspective not only of the detached social scientist, but also of men, women, and children of the society under study. Additionally, many have become politically active, fighting for the rights of oppressed minorities and traditional peoples throughout the world.

The challenges to anthropology and the discipline's response to them have caused enormous controversy. Some theorists insist that anthropology must be committed and engaged. They argue that it is the duty of anthropologists to defend the rights of the oppressed and present the views of those who have not previously been heard. Others argue that such political engagement distorts anthropological research and that anthropologists should be concerned with gathering data as objectively as possible and using it to increase our theoretical knowledge of the underlying dynamics of human society. (See D'Andrade, Scheper-Hughes, et al. 1995 for a good exploration of this debate.)

We firmly believe that anthropology benefits from lively discussion of its role and meaning. The participation of anthropologists from many backgrounds, as well as members of the communities anthropologists study, makes the discipline richer and the debate more useful.

## Anthropology and Globalization

During the early years of anthropology in the 19th and early 20th century, anthropologists usually studied societies as if each culture was a separate, well-defined, and isolated unit. Books from this era often include exhaustive descriptions of individual cultures but contain only scant mention of the relationships between cultures. For example, A. R. Radcliffe-Brown's *The Andaman Islanders,* a well-known ethnography first published in 1922, described people living on an archipelago in the Indian Ocean between India and Thailand. *The Andaman Islanders* has 500 pages of description and analysis of social organization, ceremonies, religious customs, and technology but only one or two pages describing the connections between the islands and the rest of the world.

Even in the era when Radcliffe-Brown wrote, the Andamans were only relatively isolated. The British government established a penal colony on the Andamans in the 18th century, and contacts between the islands and the outside world were well established by the time Radcliffe-Brown arrived more than a century later. In fact, Radcliffe-Brown actually did his work by interviewing people at Andaman Homes, an institution founded by a colonial clergyman that functioned as something between a prison and a boarding school (Pandya 2005.; Mukerjee 2003:50).

Today, the Andaman Islands remain remote to the rest of the world. However, you can fly from New York City to the Andamans on regularly scheduled service in under two days. You can book your vacation there through www.andamanholidays.com and stay at one of several resorts. You can join the Switzerland-based Andaman Association, and you can view more than 13,000 pictures from the Andamans on Flickr.com. However, this increased contact has not been good for all of the Islands' residents. One hundred and fifty years ago, there were perhaps 5000 to 8000 indigenous people living on the Andaman Islands. Today, the total population is almost 400,000 but there are fewer than 500 indigenous people. One indigenous group, the Jarawas, remained more or less isolated until the 1990s, when a highway extended into their territory, bringing timber companies,

tourists, poachers, and disease. Today, the Jarawa are the largest indigenous group but only about 250 remain.

One of the most compelling facts of our world is that no place is truly isolated. Today, we are connected with one another by lines of transportation and communication. Even more important, we are connected by flows of money, products, and information. Policy decisions, wars, natural disasters, fashions, and tastes in one part of the globe have profound effects on the lives of people in many parts of the world. Wars in the Middle East directly affect the lives of American servicemen and their families as well as the millions who live in areas of political instability. The consumption habits of Americans and Chinese affect each other as the price of oil moves up and down in dramatic swings. Styles in clothing in the West affect the lives of villagers in Asia and Latin America as corporations search for the cheapest and most efficient way to produce products. Migration has become so extensive that anyone living in a large Western city is likely to come into contact with people from all over the world every day. Conversely, individuals living in poverty in rural Africa, Asia, and Latin America are likely to have relatives living in large cities in the United States, Europe, or the Arab World.

Globalization has affected anthropology in at least two important ways. First, anthropologists have often worked with small, relatively isolated groups. These groups are usually virtually powerless in the modern nations that control their territory. Like the Andaman Islanders, such groups have often suffered enormously from increased contact with the outside world. They have been pushed onto smaller and smaller areas of land, decimated by disease, and exploited by corporations, governments, and even tourists. Anthropologists have responded by becoming increasingly engaged in political and social action. Anthropologists' interests in defending the rights of indigenous people has sometimes led to activist research in which anthropologists work together with the people they study to formulate strategies to end their oppression and improve their lives (Hale 2001:13).

Secondly, globalization has changed the ways in which anthropologists work and write. As we saw in the case of Radcliffe-Brown, until the late 20th century, anthropologists generally focused on the particular unique characteristics of the communities they studied. Today, they are far more likely to focus on the relationships and exchanges between those they study and the rest of the world. Anthropologists rarely write works that purport to describe an entire culture and it is unusual for their books to have titles like *The Andaman Islanders.* Instead, book titles reflect specific concerns and often focus on the connections between cultures. Some examples are *From Enslavement to Environmentalism: Politics on a Southern African Frontier* (Hughes 2006), *An Alliance of Women: Immigration and the Politics of Race* (Merrill 2006), and *Practicing Ethnography in a Globalizing*

*World: An Anthropological Odyssey* (Nash 2007). Even books that sound as if they might be descriptions of a single group emphasize global connections. Hillary Kahn's (2006) *Seeing and Being Seen: The Q'eqchi' Maya of Livingston, Guatemala, and Beyond* is a good example. It includes chapters on colonialism, the ways in which religious belief is connected to exchange with outsiders, and Q'eqchi' relations with their neighbors, the Garifuna, one quarter of whom have migrated to New York City (2006:12).

We explore the anthropology of globalization in many places in this book. The ethnographies in Chapter 6, for example, indicate how making a living in today's world ties many people to globalization. Chapter 7, "Economics," provides some additional background for understanding globalization. In Chapters 8 ("Kinship") and 11 ("Political Organization"), we examine the issues of global migration, and Chapter 10, "Gender," explores some of the new roles of women in a global economy. Religion, and art, too, now have global dimensions, which we explore in Chapters 13 and 14. Chapter 15, "Power, Conquest, and a World System," describes the historical development of economic and social links between disparate peoples, and in Chapter 16, "Culture, Change, and the Modern World," we examine many of the problems and prospects that face people in both wealthy and poor nations alike. In addition, each chapter of the book ends with a feature called "The Global and the Local," in which we offer examples of the ways in which global and local cultures interact with each other; these sections include discussion questions about this interaction.

## Why Study Anthropology?

If you're reading this book for a course at a college or university, and particularly if you are considering a major in anthropology, you've probably faced some strong questioning from friends and family members. Some may have known about anthropology and applauded your wisdom in taking this course. Others may have had no idea what anthropology is. Still others probably asked you what anthropology was good for and what you hoped to do with it. You might have told them that you want to work in one of the many aspects of applied anthropology or become a college professor, but we think there are other good answers as well.

Anthropology is, in most places, part of a liberal arts curriculum, which also generally includes English, Geography, History, Modern Languages, Philosophy, Political Science, Psychology, and Sociology, as well as other departments and programs. Some liberal arts departments have teacher training programs. If you want to teach middle school English, in most places you probably need a degree in English. Some liberal arts programs involve training in highly technical skills that are directly applicable to jobs. For example, geography departments may offer training in remote sensing, the acquisition and analysis of aerial photography, and multispectral and infrared imagery and radar imagery for use by government and business; these are highly complex skills with very specific job applications. However, the vast majority of liberal arts programs produce generalists. An undergraduate degree in psychology does not generally get you a job as a psychologist. Most people who study political science do not go on to be politicians, and few who study sociology go on to work as sociologists. In fact, survey data show that there is often little connection between people's undergraduate major and their eventual career. For example, in a survey of 3000 alumni from the University of Virginia School of Arts and Sciences, 70 percent reported that there was little such connection. And this survey included many who had majored in subjects that taught very specific technical skills (University of Virginia 2008.).

The fact is that both job prospects and the careers that people eventually pursue are about the same for students who study anthropology and those who major in other liberal arts disciplines. Like the others, anthropology graduates go on to government, business, and the professions. Some become executives at large corporations, some are restaurateurs, some are lawyers, some are doctors, some are social service workers, some sell insurance, some are government officials, some are diplomats, and yes, no doubt, some still live with their parents. And you could say the same of every other liberal arts program.

To refocus our question we might ask: What are the particular ways of thought that anthropology courses develop and that are applicable to the very broad range of occupations that anthropologists follow? How is anthropology different from other social science disciplines? Although there are certainly many ways to answer these questions, it seems to us that three are of particular importance.

First, anthropology is the university discipline that focuses on understanding other groups of people. This focus on culture is one of the most valuable contributions anthropology can make to our ability to understand our world, to analyze and solve problems.

Although America has always been an ethnically and culturally diverse place, for most of the 20th century, the reins of wealth and power were held by a dominant group: white Protestant men of Northern European ancestry. Members of other groups did sometimes become rich, and there were certainly many poor white Protestants. However, wealthy white Protestants held the majority of positions of influence and power in American society, including executive positions at most large corporations, high political offices at both state and national levels, and seats on the judiciary. As a result, if you hap-

America is once again a nation of immigrants. In 2007 about 12 percent of the U.S. population was foreign born. Here, new citizens recite the Pledge of Allegiance during naturalization ceremonies. At this ceremony at Fenway Park in Boston, more than 3,000 people took the oath of citizenship.

© AP Photo/Steven Senne

pened to be born white, Protestant, and male you had an advantage. Of course, you might inherit great wealth. But, even if (as was far more likely) you were the son of a factory hand or a shopkeeper, you were a representative of the dominant culture. The ways of the powerful were, more or less, your ways. If members of other cultural groups wanted to speak with you, do business with you, participate in public and civic affairs with you, they had to learn to do so on your terms. . . . not you on theirs. They not only had to learn to speak English, they had to learn the forms of address, body language, clothing, manners and so on, appropriate to their role in your culture. Because it was others who had to do the work of changing their behavior, you yourself were probably almost completely unaware of this disparity and accepted it simply as the way things are. *Miami Herald* columnist Leonard Pitts has pointed out that "if affirmative action is defined as giving preferential treatment on the basis of gender or race, then no one in this country has received more than white men (2007)." This is true whether such men wanted preference or even realized they were getting it.

Although the white, Protestant, Northern European male is hardly an extinct species in America (such people still today control most of the nation's wealth), by the late 20th century, their virtual monopoly on power began to break up. In America, members of minority groups have moved to stronger economic and political positions. Moreover, America increasingly exists in a world filled with other powerful nations with very different histories and traditions. It is less and less a world where everyone wants to do business with America and is willing to do so on American terms. Instead, it is a rapidly globalizing world characterized by corporations with headquarters and workforces spread across the world, by international

institutions such as the World Bank, the International Monetary Fund, and the World Trade Organization, and by capital and information flows that cross cultural boundaries in milliseconds. Americans who wish to understand and operate effectively in such a world must learn other cultures, and other ways; failure to do so puts them at a distinct disadvantage.

At home, America is once again a nation of immigrants. Until the late 20th century, most immigrants were cut off from their homelands by politics and by the expense and difficulty of communication. Under these conditions, assimilation to the dominant American culture was essential. Although politics will always be an issue, today's immigrants can, in most cases, communicate freely and inexpensively with family and friends in their homelands and may be able to travel back and forth on a regular basis. Thus, complete assimilation is far less necessary or desirable.

Some people may applaud multiculturalism, others may bemoan what they feel is the passing of the "American" way of life. What no one can really dispute is that the world of today is vastly different from the world of 1950. Given the increasing integration of economic systems, declining costs of communication and transportation, and the rising economic power of China and other nations, we can be sure that people of different ethnic, racial, and cultural backgrounds will meet more and more frequently in arenas where none has clear economic and cultural dominance. Thus, an understanding of the nature of culture and knowledge of the basic tools scholars have devised to analyze it is essential, and anthropology is the place to get it.

In addition to this first, very practical application, there is a second, more philosophical concern of anthropologists. Like scholars in many other disciplines, anthropologists grapple with the question of what it means to be a human being. However, anthropologists bring some unique tools to bear upon this issue. Within anthropology we can look for the answer to this question in two seemingly mutually exclusive ways. We can look at culture as simply the sum total of everything that humans have done, thought, created, and believed. In a sense, as individual humans, we are heirs to the vast array of cultural practices and experiences humans have ever had. Anthropology is the discipline that attempts to observe, collect, record, and understand the full range of human cultural experience. Through anthropology we know the great variety of forms that cultures can take. We know the huge variation in social organization, belief system, production, and family structure that is found in human society. This gives us insight into the plasticity of human society as well as the limits to that plasticity.

Alternatively, we can answer the question by ignoring the variability of human culture and focusing on the characteristics that all cultures share. In the 1940s, George Murdock listed 77 characteristics that he believed were common to all cultures. These included such things as dream interpretation, incest taboos, inheritance rules, and religious ritual. More recent authors (Brown 1991; Cleaveland, Craven, and Danfelser 1979) have developed other lists and analysis. Brown (1991:143) notes that human universals are very diverse and there is likely no single explanation for them. However, thinking about such commonalities among cultures may guide us in our attempt to understand human nature.

Finally, a third interest of anthropologists is in creating new and useful ways to think about culture. One particularly effective way to understand culture is to think of it as a set of answers to a particular problem: how does a group of human beings survive together in the world? In other words, culture is a set of behaviors, beliefs, understandings, objects, and ways of interacting that enable a group to survive with greater or lesser success and greater or lesser longevity. At some level, all human societies must answer this critical question and to some degree each culture is a different answer to it.

In the world today and in our own society we face extraordinary problems: hunger, poverty, inequality, violence between groups, violence within families, drug addiction, pollution, crime. . . . The list is long. However, we are not the only people in the world ever to have faced problems. At some level, all of these problems are the result of our attempt to live together as a group on this planet. Learning how other peoples in other places, and perhaps other times as well, solved their problems may give us the insight to solve our own; we might learn lessons, both positive and negative, from their cultural experiences.

In some ways the cultures of today are unique. Societies have never been as large and interconnected as many are today. They have never had the wealth that many societies have today. They have never had the levels of technology, abilities to communicate, and abilities to destroy that our current society has. These characteristics make it naive to imagine that we could simply observe a different culture, adopt their ways as our own, and live happily ever after. We can no more recreate tribal culture or ancient culture or even the culture of industrialized nations of 50 years ago than we can walk through walls. But it does not therefore follow that the answers of others are useless to us.

In Greek drama, the notion of hubris is critical. Hubris is probably best understood as excessive pride or confidence that leads to both arrogance and insolence toward others. In Greek tragedy, the hubris of characters is often their fatal flaw and leads to their downfall. Heroes such as Oedipus and Creon are doomed by their hubris.

We surely won't find that the members of other cultures have provided ready-made answers to all the problems that confront us. But to imagine ourselves as totally unique, to imagine that the experiences of other peoples and other cultures have nothing to teach us, is a form of hubris, and as in tragedy, could well lead to our downfall.

The ancient Greeks contrasted hubris with *arete.* This characteristic implies a humble striving for perfection along with the realization that such perfection cannot be reached. With the notion of *arete* in mind, we approach the study of anthropology cheerfully and with a degree of optimism. From anthropology we hope to learn new ways of analyzing, understanding, celebrating, and coming to terms with the enormous variations in human cultural behavior. We hope to be able to think creatively about what it means to be human beings and to use what we learn to provide insight into the issues, problems, and possibilities of our own culture. We hope that, with the help of such understanding, we will leave the world a better place than we found it.

# The Global and the Local: "Stone Age" Tribes versus Globalization

Introductory anthropology students often imagine that anthropologists go off to study groups that are wholly unaffected by the modern world and uncontaminated by its practices. For better or for worse, this is not the case: there have been no such groups for a long time. Members of industrialized cultures had reached virtually every group of people in the world by the time of World War I.

One exception to this occurred in the 1930s. Then, the Leahy brothers, Australian gold prospectors, made contact with the native peoples of Highland New Guinea. Although the purpose of their exploration was strictly economic, they took both still photos and movies. Their pictures as well as interviews with the brothers and the New Guineans they encountered are explored in the film *First Contact* and the book of the same name (Connolly and Anderson 1983, 1987).

Survival International, a British organization that promotes the interests of native peoples, reports that today there are about 70 tribes that choose to reject contact with outsiders. Of these, 50 live in the Brazilian Amazon (Survival International 2000). However, here, "uncontacted" is a relative term. These groups are neither unknown nor undiscovered. In many cases they have con-

Members of an "uncontacted" group in the Peruvian Amazon. Such groups are the descendants of survivors of bloody and violent contact with the outside world in the 19th and early 20th century.

tacts with neighboring tribes and in some cases members have visited the outside world. In Brazil, such groups are composed of the descendants of the survivors of bloody and violent contact with the outside world in the 19th and early 20th century. Some of them have fled after recent contact with missionaries (National Public Radio, 2008). Thus, rather than being people unaffected by the outside world, the members of uncontacted tribes are people who know of the outside world and choose to flee from it.

The current world population is approximately 6.8 billion. It is very difficult to estimate the total population of uncontacted people, but it is probably no more than 10,000, or about 1 uncontacted person for every 600,000 of world population. One of the most compelling facts of life in the 20th century is that although some groups of people are surely more isolated than others, virtually all groups are in contact with one another. Today, anthropologists are apt to find that the people they work with are well aware of events in the United States and the policies of governments around the world. They wear T-shirts with the names of American cities or professional sports teams and drink Coca-Cola. They get their news from the radio, television, and the Internet. Even in very remote locations, it is common to meet people who have traveled themselves or who have relatives living in the United States, or in Western Europe.

The successful presidential campaign of Barack Obama is a good example of the extent of global interconnections. Obama's mother was an anthropologist and this may have increased his sensitivity to the variety and complexity of culture. Obama's candidacy drew unprecedented attention not only in the United States but throughout the world. The enthusiasm generated by his campaign was demonstrated by the spontaneous appearance of Obama songs in many places. Some examples include Trinidadian Mighty Sparrow's "Barack the Magnificent," Jamaican Cocoa Tea's "Barack Obama," Ghanaian artist Blakk Rasta's "Barack Obama," and Kenyan Tony Nyadundo's 17-minute-long "Obama." Enthusiasm for Obama was not limited to the African diaspora. Irish artists Hardy Drew and the Nancy Boys sang "There's No One as Irish as Barack O'bama." The German country duo Sly'N'Boyle sang "Gimme Hope Obama." And residents of Obama, Japan, produced a song for Barack Obama called "Obama, Is Beautiful World." You can see most of these as videos on YouTube. Somewhat more seriously, American news election coverage on November 4, 2008, featured shots of jubilant crowds around the world celebrating Obama's victory, and the Kenyan government declared November 5 a national holiday.

We are connected more closely to those around the globe than we often believe. And the implication of that is that no one today is truly isolated from world events. No one lives in the Stone Age.

## Key Questions

1. What are your global connections? Do you have relatives you know who are living in other nations or are citizens of other nations? If all of your classmates answered this question, how many individuals and nations would be represented?

2. One of the consequences of global interconnections is that the economic and political policies of powerful countries like the United States affect people all over the world. Given this, should noncitizens be represented in the American political system? If so, how should such representation take place?

# Summary

1. **What is the definition of anthropology?** Anthropology is the comparative study of human societies and cultures. Its goal is to describe, analyze, and explain different cultures, to show how groups have adapted to their environments and given significance to their lives.

2. **In what ways is anthropology holistic?** Anthropology is holistic in that it combines the study of human biology, history, and the learned and shared patterns of human behavior and thought we call culture in order to analyze human groups.

3. **What are the five subdisciplines, or specializations, of anthropology?** The five areas of specialization within anthropology are cultural anthropology, linguistics, archaeology, biological (or physical) anthropology, and applied anthropology.

4. **What is the focus of study of cultural anthropology?** Cultural anthropology focuses on the learned and shared ways of behaving typical of a particular human group.

5. **What is the focus of study of linguistic anthropology?** Linguistic anthropology examines the history, structure, and variation of human language.

6. **What is the focus of study of archaeology?** Archaeologists try to reconstruct past cultures through the study of their material remains.

7. **What is the focus of study of biological anthropology?** Biological anthropologists study humankind from a biological perspective, focusing on evolution, human variation, skeletal analysis, primatology, as well as other facets of human biology.

8. **What do applied anthropologists do?** Applied anthropologists are trained in one of the other subfields. They use anthropological research techniques to solve social, political, and economic problems for governments and other organizations.

9. **Name some critical issues that concern cultural anthropologists.** Critical issues that concern all cultural anthropologists include ethnocentrism, cultural relativism, race, and globalization.

10. **What is ethnocentrism and what is its importance in the study of different cultures?** Ethnocentrism is the notion that one's own culture is superior to all others. Anthropologists find that ethnocentrism is common among almost all people and may serve important roles in society. However, anthropology also shows the problems of judging other people through the narrow perspective of one's own culture.

11. **What is cultural relativism and is it the same as moral relativism?** Cultural relativism is the belief that cultures must be understood as the products of their own histories, rather than judged by comparison with each other or with our own culture. Anthropologists note that cultural relativism differs from moral relativism; understanding cultures on their own terms does not necessarily imply approval of them.

12. **What is the anthropological perspective on race?** Anthropology demonstrates that race is not a valid scientific category, but rather an important social and cultural construct.

13. **How have anthropologists responded to the increasing interconnections among people throughout the world?** Anthropologists are deeply concerned with documenting and understanding the ways in which global economic, social, and political processes affect local culture throughout the world. Anthropologists have often been involved in advancing the rights and interests of native peoples.

14. **What is anthropology's relationship to other university disciplines and what sorts of jobs do anthropology majors hold?** Anthropology is part of the liberal arts curriculum. Both the job prospects and the careers of those who study anthropology are similar to those who study other liberal arts disciplines. Anthropology courses develop ways of thinking that are applicable to the broad range of occupations that anthropologists follow.

15. **In what ways is anthropological thinking useful in the world?** Anthropology focuses on understanding other groups of people. This is critical because people are more in contact with each other than ever before. Anthropologists grapple with the question of what it means to be a human being. Anthropologists attempt to observe, collect, record, and understand the full range of human cultural experience. Anthropology presents many useful ways of thinking about culture. Learning how other peoples in other places solved their problems may give us insight to solve our own. Additionally, we can learn lessons from their cultural experience.

# Key Terms

anomie
anthropology
applied anthropology
archaeology
artifact
biological (or physical) anthropology
biopsychological equality
cultural anthropology
cultural relativism
cultural resource management (CRM)

culture
emic (perspective)
ethnocentrism
ethnography
ethnohistory
ethnology
etic (perspective)
forensic anthropology
historical linguists
holistic/holism

human variation
indigenous peoples
linguistic anthropology
medical anthropology
paleoanthropology
prehistoric
primate
racism
society
urban archaeology

# Suggested Readings

Anderson, Barbara G. 1999. *Around the World in 30 Years: Life as a Cultural Anthropologist.* Prospect Heights, IL: Waveland Press. Anderson describes her experiences as an anthropologist in 10 cultures, including the United States, France, Thailand, Japan, Russia, and Corsica. In each chapter she highlights principles of anthropology, as well as describing both the successes and failures of life as an anthropologist in the field.

DeVita, Philip R., and James D. Armstrong. 1993. *Distant Mirrors: America as a Foreign Culture.* Belmont, CA: Wadsworth. An entertaining series of articles about the way American culture looks to foreign anthropologists. This book gives us a chance to reflect on our own cultural practices.

Grindal, Bruce, and Frank Salamone (Eds.). 1995. *Bridges to Humanity: Narratives on Anthropology and Friendship.* Prospect Heights, IL: Waveland. A collection of 14 essays by anthropologists who explore the process of anthropological research and the often very personal meaning it has for them. This book explores the ways that anthropology changes our understanding of others and of ourselves.

Malik, Kenan. 1996. *The Meaning of Race.* New York: New York University Press. A provocative and stimulating discussion of the development of the idea of race in the history and culture of Western society. Malik focuses specific attention on recent events, particularly the end of the Cold War.

As fragments of a hominid find are collected, each location where a piece is discovered is marked with a flag. Here, Yoel Rak of Tel Aviv University and the Institute of Human Origins flags the precise location of each fragment of the *Australopithecus afarensis* cranium discovered at Hadar in 1992.

Dan Johanson/Institute of Human Origins/Courtesy of National Museum of Ethiopia

**THINKING POINT:** In 1924, South African paleontologist Raymond Dart was getting ready for a wedding when he received a box containing the fossilized skull of a primate. Almost 3 months of careful chipping away at the stone revealed the face of an ancient "child." Dart called the child his "Taungs Baby" (after the place it was found) but gave it the scientific name *Australopithecus africanus*. Though few people believed Dart at the time, he had found an authentic early hominin. His discovery was critical because it showed that human ancestors had lived in Africa and that their upright posture developed before their large brains.

—[See page 32 for details.]

# {chapter 2}

# Human Evolution

In its broadest sense, evolution refers to directional change. Biological evolution, however, is something more specific. For biologists, **evolution** is descent with modification from a single common ancestor or ancestral population. Evolution is a characteristic of populations, not individual organisms. As individuals we may grow and learn. We may create inventions or alter our lifestyles. But, for a change to be evolutionary in a biological sense, it must affect the genes we pass along to the next generation. Evolution is the primary way we understand the biological history of humanity and, indeed, of all life.

Speculation about human history and the natural world plays an important role in most societies. For example, the notion that human beings came from earlier life forms was well developed among ancient European philosophers. In the 6th century BCE, the Greek thinker Anaximander of Miletus speculated that humans arose from fish. A century later, his disciple, Xenophanes of Colophon, used evidence of fossil fish from numerous places around the Mediterranean to support Anaximander's theory.

We are often asked why, in a text on cultural anthropology, there should be an extensive chapter on human evolution, normally a part of biological anthropology. We include it because although modern human behavior is almost totally learned and cultural, it rests on a biological base. It is expressed in the brains and bodies of actual human beings. These brains and bodies were shaped by the process of evolution. Evolution has shaped our behavior, our capacity for culture, and the nature of that culture. For example, we have highly accurate depth perception, hands with opposable thumbs, and the ability to manipulate objects with great precision. These features, which developed ≫

over the course of evolution, are absolutely fundamental to the making of tools and thus the cultural behavior of modern humans. Members of all cultures are adept tool users. Humans make tools ranging from fishhooks and spears to microprocessors and satellites. The use of such tools is basic to human life and helps to shape the patterns of subsistence, learning, and communication within society. Without tools, human culture would be vastly different, if it existed at all. Language, our habitual two-legged stance, and our need to reproduce are all evolved traits that are basic to human culture.

Although human cultures are vastly different, human bodies and brains are all very similar. All human beings share a common evolutionary heritage and this heritage shapes our cultures. It means that despite the impressive differences among cultures, there are powerful underlying similarities as well. Understanding our evolutionary history is vital to cultural anthropologists because it informs us about the things that all humans have in common. As we learn about evolution, we gain insight into what it means to be human, the ties that bind us to one another, and our relationship to the nonhuman world. ≪

# Darwin and Natural Selection

In the 18th and 19th centuries, scientists in Europe and North America proposed many different theories of evolution. It was Charles Darwin's theory of evolution by **natural selection,** however, that proved the most convincing scientific explanation of the variety and history of life on earth.

## The Theory of Natural Selection

Darwin's notion of natural selection is both powerful and elegant. It is a relatively simple set of ideas with profound consequences. Because it is based on things that are easily observable, such as variation among members of a species, most of its elements are easy to verify and extremely difficult to refute. As a result, Darwin's theory has been highly durable.

Darwin began by pointing out the great variety of nature. He observed that no two living things, even those of the same species, are quite alike. As later scientists discovered, variation among members of a species comes

from sources including mutation, sexual reproduction, gene flow, and gene drift.

All living things are subject to **mutations,** or random changes in genetic material. These are the ultimate source of all variation. Sexual reproduction and the movement of individuals and groups from place to place (or **gene flow**) results in the mixing of genetic material and also creates new variations. Isolation can play an important role as well. Imagine that a small number of individuals are separated from a larger population. By chance, some members of the small group have a characteristic relatively rare in the larger population—say, a sixth finger on their right hand. The descendants of this small, isolated group will have an unusually large percentage of individuals with six fingers, compared with the larger population from which they were separated. This process is known as **genetic drift.**

Darwin went on to observe that most creatures, human and nonhuman, did not survive long enough to have offspring. They fell victim to predators, contracted diseases, or perished through some defect in their biological makeup. Darwin argued that, in most cases, those creatures that survived did so for some reason. That is to

© American Museum of Natural History

**Charles Darwin as a young man. Darwin's theory of natural selection revolutionized evolutionary thought because it accurately showed how evolution occurred.**

---

**evolution** In its broadest sense, directional change. For biologists, descent with modification from a single common ancestor or ancestral population.

**natural selection** The mechanism of evolutionary change; changes in traits of living organisms that occur over time as a result of differences in reproductive success among individuals.

**mutation** A random change in genetic material; the ultimate source of all biological variation.

**gene flow** Mixing of genetic material that results from the movement of individuals and groups from place to place.

**genetic drift** Changes in the frequencies of specific traits caused by random factors.

say, their survival was not a random occurrence. There was something about them that favored survival. Perhaps they blended well with a background and so were more difficult for predators to see, or they had a bit more resistance to a disease. Perhaps their shape made them a bit more efficient at getting food, or their digestive system a bit better at processing the food they did find. (See Figure 2.1.)

Although very few animals survive to reproductive age, with the advent of modern medicine we have become used to the idea that most of our children will survive. However, before the development of sanitation in the 19th century and antibiotics in the 20th century, vast numbers of children died very young. For example, more than 40 percent of all deaths in London between 1813 and 1820 were children under 10 years old (Roberton 1827). Even today, in the world's poor nations, large numbers of children die before they reach the age of 5. In 2003, for example, more than 20 percent of children died before the age of 5 in 11 African nations. Around the world, more than 10 percent died in 45 nations (World Bank 2005). In these deaths the main culprits are surely poverty and lack of access to basics such as clean water, sanitation, and medical care.

Darwin was profoundly affected by the economic and social philosophy of his era, particularly the works of Adam Smith and Thomas Malthus. Both these philosophers emphasized the role of competition in human social life and culture. In the 1770s, Smith had argued that competition among firms increased their productivity and led to social betterment. A quarter century later, Malthus wrote that because human population levels rose much faster than agricultural production, struggles over resources were inevitable. Darwin, synthesizing these two positions, gave competition and struggle prominent roles in his theory. He argued that life involved constant struggle. Creatures competed with many others for food and with members of their own species for mates. Those who had traits that suited them well to their environment tended to win this struggle for nutrition and reproduction. Thus, Darwin combined the struggle-for-food element of Malthus's work with the notion drawn from Adam Smith that competition leads to betterment.

Darwin further argued that those who won this struggle for survival were able to pass some of the traits that led to their success to their offspring. Thus, each subsequent generation would include more and more individuals with these traits and fewer without. Darwin reasoned that, over the course of millions of years, this process could give rise to new species and all of the tremendous variation of the natural world.

Darwin's theory of evolution by natural selection is sometimes referred to as "survival of the fittest," but this phrase was coined by the social theorist Herbert Spencer (1864), not by Darwin himself. Although Darwin approved of Spencer's phrase, it is misleading for modern readers. When Spencer spoke of fitness, he thought of wealth, power, and physical strength. But when Darwin spoke of fitness, he meant reproductive success: creatures better adapted to their environment tend to succeed in the struggle for food and mates, passing on their traits, whereas those less well adapted tend to disappear. Modern readers tend to understand fitness the way Spencer did, equating it with strength or intellect. So, it sounds as if Darwin's theory actually says the strong and smart survive. But this is incorrect. Strength and intelligence do not necessarily guarantee reproductive success. They are not important for all creatures or environments. Consider the tree sloth, the famous South American tree-dwelling mammal. Sloths are neither particularly strong nor intelligent, yet their continually growing teeth, multichambered stomachs, protective coloring, and habit of sleeping most of the day and night adapt them well to their tropical forest environment. Alternatively, consider

**A   Medium ground finch**
Main food: seeds
Beak: heavy

**B   Large tree finch**
Main food: leaves, buds, blossoms, fruits
Beak: thick, short

**C   Woodpecker finch**
Main food: insects
Beak: stout, straight

**D   Warbler finch**
Main food: insects
Beak: slender

**FIGURE 2.1** The 14 species of finch Darwin found on the Galapagos Islands arose from a single ancestral species. Each species had become adapted to a different ecological niche and a different food source. Four of the species are illustrated here.

crustaceans. It's hard to imagine what advantage a barnacle might gain from increased intelligence.

Darwin understood evolution by natural selection as a slow, steady, continuous process, and there is evidence that, in many cases, evolution does operate in this way. In the 1970s, Niles Eldridge and Stephen Jay Gould proposed an alternative model of evolution called punctuated equilibrium (1972). Eldridge and Gould agreed with the basic Darwinian mechanism of natural selection. However, they argued that species tend to remain stable for long periods and then, through mutation and natural selection, change quite suddenly. Much of the fossil record, especially for large species, supports punctuated equilibrium.

## Evolution, Politics, and Religion

Although Darwin's theory is accepted by virtually all reputable scientists, opposition to this theory has been raised on religious and politically ideological grounds by some groups in the United States. The majority of the world's religions have stories about the ways in which animals and humans came to live on the earth. Evolution challenges a literal reading of these stories, and for this reason it has been strongly resisted by leaders and congregations in some religions.

Not all religious people argue against evolution though. The Catholic Church, for example, declared that evolution was compatible with Christian teachings in 1950, more than half a century ago. Pope John Paul II reaffirmed this in 1996 and in 2007 Pope Benedict XVI said the debate between evolution and creationism in the United States was an "absurdity" and that evolution can coexist with faith (Catholic News Agency 2007). Many theologians in a great variety of religions agree that evolution is consistent with the teachings of their tradition. In official publications and conference proceedings, the United Presbyterian Church, the Episcopalian Church, the Unitarian Church, the United Methodist Church, and the Central Council of American Rabbis have all supported evolution and opposed the teaching of "scientific" creationism in public schools (Lieberman and Kirk 1996).

Despite religion-based disagreement, Darwin's theory of evolution by natural selection has withstood more than 140 years of intensive scientific scrutiny. Today there is no meaningful scientific challenge to evolutionary theory. In fact, evolution has become part of the basic framework of all biological sciences. Just as it is impossible to imagine a science of physics without the theory of gravity, so too modern biology, biochemistry, and many other fields of scientific endeavor are grounded in evolution and all but unthinkable without it.

Although scientists who study biology overwhelmingly agree on the basic principles of evolution and natural selection, there are disputes among them. Scholars argue about the speed of evolution and the precise conditions under which it occurs. There is much discussion about the historic relationships of plants and animals and how they should be classified. Scientists debate the appropriate evolutionary place of specific fossil human ancestors. It is important to understand, however, that all of this debate takes place within the context of evolution. All sides in these arguments agree with the basic principles of natural selection, though they may differ about the specific applications.

# Humans and Our Nearest Relatives

When people think about human evolution, they generally associate the idea with the notion that human beings evolved from apes or monkeys. But this is incorrect. Rather, modern-day humans and modern-day gorillas and chimpanzees evolved from common ancestors. The distinction is critical. Not only is it biologically inaccurate to say that humans evolved from apes or monkeys, but it also leads to a misunderstanding of evolution.

Saying that humans evolved from gorillas or chimpanzees suggests that humans are more evolved than these animals. However, no creature can be any more evolved than another. We can only imagine that we are more evolved if we believe that intellect or ability to alter the environment is the most important criterion of evolution. However, that is an extremely human-centered way of looking at biology. We could as easily say that producing the greatest number of related species or the greatest number of individuals is the best measure of evolution. If we were to take these criteria seriously, it would be clear that insects are far more "evolved" than humans. For example, there are believed to be more than 8000 species of ants, comprising countless individuals. By contrast, there is only a single species of humans, comprising a mere 6 billion individuals.

## Our Shared Ancestor and Common Characteristics

Given that humans and our nearest relatives evolved from a common ancestor, the next question we should ask is what that ancestor was. The question is not easily answered: although there are some recent finds that are good candidates for the ancestral fossil (for example, see Moyá-Solá 2004), no agreed upon common ancestor of humans and chimpanzees or humans and gorillas has been found. However, fossils that we have found and information gained from biochemical dating techniques tell us a good deal about the creature even though we have not yet found it.

Biological anthropologists use the fossil record and a variety of techniques based on the study of DNA, blood protein, blood-clotting agents, and immunology to try and determine when the animals that were the common ancestors of humans and other primate species lived. Evidence from a variety of sources yields similar dates (see Figure 2.2). It shows that the creatures that became humans and apes split from those that gave rise to the monkeys of Europe, Africa, and Asia between 25 and 20 million years ago. We last had a common ancestor with gorillas about 8 million years ago and with orangutans about 13 million years ago. Human ancestors diverged from the ancestors of chimpanzees around 7 million years ago (Begun 2004; Brunet et al. 2002; Holmquist, Miyamoto, and Goodman 1988; Marks, Schmidt, and Sarich 1988; Pilbeam 1996; Sibley and Ahlquist 1987; Sibley, Comstock, and Ahlquist 1990; Spuhler 1989; Templeton 1985, 1986).

All **primates** originated as tree-dwelling mammals, and many of our commonalities come from this **arboreal** ancestry. To survive in the three-dimensional world of trees, primates needed grasping hands and feet

Observations of primates in their natural habitat aid our understanding of their behavior. Here Deiter Steklis observes mountain gorillas.

that could be used to climb and hold. This meant that hands and feet often had fully opposable thumbs. To live in trees, primates developed very acute eyesight; most see in great detail and in color. Additionally, tree dwellers need very accurate depth perception. Misjudging the precise location of an object, such as a branch or a piece of fruit, can easily lead to a fall and death. In primates, accurate depth perception comes from stereoscopic vision. Primates have eyes that face forward, near the front of their heads. The field of vision of each eye overlaps the other. The result is that we, and other primates, see objects close to us from two slightly different angles at once. Our brains use the **parallax,** the slight difference in the images produced by each eye, to accurately compute the distance to the object. Reliance on hand-eye coordination developed along with the expansion of the areas of the brain involved in vision, motor skills, and the integration of the two.

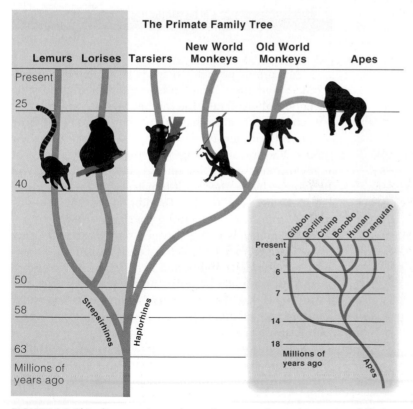

FIGURE 2.2 This diagram shows the evolutionary relationship among different primates.

**primates** A member of a biological order of mammals that includes human beings, apes, and monkeys as well as prosimians (lemurs, tarsiers, and others).

**arboreal** Tree-dwelling.

**parallax** The slight difference in the image of an object seen from two different vantage points.

Life in the trees also involved reductions in some sensory capacities. For example, among terrestrial mammals both predators and prey usually rely on a highly developed sense of smell to detect each other. In the trees, smell plays a much weaker role. Most scent molecules are heavy and tend to accumulate at ground level. Further, breezes make scent a less dependable indicator of direction than it is on the ground. As a result, primates have a reduced sense of smell compared with that of most other mammals.

## Primate Social Life

Primates, particularly apes and humans, have a larger brain compared to their body weight than do other animals, and many have extremely complicated social lives. Although human social life differs greatly from that of our closest ape relations, there are some similarities as well. By examining the characteristics of primate social lives, we may be able to find basic patterns shared by all primates, including humans. We may also learn the ways in which humans are fundamentally different from our primate relatives.

Almost all primates live in social groups, and these are arranged in several different ways. Gorillas live in groups consisting of a single adult male and numerous adult females and their offspring. Chimpanzees, on the other hand, live in groups that include several adult males and several adult females and their offspring. Gibbons, as well as several species of monkey, live in monogamous pairs, and some monkeys from Central and South America live in groupings with one female and two males (Jolly 1985).

One of the most important behavior patterns among humans and nonhuman primates, like gorillas, is the intensely close bond between mothers and their infants.

© Judith Pearson

Grooming is an essential element of social behavior in many primate species, as among these longtail macaques.

Courtesy of Meredith Small

The core of primate societies is the bond between mothers and their infant offspring. With the possible exception of elephants, the mother-infant bond is stronger among primates than any other animals. Infants spend most of their time in very close contact with their mother and travel by clinging to their mother's belly. In many primate species, if a mother dies, the offspring will be adopted by another adult female, often a family member of the deceased mother. Grandmothers may also play an important role in parenting (Fairbanks 1988).

The intense bonding between mother and offspring is an ideal ground for teaching and learning. Primates have an enormous ability and need to learn. Young primates learn initially by imitating their mother's actions. In this way, they discover where to find food and water as well as which other animals are dangerous and which can be approached safely.

As primates grow older, play becomes central to their interaction with their age-mates, and they may spend most of their waking hours in intense, repetitive, and physical play. By playing, primates refine their physical skills, explore their world, and practice solving problems. It is important to understand that primates are motivated to learn because much of learning, like play, is highly pleasurable for them (Fagan 1993).

In most primate societies, both males and females develop dominance hierarchies; that is, they are ranked as superior or inferior to one another. These hierarchies exist both within and between genders. Although such hierarchies, particularly among males, are created and maintained by shows of aggression, anthropologists believe that overall hierarchies serve to limit the amount of aggression within societies; once the hierarchy is established, lower-ranking individuals are less likely to challenge those with more status than might otherwise be the case.

The critical benefit of high rank is greater access to food, sex, and other resources. There is also evidence that high-ranking individuals reproduce more frequently than those of low rank. However, this is controversial. Although it is true that high-ranking males are frequently seen having sex, both by anthropologists and by members of their own species, there is evidence that low-ranking males also have frequent sex—they just do it covertly. Thus, even though high-ranking males have better reproductive chances, those of lower rank are not always effectively prevented from fathering offspring (Constable, Ashley, Goodall, and Pusey 2001).

Among most primates, dominance hierarchies result from a great many individual encounters. Thus, though the presence of a hierarchy prevents constant conflict, rankings are not absolutely fixed. Aggression among animals does occur, and patterns of dominance within the group may change. Furthermore, it is important to note that rank may be context specific. That is, a low-ranking female might give way to higher rank in competition for food but will defend her baby against all others, regardless of rank.

In addition to displays of aggression, primates have many means of reconciliation. One of the best known, grooming, is common among members of the same sex as well as members of different sexes. Inferior-rank animals groom their superiors, and friends groom friends. Among chimpanzees, baboons, and others, friends may hug, pat each other, or hold hands. A variety of other behaviors, including lip smacking and male–male mounting are used to establish, reestablish, or maintain friendly relations between individuals and cohesion within the group.

## Tool Use among Primates

The use of tools is fairly common among nonhuman animals. Many different animals build nests; some use rocks, twigs, or leaves to get at their prey. Sea otters, for example, use stones to crack open abalone shells. However, these capacities seem qualitatively different from the extremely complex and varied tool manufacture and use among humans. Nonhuman primates also use tools,

but in ways that seem different both from the behavior of animals such as sea otters and from humans.

Jane Goodall recorded the first tool use among non-human primates in 1960 (Goodall 1971). Since then, many additional discoveries have been made. Monkeys use sticks and branches to threaten others or defend themselves when they are threatened. Some Japanese macaques wash their food and use water to separate grains of wheat from sand (Huffman and Quiatt 1986; Strier 2000). However, the most sophisticated tool use is found among chimpanzees and bonobos. For example, Pruetz and Bertolani (2007) reported chimpanzees fashioning sticks into spears and using them to hunt bush babies (squirrel-sized nocturnal primates). Mercader, Panger, and Boesch (2002) reported that chimpanzees in Ivory Coast used hammer stones to break nuts and that stone piles and stone chips left by this process are very similar to the remains of early hominin tools found by archaeologists.

Two particularly well-documented examples of chimpanzee and bonobo tool use are termite fishing and the use of leaf sponges. **Termite fishing** involves the use of a stick or blade of grass. After carefully selecting a stick, chimpanzees modify it by stripping off leaves and any other material that might interfere with the task at hand. They place the stick in a termite mound, wait until the termites begin to feed on it, and then withdraw it to eat the termites. Chimps make leaf sponges by taking leaves, chewing them, and then using the resulting wad of material to soak up water from tree hollows and other places difficult for them to access. They also use leaves to clean their fur and pick their teeth. Both termite fishing and the use of leaf sponges are complex actions requiring foresight and planning. It is interesting that among all primates who use tools, it is females who first develop tool-using skills. Further, females generally become more adept at tool use than males (Strier 2000).

Tool use behavior among sea otters, woodpecker finches, and other nonprimates seems largely instinctive. All members of the species exhibit these behaviors. Among chimpanzees however, behaviors such as spear use, termite fishing, and leaf chewing do not appear throughout the entire species. Rather, some groups exhibit the behaviors and others do not. Almost 40 different behavior patterns, including tool use, grooming, and courtship behavior are present in some chimp communities but absent in others (Whiten et al. 1999). This implies that such practices are learned behavior passed along as part of the knowledge of the social group, very much like human culture.

**termite fishing** The learned use of twigs or blades of grass to extract termites from their mounds characteristic of some groups of chimpanzees.

# The Evolution of Humans

Human beings and our nearest ape relations have been following separate courses of evolution for the past 5 to 8 million years. In this time, our species has developed in systematic ways. Our early ancestors were relatively few in number and geographically confined to Africa. In 2009, the world's population was approximately 6.7 billion, and humans lived on every continent. The history of human evolution is thus a narrative of growth and movement. In order for this movement to take place, humans have had to adapt to living in many different climates and ecosystems.

Our early ancestors did not depend heavily on tools, and their cultures left few material remains. They were certainly able to learn, and depended on this ability for their survival. However, the range of their learning was probably small. Today, our ability to learn is vastly greater than that of our early ancestors. To live in many different ecosystems, humans had to innovate, applying our learning in new and original ways, adapting by changing our behavior. The spread of humans and our ancestors reflects our gradual acquisition of increasingly sophisticated, learned, cultural behavior.

## Naming Names

Human ancestors, like those of other species, are generally referred to by their scientific names. All human ancestors, all current-day humans, as well as gorillas, chimpanzees, and orangutans, are members of the biological family *Hominidae*. Within this family, individual ancestors are known by the names of their genus and species. A **genus** is a group of similar species.

Among living creatures, a relatively simple guideline is used to determine if similar animals are members of the same or different **species.** If a male and female are capable of producing fertile offspring, they are members of the same species. If they can produce no offspring at all, or if the offspring are infertile, they are members of different species. For example, dogs and cats cannot mate at all and are therefore members of different species. Horses and donkeys are similar and can mate, but their offspring, mules, are infertile. Therefore,

horses and donkeys also belong to different species. With extinct creatures, such as our fossil ancestors, no such test can be performed. Therefore, determining species membership is much more speculative.

Most human ancestors and modern-day people fall into two genera (the plural of genus): *Australopithecus* and *Homo*. Each of these genera includes numerous fossil species. Modern people, *Homo sapiens*, are members of the genus *Homo*. Many of our ancient ancestors are assigned to the genus *Australopithecus*. In the past decade there have been several exciting discoveries of extremely ancient human relatives. Some anthropologists argue that these represent new genera, but their precise place in the evolution of humanity is still debated. (See Figure 2.3.)

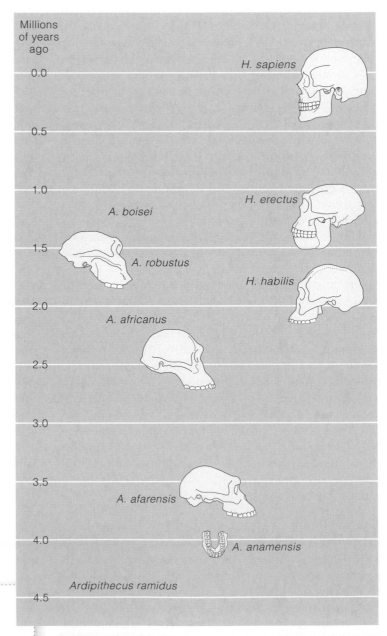

**FIGURE 2.3** A plausible view of early human evolution. A. stands for *Australopithecus*, H. for *Homo*.

**genus** In biological classification, a group of similar species.

**species** In biological classification, a group of organisms whose members are similar to one another and are able to reproduce with one another but not with members of other species.

## Finding Remains

Reconstructions of the evolutionary history of human beings are based on data. But how do anthropologists find the data, and how do they figure out when human ancestors lived?

Many of the data used to build our theories of human evolution are found in the form of fossils. Fossils may be of a great many different kinds. Sometimes they are bones; sometimes they are impressions left by bones (or, in the case of fossil footprints, by behavior). On occasion, even fossil imprints of hair, skin, and soft tissues may be found.

Fossilization of any kind is a rare event, and not all things fossilize equally well. In general, the larger and harder something is, the longer it takes to decay, and hence the greater chance it will become fossilized. Teeth are the hardest part of the body, and hence the most easily fossilized. Skulls and leg bones are large and thus found more frequently than smaller bones such as ribs. Soft tissue parts of the body, such as skin and internal organs, decay very rapidly and are rarely found.

Finding fossils involves luck, skill, and the use of careful, scientific methodology. Finding a fossil-bearing site is often extremely difficult. Anthropologists know that certain geological formations are much more likely to bear fossils than others, and they use techniques such as aerial and ground-based surveys, satellite imagery, and radar to try to locate fossils within these regions. However, luck and chance also play a large role. Experienced fossil hunters can sometimes go for many years without a major find.

Once a fossil-bearing site is found, excavation proceeds in a highly controlled manner. The area is extensively photographed and precisely mapped. Researchers usually divide it into a grid and systematically examine each section. The positions of fossils or artifacts are carefully recorded. Each item to be removed is given a number, and extensive notes are made about it. Soil is carefully analyzed for the remains of any fossilized plant or animal material that could provide clues about the ancient environment. To be sure that nothing is missed, dirt removed from the site is passed through wire screens.

One critical aspect of analyzing finds is determining their dates. Dating is a complex and highly technical procedure. Many different dating techniques are available. These include potassium/argon (K/Ar) dating, carbon 14 (C14) dating, thermoluminescence, and paleomagnetic dating. Each technique has advantages and disadvantages. It is important to note that all of these dating techniques provide date ranges rather than precise calendar dates. Dates are generally specified as plus or minus a

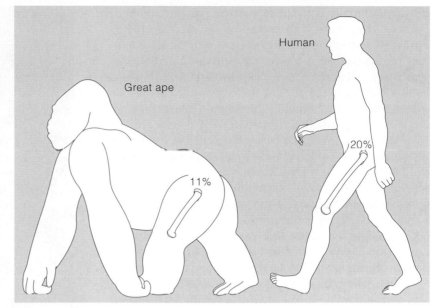

**FIGURE 2.4** Bipedalism, walking habitually on two legs, is a characteristic of all human ancestors. Bipedalism involves the lengthening of the lower limbs. The thigh accounts for 20 percent of human body height but only 11 percent of the body height of a gorilla.

certain number of years. For very ancient finds, these date ranges can be quite large.

## The Earliest Human Ancestors

From an anatomical perspective, the critical thing that differentiates humans and our ancestors from modern-day apes and their ancestors is bipedal stance and locomotion. Unlike any other primate, humans and our ancestors habitually walk on two legs. Although chimpanzees, gorillas, and some other primates are capable of walking or running on two legs for short distances, their habitual stance is on all fours. **Bipedalism** involved substantial anatomical changes (see Figure 2.4). The skulls and pelvises of bipeds are shaped differently than those of animals that walk on all fours. In addition, the feet of human ancestors are specialized for walking, whereas their hands are generalized for a wide variety of tasks. When anthropologists are able to find fossils of these bones, bipedalism is easily inferred.

Among human ancestors, bipedalism appeared far earlier in the fossil record than increased brain size or the use of stone tools. In fact, bipedalism played a critical role in the development of these features of humanity. Bipedal locomotion freed the hands, allowing our ancestors to carry things for long distances and make tools.

**bipedalism** Walking on two feet, a distinctive characteristic of humans and our ancestors.

In addition to bipedalism, particular aspects of tooth number, size, shape, and enamel are critical in tracing human ancestry. The specific qualities of teeth are important because different species have different dental characteristics and can be identified on that basis. Further, teeth are the hardest parts of the body and, for that reason, are the most frequently preserved. Hence, they are the most commonly found fossils.

The earliest evidence currently available for a creature generally considered ancestral to humans is a fossil skull between 6 and 7 million years old found in the summer of 2002. This fossil, popularly called Toumai, is far older than any previously known (Brunet et al. 2002; Vignaud et al. 2002), and is unusual not only in its age but because it was found in Chad, 1500 miles west of Africa's Great Rift Valley, where almost all other extremely ancient human ancestor fossils have been found.

The earliest, most substantial evidence for human ancestors comes from the Awash River in northeastern Ethiopia. In the early and mid-1990s, teams of anthropologists led by Tim White of the University of California discovered the remains of more than 40 individuals who lived approximately 4.4 million years ago. They named these creatures *Ardipithecus ramidus* (White, Suwa, and Asfaw 1995). These ancestors had large jaws and small brains compared with modern humans. Many of their teeth and other aspects of their jaw shape were similar to those of modern-day chimpanzees. Despite this, evidence from their pelvic bones, skulls, and forelimbs indicate that they were bipedal. Reconstructions of the environment they lived in shows a flat plain covered with open woodland and dense forests. This reinforces the notion that bipedalism first evolved in wooded areas rather than on grassy plains as many anthropologists had earlier believed (Wolde-Gabriel, White, and Suwa 1994) and suggests that these ancestors may have spent much of their time living in the trees.

## The Australopithecines

Perhaps the best known and best described of the early hominid fossils are the australopithecines. Beginning with Raymond Dart's discovery of "Taung Child" in 1924 (described in the "Ethnography" section in this chapter), more than 10,000 individual australopithecine fossil bones have been found, comprising several hundred individuals. The earliest australopithecine fossils are from northern Kenya and are between 3.9 and 4.2 million years old. The most recent, from South Africa, are only about 1 million years old. Although **australopithecines** are found only in Africa, they were a diverse and complex group of creatures.

> **australopithecines** Members of an early hominid genus found in Africa and characterized by bipedal locomotion and small brain size.

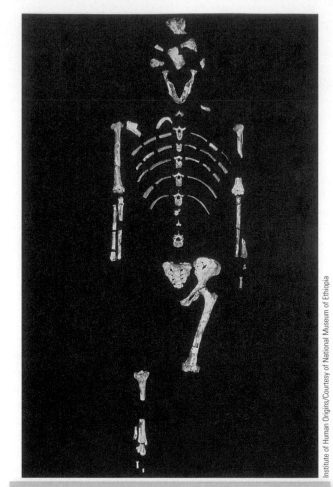

"Lucy," an unusually complete *Australopithecus* skeleton, was discovered at Hadar, Ethiopia, in 1974.

Of the many australopithecine finds, two are among the most famous in the history of anthropology. In 1974, at Hadar in Ethiopia, a team led by Donald Johanson found an australopithecine skeleton they dubbed "Lucy." "Lucy" is unusually complete; more than 40 percent of her bones are present. With such a full skeleton, anthropologists were able to answer many questions about the way australopithecines looked, stood, and moved.

The second remarkable discovery was made by Mary Leakey, at Laetoli in Tanzania. In a well-preserved 3.5-million-year-old bed of volcanic ash she and her team found two footprint trails clearly made by australopithecines. One of the trails was made by two individuals who were probably walking together. The second trail was made by three individuals; two of these were walking together and the third, a smaller individual, was walking in the footprints left by the larger of the first two.

The plethora of fossil finds reveals a great deal about the australopithecines and their lifestyles. The australopithecines of Hadar and Laetoli are called "gracile" australopithecines because they are generally small, light, and slender. They were a varied group, standing between 3.5 and 5 feet tall and weighing between 65 and 100 pounds (McHenry 1992). Their brains, at between 400 and 500 cubic centimeters, were only about one-third the size of modern human brains. Their faces protruded, and they had relatively large and slightly overlapping canine teeth. Although their hips and lower limbs were a bit different from those of modern people, they were fully bipedal.

The "gracile" australopithecines lived in a variety of arid and semiarid grasslands, bushlands, and forest environments in eastern and southern Africa. Because the remains of numerous individuals are commonly found together, anthropologists hypothesize that they were social animals living in small groups. Although they may have used tools made of wood or bone, none have survived, and there are no stone tools associated with australopithecine remains. The absence of stone tools, combined with australopithecines' relatively small size and lack of claws or very large canine teeth, strongly suggests they were **omnivores,** eating fruit and vegetable foods, insects, and small animals. They probably scavenged for remains left by larger predators, but it is unlikely that they hunted large animals.

About 2.5 million years ago, global weather turned cooler, and this seems to have resulted in the evolution of several new hominid species. One group of these new animals is called the "robust" australopithecines, though they are sometimes known by the older name *Paranthropus.* The "robust" australopithecines tended to be slightly larger than the "graciles," but the ranges of both height and weight overlap. More important, "robust" australopithecines had much heavier skulls, reinforced with bony ridges and substantially larger teeth and jaws. Such factors strongly suggest that these creatures were adapted for chewing heavy, coarse material. They were probably vegetarian. "Robust" australopithecines lived in Africa until about 1 million years ago and do not seem to be ancestral to modern humans.

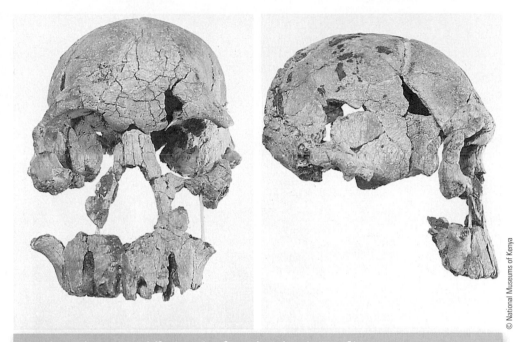

A nearly complete *Homo rudolfensis* cranium from Lake Turkana in East Africa.

© National Museums of Kenya

*Homo rudolfensis,* emerged. Although there are important technical differences between *habilis* and *rudolfensis,* they are generally quite similar. Most fossil finds of this era belong to *habilis,* and in this section we will focus on them. Several physical features distinguish *Homo habilis* from the australopithecines. Like all members of *Homo, habilis* brains were quite large compared with the size of their bodies. Their teeth were smaller than those of australopithecines, their skulls were higher, and their faces protruded less.

One thing that distinguishes *habilis* from the australopithecines is the presence of stone tools; *habilis* learned to work stone into a variety of useful shapes. The stone tools made by *habilis* are called **Oldowan tools.** New discoveries suggest that toolmaking appeared quite early. *Habilis* were making fairly sophisticated sets of tools as early as 2.3 million years ago (Steele 1999). Toolmaking was clearly a critical factor in human evolution. Human ancestors had relatively small teeth; but, by using tools, they could match the biting and chewing abilities of much larger, more powerful animals. Thus, using tools led to improvements in nutrition, which in turn favored those individuals and groups best able to make and use tools.

## Homo Habilis and Homo Rudolfensis

At roughly the same time that some "gracile" australopithecines were evolving into "robust," others gave rise to a new genus, *Homo.* Between 2.3 and 2.5 million years ago, the earliest members of this group, **Homo habilis** and

**omnivore** An animal that eats both plant and animal foods.

**Homo habilis** A species of early human found in Africa. *Homo habilis* were present between 2.5 and 1.8 million years ago.

**Oldowan tools** Stone tools made by *Homo habilis.*

# Ethnography

## Fossil Hunters

Raymond A. Dart (1893–1988) was the discoverer of "Taungs Child," the first *Australopithecus* skull to be identified. Dart was trained in England and became a professor at University of Witwatersrand in Johannesburg, South Africa. Living in what was then an academic backwater, Dart was isolated and frequently depressed. He taught anatomy, but partly to pursue his interest in anthropology and perhaps partly to relieve his boredom, he began to develop a fossil collection for the university. One way he did this was to ask his students to bring in any fossils they found. He offered a significant financial reward to whoever found the best fossil.

In early summer 1924, his only female student, Josephine Salmons, brought him the fossil skull of a baboon that had been found by a family friend in a mine at Taungs in Botswanna. Although she did not win the prize (Dart had awarded it to another student earlier), Dart was thrilled by the fossil because no primate fossils had yet been discovered in Africa south of the Sahara.

Dart rushed to see a friend who had connections at the Taungs mines and learned that the mine manager, A. E. Spires, had a collection of fossils in his office. When Spires learned of Dart's interest, he had the fossils sent to him. They arrived during a wedding held at Dart's house for which he was to be the best man. Dart, dressing for the wedding, was unable to restrain himself. He tore off his fancy dress collar and ran out to take possession of the boxes of fossils. The first box yielded nothing very interesting, but when Dart opened the second box:

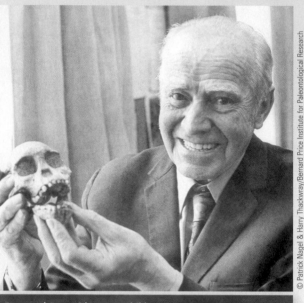

**Raymond Dart with Taung Child.**

© Patrick Nagel & Harry Thackwray/Bernard Price Institute for Paleontological Research

. . . . A thrill of excitement shot through me. On the very top of the rock heap was what was undoubtably. . . . the mold of the interior of [a] skull. Had it been only the fossilized brain cast of any species of ape it would have ranked as a great discovery, for such a thing had never before been reported. But I knew at a glance that what lay in my hands was no ordinary anthropoidal brain. Here in lime-consolidated sand was the [fossil] of a brain three times as large as that of a baboon and considerably bigger than that of any adult chimpanzee (1996:42/1959).

It took Dart 73 days, chipping away at the rock with a small hammer and his wife's knitting needles, to expose the full fossil. He wrote that when he could view the fossil from the front he could see that:

The creature which had contained this massive brain was no giant anthropoid such as a gorilla. What emerged was a baby's face, an infant with a full set of milk teeth and its first permanent molars just in the process of erupting. I doubt if there was any parent prouder of his offspring than I was of my "Taungs baby" on that Christmas of 1924 (1996:44/1959).

Dart's discovery came to be called "Taungs Child" (today, Taung Child is the more common usage). He gave it the scientific name *Australopithecus africanus* and claimed that it was a human ancestor. His assertion, however, was met with ridicule by his colleagues in Europe who were deeply committed to the authenticity of the Piltdown Man fossils, which looked nothing like Taungs Child. Piltdown Man had been "found" by Charles Dawson between 1908 and 1912. It seemed to be half ape and half human and was widely regarded as the "missing link." Piltdown, however, proved to be a fraud, and Dart lived to see his discovery vindicated.

Mary Leakey (1913–1996) was perhaps the greatest single fossil hunter of the 20th century. Among her numerous finds were the 1959 discovery of the australopithecine fossil "Zinjanthropus" and the "Laetoli footprints," the fossilized footprints of two or three ancient hominids, probably *Australopithecus africanus*.

Mary Leakey spent much of her childhood in the Dordogne in France, a region particularly rich in human prehistory. From an early age, she was fascinated by these archaeological treasures. Leakey audited courses in archaeology and geology at the University of London, but, although later in life she was to receive many honorary degrees, she never earned a university diploma.

In 1933, friends introduced her to Louis Leakey. He was the son of missionaries and had grown up in Kenya. He studied at Cambridge University and by 1930 had a Ph.D. Despite the fact that he was married, with a child and a pregnant wife, Louis and Mary began an affair. In 1935, he returned to Africa, taking Mary with him (and leaving his wife in England). In 1936, he divorced his first wife and married Mary. Mary and Louis eventually had three children. Of these, Richard and his wife, Meave, have become extremely important fossil hunters.

Louis had hoped for a job in England, but the scandal surrounding his divorce and remarriage made this impossible. From the mid-1930s until the late 1950s, Louis and Mary searched East Africa for human ancestor fossils with little success. Although Mary found the first fossil skull of an extinct primate called *Proconsul,* as well as many tools and sites, a truly big find eluded them.

On July 17, 1959, the Leakeys were waiting for their friends Armand and Michaela Denis to arrive. The Denises were naturalists who, along with their cameraman Des Bartlett, made films for British television. The Leakeys had agreed to let them film their Olduvai excavations and had paused in their research to allow them time to come to the site. Louis was sick in bed, and Mary decided to take her two dogs for a walk over to a site they were not actively working. Mary Leakey later wrote:

> There was indeed plenty of material lying on the eroded surface. . . . But one scrap of bone that caught and held my eye was not lying loose on the surface but projecting from beneath. It seemed to be part of a skull. . . . It had a hominid look, but the bones seemed enormously thick—too thick, surely. I carefully brushed away a little of the

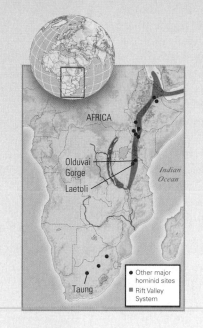

deposit, and then I could see parts of two large teeth in place in the upper jaw. They *were* hominid. It was a hominid skull, apparently *in situ,* and there was a lot of it there. I rushed back to camp to tell Louis, who leaped out of bed, and then we were soon back at the site looking at my find together (Leakey and Leakey 1996:47–48/1984).

Mary had found *Zinjanthropus,* the first australopithecine found outside of South Africa. When the Leakeys' naturalist friends and their cameraman arrived, it was the excavation of Zinjanthropus that they filmed.

Finding Zinjanthropus made the Leakeys' careers. Whereas before they had struggled along in obscurity with very limited funds, they soon found themselves international celebrities and the recipients of many grants. From the early 1960s to the early 1980s, Mary and Louis (who died in 1972) ran large and very successful projects at Olduvai and other African locations. Mary later wrote:

The reason why "Zinj" was so important to us was that he captured the public imagination. . . . If we had not had Des Bartlett and his film camera on the spot to record the discovery and excavation of the skull, this might have been much harder to achieve. Zinj made good television, and so a very wide public had the vicarious excitement of "being there when he was dug up" (Leakey and Leakey 1996:48/1984).

Louis Leakey had the academic credentials, and was a charismatic speaker with an eagle eye for outstanding publicity opportunities. Thus, until his death, he was the public face of their projects. However, it was Mary and their children who made most of the fossil finds. Mary's relationship with Louis was problematic; he had frequent affairs with other women and the couple grew apart. Looking back on their lives, it is clear that Mary was not only the better fossil finder but, despite her lack of an earned degree, her meticulous work and caution probably made her the better scientist as well.

## CRITICAL THINKING QUESTIONS

1. All anthropological research happens in a theoretical context, a political context, and a social context. Why do you think the Leakeys' fossil finds were immediately hailed as important, but Raymond Dart's gained credibility only slowly?

2. Why is fossil evidence important in understanding human ancestry?

3. How do anthropologists know that the fossils they find are indeed those of human ancestors?

Source: Excerpts reprinted by permission of Waveland Press, Inc., from Brian N. Fagan, *Quest for the Past: Great Discoveries in Archaeology,* Second Edition (Long Grove, IL: Waveland Press, Inc., 1994). All rights reserved.

The habitat of *habilis* was grassland with far fewer trees than were available to the earlier "gracile" australopithecines. Their dentition suggests that they were omnivores, competing with members of other species for both plant and animal foods. The fact that Oldowan tools are designed for cutting and bashing rather than hunting strongly suggests that *habilis* rarely killed large animals. Like their australopithecine predecessors, they probably hunted small animals and scavenged the remains of larger ones. Stone rings found at Olduvai Gorge in Northern Tanzania indicate that *habilis* probably built shelters for protection from predators and cold weather.

The earliest remains of *habilis* are from eastern and southern Africa, and it had been believed that the species was limited entirely to that continent. However, new finds cast doubt on this position (Huang et al. 1995; Swisher et al. 1994). A variety of fossils from Indonesia and China are more than 1.8 million years old, and Oldowan-style tools found in Pakistan and France have dates of between 1.6 and 2 million years ago. Skulls and other fossils that show strong similarities to *habilis* and are more than 1.75 million years old have been discovered at Damanisi in the Republic of Georgia (Abesalum et al. 2002; Lieberman 2007). If it is true that *habilis* spread out of Africa, some of our understanding of them will need revision. Such geographic dispersion would suggest that *habilis* was more adaptable, and more dependent on culture, than was previously thought.

## Homo Erectus

The earliest *Homo erectus* fossils come from northern Kenya and are about 1.8 million years old. *Homo erectus* fossils show some substantial changes from the earlier *Homo habilis.* One of the most important changes is in body size. *Erectus* were substantially larger than *habilis* and many were roughly the same size as modern-day people. For example, the 1.6-million-year-old skeleton of a 12-year-old *erectus* boy was found in the mid-1980s, at Lake Turkana in Kenya. It is estimated that, had the boy grown to maturity, he would have been at least 6 feet tall. **Homo erectus** brain size increased along with body size. The average brain volume for *erectus* is about 1000 cubic centimeters. Some had brain sizes of up to 1250 cubic centimeters, placing them within the range of modern humans.

*Erectus* was substantially more "robust" than *habilis.* Not only is the *erectus* skull larger, its bones are heavier. There is a heavy ridge of bone above the eyes, and the cranial bone is thick. The thick bones and heavy reinforcing features suggest very strong jaw muscles. Compared to modern humans, *erectus* skulls appear squat. In mod-

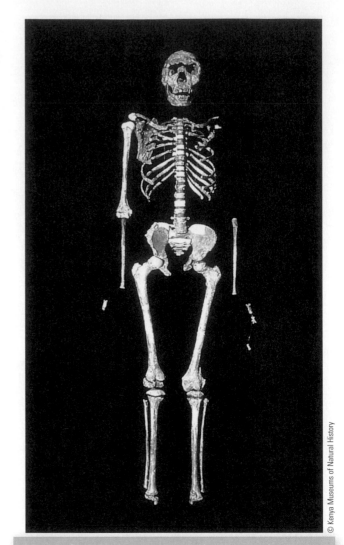

WT 15000 from Nariokotome, Kenya, is the most complete *Homo erectus* specimen yet found.

© Kenya Museums of Natural History

ern humans, the maximum width of the skull is above the ears, but in *erectus* the skull's widest point is below the ears.

The name *erectus* might seem to suggest that this species was the first human ancestor to walk upright, but as we have seen, this is not the case. Bipedalism is ancient in human ancestry; all of our ancestors, back to the australopithecines, walked on two legs. However, there is a reason this particular fossil is called *erectus*. Because the finder of a new fossil species has the right to name it, the names of the different species reflect the history of discovery. The first *erectus* fossils were found by the Dutch army surgeon Eugene Dubois in the 1890s, years before any of the australopithecines were discovered. Dubois, believing he had found the oldest human ancestor who walked upright, named his discovery *erectus*.

One reason *erectus* was found before the fossils of earlier bipedal species was that its geographic spread was much greater than that of any earlier hominid. Although

**Homo erectus** A species of early human found in Africa, Asia, and Europe. *Homo erectus* were present between 1.8 million and about 200,000 years ago.

some possible evidence of *habilis* has been discovered outside of Africa, *erectus* inhabited much of Africa, Europe, and Asia. Major *erectus* finds have been made in eastern, northern, and southern Africa, Spain, the Middle East, China, and Indonesia.

From this wide geographic dispersal, we know that *erectus* was able to adapt to life in a great variety of different ecological and climatic settings. Because much of the era of *erectus* occurred during the Ice Ages, climatic variation was probably even greater than today. In order to thrive in many different habitats, *erectus* developed an increasingly sophisticated and complex culture (see Figure 2.5).

One important window on *erectus* culture is provided by human and animal remains and artifacts found at Zhoukoudian, near Beijing, in China. Anthropologists, working in this area since the 1920s, have recovered remains from more than 40 *Homo erectus* individuals, as well as more than 100,000 artifacts. Zhoukoudian was inhabited between about 450,000 and 230,000 years ago. Its inhabitants made choppers, scrapers, points, and awls from stone. They also used deer antlers for tools, and possibly skulls for "drinking bowls" (Jia and Weiwen 1990). There are also the remains of fires. In some places, the ash layers are more than 18 feet deep. But, though most anthropologists agree that *erectus* was capable of controlling and using fire, it is not known whether they were able to make it.

*Homo erectus* almost certainly lived by hunting, scavenging, and gathering. Remains in Spain show that human ancestors were capable of hunting and butchering elephants half a million years ago. Remains of deer and wild horses have been found at Zhoukoudian. However, many of the bones at *erectus* sites show the marks of carnivore teeth as well as cut marks from tools. This strongly suggests that much of the meat consumed by *erectus* was scavenged. Debris at many other sites show that *erectus* also ate a wide variety of wild fruits, vegetables, tubers, and eggs.

Winters at many *erectus* sites were very cold, so it is likely that *erectus* made clothing of animal skins. Although no such clothing has survived, there is some evidence of needles among the bone tools found at Zhoukoudian.

Little is known about *erectus* social or religious life. The fact that they killed large animals meant that large amounts of meat had to be consumed rapidly. This suggests that social groups were relatively large and probably included complex mechanisms for distributing food, and perhaps other goods. One tantalizing if grim bit of evidence about possible religious beliefs comes from Zhoukoudian. The brains of some Zhoukoudian individuals were removed after their death, but why this was done is unknown. It could have been cannibalism; perhaps it was part of a religious ritual; or maybe individuals just wanted to use the empty skull case as a drinking vessel.

Until very recently, it had been believed that the last *Homo erectus* lived approximately 300,000 years ago. But in 2003 the paleontology world was rocked by the announcement of the discovery of a new species of hominin, *Homo floresiensis,* popularly called "The Hobbit." *Floresiensis,* discovered on the island of Flores in Indonesia, appears to be a very small variety of *Homo erectus.* It was found in association with tools, though these do not resemble other *Homo erectus* tools. Perhaps most surprising of all, *floresiensis* has been dated to as recent a time as 13,000 years ago (Brown et al. 2004). As of this writing, there is considerable controversy over *floresiensis.* Some anthropologists believe that *floresiensis* is a dwarf form of *Homo erectus.* Others believe that it evolved from a still smaller species (see Lordkipanidze et al. 2007). Still others believe *floresiensis* are simply the remains of *Homo sapiens* with diseases or congenital deformities (see Balter 2004; Culotta 2008; Powledge 2006). Recent tests have not

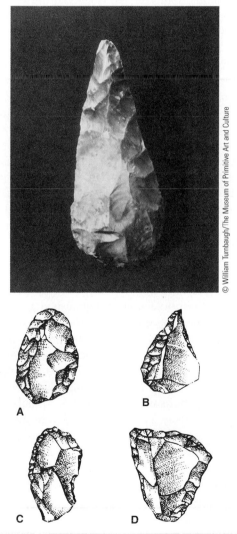

© William Turnbaugh/The Museum of Primitive Art and Culture

**FIGURE 2.5** (Top) A *Homo erectus* hand ax (biface). (Bottom) Small *Homo erectus* tools: (a) side scraper, (b) point, (c) end scraper, and (d) burin (a tool used to make grooves in wood, stone, leather, bone, or antler).

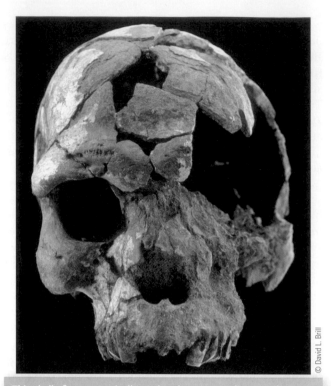

This skull of an anatomically modern human was discovered near the village of Herto in the Afar region of eastern Ethiopia. Its date of about 160,000 years ago makes it the earliest example of an early modern human.

provided clear answers. A study comparing *floresiensis* skulls with modern humans and ancient hominids found that they might be similar to either *Homo erectus* or *Homo habilis* depending on the assumptions made by the researchers (Gordon, Nevell, and Wood 2008).

## Homo Sapiens

The critical anatomical distinctions between *Homo erectus* and *Homo sapiens* lie in the volume and shape of the skull. On the average, **Homo sapiens** clearly have substantially larger brains than *erectus*. *Sapiens* skulls lack the heavy bony ridging above the eyes and the thick skull

**Homo sapiens** A species of human found throughout the world. The earliest *Homo sapiens* appeared about 500,000 years ago.

**Neanderthal** Members of a population of archaic *Homo sapiens* that lived between 130,000 and 35,000 years ago.

**multiregional model** A theory that seeks to explain the transition from *Homo erectus* to *Homo sapiens* by arguing that different populations of *Homo sapiens* are descendant from different populations of *Homo erectus*.

**replacement model** The theory that modern people evolved first in Africa and then spread out to inhabit virtually all the world, outcompeting or destroying other human populations in the process.

bone of the *erectus*. In addition, whereas *erectus* had a squat skull with a little forehead, the *sapiens* skull is high and vaulted with a large forehead.

The skeletal changes between *erectus* and *sapiens* reflect the tight interrelationship of learned behavior and biological evolution. *Erectus* tools were relatively crude. Using them in hunting required that hunters attack their quarry at close range, exposing them to substantial physical danger from the prey. In this situation, thick, heavy skull bones helped protect their brains from injury. As human ability to learn increased and weaponry improved, animals could be hunted from greater distance, and this favored the lighter-boned, bigger-brained *sapiens*.

The details of the transition from *Homo erectus* to *Homo sapiens* are complex. By about half a million years ago, some *erectus* groups were becoming more like *sapiens*. Fossil bones from locations throughout the Old World attest to ancestors who had lighter-boned, more rounded skulls than *erectus*. However, these fossils still show the bony ridging above the eyes typical of *erectus*. Between 300,000 and 100,000 years ago, this brow ridging disappeared in many of the fossils found in Africa. However, the brain size of all of these fossils is somewhat below that of modern people. About 130,000 years ago, **Neanderthals,** with brain sizes overlapping and sometimes larger than those of modern people, appeared in Europe and in some parts of the Middle East. They were present until about 35,000 years ago. About 195,000 years ago, anatomically modern people, *Homo sapiens sapiens,* appeared in Africa (McDougall, Brown, and Fleagle 2005). By about 35,000 years ago, *Homo sapiens sapiens* had spread throughout the range of all other populations of the *Homo* genus and was the only form present.

The transition from *Homo erectus* to *Homo sapiens* is a fascinating and controversial topic. Since the 1980s, there has been much debate over how this transition took place. Anthropologists have used the fossils themselves as well as molecular and genetic data to try to resolve this issue. There are two prominent theories: the **multiregional model** and the **replacement model.** Supporters of the multiregional model argue that in many places, more or less simultaneously, *Homo erectus* populations became modern *Homo sapiens* populations. Because none of these populations were isolated, individuals (and their genes) moved freely. The result was that humanity developed as a single unified species, but different populations retained substantial differences in ancestry.

Some evidence supports the multiregional hypothesis and it seems to explain some of the anatomical variation among modern human populations. Fossil finds from China include 100,000-year-old skulls that seem to have both *Homo erectus* and *Homo sapiens* traits. A modern human fossil from Australia may have mitochondrial DNA unrelated to that of current-day human populations (Adcock et al. 2001; see also Cooper et al. 2001 for a challenge to this claim). If this is true, evolution to *Homo sapiens* must have happened at least twice.

The second prominent theory used to explain the transition from *Homo erectus* to *Homo sapiens,* the replacement model, proposes that *Homo sapiens sapiens* evolved from an earlier *Homo* form in Africa about 125,000 years ago. Between that time and 35,000 years ago, this new species spread out from Africa to inhabit virtually all the world. When *Homo sapiens sapiens* ran into Neanderthals or other archaic forms of *Homo sapiens,* they outcompeted them but did not mate with them. The result was that anatomically modern people replaced all others.

Much of the data supporting the replacement theory is based on two different strands of biochemical and genetic evidence. First, there is evidence taken from the mitochondrial DNA of living humans. This has been analyzed to show that all living humans share at least one common ancestor, who lived in Africa approximately 200,000 years ago. Second, DNA extracted from the remains of archaic *Homo* populations such as Neanderthal shows that these populations were not very closely related to modern humans. Human and Neanderthal ancestral populations split 370,000 years ago, long before the emergence of anatomically modern humans (Noonan et al. 2006). Thus, modern humans could not have evolved from Neanderthals.

A third theory concerning the transition from *Homo erectus* to *Homo sapiens,* the **hybridization model,** provides a middle ground between the other two theories. It claims that *Homo sapiens sapiens* spreading out of Africa did mate with earlier archaic *Homo* populations.

Each of the theories has its proponents, and there has been acrimonious dispute among them. It is possible that no one model is correct; perhaps data from different locations can be explained by different theories. However, most data in recent years support the replacement model and this model is widely accepted in the biological sciences.

## *Homo Sapiens* Culture

Material remains show us that complex culture is not limited to modern *Homo sapiens.* Archaic forms such as Neanderthal were clearly cultural. Good evidence of this comes from burial practices. Several examples of burial of the dead by Neanderthals have been found.

One of the best-known examples is at Shanidar Cave in Iraq, where anthropologists found the remains of nine individuals, four of whom were intentionally buried. These remains are between 45,000 and 60,000 years old. They are particularly interesting, first, because high concentrations of pollen in the graves show that the bodies were buried with flowers. This strongly suggests that Neanderthals had symbolic rituals for the burial of the dead, and possibly a belief in an afterlife (Solecki 1975). Second, one of the Shanidar individuals, a male known as Shanidar 1, was severely injured during his life. He was blind in one eye, his right arm had atrophied from injury, and he would have walked with difficulty. Yet Shanidar 1 clearly survived in this condition for many years, strongly suggesting that he was supported and cared for by others. We should be careful, however, to avoid romanticizing Neanderthal life. Evidence from Moula-Guercy cave in France shows that 100,000 years ago some Neanderthals practiced cannibalism (Defleur, White, and Valensi 1999), using the same butchery techniques on game animals and other Neanderthals (Culotta 1999).

*Homo sapiens sapiens* made tools of much greater sophistication and efficiency than any prior species. For example, with a pound of flint, Neanderthals could make about 40 inches of blade; with the same amount of stone, *Homo sapiens sapiens* could make between 10 and 40 feet of blade (Bordes 1968). The tools of these early people are characterized not only by their efficiency but also by their variety: stone blades, scrapers, and chisel-like tools called burins, as well as tools of

© The Art Archive/Museo Civico Vicenza/Dagli Orti

**Venus of Willendorf, Austria. "Venus" figurines are stylized representations of women made between 40,000 and 30,000 years ago.**

**hybridization model** A theory that seeks to explain the transition from archaic to modern *Homo sapiens* by proposing that modern and archaic forms interbred.

bone, awls, needles, and tools for scraping and smoothing leather. In addition to utility, many show clear aesthetic qualities, something not true of tools made by earlier species.

One critical innovation was the compound tool, made of several wood, bone, and stone pieces bound together. Ax heads were hafted to wood or bone handles; blades of stone were set in wooden handles. One of the best-known innovations of the era was the spear thrower, or **atlatl**, a hooked piece of wood or bone used to increase the power with which a spear can be thrown (see Figure 2.6). The variety of *Homo sapiens sapiens* tools and the learning involved in their manufacture suggest that this species had much more complex culture than any earlier creature.

Although many of the best-known early tools come from Europe, some of the earliest examples come from Africa. For instance, extremely complex bone tools, probably designed to spear fish, have been found in eastern Congo. Though their dating is controversial, they are believed to be between 75,000 and 180,000 years old. If these dates are correct, the tools are considerably older than any *Homo sapiens sapiens* material found in Europe (Yellen et al. 1995).

The ability of humans to hunt using complex, efficient tools might have had a devastating effect on their environment. For example, *Homo sapiens sapiens* entered Europe during the Ice Age. At that time, much of the land was a vast tundra supporting an abundance of animal life, particularly large herd animals. Shortly after modern people appeared, more than 50 genera of large mammals became extinct. Because small mammals survived and there is no evidence of drought, it is possible that hunting by humans was responsible for these extinctions (Nentwig 2007).

In addition to tools, early people left many symbolic and artistic remains. Among the best known of these are the so-called "Venus" figurines and cave paintings. **"Venus" figurines** are small carvings of women sculpted in a variety of materials, including stone, bone, and wood, and made between 30,000 and 20,000 years ago. About 40 intact figures have been discovered, along with fragments of at least 80 more (McDermott 1996). Many depict women with exaggerated breasts and buttocks. The first of these statues was found in 1864, and controversy about their meaning and importance has raged since. They have been variously interpreted as art for art's sake (Ucko and Rosenfeld 1967), fertility magic (Burenhult

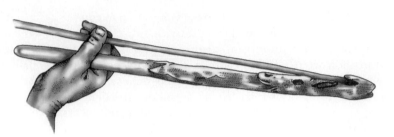

**FIGURE 2.6** *Homo Sapiens Sapiens* used spear throwers (atlatl) to increase a spear's power and range.

1993), representations of female deities (Gimbutas 1989), erotic images made for male pleasure (Guthrie 1984), ordinary women's views of their own bodies (McDermott 1996), and teaching tools used by female midwives and shamans (Tedlock 2005).

About 10,000 years ago, the last of the Ice Ages ended. As temperatures rose, the ecosystems that had supported these ancient cultures changed, and for many people new ways of living became essential. The wild animals associated with the Ice Age tundra disappeared and in some areas people turned increasingly to the domestication of both plants and animals. Dogs were domesticated between 10,000 and 14,000 years ago (Mestel 1994). People in the Middle East were beginning to use rye by about 13,000 years ago, but did not become dependent on farming until about 10,000 years ago (Pringle 1998).

The move from hunting to the domestication of plants and animals involved substantial increases in the amount of work humans had to do. Because the transition involved increased population density and increased dependence on a small number of plants, it almost certainly led to an upturn in rates of disease, increased physiological stress, a reduction in well-being, and a decline in nutrition (Larsen 1995). However, it also became possible to support a larger population than ever before. Cities, kingdoms, and empires could emerge, using domesticated plants and animals as food sources. Thus, the origin of current industrialized society lies in the move to dependence on domesticated plants and animals 10,000 years ago.

## Human Variation

As we saw in Chapter 1, the notion of race in human beings has enormous historical and sociological importance, but no biological validity. No agreed upon, scientific way to divide humanity into a set number of races, no matter how large, has ever been found. Biological analysis makes it clear that human populations are not sharply genetically distinguished from each other, and they do not constitute distinct evolutionary sublineages of humanity (Templeton 1998; Tishkoff and Kidd 2004). Further, there is no evidence that traits such as skin color

---

**atlatl** A spear thrower, a device used to increase and extend the power of the human arm when throwing a spear.

**"Venus" figurines** Small stylized statues of females made in a variety of materials by early modern humans.

commonly used to determine race are of any more significance than any of the thousands of other traits that make up a human being. Nonetheless, it is true that there is enormous variety among human beings, and the systematic variation of biological traits among human beings is an important subject for anthropological investigation. In this section we discuss a few prominent examples of variation. Some of the impacts of "race"—of constructed categories of human variation on social stratification—are discussed in Chapter 12.

Many human traits show **clinal distributions.** A cline is a geographical gradient, and a map of clines shows the systematic variation in the frequency of a trait from place to place. Blood type provides a good example. All human beings have type A, type B, type AB, or type O blood. The letters refer to the presence of specific antigens on the surface of the blood cells. Antigens are involved in the body's immune system; when foreign antigens are detected, the body attempts to eliminate them. The frequency of blood type varies geographically. In far northeastern Europe and northern Russia, between 25 and 30 percent of the population has type B blood. This number declines steadily as you move south and west. In Spain, in the far southwest, only 10 to 15 percent of the population has type B blood (Mourant, Kopec, and Domaniewska-Sobczak 1976). The pattern of blood type distribution around the world leads many anthropologists to believe that having one blood type or another gives specific advantages and disadvantages under different environmental conditions. However, no one has yet convincingly demonstrated what those advantages or disadvantages are.

The gene associated with the disease sickle cell anemia is another good example of a trait that follows a clinal distribution. The sickle cell gene is common in areas that have a high incidence of malaria, particularly certain regions of West Africa, India, and the Middle East (see Figure 2.7). Inheriting the gene from a single parent confers a degree of immunity to malaria; inheriting it from both produces sickle cell anemia. In some areas where malaria is particularly prevalent, as much as 20 percent of the population may have the trait. As one moves away from these areas, the frequency of the gene for sickle cell declines steadily.

Skin color is one of the most obvious aspects of human variation, and historically it has been the primary

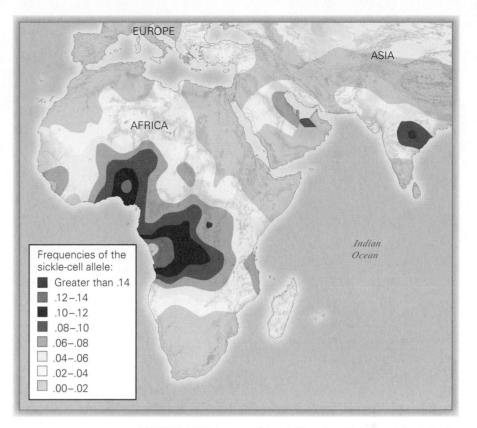

**FIGURE 2.7** This map of the sickle cell trait shows a clinal distribution.

basis for constructing systems of racial classification. Although skin color is a complex trait and we do not entirely understand it, we do know quite a bit about the geographic distribution of skin colors and their adaptive significance.

Skin color in humans, and in many other mammals, follows a clinal distribution. The darkest colors are found in bright, tropical regions, and the lightest colors in far northern or southern areas where there is much less sunlight. As one travels, for example, from equatorial Africa to northern Europe, skin color becomes progressively lighter.

The primary factor in all colors of skin is a pigment called **melanin.** Melanin is produced by special cells in the skin called melanocytes. All human beings have about the same number of melanocytes. However, the amount of melanin (and the size of melanin particles) produced by the melanocytes differs among human populations.

**clinal distribution** The frequency change of a particular trait as you move geographically from one point to another.

**melanin** A pigment found in the skin, hair, and eyes of human beings, as well as many other species, that is responsible for variations in color.

## Forensic Anthropology

Forensic anthropologists Michelle Hamilton and Kate Spradley.

Forensic anthropologists apply their knowledge of physical anthropology to the identification of skeletal or badly decomposed human remains. Their goal is to discover information that can assist in the detection of crime and the prosecution of those responsible. When human remains are found, forensic anthropologists are often called in to determine the age, sex, ancestry, and stature, as well as the manner of death of the individual. This information is used to identify the deceased and to determine whether a crime has been committed.

The work of forensic anthropologists is often vital in settling humanitarian issues. In the past two decades, forensic anthropologists have frequently been called upon to discover the identities of victims of political violence. A good example comes from Guatemala, where members of the Guatemala Forensic Anthropology Foundation are exhuming mass graves in order to identify victims and examine bones to chronicle the nation's bloody 36-year civil war. More than 40,000 individuals disappeared during the war. Most were the victims of government death squads who, in the late 1970s and early 1980s, kidnapped and murdered many whom they believed to be their opponents.

With the evidence provided by anthropologists, Guatemalans are beginning to confront their brutal past. Karen Fisher, one of Guatemala's leading human rights activists, has said, "When you've hidden secrets for years and years, the truth is going to heal your wounds, but it will take time; it won't be easy" (Moore 1998).

Forensic anthropologists played a key role in identifying the victims of the September 11, 2001, terrorist attack. Amy Mundorff, a forensic anthropologist working for the New York City Medical Examiner's office, was almost killed in the attack herself. She survived to work with a team of forensic anthropologists and other medical specialists who tried to identify the more than 16,000 body parts found at the disaster site.

Although the identification of victims of atrocities often makes the news, most forensic anthropologists work closer to home, identifying the victims of violent crime or unfortunate circumstances. Kate Spradley, a forensic anthropologist at Texas State University, conducts forensic casework in Texas and Arizona. She works with Bruce Anderson, at the Medical Examiner's office in Pima County, Arizona, to collect data on U.S.–Mexico border-crossing fatalities. Spradley and Anderson hope to use their data to improve the ability of forensic anthropologists to correctly identify the remains of individuals considered Hispanic.

---

These discrepancies in melanin production create differences in skin color.

There is a clear relationship between melanin, ultraviolet light, and skin cancer. High levels of ultraviolet light are found in tropical areas and can cause genetic mutations in skin that lead to skin cancer. Some types of skin cancer can easily spread to other parts of the body and can be fatal. Melanin in the skin absorbs ultraviolet rays and hence protects people from this form of cancer. Australia provides a good example of the relationship between skin color, cancer, and ultraviolet radiation. Australia is a largely tropical nation but, because of colonization and immigration by northern Europeans, has a majority light-skinned population. Australia has the highest skin cancer rates in the world. About one in every 54 Australians is diagnosed with skin cancer each year. By comparison, the rate of diagnosis in the United States is about one in 270 (Australian Institute of Health and Welfare 2008; Skin Cancer Research Foundation 1998).

Because human ancestors evolved in bright, tropical East Africa, they probably had very dark skin (although they did not necessarily look like dark-skinned people of today, and they are certainly no more closely related to modern-day dark-skinned people than to modern-day light-skinned people). As people moved away from areas with very high amounts of sunlight (and hence ultraviolet light), they tended to lose skin color. New research shows that much of this change was due to a single genetic mutation that appeared in the European population (Balter 2005; Lamason et al. 2005). There seems to have been very strong selection for this mutation. Following the logic of evolution, this could not have occurred simply because high

Like other forensic anthropologists, Spradley uses the data she collects from each successfully identified individual to help identify the sex, age, ancestry, and stature of other unknown skeletons.

A case begins when a law enforcement agency or medical examiner's office calls for help in discovering the identity and cause of death of an individual whose remains have recently been found. Sometimes, it turns out that the remains are nonhuman; at other times, it is determined that they are historic or archaeological; but in many cases, the remains are from a recent violent crime and therefore of forensic, or legal, significance.

The next step is the recovery of the body. Sometimes this has already been done by the law enforcement agency, but frequently anthropologists are called upon to assist and supervise the procedure. Sometimes bodies are found complete and in good preservation, but often they are found skeletonized, buried, burned, fragmentary, or in various stages of decomposition. Michelle Hamilton, a forensic anthropologist at Texas State University, reports that she has recovered bodies in caves and rock shelters, on mountaintops, in forests, down wells, under water, from burned homes, in submerged vehicles, and in many other environments. In one tricky case, Hamilton was called in to excavate underneath a house foundation where a body was reported buried. A family member who lived in this house had disappeared seven years previously. When the body was unearthed, it was still fully-fleshed and recognizable. Therefore, Hamilton concluded that it could not have been buried the entire time since the individual first disappeared. The mystery was solved when family members confessed that the individual had been killed seven years ago, but they had stored the body in a freezer and had only buried it that week.

After the body has been recovered, the anthropologist's job is to establish both the individual's identity and to aid in the interpretation of events surrounding death. To do this, the bones and any other remains are analyzed to determine the sex, age, estimated time since death, ancestry, and stature of the individual, as well as any unique identifying marks such as healed fractures or skeletal abnormalities that might be useful in making a positive identification. In some cases, facial reconstructions are made to provide a likeness of the deceased and further aid in identification.

Analysis of trauma and fracture patterns on the bones can provide information about the sequence of events that occurred at the time of death. Spradley and Hamilton have analyzed cases that showed evidence of blunt force trauma, sharp force trauma, gunshot wounds, or fire trauma.

In every case, forensic anthropologists are required to produce a report of their findings. These reports are used by law enforcement agencies to match the bodies with missing persons reports and, if foul play is suspected, to prosecute the individuals believed to be responsible. Usually the anthropologist's work ends with the delivery of the report, but on occasion a forensic anthropologist is required to testify as an expert witness in a criminal trial.

You can find additional information about forensic anthropology at the website of the American Board of Forensic Anthropology (http://www.theabfa.org).

levels of ultraviolet protection were no longer necessary. In order for there to be selection for light-colored skin, those with this trait must leave more offspring than those without it. In other words, in northern latitudes, light skin color must confer some reproductive advantage.

The most widespread theory accounting for the advantage conferred by light skin color in northern latitudes concerns vitamin D. Vitamin D plays a critical role in bone growth, particularly in infants and children. Although people get some vitamin D from food sources such as fish oils and egg yolks, most vitamin D is produced by the body and the action of sunlight on skin is basic to this process. Ultraviolet light interacts with special cells in human skin to produce chemicals critical to the body's production of vitamin D. Children with insufficient exposure to sunlight do not produce enough of these chemicals and therefore do not produce enough vitamin D. This insufficiency results in the bone disease **rickets,** which leads to deformation of the pelvis. Before modern medicine and caesarian sections were available, women with deformed pelvises often died in childbirth.

The link between ultraviolet light, vitamin D, and rickets probably plays a critical role in determining skin color. Melanin in skin protects against skin cancer by absorbing ultraviolet light. However, in so doing, melanin also reduces the amount of ultraviolet light available

---

**rickets** A childhood disease characterized by the softening and bending of leg and pelvis bones. Rickets is related to insufficiency of vitamin D and/or calcium.

to interact with the cells that produce vitamin D precursors. Thus, people with dark skin are less efficient at producing vitamin D than people with light skin. In bright, tropical areas where there is a great deal of ultraviolet light present, this inefficiency makes no difference. People are exposed to so much ultraviolet light that everyone produces adequate amounts of vitamin D. However, in far northern and southern areas, where there are few hours of daylight for much of the year and the clouds are often very dense, there is much less ultraviolet light present. In such places, efficiency at vitamin D production is at a premium, and people with light-colored skin are at an advantage; people with dark skin are more likely to get rickets.

Although there is very good evidence supporting this hypothesis (Jablonski and Chaplin 2000; Molnar 1983), it has also come in for criticism. Robins (1991), for example, argues that rickets was only a problem in urban industrial societies where people lived indoors, frequently in crowded slum conditions. This argument proposes that rickets would not have much of an effect on people who foraged or farmed outdoors, and thus it is unlikely that the disease had any effect on changes in skin coloration that happened thousands of years ago.

An alternative explanation for skin color difference is based on the reaction of different people to cold weather. Studies on soldiers from World War I through the 1950s showed that those with dark skin color were about four times more likely to suffer frostbite than soldiers with light skin (Boas and Almquist 1999:296; Post, Daniels, and Binford 1975). Thus, it might also be true that light skin color somehow confers a degree of protection against cold weather. However, if such a rela-

tionship exists, the biological mechanisms behind it are unknown.

Still another explanation involves **sexual selection.** Proponents of this approach argue that human males have a cross-cultural preference for light-skinned females (Aoki 2002; Frost 1994; Van den Bergh and Frost 1986). In very bright and sunny places, the advantage of dark skin overrides this preference. However, in regions where dark skin is less of an advantage, the male preference for light-skinned females becomes more important and, as a result, populations become light-skinned. However, Madrigal and Kelly (2007) argue that if this were the case, the difference between male and female skin color should be greater the further a population is away from the equator. However, their analysis failed to confirm this prediction.

Racial classification based primarily on skin color has been a compelling fact of human history for at least the past 500 years. On the basis of the color of their skin, some people have been enslaved, oppressed, and subjected to public scorn and humiliation. Others have been given special rights and privileges. This fact demonstrates the ability of people to create symbolic, cultural meaning around simple, biological aspects of the world. It shows the enormous power of culture. However, as we have seen, skin color is a complex trait that has to do with adaptation to environment. Much of the variation in skin color may be related to a change in a single amino acid in a single gene (Balter 2005). In and of itself, skin color has neither particular meaning nor importance. It does not serve as a good marker for other biological characteristics and has no biological connection with any particular cultural traits. The notion that the historical exposure of a population to ultraviolet light, extremes of temperature, or sexual selection has anything at all to do with cultural, intellectual, or physical superiority or inferiority is obviously ridiculous.

**sexual selection** The theory that the evolution of certain traits can be explained by competition for opportunities to mate.

# The Global and the Local: Vanishing Primates

Learning about primates is basic to understanding human evolution. Knowing how creatures are both like us and different from us helps us comprehend what it means to be a human being. Unfortunately, throughout the world, primates are increasingly endangered. Although no species of primate has become extinct in the past century, many are on the verge of disappearing today. The International Union for the Conservation of Nature reports that almost 50 percent of the world's 634 recognized species and subspecies of primates are listed as vulnerable, endangered, or critically endangered. In some regions of the world, the situation is particularly desperate. For example, in Asia, 71 percent of primates are listed as vulnerable, endangered, or critically endangered. Thirty-seven percent of African primates are so listed (International Union for the Conservation of Nature [IUCN] 2008). It is clear that without active intervention, many of these species will soon disappear.

One key factor threatening primate populations is destruction of habitat. The tropical forests where most primates live are threatened by expanding human populations and commercial exploitation. As human populations expand, people bring new lands into cultivation, destroying primate habitat as they do so. International demand for hardwoods and tropical produce also encourage the felling of forests and the establishment of agricultural plantations. In some areas, the combination of population increase and commercial demand has resulted in the destruction of more than 90 percent of the original habitat for some primates.

Primates face other problems, too. Primates have long been hunted both for food and for body parts that are used in local medicines and sometimes sold to tourists. Political turmoil can greatly increase the effects of hunting. Many nations that are home to primates suffer political instability; these include Madagascar, the Democratic Republic of Congo, and Cambodia. As farming and market systems collapse, people increasingly depend on hunted food and on the sale of anything of value, including animal body parts.

Although primates may be treasured by large numbers of people in North America and Europe, they are not necessarily equally admired by those who live among them. Primates impose significant burdens on the humans who live near them. An extensive literature details the destruction primates cause to crops (see Hill 2002 for

This orangutan from Sumatra has been trapped by local people and is being held in a rattan cage prior to being sold.

© Judith Pearson

a brief review of this literature). Primates are also an important reservoir of diseases, especially new ones. People in wealthy countries want to protect primates. This is a far more difficult position for people who live near them. These latter often view primates as pests or as sources of wealth they can exploit.

The disappearance of primates would be tragic for numerous reasons. Of course, primates are of important scientific value and studying them has contributed to our understanding of human origins, human biology, and perhaps some aspects of human behavior. Primates play important roles in their ecosystems, where they are often critical to seed dispersal (Chapman and Onderdonk 1998). Additionally, primates may have important economic and cultural value for the human communities that live around them. And, from King Kong to Zoboomafu, primates play an important role in American culture, too.

Preserving ecology in general and primates in particular is a global issue. It links the interests of people in wealthy nations to the living conditions and economic possibilities for people in poor nations. Protecting endangered species must involve much more than simply constructing preserves. Viable, politically and economically secure lifestyles must be found for the human as well as the animal populations.

## Key Questions

1. Most organizations devoted to protecting endangered species are located in wealthy nations and funded by people in those nations. Most of the species they try to protect are located in poor nations. Describe the problems and conflicts caused by this fact.

2. Many activists in wealthy nations argue that saving species is a moral imperative. However, if saving species is a moral imperative, where is such morality based and is it universally shared?

3. It is sometimes argued that eco-tourism makes preserving animals such as primates economically viable. However, because eco-tourism produces mostly low-wage jobs and because many primates are located in places that are unlikely to draw tourists, it is clearly not a general solution to the problem. What other solutions can be proposed?

# Summary

1. **What is the relationship between learned human behavior and human biology?** Although human behavior is almost entirely learned, it rests on a biological base that is the product of our evolutionary history.

2. **What is Darwin's theory of evolution by natural selection and what are its principal ideas?** Darwin's theory of evolution by natural selection shows how humans and other species came to exist. The theory notes that there is much variation among members of all species, but most that are born do not survive to reproduce. Those that do reproduce pass some of the traits that favored their survival on to their offspring.

3. **Are Darwin's ideas about evolution correct?** Although there is a great deal of religious and political controversy over Darwin's ideas about evolution, virtually all biologists and anthropologists agree that the basic elements of Darwin's theory are correct.

4. **With what other animals do human beings share common ancestry and what similarities come about as a result of this?** Human beings and other primates share common ancestry. Our closest relations are with chimpanzees and gorillas. Common ancestry gives all primates many similarities, including grasping hands and excellent three-dimensional vision.

5. **Describe the social relationship between primates, their parents, and their peer group.** Humans and other primates are highly social animals. Mothers and infants form very strong bonds, and these bonds favor teaching and learning. As primates grow, they interact more with their own age-group and play becomes essential to learning. Dominance hierarchies are extremely common in primate societies. Position within these hierarchies is decided by both birth and individual action.

6. **What are the earliest fossil remains for human ancestors and about how old are they?** The earliest fossil remains for human ancestors are between 6 and 7 million years old. Several groups of very early remains show creatures that had large jaws and small brains but were bipedal (walked on two legs).

7. **Who (or what) were the australopithecines? When and how did they live?** Between 4.2 million and 1 million years ago, a diverse group of creatures called australopithecines lived in eastern and southern Africa. Australopithecines were bipedal and small-brained. They probably lived in part by scavenging.

8. **Who (or what) were *Homo habilis*? When and how did they live?** *Homo habilis* evolved between 2.5 and 2.3 million years ago. *Homo habilis* is distinguished from the australopithecines by somewhat larger brains and the use of simple stone tools. They were probably omnivores, but it is unlikely that they were able to hunt large animals.

9. **Who (or what) were *Homo erectus*? When and how did they live?** By about 1.8 million years ago, *Homo erectus* had appeared. These creatures had large bodies and brains. Their remains are found in many places in Europe, Africa, and Asia. They made more sophisticated tools than *Homo habilis* and probably were able to control fire. They clearly had much more complex culture than earlier species.

10. **How are *Homo sapiens* distinguished from earlier human ancestors and when did they first appear?** By half a million years ago, some *Homo erectus* had become "sapienized." *Homo sapiens* are distinguished by substantially larger brain capacity and more complex culture than earlier forms. Between 300,000 and 35,000 years ago, there were several different forms of archaic *Homo sapiens,* including Neanderthals.

11. **What are the main theories of the transition from *Homo erectus* to *Homo sapiens* and which of these is currently considered most probable?** There are several theories concerning evolution from *Homo erectus* to modern *Homo sapiens sapiens*. These include the multiregional theory, the replacement theory, and the hybrid theory. Although there is some debate over these, most current evidence supports the replacement theory.

12. **How does early *Homo sapiens* culture differ from those of its predecessors? Give some examples of early *Homo sapiens* culture.** *Homo sapiens* culture is extremely complex. Neanderthals (archaic *Homo sapiens*) buried their dead and clearly had religious beliefs. "Venus" figurines and cave paintings attest to the highly developed artistic talents of human ancestors more than 30,000 years ago.

13. **Do human beings show much variability? How is the variability they show distributed?** The human species shows considerable variety. Many human traits such as blood type or the presence of sickle cell show systematic change across different geographic areas. Such a pattern is called a clinal distribution.

14. **What is the relationship between the cultural and biological importance of skin color? What is the most prominent theory proposed to account for skin color variation?** Although skin color has been of critical cultural and historical importance, it has no special biological importance. It is simply an evolutionary adaptation to ultraviolet light. The most prominent theory explaining skin

color holds that melanin protects skin from cancer in sunny areas but interferes with vitamin D production in areas with little sunlight. Hence, dark skin colors are found in sunny areas and light skin colors in areas with less sun.

15. **How does the social significance of skin color reflect the importance of culture?** The fact that skin color is implicated in so much of history is an indication of our remarkable ability to invest inherently meaningless aspects of the world with symbolic, cultural meaning and of the absurdity of racism.

# Key Terms

arboreal
atlatl
australopithecines
bipedalism
clinal distribution
evolution
genetic drift
gene flow
genus
*Homo erectus*

*Homo habilis*
*Homo sapiens*
hybridization model
melanin
multiregional model
mutation
natural selection
Neanderthal
Oldowan tools

omnivore
parallax
primates
replacement model
rickets
sexual selection
species
termite fishing
"Venus" figurines

# Suggested Readings

Gould, Steven J. 2007. *The Richness of Life: The Essential Stephen Jay Gould.* New York: W. W. Norton. From the 1970s until his death in 2002, Gould was one of the most eloquent and important authors on evolution. In addition to scientific papers and several important full-length books, Gould wrote monthly columns about evolution for *Natural History* magazine and occasional pieces for *The New York Review of Books.* This book is a collection of the best of Gould's writing spanning his entire career. It is really a "must have" for any professional or layperson interested in evolution.

Shubin, Neil. 2008 *Your Inner Fish: A Journey into the 3.5-Billion-Year History of the Human Body.* New York: Pantheon. Paleontologist Shubin examines the deep evolutionary connections between humans and other life forms in this highly readable, sometimes humorous account. Shubin offers an unusually clear discussion of evolution, the role and importance of DNA, and comparative anatomy.

Tattersall, Ian. 1998. *Becoming Human: Evolution and Human Uniqueness.* New York: Harcourt Brace. Tattersall, the curator of anthropology at the American Museum of Natural History, uses genetics, evolutionary theory, primate anatomy, and archaeology to explain the story of human evolution. This book shows the ways our ancestors adapted to their environments and the effects those adaptations had on our evolutionary history. Another Tattersall title, *The Fossil Trail: How We Know What We Think We Know about Human Evolution* (1995), examines the history of fossil discoveries and their interpretation.

Weiner, Jonathan. 1994. *The Beak of the Finch: A Story of Evolution in Our Time.* 1994. New York: Knopf. This popular account documents the work of Peter and Rosemary Grant on the Galapagos Islands. The Grants have spent more than 20 years documenting changes in populations of Darwin's finches. The Grants' work, including the documentation of DNA changes among the birds, shows the ongoing power of Darwinian evolution. Weiner's more recent work includes *Time, Love, Memory* (1999), about the science and the biologists involved in the analyses of the relationship between behavior and genetics in fruit flies, and *His Brother's Keeper: One Family's Journey to the Edge of Medicine* (2004), about medical ethics and experimental treatments for disease.

Doing ethnography requires the anthropologist not only to observe and ask questions, but also to participate in the culture and social life of a society, as with this anthropologist living among the Mentawai of Sumatra. Traditionally, these tattoos are incised with needles and vegetable dye, though these are being done with washable pigments.

**THINKING POINT:** "Anthropology is about taking people seriously. It is about trying to understand how people interpret and act in the world. Anthropologists listen to what people say; watch what they do, and then try to make sense of their words and their deeds by putting them into context. . . . this takes time, lots of it."

—(MacClancy 2002) [See page 53 and following for details.]

# {chapter 3}

# Doing Cultural Anthropology

In their attempt to understand human diversity, cultural anthropologists have developed particular methodologies for gathering data and developing and testing theories. For both technical and ethical reasons, the controlled laboratory situation of the physical sciences is of little use in cultural anthropology. Anthropologists can hardly go out and start a war somewhere to see the effect of warfare on family life. Nor can they control in a laboratory all the factors involved in examining the impact of multinational corporations on villages in the Amazon rain forest. Instead, they look to the existing diversity of human cultures. In place of the artificially controlled laboratory, anthropologists rely on ethnography and cross-cultural comparison.

**Ethnography** is the gathering and interpretation of information based on intensive, firsthand study of a particular culture (the written report of this study is also called an ethnography). Ethnographies are used as a basis for cross-cultural comparisons: the ethnographic data from different societies are analyzed to build and test hypotheses about general, or even possibly universal, social and cultural processes.

Cultural anthropology encompasses a wide range of activities and specialties: solitary fieldwork in a remote location, delving into historical archives, testing hypotheses using statistical correlations from many different societies, formal and informal questionnaires, recording life histories, making ethnographic films, curating museum exhibits, and working with indigenous peoples as advocates in cultural and political projects. But all of these diverse activities have their roots in fieldwork, which is not only the major source of anthropological data and theory, but ≫

also an important part of most anthropologists' experience. In this chapter, we explore some of the history and practice of fieldwork. We examine fieldwork techniques and different trends in anthropological data collection and styles of ethnographic writing and discuss some of the ethical issues raised by the practice of anthropology. «

# Anthropology in Historical Perspective

Anthropology was not always based around fieldwork. The first scholars who called themselves anthropologists worked in the second half of the 19th century. Among the most famous of them were Sir Edward Burnett Tylor and Louis Henry Morgan. Both were brilliant men and had traveled widely (Tylor in Mexico and Morgan in the western United States), but they saw themselves as compilers and analysts of ethnographic accounts, rather than field researchers. For their data they mostly relied on the writings of amateurs—travelers, explorers, missionaries, and colonial officers—who had recorded their experiences in remote areas of the world. Because of this, their critics sometimes referred to them as "armchair anthropologists."

Morgan and Tylor were deeply influenced by the evolutionary theories of Charles Darwin and Herbert Spencer. They assumed that such theories could be applied to human society and used data from archaeological finds and colonial accounts of current-day peoples to produce evolutionary histories of human society. Nineteenth-century anthropologists sometimes referred to simpler societies as "living fossils," a term borrowed from biology and paleontology. For biologists, living fossils are currently existing plants or animals that closely resemble their fossil ancestors. For anthropologists of this era, "living fossils" were societies they believed to be unchanged for thousands of years. Anthropologists believed that these societies were living, "fossilized" examples of earlier states of their own society. Morgan, Tylor, and others claimed that by carefully and comparatively examining such societies, they could show how society evolved from its most simple and primitive state to the most complex current societies. As they analyzed societies, they used technology as well as social institutions such as family and religion to place each society on an evolutionary scale of increasing complexity. Their scale began with simple, small-scale societies (classified as "savages"), passed through various chiefdoms (usually classified as

"barbarians"), and ended with societies such as their own (classified as "civilization"). Although Morgan and Tylor were deeply critical of many aspects of their own societies, they were also convinced that they lived in the most highly evolved society that had ever existed.

There were numerous problems with Morgan and Tylor's evolutionary anthropology. Explorers, colonial officials, and missionaries had particular interests in playing up the most exotic aspects of the societies they described. Doing so increased the fame of the explorers (and the number of books they were able to sell). It made the native more in need of good government or salvation from the perspective of the colonial official and missionary. Further, the societies that anthropologists believed were "living fossils" were, in fact, often of recent origin. Sometimes they were created by the processes of colonialism and Western expansion itself. Perhaps most important, the evolutionists were so sure that they had properly formulated the general evolutionary history of society that they twisted and contorted their data to fit their theories. Tylor, for example, wrote that his theoretical perspective was so well established that he could ignore any data that did not fit with the surety that such data was inaccurate (Tylor 2004:46/1871).

## Franz Boas and American Anthropology

Problems such as these led to a radical reappraisal of evolutionary anthropology at the end of the 19th century. The most important critic of evolutionism was Franz Boas. Born in Minden, Germany, Boas had come to the United States after completing his doctorate in geography and living among the Inuit on Baffin Island in the Canadian Arctic. In the late 1890s he became the first professor of anthropology at Columbia University in New York City. From there, he was critically involved in the training of many students, including A. L. Kroeber, Ruth Benedict, Margaret Mead, and Edward Sapir who became the leading anthropologists of the first half of the 20th century. As a result, Boas's ideas had a profound impact on the development of anthropology in the United States.

Boas's studies as well as his experiences among the Inuit convinced him that evolutionary anthropology was both intellectually flawed and, because it treated other people and other societies as inferior to Europeans, morally defective. He was deeply critical of the data-gathering techniques and the reasoning of Morgan, Tylor, and others. Boas argued that anthropologists should not be mere collectors of tales and spinners of theories, but rather should devote themselves to fieldwork, to objective data collection. Anthropologists must live among the people they studied, both observing their culture and, where possible, participating in it. They should record the cultural patterns of the group, their language, their material

**ethnography** The major research tool of cultural anthropology; includes both fieldwork among people in society and the written results of fieldwork.

In the first half of the 20th century, Franz Boas had a huge impact on anthropology in the United States. He emphasized fieldwork and cultural relativism.

goods, and their religion. Anthropologists should investigate the group past using archaeology and historical archives. They should collect statistical measures of the bodies of those they studied. Boas's style of fieldwork became known as participant observation and has been the hallmark of American anthropology. Although few anthropologists today would investigate society in precisely the same way as Boas (today, for example, archaeology and body measurements are left to archaeologists and biological anthropologists), almost all anthropologists do fieldwork in which they both observe members of a culture and participate with them to the greatest extent possible.

One of Boas's core beliefs was that cultures are the products of their own histories. He argued that a culture's standards of beauty and morality, as well as many other aspects of behavior, could be understood only in light of that culture's historical development. Because our own ideas were also the products of history, it was inappropriate to use our standards to judge other cultures. Evolutionists had failed, in part, because they had made just this mistake. They assumed, incorrectly, that the more a culture's values approached those of Europeans, the more

evolved it was. In other words, the evolutionists failed because of their own ethnocentrism. In one sense, **ethnocentrism** is simply the belief that one's own culture is better than any other. In a deeper sense, it is the application of the historical standards of beauty, worth, and morality developed in one culture to all other cultures.

Boas insisted that anthropologists free themselves, as much as possible, from ethnocentrism and approach each culture on its own terms, in light of its own notions of worth and value. This position came to be known as **cultural relativism** and is one of the hallmarks of anthropology. Boas and his followers maintained that anthropologists must suspend judgment in order to understand the logic and dynamics of other cultures. Researchers who view the actions of other people simply in terms of the degree to which they correspond to their own notions of the ways people should behave systematically distort the cultures they study.

Boas was a tireless campaigner for human rights and justice. He argued that all human beings have equal capacities for culture, and that although human actions might be considered morally right or wrong, no culture was more evolved or of greater value than another. He was an unwavering supporter of racial equality. His work and that of his students, notably Ruth Benedict and Margaret Mead, were widely used by Americans who argued for the equality of men and women, the rights of African Americans, immigrants, and Native Americans. He was, in a sense, the first activist anthropologist. Today, virtually all anthropologists rely on Boas's basic insights.

## From Haddon to Malinowski in England and the Commonwealth

While Boas was forming his ideas in America, a separate fieldwork tradition was developing in Britain. In the late 19th century, Alfred Cort Haddon mounted two expeditions to the Torres Straits (between New Guinea and Australia). Haddon was originally a biologist, but his travels turned his interest to ethnography, the gathering and interpretation of information based on intensive, firsthand study. Haddon's second expedition included scholars from several different fields. Haddon and his colleagues became professors at Cambridge and the London School of Economics, where they trained the next generation of British Commonwealth anthropologists. Like Boas, their understandings were based in fieldwork and they made it a basic part of their students' training.

**ethnocentrism** Judging other cultures from the perspective of one's own culture. The notion that one's own culture is more beautiful, rational, and nearer to perfection than others.

**cultural relativism** The notion that cultures should be analyzed with reference to their own histories and values, in terms of the cultural whole, rather than according to the values of another culture.

Bronislaw Malinowski, one of the pioneers of participant observation, worked in the Trobriand Islands between 1915 and 1918.

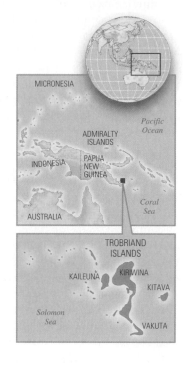

The Trobriand Islands

lands until the end of the war. Thus, what he had intended as a relatively short fieldwork expedition became an extremely long one.

Malinowski's time on the Trobriands was a signal moment in British Commonwealth anthropology. The Torres Straits scholars had studied culture at a distance, observing it for a short time, and then describing it. Malinowski spent years with native Trobrianders, learning their language, their patterns of thought, and their cultural ways. A diary he kept during those years shows he was frequently lonely, frustrated, and angry. Despite these problems, he developed a form of ethnography centered on empathic understandings of native lifeways and on analyzing culture by describing social institutions and showing the cultural and psychological functions they performed. Malinowski also stressed the interrelations among the elements of culture.

In an era when non-Europeans were often considered incomprehensible and illogical, Malinowski forcefully promoted the idea that native cultural ways were logical and rational. For example, in a famous essay on science and magic, he argued that natives used magic only for goals they were unable to attain by more rational means (such as controlling the weather). He argued that magic was like science in that it had "a definite aim intimately associated with human instincts, needs, and pursuits." Like science, magic was "governed by a theory, by a system of principles which dictate the manner in which the act has to be performed in order to be effective" (1948).

Malinowski's and Boas's anthropology were quite different. Boas and his students focused on understanding cultures with respect to their context and histories. Malinowski and his students emphasized the notion of function: the contribution made by social practices and institutions to the maintenance and stability of society. However, both developed traditions of fieldwork and participant observation. Both traditions have strong histories of opposition to racism. Both see other cultures as fully rational and neither superior nor inferior to their own. There have been a great many new approaches in anthropology since the days of Boas and Malinowski. However, these fundamental insights and principles remain basic to current-day anthropology.

Bronislaw Malinowski was one of the most prominent students of the Torres Straits scholars. Malinowski grew up in Krakow, then part of the Austro-Hungarian Empire (now in Poland). He came to England to study ethnography and his mentor, Charles Seligman, sent him to do fieldwork on the Trobriand Islands (in the Torres Straits). Malinowski arrived in the Trobriands in 1914, as World War I broke out. Because the Trobriands were governed by Australia and Malinowski was a subject of the Austro-Hungarian Empire, he was considered an enemy national. As a result, he was unable to leave the is-

## Anthropological Techniques

Today anthropologists work for a wide variety of employers including universities, businesses, and governments. You find them investigating topics as different as the way people hunt in Paraguay (Blaser 2009), kinship relations in Ethiopia (Ellison 2009), the ways in which residents of Rio de Janeiro use slang (Roth-Gordon 2009), the ways in which Americans bargain at garage sales (Herrmann 2003), and the ways in which people relate to their computers (Harkin 2001). Because of the multiplicity of anthropologies, it would be impossible to describe all of the different settings in which anthropologists work and the different ways they go about their work. However, almost all do have some similarities.

Since the days of Boas and Haddon, fieldwork has been the cornerstone of anthropology. Most anthropological data are generated through fieldwork and virtually all anthropologists do fieldwork as part of their graduate training. For most, doing fieldwork continues as a basic element of their careers. Some anthropologists return to the same fieldwork location year after year, creating a record of the community throughout their lifetime. Others may change their fieldwork location and the research problems that concern them every few years.

**Fieldwork** is the firsthand, intensive, systematic exploration of a culture. Although fieldwork includes many techniques, such as structured and unstructured interviewing, mapping space, taking census data, photographing and filming, using historical archives, and recording life histories, the heart of anthropological fieldwork is **participant observation.** Participant observation is the technique of gathering data on human cultures by living among the people, observing their social interaction on an ongoing daily basis, and participating as much as possible in their lives. This intensive field experience is the methodological hallmark of cultural anthropology. In other social science disciplines such as psychology, sociology, and economics, the key methodological tools tend to be laboratory experimentation, large-scale survey, close readings of archives, or analysis of statistical information. Anthropologists believe that only by living with people and engaging in their activities can we begin to understand the interrelated patterns of culture. The anthropologist observes, listens, asks questions, and attempts to find a way in which to participate in the life of the society over an extended period of time.

Participant observation has both advantages and limitations. Perhaps the key advantage is that anthropologists are on the job 24/7. Anthropologists observe people at work, at play, and sleeping. They share the good times of the communities where they work and frequently the tragedies as well. Regardless of their specific interests, the constant attempt to participate in another culture gives anthropologists a depth of understanding that is almost impossible to achieve in any other way. An important limitation of participant observation is that anthropologists necessarily work with a limited number of individuals. A sociologist carrying out a carefully constructed survey of several thousand individuals may be able to describe certain aspects of a large community accurately. Anthropologists rarely work with more than 50

Anthropologist Nadine Peacock does participant observation among the Efe.

individuals and it is sometimes difficult to say how well these represent larger communities.

Fieldwork is often funded by grants given by universities, government agencies, and nonprofit organizations that promote social science research. Sometimes, anthropologists will pay for their research themselves, although because research frequently involves extended stays in distant places, doing it is fairly expensive. In most cases, anthropologists are required to submit their research proposals to **institutional review boards (IRBs).** These are committees organized by universities and other research institutions that approve, monitor, and review all research that involves human subjects. Their goals are to protect the rights and welfare of the research subjects, the research institutions, and the researchers themselves. IRBs were originally started to review medical research but in most places have expanded their scope of operations to include all research involving living people.

Decisions about which communities anthropologists investigate are based on a large number of factors. Some of these include personal history, geographical preferences, political stability, cost, physical danger, and con-

**fieldwork** The firsthand, systematic exploration of a society. It involves living with a group of people and participating in and observing their behavior.

**participant observation** The fieldwork technique that involves gathering cultural data by observing people's behavior and participating in their lives.

**institutional review board (IRB)** A committee organized by a university or other research institution that approves, monitors, and reviews all research that involves human subjects.

nections their professors and other mentors may have. However, the most critical aspect of choosing a location has to do with the particular research questions that the anthropologist wishes to answer.

In the early 20th century, anthropologists studying relatively small groups often attempted to write complete descriptions of societies. Their books, with titles such as *The Tiwi of Northern Australia* (Hart and Pilling 1960), *The Sebei: A Study in Adaptation* (Goldschmidt 1986) or *The Cheyennes: Indians of the Great Plains* (Hoebel 1960), had chapters on the whole range of culture and society, including subjects such as family, religion, farming, and legal affairs. In a sense, it did not matter much where they chose to work; any small-scale community or society could be described.

Today, few anthropologists attempt to write such descriptions. This is partly because most feel that societies are so complex they cannot be adequately described in a single work. But more important, although societies were never really isolated, today they are so interconnected and so changed by these connections that they must be seen in regional and global context. Current ethnographies focus on specific situations, individuals, events, and frequently on culture change. Some recent examples describe Native Americans and casino gambling (Darian-Smith 2004), the relationship between indigenous peoples and national parks (Igoe 2004), or the ways in which immigrant communities cope with new customs and values (Stepick 1998). As research questions have narrowed, both the questions anthropologists ask and the conditions and locations where they can be answered have become more specific.

After they have identified an area of general interest, anthropologists spend a great deal of time reading the existing research on their subject. It is no exaggeration to say that most researchers spend several hours reading for each hour they spend actually doing active field research. From their studies, they gain an understanding of the geography, history, and culture of their chosen area. They find out what is known and what remains to be learned about the subjects of their interest. They try to design projects that help to close the gaps in existing knowledge. It is a bit like filling in pieces of a jigsaw puzzle, with one important exception: you can finish a puzzle but good research leads to the posing of interesting questions, and thus, more research.

The opportunity to do participant observation, to live a life and understand a culture very different than the one in which the anthropologist grew up, is one of the key factors that brings people to anthropology. However, arriving at a field location can be a difficult and disorienting experience. Often, the anthropologist will have made a brief trip to the field location to arrange logistics such as obtaining the necessary research clearances and finding a place to stay. Despite this, and a great deal of other preparation, for most people, living in another culture and trying to learn its ways is difficult. Culture is learned behavior and we have been learning our culture since the moment of our births. When we move to a radically different culture much of that learning is no longer relevant.

Anthropologists arriving in new cultures are in many ways like children. Their language skills are often weak and their speech is sometimes babyish. Their social skills are undeveloped. They are ignorant of many aspects of their environment and their new culture. One common result of this is the syndrome often called **culture shock;** the feelings of alienation, loneliness, and isolation common to one who has been placed in a new culture. Most all researchers experience some degree of culture shock. For graduate students, sometimes the journey stops there. You can be an outstanding scholar—well versed in literature and able to think and write creatively—yet be unable to do fieldwork. Sometimes aspiring anthropologists return after a few weeks of fieldwork and pursue other fields of study.

Getting past culture shock is a process of learning: learning language, customs, social organization—the fundamental grounding knowledge that it takes to be an adult in a different culture. It is probably accurate to say most anthropologists never feel like they are truly members of the cultures they study. We are separated from our subjects by our backgrounds, education, and sometimes the color of our skins. Perhaps most importantly, we're separated by the knowledge that our time in the field is temporary and we will leave to rejoin our other lives. However, in our best moments, anthropologists do come close to acting and feeling like members of the cultures we study.

Although almost all anthropologists rely on participant observation, within this general technique there are numerous different styles of anthropological research. The research techniques and tools that anthropologists use depend on the type of research they do and the sorts of questions they want to answer. Anthropological research styles are sometimes characterized as either emic or etic, terms drawn from the study of language. Anthropologists using the **emic perspective** seek to understand how cultures look from the inside. The aim of emic research is to enable cultural outsiders to gain a sense of what it might be like to be a member of the culture. Anthropologists using an **etic perspective** seek to derive principles or rules that explain the behavior of members of a culture. Etic analysis may produce conclusions that con-

**culture shock** Feelings of alienation and helplessness that result from rapid immersion in a new and different culture.

**emic perspective** Examining a society using concepts and distinctions that are meaningful to members of that culture.

**etic perspective** Examining societies using concepts, categories, and rules derived from science; an outsider's perspective which produces analyses that members of the society being studied may not find meaningful.

flict with the ways in which people understand their own culture. However, etic research is judged by the usefulness of the hypotheses it generates and the degree to which it accurately describes behavior, not by whether or not members of the culture studied agree with its conclusions.

Some anthropological research follows a model drawn from the natural sciences. In this sort of research, anthropologists propose a hypothesis and collect empirical data to determine whether or not the hypothesis can be supported. For example, in a recent study, Wendy Phillips (2005) analyzed pregnancy beliefs among women of African descent in three communities in the United States. The communities differed in the degree and extent of their contact with the dominant American culture. Phillips hypothesized that women who have historically had the least contact with the dominant culture would report more traditional practices. She interviewed thirty-six mothers with children under the age of 5, twelve from each community. Her analysis of her interview data largely confirmed her hypothesis, although she found that some West African beliefs persisted even among members of the community with the greatest contact with the dominant culture.

Some anthropological research is more highly interpretive and uses techniques drawn from the study of history and literature. For example, Allison Truitt (2008) recently studied the important role of motorbikes in current-day urban Vietnam. Her study has no formal hypothesis. Instead, she uses data from interviews, advertisements, observations of traffic patterns, and legal codes to analyze the value and meaning of motorcycles in current-day urban Vietnamese culture. She explores both the practical and symbolic importance of motorcycles, showing how motorcycles are markers of social and economic mobility and of middle-class identity. Her work describes the ways in which motorcycles have become key symbols in a political struggle that pits consumer demand against government attempts to control production and consumption.

Regardless of their style of research, in most cases, as anthropologists begin to observe and participate in new cultures, they develop networks of friends and contacts. These are often the people who both guide them in their new surroundings and offer insights into the culture. Traditionally, in anthropology, these are called **informants** though the word has fallen somewhat out of use (to some, it sounds too much like spying). More modern words are respondents, interlocutors, and consultants. These words emphasize the collaborative nature of fieldwork and suggest that the people who work with the anthropologist are active and empowered. Much of what anthropologists know they learn from such people, who frequently become enduring friends. In some cases, an-

© Joan Gregg

Allison Truitt used data from interviews, advertisements, observations of traffic patterns, and legal codes to understand the importance of motorcycles in current Vietnamese urban culture.

thropologists work with a few individuals (sometimes called "key informants") who they believe are well informed and eager to talk with them. Alternatively, they may construct statistical models and use techniques such as random sampling to choose their consultants. Sometimes, they are able to interview all members of a community.

Anthropologists often develop deep rapport with some of their informants, and even lifetime friendships (Grindal and Salamone 1995). These informants are essential not only for explaining cultural patterns but also for introducing anthropologists to the community and helping them establish a network of social relationships. In the early stages of fieldwork, the anthropologist may just observe. Within a short time, however, he or she will begin to participate in cultural activities. Participation is the best way to understand the difference between what people say they do, feel, or think and what they actually do. It is not that informants deliberately lie (although they may), but rather that anthropologists and informants have particular interests and individual ways of looking at issues. People wish to present their lives, their families, and their communities in a certain light. No one, including the anthropologist, can present a

**informant (consultant)** A person from whom an anthropologist gathers data.

## Anthropologists and Drug Use

Anthropologists have an important contribution to make to our understanding of the use and abuse of controlled substances. In the 1960s and 1970s, the identification of a drug addict subculture drew anthropologists into the world of substance abuse and addiction (Schensul 1997). Ethnography was a particularly suitable methodology for studying street drug scenes and their participants.

Medical models of drug use emphasize its psychological and biochemical elements. Most social science models of drug use and distribution treat drug users and sellers as "deviants," separate from the larger population and operating outside of its social networks and cultural norms. Anthropologists, on the other hand, in keeping with their broader holistic perspective, have introduced models that aim at connecting individual drug users and sellers with the larger, structural features of the society, and economy. For example, in the 1990s, Hamid (1998, 1992, 1990) demonstrated that patterns of drug-related violence vary as a result of the ways in which political decisions and economic processes impact on neighborhoods, families, and kinship networks. Hamid's work showed that drug use and distribution are integrated with larger economic and political issues, particularly those affecting the transformation of minority neighborhoods.

Anthropologist Kojo Dei, in his ethnography of Southside, a lower-class African-American neighborhood in a suburban county in the Northeast, found that the residents of this community view drugs quite differently than both the law and the cultural norms of middle-class America. In this community, smoking marijuana is common. Although in public most adult residents of Southside give lip service to the view that "drugs are a major social problem," in private they express different views. Many Southside residents note that alcohol and nicotine—two legal addictive drugs—do more harm than marijuana. The community's view of a "drug addict" is a person who cannot function because of his or her drug use—a definition different from that of the social service and medical professions, which define addiction in terms of physical withdrawal symptoms. And, unlike those with law enforcement perspectives, the community's main concerns are the violence and other criminal activities associated with the use and distribution of both illegal drugs and alcohol rather than the use and distribution of illegal drugs as such (Dei 2002). Jagna Sharff's (1997) study of a Puerto Rican neighborhood in New York shows that sometimes the sale of illegal drugs may be seen as just one possible option in a range of economic survival strategies that span the spectrum from legal to underground jobs. Indeed, many of the young men Dei studied viewed selling drugs as a legitimate, if not legal, path to achieving the American Dream through the capitalist model of entrepreneurship. In addition to appreciating the money, many of these young men prefer selling drugs to "working for the white man." Unlike the inner-city youth in Katherine Newman's (1999b) study, who are willing to work in dead-end jobs in the fast-food sector of the economy in order to get ahead, Dei's consultants in Southside consider these jobs "kid stuff."

fully accurate and unbiased portrait of a culture. Participation, however, forces the researcher to think more deeply about culture and gives greater context and depth to the information they glean through interviews and observation.

Working with consultants is often informal, but anthropologists also use an arsenal of more formal tools depending on their theoretical interests. Much of anthropology is done by interviewing and there are many different interview techniques. Some anthropologists prepare exhaustive inventories and questionnaires; however, more frequently they design a series of open-ended questions that allow their subjects to talk freely and extensively on a topic. Occasionally, they use a structured interview, a technique designed to help identify the objects and ideas that their consultant thinks are important. Because kinship structures are important elements of many societies, anthropologists also become adept at gathering genealogical information.

In addition to interviewing, anthropological data gathering also includes mapping, photography, careful silent observation of a wide range of activities, measurements of various kinds of production, and in some cases, serving apprenticeships. It all depends on the nature of the problem the anthropologist is investigating.

As with the techniques used, the analysis of data also depends on the questions being asked and the theoretical perspective of the researcher. Anthropological data generally comes in the form of extensive field notes, tape recordings, and photographs. In most cases, organizing data presents substantial challenges. Notes have to be indexed, recordings transcribed, and data entered in spreadsheets. Aspiring anthropologists should keep in mind that, as with background research, successful anthropologists often spend more time working with their data than they did collecting it in the first place. Recording an interview may take only an hour or two. Transcribing and indexing that recording may take several days.

Courtesy of Kojo A. Dei

Kojo A. Dei (right) does ethnographic field-work among African-American youth in a major American city. He focuses on the ways that the cultural meanings of drug use within inner-city communities both support and diverge from those in the larger society. In this picture he is seen with Prince Afrika, one of his key consultants.

Much "drug scene" ethnography by anthropologists has been used in formulating more effective services and risk reduction programs for those using drugs. Merrill Singer's work has been instrumental in this regard. Singer and his colleagues have been studying drug use in Hartford, Connecticut, since the mid 1980s. They have made important contributions to AIDS prevention education and shown the effectiveness of needle-exchange programs in preventing AIDS (Singer 2000). Some of their recent work has focused on the connection between drugs and alcohol. In most studies illegal drugs and alcohol are treated separately. However, in a recent study Singer, Salaheen, Mirhej, and Santelice (2005) found that more than 80 percent of the drug users they interviewed mixed alcohol with other drugs and they did so for a variety of reasons. For example, they found a close relationship between cocaine and alcohol use. People used alcohol to "come down," that is, to lessen the effects of cocaine, but they also used cocaine to stay awake and consume more alcohol. The re-

searchers also found that alcohol was both a "gateway drug" and a "gateway-back." That is, alcohol tended to be the first drug used by almost all people who went on to use illegal drugs. And for about one third of people who had stopped using drugs for 6 months or more but later relapsed, alcohol was the drug that led them back to illicit drug use. These findings have clear use in designing and implementing programs to help drug users.

Ethnography also reveals where anti–drug-use programs are ineffective. In Southside, for example, the Drug Abuse Resistance Education (DARE) program, run by the school district, is largely ineffective because it is taught by police officers in uniform, whom the black community generally distrusts.

Anthropology, then, through its holistic perspective on the individual, its ethnographic methodology, and its multilevel analysis of culture and society, has much to contribute to drug policies in the United States.

## Ethnographic Data and Cross-Cultural Comparisons

Boas and his students were interested in describing cultures in their contexts. Because they understood each culture as the product of its unique history, they did not attempt systematic comparison of one culture to another and were not very interested in discovering laws or principles of cultural behavior. However, some level of comparison has always been implicit in anthropology. One goal of the Boasians, for example, was to use their research to cause Europeans and Americans to compare their own societies with the societies anthropologists described. Anthropologists hoped that this would help people think about their own societies in a new light and help change them for the better.

British and European anthropologists were more explicitly interested in **ethnology,** the attempt to find general principles or laws that govern cultural phenomena. They compared societies in the hope of deriving general prin-

ciples of social organization and behavior. Starting in the 1860s, Herbert Spencer began to develop a systematic way of organizing, tabulating, and correlating information on a large number of societies, a project he called Descriptive Sociology. The American scholar William Graham Sumner, his student Albert Keller, and Keller's student George Murdock brought Spencer's ideas about cross-cultural comparison to the United States. In the late 1930s, Murdock and Keller created a large, indexed ethnographic database at Yale University. First called the Cross Cultural Survey, in the late 1940s the project was expanded to include other universities and its name was changed to the **Human Relations Area Files** (or **HRAF**).

**ethnology** The attempt to find general principles or laws that govern cultural phenomena.

**Human Relations Area Files (HRAF)** An ethnographic database that includes descriptions of more than 300 cultures and is used for cross-cultural research.

The HRAF is an attempt to facilitate cross-cultural analysis. It provides a single index to ethnographic reports and other sources on 710 numbered subject categories. Some examples of categories are 294, techniques of clothing manufacture and 628, traditional friendships and rivalries within communities. Using the HRAF, a researcher can find information on these and many other topics for a wide range of current and historic societies.

The HRAF frequently comes under fire; critics charge that the project takes cultural data out of context and therefore corrupts it. They say that the works indexed in the HRAF were written from different perspectives, for different purposes, and in different eras. Because of this, indexing is often inconsistent or inappropriate and therefore analyses based on it are suspect. Despite these problems, work based on the HRAF is often both interesting and insightful. For example, back in the 1950s, the rising divorce rate in the United States was causing alarm. Was divorce truly something new and different, a product of modernity? Murdock used the HRAF to show that almost all societies had some form of divorce and that the divorce rate in America (in the 1950s) was lower than average. Thus, his use of the HRAF allowed people to think about divorce in a comparative context. In recent years, the HRAF, now available online and in computer searchable formats, has been used to consider a wide variety of issues. These include family violence (Levinson 1989), corporal punishment of children (Ember and Ember 2005), patterns of cultural evolution (Peregrine, Ember, and Ember 2004), and adolescent gender and sexuality (Schlegel and Barry 1991).

Of course not all cross-cultural research involves the use of the HRAF. Much research is done by a single investigator working in two or more locations or by teams using the same techniques in multiple locations. Some examples include cross-cultural studies of violence (Aijmer and Abbink 2000), of economics (Durrenberger and Marti 2006; Henrich et al. 2004), and of language and cognition (Wierzbicka 2003). Medical anthropology is a particularly rich area of cross-cultural research. The delivery of effective medical services to members of different cultures is a critical area of interest for applied medical anthropologists. Doing this effectively involves a thorough knowledge of the ways in which different groups of people understand diseases. Medical anthropologists need to know how people in different cultures understand the causes, symptoms, and cures for different diseases. For example, Carod-Artal and Vázquez-Cabrera (2007) recently investigated migraine headache symptoms among three different groups of Native Americans: the Tzeltal Maya of Mexico, the Kamayurá of Brazil, and the Uru-Chipaya of Bolivia. They found that all three groups had named syndromes whose symptoms matched migraines. However, their understandings of the origins of such headaches and how to treat them differed greatly from each other and from our own.

Another example of cross-cultural research is a study of preschools in China, Japan, and the United States carried out by a team of anthropologists and educators. The aims of the study were to examine preschools comparatively, but also to examine these three different cultures through a focus on their preschools, linking the findings on preschools to larger cultural and social concerns, particularly social change. The study hoped to go beyond statistical measures, such as teacher/child class ratios, and instead elicit the cultural meanings embedded in preschools—what they are meant to do and to be (Tobin, Wu, and Davidson 1989). Inspired by methods in visual anthropology, in which the subjects of ethnographic films were asked to comment on the completed film, the researchers in this study used videotapes in their ethnography and then showed the tapes to audiences both from the filmed culture and from the two other cultures. This method thus not only documented the diversity of human cultures, but in good anthropological tradition, used the study of other cultures to achieve insights about the researchers' own cultures.

## Changing Directions and Critical Issues in Ethnography

In one example of cross-cultural research, anthropologists examined preschools in China, Japan, and the United States. They hoped to link their findings about these schools to larger social concerns, particularly culture change.

© Joan Gregg

### Feminist Anthropology

By the 1960s, the role of fieldwork in anthropology was extremely well established. Additionally, the position of women within academic anthropology was relatively good, particularly in comparison to other areas of the university. Franz Boas had trained several female anthropologists, and these had gone on to become well known within the discipline. One, Margaret Mead, had become a household name outside of anthropology as well. Despite this (or perhaps because of it), the political movements of the 1960s, particularly the civil rights movement and the feminist movement, caused anthropologists to begin to think about gender and their discipline in new ways.

Feminists soon discovered that the presence of some very high-profile women within anthropology did little to counteract the fact that the overwhelming majority of anthropologists were men and their areas of interest tended to focus on the social roles, activities, and beliefs of men in the societies they studied. There were several reasons why anthropologists had focused on men. First, in many societies, men and women live quite segregated lives. Because they were men, most anthropologists had little access to the lives of women. Second, anthropologists tended to assume that men's activities were political and therefore important whereas women's activities were domestic and therefore of less importance (see page 226 in Chapter 10, "Gender"). Third, in most societies, men's activities were far more public than women's activities. Anthropologists tended to assume that what was public and visible was more important than what was more behind-the-scenes and less visible. However, this is clearly not always (or even often) the case.

The result of taking men more seriously than women was a systematic bias in anthropological data and understandings. Anthropologists had often reported with great detail and accuracy about men's social and cultural worlds, but they had barely scratched the surface of women's worlds. Further, the assumption, frequently implicit in ethnographies, that men spoke for all of society often made cultures appear more harmonious and homogeneous than they actually were.

Starting in the 1970s, increasing numbers of women joined university anthropology faculties. By the late 1990s, more than 50 percent of new anthropology Ph.D.'s and more than 40 percent of all anthropology professors were women (Levine and Wright 1999). They began paying greater attention to women's lives in the societies they studied and to the nature of sexuality and gender, issues addressed more fully in Chapter 10.

## Postmodernism

Ultimately, the issue of women in anthropology focused on different ways of knowing. Feminists argued persuasively that male anthropologists had missed vital dimensions of society because their gender, and their academic interests predisposed them to see certain things and not others. These ideas dovetailed well with postmodernism, a critique of both natural and social sciences that gained prominence in the 1980s. **Postmodernists** hold that all

knowledge is influenced by the observer's culture and social position. They claim fieldworkers cannot discover and describe an objective reality, because such a thing does not exist (or exists but cannot be discovered or comprehended by human beings). Instead, postmodernists propose that there are only partial truths or cultural constructions and that these depend on frame of reference, power, and history.

Postmodernists urged anthropologists to examine the ways they understood both fieldwork and the work of writing ethnographies. They demanded that anthropology become sensitive to issues of history and power. Some postmodernists challenged the ethnographer's role in interpreting culture, claiming that anthropological ethnographies were just one story about experienced reality, and the ethnographer's voice only one of many possible representations.

The publication of Edward Said's *Orientalism* in 1978 was a critical moment in opening anthropology to postmodern ideas. The "orient" of Said's title refers to the colonial British name for what is now called the Middle East. Said argued that European art and drama as well as anthropology and other social sciences gave a simplified, distorted, and romanticized view of Middle Eastern cultures, portraying them as timeless societies full of savagery and exotic wonder. Said believed that this portrayal was politically and culturally motivated, demonstrating Western European superiority and justifying military conquest and colonization. Moreover, it also drew attention from the area's actual history, economics, and politics. It particularly ignored the roles the British and other colonizers had played in shaping Middle Eastern politics and culture. One area of Western fascination was gender and sexuality. Because they focused on multiple wives, the harem, and the role of Islam, Western observers almost entirely misunderstood the actual lives of Middle Eastern women. (For more detail, see page 331 in Chapter 14, "Creative Expression: Anthropology and the Arts").

During the 1990s, reflection on the nature of fieldwork and the anthropological enterprise became a central focus of writing in anthropology. Work such as Said's encouraged anthropologists to think about the ways in which their own status, personality, and culture shape their view of others, and how the ethnographer interacts with members of other cultures to produce data. In many cases, anthropologists turned from writing about culture to writing about anthropology itself and critical analyses of earlier anthropological literature became common. In other cases, rather than trying to describe culture or find principles

**postmodernism** A theoretical perspective focusing on issues of power and voice. Postmodernists suggest that anthropological accounts are partial truths reflecting the background, training, and social position of their authors.

underlying cultural practices, anthropologists wrote about their own experience of living in other cultures.

The claims of postmodernists have been a subject of intense debate in anthropology. Few anthropologists accept the postmodern critique in its entirety. To do so would be to understand anthropology as a rather peculiar sort of travel writing or a school of literary criticism. However, some of the ideas of postmodernism have become part of the mainstream. For example, almost all anthropologists today agree that ethnographers need to reflect critically on their positions as observers and be aware of the moral and political consequences of their work. Most ethnographies now include information about the conditions under which the fieldwork was carried out, and the nature of the relationships between the anthropologist and his or her consultants. Most are sensitive to issues of voice and of power and the ways anthropology is written.

## Engaged and Collaborative Anthropology

Engaged and **collaborative anthropology** reflect some of the concerns just noted. Collaboration is the process of working closely with other people and in a sense describes all anthropological research. Collaborative anthropologists, however, highlight this aspect of their work. They consult with their subjects about shaping their studies and writing their reports. They attempt to displace the anthropologist as the sole author representing a group, turning research into a joint process between researcher and subject. The work of James Spradley (1933–1982) is an important contribution to collaborative, engaged anthropology. His classic ethnography *You Owe Yourself a Drunk* (1970) was aimed at getting the public to understand and help the homeless alcoholics who were the subject of the book.

Erik Lassiter, an anthropologist inspired by Spradley, has done several collaborative projects. While still a student, he began collaborative work with Narcotics Anonymous, a drug addiction and recovery group. Based on his observations of their meetings, Lassiter worked with his consultants to develop an ethnography focused on the experience of drug addiction and recovery that could be given to drug addicts considering joining the program. In a later project Lassiter constructed a collaborative project with the Kiowa Indians in Oklahoma. The Kiowa were particularly interested in an ethnography of Kiowa song, and stipulated that it be written so that it could be read and understood by the Kiowa people themselves, and

that they would be acknowledged for their contributions. Lassiter emphasizes that a critical aspect of his collaboration with the Kiowa was to give the highest priority to representing the Kiowa cultural consultants as they wished to be represented, even if this meant adding or changing information or changing his interpretations. For Lassiter (2004), collaborative ethnography is not just eliciting the comments of the cultural consultants but, even more important, integrating these comments back into the text.

**Engaged anthropology** moves from the production of texts to political action. Most anthropologists would like their work to further a deep understanding of the human condition. Most also feel a deep sense of connection with the people among whom they work. In many cases, the communities in which anthropologists work are poor, and in some cases they face political oppression as well. In these circumstances, it is not surprising to find that many anthropologists believe that for anthropology to be relevant and meaningful it must be involved in political and social efforts to improve the life chances of people in these communities. Engaged anthropologists move from describing and analyzing the communities they study to actively promoting their interests and welfare.

Vincent Lyon-Callo (2004), an anthropologist who studies social services for homeless people, is a good example of an engaged anthropologist. Lyon-Callo hopes to understand homelessness but also to move attention on its causes to the center of American culture and politics. Lyon-Callo believes that most homelessness in the United States results from a cultural and political philosophy that embraces the free markets and private initiative as the solution to social problems. He argues that most Americans have a "social services" orientation to homelessness. They believe the problem can be solved through

Engaged anthropologists promote political action. Lyon-Callo both studied the homeless and advocated political change on their behalf. Pictured here, a homeless man near a soup kitchen.

© A.T. Willett/Alamy

**collaborative anthropology** Ethnography that gives priority to informants on the topic, methodology, and written results of research.

**engaged anthropology** Anthropology that includes political action as a major goal of fieldwork.

charity or services aimed at reforming homeless people, who are seen as deviant or disabled. This understanding undercuts attempts to see homelessness as a result of systemic inequalities such as increasing unemployment, declining relative wages, and exploitation of workers. Lyon-Callo argues that by distracting action from these issues, the social services orientation actually helps to maintain homelessness.

Working in collaboration with community members and homeless people in Northampton, Massachusetts, Lyon-Callo promoted new understandings of homelessness. His emphasis on structural causes of homelessness such as lack of jobs and lack of housing led to the creation of a winter-cot program in community churches, a living-wage campaign, as well as new job opportunities for the homeless.

Lyon-Callo suggests that anthropological analysis can challenge routine understandings, raise new questions, and get people to think in new ways. He argues that in the absence of political efforts to transform the economy, caring and helping cannot themselves end homelessness. Anthropologists must work in public political forums to expose the connections between social problems, political ideologies, and inequality. However, promoting profound change is slow and discouraging work. Even those who basically agree with Lyon-Callo note that the current social service approach at least offers a degree of immediate hope and help for homeless people.

Although many anthropologists practice some elements of both collaborative and engaged anthropology, these approaches raise important issues. Collaborative anthropologists propose that an anthropologist's primary job is to write and say what his or her consultants want. However, most anthropologists also believe they have an obligation to accurately report what people say and do to the best of their ability. They have a further obligation not to knowingly falsify information. These obligations may frequently conflict with the goal of producing the work the consultants desire. Further, communities are rarely so homogenous that they speak with a single voice. Collaborative anthropology may give voice and legitimacy to one element of a community over another. Often, writing what consultants want really means choosing their side in a political contest.

Engaged anthropologists have no difficulty in choosing sides in political contests. This, however, raises other problems. In the wake of postmodernism, anthropologists have acknowledged that objectivity and subjectivity are problematic concepts. It is impossible to achieve complete neutrality. Personal history, particular interests, and chance all play important roles in what anthropologists observe and report. Nevertheless, anthropologists who pursue specific political and social agendas face particular problems in this regard. As we noted earlier, anthropologists have an obligation to report what people say and do to the best of their ability and a further obligation not to falsify data. Can engaged anthropologists do this if what their collaborators say and do does not promote their political agenda? Even if the answer is yes, political opponents are unlikely to give much weight to data and analysis generated by engaged anthropology.

## Studying One's Own Society

When most people think of anthropologists they imagine researchers who study others in exotic locations, but since the early 20th century anthropologists have also studied their own societies. W. Lloyd Warner, Solon T. Kimball, Margaret Mead, Zora Neale Hurston, and Hortense Powdermaker were all American anthropologists who wrote about American culture. Kenyan anthropologist (as well as freedom fighter and first president of Kenya) Jomo Kenyatta wrote about the Gikuyu of Kenya in 1938, and Chinese anthropologist Francis Hsu wrote extensively on Chinese society. Anthropologists who study their own society are sometimes

It is increasingly common for anthropologists to study their own societies. Here, Louis Tepardjuk, an Inuit, records the stories of Piugaatuk, an Inuit elder from Igloolik, Nunvut, Canada.

called **native anthropologists.** In recent years, native anthropologists have become even more common. This trend is driven by many factors, including the training of more anthropologists from more different cultures, the increasing total number of anthropologists, the rise of interest in ethnicity in America and Europe, as well as the dangers of violence and political instability, and the corresponding difficulty in getting access to and funding for work in some areas where anthropologists have studied in the past.

The emphasis on more reflective fieldwork and ethnography affects all anthropologists but particularly those who study their own societies. Traditionally, anthropologists doing fieldwork try hard to learn the culture of the people with whom they are working. In a sense, anthropologists working in their own culture have the opposite problem: they must attempt to see their culture as an outsider might. This is challenging because it is easy to take cultural knowledge for granted. In addition, it may be as difficult to maintain a neutral stand in one's own culture as it is in a different one. As Margaret Mead once noted, it may be easier to remain culturally relativistic when we confront patterns, such as cannibalism or infanticide, in other cultures than when we confront problematic situations such as child neglect, corporate greed, or armed conflict in our own.

Some of the problems and the rewards of studying one's own culture can be seen in Barbara Myerhoff's books and films. Myerhoff contrasted her work with the Huichol of northern Mexico (1974) with her work among elderly Jewish people in California (1978). She notes that in the first case, doing anthropology was "an act of imagination, a means for discovering what one is not and will never be." In the second case, fieldwork was a glimpse into her possible future, as she knew that someday she would be a "little old Jewish lady." Her work was a personal way to understand that condition and contemplate her own future. It was, tragically, a future that never arrived. Myerhoff died of cancer when she was only 49.

The issues and problems raised by engaged anthropology may be particularly poignant for native anthropologists. On the one hand, nothing about being a native requires an individual to take a specific political position. On the other, in some cases it may be particularly difficult for a native anthropologist to avoid politics. Delmos Jones, an African-American anthropologist who worked in the United States, provides a case in point. Jones was deeply concerned with improving the position of African Americans. He studied voluntary organizations whose goal was to create political and social change in African

American urban communities (1995). He was able to get access to such organizations both because he was an African American and because he shared their goals. However, one of his important findings was that, for a variety of reasons, there was considerable dissent between the leadership and the rank and file in the groups he studied. Further, he found that leaders used a variety of means to stifle this dissent. Jones's findings left him with a variety of unpleasant choices. If he publicized problems within the organizations he risked both alienating the leaders who had befriended him and potentially damaging causes in which he believed deeply. On the other hand, if he failed to publicize such problems he would be omitting an important aspect of his findings and supporting leadership practices he considered troubling.

Reflecting on his research experience, Jones concluded that although being a cultural insider offers certain advantages such as access to the community, it also poses special dilemmas, particularly when the group being studied has been oppressed by the larger society. Indeed, he noted that the very concept of a native anthropologist is problematic. An individual has many identities, including race, culture, gender, and social class. Being a native in one identity does not make one a native in all one's identities (Cerroni-Long 1995; Narayan 1993).

# Ethical Considerations in Fieldwork

Delmos Jones's position as a native anthropologist involved him in a delicate ethical situation. This is not at all unusual. Ethical issues frequently arise in anthropological research. Anthropologists have obligations to the standards of their discipline, to their sponsors, to their own and their host governments, and to the public. However, their first ethical obligations are to the people they study and to the people with whom they work. Under some circumstances, these obligations can supersede the goal of seeking new knowledge. According to the American Anthropological Association Statement on Ethics (1986), "Anthropological researchers must do everything in their power to ensure that their research does not harm the safety, dignity, or privacy of the people with whom they work. . . ." This includes safeguarding the rights, interests, and sensitivities of those studied; explaining the aims of the investigation as clearly as possible to the persons involved; respecting the anonymity of informants; not exploiting individual informants for personal gain; and giving "fair return" for all services. It also includes the responsibility to communicate the results of the research to the individuals and groups likely to be affected, as well as to the general public.

Informed consent is a critical aspect of anthropological ethics. Generally, obtaining the informed consent of

**native anthropologist** An anthropologist who does fieldwork in his or her own culture.

study participants requires anthropologists to take part in ongoing and dynamic discussion with their consultants about the nature of the study as well as the risks and benefits of participation in it (Clark and Kingsolver n.d.). In particular, **informed consent** means that study participants should understand the ways in which their participation in the study and the release of the research data are likely to affect them. Further, individuals must be free to decide whether or not they will participate in the study.

Anthropologists also have obligations to the discipline of anthropology. Two of these obligations seem both particularly important and particularly problematic. First, anthropologists should conduct themselves in ways that do not endanger the research prospects or lives of other anthropologists. Anthropologists who violate the mores and ethics of the communities where they work make it unlikely that those communities will accept other anthropologists in the future. Anthropologists who become involved with and identified with governments, military forces, or political platforms may endanger not only their own lives but the work and lives of others. People may come to believe that because some anthropologists are identified with specific political actors, all are.

Second, many anthropologists believe that the primary purpose of research is to add to the general store of anthropological knowledge. Because of this, anthropologists have an obligation to publish their findings in forms that are available to other anthropologists and to the general public. Publishing usually involves review of the work by other anthropologists and this helps ensure the validity and quality of research. Anthropologists acknowledge that certain forms of secrecy are acceptable, and, on occasion, even required. For example, to protect both the communities where they work and the individuals with whom they work, anthropologists may decide not to reveal the precise location of their research or the actual names of the individuals they discuss. However, research in which the methods and findings are secret is a far greater problem. Not only does it fail to contribute to anthropological knowledge but the scientific community has no way of assessing its validity.

The obligations to protect other anthropologists and to publish research findings both pose dilemmas. The engaged anthropologists described earlier believe that anthropologists must work for the communities they study. However, this may make it impossible for future anthropologists to work at all. For example, governments may not grant anthropologists research visas and organization may not allow research if they believe anthropologists will promote political action against them. Applied anthropologists wish to work for businesses and governments. Often anthropological findings have greatest value for these entities when they are not shared with other businesses or the general public. There may be very few jobs available for applied anthropologists who

insist on the right to publish all of the results of their research.

Numerous projects have tested the boundaries of ethics in anthropology, both in regard to the people anthropologists study and to the discipline itself. One of the best known of these was "Project Camelot," a mid-1960s attempt by the Army and Department of Defense to enlist anthropologists and other social scientists in achieving American foreign policy goals. Project Camelot's purpose was to create a model for predicting civil wars but it was also implicated in using military and cultural means to fight insurgency movements and prop up friendly governments (Horowitz 1967). When Project Camelot was made public in 1965, the United States had recently invaded the Dominican Republic and was escalating the Vietnam War.

Project Camelot created controversy both inside and outside of anthropology. In countries where anthropologists worked, people began to see them as spies whose presence presaged an American invasion. At the American Anthropological Association, Project Camelot led to vitriolic debate; members raised concerns for the integrity of research, the safety of anthropologists in the field, and the purposes to which anthropological knowledge might be put. These concerns eventually led to the issuing of the first official statement on anthropological ethics in 1971.

## Anthropology and the Military

Recently concerns similar to those raised by Project Camelot have recurred over the engagement of some anthropologists with the American military. Anthropologists and other social scientists are involved with the military in two different ways. Some anthropologists have worked at military colleges and bases providing anthropological training for officers or analyses of the culture of the military itself. Other anthropologists and social scientists have worked on the ground collecting data in zones of active conflict. Most of these individuals work for a program called Human Terrain Systems (HTS). As of this writing (June 2009), three social scientists working in this program have been killed.

The use of anthropologists in the training of military officers is the less controversial of the two forms of engagement. Anthropologists who favor this form of working with the military argue that such anthropologists generally present information that is publically available. Military personnel are free to enroll in anthropology courses at public and private universities. Presenting an-

**informed consent** The requirement that participants in anthropological studies should understand the ways in which their participation and the release of the research data are likely to affect them.

# Ethnography

## Dangerous Field

Throughout much of the history of anthropology, researchers assumed that they would be safe in the field. Most students are drawn to anthropology at least partially by the chance to do work in interesting places—to live with people, learn their ways of life, and become friends with them (Chagnon 1997). Fieldwork conjures images like the one of Bronislaw Malinowski peacefully learning about music on page 52 or Margaret Mead, seen greeting friends in Bali in the photo in this box. Anthropologists have generally assumed that they will work under conditions of stability, trust, quietude, security, and freedom from fear. Although anthropologists today do often work in places where these conditions are possible, in many other places, anthropology, if it is done at all, is done under conditions of instability and violence.

**Margaret Mead visits friends in Bali in 1957.**

© Associated Press

A 1990 study of dangers to anthropologists in the field identified malaria, hepatitis, and vehicle crashes as the three greatest risks anthropologists face (Howell 1990). However, the study also notes a surprisingly high rate of encounters with violence, criminality, and political instability. For example, at least 42 percent of anthropologists experienced "criminal interpersonal hazards" and 22 percent reported living through political turmoil such as war, revolution, and rioting.

J. Christopher Kovats-Bernat points out that the conditions under which Malinowski, Mead, and many other anthropologists operated were, in many cases, artificially peaceful. Anthropologists worked in areas that were controlled by colonial governments or were American protectorates. In these cases, hostility among groups was suppressed and managed by colonial authorities. Anthropologists themselves, regardless of who they worked for, were protected by these authorities, and natives could expect that violence against anthropologists would be punished rapidly and harshly.

The world of colonial anthropology is gone and today, in many cases, anthropologists work in conditions of danger and physical risk to themselves and those who work with them. Kovats-Bernat has worked on the streets of Port-au-Prince, Haiti, in an area of the city often called "Kosovo" because of the prevalence of gangsterism, political gunplay, and drug terrorism. Most of the street kids in the area sniff glue and some carry razors. Kovats-Bernat reports that he has at various times "been present at street shootings, threatened, searched, suspected of subversion, and in the midst of crossfire" (2002:209). His experiences are not particularly unusual. Anthropologists have faced danger and physical violence during fieldwork in many parts of the world. For example, Danny Hoffman, a photojournalist turned anthropologist, writes about his experiences of civil war in Sierra Leone. He recounts an incident at a UN disarmament center when tensions increased as the number of armed combatants grew beyond the ability of the UN monitors to control them. Finally, one of the combatants threw a grenade into the crowd. Fortunately, the grenade did not explode and Hoffman reports that he was able to "observe. . . . the dynamics of a crowd at an instant of intense violence and confusion and to understand the accounts we later gathered through the prism of our own experience of the event" (2003:12). Monique Skidmore did field research in Burma. She writes that anthropologists and

thropology courses as part of military training is no different. Additionally, supporters of such engagement argue that soldiers of all ranks who understand the dynamics of culture, the importance of critical meanings and symbols, and the structure and distribution of power within a society are liable to be more successful and less destructive than those who do not. Where are they to get this knowledge if not from anthropology? However, such engagement also raises important questions. No professor can ever control the uses to which students put the information and skills received in classes. However, the military's interest in anthropological knowledge is re-

informants inevitably share experiences and that in her case these included being frightened, confused, and disoriented, and suffering from a general loss of perspective (Skidmore 2003:6).

Kovats-Bernat, Hoffman, and Skidmore are drawn to the ethnography of violent places for different reasons but all believe the risks they and their informants take are worthwhile. Skidmore considers herself "an activist by proxy" determined to write against terror (2003: 6). Hoffman (2003: 9–10) notes that media conglomerates are increasingly unwilling to support correspondents in out-of-the-way places. Reporters sent to locations of violence are usually only briefly there. They depend on governments for access and thus tend to report news that governments allow. Their reporting generally follows the governments' interests and understandings. Given this, anthropologists are often among the very few who witness dangerous events and have the depth of knowledge to understand and analyze them. Kovats-Bernat writes that doing the ethnography of violence can make a critical contribution to anthropological theory. For him, violence is not something that covers and contaminates society but rather, in many cases, it is the stuff of social relationships, inseparable from kinship, market activities, language, and other aspects of culture (2002:217).

Doing fieldwork in dangerous locations raises important ethical questions. Kovats-Bernat writes that he has often found the American Anthropological Association's "Code of Ethics" to be "irrelevant, naïve, or insufficient to guide [his] actions" (2002:214). For example, the AAA's "Principles of Professional Responsibility" states that "Anthropologists must do everything in their power to protect the physical, social, and psychological welfare. . . . of those studied. . . . It is axiomatic that the rights, interests, and sensitivities of those studied must be safeguarded" (AAA 1986:1). Kovats-Bernat questions how this can be done under conditions of violence and lawlessness. The AAA statement assumes that it is the researcher who has the knowledge and power to look after the subject of the research, yet in real field situations, the reverse is often true. It is the subjects of research who have the local knowledge necessary to survival; they are in the best position to understand their own interests and the dangers they face. In reality, it is often the subjects of research who must protect the researcher rather than the other way around.

In situations of instability, activities basic to research may be fraught with danger. For example, even the most innocuous of field notes may, under certain conditions, mean the difference between life and death for anthropologists and their subjects. Efforts at encrypting notes or locking them up are often futile. The "Code of Ethics" and "Principles of Professional Responsibility" urge anthropologists to maintain transparency and avoid deception. However, in violent societies, trying to explain what an anthropologist is and does could, in some cases, lead to arrest or worse. Kovats-Bernat writes that at times he found it necessary to give the impression that he was concealing a firearm. So doing facilitated his survival in situations in which not having a weapon would have put him in the minority and made him vulnerable (2002:215).

Kovats-Bernat writes that when anthropologists do research under conditions of violence, they invite the possibility of victimization and violence on both themselves and their informants. If anthropologists and informants accept that such research is worthwhile, we must understand the relationship between anthropologists and their subjects in a new way. Our relationship needs to be "one of *mutual responsibility*. . . . all participants in the research must. . . . willingly accept the possibility that *any* involvement in the study could result in intimidation, arrest, torture, disappearance, assassination, or a range of other, utterly unforeseeable dangers" (Kovats-Bernat 2002:214; italics in the original).

## CRITICAL THINKING QUESTIONS

1. Given the ethical problems of conducting research in violent locations, should anthropologists ever be involved in such research? If not, will their analyses of society be biased in favor of seeing violence as an aberration?

2. The AAA "Code of Ethics" and "Principles of Professional Responsibility" make moral demands on researchers. These may have costs in terms of personal safety and limit the types of information anthropologists may collect. What level of danger should anthropologists be ready to accept to remain true to these professional codes? Are some research topics off limits to anthropologists?

3. Anthropologists who work in violent locations are motivated by intellectual goals and professional advancement. What motivates informants to take the risk of working with the anthropologists?

lated to conquest, domination, and control of other populations. Some anthropologists argue that engagement with the military is wrong because it actively promotes such ends. David Price (2009) notes that although anthropologists working in universities and in the military face similar issues, at least in theory anthropologists in universities seek knowledge for its own sake whereas those working for the military seek it for victory, security, and defense.

The use of anthropologists and other social scientists as part of HTS teams on the ground raises much deeper problems than their presence in military training. Starting in early 2007, the Pentagon has employed HTS teams to help its combat brigades. According to some military analysts, this program has been very successful. For example, the obituary of Michael Bhatia, one of the HTS members who died while performing their duties, reports that Bhatia's work helped save the lives of both U.S. soldiers and Afghan civilians. Colonel Martin Schweitzer testified before Congress that "the HTS team helped the 4-82 Airborne Brigade reduce its lethal operations by 60 to 70 percent, increase the number of districts supporting the Afghan government from 15 to 83, and reduce Afghan civilian deaths from over 70 during the previous brigade's tour to 11" (Fondacaro and McFate 2008). However, David Price (in press, 2009) reports that Schweitzer had no data to back up his claim and that it was simply Schweitzer's own judgment of how it seemed.

Whether the use of anthropologists by the military is effective or not, most anthropologists find it extremely problematic. A recent American Anthropological Association report notes that engagement with the military raises concerns about obligations to those whom anthropologists study; perils for the discipline, one's colleagues, and the broader academic community; and issues of secrecy and transparency (Peacock et al. 2007).

It is indeed difficult to see how many of anthropology's ethical requirements can be met under conditions of warfare. How, for example, are participants to give coercion-free consent while subject to military occupation? How can anthropologists honestly inform participants about the ways the research data will be used and are likely to affect them? Are individuals in a conflict ever really free to decide whether or not they will participate in a study? Can anthropologists working under such circumstances ensure, within reason, that the information they supply will not harm the safety, dignity, or privacy of the people with whom they work? Isn't the point of their work sometimes just the opposite of that? What of anthropologists' obligations to publish their research? Aren't the results of this sort of research necessarily secret? Historically, anthropologists have been concerned with protecting the rights and safety of the people they study. The primary concern of anthropologists working in HTS must be the safety, security, and goals of their employers instead.

Given all of the problems with HTS, it is probably safe to say that a strong majority of anthropologists oppose this use of anthropology. Anthropologists voiced opposition to HTS and other forms of involvement with the military at the annual meetings of the American Anthropological Association (AAA) in 2007 and 2008. It seems very likely that, in the next few years, the AAA will revise its code of ethics to take a stronger position against this kind of anthropology. However, ultimately, ethical behavior is the responsibility of each individual anthropologist. The members of the American Anthropological Association are supposed to subscribe to its code of ethics. Universities and some other research organizations have institutional review boards that examine all research involving human subjects for ethical violations. However, not all anthropologists are subject to the AAA or to institutional review boards. Lawyers who behave unethically can be disbarred. Doctors can have their medical licenses revoked. In both cases, they violate laws and can be punished if they continue to practice. There is no comparable sanction for anthropologists (and, indeed, for members of most disciplines). Therefore, there will always be a great diversity of anthropological practice.

# New Roles for the Ethnographer

Although there have been native anthropologists for a long time, until the 1970s, the prevailing model of fieldwork was a European or North American ethnographer visiting a relatively isolated and bounded society and reporting on that society to other Europeans and North Americans. In the past several decades this model has become unrealistic. Immigration, inexpensive communication, and relatively cheap airfare have altered the world and the nature of the anthropologist's job.

Whether working in cities, villages, or with tribal groups, almost all ethnographers must take into account the interaction of these local units with larger social structures, economies, and cultures. Such connections may extend from the region to the entire world. Thus, research may mean following consultants from villages to their workplaces in cities or collecting genealogies that spread over countries or even continents. In addition to expanding the research site, contemporary ethnographers must often use techniques such as questionnaires, social surveys, archival material, government documents, and court records in addition to participant observation.

Brazilian Indians demonstrate in Brasilia in 2009. They want indigenous issues to receive more government attention.

The deep connections among cultures and the global movement of individuals means that we must constantly reevaluate the nature of the cultures we are studying, their geographical spread, their economic and political position, and their relation to each other.

Today, not only are native anthropologists much more common, but the people anthropologists study generally have far greater knowledge of the world than they did in earlier times. Often, they understand what anthropology is and what anthropologists do, something not true in the past. In some cases, this has led to difficulties as people struggle over the question of who has the right to speak for a group. In other cases, people from the groups that anthropologists have described have publicly taken issue with their analysis. For example, in the early 2000s, a fierce controversy broke out over anthropological descriptions of the Yanomamo, an often studied Amazonian group. Had their primary ethnographer, Napoleon Chagnon, portrayed them accurately? Was the research team that he was part of responsible for spreading disease and decimating Yanomamo villages? Anthropologists, journalists, and Yanomamo tribe members debated these questions at meetings and in the popular press (for a review of the debate see Borofsky 2005).

Despite controversies, for the most part, natives' increased knowledge of the outside has resulted in closer relations among anthropologists and the people they study as well as more accurate ethnography. Ethnographic data are often useful to a society. Sometimes they serve as the basis for the revitalization of cultural identities that have been nearly effaced by Western impact (Feinberg 1994). Sometimes they play important roles in establishing group claims to "authenticity" and are useful in local political and economic context. For example, when Kathleen Adams (1995) carried out her fieldwork among the Toraja of Sulawesi, Indonesia, she became a featured event on tourist itineraries in the region. Toraja tour guides led their groups to the home of her host, both validating his importance in the village and bolstering the tourists' experience of the Toraja as a group sufficiently "authentic" and important to be studied by anthropologists.

In the past, anthropologists sometimes worried about their subject disappearing. They argued that the main thing anthropology was designed to study was small-scale, relatively isolated "primitive" society. They worried that as economic development spread around the world, such societies would go out of existence and the job of anthropology would essentially be finished. In a small sense they were right, but in the larger sense they were wrong. Any anthropologist looking today to study a society untouched by the outside world would be out of luck. No such societies have existed for a long time. On the other hand, the forces of globalization have been as productive of diversity as they have been of homogeneity. Economic, political, and social forces bring groups of people together in new ways, in conflict and in cooperation. New cultural forms are created and old ones modified. Human cultural diversity, imagination, and adaptability show no signs of dying out and, thus, anthropologists will always have material to study. Wherever human cultures exist and however they change, anthropologists will be there, devising means to study, understand, and think about them.

# The Global and the Local: Rights, Ethics, and Female Genital Operations

What could be more obvious than that anthropologists should support human rights and be actively engaged in their promotion? Doubting the value of human rights is like arguing against freedom of speech or claiming that children are not important. Yet, human rights pose ethical dilemmas for anthropologists. Almost all anthropologists believe firmly our duty to promote human rights in our own society. Many also believe that they have an obligation to promote the interests of those they study. For example, Laura R. Graham writes that "Our privileged position, specialized training, and unique skills. . . . carry with them specific ethical obligations to promote the well-being of the people who are collaborators in our anthropological research and in the production of anthropological knowledge" (2006:5). Ida Nicolaisen points out that standing for human rights is often a matter of life and death. She notes, for example, that in the Philippines, between 2005 and late summer 2006, at least 73 indigenous people were "subjected to extra-judicial killings" and concludes that "We owe it to indigenous peoples and other marginalized groups to stand up for their basic human rights when needed" (2006:6).

But there are often difficulties in determining exactly what rights are. Laura Nader writes that ideas about human rights were developed in a largely Western European context and are often conceived of as "something Euro-Americans take to others (2006:6)." Promoting Western notions of human rights may mean denying people in other societies what they consider to be their rights to pursue individual and cultural choices. Female genital operations are a good example.

Approximately 100 million females in the world today, mainly in Africa and the Middle East, have undergone some form of female genital operation (FGO), the ritual cutting of a girl's genitals. These practices vary in intensity from a ritualized drawing of blood, to infibulation, the removal of almost all of the genitals, stitching together of the wound, and leaving only a small opening for passing urine and menstrual flow. Where they are traditionally practiced, these operations are considered essential and are intended to preserve a girl's virginity before marriage, to symbolize her role as a marriageable member of society, and to emphasize her moral and economic value to her patrilineage (Barnes and Boddy 1994; Walley 1997).

Almost everything about FGO is controversial, beginning with the debate about whether or not it is medically harmful. A study by the World Health Organization published in 2006 showed that such operations increased the likelihood of the death of both mothers and children during childbirth. However, this finding is contradicted by other studies (for example, Morison et al. 2001; Obermeyer 2003). All of these studies are controversial and both their methodology and findings have been critiqued (see Shell-Duncan 2008, Tierney 2008). The name of the rites is itself politically loaded. Are they female genital operations, a rather neutral term; female genital mutilations, a term that implies that these rituals are wrong; or female circumcision, a name that makes them sound similar to male circumcision, clearly a less invasive and less painful practice?

There is no doubt that the female genital operations of African and Middle Eastern cultures offend the sensibilities of many people in the wealthy nations of America and Europe. Amnesty International (2005) considers such operations to be "a grave violation of human rights." UNICEF, the World Health Organization, and other groups carry out campaigns against them, and many anthropologists oppose them (Fluehr-Lobban 1998; Shell-Duncan 2008). However, others urge that these practices be examined carefully in their cultural contexts. Indeed, from the perspective of some women in some African societies, female genital cutting is an affirmation of the value of women (Merwine 1993; Walley 1997). Fumbai Ahmadou has recently written: "What western audiences rarely see. . . . is the fact that many circumcised women who support their tradition, are healthy, . . . lead sexually fulfilling lives, and. . . . quite like their circumcised bodies (in Tierney 2008). Ahmadou goes on to argue that some of the problems associated with FGO, such as sexual dys-

function and feelings of shame, disfigurement, and inferiority, are really caused by Western condemnation of it.

Today, many women from societies where female genital rituals are practiced are migrating to Europe and the United States, giving this once local cultural pattern a global dimension. Although some women have fled their countries for fear of being forced to undergo some form of genital cutting, others wish to preserve this practice in their new countries. However, these practices have been outlawed by several European countries and the United States.

While some women from societies that practice female genital operations defend it, others from those cultures speak out against it (El Saadawi 1980). However, many who oppose the practice also think Western interest in eliminating it is unwarranted interference in their right to determine their own culture. They point to a double standard: Westerners, and Americans in particular, see such practices as "barbaric" while ignoring similar practices in their cultures. The only place where female genital operations are currently increasing is in the world's wealthy nations. Conroy has pointed out that "'Designer laser vaginoplasty' and 'laser vaginal rejuvenation' are growth areas in plastic surgery. . . . [In these operations] women are being mutilated to fit male masturbation fantasies, in what Faith Wilding calls 'the full-scale consumer spectacle of the cyborg porn babe.'"(Conroy 2006)

## Key Questions

1. Given the diversity of culture and the anthropological importance of cultural relativism, can there be such a thing as universal human rights?
2. If anthropologists have moral obligations to the people with whom they work, should they ever work with people whose beliefs and practices they disapprove of? If yes, then what obligations do they have to such people? If no, how are we to accurately represent such people?
3. What sorts of things do you consider to be universal human rights? How good is our society at ensuring the rights you have identified? Do you think there is a core set of universal rights upon which most people could or should agree?

# Summary

1. **When did anthropology begin as an academic discipline and what were the methods and goals of early anthropologists?** Anthropology began in the 19th century. In that era, anthropologists were compilers of data rather than fieldworkers. Their goal was to describe and document the evolutionary history of human society. There were numerous problems with their data and methods.

2. **Who was Franz Boas and what role did he play in American anthropology?** Franz Boas was a German trained social scientist. In the United States, Franz Boas established a style of anthropology that rejected evolutionism. Boas insisted that anthropologists collect data through participant observation. He argued that cultures were the result of their own history and could not be compared to one another, a position called cultural relativism.

3. **Who was Bronislaw Malinowski and what role did he play in anthropology?** Bronislaw Malinowski was a British trained anthropologist whose approach and fieldwork were critical in establishing anthropology in Britain. Although the focus of Malinowski's work was different from Boas's, both emphasized participant observation and both saw members of other cultures as fully rational and worthy of respect.

4. **How is research in anthropology today different from research in the early 20th century?** Almost all anthropologists today do fieldwork, and many continue to work in small communities. Most focus on answering specific questions rather than describing entire societies. Anthropological techniques include participant observation, interviews, questionnaires, and mapping.

5. **What is participant observation?** Participant observation is the technique of gathering data on human cultures by living among the people, observing their social interaction on an ongoing daily basis, and participating as much as possible in their lives. This intensive field experience is the methodological hallmark of cultural anthropology.

6. **What are the emic and etic perspectives?** Anthropological research styles are sometimes characterized as either emic or etic. Anthropologists using the emic perspective seek to understand how cultures look from the inside. Their goal is to enable cultural outsiders to gain a sense of what it might be like to be a member of the culture. Anthropologists using an etic perspective seek to derive principles or rules that explain the behavior of members of a culture. Etic research is judged by the usefulness of the hypotheses it generates and the degree to which it accurately describes behavior, not by whether or not members of the culture studied agree with its conclusions.

7. **What is the Human Relations Area Files (HRAF) and what is it used for?** The HRAF is a database of information on more than 300 cultures. It is used for cross-cultural research. Cross-cultural researchers attempt to compare cultures to derive laws or principles that can be applied to many different cultures.

8. **What is feminist anthropology and what is its importance in the development of anthropological thinking?** Most anthropology before the late 1960s focused on men's lives. In the 1960s feminist anthropology was a movement to change the focus of anthropology to include all people and to increase the number of female anthropologists. Feminist anthropology began a trend of thinking about both the structure of anthropology as a discipline and the role of gender, power, and voice in society.

9. **What is postmodernism and how did it affect anthropology?** Postmodernism is a theoretical position focusing on the role of power and voice in shaping society and research. Postmodernists urged anthropologists to become more sensitive to these issues. Postmodernists also held that the objective world was unknowable and anthropologists' voice uncertain. Postmodernism created intense debate within anthropology but ultimately enriched ethnography.

10. **What are engaged and collaborative anthropology?** Engaged and collaborative anthropology place special emphasis on some of the issues raised by postmodernism. Collaborative anthropologists take great pains to involve members of the groups they study in the production of ethnographic knowledge. Engaged anthropologists place special emphasis on the political dimensions of their work and combine fieldwork with political and social activism.

11. **What are native anthropologists and what special advantages and problems do they have?** Native anthropologists are those who study their own society. Native anthropologists may have advantages of access and rapport. However, in some cases, they also experience burdens more intensely, such as whether to expose aspects of the culture that may be received unfavorably by outsiders.

12. **What are some ethical dilemmas that face anthropologists?** Anthropological ethics require protecting the dignity, privacy, and anonymity of the people one studies as well as obtaining their informed consent. However, it is not clear that this can be accomplished in all cases. In places of violence and instability, anthropologists

may not have the knowledge or power necessary to provide such protection. The use of anthropologists in the military presents an extremely difficult ethical issue for many anthropologists.

13. **What is the importance of anthropology in an increasingly globalized world?** Anthropologists are increasingly enmeshed in a global society. Those they study are rarely isolated and are often quite knowledgeable about anthropology. Anthropological knowledge is often important in the ways people understand their identity and, as such, is increasingly political.

# Key Terms

collaborative anthropology
cultural relativism
culture shock
emic perspective
engaged anthropology
etic perspective

ethnocentrism
ethnography
ethnology
fieldwork
Human Relations Area Files (HRAF)
informant (consultant)

informed consent
institutional review board (IRB)
native anthropologists
participant observation
postmodernism

# Suggested Readings

Angrosino, Michael V. 2002. *Doing Cultural Anthropology: Projects for Ethnographic Data Collection.* Prospect Heights, IL: Waveland. A brief book for beginning anthropology students; covers such topics as life histories, archival research, using museums as ethnographic resources, designing questionnaires for cross-cultural research, and working with numerical data.

DeVita, Philip R. (Ed.). 2000. *Stumbling Toward Truth: Anthropologists at Work.* Prospect Heights, IL: Waveland. An anthology of original and often amusing articles by anthropologists who have been taught some important lessons by their consultants in the process of doing fieldwork.

Gardner, Andrew M., and David Hoffman. 2006. *Dispatches from the Field: Neophyte Ethnographers in a Changing World.* Prospect Heights: Waveland. A collection of essays by graduate students conducting research under challenging conditions. Focuses on the issues raised by doing research in a globalized world.

Kidder, Tracy. 2004. *Mountains Beyond Mountains.* New York: Random House. An absorbing portrait of Paul Farmer, a medical doctor and anthropologist, and his quest to cure infectious diseases in some of the poorest places on earth. Dr. Farmer's work illuminates the conditions that contribute to global health problems.

The many dimensions of culture are expressed in the special ritual dress of this male initiate from the Basotho of South Africa: the stick he carries is a phallic symbol; the blankets are given by his family as a sign of his changed status; the mirrors symbolize the enlightenment that comes with changing status; the (plastic) combs symbolize beauty; the color white is for purity; the sunglasses prevent directly gazing on the sun, which is considered the creator.

**THINKING POINT:** Sometimes we think that culture is like a watch; a thing composed of many parts that fit precisely together to operate in a smooth, consistent fashion. Many current anthropological theorists agree that culture is composed of different elements, but some say these cultural elements don't necessarily fit together very well; instead of running smoothly, the different parts grind against each other. If culture was a watch, we'd never know what time it was.

—[See page 83 for details.]

# {chapter 4}

# The Idea of Culture

Although culture is not easy to define precisely, practically everything humans perceive, know, think, value, feel, and do—in short, almost everything that makes us human—is learned through participation in a sociocultural system. Even things that strike us as natural often are cultural. Culture is so much a part of our being that it is sometimes difficult to think about. In a sense, trying to teach people about culture is like trying to teach fish about water. Water is the fundamental assumption for the life of a fish. If fish could think abstractly, it would be very difficult for them to fully imagine a life without water. Similarly, culture is so basic to human society that it is difficult to imagine what human life would be without it. We might come close, however, by considering autism.

Autism is a developmental disorder characterized by difficulties in both verbal and nonverbal communication, impairment of social interaction, and a host of other symptoms. It is generally diagnosed in children between the ages of 18 and 36 months. Autism may affect as many as one in 150 children. As a result, it is likely that you either know or know of someone with some form of autism.

Autism can occur in many different levels of severity. Some with profound autism are silent and withdrawn. However, there are many others who have a mild to moderate form of autism called Asperger's syndrome. People with Asperger's are able to master language and learn to participate in society.

Some people with autism or Asperger's have exceptional intellectual skills; Dr. Temple Grandin is among the best known of these. Dr. Grandin, an associate professor of animal science at Colorado State University, has written extensively about her experience of autism and the ways in which she has learned to interact with other people. ≫

As Grandin and psychologist Oliver Sacks explain it, autistics think in extremely concrete terms and have profound difficulty understanding social conventions and unwritten cultural rules of every sort. Grandin has learned to relate to others in ways that are fundamentally different from most people. Writing about her, Sacks says that Grandin lacks "The implicit knowledge, which every normal person accumulates and generates throughout life on the basis of experience and encounters with others." As a result, she must "'compute' others' intentions and states of mind, to try to make ... explicit, what for the rest of us is second nature" (Sacks 1995:270).

Grandin has often described herself as an "anthropologist on Mars." To her, being in human society is like being on a different planet. She is an outsider confronted with a wholly different way of life. She can observe what people do, but their actions make no sense. She has no intuitive feel for the things going on around her. In other words, for Grandin, other people have this thing that we call "culture." She either lacks culture or her culture is enormously different from what other people have. Grandin has been very successful because she has learned to imitate culture; that is, she has learned when she needs to say certain things and perform certain actions in order to appear normal. But, despite her success, Sacks reports that Grandin does not think she understands others (Sacks 1995:286). Describing this condition, the classical music critic Tim Page, who also has Asperger's, has written: "I am left with the melancholy sensation that my life has been spent in a perpetual state of parallel play, alongside, but distinctly apart from, the rest of humanity" (2007:36).

Accounts of autistic individuals such as Grandin and Page show that it is extremely difficult for them to become functioning members of society. Grandin's experiences as well as her notion of herself as an anthropologist on Mars strongly suggest that she does not participate in culture in the way that most people do. Such cases make it clear that if we do not internalize the constraints, assumptions, and patterns imposed by culture, it is extraordinarily difficult to express our human qualities and abilities. But what is culture? <<

# Defining Culture

In 1873, Sir Edward Burnett Tylor introduced the concept of culture as an explanation for the differences among human societies. Tylor defined culture as the "complex whole which includes knowledge, belief, art, law, morals, custom, and any other capabilities acquired [learned] by man as a member of society" (1920:1), and he defined anthropology as the scientific study of human culture.

Today, anthropologists generally agree that all cultures share, in some degree, the following six characteristics:

1. Cultures are made up of learned behaviors. People are not born knowing their culture. They learn it through a process called **enculturation.** Learning culture is a continuous process. We start learning our culture the day we are born, and we are still learning things at the time of our death.

2. Cultures all involve symbols. A symbol is simply something that stands for something else. People manipulate, invent, and change symbols. All cultures have language, a complex symbolic system. Using symbols helps people create meaning, including statements about the way the world should be. However, many different statements are likely to be found within any culture.

3. Cultures are to some degree patterned and integrated. That is, the elements of culture stand in some logical relationship to one another. However, as we see later in the chapter, the degree of coordination among elements of culture is hotly disputed.

4. Cultures are in some way shared by members of a group. Every human being has an individual personality. Studying that is the domain of psychology. Each person must also interact with others and thus must share a framework of meaning and behavior with them. Studying that framework is the domain of cultural anthropology.

5. Cultures are in some way adaptive. That is, cultures contain information about how to survive in the world. Cultures also contain much that is maladaptive.

6. All cultures are subject to change. Whether propelled by its internal dynamic or acted upon by outside forces, no culture remains static. However, the speed with which cultures change may vary enormously from place to place and time to time.

Based on this list, we might define culture as the learned, symbolic, at least partially adaptive, and ever-changing patterns of behavior and meaning shared by members of a group. Although anthropologists might agree to this broad definition, such accord would cover up important disagreements over what the definition really means. These disagreements occur because anthropologists have different ideas about which aspects of culture are fundamental and the ways in which culture should be studied. These different ideas represent different theoretical positions. Theory lies at the heart of anthropology. Each theoretical position directs those who adopt it to study different aspects of society and, in many cases, use different techniques.

**enculturation** The process of learning to be a member of a particular cultural group.

The notion of culture is like a window through which one may view human groups. Just as the view changes as one moves from window to window of a building, so the anthropologist's understanding of society changes as he or she moves from one definition of culture to another. And just as two windows may have views that overlap or views that show totally different scenes, definitions of culture may overlap or reveal totally different aspects of society. In this chapter, we explore some aspects of anthropological theory by examining each of the six points of our definition of culture. Each of these characteristics of culture tells us something about what it means to be human. We examine culture as a system of learned behaviors, and explore the ways that humans use it to organize and give meaning to the world around them. We discuss the debate over the degree to which cultures are integrated systems and examine the question of whether all members of a culture really share values and norms. We explore the relationship between culture and human adaptation to the world. Finally, we discuss some of the ways cultures change. This discussion is not meant to be an exhaustive description of the ways anthropologists see the world. Rather, it is intended to give some of the flavor of the lively debate among anthropologists about the nature of human society and allow you to reexamine some of the ideas and ways of behaving that we perhaps take for granted in our own and other societies.

Table 4.1 provides a very brief list of key theoretical schools in anthropology and their understanding of culture. (For more detailed summaries of these schools and lists of key works within them, see the Appendix.)

**TABLE 4.1 Some Major Anthropological Schools of Thought and Their Understanding of Culture**

| THEORY NAME | UNDERSTANDING OF CULTURE | CRITICAL THINKERS |
|---|---|---|
| Nineteenth-century evolution | A universal human culture is shared, in different degrees, by all societies | E. B. Taylor (1832–1917) <br> L. H. Morgan (1818-1881) |
| Turn-of-the-century sociology | Groups of people share sets of symbols and practices that bind them into societies. | Emile Durkheim (1858–1917) <br> Marcel Mauss (1872–1950) |
| American historical particularism | Cultures are the result of the specific histories of the people who share them | Franz Boas (1858–1942) <br> A. L. Kroeber (1876 1960) |
| Functionalism | Social practices support society's structure or fill the needs of individuals. | Bronislaw Malinowski (1884–1942) <br> A. R. Radcliffe Brown (1181–1995) |
| Culture and personality | Culture is personality writ large. It both shapes and is shaped by the personalities of its members. | Ruth Benedict (1887–1948) <br> Margaret Mead (1901–1978) |
| Cultural ecology and neo-evolutionism | Culture is the way in which humans adapt to the environment and make their lives secure. | Julian Steward (1902–1972) <br> Leslie White (1900–1975) |
| Ecological materialism | Physical and economic causes give rise to cultures and explain changes within them. | Morton Fried (1923–1986) <br> Marvin Harris (1927–2001) |
| Ethnoscience and cognitive anthropology | Culture is a mental template that determines how members of a society understand their world. | Harold Conklin (1926– ) <br> Stephen Tyler (1932– ) |
| Structural anthropology | Universal original human culture can be discovered through analysis and comparison of the myths and customs of many cultures. | Claude Levi Strauss (1908– ) |
| Sociobiology | Culture is the visible expression of underlying genetic coding. | E. O. Wilson (1929– ) <br> Jerome Barkow (1944– ) |
| Anthropology and gender | The roles of women and ways societies understand sexuality are central to understanding culture. | Sherry Ortner (1941– ) <br> Michelle Rosaldo (1944?–1981) |
| Symbolic and interpretive anthropology | Culture is the way in which members of a society understand who they are and give lives meaning. | Mary Douglas (1921–2007) <br> Clifford Geertz (1926–2006) |
| Postmodernism | Because understanding of cultures most reflect the observer's biases, culture can never be completely or accurately described. | Renato Rosaldo (1941– ) <br> Vincent Crapanzano (1939– ) |

Note. Theoretical positions in anthropology represent sophisticated thinking and cannot be summed up in a single line. You will find detailed information on each of the theories listed in this table in the appendix: A Brief Historical Guide to Anthropological Theory, starting on page 382. There are many outstanding books about anthropological theory, including McGee and Warms (2004), *Anthropological Theory: An Introductory History*.

## Culture Is Made Up of Learned Behaviors

Just about everything that is animate learns. Your dog, your cat, even your fish show some learned behavior. But, as far as we know, no other creature has as much learned behavior as human beings. Almost every aspect of our lives is layered with learning. Our heart beats, our eyes blink, and our knees respond reflexively to the doctor's rubber mallet, but to get much beyond that, we need learning. Food is a good example. Humans must eat; that much is determined biologically. However, we don't just eat; our culture teaches us what is edible and what is not. Many things that are nutritious we decline as not-food. Many insects, for example, are perfectly edible. The philosopher Aristotle was particularly fond of eating cicadas, and some species of beetles were eaten in Northern Europe well into the 19th century. Yet most Americans have learned that insects are not-food and will go hungry, to the point of starvation, before eating them. Further, we eat particular things at particular times, in particular places, and with particular people. For example, although it is perfectly acceptable to eat popcorn at the movies, you would be unlikely to have lamb chops and asparagus there, or a nice stir-fry.

As a way of adapting to a harsh environment, Inuit children are taught to be autonomous at an early age.

We sometimes think of learning as an aspect of childhood, but in every society, human beings learn their culture continuously. We are socialized from the moment of our births to the time of our deaths. Although in many societies large demands for labor and responsible behavior may be placed on children, all humans remain physically, emotionally, and intellectually immature well into their teen years and perhaps into their early 20s. This lengthy period of immaturity has profound implications. First, it allows time for an enormous amount of childhood learning; this means that very few specific behaviors need be under direct genetic or biological control. Second, it demands that human cultures be designed to provide relatively stable environments that protect the young for long periods of time.

Human infants become adults in a particular human society. Thus, the infant grows into a child and later into an adult not simply as a human, but as a particular kind of human: a Kwakiutl, Trobriand Islander, Briton, or Tahitian, for example. Each society has both informal and formal means of enculturation, or transmitting its culture, so that children grow up to be responsible and participating adults and so that the society is reproduced socially as well as biologically.

The biological processes of conception, birth, maturation, and death are the same for all human beings, although these may be affected by environmental factors such as nutrition and disease. However, in all societies, such biological processes are less important than the social understandings involved. Consider our own society. When does a child become an adult? When he or she reaches puberty? Gets a driver's license? Graduates from high school or college? Gets married? Has a child? Although some of these are clearly biological events, culture, not biology, provides the answers.

The question of when a child becomes a human being is another good example of the cultural nature of growth. Birth is a biological event, but being born does not necessarily make an individual a human. Social birth refers to the point at which one is considered a human being and a member of human society (Morgan 1996). There is much variability in when cultures recognize a fetus, an infant, or a child as a social person and this is linked to factors including the productive basis of society, the relations between the sexes, the social stratification system, the culturally defined divisions of the life cycle, attitudes toward death, and particularly, infant mortality rates.

In northeastern Ghana, for example, some newborns are believed to be *chichuru*, "spirit children," not real children but spirits who come to the world to play and cause distress to their communities (Allotey and Reidpath 2001). A newborn may be a "spirit child" if it has physical abnormalities, if its birth is followed by tragic events, if it cries constantly, or if there were irregularities in the mother's sexual behavior or her pregnancy. A child identified as a "spirit child" is killed and buried without a funeral ceremony. Its family must perform a series of sacrifices in order to be cleansed. A study found that in this area of Ghana, almost 15 percent of the deaths of children younger than 3 months old were considered deaths of *chichuru* (Allotey and Reidpath 2001).

Often, it is social birth rather than biological birth that is marked by ritual. Among the Toda of India, for example, the newborn is not considered a person until the age of 3 months, after which a "face opening" ceremony takes place. The infant is brought outdoors, its face is unveiled at dawn, and it is introduced to the temple, to nature, to buffaloes, and to its clan relatives (Morgan 1996:28).

In the poverty-stricken region of northeastern Brazil, a child is not considered a social person until it shows physical and emotional signs of being able to survive (Scheper-Hughes 1992). Children are raised under extremely harsh conditions. The need for both adults and children to work to avoid starvation results in babies frequently left at home during the day, a condition under which many weaker babies die. Infants who are small and sickly are believed to have an "aversion to living." If they develop acute symptoms, such as convulsions, they are left to die. Their deaths are viewed as "nature taking its course" or as indicating that the child "wants to die." Mothers learn to distance themselves emotionally from such infants and believe that allowing their deaths is cooperating with God's plan. Dead infants are buried in unmarked graves with little ceremony, and mothers are strongly discouraged from crying or grieving for them.

These examples from northeastern Ghana, the Toda, and northeastern Brazil contrast sharply with American understandings and shed new light on the intense debate over abortion policy. Most people involved in the abortion debate are not particularly concerned about the deaths of nonhumans. So, the American abortion debate is really about when one becomes a human, that is, a social person, not when something is alive. As we have seen in the examples above, humanness is a cultural, not a biological designation. Almost all Americans agree that a newborn child is a member of society and has certain rights. However, they disagree about whether the same is true of a blastula, embryo, or fetus. Many abortion opponents argue that a social person is created at the act of conception or shortly thereafter. Those who favor legal abortion argue that a social person is not created until the fetus can survive outside the womb. All sides in this debate cite deeply held beliefs. However, it is important to understand that the debate is cultural, not biological or scientific. Science can identify the moment of conception or the hour of birth but only culture can determine when a human being comes into existence.

The recognition of human status is the beginning phase in human development. Beginning with birth, all humans pass through developmental phases, each characterized by an increase in the capacity to deal with the physical and social environment. At each phase, the bio-logically based physical, mental, and psychological potentials of the individual unfold, within a specific cultural context.

Child-rearing practices in all cultures are designed to produce adults who know the skills, norms, and behavior patterns—the cultural content—of their society. But the transmission of culture involves more than just knowing these things. It also involves patterning children's attitudes, motivations, values, perceptions, and beliefs so that they can function in their society (which itself adapts to external requirements of the physical and social environment). The process of learning to be a member of a particular cultural group is called enculturation.

As an example, we will take a closer look at child rearing among the Inuit, a hunting people of the Arctic. The Inuit teach their children to deal with a world that is a dangerously problematic place, in which making wrong decisions might well mean death

The Inuit

(Briggs 1991). To survive in this harsh environment, Inuit must learn to maintain a "constant state of alertness" and an "experimental way of living." Therefore, developing skills for solving problems quickly and spontaneously is central to Inuit child rearing. Children are brought up to constantly test their physical skills, in order to extend them and to learn their own capacity for pain and endurance (Stern 1999).

Inuit children learn largely through observing their elders. Children are discouraged from asking questions. Rather, when confronted with a problem situation, they are expected to observe closely, to reason, and to find solutions independently. They watch, practice, and are then tested, frequently by adults asking them questions. For example, when traveling on the featureless, snow-covered tundra, an adult may ask a child "Where are we? Have you ever been here before?"

Play is a critical part of Inuit child rearing. Inuit games prepare children for the rigors of the arctic environment by stressing hand-eye coordination, problem solving, and physical strength and endurance. Some games involve learning by taking objects apart and trying to put them back together. This develops careful attention to details, to relationships, to patient trial and error, and to a mental recording of results for future reference. Many games stress the body and test the limits of the individual's psychological and physical endurance (see Nelson 1983). In the ear pull game, for example, a thin loop of leather is positioned behind the ears of each of two competitors who then pull away from each other until one gives up in pain (Canadian Broadcasting Company 1982).

The emphasis on experiential learning means that Inuit children are less physically restrained or verbally reprimanded than children in many other cultures. Inuit mothers are willing to permit a child to experiment with potentially harmful behavior so that the child learns not to repeat it.

In addition to being physically adept and independent, Inuit children must learn to be cooperative and emotionally restrained. Under the conditions of their closely knit and often isolated camp life, expressions of anger or aggression are avoided. The Inuit prize reason, judgment, and emotional control, and these are thought to grow naturally as children grow.

The Inuit believe that children have both the ability and the wish to learn. Educating a child thus consists of providing the necessary information, which sooner or later the child will remember. Scolding is seen as futile. Children will learn when they are ready; there is no point in forcing a child to learn something before he or she is ready to remember it. Inuit elders believe that frequent scolding makes children hostile, rebellious, and impervious to the opinions of others.

The study of enculturation has a central place in the history of anthropology and gave rise to some of its classic works. Margaret Mead's 1928 book *Coming of Age in Samoa* was a bestseller and a landmark work that changed how Americans looked at childhood and culture. Mead and others who studied childhood learning are known as **culture and personality theorists.** Culture and personality theorists held that cultures could best be understood by examining the patterns of child rearing and considering their effect on adult lives and social institutions. Culture and personality theory was extremely influential from the 1920s until the 1950s. Although few anthropologists today would use the phrase "culture and personality theorist" to describe themselves, enculturation remains an important topic of anthropological research.

# Culture Is the Way Humans Use Symbols to Classify Their World and Give It Meaning

As human beings, we are unable to see everything in our environment. Instead, we pay attention to some elements of our surroundings and disregard others. For example,

when you walk into a classroom, you notice friends and other students, the professor, video equipment, and so on. You might spend an entire semester without ever seeing the cracks in the ceiling, the pattern of the carpeting, or the color of the walls. Yet these things are as physically present as the chairs and your friends.

You see certain things in the classroom and overlook others because you mentally organize the contents of the classroom in respect to your role as a student. In that context, some of the things in the room, such as professors and friends, are relevant and others, such as the color of the walls, you discount and may not notice at all. It is virtually impossible to see things without organizing and evaluating them in some manner.

If you paid as much attention to the cracks in the wall, the patterns on the floor, and the humming of the ventilation system as you did to the professor's lecture, you would not only be likely to fail the class, but you would live in a world that was overwhelming and impossibly confusing. Only through fitting our perceptions and experiences into systems of organization and classification can we comprehend our lives and act in the world. A human without this ability would be paralyzed, frozen by an overwhelming bombardment of sensations. Indeed, this is one of the problems that autistic people such as Temple Grandin often experience.

Methods of organizing and classifying are products of a group. You are not the only one who thinks that the students and professors in a classroom are more important than the ceiling tiles; that perception is probably shared by all students and professors. Anthropologists have long proposed that culture is a shared mental model that people use to organize, classify, and ultimately to understand their world. A key way this model is expressed is through language, a symbolic system.

Different cultures have different models for understanding and speaking about the world, and the ways people classify elements of their environment provide many examples. For instance, Bamana children in Mali classify some kinds of termites as food. Americans think of all termites as pests. In English, the verb *smoke* describes the action of ingesting a cigarette and *drink* describes the action of consuming a liquid. However, in the Bamana language, you use the same verb, *min,* for smoking and drinking. Americans classify rainbows as objects of beauty and take pleasure in pointing them out to each other. Lacondon Maya in southern Mexico classify rainbows as dangerous and frightening, and it is highly inappropriate to point one out to another person (McGee, personal communication).

One way of thinking about culture is as a codification of reality—a system of meaning that transforms physical reality, what is there, into experienced reality. Dorothy Lee (1987), an anthropologist interested in the different ways people see themselves and their environments, described her perception of reality as she looked

**culture and personality theory** An anthropological perspective that focuses on culture as the principal force in shaping the typical personality of a society as well as on the role of personality in the maintenance of cultural institutions.

Understandings of health and sickness as well as medication vary among cultures. Here, street merchants in Tanzania sell traditional medications.

ent cultures to isolate common patterns. They believe that these reflect a universal underlying patterning of human thought: the tendency to divide everything into two opposing classes (male/female, good/bad, right/left), as well as a third class that crosses the boundary between these two.

Human beings not only classify the world, but they also fill it with meaning. Members of every culture imbue their world with stories and symbols. Ideas, words, and actions have not only practical value but symbolic meaning and emotional force. Human behavior signifies something. The central histories, legends, and lore of religions and cultures are not simply stories; they have powerful emotional resonance for us. People are literally willing to fight and die for their religious and moral beliefs expressed in symbols. Actions that challenge the central meanings of our culture, such as flag burning or the desecration of religious symbols, often bring immediate and passionate response. As anthropologist Clifford Geertz puts it, a human being is "an animal suspended in webs of significance which he himself has spun"(Geertz 1973:30). To put this another way, a culture is a story people tell themselves about themselves. Culture is the way people understand who they are and how they should act in the world. It is the context within which human actions can be understood.

Symbols are the key mechanism people use to fill their world with meaning. The simplest definition of a **symbol** is something that stands for something else. Words (both spoken and written), objects, and ideas can all be symbols. Symbols enable us to store information. The book you are currently holding, for example, contains a huge amount of information all stored symbolically. Nonhuman animals must learn through experience or imitation. Because humans can store information symbolically, as stories and teachings passed from generation to generation, or as written words, their learning is not so limited. Human cultures can be endlessly large.

out the window of her house: "I see trees, some of which I like to be there, and some of which I intend to cut down to keep them from encroaching further upon the small clearing I made for my house." But she noted that Black Elk, a holy man of the Oglala (Sioux) "saw trees as having rights to the land, equal to his own. He saw them as the standing peoples, in whom the winged ones built their lodges and reared their families."

Anthropologists who are particularly interested in describing the systems of organization and classification used by individual cultures often use a theoretical perspective called **ethnoscience.** Generally these anthropologists are interested in capturing the understanding of members of a culture. Ethnoscience is one position or technique within a broader perspective called **cognitive anthropology,** which focuses on the relationship between the mind and society. Understanding classification systems is also extremely important for scholars interested in **ethnobotany** and **ethnomedicine.** Ethnobotany focuses on the relationship between humans and plants in different cultures. Ethnomedicine examines the ways in which people in different cultures understand health and sicknesses as well as the ways they attempt to cure disease. In each case, discovering how people classify and organize their world is a key focus of research.

Other anthropologists believe that although the details of a system of classification may be unique to individual cultures, there are grand overall patterns to these systems that are common to all humanity. The study of this aspect of culture is generally called **structural anthropology.** Perhaps the most important scholar in this school is the French anthropologist Claude Levi-Strauss. Levi-Strauss and his followers compare the myths and beliefs of differ-

**ethnoscience** A theoretical approach that focuses on the ways in which members of a culture classify their world and holds that anthropology should be the study of cultural systems of classification.

**cognitive anthropology** A theoretical approach that defines culture in terms of the rules and meanings underlying human behavior, rather than behavior itself.

**ethnobotany** A field of anthropological research focused on describing the ways in which different cultures classify and understand plants.

**ethnomedicine** A field of anthropological research devoted to describing the medical systems and practices of different cultures.

**structural anthropology** A theoretical perspective that holds that all cultures reflect similar deep, underlying patterns and that anthropologists should attempt to decipher these patterns.

**symbol** Something that stands for something else.

## Culture and HIV

For the past 25 years, anthropologists have used a variety of theories and methods to understand and address the HIV/AIDS epidemic. These include long-term ethnographic research and focused interdisciplinary teamwork (Feldman 2008, 2009). More recently anthropologists have developed an approach to improving human health that stresses the importance of understanding the ways in which ecosystems, local and global political economies, cultural systems, biological factors, and malnutrition contribute to disease, including AIDS, particularly among disadvantaged populations (Himmelgreen and Romero-Daza 2008; Singer 2008). These understandings help formulate more effective interventions by government and nongovernmental agencies (NGOs).

The most significant forms of behavior implicated in the transmission of HIV/AIDS are heterosexual and same-sex sexual relations. As a result, many preventive interventions target sexual relationships, incorporating abstinence, sexual fidelity, and condom use, alone or in

AIDS is an international scourge. Notice that in this AIDS prevention billboard in Malaysia, the emphasis is on avoiding promiscuity rather than using condoms, a message consistent with the cultural emphasis promoted by the Malaysian government.

combination. As anthropology makes clear, these intimate relationships are shaped both by culture and by the political economy. For example, there is overwhelming

evidence that condom use inhibits the spread of AIDS. But condom use is significantly shaped by cultural values and norms regarding intimate relationships such as marriage, long-term love affairs, or relationships focused on sexual exchanges. Anthropologist Eric Ratliff (1999) found in the Philippines, for example, that exotic dancers who exchanged sex for money considered these transactions "sex work" only in relation to first-time sexual encounters. When engaging in sex as work, the women were willing to demand that their clients use condoms. But repeated sexual encounters with a particular client were experienced not as merely a job, but as a potential love relationship that might lead to marriage and away from prostitution. In these circumstances the women were unlikely to demand that their partners, or "boyfriends" as they now defined them, use condoms. Ratliff's conclusion that condom use can be an effective AIDS intervention strategy between sex workers and their clients, but is less effective in long-term intimate rela-

Alejandro Toledo rose from humble origins to become President of Peru from 2001 to 2006. During his election campaign he made extensive use of symbols of Peruvian culture. He appeared frequently in traditional clothing and stressed comparisons between himself and the Inca emperor Pachacútec. In this picture, he wears the Inca flag around his neck. Toledo is married to anthropologist Elaine Karp.

Symbols also have the ability to condense meaning. People may take a single symbol and make it stand for an entire constellation of ideas and emotions. Religious symbols and national symbols often have this characteristic. The meaning of a national flag or a religious symbol cannot be summed up in a word or two. These stand for vast complexes of history, ideas, and emotions.

Symbolic anthropologists try to understand a culture by discovering and analyzing the symbols that are most important to its members. These often reflect the deep concerns of the culture's members in ways that may be difficult for them to articulate. For example, among the Ndembu of East Africa, the mudyi tree is a central symbol and plays an important role in girls' puberty rites. The tree has a white, milky sap, which symbolizes breast-feeding, the relationship between mother and child, inheritance through the mother's family line, and at the most abstract level, the unity and continuity of Ndembu society itself. It is unlikely that all Ndembu think deeply about all of these meanings during girls' puberty rites. However, this complex symbolism helps hold Ndembu society together by

tionships, is confirmed by much cross-cultural evidence (McCombie and Eshel 2008) and applies to both heterosexual and same sex relationships (Feldman 2009).

Ratliff's study focused on meaning and values. Anthropologists also focus on the social, economic, and political factors implicated in the spread of AIDS. One important context is gender inequality. Where women are near powerless or economically dependent on men, they are less likely to insist on behavioral changes, such as marital fidelity or condom use, that inhibit the spread of AIDS. Thus, in southern Africa, where AIDS infection rates are extremely high, 55 to 60 percent of AIDS victims are women. The Ju/'hoansi people of Namibia are an exception to this statistic. According to anthropologists Richard Lee and Ida Susser (2008), the significantly lower rate of AIDS among Ju/'hoansi women is due to their economic autonomy. Ju/'hoansi women assertively declared that they would have no hesitation in refusing to have sex with a man who would not wear a condom. Lee and Susser note, however, that as a changing economy introduces more outsiders into the formerly somewhat isolated Ju/'hoansi area, AIDS infection, though still low, has increased.

A materialist perspective also reveals how AIDS may be spread in particular subcultures, and thus points the way to more effective interventions. Among intravenous drug users in the United States, for example, needle sharing is a significant cause of AIDS infection. Intravenous drug users share needles because clean needles are frequently unavailable and many cannot afford to buy their own "works" (syringes and related paraphernalia). In addition, in the many states where owning a needle without a prescription is illegal, drug users are afraid to carry their own works. Anthropologists point out that an effective AIDS intervention is to make clean needles available to intravenous drug addicts (Carlson et al. 1996). Clean needles, distributed by the government or NGOs, would inhibit addicts from borrowing needles from friends or renting them in "shooting galleries," both of which increase the transmission of HIV (Singer, Irizarry, and Schensul 1991).

Although, based on the recommendation of applied anthropologists, many major American cities recommended and some implemented free needle distribution, political opposition became fierce (Heimer et al. 1996). Local politicians blamed these programs for many local drug-related problems, an accusation that was proved false when dismantling the programs did not result in improvement in a city's drug problems. Rather, syringe sharing increased and a black market in syringes emerged, increasing the spread of AIDS (Broadhead, Van Hulst, and Heckathorn 1999).

The examples of the needle sharing and AIDS prevention programs demonstrate both the benefits of a holistic anthropological approach and the difference theoretical positions make. In these cases, effective solutions to problems could only be proposed after fieldwork allowed anthropologists to understand the cultural context of behavior as well as what people actually did, thought, and said. However, this did not lead to a single type of proposal. Instead, the anthropologists were guided by different theoretical perspectives to generate very different plans for improvement.

reaffirming its central tenants (Turner 1967). For anthropologists, understanding the meaning of the mudyi tree and the role it plays in Ndembu society is to have penetrated deeply into the Ndembu view of the world.

Culture can also be analyzed using the tools of literature and this is the job of **interpretive anthropology.** Clifford Geertz, one of the best known interpretive anthropologists said that in a sense, culture is like a novel. It is an "ensemble of texts. . . . which the anthropologist strains to read over the shoulders of those to whom they properly belong (2008:574)." Like all good stories, culture engrosses us and helps us understand the nature and meaning of life. It comments on who we are and how we should act in the world. Interpretive anthropologists often find these cultural texts in public events, celebrations, and rituals. Analyzing them gives us clues and insights into the meaning of culture for its participants.

Consider the American fascination with football. American football has little appeal outside the United States, but here it draws more fans than any other sport. In order to explain its popularity, analysts have studied the key themes of the game. They point out that the game is heavily laden with sexuality. Dundes (1980) notes that the vocabulary of football is full of sexual overtones (ends, making a touchdown in the end zone, scoring, going all the way). Football uniforms accentuate the male physique: enlarged head and shoulders, narrow waist, and a lower torso "poured into skintight pants accentuated only by a metal codpiece" (Arens 1975). Dressed this way, men tackle each other, hold hands, hug each other, and pat each other's bottoms. But sexuality is not the only important aspect of the sport. Football is, in Geertz's terms, "playing with fire" (1973b). It attracts us because, more than other sports, it displays and manipulates topics such as the violence and sexuality underlying competition between men, the social role of women, the relationship of the individual to the group,

**interpretive (symbolic) anthropology** A theoretical approach that emphasizes culture as a system of meaning and proposes that the aim of cultural anthropology is to interpret the meanings that cultural acts have for their participants.

Football in the United States and bullfighting in Spain are both popular because they illustrate important themes of their respective cultures. They are exciting in part because they tell stories loaded with cultural meaning.

rules and their infringement, gaining and surrendering territory, and racial character (Oriard 1993:18). As we watch football, we see these issues displayed and manipulated or implied. Football is just a game, but so is checkers. Millions watch football because it is meaningful in ways that checkers is not. For interpretive anthropologists, football's meaning derives from the ways in which it explores and comments on critical themes in American culture. It is a text that we read, and those who would understand Americans must learn to read it as well (see also our discussion of deep play and the Balinese cockfight on page 325 in Chapter 14).

Interpretive and symbolic anthropologists use methods drawn from the humanities rather than the sciences to uncover and interpret the deep emotional and psychological structure of societies. Their goal is to understand the experience of being a member of a culture and to make that experience available to their readers (Marcus and Fischer 1986).

## Culture Is an Integrated System—Or Is It?

Consider a biological organism. The heart pumps blood, the lungs supply it with oxygen, the liver purifies it, and so on. The various organs work together to create a prop-

**functionalism** The anthropological theory that specific cultural institutions function to support the structure of society or serve the needs of individuals in society.

erly functioning whole. An early insight in anthropology was that it is useful to compare societies to organisms. The subsistence system provides food, the economic and political systems determine how it is distributed, religion provides the justification for the distribution system, and so on. Societies, like bodies, are integrated systems.

This organic analogy has strengths and weaknesses. It allows us to think about society as composed of different elements (such as kinship, religion, and subsistence) and it implies that anthropologists should describe the shape and role of such elements as well as the ways in which changes in one affect the others. For example, subsistence and social structure are two identifiable social elements and are related to each other. Foraging is an activity most often done in small groups and requiring little direction or coordination. People who forage for their food will probably have relatively loosely defined social groups with changing membership. Farming requires more coordination than foraging and therefore people who farm will likely have a society with a more rigid structure and a more stable membership. If a group was to move from foraging to farming, we would expect it to develop an increasingly well-defined social structure.

Anthropologists drawn to the study of the relationships among different elements of culture and the ways in which these elements support one another are called **functionalists.** These anthropologists often sought to find laws of cultural behavior. In the first half of the 20th century, functionalists such as A. R. Radcliffe-Brown and Bronislaw Malinowski searched for such laws in the mutually supportive relationships among kinship, religion, and politics. For example, Radcliffe-Brown argued that religion supports social structure by giving individuals a sense of dependence on their society (1965:176/1952).

More recently, **ecological functionalists** have focused on the relationship between the environment and society. Rather than seeing cultures as being like organisms, these anthropologists view social institutions and practices as elements in broader ecological systems. They are particularly concerned with ways cultural practices both altered and were altered by the ecosystem in which they occur. For example, Marvin Harris's (1966) classic explanation of the Hindu taboo on eating beef focuses on the effect of cattle in the Indian environment rather than on the Hindu belief system. Harris notes that despite widespread poverty and periodic famine in India, Hindus refuse to eat their cattle. Although superficially this seems unreasonable, it makes good ecological sense. Cows are important in India because they provide dung for fertilizer and cooking fuel, and give birth to bullocks, the draft animals that pull plows and carts essential to agriculture. If a family ate its cows during a famine, it would deprive itself of the source of bullocks and could not continue farming. Thus, the Hindu religious taboo on eating beef is part of a larger ecological pattern that includes the subsistence system. It functions to keep that system stable.

Functionalism is a powerful way of thinking about society and provides important insights. However, the comparison of societies to organisms has some critical problems. The organic analogy implies that properly functioning societies should be stable and conflict free. The parts of a biological organism work together to keep the entire being alive and well. The lungs do not declare war on the liver. If such conflict occurs (an auto-immune disease, for example), we understand that the organism is not functioning properly and if steps are not taken to restore the system, the result will be sickness or death. Thinking of cultures as systems may similarly suggest that their parts should work in harmony and that conflict and struggle are deviations from normality that need correction. But are cultures really like that? Do their elements really fit well together?

Many anthropologists today, although accepting that cultures are patterned systems, argue that the elements of these systems never fit together perfectly. Because of this, conflict and struggle are fundamental parts of all cultures rather than problems needing remedies. This position often reflects the deep influence of the work of Karl Marx and the early 20th century sociologist Max Weber. Both Marx and Weber saw conflict in society as a key factor driving social change. Anthropologists who rely on their insights are often referred to as **neo-Marxists.**

Consider the relationship between the American family and the workplace as an example of conflict in society. Does the family system really fit well with the demands made by jobs? Most Americans probably want to maintain long-term marriage commitments, raise families, and live middle-class lifestyles. Most jobs in the United States provide inadequate income for this purpose. Furthermore, jobs often require mobility, long hours, and flexibility, conflicting with the demands of the family. Americans must negotiate the conflicts among the lifestyle they desire, the demands of their families, and the requirements of their jobs. For most people, there is no way to satisfy all of these demands simultaneously. Some interests are always sacrificed to others.

In socially stratified societies, different groups have different and often opposing interests, and this creates conflict. Institutional arrangements within and between societies may favor one group over another. Societies may be divided into castes, or individuals of a particular ethnic origin may be relegated to undesirable positions. For example, consider a modern factory. Both the workers and the owners want the company to do well, but within this context, the owners hope to maximize their profit and the workers want to maximize their pay. Because increases in the cost of labor come at some expense to profits, there is a structural conflict between the owners and the workers. This conflict does not occur because society is not working properly. Rather, it is a fundamental condition of capitalist society. The conflict between workers and owners has the potential to erupt in violence. In the late 19th and early 20th century, labor strikes in the United States repeatedly resulted in death and injury as security forces, police, the National Guard, and the army battled strikers. Even during World War II, a time we usually think of as characterized by great internal solidarity, the United States experienced 14,471 strikes involving 6,774,000 workers (Brecher 1972).

There is nothing uniquely American or modern about contradiction and conflict within culture. Although conflicts are exacerbated in socially stratified societies, social life in all societies is characterized by conflict as well as concord. People in nonindustrialized societies must also handle conflicting commitments to their families and other social groups, such as secret societies or religious associations. Even in societies that lack social groups beyond the family, the interests of men and women may differ, or those of the old and young. Culture is certainly patterned and surely a system, but its parts rub, chafe, and grind against each other.

**ecological functionalism** A theoretical perspective that holds that the ways in which cultural institutions work can best be understood by examining their effects on the environment.

**neo-Marxism** A theoretical perspective concerned with applying the insights of Marxist thought to anthropology; neo-Marxists modify Marxist analysis to make it appropriate to the investigation of small-scale, non-Western societies.

# Culture Is a Shared System of Norms and Values—Or Is It?

What would a person with their own private culture be like? Perhaps they would be like Temple Grandin, Tim Page, or other high-functioning autistics; able to exist in the social world, but unable to "get it." Alternatively, such a person might live in a world in which everything would have one set of meanings to them, but different meanings to everyone else. People with certain forms of schizophrenia seem to have just this problem; they live in worlds filled with symbols that are of meaning only to themselves. In either case, it would be very difficult for such people to interact with others; they would probably be isolated and in some cases, clearly insane. It is clear, then, that at some level, members of a culture must share ways of thinking and behaving. Often, we refer to these as norms and values.

Norms and values are two sorts of ideas that members of a culture might share. **Norms** are the ideas members of a culture share about the way things ought to be done. For example, shaking hands rather than bowing when introduced to a stranger is an American norm. **Values** are shared ideas about what is true, right, and beautiful. For example, the notion that advances in tech-

nology are good is an American value; most Americans agree that humans can and should transform nature to meet human ends. Norms and values are often embedded in rules of behavior that reflect and reinforce culture. In many cases they seem to cluster around certain identities, roles, or positions in society. Members of all cultures have ideas about how people such as parents, politicians, or priests ought to think and behave.

Human behavior is not always consistent with cultural norms or values. What people do and what they say they do are not exactly the same. For example, among upper-middle-class Hindus living in large cities in India, the norm of social equality among all classes of society is widely accepted. However, this norm is considerably different from actual behavior, which rarely involves social interaction between people of the highest and lowest castes on a basis of equality.

Norms may also be contradictory and can be manipulated for personal and group ends. For example, in India people believe that women should be in their home and not "moving about" with their friends. They also believe that women should spend a lot of time in religious activities. Modern Indian women use the second of these ideals to get around the first. By forming clubs whose activities are religious, they have an excuse to get out of the house to which their elders cannot object too strongly.

These examples raise important questions about norms and values. How do we determine the norms and values of any society? Do all people in society agree on these things? How many people must agree on something before it is considered a norm or a value? Who gets to decide these sorts of things? Historically, anthropologists tended not to worry much about these issues, assuming that the small non-Western societies they studied were homogeneous. It followed that people in such societies always acted in the same way in the same situation and attached the same meanings and values to cultural patterns. As early as 1936, however, Ralph Linton, an important American anthropologist, noted that not everyone participates equally in a culture (Linton 1936).

Research shows that even in small societies, norms are not always followed and values are not universal. Individuals differ in their knowledge, understanding, and beliefs. For example, one might expect that in a small fishing society all members would be able to agree on the proper names for different kinds of fish, but on Pukapuka, the small Pacific atoll studied by Robert Borofsky (1994), this is not the case. Even experienced fishermen disagreed about fish names much of the time.

Differences among individuals or groups within a society may be significant when values and beliefs are at issue. A close look at societies with significant sex segre-

Not everyone in a culture must conform. While cultures demand a certain amount of consensus, members of a single culture often show great variability in knowledge, style, and beliefs.

**norm** An ideal cultural pattern that influences behavior in a society.

**value** A culturally defined idea of what is true, right, and beautiful.

gation, such as those in Papua New Guinea (Hammar 1989) and the Amazon (Murphy and Murphy 1974), makes it clear that men and women do not attach the same meanings to many of the myths and rituals that maintain the system of male dominance.

The degree to which people do not share a single culture is even more obvious in larger societies. Sometimes the term **subculture** is used to designate groups within a single society that share norms and values significantly different from those of the dominant culture. The terms dominant culture and subculture do not refer to better and worse, superior and inferior, but rather to the idea that the dominant culture is the more powerful in a society.

Dominant cultures retain their power partly through control of institutions like the legal system, criminalizing practices that conflict with their own (Norgren and Nanda 2006). In contemporary society, public schools help maintain the values of the dominant culture, and the media play an important role in encouraging people to perceive subcultures in stereotypical (and usually negative) ways. For example, in a study that focused on television news and reality shows, Oliver (2003) found that images of race and crime systematically over-represent African Americans as criminal. Further, such shows tended to portray black men as particularly dangerous and present information about black suspects that assumed their guilt.

Although in some situations domination of one group by another may be extreme, it is rarely complete. People contest their subjugation through cultural, political, economic, and military means. Sometimes, when domination is intense, they are able to do so only through religious faith and tales that cast themselves in positions of power and their oppressors in weak roles (Scott 1992).

The result of struggles between groups in society is that norms and values, ideas we sometimes think of as timeless and consensual, are constantly changing and being renegotiated. This dynamic process involves conflict and subjugation as well as consensus. Understanding that norms and values are the result of such processes is critical because such cultural ideas influence and are influenced by real issues of wealth, power, and status.

In the United States, for example, do we see individuals as responsible for their own destinies or as the product of social circumstances? The question is extremely complicated and has very important political ramifications. In the standard version of the American Dream, people compete with one another and the most talented and hardest working individuals achieve material success. But is this really how America works? For people's hard work and talent to be justly rewarded, everyone must start out with a more-or-less equal chance for success. Some Americans insist that because people do start out with approximately equal chances, failure is the result of lack of talent, poor individual choices, and

© Martha Oppersdorff/Photo Researchers, Inc.

The Amish are members of an American subculture. They have customs, language, and values different from those of most Americans.

incorrect actions. If this is the case, society bears little responsibility for helping people to succeed. Other Americans reject this notion, proposing instead that success or failure depends to a considerable extent on accidents of birth and the many forms of prejudice institutionalized in American society. If this is the case, it follows that society has an obligation to provide services and programs that benefit historically oppressed groups. This point of view is common among the poor and among members of minority groups (Hochschild 1995). For example, a 2003 poll showed that most African Americans believed that racism was a big problem in the United States and nearly half said that they experienced some form of discrimination in the past 30 days. Whereas 61 percent of whites believed that blacks have achieved the same job opportunities as whites, only 12 percent of African Americans agreed (AARP, Gallop poll 2004). These issues are more fully discussed in Chapter 12.

Believing either that blame for failure is individual or that family and ethnic background plays the most important roles in social advancement does not make one individual more or less "American" than another. However, which of these notions is held by those in

**subculture** A system of perceptions, values, beliefs, and customs that are significantly different from those of a larger, dominant culture within the same society.

power is critical. It determines public support for social welfare programs that, for good or ill, have direct economic impact on the lives of many Americans.

To avoid the predicament of the people with schizophrenia described at the beginning of this section, members of a culture must have a great deal in common. However, determining exactly what they share is not easy. Anthropologists have generally assumed that people need to share information in order to form a society (Borofsky 1994). It may well be, however, that people share certain information because they have learned how to interact with one another. In other words, shared ideas and the sense of community may be the result of human interaction rather than its cause.

Historically, the notion of culture as a shared set of norms and values was associated with American anthropology in the first half of the 20th century. Many of the pioneering anthropologist Franz Boas's students, such as A. L. Kroeber, Paul Radin, Robert Lowie, Ruth Benedict, and Cora DuBois, saw shared norms and values as central to culture and tried to identify and describe the beliefs, values, and psychological characteristics that were central to individual particular cultures. In contrast, some contemporary neo-Marxist, postmodern, and feminist anthropologists hold that culture is a context in which norms and values are contested. Rather than assuming a cultural core of shared beliefs and values, these anthropologists try to describe the processes through which norms and values are both subverted and maintained. They often focus on the role of governments and other institutions in that process. This issue is examined in more detail in Chapters 11, 12, and 13.

# Culture Is the Way Human Beings Adapt to the World

All animals, including human beings, have biologically based needs. All need food and a place to live, and each species must reproduce. All creatures are adapted to meet these needs. **Adaptation** is a change in the biological structure or life ways of an individual or population by which it becomes better fitted to survive and reproduce in its environment. Nonhuman animals fill their needs primarily through biological adaptation. Lions, for example, have a series of biologically based adaptations that are superbly designed to enable them to feed themselves (and their mates). They have large muscles for speed as well as sharp teeth and claws to capture and eat their prey.

In many societies, housing is well adapted to environment. The Dolgon of Siberia build houses on runners which can then be moved from place to place by reindeer teams.

Humans are different. We are lacking in offensive biological weaponry and if left to get our food like the lion, we would surely starve. There is little evidence that we have an instinct to hunt or consume any particular kind of food, to build any particular sort of structure, or to have a single fixed social arrangement. Instead, human beings, in groups, develop forms of knowledge and technologies that enable them to feed themselves and to survive in their environments. They pass this knowledge from generation to generation and group to group. In other words, human beings develop and use culture to adapt to the world.

Most of a lion's adaptation to the world is set biologically. The growth of its teeth and claws, its instinct to hunt, and the social arrangement of a pride are largely expressions of the lion's genetic code. Humans also have a biological adaptation to the world; the ability to learn the specifics of a culture. All humans automatically learn the culture of their social group. The only exceptions are people with profound biologically based difficulties (such as autism) and, sometimes, victims of extreme abuse. The fact that humans universally learn and use culture strongly suggests that such learning is a manifestation of our genetic code.

Although our biology compels us to learn culture, it does not compel us to learn a particular culture. The range of human beliefs and practices is enormous. Despite this variation, culture must do certain things. People everywhere learn to fill their basic needs such as food and shelter through cultural practices. Therefore, culture everywhere must, to some extent, be adaptive.

Cultural adaptation has some distinct advantages over biological adaptation. Because humans adapt through learned behavior, they can change their approach to solv-

---

**adaptation** A change in the biological structure or lifeways of an individual or population by which it becomes better fitted to survive and reproduce in its environment.

ing problems more quickly and easily than creatures whose adaptations are primarily biological. Furthermore, biological or evolutionary change is based on the presence of more highly adapted variations within the gene pool of a species. These variations occur as chance mutations. If the variations happen not to be present, no change is possible. For example, imagine a species of fish living in a pond of fresh water. If the pond is polluted by industrial waste, all will die except those that, by chance, have a genetic makeup that allows them to survive in polluted water. These will go on to give birth to the next generation of fish. If such a variation does not exist, none will survive and the fish will become extinct. There is no way a fish can learn how to live in the polluted water. Either the genetic variation that allows some of them to survive is present or it is not. Human beings, on the other hand, can learn to live in polluted environments. They can develop ways to clean the environment or mechanisms to enable their survival within it. People can teach these things to others. No biological change is necessary.

Lions hunt and eat today in much the same way as they have for tens of thousands of years. The vast majority of human beings today do not live like humans of three or four generations ago, let alone our distant ancestors. Our means of feeding ourselves, our culture, has changed. **Plasticity**—the ability to change behavior in response to a range of environmental demands—has allowed human beings to thrive under a wide variety of ecological conditions.

Cultural adaptation has some disadvantages too. Misinformation, leading to cultural practices that hinder rather than aid survival, may creep into human behavior. For example, before 1820 most Americans considered the tomato to be poisonous and therefore did not use this valuable food source. Cultural practices that encourage overpopulation, or destructive depletion or contamination of natural resources, may lead to short-term success but long-term disaster. Further, it is clear that many human practices are not adaptive, even in the short run. Political movements such as policies of ethnic cleansing and genocide that urge people to murder their neighbors may benefit their leaders, but it is hard to see any meaningful way in which they are adaptive. A normal lion will always inherit the muscle, tooth, and claw that let it survive. Normal humans, on the other hand, may inherit a great deal of cultural misinformation that hinders their survival.

Anthropologists who view culture as an adaptation tend to be concerned with people's behavior, particularly as it relates to their physical well-being. They ask questions about subsistence technology and its relationship to family structure, religion, and other elements of society. They investigate the ways in which cultures adapt to specific environments and the ways in which cultures have changed in response to new physical and social environments. Such anthropologists may identify themselves as belonging to theoretical schools including **cultural ecology, cultural materialism, neo-evolutionism,** neo-Marxism, and **sociobiology** (McGee and Warms 2008).

# Culture Is Constantly Changing

In the popular press or movies, one often hears of "Stone Age peoples." The implication is that a group of people has been living in precisely the same way for thousands of years. This romantic notion is, as far as we know, incorrect. All cultures have histories of change, and no one belongs to a culture that is stuck in time. Cultures are constantly changing and change often involves issues of conflict and oppression as well as consensus and solidarity. Cultures change because of conflict among different elements within them. They change because of contact with outsiders. Innovation, population growth, disease, climate change, and natural disaster all drive culture change. However,

Innovation often involves crafting familiar things from new materials. In Niger, a craftsman fashions sandals from old tires.

**plasticity** The ability of humans to change their behavior in response to a wide range of environmental demands.

**cultural ecology** A theoretical approach that regards cultural patterns as adaptive responses to the basic problems of human survival and reproduction.

**cultural materialism** A theoretical perspective that holds that the primary task of anthropology is to account for the similarities and differences among cultures and that this can best be done by studying the material constraints to which human existence is subject.

**neo-evolutionism** A theoretical perspective concerned with the historical change of culture from small-scale societies to extremely large-scale societies.

**sociobiology** A theoretical perspective that explores the relationship between human cultural behavior and genetics.

# Ethnography

## Building a House in Northwestern Thailand

One way of thinking about culture is to see it as an adaptation to the environment. All living things are biologically adapted to their environments and all use these adaptations to survive and reproduce. For example, the giraffe's long neck allows it to feed on leaves that other creatures cannot reach; the polar bear's white fur protects it from the cold and allows it to blend into its environment and more easily catch its prey. Human beings are also adapted to the environment in many ways. Our bodies were shaped in the evolutionary process of adaptation. The necessity for humans to learn a culture is a biologically based aspect of the human brain. Culture itself can function for humans in the same way that long necks and fur function for giraffes and polar bears. That is, it can protect us and allow us to get our food in specific environments. The adaptive aspects of culture can often be seen in the ways in which humans satisfy their basic needs for food, shelter, and safety.

Anthropologist James Hamilton found out about the adaptive nature of traditional shelter the hard way when he tried to build a house for himself while doing fieldwork among the Pwo Karen of northwestern Thailand (Hamilton 1987).

To learn about house construction, Hamilton carefully observed the details of building a house. Karen houses are essentially wooden-post structures, raised about 6 feet off the ground, with bamboo walls, peaked roofs, and a veranda. There are no windows; the space between the thatch of the roof and the height of the walls serves for light and ventilation. The kitchen is in the house, with a water storage area on one side of the veranda. This is an important feature of a house because Karen customs of sociability require that visitors and guests be offered water.

Although Hamilton knew a great deal about Karen house construction, when he went to build his own home he decided to incorporate his own, American notions of what a proper, comfortable house should be. First of all, because the climate was very hot, he insisted that his house be in a shaded area under some tall trees. The Karen villagers suggested that this was a bad location but failed to dissuade him. Like most Americans, Hamilton also liked his lawn—a wide grassy area in front of his house—and protested when the villagers started pulling up the grass. He said he was not concerned about the snakes and scorpions that might be in the grass; besides, he had a flashlight and boots in case he had to go out at night. In a traditional Karen house, a person cannot stand up straight because

the side walls are less than 5 feet high. In order to accommodate his belief that people ought to be able to stand up in their houses, Hamilton lowered the floor to about 2 feet off the ground. Furthermore, because the Karen house is dark and, to Americans, rather small, Hamilton decided to have his kitchen outside the house. Despite Karen grumbling that this was not the proper way to build a house, he built an extension on one side of the house with a lean-to roof covering made of leaves, and this became his kitchen. Finally, when the Karen started to cut off the long overhanging thatch from the roof, Hamilton asked that they let it remain, because it gave him some privacy

---

cultures do not always change at the same speed. Cultural change may happen in small increments, or it may happen in revolutionary bursts. Historically, in most places and at most times, culture change has been a relatively slow process. However, the pace of change has been increasing for the past several hundred years and has become extremely rapid in the past century.

Since the 16th century the most important source of culture change has been the development of a world economic system based primarily in the wealthy nations of Europe and Asia. This has involved invasions, revolutions, and epidemic diseases. These historic processes and the resultant global economic system are the primary topics of Chapters 15 and 16. In this chapter, we focus on some of the more traditional ways anthropologists have examined culture change.

Anthropologists usually discuss cultural change in terms of innovation and diffusion. An **innovation** is a new object, way of thinking, or way of behaving that is qualitatively different from existing forms (Barnett 1953:7). Although we are likely to think of innovations as technological, they are not limited to the material aspects of culture. New art forms and new ideas can also be considered innovations.

Some innovations seem to be genuinely new and different. Anthropologists sometimes call these primary innovations. Primary innovations are often chance discov-

**innovation** A new variation on an existing cultural pattern that is subsequently accepted by other members of the society.

from eyes peering over the wall, which did not meet the top of the house.

After the house was finished and Hamilton had lived in it for a while, he found out why the Karen did not like the alterations he had made to their traditional design. This part of Thailand has a heavy rainy season. Because the house was under the trees, the roof could not dry out properly and it rotted. In addition, so many twigs and branches fell through the roof that it became like a sieve, barely providing any protection from the rain at all. The slope of the lean-to over the kitchen was not steep enough; instead of running off, the water came through the roof. The roof on that whole side of the house had to be torn off and replaced with a steeper roof, made of sturdier and more expensive thatch.

The nice lawn combined with the reachable thatch of the roof offered too great a temptation for the local cows, who tried to eat it. One morning Hamilton woke to find his lawn covered with piles of cow dung, with hundreds of dung beetles rolling little balls of dung all around the yard. He cut off the thatch overhang that was left under the trees and pulled up all the grass.

Because the house had been built low to the ground (by Karen standards) in a shady, cool, wet area, there was insufficient ventilation and drying in and around the house to prevent mildew. This meant that Hamilton had to sweep the walls and wipe all leather objects once a week and tightly seal all his anthropological tools, including field notes, camera, film, tape recorder, and typewriter.

People in the United States and other wealthy nations generally think of housing design as reflecting personal taste and being constrained by personal budget. Our ability to harness electricity and fossil fuels for light, heating, and cooling, as well as the development of high-tech building materials, allows us to build almost anything almost anywhere (providing we have the money to do so). Hamilton learned that for people without access to these things, housing choices were much more constrained. However, through culture, people have developed forms of shelter well adapted to their environments. Although the Karen house did not match Hamilton's ideas of what a house should be, it worked extremely well in the Karen environment and its design was not easily tinkered with.

### CRITICAL THINKING QUESTIONS

1. James Hamilton's experience shows that even though traditional Karen housing ideals did not match American notions of housing, they were well adapted to their environment. What particular design features of housing are adaptations to the environment where you live?

2. Is housing in the United States generally well adapted to the environment? Consider both modern and older construction. Is modern construction better adapted to the environment than older construction?

3. Because it is a physical object, it is easy to see a house as an adaptation. But intangible things such as social structure and family type can also be adaptations. For example, the Shoshone Indians lived in the deserts of the American West and supported themselves by hunting animals and gathering plants. They lived in family groups of fewer than 20 people. In what way was living in such small groups an adaptation to their environment?

Source: Adapted from James W. Hamilton, "This Old House: A Karen Ideal." In Daniel W. Ingersoll Jr. and Gordon Bronitsky (Eds.), *Mirror and Metaphor: Material and Social Constructions of Reality.* Lanham, MD: University Press of America, 1987. Courtesy of James Hamilton.

eries and accidents. In our own society, some examples of primary innovations include penicillin, discovered when British researcher Alexander Fleming noticed that bacteria samples he had left by a window were contaminated by mold spores, and Teflon, discovered by Roy Plunkett, who was trying to find new substances to use in refrigeration. Microwave ranges were invented by Percy Le Baron Spencer while he was working on radar. And the artificial sweetener NutraSweet was discovered by James Schlatter, who was trying to develop a drug to treat ulcers. Of course, such accidental discovery is not limited to our own society or time. For example, the fact that clay hardens and becomes durable when it is fired was probably accidentally discovered in many different cultures.

Primary innovations are sometimes called inventions. We resist this term, however. The idea of invention seems to imply something wholly new and completely different, but no innovation is really totally new. Even the examples listed above happened within a cultural context that provided the background, critical ideas, and history that made them possible. For example, although it is true that Fleming discovered penicillin by "accident," it is also true that Fleming was able to understand the importance of penicillin mold because he was a trained bacteriologist who had been looking for a substance to fight infection for more than a decade. The effects of mold on some forms of bacteria had been noted several times in the late 19th century: by Lister in 1871, Tyndale in 1875, Pasteur and Joubert in 1877, and Duchesne in 1897 (Macfarlane 1985). Fleming was aware of all of this research. It does not diminish his achievement to point out that he, like every other inventor or discoverer, did not create something totally new. He realized the critical importance of new combinations of things that already existed. His culture provided him with the training, tools, and context in which his discovery could be made.

All innovations involve human ingenuity and creativity, and these exist in the same quantity in all societies. However, even geniuses are limited by the nature of their cultures. Had Einstein been born among a group that did not have Western notions of science, he could never have "invented" the theory of relativity. If Beethoven had been a Bororo (a member of a Brazilian hunting, gathering, and gardening group), he would never have composed a symphony. An old cliché has it that we all stand on the shoulders of giants. This means that everyone in a culture builds on what has gone before.

Innovations tend to move from one culture to another. This process is known as **diffusion.** Diffusion can happen in many ways; trade, travel, and warfare all promote it. Direct contact among cultures generally results in the most far-reaching changes. That is why cultures located on major trade routes tend to change more rapidly than those in more isolated places. However, because no human society has ever been isolated for a long time from all others, diffusion has always been an important factor in culture. This implies that "pure" cultures, free from outside influences, have never existed.

Innovation and diffusion are not simple processes. People do not "naturally" realize that one way of doing things is better than another or that one style of dress, religion, or behavior is superior. In order for innovation and diffusion to occur, new ideas must be accepted, and that is a very complex process. The discovery of penicillin again provides a good example. Although Fleming understood some of the importance of his discovery in 1928, he was not able to purify the drug; that was done by Howard Florey and Ernest Chain. Fleming himself did not advocate human trials with penicillin until 1940. Penicillin was used extensively to treat wounded servicemen in the later years of World War II, but it was not commonly prescribed by American physicians until the mid-1950s to the late 1950s. The commercial process to manufacture large quantities of the drug was developed by John Sheehan in the late 1950s. The drug companies played critical roles in popularizing penicillin and promoting its acceptance by often reluctant physicians in America and elsewhere (Sheehan 1982; Williams 1984).

As the example of penicillin shows, even when the desirability of an innovation is very clear, gaining its acceptance is often far from straightforward. Part of the problem may be comprehension. People may not fully understand the new idea or its implications. But more frequently other factors lead to slow acceptance of inno-

vation. First, people vary in their willingness to adopt change; some are, by temperament and personal history, early adopters of change. Others are much more conservative. Additionally, innovations do not necessarily benefit all segments of a society and rarely do they benefit all segments equally. New agricultural techniques, for example, may benefit the wealthy landowner but impoverish small family farms. An examination of the Green Revolution (the use of highly productive and technological farming techniques) shows that it did raise yields in many poor nations but also had other less desirable effects. Dependence relations between landowners and laborers were undermined. Large landowners received the greater part of the benefit. Laborers, many of whom were landless, were often impoverished (Das 1998). Additionally, Norman Borlaug, one of the architects of the Green Revolution, notes that although food supplies worldwide have increased, tens of millions go hungry because they lack the resources to purchase food (Borlaug 2000).

Change is often promoted or resisted by powerful forces. Innovations that have strong political, economic, or moral forces behind them may be rapidly accepted. But, when those forces are arrayed against an innovation, it can be profoundly delayed. New technologies may face powerful resistance from those who have invested heavily in older ones. For example, FM radio broadcasting is clearly superior to AM broadcasting; it has greater fidelity and is much less susceptible to static and interference. FM broadcasting was invented in 1933, but because of the resistance of CBS, NBC, and RCA, extremely powerful corporations heavily invested in AM technology, FM did not gain popularity until the late 1960s (T. Lewis 1991).

Innovations are often altered to fit new cultural settings. Thus, cultural elements that move from one society to another frequently undergo changes in both form and meaning as they become part of an existing cultural pattern. For example, American football had its origins in British rugby. Football was born when American colleges modified rugby rules in the late 19th century (Oriard 1993:26–27). The game took on new meanings and has become a central symbol of American culture. Rugby is not nearly as important in British society. Changes in the meanings of cultural elements are of particular interest to archeologists. Archaeologists who find the same material item in two different cultures cannot assume that it has the same meaning in both.

Like innovation, diffusion is often accompanied by conflict. Cultures often confront one another in war, and people who are captured or colonized by others are forced to assume new cultural practices. New rulers may require that traditions be abandoned. Economic demands by governments or creditors often compel the adoption of new technologies and practices. Although these processes happen in most places where cultures confront one another, they have been particularly important in the past 500 years. During this time, cultures have been in-

**diffusion** The spread of cultural elements from one culture to another through cultural contact.

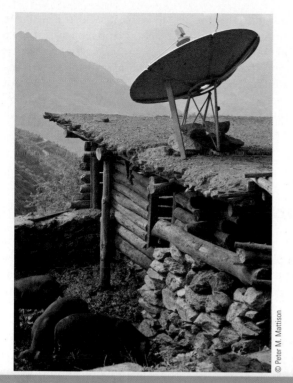

In today's global economy, traits spread rapidly from one culture to another. All cultures are affected by capitalism and mass communication. This photo was taken in a small village in Yunnan Province, China, where TV is increasingly common. Electricity is available only at night, but villagers gather to watch TV (often Korean soaps) with one of the families fortunate enough to own their own TV.

creasingly tied together in an economic system centered in northern Europe, North America, and Japan. The expansion of powers located in these regions has involved the diffusion of many cultural traits to all areas of the world. Such diffusion has sometimes been peaceful, but often it has involved conflict and unspeakable violence (E. Wolf 1982). We examine this process more fully in Chapter 15.

The rapid pace of cultural change and diffusion, particularly in the past 100 years, raises the question of cultural homogenization. Are cultural differences being erased? Are we all being submerged in a single global culture? There is no simple answer to these questions. On one hand, modern technological culture now penetrates virtually every place on earth. People in almost every country have access to radio, telephones, e-mail, television, and other aspects of modern technology. On the other hand, this access is extremely uneven.

The world may be a global village, but not all parts of it are equally close to the center. The vast majority of electronic communication, for example, is located in the industrialized nations. People in rural African villages may have radios, but they are unlikely to be connected to the Internet any time soon.

The world dominance of industrialized nations has affected cultures everywhere, but rather than annihilat-

ing local culture, the result may be what Ortiz (1947) has described as **transculturation.** Cultural traits are transformed as they are adopted, and new cultural forms result. Radio is again a good example. Developed by industrialized societies, it has spread throughout the world, promoting the culture of consumption through advertising. But radio can be used to broadcast messages of resistance and cultural preservation as well as the messages of the society where it originated. Osama bin Laden as well as insurgents and jihadists in Iraq and elsewhere have made extensive use of radio, television, cell phones, and the Internet in their campaign against Western technological society. In 2009, Facebook and Twitter, social networking tools designed originally for young Americans, were critical in organizing mass demonstrations following the presidential elections in Iran, and in showing the repression of those demonstrations to the outside world.

Anthropologists have traditionally worked in tribal and peasant societies. Because such cultures have been profoundly affected by their contact with industrial societies, anthropologists of most theoretical orientations have been interested in change. The study of cultural change has special interest for applied anthropologists, particularly those who investigate issues related to the economic development of poor nations.

# Culture Counts

Culture is many different things. It is learning, symbolism and meaning, patterns of thought and behavior, the things we share with those around us, the ways in which we survive in our world, and dynamism and change. It incorporates both consensus and conflict. Culture makes us human and ties us to others everywhere. Ultimately, because all societies are based around fundamental patterns of culture, no society is utterly incomprehensible to members of another. On the other hand, enormous variability is also built into these patterns. The fact that human lifeways are shared, learned, and symbolic, that we don't simply adapt to our environment but fill it with meaning, results in extraordinary differences in human cultures.

In the opening paragraphs of this book, we defined culture as the answer people have devised to the basic questions of human social life. These questions concern things such as how to feed oneself, how to live with other groups, and how to lend meaning to life. In considering ways to explore and understand these cultural answers, anthropologists have looked at different aspects of cul-

**transculturation** The transformation of adopted cultural traits, resulting in new cultural forms.

ture. The studies they have done reflect the facets of culture they chose to explore. In this chapter, we have described some of these different ways of looking at culture. Taken together, they do not make up a unified whole but rather involve contending views of what it means to be human.

Anthropologists are always involved in fractious debate over the nature of culture and the proper ways to study and describe it. However, as Geertz has written, "Anthropology. . . . draws the greater part of its vitality from the controversies that animate it. It is not much destined for secured positions and settled issues" (1995:4). By thinking about the nature of culture, we arrive at new understandings of ourselves and our subject matter. We come to a keener appreciation of the nature of culture and, ultimately, what it means to be human.

# The Global and the Local: Understanding 9/11

On September 11, 2001, the United States came under terrorist attack. In New York City and Washington, D.C., tens of thousands of people witnessed the events in person. Millions throughout the world sat by radios and televisions, often in stunned silence, as planes crashed, buildings fell, and thousands died.

As tragedies go, the number of people who died in 9/11 was not particularly large. About 3,000 people died on that day, but that number pales before those killed worldwide by natural disaster and acts of war. For example, in May 2008 almost 70,000 people died in the Sichuan earthquake in China. It is estimated that genocide, tyranny, military and civilian warfare deaths, and manmade famine killed between 150 million and 200 million people in the 20th century alone. These disasters often seem remote, but our own sense of grief and our search to understand 9/11 now connect us to those everywhere who have suffered.

When anthropologists are confronted with disaster, they search for ways to understand it. In numerous articles and books anthropologists ponder questions such as: Why were we attacked? What should we do to prevent future attacks? How do we remember and honor those who died, those who labored to save them, those who came together to pick up the pieces? What effects have the attacks had on our national political discourse? How have the attacks changed the incidence of both physical and psychological disease? (Hefner 2002; Hinton, Nguyen, and Pollack 2007; Greenhouse 2005; Jacobs-Huey 2006; Matthews-Salazar 2003; Mattingly, Lawlor, and Jacobs-Huey 2002).

Whether we realize it consciously or not, when we think about such things we are searching for theories and trying to apply them. For example, we might take a materialist or adaptationist approach to understand the events of 9/11. In so doing, we would focus on the economic forces at work and the conditions of life in the Middle East and in New York. We would examine the roles of poverty and wealth, the ways in which the United States and the Soviet Union battled over Afghanistan in the 1980s, and the involvement of the United States in the Persian Gulf conflict of the early 1990s. We would try to understand how these events created an environment in which hatred of the United States could flourish and individuals could be trained and equipped to act upon that hatred.

Alternatively, we may take the idealist view, focusing our attention on the ways in which the people involved in the attack came to understand and organize their worlds: what violence against America symbolized and

© Judith Pearson

The 9/11 bombing of the World Trade Center was interpreted in different ways. In New York City, an important reaction centered on grief and mourning for the victims and the heroism of those who tried to save them.

what their acts meant to them. If we took that approach, we might focus on examining the history of peace and violence in Islam. We would want to know how Osama bin Laden and the members of Al Qaeda understood the world and how the United States and the attacks fit into their understanding. To comprehend the impact of the disaster in the United States and our responses to it, we might examine the symbolic role that New York City and the World Trade Center towers play in American thinking. We might focus on the importance of key symbols such as American flags and firefighters, and explore the ways in which the attacks drove us to a new understanding of ourselves as Americans.

Many other theoretical perspectives are available to us. We could explore the ways in which the attacks fit into larger integrated patterns of culture, the role of diffusion of ideas and technologies, the history of conflict between the United States and the Middle East or Islam and the West, the intricacies of subcultures in the Middle East or in the banking communities of New York City, or the relationship between the cultures of the Middle East and the personalities of terrorists.

We can draw several conclusions from this discussion of theoretical perspectives. First, when we think about an issue such as 9/11, we rarely begin by saying "well, I think I'll take such and such a theoretical perspective." Nonetheless, we clearly do take theoretical perspectives, whether consciously or not. Second, different theoretical positions represent different types of questions and answers about world historical events. People who take a materialist or adaptationist approach want to know different things about culture and society than those who take a symbolic or cognitive approach. Being aware of, and knowledgeable about, our theoretical perspectives allows us to achieve deeper understandings. It points the way to additional questions we need to ask. Third, no one perspective can supply all our questions and answers. Fully understanding an issue requires contributions from different kinds of thinkers. And, finally, although theory can guide us to ask the questions that deepen our understanding, it provides no ultimate answer. No matter how deeply we probe and how many different perspectives we employ, for most Americans, there will probably always be a fundamental incomprehensibility about the events of September 11 and our thoughts and feelings on that day.

## Key Questions

1. When you think about incidents such as 9/11, what theoretical approach do you generally take?

2. Do you take the same approach to thinking about incidents such as 9/11 as you do to thinking about problems such as homelessness or drug use?

3. Try to think about an event or a social problem using a theoretical approach different than the one you generally use. What different conclusions do you come to by taking a different theoretical approach?

# Summary

1. **What might human beings without culture be like?** No humans can truly be said to be without culture but people with autism and Asperger's syndrome give us insight into what having culture differently than others might be like.

2. **Define culture.** Culture is the learned, symbolic, at least partially adaptive, and ever-changing patterns of behavior and meaning shared by members of a group.

3. **Describe the importance of learning in human cultural behavior.** At a basic level, culture is learned behavior. For humans, almost all behavior is at least partially learned, even those things, such as eating, that are biological necessities involve cultural learning. Anthropologists interested in the ways in which culture is learned often study cross-cultural variation in child rearing.

4. **Describe the importance of symbols in human cultural behavior.** Cultures are symbolic systems, mental templates for organizing the world. Every culture has a system of classification through which its people identify and organize the aspects of the world that are important to them. Culture is also a collection of symbols and meanings that permit us to understand others, understand ourselves, and experience our humanity. It is the web of significance that gives meaning to our lives and actions.

5. **In what ways are cultures like biological organisms and what are the problems with this organic analogy?** Cultures, like biological organisms, can be thought of as systems composed of interrelated parts. Changes in one aspect of culture result in other changes as well. However, unlike biological organisms, conflicts between different elements of culture are found in all cultural systems. If culture is a system, its parts do not fit together easily or well.

6. **What are norms and values? Do people within a culture agree upon them?** Norms are shared ideas about the way things ought to be done. Values are shared ideas about what is true, right, and beautiful. Norms and values are not necessarily consistent and may not be

shared in the same way by all members of a culture. Individuals and groups manipulate them, renegotiate them, and battle over them. Norms and values involve conflict and subjugation as well as accommodation and consensus.

7. **How is culture similar to the biological adaptations of non-human animals to their environments?** Many anthropologists understand culture as the major adaptive mechanism of the human species. Whereas other animals adapt primarily through biological mechanisms, humans satisfy their needs for food, shelter, and safety largely through the use of culture. Cultural adaptation has advantages of speed and flexibility but disadvantages of misinformation and maladaptive practices.

8. **Are there any cultures that are static and unchanging?** Cultures are constantly changing. There have been no "Stone Age people" since the Stone Age. Cultural change often occurs as part of the domination of one culture by another. This process has occurred throughout human history, but it has been particularly important in the past few centuries.

9. **Define innovation and diffusion and describe their importance to culture.** An innovation is a new variation on an existing cultural pattern. Diffusion is the spread of elements from one culture to another. Both are present in all cultures. However, both depend on cultural context. New cultural traits build upon older traits, and the use and meaning of symbols and objects may change as they move among cultures. Within society, new traits may favor some groups and be opposed by others.

10. **Do anthropologists agree on the definition and meaning of culture?** Anthropologists argue frequently over the proper definition of culture and the right ways to study and understand it. Our understanding of culture progresses through such discussion and debate.

# Key Terms

| | | |
|---|---|---|
| adaptation | ethnobotany | norm |
| cognitive anthropology | ethnomedicine | plasticity |
| cultural ecology | ethnoscience | sociobiology |
| cultural materialism | functionalism | structural anthropology |
| culture and personality theorists | innovation | subculture |
| diffusion | interpretive (symbolic) anthropology | symbol |
| ecological functionalism | neo-evolutionism | transculturation |
| enculturation | neo-Marxism | value |

# Suggested Readings

Harris, Marvin. 1968. *The Rise of Anthropological Theory: A History of Theories of Culture.* New York: Harper & Row. Well known analysis of the history of anthropological theory. Harris writes to promote his own theoretical position, cultural materialism, therefore, the book must be read critically. Harris has also written a series of popular books on anthropology, including *Cows, Pigs, Wars, and Witches* (1974), and *Cannibals and Kings* (1977).

Marcus, George E. (1998). Ethnography Through Thick and Thin. Princeton, NJ: Princeton University Press. Charts changes in the ways anthropologists have pursued anthropology from a postmodern perspective. Part of a series of influential books written or edited by Marcus, including *Anthropology as Culture Critique* (1986), and most recently *Design for an Anthropology of the Contemporary* (2008, with Paul Rabinow and Tobias Rees).

McGee, R. Jon, and Richard L. Warms (Eds.). 2008. *Anthropological Theory: An Introductory History* (4th edition). New York: McGraw Hill. A comprehensive introduction to theory in anthropology, this edited volume contains essays by critical theoretical thinkers as well as detailed annotations and commentary by McGee and Warms.

Moore, Jerry D. 2004. *Visions of Culture.* Walnut Creek, CA: Alta Mira. A series of essays about critical thinkers in anthropology from the mid-19th century to the 1990s. The essays briefly explore the biography and critical ideas of major theorists and provide a useful bibliography of their most important works. A very readable introduction to theory designed for undergraduate students.

Human language consists of words and gestures, as illustrated in this interaction between Israeli Bedouin in a marketplace.

Courtesy of Serena Nanda

**THINKING POINT:** Many people have pondered the origins of language. According to the Ancient Greek historian Herodotus, around 600 BCE, the Pharaoh Psammetichus ordered two children to be raised by shepherds in a place where they could hear no human voices. Psammetichus reasoned that because they had no outside influence, these children would speak the original human language. Similar experiments were reportedly conducted by Frederick II of Germany in the 1200s and James IV of Scotland around 1500.

—Find the results of these experiments on page 99.

# {chapter 5}

# Communication

**Communication** is the act of transmitting a message that influences the behavior of another organism. Communication, and hence interaction, in all animal species depends on a consistent set of signals by which individuals convey information. These signals are channeled through visual, olfactory, auditory, and tactile senses.

Many animals use sounds and movements to share information. Such communication can be quite complex. For example, a scout honeybee uses stereotyped and patterned movements to communicate information about the direction and distance of a field of pollen-bearing flowers to others in its hive. But although bees can say a lot about where flowers are, they cannot say much about anything else. Crows caw as a signal of danger, and crickets chirp when they are ready to mate. Dolphins have "signature whistles" that enable them to identify each other as individuals (Janik and Slater 1998). Among primates, far greater amounts of information can be transmitted about many more subjects.

Although communication among nonhuman animals is critical to their survival, it is quite limited compared with human language. Animal systems of verbal communication are referred to as **call systems.** They are restricted to a set number of signals generally uttered in response to specific events. Human language, on the other hand, whether spoken, signed, or written, is capable of re-creating complex thought patterns and experiences in words. Our linguistic abilities allow enormous variety in how we act, think, and adapt to our surroundings.

Human language is distinct from other animal communication system in three ways: conventionality, productivity, and displacement. ≫

**Conventionality** describes the association between a meaningful sequence of sounds and an object, action, or idea. In human languages, a limited number of sounds (hardly any language uses more than 50) are combined to refer to thousands of different things and experiences. Words are symbols, and they stand for things simply because speakers of a language agree that they do. An animal is no more a dog than it is a chien (French), a perro (Spanish), or a kutta (Hindi). Without conventionality—the capacity to separate the vocal symbol from its referent—we would have to use a unique sound for every item of meaning. This would result in either a very small vocabulary (like an animal call system) or an impossibly large number of sounds. It is the ability to recombine sounds to create new meanings that makes human language such an efficient and effective communication system.

Not only is human language efficient, it is also infinitely **productive.** Humans constantly forge new combinations of words. Speakers of any human language can generate an almost infinite number of new words and combine these into different sentences. The productive capacity of human language, sometimes called openness, makes it a flexible instrument for communication, capable of conveying new information.

The third distinguishing characteristic of human language is **displacement**—the ability of language to convey information about something not in the immediate environment. We can describe things that happened in the past, will or may happen in the future, exist only in the mind, or may not happen at all.

Among other animals, communication is generally about the present and the particular: a particular threatening object is in a particular place at this particular time. Human language generalizes; it categorizes some objects and events as similar and other objects and events as dissimilar. Humans can talk about a particular tree ("The tree in front of my house needs trimming.") and also about trees in general ("I think that I shall never see a poem lovely as a tree.").

These qualities of human language—conventionality, productivity, and displacement—allow people to make plans, understand and correct mistakes, and coordinate their activities. They give our species a distinct advantage over other animals. By translating experience into language, humans build up a storehouse of knowledge that can be transmitted to new members of the group. Although one may learn simple tasks by imitation, complex human behavior patterns could not exist without the symbolizing capacity of human language. Without language, it would be impossible to socialize children into the intricate workings of their cultures, to teach others how to make anything but very simple tools, or to pass on the traditions, rituals, myths, and religious beliefs that instill a sense of group identity and maintain social order. <<

**communication** The act of transmitting information.

**call system** The form of communication among nonhuman primates composed of a limited number of sounds that are tied to specific stimuli in the environment.

**conventionality** The notion that, in human language, words are only arbitrarily or conventionally connected to the things for which they stand.

**productivity** The ability of humans to combine words and sounds into new meaningful utterances.

**displacement** The capacity of all human languages to describe things not happening in the present.

# Origins and Acquisition of Human Language

Like the communication systems of all animals, human language reflects the particular character of our adaptation. Language and human culture probably evolved together. The more elaborate the culture of human ancestors grew, the more complex the system of communication among people had to become. Conversely, increases in the sophistication of communication led to increases in the complexity of culture (Salzmann 1993:88).

No one really knows how human language originated, but in the early 1970s, Charles Hockett suggested that language evolved in two steps. The first step, which he called blending, occurred when human ancestors began to produce new calls by combining old ones. Although a communication system based on blending greatly increases the number of possible messages in a call system, it is still limited compared with modern language.

Hockett called the second step in the evolution of language duality of patterning. At this stage, human ancestors acquired the ability to produce different arrangements of blended sounds and to combine these sounds into a virtually limitless number of utterances (Hockett 1973:106). Although early language sounded nothing like modern language, we can use current-day English to get a sense of blending and duality of patterning. Blending would be like combining two words to make a third word (for example, combining *breakfast* and *lunch* to make *brunch*). Duality of patterning would be like combining the sound units that compose the words *breakfast* and *lunch* to make a great many different new words, such as *bench, bunch, chest, fun, less, lust,* and so on (Salzmann 1993:84).

Estimates of when language emerged vary tremendously. Certainly our most distant ancestors communicated, but they probably used call systems similar to modern-day primates. Some believe that language might have begun as early as 2 million years ago, at the time of the emergence of the genus *Homo* (see Schepartz 1993:119), but most anthropologists think that language has been limited to members of our own species. Because the earliest *Homo sapiens* date from about 200,000 years ago, language may well have emerged at that time. A third position holds that language emerged about 50,000 years ago, in connection with a big jump in the sophistication of human toolmaking and symbolic expression (Bickerton 1998).

Whichever date is correct, anthropologists generally agree that language is part of our biological adaptation, more than simply a capacity or ability. For example, people have the capacity or ability to learn algebra or ice skating. They may do it or not as their culture and their individual choices dictate. Language is different. Unless prevented by total social isolation or physical incapacity, all humans learn a first language as part of the developmental process of childhood. All go through the same stages of language learning in the same sequence and at roughly the same speed regardless of the language being learned. Although in any culture some people talk with greater or lesser artistry than others, all physiologically normal individuals in every culture develop adequate language skills.

Our use of language rests on certain features of human biology. The visual and auditory areas of human brains are directly connected to each other and both are connected to the brain region concerned with touch. Thus, human children are able to make the association between the visible image, the feel of an object, and the sound pattern or word used to designate it. Furthermore, the structure of human air and food tracts is different from that of our closest ape relations. Among apes, food and air pass through separate passageways. As anyone who has ever tried to speak while eating knows, in humans the food and air tracts are connected. This increases the possibility of choking but also greatly expands our ability to make different sounds (see Figure 5.1).

Humans have what Steven Pinker (1994) calls a "language instinct." Pinker points out that the language "instinct" in humans is very different from instinctive communication in other animals. Among animals the instinct for communication means that patterns of communication are the expression of underlying genetic codes. Dogs do not *learn* to wag their tails when they are content and growl when they are angry: these things are dictated by canine biology. Dog behavior is species-wide. A growl means the same thing to a dog in Vladivostok as it does to a dog in Manhattan. But language is not instinctual in this way. The human "instinct" is to learn the language of the group into which the individual is socialized. There is no biological basis for learning one language over another: for example, an infant born to French-speaking parents but raised in an English-speaking family has no predisposition to speak French.

If you are wondering what language a human being would speak if he or she were not taught any particular language, several anecdotes report historical experiments in which just this was done. Herodotus, the ancient Greek historian, wrote that the Egyptian pharaoh Psammetichus ordered two infants reared where they could hear no human voices in order to learn the original language of humankind. Psammetichus assumed that the children would "naturally" speak in the language of their ancestors. To his ears, their babbling sounded like Phrygian, which he concluded was the original human language. King James IV of Scotland supposedly tried a similar experiment, and he claimed that the two infants spoke Hebrew. Biblical scholars of his time asserted that Adam and Eve had spoken Hebrew, and people believed that it was the original, natural language of all humans. Although Psammetichus interpreted what he heard as Phrygian and James IV interpreted what he heard as Hebrew, all modern evidence shows that such children would not speak any intelligible language.

Although it has a clear biological basis, speech must be learned as part of a **speech community,** a group of people who share a set of norms and rules for the use of

---

**speech community** A group of people who share a set of norms and rules for the use of language.

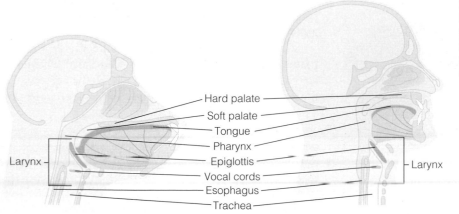

**FIGURE 5.1** The human vocal tract is different from that of our nearest ape relations. The lower position of the larynx in humans allows us greater flexibility in making sounds but at the cost of increased hazard of choking.

Hard palate
Soft palate
Tongue
Pharynx
Epiglottis
Vocal cords
Esophagus
Trachea

Larynx

Larynx

# Anthropology Makes a Difference

## Can Nonhumans Speak?

Since the mid-20th century, many claims have been made about the ability of nonhuman animals to understand and use human languages. Such claims can play an important role in debates about the rights of animals and the degree to which humans are unique (see Partridge 1984, Regan 1982, Singer 1979, and Wise 2002 for examples). Researchers have examined the linguistic abilities of gorillas, chimpanzees, parrots, dolphins, and whales. There is no question that these creatures have complex communication abilities. For example, baboons in the wild transmit information to one another by lip smacking, grunts, stares, poses, and screams. Alex, an African Gray parrot raised in captivity, had a vocabulary of about 100 words, and researcher Irene Pepperberg (2000) claimed that the bird could use these words in ways that showed productivity, the use of syntax, and an understanding of meaning.

Parrots and humans last shared a common ancestor more than 300 million years ago. Therefore, the biologies of human and

Some physical anthropologists study the behavior of our nearest primate relations. In this picture, the chimp signs "double apple" to his trainer, Joyce Butler, at Colorado University.

*Courtesy of Colorado University*

parrot communication are likely to be very different. Chimpanzees, on the other hand, are among humans' closest relations. We shared a common ancestor with them about 6 million years ago. Because of this close connection, chimp communication is

of great interest to anthropologists. Wild chimpanzees exhibit a wide variety of communicative behaviors. However, a primate call system is not the same as human language. Chimp calls signal only their immediate physical environment or emotional state. Chimpanzees have vocal apparatus capable of making many of the sounds of human languages, even simple words, but despite the fact that captive chimpanzees have been raised in close proximity to humans, no chimp has ever produced voluntary speechlike verbalizations (Lieberman 2003).

One famous research strategy involved attempting to teach chimpanzees a version of sign language; studies using this strategy show them capable of much more complex communication than they demonstrate in the wild. For example, Allen and Beatrice Gardner attempted to teach sign language to a chimp they called "Washoe." The Gardners claimed that after learning 10 signs, Washoe spontaneously began to produce new combinations of signs (Gardner and Gardner 1969). Other re-

*© Myrleen Ferguson Cate/PhotoEdit*

Interaction between infants and others is critical to learning language. By the time children are 6 months old, their babbling includes many of the sounds and sequences of the language that surrounds them.

language (Romaine 1994:22). The need for community is illustrated by cases of children brought up in isolation. For example, Genie, a child discovered in the 1970s by social workers in California, had been locked in an attic for the first 12 years of her life. With training and good living conditions, she rapidly acquired a large vocabulary but never mastered English syntax. For example, she spoke in sentences like "Genie have Momma have baby grow up" (Pinker 1994:292).

Cases such as Genie's imply that there is a critical period of language development for humans. All children are capable of learning language before the age of 6, but thereafter it becomes increasingly difficult, and after pu-

searchers argued that Washoe was ultimately able to master more than 85 signs and that, without human intervention, Washoe taught more than 50 of these signs to her adoptive son, Loulis (Fouts and Fouts 1989). Researcher Sue Savage-Rumbaugh taught Kanzi, a bonobo chimpanzee, a vocabulary of about 150 signs. She claims that he is able to arrange these signs into sentencelike strings. Researchers argue that Kanzi has responded appropriately to more than 500 sentences of spoken English (Savage-Rumbaugh, Shanker, and Taylor 1998).

Although the data from the sign language experiments are certainly impressive, they are also controversial. It is not clear whether the achievements of these animals reflect true language abilities or simply training, unconscious cuing, and projection on the part of researchers. Some researchers report little success in demonstrating language skills in chimps. For example, Terrace (1983) believed that his attempts to train a chimp did not result in any true humanlike language abilities. Seidenberg and Petitto's (1987) analysis of material from Kanzi concluded that the animal probably did not have mental representations of ob-

jects or events. They wrote: "Our view is that Kanzi's behaviors are more like the use of tools than the human use of language. Tools are the instruments by which we attain certain outcomes. They are not symbols" (1987:284). Savage-Rumbaugh (1987) and others hotly dispute this analysis.

The difference between a tool and a symbol is critical. Human use of symbols is essential to our ability to think about the past or future, reflect on our own condition, and pass knowledge to others. The use of tools does not necessarily imply these abilities. Our ability to use symbols is expressed in language. If other creatures can use language symbolically, their thinking may be more similar to our own than previously recognized. Experiments on animal communication suggest that the answer to this is complicated and equivocal. On the one hand, the results suggest that some animals have much greater linguistic abilities than previously recognized. On the other hand, despite enormous effort in training, no researcher has argued that any nonhuman animal has ever developed greater linguistic skill than a very young child. There are two possible explanations.

Perhaps chimps are learning language in ways that are similar to those used by humans, and they have simply reached the limit of their linguistic ability. If so, then language and symbolic behavior is a continuum: chimps and humans are similar in the nature of their abilities; humans just have much more of those abilities. Alternatively, perhaps chimps learn language poorly because they must learn it in ways fundamentally different from those used by people. Human infants learn language spontaneously because their biology compels them to learn it. Other animals may learn by rote memorization. If that is the case, then their linguistic abilities are not only different in quantity but different in kind from our own.

One thing is clear: human language is the result of our own particular evolutionary history. Human language is unique in terms of its great complexity and the importance of its role in human adaptation. We may be able to teach other animals simple humanlike languages, but these languages are not essential to them. In contrast, the use of highly complex language is fundamental to human culture.

berty it is very rare (Pinker 1994:293). You have probably experienced the time-limited nature of human ability to learn language. All college students (and indeed all people) speak the language they learned as children with ease and fluency. Most students, however, struggle to learn a second language and very few will ever learn to speak one with the proficiency of a native speaker.

Studies of how children learn language show that they recognize the sounds of their language within days of birth. By the time children are 6 months old their babbling includes consonant and vowel sequences and repetitive patterns. Surrounded by the flow of sounds, words, and intonations, they imitate these and form combinations of words they have not heard before but that are consistent with the rules of the language. Even when children do not understand what they are saying, they can speak grammatically, using the different parts of speech in correct relation to one another.

The universality of the process of learning a first language as well as the underlying similarities that unite all human languages led Noam Chomsky and many others to propose that there is a **universal grammar**—a basic set of principles, conditions, and rules that form the foundation of all languages (Chomsky 1975). Children learn language by applying this unconscious universal grammar to the sounds they hear. They process the sequences of words in their parents' speech to figure out their language's grammar. They model their utterances to those they hear until their version matches, or almost matches, the one being used around them (Pinker 1994).

One good way to understand universal grammar is by using the analogy of computer languages. A computer language is a set of symbols and rules in which instructions for a computer to follow are written (see Figure 5.2). Some examples are FORTRAN, Pascal, C, and BASIC.

**universal grammar** A basic set of principles, conditions, and rules that underlie all languages.

Such languages are used to write programs. Many different kinds of programs can be written using a single computer language. However, because they all ultimately derive from the same set of principles and rules, the programs will have certain fundamental similarities. In the same way, Chomsky and his followers argue, each individual is born with an instinctive universal grammar, analogous to a programming language. A child "programs" his or her language by interacting verbally with other people. The result is that, although humans speak many different languages, they all share fundamental underlying similarities.

```
TYPE STRING = PACKED ARRAY[1..40] OF CHAR;
     PART = RECORD
               DESCR : STRING;
               ID : INTEGER;
               COST : REAL
               END; (*RECORD*)
     NAME = ARRAY[1..20] OF CHAR;

VAR INFILE, OUTFILE : TEXT;
     MAIL : FILE OF NAME;
     WORDS : FILE OF STRING;
     INVTRY : FILE OF PART;
     LETTER : NAME;
     WORD : STRING;
     APART : PART;
```

**FIGURE 5.2** Many sorts of computer programs may be written in a single language such as Pascal. Though such programs may be very different, they will share underlying resemblances. Similarly, all human languages may share characteristics of an underlying universal grammar.

The computer analogy is not perfect. Programming a computer is a conscious, voluntary task. Children learn language automatically, without conscious effort. Furthermore, no computer application has yet been able to equal the subtlety and complexity of human language.

Anthropologists point out that speaking is far more than simply learning words and grammar. Children must learn the social rules about how to use language to participate in their society. These rules include when to speak and when not to speak, whom to speak to and in what manner, what to talk about, and many other aspects of participation (Duranti 1997:20–21). Ochs and Schieffelin (1984) examined language acquisition among white middle-class Americans, Samoans, and the Kaluli of Papua New Guinea. They found that parents relate to infants very differently in these cultures. American parents spend a great deal of time talking with their infants, using simplified "baby talk" and encouraging them to speak. They believe that their young children's utterances are very important. The Kaluli, on the other hand, rarely talk to their infants at all, except for an occasional rebuke. They do not consider the utterances of young children to have any importance. Samoans talk to their children using adult speech, frequently rebuking them. Like the Kaluli, they do not attribute any importance to the speech of young children. In all three societies, children learn to speak at the same speed and with the same level of competence. However, in each society children learn different rules about when to speak, who to speak to, their responsibility for the words they say, and other aspects of communication. Thus, although the actual process of learning to produce grammatical speech is largely a function of biology, learning to be a member of a speech community is clearly a function of culture.

**descriptive or structural linguistics** The study and analysis of the structure and content of particular languages.

**phonology** The sound system of a language.

**morphology** A system for creating words from sounds.

**syntax** The part of grammar that has to do with the arrangement of words to form phrases and sentences.

**semantics** The subsystem of a language that relates words to meaning.

**phone** A sound made by humans and used in any language.

**International Phonetic Alphabet (IPA)** A system of writing designed to represent all the sounds used in the different languages of the world.

## The Structure of Language

Every language has a structure: an internal logic and a particular relationship among its parts. The study of the structure and content of specific languages is called **descriptive or structural linguistics.** Descriptive or structural linguists study language separately from the social context in which speaking takes place. Their work suggests that the structure of any language consists of four subsystems: **phonology** (a system of sounds), **morphology** (a system for creating words from sounds), **syntax** (a system of rules for combining words into meaningful sentences), and **semantics** (a system that relates words to meaning).

### Phonology

People use hundreds of different sounds in their various languages. The total set of sounds that are used in all of the world's languages are called the set of **phones.** A system of writing, called the **International Phonetic Alphabet (IPA),** has been devised to represent the sounds of all of the world's languages. Although you may have experienced great difficulty in correctly producing the sounds of a language you are learning, all humans are biologically capable of making all of the sounds of the world's languages. However, any particular language uses only a relatively small number of phones and those are the ones its speakers learn to make and recognize.

Sounds used in one language may be absent in other languages. English, for example, does not use the click sound of the language of the Ju/'hoansi (!Kung) of southern Africa or many of the tonal sounds of Chinese. Furthermore, combinations of sounds are used in different ways in different languages. For example, an English speaker can easily pronounce the *ng* sound in *thing* at the end of an utterance but not at the beginning; however, this sound is used in the initial position in Bambara, a language of Africa (compare the ease of saying *thing* with the difficulty of saying *ngoni,* the name of a musical instrument in Bambara).

The set of phones used in a particular language is referred to as the phonemes of the language. A **phoneme** is the smallest sound unit that distinguishes meaning within a given language. An example will help to make this clear. In **Standard Spoken American English (SSAE),** the English accent you generally hear on network news broadcasts, the sound /d/ in the English word *den* and /th/ in *then* are phonemes. The words *den* and *then* have different meanings, and this difference in meaning is indicated by the initial consonant sound (/d/ or /th/). Spanish also uses these sounds, but in Spanish these two sounds are **allophones;** that is, both phones indicate only one phoneme. In Spanish, the sounds /d/ and /th/ may be slightly different, but they do not distinguish words from one another. Rather, these sounds are used in different contexts (/d/ at the beginning of a word and /th/ in the middle of a word). A person who says *día* (Spanish for "day" and a word beginning with the /d/ phoneme) using the consonant sound in *nada* will still be understood to be saying "day," although people may think the accent is "wrong" or "foreign." Like Spanish, English has many cases in which a single phoneme may be indicated by many phones. For example, the English phoneme /t/ includes at least six different phones (Ladefoged 1982). Consider the /t/ sounds in *stick, tick,* and *little.* The /t/ sound in each of these words is different. As you say the /t/ sound in one word after another, you can feel your tongue change position. Now, hold your hand in front of your mouth and say *stick* and then *tick.* You will feel a puff of air as you say the /t/ in *tick* but not when you say *stick.* This demonstrates that the sounds are different, even though you may have a difficult time describing the precise difference.

Because different speakers have different accents, calculating the precise number of phonemes in any language is difficult and controversial. Most of the world's languages have between 20 and 40 phonemes. There are, however, some radical departures from this. The languages with the smallest number of phonemes may have only 11 or 12. Mura, an indigenous language from Brazil, is one of these. At the other end of the spectrum, some languages have well over 120 phonemes. For example, some of the Khoisan "click" languages of southern Africa have over 140. English is believed to have between 40 and 45 phonemes (Clark, Yallop, and Fletcher 2007: 118–124). Perhaps surprisingly, there is no relationship between the number of phonemes in a language and the number of things that can be said in that language. Anything that can be said in Khoisan can also be said in Mura.

## Morphology

The smallest unit of a language that has a meaning is called a **morpheme.** In English, -s, as in *dogs,* means "plural"; un-, as in *undo,* means "negative"; -er, as in *teacher,* means "one who does." Because -s, un-, and -er are used not by themselves but only in association with another unit of meaning, they are called **bound morphemes.** A morpheme that can stand alone, such as giraffe, is called a **free morpheme.**

A **word** is the smallest part of a sentence that can be said alone and still retain its meaning. Some words consist of a single morpheme. *Giraffe* is an example of a single-morpheme word. *Teacher* has two morphemes, teach and -er. *Unlocks* has three morphemes: un-, lock, and -s.

Languages differ in the extent to which their words tend to contain only one, several, or many morphemes, as well as in their rules for combining morphemes. Some languages, such as English and Chinese, are isolating. They have relatively few morphemes per word, and the rules for combining morphemes are fairly simple. Agglutinating languages, such as Turkish, allow a great number of morphemes per word and have highly regular rules for combining them. Synthetic languages such as Mohawk or Inuktitut (an Arctic Canadian language) have words with a great many morphemes and complex, highly irregular rules for their combination. In agglutinating or

---

**phoneme** The smallest significant unit of sound in a language. A phonemic system is the sound system of a language.

**Standard Spoken American English (SSAE)** The form of English spoken by most of the American middle class.

**allophones** Two or more different phones that can be used to make the same phoneme in a specific language.

**morpheme** The smallest unit of language that has a meaning.

**bound morpheme** A unit of meaning that must be associated with another

**free morpheme** A unit of meaning that may stand alone as a word.

**word** The smallest part of a sentence that can be said alone and still retain its meaning.

synthetic languages, translating a single word may require an entire English sentence. For example, the Inuktitut word *qasuirrsarvigssarsingitluinarnarpuq* contains 10 morphemes and is best translated as "someone did not find a completely suitable resting place" (Bonvillain 1997:19).

In all languages, the rules used to combine morphemes into words can be quite complex. For example, one of the rules of English morphology is that a plural is formed by adding the morpheme -s following the element that is being pluralized. However, there are many exceptions. The plural of *dog* is made by adding -s, but the plural of *child* is made by adding -ren. A description of morphology must specify both the general rules for the combination of morphemes and their exceptions in any particular language.

## Syntax

Syntax is the arrangement of words to form phrases and sentences. Languages differ in their syntactic structures. In English, word order is important because it conveys meaning. The syntax of the English language gives a different meaning to these two sentences: "The dog bit the man." and "The man bit the dog." However, word order is not equally important in all languages. In Latin, for example, the subject and object of a sentence are indicated by word endings rather than word order.

When they analyze the syntactic structure of a language, descriptive linguists establish the different form classes, or parts of speech, for that language. All languages have a word class of nouns, but different languages have different subclasses of nouns, frequently referred to as genders. Gender classification can apply to verbs, indefinite and definite articles, and adjectives, all of which must agree with the gender classification of the noun.

Many Americans have some experience of Spanish, French, or another Romance language. In these languages, nouns are classified as either masculine or feminine so using the word "gender" seems logical. However, the use of "gender" in linguistics has nothing to do with sex roles. Many languages have genders that are in no way related to ideas about masculine or feminine. For example, German and Latin have a neuter subclass and Kivunjo, a language spoken in East Africa, has 16 genders (Pinker 1994:27). Papago, a Native American language, has only two genders but rather than masculine and feminine they are "living things" and "growing things." Living things include all animated objects, such as people and animals; growing things refer to inanimate objects, such as plants and rocks.

Applying the rules of grammar turns meaningless sequences of words into meaningful utterances, but sometimes grammar seems to have a meaning of its own. We can recognize a sentence as grammatical even if it makes no sense. To use a now classic example (Chomsky 1965), consider the following sentences: "Colorless green ideas sleep furiously." "Furiously sleep ideas green colorless." Both sentences are meaningless in English. But the first is easily recognized as grammatical by an English speaker, whereas the second is both meaningless and ungrammatical. The first sentence has the parts of speech in English in their proper relation to each other, so it seems as if it should make sense. The second sentence does not.

## Semantics: The Lexicon

The total stock of words in a language is called a **lexicon.** Because the lexicon of any culture reflects many of the objects and ideas that are important to that culture, lexicons illustrate the relationship between culture and language. For example, whereas the average American can name only about 50 to 100 species of plants, members of societies based on hunting and gathering or on gardening can typically name 500 to 1000 species of plants (Harris 1989:72). Such lexical specialization is not limited to nonindustrial societies. Germans in Munich have a vocabulary of more than 70 words to describe the strength, color, fizziness, clarity, and age of beer (Hage 1972, cited in Salzmann 1993:256).

The lexicon gives us clues to the ways members of a culture understand their physical and social environments. Sometimes, knowing how people use language to classify their world can give us an insider's view of their understandings. This is particularly true concerning fam-

Languages build vocabularies around ideas and things important to their speakers. Germans in Munich have more than 70 words to describe beer.

© Reuters/Corbis

---

**lexicon** The total stock of words in a language.

ilies and kinship systems. In English, for example, the term *brother-in-law* can include one's sister's husband, one's spouse's brother, and the husbands of all one's spouse's sisters. The use of a single term for all of these relations reflects the similarity of our behavior toward the men in those different kinship statuses. Hindi, a language of North India, has many separate terms for brother-in-law. Which term one uses depends first on whether the speaker is male or female. For women, a sister's husband is *behnoi*, a husband's elder brother is *jait*, a husband's younger brother is *deva*, and the spouses of one's husband's sisters are *nandoya*. The variety of words in Hindi reflects the fact that a woman treats the members of each of these categories differently. (For more detail, see page 180 in Chapter 8, "Kinship.")

# Language and Culture

We have been describing the structure of language. However, language is much more than its structure. In the early years of the 20th century, the Swiss linguist Ferdinand de Saussure theorized that language could be best understood by separating it into language (*langue*) and speech (*parole*). He argued that *langue* was an arbitrary and abstract system of signs that existed independently of any speaker. *Parole* was the actual performance of language by an individual speaker. In the sections you have just read, we have been examining *langue*, language as an abstract system. However, anthropologists are also interested in understanding *parole*: the actual encounters that involve verbal (and also accompanying nonverbal) communication between human beings. Consider the following example of *parole*:

> *Scene: It's a clear, hot evening in July. J and K have finished their meal. The children are sitting nearby. There is a knock at the door. J rises, answers the knock, and finds L standing outside.*

THE WESTERN APACHE.

*J:* Hello, my friend! How're you doing? How are you feeling, L? You feeling good? *(J now turns in the direction of K and addresses her.)*

*J:* Look who here, everybody! Look who just come in. Sure, it's my Indian friend, L. Pretty good, all right. *(J slaps L on the shoulder and, looking him directly in the eyes, seizes his hand and pumps it wildly up and down.)*

*J:* Come right in, my friend! Don't stay outside in the rain. Better you come in right now. *(J now drapes his arm around L's shoulder and moves him in the direction of a chair.)*

*J:* Sit down! Sit right down! Take your loads off you ass. You hungry? You want crackers? Maybe you want some beer? You want some wine? Bread? You want some sandwich? How about it? You hungry? I don't know. Maybe you sick. Maybe you don't eat again long time. *(K has now stopped what she is doing and is looking on with amusement. L has seated himself and has a look of bemused resignation on his face.)*

*J:* You sure looking good to me, L. You looking pretty fat! Pretty good all right! You got new boots? Where you buy them? Sure pretty good boots! I glad. . . . *(At this point, J breaks into laughter. K joins in. L shakes his head and smiles. The joke is over.)*

The joke is over. . . . So what was the joke? This joke, from the Western Apache, recorded by Keith Basso (1979), is about how the Apache see white people as communicating with them and with each other. In the joke, J pretends he is a white man. The joke is that white speech, as J presents it, is highly inappropriate and offensive. For starters, you do not publicly call someone a friend or ask how they are feeling. For the Western Apache, these are very personal statements and questions. To use them in a highly public way as J does here conveys insincerity. The Apache believe that one should enter and leave a room as unobtrusively as possible, so J making a big to-do about L coming into the room is inappropriate as well. Actions such as putting an arm around another man's shoulder or asking repeatedly if he wants something to eat are understood as both violations of individual dignity and overwhelming bossiness. To the Apache, such actions suggest that the speaker thinks the person they are talking to is of no account and that his wishes can be safely ignored. Perhaps worst of all is suggesting that another might be sick. Not only is this a violation of privacy; the Apache fear that talking about misfortune may well bring it on.

Knowing only the technical grammatical aspects of language would not help much in understanding J and L's speech. Their speech embeds critical cultural concepts and values. Without understanding their culture, an observer cannot possibly get the joke. Language is so heavily freighted with culture that understanding one is almost always a key to understanding the other.

**Sociolinguistics** is the study of the relationship between language and culture. The sociolinguist attempts

---

**sociolinguistics** A specialization within anthropological linguistics that focuses on speech performance.

# Ethnography

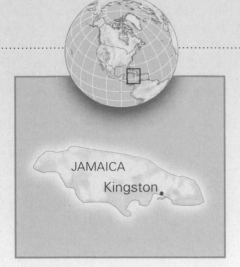

## Cell Phone Use in Jamaica

There is no question that the past 10 years have seen a revolution in communication. The Internet, instant messaging, digital television, and other technologies have changed the way we communicate. However, the cell phone has probably been the most important part of this revolution. Sometime in 2006 or 2007, the number of cell phone subscriptions worldwide reached 3.3 billion, half of the world's population. Some people had more than one subscription, and in some places cell phones were rare. However, many of the statistics are surprising. Some of the biggest markets for cell phones are in poorer countries. By the end of 2008, China alone had more than 600 million cell phones and India almost 300 million (International Telecommunications Union 2008). Even some very poor areas of the world have large numbers of cell phones. For example, Chad, one of the world's poorest countries, has more than 200,000 cell phone subscribers and Uganda has close to 5 million. At the end of 2007, Africa had more than 280 million cell phone subscribers (Smith 2009).

Jamaica is a good example of the success of cell phones. In 2004, the population of the island was about 2.6 million and there were 2 million cell phone subscriptions. It was estimated that 86 percent of Jamaicans over age 15 owned a cell phone. By comparison, relatively few Jamaicans had access to landline telephones—only about 7 percent of families in 2004 (Horst and Miller 2006:19). The popularity of cell phones is particularly impressive because making calls

on cell phones is, in most cases, far more expensive than making the same calls on landlines. Despite this, families claimed that they used cell phones to save money.

Anthropologists Heather Horst and Daniel Miller investigated cell phone use among two low-income Jamaican communities, urban Marshfield and rural Orange Valley. The average family they studied had three cell phones. Horst and Miller were interested in how these phones were used and whether or not their use provided an economic benefit. They argue that these questions could only be answered in relation to the economic and cultural context of the communities they studied. Several elements of background knowledge are necessary. First, although Jamaicans are highly individualistic, they place a great emphasis on social connectedness. Jamaicans retain close connections not only with their families but also with large numbers of unrelated individuals. Second, the people among whom Horst and Miller worked have highly irregular access to sources of income and support. In Marshfield, only 20 percent of households had members with regular jobs. In rural Orange Valley, the number was even less. In both, other sources of income included remittances from family members abroad and in other communities, and payments from the government or aid agencies. However, all of these were extremely undependable.

Horst and Miller originally set out to analyze the content of phone conversations. However, they found that most con-

versations were very short and uninteresting. For example, a complete conversation might consist of a question like "Hi, how is everything" and the response "Oh, I'm OK, I'm just enjoying the summer." Although people do make some longer calls, the average length of a cell call in Jamaica is only 19 seconds (2006:96). The short length of phone calls is counterbalanced by the number of contacts that individuals keep and the frequency with which they call them. Horst and Miller found that most of the 100 people they interviewed knew exactly how many names they had on their phone's contact list. Although some had as few as 13, many had more than 100 and the average was 95. Two things were of further interest about these phone lists. First, although Jamaicans do keep in close contact with their kin, relatively few of the names on the phone lists were relatives, on the average only 13 of the 95. Second, people put a great deal of effort into keeping the lists up to date and active. They made brief calls to a high percentage of the people on their list at least every couple of weeks, a

to identify, describe, and understand the cultural patterning of different speech events within a speech community. The ways in which people actually speak are highly dependent on the context of their speech. For example, a political speech has different purposes and is limited by different norms from those for a political discussion among friends. And different cultures have different norms regarding political speeches: who can participate as speaker and audience, the appropriate topics for such a speech, what kinds of cultural themes can be used,

where such speeches can take place, the relationship between the speaker and hearer, the language used in a multilingual community, and so forth.

Sociolinguists are interested in the ways in which speech varies depending on a person's position in a social structure or social relationship. In some cultures, different speech forms are used depending on whether the speaker and hearer are intimate friends, acquaintances on equal footing, or people of distinctly different social statuses. French, German, and Spanish, among

style of communication that Horst and Miller call "linking-up" (2006:96-97).

So, why do Jamaicans "link-up?" There are clearly functional advantages to these large name lists. They create wide webs of resources that individuals can call on for gifts of money or aid in times of need. These webs stretch out from Jamaica to include people living throughout the world. For example, Keisha, a 33-year-old living in Marshfield, decided that she wanted to go back to school but required significant financial help to do so. She used her phone list to call 14 people, each of whom she asked for help in paying for the books and clothing she needed for school. Some of those were local, others lived in nearby cities, and some lived in the United States. Although only some of those she contacted helped her, she was able to acquire enough money to return to school (Horst and Miller 2006:109–110). Many Jamaican families meet their daily requirements by asking others for money and help. In Orange Valley, for example, 34 percent of households have no regular income and meet their daily needs exclusively through asking for money from others. The cell phone greatly facilitates the ease and efficiency with which this can be done.

In some cases, people successfully begged for money and favors from relatives. However, the majority of requests made and granted were from friends and acquaintances. In most cases, the person who gave was not returning an earlier favor. Neither did the person who received the money feel that they owed a return favor to the giver.

This lack of direct reciprocity leads to an interesting question: what motivates people to give to others? Two factors help explain this. First, although givers do not necessarily expect to receive a return directly from the person to whom they give, they do know that in an uncertain economy, they will probably have to beg someone in the future. Although they may never receive money from the person to whom they have given, being known to many people, and being known as a person who gives, certainly increases their chances of receiving money or favors. Perhaps more important, Horst and Miller argue that constantly giving gifts enables those who do it to expand their social networks. Giving is a further opportunity to create or reinforce link-ups. In creating such link-ups, Jamaicans create a "a kind of demonstrable expansion of the self, distributed and confirmed by one's presence in the lives of others" (Horst and Miller 2006:121). This was an important goal in its own right. Ultimately, although there are vital economic components to Jamaican use of cell phones, their popularity cannot be understood apart from the desire for these rich and deep networks of social connection.

Horst and Miller point out that for low-income Jamaicans, the phone is not a luxury but an essential survival tool. It may cost money, but it enables them to reach and activate extensive networks of people who provide them with physical, financial, and emotional aid. In this sense, it has improved the quality of their lives. However, cell phones come with problems too. For exam-

ple, cell phones have become an "absolute priority" among Jamaican teens and distract them from education. Educational achievement in Jamaica has declined as cell phone usage has increased (2006:147, 151). Although cell phones can sometimes be used in preventing crime, they may also be used to plan crime. In fact, one of the common responses Horst and Miller found to the question "What do people use cell phones for?" was "Men use them to target the people they are going to shoot" (2006:129). Finally, although the cell phone did not cause Jamaicans to beg for money, it has enabled them to ask more people faster than ever before. Thus, any money in the community is rapidly redistributed. This makes it very difficult for any community member to accumulate enough capital to escape from poverty (2006:165–166).

## CRITICAL THINKING QUESTIONS

1. Jamaicans create large lists of phone contacts. Do some Americans do the same thing? What factors motivate Americans to create large cell phone contact lists?

2. The "link-up" described here is only one use of the cell phone in poor countries. What are other ways that cell phones might improve the quality of life for people in poor nations? What things in your life would be different if you had no access to telephones?

3. Describe some of the problems cell phones create. Do they create different problems in wealthy and poor nations?

other languages, have formal and informal pronouns and conjugations that are not found in English. The rules for their use vary from culture to culture. In France, parents use the informal term *tu* to address their children, but children use the formal term *vous* to their parents. In the Spanish spoken in Costa Rica, many people use three forms: the informal *tú* may be used by an adult speaking to a child (or lover), the formal *usted* is used among strangers, and an intermediate term, *vos,* may be used among friends. Historically,

English had this same distinction. The words *thee* and *thou* are the singular and informal forms of the more formal, plural term, *you.* Thus, if we recite the Lord's Prayer (Our father who art in heaven, hallowed be thy name) we address God informally (*thy* is the possessive form of *thou*). Quakers used the informal words *thee* and *thou* (or in some cases only *thee*) to express their belief in the radical equality of all people. Their refusal to use the word *you* to address the clergy or aristocracy was an act of political and religious defiance.

In many speech communities, the ordinary person knows and uses more than one language. Sociolinguists are interested in the different contexts in which one or the other language is used. The language a person chooses to use can be a way of solidifying ethnic or familial identity or of distancing oneself from another person or group.

## Language and Social Stratification

From a linguistic perspective, all languages are equally sophisticated, serve the needs of their speakers equally well, and every human being speaks with equal grammatical sophistication. Despite this, in complex, stratified societies such as the United States, some speech is considered "correct" and other speech judged inferior.

So, what is good English? Consider the example of the double negative. Almost everyone reading this book has heard someone (perhaps a teacher) claim that a double negative is really a positive. Thus, saying "I don't want no" is really saying I want some. This is simply incorrect. When Mick Jagger sings "I can't get no satisfaction" no native English speaker believes he is saying how satisfied he is. And no one imagines that the kids singing in Pink Floyd's *The Wall* are telling us how much they want to go to school.

But sometimes two negatives do make a positive, as when a child who refuses to do her homework says: "I won't not do my homework if you buy me some ice cream." And two or more positives can sometimes make a negative, as in:

Speaker A: "Yes, I will do it."

Speaker B: "Yeah, yeah, yeah, sure you will."

The point is that from a linguistic perspective, one way of speaking is as good as the next. There is no reason to prefer "I don't have any money" to "I ain't got no money," and there is no reason that saying "I'm about to go get lunch" is better than saying "I'm fixin' to get me some lunch." All the statements are fully logical, comprehensible, and communicate the information the speaker desires.

In hierarchical societies, the most powerful group generally determines what is "proper" in language. Indeed, the grammatical constructions used by the social elites are considered language, whereas deviations from them are often called **dialects.** Because the power of the speaker, rather than any inherent qualities of a speech form, determines language's acceptability, linguist Max Weinreich has defined a language as "a dialect with an army and a navy" (quoted in Pinker 1994:28).

The relation of language usage to social class and power is reflected in the speech of different social classes in the United States. In a classic study sociolinguist William Labov (1972) noted that elites and working-class people have different vocabularies and pronounce words differently. The forms associated with higher socioeconomic status are considered "proper," whereas forms spoken by those in lower socioeconomic statuses are considered incorrect and stigmatized.

Labov found that speakers often vary their vocabulary and pronunciation in different contexts and that the degree of such variation is related to their social class. At the bottom and top of the social hierarchy there is little variation: Elites use privileged forms of speech and the poor use stigmatized forms. However, members of the lower-middle class often use stigmatized forms in casual speech but privileged forms in careful speech. One interpretation is that people at the bottom and top of the social hierarchy do not vary their speech because their social position is stable; the very poor do not believe they have much chance to rise, and the wealthy are secure in their positions. Members of the lower-middle class, however, are concerned with raising their social position and in consequence copy the speech patterns of the wealthy in some social situations. However, they are also concerned with maintaining connections to family and friends, and therefore use stigmatized speech with them.

Labov's study makes clear what many of us know but do not like to admit: we do judge a person's social status by the way he or she speaks. What we say and how we say it are ways of telling people who we are socially or, perhaps, who we would like to be.

**Ebonics** Although there are many stigmatized variants of American English including Appalachian English, Dutchified Pennsylvania English, Hawaiian Creole, Gullah, and emergent Hispanic Englishes, the most stigmatized is **African-American Vernacular English (AAVE),** also called **Ebonics.** AAVE is simply a variant of Standard English, neither better nor worse than any other. Further, from Mark Twain and William Faulkner to Toni Morrison and Maya Angelou, from George Gershwin to Public Enemy and Run DMC, Ebonics has had deep influences on American art, speech, literature, and music.

AAVE has deep roots in the African-American community, particularly among rural and urban working-class blacks. Although not all Americans of African origin speak it, AAVE has become emblematic of black speech in the minds of many Americans.

---

**dialect** Grammatical constructions that deviate from those used by the socially dominant group in a society.

**African-American Vernacular English (AAVE)** A form of English spoken by many African Americans, particularly among those of rural or urban working-class backgrounds. Also known as Ebonics.

**Ebonics** A form of English spoken by many African Americans, particularly among those of rural or urban working-class backgrounds. Also known as African-American Vernacular English.

From the 1950s to the 1970s, a group of linguists, psychologists, and educators called cultural deficit theorists argued that African-American children did poorly in school because of general cognitive deficiencies, in which language played a key role. They argued that the poor speech of these children, which they characterized as coarse, simple, and irrational, was due to a culturally deprived home environment (Ammon and Ammon 1971). They proposed that if people could be taught to speak Standard English they would be able to think more logically, and this would help lift them from poverty (Bereiter and Engelmann 1966; Engelmann and Engelmann 1966).

The work of William Labov and others was central to countering the arguments of the deficit theorists. Through analysis of dialogues Labov showed that inner-city black speech, particularly the speech of children of poverty, was no more or less complex, rational, or orderly than that of other English speakers. It simply followed different rules, many of which were also found in other languages. For example, where SSAE uses the word *there* as a meaningless subject (as in "If there is a God. . . ."), AAVE uses the word *it* (as in "If it is a God. . . ."). Like SSAE, AAVE allows certain kinds of contractions. For example, in both you may contract the verb "to be." However, you do it in different ways. In SSAE, for instance, "you are" may be replaced with "you're," or "I am" may become "I'm." In AAVE, the verb "are" may be left out entirely. Thus, "If you are bad" may be replaced with "If you bad" (Pinker 1994:30). Labov demonstrated that AAVE was just a different way of speaking, and from a linguistic point of view, neither better nor worse than any other.

Since the 1970s, controversy over Ebonics has continued, sometimes becoming politicized. For example, in the mid-1990s, the Oakland, California, school board encouraged its teachers to make use of Ebonics in teaching Standard English (Monaghan 1997). Many Americans misunderstood the Oakland School Board as encouraging the teaching of Ebonics, and this misunderstanding ignited a national furor; a North Carolina legislator denounced Ebonics as "absurd," an *Atlanta Constitution* editorial referred to "the Ebonic plague," and laws banning it being taught were introduced in several state legislatures (Matthews 1997; Sanchez 1997).

Despite the fact that objectively AAVE is simply a language like any other, it is stigmatized in American society. Marcyliena Morgan (2004) notes that people in

William Labov's work was critical in establishing the relationships among language, social class, and ethnicity. Labov demonstrated the sophistication of African-American Vernacular English.

*Courtesy of Dr. William Labov, University of Pennsylvania*

families that speak both AAVE and SSAE don't necessarily value one over the other. In fact, AAVE may deliver "formal and informal knowledge as well as local knowledge and wisdom." On the other hand, they are aware that in the dominant cultural system AAVE is stigmatized and symbolizes deviance and ignorance. SSAE, on the other hand, symbolizes normality and intelligence. Most speakers of AAVE, through school, exposure to mass media, and the need to work in the world outside the local community, become effective speakers of several varieties of English. Like others who are bilingual, they must engage in code switching. **Code switching** is the ability of speakers of two languages to move seamlessly between them. Those who code switch use each language in the setting that is appropriate to it. To successfully navigate both their own communities and the dominant community, they must be acutely aware of the politics of language.

The study of AAVE shows the advantages of an anthropological approach. Much of the misunderstanding of AAVE occurred because it was studied in schools and in laboratory situations—places representing the dominant SSAE culture and often viewed as hostile by AAVE speakers. Linguists could get an accurate appreciation of AAVE only when they studied it within its own cultural context.

## The Sapir-Whorf Hypothesis

The close relationship between culture and language raises interesting questions about the connections between language and thought. In the previous section, we pointed out that in the 1950s and 1960s some social scientists believed, incorrectly, that AAVE was less logical than SSAE and that as a result AAVE speakers thought illogically. In so doing, they assumed a strong relationship between speaking and thinking. The existence of such a relationship is an old and controversial idea in anthropology. It is often associated with the work of Edward Sapir and his student Benjamin Lee Whorf. Sapir and Whorf believed that languages had a compelling influence on thought. Sapir wrote:

**code switching** The ability of individuals who speak multiple languages to move seamlessly between them.

Human beings do not live in the objective world alone. . . . but are very much at the mercy of the particular language which has become the medium of expression for their society. . . . The fact. . . . is that the "real world" is to a large extent unconsciously built up on the language habits of the group. No two languages are ever sufficiently similar to be considered as representing the same social reality. The worlds in which different societies live are distinct worlds, not merely the same world with different labels attached (1949b:162).

In other words, he believed that language played a critical role in determining the way people understand the world. It then followed that people who spoke different languages must understand the world in different ways. Sapir and Whorf proposed that concepts such as time, space, and matter are not the same for all people but are conditioned by the structure of our language. Thus, we perceive the world in certain ways because we talk about the world in certain ways. Further, cultural ideas and behavioral norms are encoded in language. Thus, we act the way we do because we speak a certain language. These ideas came to be known as the **Sapir-Whorf hypothesis.**

There are unquestionably some connections among language, perception, and thought. We clearly choose our words to guide and direct others' thoughts. Politicians, for example, routinely search for derogatory words and phrases to characterize their opponents. Or consider the term "side-effect." A side-effect is an unwanted consequence of something such as a drug. However, the phrase *side effect* encourages us to think of it as off to the side, and therefore less important than the "central" *effect* of the drug.

The use of the term *side-effect* encourages us to think in a certain way. But, does it force us to think in that way? In the late 1950s and early 1960s thalidomide was prescribed to calm the stomachs of pregnant mothers. The drug was effective but had the horrible side-effect of causing severe deformities in babies born to those mothers. Calling the deformities *side-effects* did not prevent people from thinking that they were more important than the drug's effect. In fact, the thalidomide case led to special testing of drugs prescribed during pregnancy. The thalidomide example shows us that words cannot force people to think in one way or another. Even a government that controlled all the words people used could not control their thoughts. People merely invent new words or give the old ones new and ironic meanings.

The Sapir-Whorf hypothesis went well beyond the issue of word choice. They argued that the grammatical structure of languages compelled their speakers to think and behave in certain ways. Whorf claimed, for example, that because tenses in the Hopi language were very different from tenses in English, Hopi speakers necessarily understood time in ways very different from English speakers (Whorf 1941). This position is sometimes called "strong determinism," and it has some deep problems. For example, consider the differences in the way we speak about missing a person in English and French. In English, we say "I miss you." "I," the person doing the missing, is the subject and "you," the person being missed, is the object. In French, however, the order is reversed: you say "Tu me manques." The person being missed is the subject and the person doing the missing the object. Literally translated, the French sentence appears to mean "you miss me." A strong determinist would expect this structural difference to indicate that speakers of French and English have different understandings of missing a person. However, there is no evidence to suggest that this is so.

Anthropologists have attempted to test the Sapir-Whorf hypothesis with mixed success. For example, Harry Hoijer (1964) applied it to the Navajo. Many aspects of Navajo grammar (such as the conjugation of active verbs and the reporting of actions and events) emphasize movement. Hoijer found parallels to this linguistic emphasis on motion in many aspects of Navajo culture. In Navajo mythology, for example, gods and cultural heroes restlessly move from one place to another, seeking by their motion to perfect the universe. However, this sort of evidence is quite weak. Consider that like their Navajo counterparts, Greek cultural heroes such as Odysseus move restlessly from place to place, but the Greek language is utterly different from Navajo. Bowerman (1996) argued that space is understood differently in English and Korean, and, more recently, Gordon (2004) reported that members of the Brazilian tribe he studied have difficulty understanding and recalling numbers for which they have no words. However, these examples are all controversial. The relationship between language and thought seems both fairly weak and related primarily to the vocabulary rather than the structure of language.

Beyond the technical difficulties with tests of the Sapir-Whorf hypothesis, the idea itself seems to miss one of the most compelling aspects of human communication. Although scholars often argue about the subtleties and poetics of translation, all languages are sufficiently similar that anything said in one language can be translated into every other human language. It is true that sometimes a single word in one language requires many words in another. Additionally, a great deal of study may be required to fully appreciate the meaning of a foreign term (but the same may be true of fully understanding a

**Sapir-Whorf hypothesis** The hypothesis that perceptions and understandings of time, space, and matter are conditioned by the structure of a language.

Edward Sapir and Benjamin Lee Whorf argued that Native American languages such as Hopi compelled their speakers to understand the world in a way different from native English speakers. Above, a Hopi priest.

word in one's own language[1]). However, no one has ever found a meaning in one language that was simply incomprehensible to speakers of other languages.

# Nonverbal Communication

Before returning to our discussion of spoken language, it is important to note that anthropologists also study the nonverbal ways in which humans communicate. Our use of our bodies, interpersonal space, physical objects, and even time can communicate worlds of information. In the words of Edward Hall (1959), an influential analyst of nonverbal behavior, "Time talks" and "space speaks." Nonverbal communication includes artifacts, haptics, chronemics, proxemics, and kinesics.

In the context of nonverbal communication, artifacts such as clothing, jewelry, tattoos, piercings, and other visible body modifications send messages. For example, among the Tuareg, a people of the Sahara, men often wear veils and use their position as an important part of nonverbal communication (R. Murphy 1964). A Tuareg man lowers his veil only among intimates and people of lower social status. He raises it high when he wishes to appear noncommittal. In the United States, we are very aware of the use of artifacts to send messages about ourselves. A pierced ear means something different from a pierced lip or tongue. Some students come to class in torn jeans and T-shirts; others wear designer labels or a white shirt and tie. All are trying to send messages about who they are.

**Haptics** refers to the study and analysis of touch. Handshakes, pats on the back or head, kisses, and hugs are all ways we communicate by touch. Many American males, for example, believe that the quality of a handshake communicates important information. Strong, firm handshakes are taken to indicate power, self-confidence, and strength of character, whereas limp handshakes may be interpreted as suggesting lack of interest, indecisiveness, or effeminacy. Americans generally feel free to use their left hands for virtually anything, but in many cultures, particularly in the Middle East, people scrupulously avoid the use of their left hands for eating, handling money, and many other social interactions. The left hand is considered unclean, and using it is generally unacceptable.

Some anthropologists suggest that societies can be divided into "contact" cultures, where people tend to interact at close distances and touch one another frequently, and "noncontact" cultures, where people tend to interact at greater distance and avoid touching (E. Hall 1966; Montagu 1978). Contact cultures are common in the Middle East, India, the Mediterranean, and Latin America. Noncontact cultures include those of northern Europe, North America, and Japan. But this dichotomy is too simplistic: India, for example, may be a contact culture between equals, but is very much a noncontact culture between persons regarded as socially unequal. In the United States, in public social relationships, the person who touches another is likely to have more power than the person who is touched. Bosses touch their subordinates, but subordinates rarely touch their bosses (Leathers 1997:126).

**Chronemics** refers to the study of cultural understandings of time. For example, in North American culture, what does it say when a person shows up for an appoint-

[1]For example, in *Democratic Vistas* (1871), Walt Whitman puzzled over the true meaning of the word democracy. "We have frequently printed the word Democracy. Yet I cannot too often repeat that it is a word the real gist of which still sleeps, quite unawaken'd. . . . It is a great word, whose history. . . . remains unwritten, because that history has yet to be enacted. It is, in some sort, younger brother of another great and often-used word, Nature, whose history also waits unwritten."

**haptics** The analysis and study of touch.

**chronemics** The study of the different ways that cultures understand time and use it to communicate.

ment 40 minutes late? Does it mean something different if he or she shows up 10 minutes early? Is a Latin American who shows up late for an appointment saying the same thing?

Edward Hall (1983) divided cultures into those with monochronic time (M-time), such as the United States and northern European countries, and those with polychronic time (P-time). Hall argued that in M-time cultures time is perceived as inflexible and people organize their lives according to schedules. In P-time cultures, time is understood as fluid; the emphasis is on social interaction and activities are not expected to proceed like clockwork. Thus, being late for an appointment in P-time cultures does not convey the unspoken messages that it would convey in an M-time culture (Victor 1992).

Like the contact/noncontact dichotomy, M-time and P-time seem to capture a basic truth about cultural variation but fail to account for the enormous variability within cultures. For example, how long an individual is kept waiting for an appointment may have more to do with power than with cultural perceptions of time. People are more likely to be on time for their superiors but can keep their subordinates waiting.

**Proxemics** is the social use of space. Hall (1968) identified three different ranges of personal communicative space. Intimate distance, from 1 to 18 inches, is typical for lovers and very intimate friends. Personal distance, from 18 inches to 4 feet, characterizes relationships among friends, and social distance, from 4 to 12 feet, is common among relative strangers. However, these distances are also affected by circumstances, culture, gender, and aspects of individual personality. We speak to strangers at a much closer distance in a movie or a classroom than we would in an unconfined space. In the United States, women and mixed-gender pairs talk to each other at closer distances than do men. In Turkey, on the other hand, men and women talk at close distances with members of their own sex but at very large distances with members of the opposite sex (Leathers 1997).

Finally, **kinesics** is the study of body position, movement, facial expressions, and gaze. We use our posture, our visual expression, eye contact, and other body movements to communicate interest, boredom, and many additional things. Virtually all body movements can have significance. But, of course, not all do. Clifford Geertz (1973b) famously suggested that the job of an ethnographer was learning to tell the winks from the twitches—that is, to tell the meaningful communication from the

© Jeff Greenberg/PhotoEdit

In addition to speaking, people use hands and facial expressions, as well as interpersonal space to communicate.

meaningless. Geertz meant this metaphorically, but those who study kinesics do it literally.

The case of smiling is a particularly interesting example of kinesic research. It is likely that smiling, and some other facial expressions, are biologically based human universals. There are no societies in which people do not smile. In fact, smiling is also found in chimpanzees and gorillas, our nearest nonhuman relations. Moreover, some aspects of smiling seem to transcend cultural variation. In any society, social interactions are more likely to have a positive outcome if people are smiling than if they are frowning or scowling.

But smiling also shows the powerful effects of culture on biology. A smile does not mean the same thing in all cultures. Americans generally equate smiling with happiness, but people in many cultures smile when they experience surprise, wonder, or embarrassment (Ferraro 1994). A recent guide book on international business advises American managers that the Japanese often smile to make their guests feel comfortable rather than because they are happy (R. Lewis 1996:267). Despite this, Japanese and Americans agree that smiling faces are more sociable than neutral faces (Matsumoto and Kudoh 1993), and most often interpret smiles in the same way (Nagashima and Schellenberg 1997).

## Language Change

Fæder ure þu þe eart on heofonum
Si þin nama gehalgod
to becume þin rice
gewurþe ðin willa
on eorðan swa swa on heofonum.

---

**proxemics**  The study of the cultural use of interpersonal space.

**kinesics**  The study of body position, movement, facial expressions, and gaze.

urne gedæghwamlican hlaf syle us todæg

and forgyf us ure gyltas

swa swa we forgyfað urum gyltendum

and ne gelæd þu us on costnunge

ac alys us of yfele soþlice

This 11th-century version of the Lord's Prayer shows how much English has changed in the past thousand years. All language is constantly changing on many levels, such as sound, structure, and vocabulary, and some of the change happens in patterned ways.

Consider sound. When we imagine people speaking English hundreds of years ago, we often think of them using different words than we do, but otherwise sounding pretty much like us. But this is incorrect. English spoken in the 14th century sounded very different from the English of today. Between 1400 and 1600 there was a change in sound of English that is called the Great Vowel Shift. A correct reading aloud of the Lord's Prayer at the start of this section would require speaking with the sounds used in English more than 600 years ago. For example, the fifth word of the last line, *yfele,* gives us the modern English word "evil." The medieval pronunciation is close to "oo-vah-la." Shifting sounds are not just something out of the past. Language sounds are constantly changing. For example, since about 1950 some vowel sounds in U.S. cities around the Great Lakes have been changing, a process linguists call the northern city shift (Labov 2005).

The grammatical structures of a language (its syntax) also change. For example, as we have seen, meaning in modern English is tightly tied to word order. But in Old English, as in Latin, the endings of nouns indicated whether they were subjects or objects, making word order within sentences less important. Thus, in Old English, the two sentences "The dog bit the child" and "The dog the child bit" would have the same meaning and be equally grammatical.

Vocabulary is the most noticeable aspect of language change, and this is easily seen in slang. Consider slang terms from the 1950s and 1960s such as "boss" to mean great (as in "The new Little Richard album is really boss") or "bag" to mean something that an individual likes (as in "What's your bag" or "Reading anthropology is really my bag"). Many of us still understand the slang expressions of the 1960s, but terms from the 19th and early 20th century are almost entirely lost: would you know what "ramstuginous" or "kafooster" mean?

New words are constantly added to language. In the past 10 to 20 years, for example, an entire vocabulary has grown up around computers and the Internet. Words such as software, dot-com, disk drive, gigabyte, and e-mail would have been unintelligible to most people in 1980. WiFi, spyware, domain name, text message, and many others would have been meaningless to people in the mid-1990s. In the past few years, gaming, instant messaging, and cell phones have spawned a new vocabulary of acronyms and abbreviations such as IMHO, LOL, nube, and TTYL.

## Language and Culture Contact

The meeting of cultures through travel, trade, war, and conquest is a fundamental force in linguistic change. Languages thus reflect the histories of their speakers. Current-day English has French words such as "reason," "joy," "mutton," and "liberty" that came into the language after the Norman Conquest of England in the 11th century. Other words speak of more recent political events. For example, "cot," "pajamas," and "jungle" come from Hindi and reflect the British colonization of India. "Gumbo," "funky," and "zebra" come from Kongo, and reflect the slave trade. Nahuatl, a language spoken in Mexico and Central America, gives us "tomato," "coyote," "shack," and "avocado." Most Americans in 1970 probably did not know what words like "sunni," "muhajadin," or "fatwa" meant. Today, we do.

When societies where different languages are spoken meet, they often develop a new language that combines features of each of the original ones. Such languages are called **pidgins.** No one speaks a pidgin as a first language, and the vocabulary of pidgins is often limited

**pidgin** A language of contact and trade composed of features of the original languages of two or more societies. (Compare with *creole.*)

Pidgins develop when people who speak different languages come together. This church banner, in Papua New Guinea where people speak more than 750 different languages, means "Jesus is Lord."

to the words appropriate to the sorts of interactions engaged in by the people speaking it.

As culture contact deepens and time passes, pidgins are sometimes lost, and people speak only the language of the dominant power. Or pidgin languages may become creoles. A **creole** is a language composed of elements of two or more different languages. But, unlike a pidgin, people do speak creoles as their first languages and the vocabulary of these languages is as complex and rich as any others.

Many creoles were formed as Europeans expanded into Asia and the Americas. Often, in countries that were colonized, upper classes speak the language of the colonizing power, and the lower classes speak creoles. In Haiti, for example, from 70 to 90 percent of the population speaks only Creole but almost all governmental and administrative functions are performed in French, the language of the elite.

## Tracing Relationships among Languages

**Comparative linguistics** is a field of study that traces the relationships of different languages by searching for similarities among them. When such similarities are numerous, regular, and basic, it is likely that the languages are derived from the same ancestral language.

Linguists have identified a core vocabulary of 100 or 200 words such as *I, you, man, woman, blood, skin, red,* and *green* that designate things, actions, and activities likely to be named in all the world's languages. Many believe that core vocabularies change at a predictable rate (about 14 percent per 1000 years). **Glottochronology** is a statistical technique that uses this idea to estimate the date of separation of related languages. For example, if linguists examined the core vocabularies of two related languages and found they were 28 percent different, they would propose that the languages separated from each other 1000 years ago (because both languages are changing, the total change must be divided in half). Using glottochronology, linguists can discover the historic relationships among languages and use that knowledge to group languages into families. However, the accuracy of the technique has long been controversial and many modifications have been employed to improve it (Renfrew, McMahon, and Trask 2000).

Considering the history of language raises two interesting questions: First, was there at any point a single,

original human language? And second, will there be, in the future, a world with one language? Neither of these questions is fully answerable, but we can speculate about each of them.

We do not know if there was a single original human language. The agreed-upon techniques of comparative linguistics can tell us a great deal about the history of languages in the past several thousand years. There are, however, no accepted techniques for establishing the patterns and content of language that reach back tens of thousands of years. Some anthropologists, biologists, and linguists looking at this question claim they can describe the original human language (Ruhlen 1994; Shevoroshkin and Woodford 1991). For example, Alec Knight and his colleagues (2003), using techniques from both comparative linguistics and biology, argue that there was an original language and it had many of the characteristics associated with modern-day African "click" languages. Such claims are extremely controversial and, for the moment, not widely accepted. However, the development of language almost certainly involved specific genetic changes. Such changes probably happened in a single small group. If this is the case, an original language probably did exist.

The question of whether a single world language is emerging is provocative. We are clearly moving toward linguistic homogenization. The total number of languages in the world has clearly declined. About 10,000 years ago there may have been as many as 15,000 different languages. Today there are only about 6500, and half of these are under threat of extinction in the next 50 to 100 years (Krauss 1992). Today, 95 percent of the world's languages are spoken by only 5 percent of the world's total population. Almost one third of the world's languages are each spoken by fewer than 1000 people. At the same time, more than half of the world's population speaks one of the 20 most common languages (Gibbs 2002).

Languages may disappear for various reasons. All their speakers may be killed by disease or genocide. Government policies may deliberately seek to eliminate certain languages. For example, in 1885 the American government explicitly forbade the use of Indian languages in Bureau of Indian Affairs schools. Children were beaten and otherwise punished for speaking their tribal languages (Coleman 1999).

Nation-states often try to suppress linguistic diversity within their borders, insisting that government, the court system, and other aspects of public life be conducted in the language of the most numerous and politically powerful groups. Global trade favors people who speak the languages of the wealthiest and most populous nations. Similarly, the vast majority of television and radio broadcasts, as well as the Internet, are in a very few languages. In the face of such forces, people who are members of linguistic minorities often abandon their

---

**creole** A first language that is composed of elements of two or more different languages. (Compare with *pidgin*.)

**comparative linguistics** The science of documenting the relationships between languages and grouping them into language families.

**glottochronology** A statistical technique that linguists have developed to estimate the date of separation of related languages.

Words that refer to technology can charge very rapidly. But words that designate basic objects or actions may change quite slowly.

© AP Photo/Katsumi Kasahara

ment toward fewer languages is also troubling. There is generally a strong connection between language and ethnic identity. Language is often rooted in culture and entwined with it. As language is lost, so are important elements of cultural identity. Additionally, the disappearance of languages reduces our ability to understand the underlying structures of language and the range of variability these enable.

Not all global forces lead toward language homogenization. First, there is no language spoken by the majority of the world's people. Mandarin Chinese, with more than 1 billion speakers, is by far the most commonly spoken language, while hundreds of millions of people speak English, Spanish, Russian, French, Hindi/Urdu, Arabic, Portuguese, and several others. None of these languages seem likely to disappear in the foreseeable future. Second, although the number of languages spoken in the world has diminished, the diversity within each language has increased. People in New York City, Kingston, Jamaica, Glasgow in Scotland, and Mumbai, India, may all speak English, but that does not necessarily mean they can understand each other. Perhaps more important, the nature of language—the human ability to create new meanings, new words, and new grammatical structures—means that language adapts to the needs, interests, and environments of its speakers. Thus, even as globalizing forces move humans toward cultural and linguistic homogeneity, spaces are created in which linguistic and cultural diversity can also flourish.

languages because they find it more convenient, prestigious, or profitable to speak the languages of wealth and power.

In some senses, linguistic homogenization is a positive development. Today, more people are able to speak to each other than ever before. In the future, this may be true to an even greater extent. However, the global move-

# The Global and the Local: English Only

According to the Center for Immigration Studies, in 2007 about one in eight U.S. residents was an immigrant. This is the highest percentage since the early 20th century. Nationally, about one in five children in American schools (kindergarten through grade 12) had at least one immigrant parent (Fix and Capps 2005). The result of high immigration is that in many places, the United States has truly become a multilingual society. New York currently translates educational documents for parents into the eight most common non-English languages spoken by its school students: Arabic, Bengali, Chinese, Haitian Creole, Korean, Russian, Spanish, and Urdu.

The close connection between language and cultural identity has made multilingualism an important topic in America. On the one hand, immigrants wish to preserve many aspects of their own cultures and consider using

their own language and keeping it alive for their children critical to their identity. Others, though not immigrants themselves, celebrate the diversity of multilingualism. On the other hand, critics of multilingualism point out that just as immigrants' use of their own language is central to their ethnic identity, so too English is central to American ethnic identity. They argue that a strong American identity must ultimately be tied to the English language. Although they may support learning foreign languages, they reject the idea that the United States should be a multilingual nation.

The linkage of English and American identity is powerfully attractive to many. As of 2007, thirty states have enacted legislation to make English their state's official language. Both the U.S. House and Senate have voted to make English the national language or require the federal government to conduct all its official business in English. Although no federal bill making English the national language has yet passed both chambers of Congress and become law, a recent survey suggests that 85 percent of Americans believe English should be the official national language (Rasmusen Reports 2006).

U.S.English, Inc., a lobbying group that promotes English Only legislation, claims to have 1.8 million members. According to U.S.English, "Official English benefits every resident of this wonderful melting pot called America. The melting pot works—because we have a common language. English is the key to opportunity in this country. It empowers immigrants and makes us truly united as a people. Common sense says that the government should teach people English rather than provide services in multiple languages. What would happen if our government had to provide services in all 322 languages spoken in the U.S.? Without a common language, how long would we remain the 'United' States?" (usenglish.org 2007)

Many anthropologists, perhaps most, believe the legislative program of groups like U.S.English is misguided and their claims inaccurate. Graham, Jaffe, Urciuoli, and Valentine (2007), for example, say that when people talk about language they are really talking about race: "People in positions of social advantage feel free to say things about the language of stigmatized groups that they would never say about race or ethnicity." Further, Graham and colleagues claim that promoters of English Only assume that difficulties in communication are caused by people speaking many languages, ignoring the simple fact that sharing the same language does not create effective communication. Finally, critics of English Only say that the idea that requiring official English will unify the nation and help provide answers to problems of racism gets things backward. The underlying problem is not language, it is inequality. Official English, in the name of promoting unity and opportunity, actually disadvantages the poor and powerless, making it harder for them to gain access to education and public services.

## Key Questions

1. Do you speak a language other than English as a first language? If so, do you want your children and grandchildren to speak that language? If English is your first language, did your parents or grandparents speak a different first language? How do you feel about your abilities (or lack of ability) in that language?

2. In the United States, how closely is language linked both to American identity and to ethnic identity? To what degree can one be a full citizen of America without speaking English as a primary language?

3. The United States has never had an official national language. Are there good reasons why this should change? Multiple languages are a great asset in the global economy. Instead of mandating English only, would it be better to mandate increased second-language training for Americans?

# Summary

1. **In what ways is human language distinct from animal communication?** All animals communicate. However, human communication differs from that of other animals in its flexibility and its ability to convey new ideas and abstract concepts. Some key elements believed to be unique to human language are conventionality, productivity, and displacement. All of these are related to the human use of symbols. Some animals may be trained to use language in humanlike ways. However, language is a fundamental part of human adaptation. As far as we know, it does not play this role for any other species.

2. **When did human language originate?** Anthropologists disagree about the origins of language. Human ancestors certainly communicated with each other. However, the linguistic abilities of current-day *Homo sapiens* may have emerged as recently as 50,000 years ago.

3. **How do children learn language?** In all cultures, children go through the same stages of language learning in the same sequence and at roughly the same speed regardless of the language being learned. This suggests that humans have an innate language-learning capacity. However, this potential for speech is realized only through social interaction with other humans. Children deprived of such interaction do not learn language.

4. **What are the principal components of all human language?** The components of a language are a sound system (phonology), rules that pattern word formation (morphology), a system for combining words into meaningful utterances (syntax), and linkages between words and their meanings (lexicon).

5. **What is the relationship between the rules of language and the performance of language?** Language can be described by a series of rules, but actually speaking and understanding language requires deep understanding of culture.

6. **Are some forms of speech better than other forms?** Stratified societies often have many different forms of language. When this is the case, some forms are often considered to be correct and others improper or inferior. Although society may stigmatize some forms of speech, there is no scientific sense in which one grammatical pattern or accent is better or worse than another.

7. **Define and describe Ebonics or African-American Vernacular English (AAVE).** Ebonics, or AAVE, is the speech pattern common to rural and urban working class African-American communities. Historically highly stigmatized, Ebonics uses grammatical rules that are different from but no less logical than Standard Spoken American English. Much of American literature, poetry, and music has been strongly influenced by Ebonics.

8. **What is the Sapir-Whorf hypothesis?** The Sapir-Whorf hypothesis is the notion that grammar and vocabulary influence perception of the environment, and therefore speakers of different languages perceive their worlds in different ways. Although some evidence supports the Sapir-Whorf hypothesis, most linguists argue that the similarities among languages far outweigh their differences and that language does not have a systematic effect on thought or perception.

9. **What forms of nonverbal communication are used in human societies?** Humans everywhere communicate nonverbally as well as verbally. In every society, people use gestures, facial expressions, posture, and time to communicate with one another. However, the meaning of a gesture or expression may vary greatly from culture to culture.

10. **Describe two key ways in which language changes.** Both the sound and vocabulary of languages change over time. For example, many sounds of medieval English do not exist in current English. New words enter vocabulary through innovation as well as contact between cultures. Vocabularies reflect histories, frequently including conquest and submission.

11. **Was there ever a single human language?** Linguists have developed techniques to trace the histories of languages and relationships among them. However, these techniques cannot determine if there was ever a single human language. The development of language involved genetic changes and these are likely to happen in a single small group. Hence, there probably was a single original language.

12. **Are we moving toward a world with only a single language?** Linguistic diversity has decreased dramatically, and many languages face the threat of extinction. However, many languages have millions of speakers and are unlikely to disappear. As languages expand to include more speakers, the diversity within them may increase. People who speak the same language may not understand one another.

# Key Terms

African-American Vernacular English (AAVE)
allophones
bound morpheme
call system
chronemics
code switching
communication
comparative linguistics
conventionality
creole
descriptive or structural linguistics
dialect

displacement
Ebonics
free morpheme
glottochronology
haptics
International Phonetic Alphabet (IPA)
kinesics
lexicon
morpheme
morphology
phone
phoneme
phonology

pidgin
productivity
proxemics
Sapir-Whorf hypothesis
semantics
sociolinguistics
speech community
Standard Spoken American English (SSAE)
syntax
universal grammar
word

# Suggested Readings

Brenneis, Donald, and Ronald K. S. Macauley (Eds.). 1996. *The Matrix of Language.* Boulder, CO: Westview. A collection of essays that covers debates in the study of language and culture. Brenneis and Macauley's volume introduces students to current work in language and socialization, gender, the ethnography of speaking, and language in social and political life.

McWhorter, John H. 2001. *The Power of Babel: A Natural History of Language.* New York: Times Books/Henry Holt. In this popular account, McWhorter explores the origins of language and the ways in which it changes, with particular focus on the effects of politics and economics. McWhorter targets those who claim that language has more and less perfect forms.

Pinker, Steven. 1994. *The Language Instinct.* New York: William Morrow. A readable introduction to the highly technical field of linguistics. Pinker explains Noam Chomsky's theory of language and provides evidence for the innateness of language.

Rickford, John Russell, and Russell John Rickford. 2000. *Spoken Soul: The Story of Black English.* New York: Wiley. In this lively account by a linguistics professor and a journalist, the authors trace the history of Black English and explore the issues and controversies surrounding Ebonics and the Oakland School Board case.

The key to human survival is extracting food from the environment. This man is fishing with a butterfly net in Lake Patzcuaro, Mexico.

© Joan Gregg

**THINKING POINT:** Matthew Gilbert, an anthropologist and member of the Gwich'in, a Native Alaskan people, writes that nature is the fabric of Gwich'in lives and that because of this: "we cannot really separate 'the climate' from our human selves. . . . So when we talk about the environment and especially about the decline of caribou, we are talking about who we are and who we want to continue to be. It is a question of our very survival as a people."

—[See pages 126–127 for details.]

# {chapter 6}

# Making a Living

All societies survive by using their environments to provide people with the basic material requirements of life: food, clothing, and shelter. In this chapter, we focus on the different **subsistence strategies,** or ways in which societies transform the material resources of the environment into food.

Anthropology, particularly ecological anthropology, has always been interested in the interactions between human cultures and their environments. Ecological anthropologists seek to understand the effects of the physical environment on human activities and cultures, the effects of human cultures on the physical environment, the interrelationships among human cultures within a physical environment, and how human cultures change their subsistence strategies in response to challenges and threats to their livelihood (Bates and Lees 1996: Introduction). Although we are used to thinking about the physical environment as "natural," it is important to keep in mind that the natural environment is also a cultural construction (Igoe 2004). <<

# Human Adaptation and the Environment

Human beings, unlike most other animals, live in an extremely broad range of environments. Some, such as the Arctic or the Great Australian Desert, present extreme challenges to human existence and are relatively limited in the numbers of people and types of subsistence strategies they can support. The productivity of any particular environment, however, is related to the type of technology used to exploit it. In aboriginal America, for example, the Great Plains supported a relatively small population, which survived mainly by hunting bison. With intensive mechanized agriculture, the same region today can support millions of people. In the same way, a desert area that can support very small numbers of people without irrigation can support much larger populations with irrigation agriculture.

Technological development has enabled humans to transform a wide range of materials into sources of usable energy. As a result, humans have been able to create many kinds of artificial environments, such as farms and cities, and many different economic systems and forms of social organization. These human technologies and cultural adaptations have led to great increases in population density, which in turn have greatly intensified the human effects on the environment.

Up until about 10,000 years ago, all humans lived by **foraging**—fishing, hunting, and collecting vegetable food. As tools improved, foragers spread out into many environments and developed diverse cultures, arriving in the Americas and Australia about 25,000 years ago. Foraging sets limits on population growth and density and, consequently, on the complexity of social organization in these societies.

About 11,000 to 10,000 years ago, human groups in the Old World began to domesticate plants and animals, a change that occurred about 1000 years later in the New World (Bryant 2003). The transition to food production was actually very gradual, more like evolution than revolution, but it was revolutionary in the possibilities it opened up for the development of complex social organization.

With the increased populations that could be supported by the domestication of plants and animals, **seden-** tary village life became widespread. More intensive means of cultivation and animal management developed, and human labor was more closely coordinated and controlled, leading eventually to complex social forms such as the state. Within this general outline of growing control over the environment and increasing human population, specific environmental and historical conditions explain the exact sequence of events in any particular place.

The question of why cultivation did not arise everywhere—and why some populations, such as the aboriginal peoples of Australia or the Inuit, never made the transition from foraging to food production—has several answers. In some cases, such as in the Arctic, climate and soil composition precluded agriculture. In other cases, such as the fertile valleys of California, aboriginal foraging was so productive there was little pressure to make the transition to food production. Sometimes foraging strategies were actually more dependable than cultivation or animal husbandry, which are more adversely affected by extreme drought. For example, with the introduction of the horse by the Spaniards in the 16th century,

© Judith Pearson

In many tropical forest horticultural societies, like the Huli of New Guinea, domestic pigs add an important protein component to the diet, and are also an essential part of ritual feasting.

**subsistence strategy** The way a society transforms environmental resources into food.

**foraging (hunting and gathering)** A food-getting strategy that does not involve food production or domestication of animals and that involves no conscious effort to alter the environment.

**sedentary** Settled, living in one place.

some Native American Plains cultures, such as the Cheyenne, did so well with bison hunting that they gave up their traditional cultivation strategy. Even today, many foraging and pastoral populations resist abandoning these occupations for cultivation because they prefer the economic, social, and psychological satisfactions of a foraging or pastoral way of life. In these societies, hunting and pastoralism are highly valued occupations, intimately connected to a people's cultural identity, and in some circumstances more productive than agriculture. For many Americans today, hunting, fishing, and gathering wild foods are not only recreational pastimes but often an important contribution to the family diet as well.

**Industrialized agriculture,** the replacement of human and animal energy by machines and the use of chemical pesticides and fertilizers in food production, has greatly increased productivity. In a typical nonindustrial society, more than 80 percent of the population is directly involved in food production. In the United States today, only 1 percent of the population claims farming as a primary occupation and only 2 percent of the population lives on farms (United States Environmental Protection Agency 2007). At the same time, increasingly complex technology and industrialism have brought new problems, particularly in their impact on the environment.

Many nonindustrial societies made entirely satisfactory adaptations to their environments without modern science and with simple but ingenious technology. This success is partly due to the vast knowledge and understanding these societies have of their environment. In the enormous Amazon **rain forest,** for example, people commonly know the names of hundreds of diverse species of plants and trees and the specific uses of each (Carneiro 1988:78). They also know the place of each species in the web of forest life and the importance of sustaining the vegetal diversity that provides different animal species with their specialized, preferred foods. Indigenous peoples of the Amazon forest manage their food resources in diverse, complex, and sophisticated ways. The Kayapo of the Xingu River basin in South America, for example, carefully manage the soil, protect the ground cover, control humidity, and manage pests in their gardens, all based on their deep understanding of soil, the properties of fire, the relation of the seasons to plant growth, and the impact of human food-getting activities on the environment. They use this knowledge in efficient ways as they exploit various forest resources for food, medicine, and other necessities of life. In South Africa, also, knowledge about the medicinal properties of the different parts—roots, leaves, bulbs, and bark—of over 30 plants, are used by the pastoral Dikale to cure common problems such as headaches, stomachaches, sores or colds, toothache, and intestinal parasites (Rankoana 2001).

The environmental problems resulting from industrial and postindustrial society have led to a reawakened interest in and respect for the many ways by which nonindustrial people have adapted to their environment. In the modern technological age, we too frequently forget that technology must be used to human ends and that economic efficiency is only one of many important values. Consumer desires and energy needs of industrialized and industrializing nations are central sources of environmental degradation today. Almost from the moment of European contact with other parts of the world, European culture affected the environment. For example, when domestic animals—cattle and sheep—were introduced, they consumed the crops of the indigenous peoples of Peru; the Inca Empire had depended on these crops (Scammel 1989:125). The European fashion for furs almost denuded North America of fur-bearing animals such as the beaver, and today European consumer demands for tropical hardwoods are leading to devastating logging in tropical forests (Brosius 1999). The European demand for sugar and tobacco resulted in huge areas of monocrop agriculture, which not only transformed the physical environment of the Americas but, with the introduction of African slavery, its social environment as well (Mintz 1985). In the Pacific Northwest of the United States, dam building has affected the ability of salmon to spawn, a concern not only of conservationists but also of Native Americans in this area, for whom salmon are not only an important food but an object of religious awe (Duncan 2000). Global warming, too, resulting from oil consumption and carbon emissions, has had deleterious effects on many traditional subsistence strategies and potentially catastrophic effects on the environment.

# Major Types of Subsistence Strategies

Anthropological understanding of the interactions among culture, making a living, and the environment can be approached using a typology of subsistence strategies. Each strategy uses the environment in different ways, and each has a different impact on the environment. The five basic subsistence strategies identified by anthropologists are foraging, pastoralism, horticulture, agriculture, and industrialism (Y. Cohen 1971). Each of these strategies is an ideal type; in reality, due to the many changes that always occur in human societies, and particularly those that have occurred in the last 500 years, most societies

---

**industrialized agriculture** A production technology that adapts mechanized manufacturing processes in production, processing, and distribution of food.

**rain forest** Tropical woodland characterized by high rainfall and a dense canopy of broad-leaved evergreen trees.

actually practice a combination of strategies in order to survive.

Foraging depends on the use of plant and animal resources naturally available in the environment. **Pastoralism** primarily involves the care of domesticated herd animals, whose dairy and meat products are a major part of the pastoralist diet. **Horticulture** refers to the production of plants using a simple, nonmechanized technology. **Agriculture** (intensive cultivation) involves the production of food using the plow, draft animals, and more complex techniques of water and soil control so that land is permanently cultivated and needs no fallow period. Finally, industrialism involves the use of machine technology and chemical processes for the production of food and other goods. Within these basic types of subsistence strategies, however, there is much diversity.

Each subsistence strategy generally supports a characteristic level of **population density** (number of persons per square unit of land), and has a different level of **productivity** (yield per person per unit of land) and **efficiency** (yield per person per hour of labor invested). These criteria, in turn, tend to be associated with characteristic forms of social organization and certain cultural patterns. For example, where local technology allows only limited exploitation of the environment and where safe and reliable methods of artificial contraception are unknown, population growth may be limited by cultural practices that function to space births. These include sexual abstinence, abortion, infanticide, late weaning, and prohibitions on sexual intercourse while a child is breast-feeding.

In addition to limiting population, a society can extend its resource base by trading. Trade occurs in all types of societies, including foragers. In the Ituri rain forest in Central Africa, Mbuti foragers have complex, hereditary exchange relationships with the Lese, their horticultural neighbors. In exchange for meat, mushrooms, honey, building materials, medicine, and agricultural labor, the Mbuti receive manioc, plantains, peanuts, and rice, which together form more than 50 percent of their diet. The Lese also provide the Mbuti with metal for knives and arrowheads; cotton cloth, which is stronger and more colorful than traditional Mbuti bark cloth; and

aluminum cooking pots, which are more durable than traditional Mbuti clay pots (Wilkie 1988:123). Trade, of course, also forms the basis of the historical and contemporary global economy, incorporating peoples all over the world engaging in many kinds of food production and manufacturing.

## Foraging

Foraging is a diverse strategy that includes the hunting of large and small game, fishing, and the collecting of various plant foods. Foragers do not produce food, either directly by planting or indirectly by controlling the reproduction of animals or keeping domestic animals for consumption of their meat or milk. In most cases, foragers use simple tools including digging sticks, spatulas, spears, and bow and arrow. However, in some places, such as the Arctic, foraging technology can be quite complex. Because foragers do not consciously alter their surroundings in order to produce food, in most cases they have little impact on the environment.

At one time, perhaps 10,000 years ago, all human beings lived by foraging. However, as other forms of production developed, foragers were increasingly pushed to marginal areas such as deserts, Arctic tundra, and deep forests.

Foragers use a variety of strategies. In some extreme environments, such as the Arctic, they may depend almost solely on hunting. However, in most cases they rely primarily on gathered vegetable foods and in most cases women are responsible for gathering. Successful foraging requires extensive and highly detailed knowledge of the environment. Studies among Ju/'hoansi foragers show that women can identify more than 150 species of edible plants and men recognize more than 40 species of edible animals (Lee 1979)

Foraging strategies vary in productivity, however; in most cases foraging can only support a low population density. Foragers generally live in communities of from 20 to 50 individuals. Even at this low density, few of the marginal areas where current-day foragers are found can support a year-round human population. Therefore, foraging almost always involves seasonal movement to gain access to water or food. Thus, foraging requires independence and mobility. For this reason foraging bands tend to have highly flexible social arrangements. Seasonal movement is also a strong disincentive for the accumulation of material goods. Because they must transport everything they own frequently, the material possessions of foraging peoples tend to be limited to items essential to their survival.

In some environments (see the descriptions in this chapter of the Inuit and Pintupi), foraging is unquestionably a harsh and dangerous way of life. However, in less demanding environments, foragers often live in relative abundance. Further, the extreme flexibility of forager so-

---

**pastoralism**  A food-getting strategy that depends on the care of domesticated herd animals.

**horticulture**  Production of plants using a simple, nonmechanized technology; fields are not used continuously.

**agriculture**  A form of food production in which fields are in permanent cultivation using plows, animals, and techniques of soil and water control.

**population density**  The number of people inhabiting a given area of land.

**productivity**  Yield per person per unit of land.

**efficiency**  Yield per person per hour of labor invested.

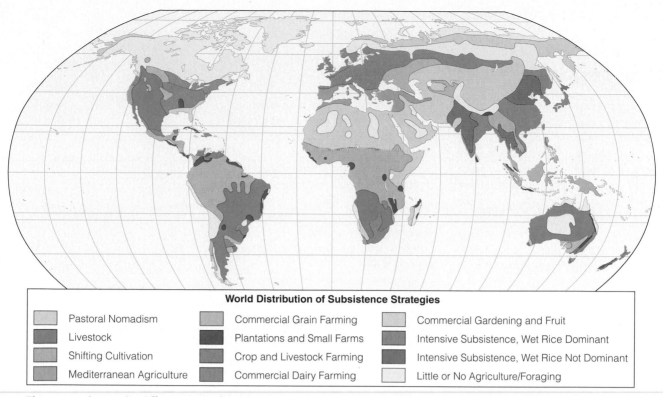

**World Distribution of Subsistence Strategies**

| | |
|---|---|
| Pastoral Nomadism | Commercial Grain Farming | Commercial Gardening and Fruit |
| Livestock | Plantations and Small Farms | Intensive Subsistence, Wet Rice Dominant |
| Shifting Cultivation | Crop and Livestock Farming | Intensive Subsistence, Wet Rice Not Dominant |
| Mediterranean Agriculture | Commercial Dairy Farming | Little or No Agriculture/Foraging |

This map indicates the different ways of making a living through cultivation and animal husbandry as they are found in different environments.

cial arrangements means that there is very little hierarchy in foraging societies.

Only a very small proportion of the world's people currently live by foraging, mainly in marginal areas such as deserts and Arctic tundra into which they have been pushed by expanding, militarily superior agricultural peoples and states. In the past, however, foragers occupied many diverse environments, including fertile plains and river valleys.

A wide variety of plant foods and small animals permits people to survive in the harsh environment of the Great Sandy Desert.

*© David Austen/Stock, Boston LLC*

**Australian Foragers** The Pintupi people of the Great Sandy Desert of Australia are more typical of foraging than the Inuit described in the "Ethnography" box that accompanies this section. In the Great Sandy Desert, a wide range of vegetal foods provided most of the diet. As with other foraging peoples, the unreliability of water supplies posed a fundamental challenge to the Pintupi. The key to their adaptation was the use of a wide variety of seasonally available plant and animal foods and their detailed knowledge of their environment. Even with simple technology, this made foraging a reliable strategy, though at certain seasons a very difficult way of life.

These Australian foragers have an intimate knowledge of their environment. They recognize and can name 126 plants serving 138 different social, economic, and medicinal functions. They use more than 75 different plants for edible seeds. Their diet also includes tubers, fruits, nectars, sap, and edible insects as well as birds, bird eggs, and small mammals. The main constraint on population growth is the scarcity of water during the driest and hottest months. Thus, the Western Desert societies consist of small, isolated family groups, and have a population density as low as one person per 150–200 square miles.

# Ethnography

## Global Warming and the Inuit Foraging Strategy

All foragers exploit the diversity of their environments. In spite of the popular stereotype of the prehistoric hunter, most foragers actually rely more on collecting vegetable food than on hunting. One exception is the Inuit of the Arctic Circle, whose traditional hunting strategy includes almost no collecting of plant food, which is virtually absent in their environment. However, as is typical for most foragers, the Inuit food quest does follow the seasonal variation of their climate—a long, cold winter during which the water areas become sheets of ice, and a short, cool summer.

For 6000 years the Inuit of the Arctic hunted large land and sea animals: bowhead whales, walrus, caribou, and seal. Even in their harsh environment, Inuit knowledge and ingenious technology enabled them to be successful hunters, as they followed the seasonal availability of animals and birds. Inuit culture and social organization are also adapted to their foraging strategy. Their cultural values emphasize cooperation and mutual aid; their religious rituals provide effective outlets for the isolation and tension of the long dark winters; and their flexible kinship organization allows local populations to expand and contract in response to the seasonal variation in resources.

As with many other foragers, however, the 20th and 21st centuries have brought great changes in Inuit subsistence strategies (Condon et al. 1996; Chance 1990). Most Inuit now base their livelihoods on a combination of cash income from a variety of sources while maintaining their traditional subsistence foraging. By the early 20th century, the Western demand for furs significantly replaced the Inuit subsistence hunting with commercial trapping, providing many Inuit with guns and cash, which they then used to buy food, tobacco, tea, canvas tents, and clothing. Other nontraditional sources of Inuit income today are handicrafts, tourism, various kinds of government subsidies, and for the Alaska Inuit, payments from the Alaska Native Claims Settlement Act.

Subsistence hunting and traditional uses of wildfoods, such as moose, caribou, whales, ducks, fish, and other wildlife continue to provide half or more of the Inuit diet. At the same time, this traditional foraging makes significant use of modern technology such as snowmobiles, gasoline, fishing nets, and sleeping bags. Many Inuit households enjoy modern conveniences, and the costs of these conveniences require household members to work full time or seasonally in the cash economy (Kofinas 2007.)

Global warming is yet another change to which the Inuit must adapt. Essential to the Inuit traditional livelihood is the transformation of water areas into ice during the long, cold winters. Sea ice is used as a highway, formerly for dog sleds and now for snowmobiles, for building materials, and for hunting platforms. However, winter ice is disappearing. Danny Gordon, a 70-year-old Inuit man from the Yukon in Canada, said:

> In the summer 40 years ago, we had lots of icebergs, and you could land your boat on them and climb on them even in summer. . . . Now in the winter they are tiny. The weather has changed (in Myers et al. 2005).

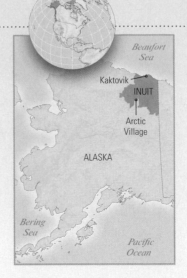

With global warming, icebergs and the permafrost are melting at an accelerating rate, making it more difficult for Inuit marine hunters to maintain their cultures and traditional ways of making a living. The shrinking ice makes it harder for polar bears to fatten up on seals and the bears are becoming emaciated. Alaskan whale hunters in the open seas have seen walruses try to climb onto their white boats, mistaking them for ice floes. The pelts of fox, marten, and other game are thinning, and even seasoned hunters are falling into water that used to be ice.

The Gwich'in are one of the many foraging groups in northeastern Alaska and northwestern Canada that have been affected by global warming. "Gwich'in elders long ago predicted that a day would come when the world would warm and things would not be the same with the animals. That time is now. . . ." says Matthew Gilbert, a member of the Gwich'in. "The lakes, the rivers, the waterfowl and, most of all, the caribou that we depend on are under threat" (Gilbert 2007).

---

Climatic changes are extreme. Summer temperatures reach 120 degrees, and winter temperatures average around 72 degrees. Most critically, rainfall is very low, unpredictable, and evaporates quickly. The availability of food, and particularly water, is the most important influence on the distance people travel, the places they camp, and the length of time they stay in one place. In the wet season, December through February, water is available and families spread across the desert. They move great distances to search for food and to attend ceremonies. Although water is easily available, food is scarce at this time of year, limited mainly to foods left over from the previous year. Men and women gather lizards and edible toads, which are relatively easy to collect. At this season, kangaroo, the most common mammal, are so widely spread across the desert that they are rarely encountered.

The 8000 Gwich'in live in small villages spread across the huge sub-Arctic tundra and forest, which contains thousands of lakes and scores of rivers. The main source of Gwich'in subsistence are the caribou herds that also occupy this area. The Gwich'in also hunt small animals for their pelts, which they sell for cash. Global warming has negatively affected the sources of Gwich'in subsistence. Recently, two immense forest fires laid waste millions of acres, driving the marten (a small furbearing animal) north of their traditional habitat, making it harder for the Gwich'in to trap them. This has resulted in a loss of fur for clothing and a loss of cash income from the sale of marten pelts. The warmer weather also means that creeks take longer to freeze and the ice is often too thin to take heavy loads. Thus, getting firewood in the early winter becomes difficult and dangerous.

Most important, climate change has decreased the number of caribou, which are also less healthy than they were formerly. Because of early river thaws, many caribou calves are drowned crossing the rushing river waters; the glaciers and snow pockets that provide essential resting places for mothers and their calves are disappearing; and the caribou must move farther north, out of their usual territory. This makes it harder for the hunters to find them, and hunting has to begin later in the season than normal.

Oil exploration in the Arctic is another threat facing the Gwich'in. Some (though not all) of the Inuit have become locally active in resisting oil exploitation of the Arctic

Polar bear crossing from one ice floe to another in summer pack ice. The warmer water due to climate change has led to the starvation of many polar bears.

Wildlife Refuge and other Arctic areas where oil companies are now able to exploit offshore energy resources revealed by global warming (Matthiessen 2007).

Most of the economic activities that are the likely cause of global warming are located far from the Arctic and the Gwich'in can do little about global climate change. However, it is clear that Gwich'in culture will be deeply affected by the warming of the planet. Gilbert (2007) notes that nature is the fabric of Gwich'in lives and that because of this: "we cannot really separate 'the climate' from our human selves. . . . So when we talk about the environment and especially about the decline of caribou, we are talking about who we are and who we want to continue to be. It is a question of our very survival as a people." A Canadian

Inuit sadly noted: "The next generation. . . . is not going to experience what we did. . . . We can't pass the traditions on as our ancestors passed them on to us" (Kofinas 2007).

### CRITICAL THINKING QUESTIONS

1. What are the main traditional food-getting strategies of Arctic peoples?
2. Describe some major changes in Arctic food-getting strategies due to Western contact.
3. How does global warming affect traditional Arctic food-getting strategies?

At the end of the wet season, when temperatures moderate, families move near the large surface water holes. June and July bring the greatest material prosperity; tubers, fruits, and grass seeds are all abundantly available. Edible fruits are collected from 12 different plants and stored for the "hungry time." People live around the water holes until August, when food availability decreases and temperatures rise steadily, reaching over 100 degrees. The landscape begins to dry out and people fall back to large rock holes where there is water. They set fires on the plains to attract game and to stimulate the growth of new grass seeds and tubers for the following year. Both men and women spend most of the day in the food quest, hunting monitor lizards and kangaroos and gathering fruits, bulbs, tubers, and grass seeds, which are both eaten and stored. In November, temperatures continue to rise, sometimes reaching 120 degrees. This is the harshest time of year, called the "hungry time." Families travel to the largest rock holes for water, but even these occasionally run dry. Food becomes less available, and many seeds and tubers run out completely. If the rain has not come by December, foraging ceases almost entirely. People try to take it easy to conserve food and water. Women remain in camp looking after the children and the elderly while the men search for food, sometimes traveling as far as 12 miles a day from camp. Average daily intake may be reduced to 800 calories per person. Heat stress and the shortage of water prevent the whole camp from moving to areas where food might be more available, and people are thus "trapped" in the areas around the larger water holes. Under conditions of starvation, weak individuals may be fed blood from healthier people to get them through the worst weeks.

The Pintupi and other Australian foragers demonstrate the extraordinary ability of human beings to adapt to the most extreme environments. Though constrained by their simple technology, foragers' detailed knowledge of their environment has permitted them to survive for thousands of years, as well as to develop highly complex ceremonial, religious, kinship, and artistic cultural patterns. These Australian tribes survived using traditional foraging strategies until the mid-20th century. Beginning in the 1920s, because of prolonged drought, the Pintupi began moving to mission stations, cattle stations, government settlements, and towns around the desert fringe. The last Pintupi left the Western Desert in 1966 (Myers 1986). From their point of view, food was easier to get elsewhere.

The Pintupi subsistence strategy demonstrates that in extreme environments foraging can be a harsh existence with periods of desperation. However, in less extreme environments where predictable vegetal foods can be supplemented by hunting, foragers may experience abundant leisure time and generally good health. For example, Richard Lee estimated that an adult Dobe Ju/'hoansi of the Kalahari Desert in southern Africa spends an average of only two-and-a-half 6-hour days per week in subsistence activities, and a woman can gather enough in one day to feed her family for three days (1984:50–53).

Today, like the Pintupi, most foragers have moved to permanent settlements, either by choice or as the result of government pressure. Old trading relationships between foragers and nonforaging people have, in most places, disappeared or become greatly diminished. Although throughout the world, people continue to forage for food when they can, members of contemporary foraging bands rely on the market for much of their food.

## Pastoralism

Pastoralism is a specialized adaptation to an environment that, because of hilly terrain, dry climate, or unsuitable soil, cannot support a large human population through agriculture, but can support enough vegetation for animals if they are allowed to range over a large area. Because human beings cannot digest grass, raising animals that can live on grasses makes pastoralism an efficient way to exploit semiarid natural grasslands. Unlike ranching (commercial animal husbandry), in which livestock are fed grain to produce meat or milk, pastoralism does not require direct competition with humans for the same resources (Barfield 1993:13).

Pastoralists may herd cattle, sheep, goats, yaks, or camels, all of which produce both meat and milk. The major areas of pastoralism are found in East Africa (cattle), North Africa (camels), southwestern Asia (sheep and goats), central Asia (yak), and the sub-Arctic (caribou and reindeer). Because, with the exception of the llama and alpaca in Peru, the herd animals found in the Americas were not easily domesticated, pastoralism did not develop as a New World subsistence strategy.

Pastoralism can be either transhumant or nomadic. In **transhumant pastoralism,** found mostly in East Africa, people establish permanent villages. Men and boys move the animals to different areas as pastures become available at different altitudes or in different climatic zones. Women, children, and some men remain at the permanent village site. In **nomadic pastoralism,** the whole population—men, women, and children—moves with the herds throughout the year, and there are no permanent villages.

Pastoralism involves complex interactions among animals, land, and people. With domestication, animals became dependent on their human keepers for pasture, water, breeding, shelter, salt, and protection from predators. Pastoralists, therefore, must be highly knowledgeable about the number of animals their land can support, as well as the number needed to provide subsistence for the human population (Barfield 1993:6).

Pastoralism is actually a mixed subsistence strategy. It is extremely difficult for humans to survive solely on the products of herds. Therefore, most pastoralists have access to grains and other foods as well. In some cases, pastoralists' survival depends upon relationships with their sedentary neighbors, with whom they trade meat animals, wool, milk products, and hides for grain and manufactured goods. In other cases, pastoralists spend part of the year raising grain and other crops.

The key to the pastoralist economy is herd growth, which depends primarily on reproduction by female ani-

**transhumant pastoralism** A form of pastoralism in which herd animals are moved regularly throughout the year to different areas as pasture becomes available.

**nomadic pastoralism** A form of pastoralism in which the whole social group (men, women, children) and their animals move in search of pasture.

mals. The number of animals needed to support a family is a perennial focus of decision making in pastoralist societies. Eating or selling too many animals in a single year may lead to insolvency, so pastoralists must always balance their present needs against future herd production. Pastoralism is a risky business; weather disasters such as drought or storms, disease, or theft can easily decimate a herd.

Nomadic pastoralist societies tend to be based on **patrilineal** kinship. In Southwest Asia, their characteristic political organization is supratribal confederations, with powerful leaders allied in regional political networks. In the past, they were subordinated to various empires on the Iranian and Anatolian plateaus, which had little success in controlling them. For the past 200 years, however, pastoralists have had to adapt to the policies set by distant governments of centralized nation-states, losing much of their political and military autonomy (Barfield 1993:206).

### The Yarahmadzai: Nomadic Pastoralists

The Yarahmadzai, who live in the southeastern corner of Iran known as Baluchistan provide an example of a mixed pastoralist adaptation that has undergone changes due to both a global economy and the restraints of adapting to the control of the national state (Salzman 2000). Yarahmadzai tribal territory occupies a plateau at 5000 feet above sea level where their chief problem is finding adequate water and pasture year round. They solve this by moving to seek pasture according to the seasons. The Yarahmadzi live in small camps of between five and twenty families. When information about good pasture becomes available, the whole Yarahmadzai camp migrates. Because even good pasturage quickly gets exhausted, the camp migrates frequently, anywhere from 5 to 25 miles in each move.

Most of the 6-inch annual rainfall occurs in the winter. This means that there is good pasturage on the Yarahmadzai's high plateau in the spring. However, by June and July, the animals have eaten all of the spring's growth and the season has turned very dry and hot. In response the Yarahmadzai migrate to areas served by government irrigation projects to earn money by harvesting grain. They remain there until the harvest ends in early autumn. Then they migrate to the lowland desert where there are groves of date palms, leaving their tents, as well as their goats and sheep on the plateau in the care of young boys. During this time they harvest dates and preparing date preserves for the return journey to their winter camps. Those who also farm plant grain, and many women work for cash in nearby towns. In November, the Yarahmadzai return to their winter camps. At this time the Yarahmadzai plateau is almost completely barren and there is very little for the animals to eat. They live on their accumulated fat and small quantities of roots, grains, dates, and processed date pits their keepers provide. The people depend on food stores from the pre-

In cultures like the Yarahmadzai, which are based on the nomadic pastoralism, all members of the group—men, women, and children—move with their herds throughout the year, and there is no permanent settlement. Women are responsible for the water supply and take care of the processing of daily food, while men herd the animals.

vious year, but because winter is the rainy season, water is normally available.

Milk is the staple food of the Yarahmadzai and is consumed in many different forms, both fresh and preserved as dried milk solids and butter. Milk and milk products are also sold and exchanged for grain. Milk is the main source of protein, fat, calcium, and other nutrients; the Yarahmadzai, like most other pastoral peoples, do not eat much meat. Their flocks are their capital and the Yarahmadzai hope increase their size. Since killing animals for food works against this objective, the Yarahmadzai rarely do it (Salzman 1999:24).

Like most contemporary pastoralists, then, the Yarahmadzai combine herding with other subsistence strategies in order to earn a living. Many pastoralists today now depend less on consuming the direct products of their herds—meat, wool, milk—and more on the sale of animals and animal products for cash. In this sense, many nomadic pastoralists are becoming ranchers: pastoral specialists in a cash economy.

Pastoralists today are often successful in adapting their products to local and even global markets. Nomads in Afghanistan and Iran, for example, are highly inte-

**patrilineal** A society that reckons descent through the male line.

## The Maasai of East Africa: A Transhumant Pastoral Adaptation

The Maasai, one of the many "cattle cultures" of East Africa, live in the semiarid grasslands (savanna) of southern Kenya and northern Tanzania, an area characterized by many different microenvironments. Like other cattle herding groups in the region, traditionally the Maasai's diet consisted primarily of the blood and milk of their cattle, supplemented by other resources such as grain or fish. In recent years, it has become increasingly difficult for the Maasai to maintain this diet because the loss of pasture and water has so decreased their herds. Cattle are considered sacred in Maasai culture, and traditionally were never sold and were slaughtered only for important ritual occasions. Today, more Maasai are forced to sell and slaughter their cattle just to survive.

The traditional Maasai subsistence strategy is determined by various environmental factors such as elevation, the distribution of lakes and rivers, seasonal rainfall, vegetation, and the presence of tsetse flies and malarial mosquitoes, but the most important factor is seasonal rainfall. The rainy season generally lasts from about November through May and the dry season from June through October. The Maasai environment is full of uncertainties. The droughts that occur every 7 to 10 years kill crops as well as livestock. The Maasai have survived by developing an economy adapted to the difficulties of their environment, including the periods of relative scarcity. The Maasai subsistence strategy features the flexible exploitation of multiple ecological niches and includes measures to deal with environmental unpredictability and even occasional catastrophes.

Maasai resource management is a system of specialized herding well suited to

East Africa's savanna. Maasai livestock rely on the varieties of palatable grasses seasonably available, depending on rainfall. The seasonal rainfall dictates where herders move their livestock. During the dry season, the Maasai and their livestock concentrate around permanent water sources such as lakes and rivers. During the wet season they disperse in search of fresh pasture and temporary sources of water that has collected in low-lying areas following the rains. Whereas the dry season is often a period of hunger and scarcity, the wet season brings malaria and other illnesses and makes the roads impassable and travel uncertain.

The Maasai knowledge of their environment is passed down from fathers to elder sons and from elder to younger brothers. This complex knowledge focuses on information most necessary to effectively move their livestock, particularly information about the most likely areas of rainfall. Maasai women also have detailed knowledge of their environment, particularly about types of medicinal plants and the availability of water. Up-to-date information about the different areas in the region is shared through extended kin and trading networks, and at markets and ritual celebrations; and now, cell phones can communicate information about pasturage within a several-hundred-mile radius (Mason 2007).

The movement of livestock between wet and dry season pastures generally stays the same from year to year (exceptions occur when rain fails in one area and herders are forced to move their animals to areas where rainfall is more abundant). In the dry season, a Maasai community and its livestock concentrate around a permanent water point. Permanent homesteads are built

around this area so that everyone has equal access to it, but are built far enough away from each other to reduce the likelihood of overgrazing. Cattle are permitted to drink only according to the elaborate rotation schedules set up by the elders.

The number of animals concentrated around permanent water during the dry season often runs into several thousand, so that the Maasai water their animals on alternate days. On days that livestock are watered they are taken to the queuing area in the morning and, after being watered, they are moved beyond the permanent homestead into the dry-season pasture. They graze here and return home in the evening. On alternate days the livestock are herded away from the permanent water source to a different part of the dry-season pasture, where they graze for the entire day.

When the rains begin, usually in November or December, the young men take the mature and healthy stock to the wet-season pasturage areas, where they live in temporary camps and there is an abundance of seasonal water sources and mineral-rich pasture. This allows the dry-season pasture to recover. Most of the women, children, and elder men remain in the permanent homesteads with the sick,

grated into national and international trade networks. They specialize in selling meat animals to local markets, lambskins to international buyers, and sheep intestines to meet the huge German demand for natural sausage casings (Barfield 1993:211).

Critics of nomadic pastoralism claim that the individual pastoralist's desire to increase the size of his herds inevitably leads to collective overgrazing and the destruction of grasslands. In fact, however, pastoralists are aware of this potential problem and in varied ways restrict ac-

immature, and lactating animals. Household heads check on their sons and herds periodically. At the end of the wet season, in May or June, the young men return with the livestock to the permanent homesteads and a new cycle begins.

A critical adaptive feature of the Maasai strategy is the drought reserve, the setting aside of relatively large areas of water and pasture that never dry up, even during the worst years of drought. These areas are usually swamps, lakes, or mountain springs at relatively high elevations. During normal years, the Maasai do not bring their herds to these areas. When a drought occurs, however, herders will come from as far as a hundred miles away. Although animals do die during severe droughts, the drought reserve permits enough to survive so that the herd can recover in less than 5 years.

The Maasai also build flexibility into their adaptive strategy by treating land as common property. Access to pasture and water are regulated and negotiated by a council of local elders representing the community. Kinship, clan membership, and membership in the age grade system (see Chapter 11, "Political Organization") build extensive social networks that ensure maximum flexibility, giving a herder multiple options as to where he can move his herds. The flexibility of the Maasai adaptation also depends on exchange; in some areas the Maasai exchange small stock and milk for honey, gathered by local foraging groups, which is an essential ingredient in the honey beer used on all Maasai ceremonial occasions. Some Maasai also encourage farmers to settle among them. Where small farmers have settled on riverbanks, they exchange fish, as well as grains, fruit, and vegetables with the Maasai. When the farmers earn cash by selling their products in the markets, they use it to buy livestock and milk from the Maasai, who in turn use the cash to buy clothing, aluminum cooking pots, iron spearheads, and veterinary medicine.

The Maasai lived successfully in the Great Rift Valley region for hundreds of years, but since the late 19th century it has become more and more difficult for them to practice their transhumant pastoralist strategy. Much of their best grazing land, as well as their drought reserves, was also suitable for forestry, intensive farming, and stall-fed livestock. These areas were taken over by the Europeans during the colonial period and much of this land is still owned by Europeans. After World War I, and increasingly after independence, Kenya and Tanzania looked for new ways to improve their economies. Inspired by the wildlife conservation movement, the government began to set aside huge tracts of land for national parks and game reserves to attract tourism. Many Maasai were evicted from this land and their herding areas narrowed substantially. As Maasai herding has increasingly been circumscribed by other land uses, much herding knowledge has been lost. Although the Maasai had coexisted with wild grazing herds and indeed imitated the seasonal patterns of the herds, today they are largely shut out of conservation policy making. Development planners often regard them

In east African cattle cultures, like the Maasai, the blood and milk of cattle are the major dietary elements. Cattle are killed for meat only on very special ceremonial occasions.

as obstacles to the most effective use of their own land. The changing Maasai subsistence strategy illustrates the effect of global economics and global values, such as wildlife conservation, on local communities.

### CRITICAL THINKING QUESTIONS

1. What are the main things the Maasai have to know to adapt to their environment?

2. How do the Maasai build flexibility into their subsistence strategy?

3. How can the needs of the Maasai, the economic development of Kenya, and the ideology of wildlife conservation be reconciled as these interact in the African savannah?

Source: Based on Jim Igoe, *Conservation and Globalization: A Case Study of Maasai Herders and National Parks in East Africa*. Belmont, CA: Wadsworth, 2004.

cess to common pasture (Barfield 1993:214). Indeed, it is more often government policies that restrict nomadic use of pastoralist territories in an attempt to make them productive for agriculture that directly and indirectly exacerbate environmental degradation.

Pastoralism cannot support an indefinitely increasing population, and many pastoralists have already become sedentary. But with their knowledge of their environment, their creative use of multiple resources, and global demand for their products, pastoralism as a subsis-

## The Lua': Swidden Cultivators in Thailand

The traditional livelihood of the Lua' people, who live in the mountains of northern Thailand, is swidden cultivation. After using a block of land for 1 or 2 years, villagers allow it to lie fallow for about 9 years because they understand that in 2 years the soil loses its fertility and becomes overgrown by weeds. Swidden blocks around the village are cultivated in a regular rotational sequence. Each household normally returns to the same field it cultivated 10 years before, marking their swidden field boundaries with charred logs.

In January, village elders inspect the swidden blocks they expect to use the following year to confirm that the forest regrowth is adequate for cultivation and that fire has not depleted the soil's fertility. Using long steel-bladed knives, the men clear their fields by felling small trees, leaving stumps about 3 feet high. They leave strips of trees along watercourses and at the tops of ridges to prevent erosion and provide seed sources for forest regrowth during the fallow period. They leave taller trees standing, but trim their branches so they will not shade the crops.

The fields cleared in January and February are allowed to dry until the end of March, the driest time of the year. In consultation with ritual leaders and village elders, a day is chosen to burn the fields. First a firebreak is cleared around the swidden block so that fire does not accidentally spread into the forest reserved for future cultivation or into the village. Then the swidden is burned. The men burning the swiddens usually carry guns, hoping game animals such as boar or barking deer will run toward them out of the burning fields, although this happens less today than in the past.

The cultivators first plant cotton and corn, which they sow on the slopes of the fields, and plant yams on the lower, wetter portions. For the next 2 weeks they prop up unburned logs along the contour of the fields to reduce erosion. They mark the boundaries, gather larger logs for firewood, and build fences to keep livestock out of the field. By mid-April they begin to plant the main subsistence crop, upland rice, jabbing the earth loose with 10-foot iron-tipped planting poles. They hope the rice will take root and sprout before the heavy monsoon rains come. Different types of rice are sown in different areas of the field. Quick-ripening rice is planted near the field shelter, where it can be easily watched. Drought-resistant varieties are planted on the drier, sandier tops of the slopes, along with millet.

Each household plants tall-growing sorghum (a cereal grass) to mark out their fields from their neighbors'. Mustard greens, peppers, several varieties of beans, and other vegetables are grown in gardens near the field shelters. Vine plants are grown along the creases in the hillside fields, which are more vulnerable to erosion. By May, weeding begins, with mainly women and older children using a short-handled tool to scrape and hack at the weeds on the surface; weeds are not dug or pulled out by the roots.

Both men and women harvest the rice, using small, handheld sickles, cutting the stems of each bunch of rice close to the ground. The 3-foot-long stalks are laid out to dry for a few days before threshing, when women gather large bundles of rice stalks on a threshing floor leveled on the hillside. Young men beat the rice stalks against a threshing mat laid on the floor to knock the rice grains loose; other men beat the broken straw with bamboo threshing sticks to separate the rice grains as completely as possible. As the grain and chaff piles grow, the men shuffle through with their feet, fanning with a woven bamboo winnowing fan to blow away as much dirt as possible. After a second winnowing, the cleaned rice is loaded into baskets and kept in a temporary barn near the field shelter.

Like most horticulturalists, the Lua' maintain a pattern of varied vegetation zones around the village. The villagers are forbidden to cut lumber or make swiddens or gardens in mature forests, which are thus preserved. Uncut forest strips are also maintained between swidden blocks, around the village, along streamcourses and headwaters, and at the tops of ridges, all of which reduce erosion. Villagers use the plants that grow on fallow fields for grazing and as traditional medicines, dyes for homespun clothing, and material for weaving baskets and building houses. The wild fruits and yams that grow on fallow land are particularly important during food shortages.

The Lua' also keep pigs, water buffalo, cattle, and chickens, which may be sold at local markets for cash. Before the 1960s, when the big fish in the streams were killed by pollution from chemical dumping of agricultural waste and malaria eradication pesticides, fish were also important in the Lua' diet. Hunting also has declined. Since World War II, there has been little game in the forests, although occasionally a forest animal will fall into a trap set in the fields to catch birds and rats, which can destroy a crop.

Lua' adaptation worked well with its relatively stable population, which until the 1960s was held in check by a high mortality rate (caused largely by smallpox and malaria) and a delayed age of marriage. With a limited amount of cultivable land, large families were not seen as an advantage, and the number of women who migrate to the village as brides was generally balanced by the number who moved out.

The stability of Lua' land use patterns and population has been changing since the early 20th century, when other ethnic groups entered the area and paid rent to the Lua' to farm on their land. By the mid-20th century, still other ethnic groups, including the Hmong, began to settle in the area. These newer settlers were less careful about their swidden practices than the Lua' and the quality of the land began to deteriorate. Like many governments today, the Thai government claims ownership of all forested land and, without distinguishing between good and bad swidden practices, has generally discouraged swidden. Since the late 1990s, government officials have applied heavy pressure on the Lua' to limit their use of swiddens. (Delcore 2007:96).

The Lua' were familiar with more intensive methods of agriculture, including permanently irrigated fields, and some Lua' had already switched to agriculture before the end of the 19th century. The pressure to substitute intensive cultivation for horticulture has increased, and today, instead of maintaining the diversity of their environment with their swidden-rotation system, the Lua' are homogenizing their land use with irrigated, terraced agriculture. With the increase of cattle and human population in the area, sorghum and millet are no longer

Swidden, or slash and burn, horticulture, as practiced traditionally in northern Thailand, is based on a deep understanding of the forest environment. All the features of the landscape are taken into account as Lua' build their houses and plant their fields with a variety of crops used for subsistence, for cash, and for animal fodder.

grown. Fields planted with cotton have also declined, and now the Lua' usually buy thread for weaving and cotton clothes. Cattle graze on the fallow land and this means less grass is available for house construction and more Lua' now roof their houses with leaves or with corrugated metal if they can afford it. The increase of cash cropping in soybeans has transformed the previously clear and free-flowing streams to muddy, polluted pools, which the Lua' now consider too dirty to wash their clothes in, and year-round irrigation has brought in year-round mosquitoes. Although the Lua' have not been subject to the severe dislocations of some neighboring ethnic groups, such as the Hmong, these changes in Lua' food

production have brought about substantial changes in their economic, social, and ritual lifestyle.

### CRITICAL THINKING QUESTIONS

1. What do the Lua' need to know about their environment in order to be successful farmers? What do you need to know about your environment in order to be successful?
2. Compare the effects of environmental pollution on the Lua' with its effects on your own life.
3. What changes have impacted the Lua' subsistence strategy?

# Ethnography

## Musha: A Peasant Village in Egypt

Musha is an agricultural village about 250 miles south of Cairo in the Nile Valley, a fertile agricultural strip between the riverbanks and the desert. Musha's farmers practice a 2-year crop rotation system based on summer crops of cotton, maize, and sorghum, and winter crops of wheat, lentils, chickpeas, and millet. The cycle begins with cotton in the first summer, followed by wheat in the following winter. Maize or sorghum follows in the second summer, or the land may be left fallow. The cycle is completed in the second winter with millet, lentils, and chickpeas. In addition, farmers grow grapes and pomegranates and raise onions, peppers, watermelons, and other vegetables on small patches for home consumption. Small farmers also depend heavily on the milk, cheese, and butter from water buffalo and the cheese from cows, sheep, and goats. Only water buffalo are regularly eaten and sold.

Traditional Musha farmers relied on either animal power or human effort and a few basic wooden tools, including a short-handled hoe for weeding and irrigation, a small sickle for harvesting, and a digging stick for planting cotton. Shallow plows and threshing sleds were pulled by cows. Winnowing relied on the wind and a winnowing fork and sieves for the final cleaning. Donkeys carried small loads for short distances; camels were used for larger loads and longer distances and for bringing the crops in from the field.

Many changes, starting in the 1950s, have occurred in Musha. By 1980 almost all farmers were using machines at least some of the time. These include tractors which are used to pull wagons that transport fertilizer and crops as well as to power threshing machines. In addition, farmers now depend on chemical fertilizers and pesticides as well as animal manure.

Individual farmers now use pumping machines to lift the groundwater to supplement the Nile floodwater for part of the year, which makes double cropping and cotton cultivation possible. Land values have increased, leading to the creation of large land holdings and increased demand for labor. In the 1960s, when the completion of the Aswan High Dam brought an end to the flooding of the Nile, the government constructed feed canals and these became the main source of water for the fields. Water must be raised from the canals to the level of the fields. Pumps that perform this task are generally owned by several people, who share the work of guarding and maintaining the pumps, maintaining the ditches that bring the water from the canals to the fields, arranging for the distribution of water to the farmers' fields, and keeping accounts. Each farmer provides the necessary labor to open a break in the ditch band so that the water will flow into his field. The farmer pays the owner of the pump a set fee per watering and also pays the pump guard an annual fee. The government is responsible for maintaining the feeder canals and cleans them once a year. After arranging for the distribution of water to his fields, the farmer must hire a driver and tractor to plow the fields if he, like many small farmers, does

not own one. Fertilizer and seed are hauled from the village bank to the farmer's home and from his home to the field. The fertilizer is then spread by hand.

Wheat is one of the most important crops in Mushu. It is planted in November and harvested in May and June, and is used for both grain and straw. Hired laborers usually harvest wheat using a small sickle. The reaped wheat is bundled into sheaves, which are transported by camel or wagon to the threshing ground at the edge of the village. A five-member team hand feeds sheaves to the machine and the threshed grain is winnowed and sifted by specialists who are paid piece rates, supervised by the farmer. Finally, the grain and straw are hauled from the threshing ground back to the farmer's storeroom.

In deciding on their strategies for making a living, Musha farmers must adapt not only to the physical environment but also to the government policies. At one time, the government controlled prices for key crops such as wheat and cotton. Much of this direct intervention either ended or was greatly reduced following reforms in the

---

tence strategy has a strong future in exploiting the planet's large arid and semiarid zones.

## Horticulture

Horticultural societies depend primarily on the production of plants using simple, nonmechanized technology. In horticulture, cultivated fields are not used year after year, but remain fallow for some time after being culti-

vated. This is an important contrast between horticulture and agriculture. Horticulturalists plant and harvest with simple tools, such as hoes or digging sticks, and do not use draft animals, irrigation techniques, or plows. Generally speaking, horticulture produces a lower yield per acre and uses less human labor than agriculture. Traditionally, horticulturalists grow enough food in their fields or gardens to support the local group, but they do not produce surpluses that involve the group in a wider mar-

1980s and 1990s. However, the government is still heavily involved in agriculture. Indeed, through investments in irrigation systems and other infrastructure, the government has remodeled the very landscape on which the farmer works. Government organizations, such as the Principal Bank for Development and Agriculture and the General Authority for Food Commodities, make loans to farmers, distribute agricultural inputs such as seed and fertilizer, subsidize the production of particular agricultural products, and buy some of the farmers' crops. State policies, such as importing wheat from the United States, affect the prices received by farmers. The state sets land ownership policy and makes rules governing land tenancy. The state affects the labor market through policies that encourage migration.

The household is central in Musha cultivation, with extra laborers hired as needed. Household members also may work outside the agricultural sector. Women do not work in the fields, but keep house, care for animals, and make cheese. Children, recruited by labor contractors, cut clover for animals and help harvest cotton. The household head plays a key managerial role in Musha, supervising others, making agricultural purchases, hiring labor, scheduling the use of machinery, and arranging for the water flow into his fields.

Profits from farming are uncertain, and most families have several sources of income. Animals are sold in weekly markets through professional brokers who have established trusted relationships built on per-

sonal contact. Fruits and vegetables are sold either in the fields or to merchant brokers. In fact, 70 percent of village households derive their major income from activities other than farming: day labor, government jobs, craft trades, specialist agricultural work, as well as remittances from family members who have migrated, or from rents and pensions.

Thus, farmers must interact with family members and government officials. They must negotiate with the owners of tractors, day laborers, recruiters for child labor, neighbors, contractors for transport animals, and merchants. The farmer must supervise the agricultural work and manage a wide range of activities, making important decisions at every step. With the increasing monetization of agriculture, farmers now consciously orient themselves to the market and have become sophisticated in dealing with it. Peasant farmers in Musha today are part of a world economy.

### CRITICAL THINKING QUESTIONS

1. Discuss the role of technological change on the working environment in Musha.

In peasant villages in Egypt, a farmer makes important decisions regarding the allocation of household and extradomestic labor, purchases necessities for agriculture, schedules the use of machinery, and may negotiate with the government for the sale of his crops.

© Robert Caputo/Stock, Boston LLC

2. Compare the impact of the state on your work life with the impact of the state on farmers in Musha.

3. How has globalization affected agriculture in Egypt compared with industrialized agriculture in the United States? (See "The Global and the Local" section in this chapter.)

Source: Adapted from Nicholas Hopkins, "Mechanized Irrigation in Upper Egypt: The Role of Technology and the State in Agriculture." In B. Turner II and Stephen B. Brush (Eds.), *Comparative Farming Systems*. New York: Guilford Press, 1987, pp. 223–247. Reprinted with permission.

ket system with nonagricultural populations. Population densities among horticultural peoples are generally low, usually not exceeding 150 people per square mile (Netting 1977). Despite this, horticultural villages may be quite large, ranging from 100 to 1000 people.

Horticulture may be practiced in dry lands, such as among the Hopi Indians of northeastern Arizona, who cultivate maize, beans, and squash, but is typically a tropical forest adaptation found mainly in Southeast

Asia, sub-Saharan Africa, some Pacific islands, and the Amazon Basin in South America. In these environments, people practice **swidden,** or **slash and burn, cultivation.** In slash and burn cultivation, a field is cleared by felling the

**swidden (slash and burn) cultivation** A form of cultivation in which a field is cleared by felling the trees and burning the brush. Typical of horticulture.

# Anthropology Makes a Difference

## A Successful Agricultural Intervention in Bolivia

With food shortages increasing among poor peoples the world over, food scientists are proposing new solutions. One of these is the expansion of potato cultivation, which could supplement or even replace grains that are most often shipped to poor nations from far away and are subject to severe price fluctuation in world markets. Peru is among the many governments worldwide that are now urging growing and eating potatoes as a way to ensure food security and build rural income (Rosenthal 2008). In highland South America, potatoes were traditionally a significant part of the diet. Potatoes are a good source of nutrients, proteins, and vitamins and require less energy and water to grow than wheat, but are best suited as a local, subsistence crop because they do not travel well.

The holistic approach of anthropologists can make a big difference in improving the quality and quantity of food production. This is demonstrated by the work of Alan Kolata, an archaeological anthropologist who, with agronomists and local farmers in a high plateau region of the Andes Mountains in Bolivia, is reviving an ancient system of agriculture with the potato as the central crop.

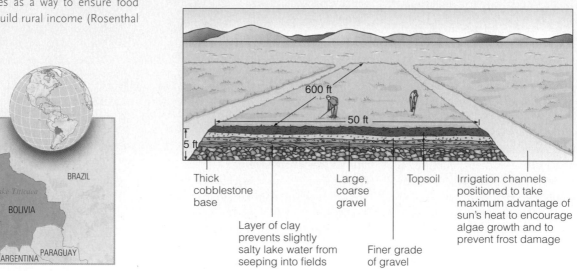

Thick cobblestone base

Layer of clay prevents slightly salty lake water from seeping into fields

Large, coarse gravel

Finer grade of gravel

Topsoil

Irrigation channels positioned to take maximum advantage of sun's heat to encourage algae growth and to prevent frost damage

trees and burning the brush. The burned vegetation is allowed to remain on the soil, which prevents its drying out from the sun. The resulting bed of ash acts as a fertilizer, returning nutrients to the soil. Fields are used for 1 to 5 years and then allowed to lie fallow for a longer period (up to 20 years) so that the forest cover can be rebuilt and fertility be restored. Swidden cultivators require five to six times as much fallow land as they are actually cultivating. Swidden cultivation *can* have a deteriorating effect on the environment if fields are cultivated before they have lain fallow long enough to recover their forest growth. Eventually, the forest will not grow back, and the tree cover will be replaced by grasslands. Because of the possibility of irreversible ecological deterioration, swidden cultivation is considered both inefficient and destructive by governments in developing nations. However, it is modern industrial strategies such as logging and giant agribusiness, not swidden cultivation, that is mainly responsible for the deterioration and disappearance of tropical forests (Sponsel 1995).

Horticulture is also a mixed subsistence strategy. Most swidden cultivators grow several crops. Because their gardens do not provide all the necessary proteins for human health, they may also hunt and fish or raise some domestic animals. In Papua New Guinea, for example, domestic pigs are an important source of protein. The horticulturalist Kofyar of Nigeria keep goats, chickens, sheep, and cows. The Yanomamo of the Amazon rain forest hunt monkeys and other forest animals.

Because of the very diverse environments of swidden cultivation, horticulturalists have diverse cultures. Most horticulturalists shift residences as they move their fields, but some occupy villages permanently or at least on a long-term basis.

## Agriculture (Intensive Cultivation)

In agriculture, the same piece of land is permanently cultivated with the use of the plow, draft animals, and more complex techniques of water and soil control

This region, on the shores of Lake Titicaca, was the site of an ancient culture called the Tiwanaku. By around 1500 BCE, local farmers had developed a system of agriculture that was ingenious in taking advantage of the particular resources of this area while compensating for its deficiencies.

Lake Titicaca, which has the highest elevation of any commercially navigable lake in the world, is slightly salty. The area around it receives intense sunlight during the day, but during the growing season is subject to severe temperature drops in the evening. Successful farming in this area required cushioning the growing area from these temperature extremes and preventing the seepage of brackish water into the cultivated area.

To adapt to the opportunities and drawbacks of the region, the Tiwanaku farmers constructed a system of raised-bed agriculture. They made a series of platforms, beginning with a foundation layer of cobblestones. Next they added a layer of clay that prevented the salty lake water from seeping into the topsoil. Above the clay was a layer of sand and gravel that promoted drainage, and above that was the fertile soil in which the crops were grown. Surrounding the platforms were canals, filled with water from a river that the farmers rerouted from its natural bed. This water trapped the radiant energy from the intense Andean sunlight, so that an insulating blanket of warm water seeping into the growing soil from the canals protected the crops from evening frosts. These canals of standing water also became an environment for plants, insects, and other organisms that enriched the soil.

After the Spanish conquest in the 16th century, the raised fields fell into disuse as the farmers adopted European farming methods. The platforms deteriorated into marshy pasture, although the mounds were still visible around the lake.

In 1979, Kolata noted the mounds while investigating the remains of the ancient culture in the area. His research indicated that this area had once supported a much larger population than it does today. This led Kolata to think about whether reviving this earlier system of agriculture might prove more productive for local farmers than their present methods. Kolata's idea was positively received by local development experts, who were beginning to believe that industrialized, capital-intensive, irrigation-based agriculture was not the only solution to problems of food production in developing nations and were looking for new alternatives more suited to local conditions. By 1987, Kolata was supervising five experimental raised-bed fields to compare their yields with those produced by traditional postconquest farming methods.

The potato yield in the experimental fields was much higher than in the traditional plots, and the experimental fields survived a crucial test: when potatoes and other crops were nearly destroyed by a frost late in the growing season, the crops in the raised-bed fields escaped almost undamaged. Kolata is now spearheading a project to reclaim more land on which to revive this ancient system of agriculture that has proven to be so effective (Kolata 1996). In such ways, basic research in anthropology can be applied to solve human problems.

than are used by horticulturalists. Plows are more efficient at loosening the soil than are digging sticks or hoes. The turning of the soil brings nutrients to the surface. Plowing requires a much more thorough clearing of the land, but it allows land to be used year after year.

Irrigation is also important in intensive cultivation. Although some horticulturalists practice simple methods of water conservation and control, agriculture in dry areas can be carried out only with sophisticated irrigation techniques. In hilly areas, agriculture requires some form of terracing in order to prevent crops and good soil from being washed down the hillside. Preindustrial agriculture also uses techniques of natural fertilization, selective breeding of livestock and crops, and crop rotation, all of which increase productivity. Whereas horticulturalists have to increase the amount of land under cultivation in order to support a larger population, agriculture can support population increases by more intensive use of the same piece of land.

Intensive cultivation generally supports higher population densities than horticulture. In Indonesia, for example, the island of Java, which makes up only 9 percent of the Indonesian land area, supports more than two-thirds of the Indonesian population through intensive wet rice cultivation using elaborate irrigation terraces. The Javanese population density of well over 2000 people per square mile (Indonesia 1997) contrasts sharply with the maximum population density of swidden areas in Indonesia, which is about 145 persons per square mile (Geertz 1963:13).

The greater productivity of agriculture results also from more intensive use of labor. Farmers must work long and hard to make the land productive. For example, growing rice in an irrigated paddy requires about 233 person days of labor per year for each hectare (a hectare is about 2.5 acres) (Barker, Herdt, and Rose 1985:128). Agriculture also requires more capital investment than horticulture; apart from the cost of human labor, plows must be bought and draft animals raised and cared for.

## The American Beef Industry

The American beef industry is a good if disturbing example of industrialism. Americans have long had a love affair with beef. Because during much of America's past meat was expensive for the average family, beef became both the symbol and the substance of having made it into the middle class. Immigrants to the United States viewed the regular eating of steaks and chops as a symbol of their upward mobility. For Americans steak is symbolic of manliness, and "meat and potatoes" are still considered the iconic American meal, despite the scientific conclusion that beef consumption increases obesity and the chance of heart disease.

After World War II, disposable income rose in the United States, wives began working, suburban commutes lengthened the working day, and busy schedules splintered American family togetherness. These changes led to changes in American food culture, which became marked by the consumption of packaged convenience meat and poultry; these foods were "grazed" on at home, in drive-ins or at fast food restaurants, or taken on the run as mobile "fist food."

As the standard of living in the United States rose after World War II, so did the demand for inexpensive beef, pork, and poultry. The postwar era also brought the rise of the suburbs and, particularly after 1960, the entry of large numbers of women into the workforce. These developments increased the complexity of American family life and reduced the amount of time available for cooking and dining together, thus people began to favor packaged convenience foods and meat that could be rapidly prepared. Additionally, the expansion of the fast food industries beginning in the 1960s greatly increased American consumption of hamburgers and hence increased the demand for beef. In 2007, McDonald's alone purchased close to 1 billion pounds of beef in the United States (Roybal 2007). American dinner tables had been supplied with meat that came through a production chain that started with the livestock on a family farm and ended in the neighborhood retail butcher shop. However, this system of production could not generate the levels of supply that were now demanded by families and the fast food industry.

America's love affair with cheap beef and poultry came at a significant price to the nation's rural culture and environment. The high demand for inexpensive meat favored large corporations that could employ mass production technologies over small family-owned farming operations. By the late 1980s, most family farms were no longer economically viable and many small farmers lost their land through sale or foreclosure. Rural America became dominated by large farming operations, many of them tied to multinational corporations. Rural poverty increased and young, would-be farmers saw little future for themselves. Some remained in America's rural areas and took the dangerous and poorly paid jobs offered by the corporate meat and poultry processing industry; others left the countryside altogether. Local governments recruited agribusiness with free land and tax breaks, putting a greater revenue burden on farmers and small town residents already in a downward economic spiral.

The cost of labor is a significant factor in the production of meat. Through the 1970s and 1980s, meat processors led by Iowa Beef Processors Inc. (the predecessor of the current day corporation Tyson Fresh Meats) succeeded in driving down the wages paid to workers. The key to this was their use of non-union workers and these were frequently immigrants from Latin America and Southeast Asia. Such workers were not easily (or very willingly) absorbed into tightly-knit farm communities and small towns. As the rural economy declined, resentment of immigrants increased, as did social problems such as crime and child abuse. There were strains on health care and other social services and school environments often became unstable as host communities dealt with the rapid turnover and limited English language proficiency of many agricultural workers (Artz, Orazem, and Otto 2007). These factors led to deep poverty and loss of population in many rural communities (Warren 2007).

In many cases, large-scale meatpacking industry had disastrous environmental impacts. U.S. livestock production creates about 900 million tons of waste annually. In Iowa, hog farming alone produces 50 million tons of manure annually. This waste often seeps into local streams and groundwater supplies, polluting critical resources (Bittman 2008). Thus, although some rural regions experienced short-term job increases from the meatpacking and poultry processing industries, there was a hidden

And although agriculturalists may have more control over food production than horticulturalists, they are also more vulnerable to the environment. When people depend on the intensive cultivation of one or two crops, one crop failure or a disease that strikes draft animals may become an economic disaster.

Agriculture is generally associated with sedentary villages, the rise of cities and the state, occupational diversity, social stratification, and other complex forms of social organization, although some states, in Africa for example, were built on horticulture. And in contrast to horticulturalists, who grow food mainly for the subsistence of their households, farmers (agriculturalists) are enmeshed within larger complex societies. Part of their food production is used to support non–food-producing occupational specialists, such as religious or ruling elites.

cost and a long-term downside for rural communities (Stull and Broadway 2004).

The cost efficiency of assembly line beef processing has high human costs. The meatpacking industry has a long history of horrific working conditions. In 1906, Upton Sinclair described the deeply impoverished lives, terrible working conditions, and hopelessness of workers in Chicago's slaughterhouses. Although the meatpacking industry today is vastly different from the industry of 100 years ago, in many cases working conditions are still deeply disturbing. The low costs and high availability of American meat is made possible only by cheap labor and getting the maximum product out the door 24/7/365. "On the floor" this translates into a large proportion of unskilled, poorly trained, low-paid hourly workers; a speeded-up "disassembly" line; an insufficiency of lunch and bathroom breaks; and no-paid "donning and doffing" time when workers can clean off the blood which bespatters them and change their clothing at the end of their shift. Work in the meatpacking industry is difficult and dangerous even in the best plants. The processing operations on the line involve thousands of panicked animals moving through a treadmill to be stun-gunned by a "knocker," axed in half by "splitters" on a moving platform, and deboned and cut up with sharp knives wielded by an assortment of specialists such as "stickers," "gutters," "tail rippers," and "head droppers," whose names suggest their roles in the process—and the possibilities for injuries. The blood, intestines, ears, hooves, and other animal by-products used for making perfumes, bone-meal, paintbrushes, and hundreds of other items are supposed to be continually cleaned up or removed to separate locations for later use, but are sometimes left to decay, emitting noxious fumes. The working conditions of meat processing affect not only the health of the workers, but also the quality of the product. This was dramatically demonstrated in early 2008, when the Westland/Hallmark meatpacking company recalled 143 million pounds of meat, some of which was used in school lunch programs! The working conditions of this sector of American agribusiness are so severe that Human Rights Watch has deemed them in violation of international standards and basic human rights. Despite this, demand for inexpensive beef remains high and meaningful reform of the industry does not seem likely in the near future.

Many cultural changes are the result of the industrialization of the beef industry in rural America. Thousands of workers, mainly immigrants, must adjust to the pressures and safety hazards of the work floor, while rural communities must also adjust to the replacement of family farms with the new subsistence pattern of industrialism.

© Ed Lallo/ZUMA/Corbis

## CRITICAL THINKING QUESTIONS

1. What are the main features of the beef industry in the United States?
2. How has the industrial processing of beef affected the small Midwestern towns in which these factories are located?
3. What are some connections between American food culture and other social and economic values, and the industrial processing of beef?

Rural cultivators who produce for the subsistence of their households but are also integrated into larger, complex state societies are called **peasants.**

Musha, the Egyptian village described in the accompanying "Ethnography" box, exhibits many of the general characteristics of peasant villages, including the importance of the household in production, the use of a supplementary labor supply outside the household, the need of many farmers to depend on part-time work to supplement their income, and the surplus extracted from the cultivator by the state in the form of rent, taxes, and free

**peasants** Rural cultivators who produce for the subsistence of their households but are also integrated into larger, complex state societies.

labor. Although Egypt has a particularly long and well-documented history of state intervention in agriculture, the intervention of the state in Musha is typical of peasant societies generally. The multiple strategies for making a living in Musha highlight the ways in which both physical and social environments provide opportunities but also constrain human choices and shape culture and society.

## Industrialism

In **industrialism,** the focus of production moves away from food to the production of other goods and services. Investments in machinery and technologies of communication and information become increasingly important. In foraging, pastoralism, horticulture, and agriculture, most of the population is involved in producing food. Although the food industry is very large in industrial societies, only a very small percentage of the population is directly involved in food production. In the United States, for example, in 2005, fewer than one million people, less than one half of 1 percent of the population, had farming as their primary occupation (United States Census Bureau 2008).

Industrialism has an explosive effect on many aspects of economy, society, and culture. It has led to vastly increased population growth, expanded consumption of resources (especially energy), international expansion, occupational specialization, and a shift from subsistence strategies to wage labor. In every industrialized society, most people work for wages, which they use to purchase food, goods, and services. Although cash transactions are found in other production systems, in industrial economies, almost all transactions are mediated by money.

Industrial economies are based on the principles that consumption must constantly expand and material standards of living must always rise. This contrasts with economies created by the production systems previously discussed, which put limits on both production and consumption and thus make lighter demands on their environments. Industrialism today has vastly outgrown national boundaries. The result has been great movement of resources, capital, and population, as the whole world has gradually been drawn into the global economy, a process we call **globalization.**

**industrialism** The replacement of human and animal energy by machines in the process of production.

**globalization** The integration of resources, labor, and capital into a global network.

Contemporary industrial and postindustrial societies are characterized by well-coordinated specialized labor forces that produce goods and services and much smaller elite and managerial classes that oversee day-to-day operations of the workplace and control what is produced and how it is distributed. Government bureaucracies become important economic and social strata. Increasingly, mobility, skill, and education are required for success.

Because industrialized societies generate much higher levels of inequality than societies based on foraging, pastoralism, or horticulture, and because industrial systems require continued expansion, wealth and poverty become critical social issues. The unequal distribution of opportunity, economic failure, illness, and misfortune limit the life chances of vast numbers of people in industrialized society. Poverty punishes weakness, failure, or ill fortune in a way that is less true of the subsistence strategies of foraging, pastoralism, horticulture, and agriculture. Conversely, economic success creates lifestyles well above poverty for large numbers and conditions of truly extraordinary wealth for a very small number. Inequalities characterize relations among as well as within nations. The creation of complex global systems of exchange between those who supply raw materials and those who use them in manufacturing, as well as between manufacturers and consumers, has resulted in increasing disparities of wealth both within and among nations around the world.

## The Global Marketplace

The contemporary world is characterized by connectedness and change of a magnitude greater than anything seen earlier. For some people, the expansion of the global economy has meant new and more satisfying means of making a living. However, these opportunities are not equally available to all peoples or to all individuals within a culture. For many peoples the promise of prosperity offered by the global economy has yet to be fulfilled.

Anthropology is particularly sensitive to the complex linkages between local, regional, national, and global contexts that structure the modern world. Anthropologists today can play an important role in shaping government and global economic policies that take into account the environmental impact of different ways of making a living, the values and practices of local cultures, international plant and animal conservation efforts, and corporate- and state-driven efforts to participate in global markets. In the postindustrial, globalized society, new responses are called for, by individuals, governments, and business, as they adapt to significant changes in the production and distribution of goods. We explore some of these changes in the next chapter on economics.

# The Global and the Local: Globalization and Food Choice

In the recent past (in fact, during the childhoods of the authors of this book), much of the food on American tables was locally produced and seasonally available. Strawberries arrived in the spring and fresh sweet corn was a special treat for a few weeks in the fall. For most Americans today, that world is gone. Although prices fluctuate seasonally, almost everything we eat is available all year long. This is made possible by the globalization of agriculture. Most of the foods we eat today are produced on large farms located in rich agricultural regions thousands of miles away from the populations they serve. For example, more than half of all fruit produced in the United States comes from California, and that state together with Washington and Florida account for 80 percent of U.S. fruit production (Perez and Pollack 2008). However, our culinary net spreads far wider than the United States. In fiscal year 2007, the United States imported $70 billion worth of agricultural products. Although the largest single source of these goods was the member states of the European Union, imports from Mexico accounted for $10.3 billion and included $3.3 billion worth of fresh vegetables, $1.9 billion of fruit, and $1.6 billion of beer (USDA 2009).

The presence of so much food from distant places is one of the great triumphs of globalization. The variety and convenience available to consumers in wealthy nations is stunning. We dine on frozen Indian meals actually prepared in India and accompany them with water from Fiji and fruit from Chile. However, this global food network also extracts a high price. Although determining the carbon footprint of individual products is extremely difficult (*Economist* 2007), moving food around the world may have high environmental costs. For example, the average tomato imported into Canada has traveled almost 3000 miles. Transportation of such tomatoes involves the production of more than three times the carbon dioxide than transportation of locally grown tomatoes (Brandt 2008:26). As our dependence on imported food increases, so does our reliance on the fuel necessary to move it. This means that changes in the price of oil can result in large jumps in the price of food. Because spikes in the price of oil are usually related to economic and political instability, our dependence on globalized food means that our food supply is more vulnerable than ever to global economics and politics.

Dependence on food shipped long distances also favors the emergence of varieties of food that look pretty and are easy to ship but may have less taste and nutritional value than foods grown closer to home. Along with this comes the loss of indigenous and traditional varieties. Although estimates about the percentage of plant species that have disappeared vary, a study of 75 different types of vegetables found that 97 percent of the varieties on a U.S. Department of Agriculture list from the early 20th century are extinct today (Brandt 2008:56). The varieties that are extensively grown, along with the fertilizers and pesticides necessary to grow them, are produced by large multinational corporations such as Monsanto, ADM, Cargill, DuPont, and Bayer. These companies make huge profits but sometimes at the expense of workers. For example, according to the United Nations Environmental Programme (2004), between 1 million and 5 million people are poisoned by pesticides yearly and as many as 20,000 of these die (World Bank 2006). Poor nations account for only 25 percent of the world's pesticide use but 99 percent of the deaths from pesticide poisoning.

Buying globally means less work for local producers and hence contributes to rural poverty. It does provide jobs for agricultural workers around the world, but working conditions in such jobs are often harsh and the key beneficiaries are the corporations that organize food production and transportation.

In recent years, food alternatives that were once on the margins are becoming more mainstream. These include vegetarianism, the slow food movement (an organization devoted to counteracting fast food and encouraging traditional cuisines as well as interest in how our food choices affect the world.), community-supported and local agriculture, and small-scale organic foods. All of these are probably healthier for both individuals and the environment than large-scale globalized food production (Wilk 2006). However, thus far they affect relatively few people in wealthy nations, often cost more than alternatives, and involve the difficult task of changing culturally ingrained food habits.

## Key Questions

1. Discuss some of the cultural patterns and values that you think underlie America's food choices and the ways in which they affect your own food choices (consider prestige, nutrition, religious beliefs, working conditions, and other factors).

2. Do you believe movements in favor of local agriculture, organic foods, and slow foods are likely to have success in America? What factors might favor or retard their success?

# Summary

1. **What is the relationship between the environment and subsistence (food-getting) pattern of a society?** Different physical environments present different problems, opportunities, and limitations to human populations. The subsistence (food-getting) pattern of a society develops in response to seasonal variation in the environment and environmental variations such as drought, flood, or animal diseases. As populations have increased and more complex forms of social and economic organization have developed, humans have had increasingly intensive impacts on their environments.

2. **What are the major subsistence strategies of human populations?** The five major subsistence patterns of human populations are foraging (fishing, hunting, and gathering), pastoralism, horticulture, agriculture, and industrialism. As a whole, humankind has moved in the direction of using more complex technology, increasing its numbers, and developing more complex sociocultural systems.

3. **What is foraging? How has the Inuit foraging strategy been affected by global warming?** Foraging is reliance on food naturally available in the environment and acquired through hunting, gathering, and fishing. It was the major food-getting pattern during almost all of the time humans have been on earth. Although this way of life is rapidly disappearing, foraging is still a useful adjunct to other subsistence strategies for many societies. With the gradual decrease in Arctic ice, many Inuit have had to change the timing and focus of their traditional foraging strategy and seek alternative ways of getting food.

4. **What are the different kinds of pastoralism? How is pastoralism affected by its inclusion in state societies and the global economy?** Pastoralists rely on herd animals. Nomadic pastoralists move with their herds. Transhumant pastoralists establish permanent villages and part of the population moves with the herds. Animals alone cannot provide the all the necessary ingredients for an adequate human diet so supplementary foods such as grains are required. Therefore, pastoralists cultivate crops or develop trading relations with food cultivators. In state societies, pastoralists are often under pressure to conform to state goals that often aim at moving pastoralists into agriculture. At the same time, the global economy provides markets for animal products.

5. **What are the major values and strategies in the Maasai transhumant pastoralist society? What are some important challenges to their traditional subsistence strategy?** The Maasai subsistence strategy heavily depends on their extensive knowledge of their environment and features the flexible exploitation of multiple ecological niches. In addition to herding cattle, they trade small animals for honey, fish, grains, fruit, and vegetables. The Maasai strategy is challenged as their herding grounds give way to conservation and national parks, an important source of tourist income for Kenya.

6. **What are the major dimensions of horticulture as a subsistence strategy?** Horticulturalists rely on gardens and fields. Horticulture is typically (though not exclusively) a tropical forest adaptation and requires the cutting and burning of jungle to clear areas for cultivation. Gardens are used for several years then allowed to lie fallow for long periods to restore fertility.

7. **Describe the subsistence strategy of the Lua' of Thailand. How have Lua' swidden practices been modified by their contact with other groups?** The Lua' are swidden cultivators in the mountainous region of northern Thailand. Their major crops are cotton, corn, yams, rice, and sorghum; they also grow vegetables and keep pigs, water buffalo, cattle, and chickens. In addition to relying on their gardens, they also sell products at local markets. Thus, they are becoming more enmeshed in the local and global economies. This is increasingly typical of horticulturalists in the modern world.

8. **What are the major characteristics of the agricultural subsistence strategy?** Agriculturalists farm on stable fields using crop rotation and fertilization to maintain land fertility. Agriculture may involve the use of irrigation, animal-drawn plows, and other technology. This food-getting pattern generally supports greater population densities than all but industrial patterns. It is associated with sedentary village life and the rise of the state.

9. **How does Musha, an Egyptian village, illustrate a typical peasant economy? In what ways does the state impact on the economic and social life of this peasant community?** Peasants like those in Musha are cultivators who produce mainly for the subsistence of their households and who are part of larger political entities, such as the state. For peasants, agriculture is the main source of subsistence, but they also participate in the larger cash economy of the state, engage in wage labor, and have some occupational specialties. Peasant farmers make important decisions about their work within a larger economic and regulatory structure imposed by the state, landlords, and others to whom they may be in debt.

10. **What are the main characteristics of industrialism? How is industrialism related to the global economy?** Industrialism is a system in which mechanical and chemical processes are used for the production of goods. In industrialized societies, very small agricultural populations are able to support vast numbers of people who are not directly engaged in agriculture. Industrialism requires a large, mobile labor force. The global economy links markets into a worldwide network resulting in the movement of goods, capital, and people among widely disparate locations. Industrialism has resulted in great material prosperity for many people, but at the cost of high levels of inequality and environmental destruction.

11. **What are some of the economic and cultural factors associated with the rise of the American beef industry? What are the major characteristics of this form of production?** The American preference for beef is related to the association of meat eating with social status, and the increased use of packaged convenience meat and poultry, especially after World War II. This industrial strategy used by the beef industry is associated with a high use of immigrant labor, a difficult and dangerous production assembly line, the spoiling of local soil and water, and social change and conflict in rural communities. Propelled in part by American agribusiness and fast food chains, the taste for beef is increasingly international. Because beef production requires a high level of resources, this may have profound environmental implications.

# Key Terms

| | | |
|---|---|---|
| agriculture | industrialized agriculture | productivity |
| efficiency | nomadic pastoralism | rain forest |
| foraging (hunting and gathering) | pastoralism | sedentary |
| globalization | patrilineal | subsistence strategy |
| horticulture | peasants | swidden (slash and burn) cultivation |
| industrialism | population density | transhumant pastoralism |

# Suggested Readings

Denslow, Julie Sloan, and Christine Padoch. 1988. *People of the Tropical Rain Forest.* Berkeley: University of California Press. A beautifully illustrated, sensitive portrayal of the many peoples who inhabit the tropical rain forests in different parts of the world. The book includes essays on what we can learn from tropical forest peoples and the impact of the modern global economy on their subsistence economies and environments.

Harris, Marvin. 1998/1985. *Good to Eat: Riddles of Food and Culture.* Prospect Heights, IL: Waveland. This classic, in Harris's typically engaging style, examines the diversity of food habits and the cultural values that support them, persuasively demonstrating that what seem to be irrational dietary customs have been shaped by practical economic or political considerations.

Schlosser, Eric. 2005. *Fast Food Nation: The Dark Side of the All-American Meal.* New York: Harper Perennial. A thoroughly researched and serious book that examines the fast food process from meat to marketing and the consequences for Americans and the world. With a particular focus on McDonald's, this book tells you everything you might need to know about that authentic example of American culture: the hamburger and how you get it "your way."

Stull, Donald D., and Michael Broadway. 2004. *Slaughterhouse Blues: The Meat and Poultry Industry in North America.* Belmont, CA: Wadsworth. This model of interdisciplinary, applied social science written by a social geographer and an anthropologist highlights the ways in which the meat industries, with their diverse immigrant labor forces, are changing the face of rural America.

Specialization and the creation of markets is a critical aspect of the development of a large-scale economy. In earlier times, cheeses were made and consumed locally. Now, they are part of a network of international trade. The Amsterdam cheese market, pictured here, is an important node in that network.

**THINKING POINT:** In many noncapitalist societies, a person does certain work and receives certain benefits because of his or her membership in a family or because of kin links to others. In capitalist societies, most individuals work for impersonal firms and receive wages. Sometimes, capitalist relations of production are masked by kinship and friendship. People believe that they do certain work and receive certain pay because of their kin connections but impersonal capitalist relations lie just beneath the surface.

—[See page 160 for details.]

# {chapter 7}

# Economics

All human societies have economic systems within which goods and services are produced, distributed, and consumed. In one sense, the economic aspect of culture is simply the sum of the choices people make regarding these areas of their lives. Such choices have important ramifications. For example, choosing to become a farmer rather than an insurance broker may determine where you live, who you are likely to meet, and the sorts of behaviors you will expect in your spouse and offspring. However, such choices are not unlimited; rather, they are constrained by our cultures, traditions, and technologies. Furthermore, our environments set the boundaries within which choices about the production, distribution, and consumption of goods and services are made.

Every society must have an **economic system** in the sense that each group of people must produce, distribute, and consume. Economics deals partly with things—with the tools used to produce goods and the goods themselves. More important, it deals with the relationship of things to people and people to one another in the process of producing, distributing, and consuming goods. Anthropologists are interested in understanding the relationship between the economy and the rest of a culture. One aspect of this relationship is that culture defines or shapes the ends sought by individuals and the means of achieving those ends. Society and economy are interdependent in other ways. The way in which production is organized has consequences for the institution of the family and for the political system. For example, in southern Mali, where most people live by agriculture and where land is abundant, children can help farm when they are very young. Thus, families tend to have as many children as they possibly can. Large families can cultivate more land and therefore are generally wealthier than small families. Their leaders acquire the political power and social prestige that derives from having wealth and numerous relations. ≫

Although economists often attempt to do so, it is difficult to separate the economic system from the rest of culture. Economics is embedded in the total social process and cultural pattern. In nonindustrial and kin-based societies, for example, few groups are organized solely for the purpose of production; their economic activities are only one aspect of what they do. Production is carried out by groups such as families, larger kinship groups, or local communities. The distribution, exchange, and consumption of goods is thus embedded in relationships that have social and political purposes as well as economic ones. <<

# Economic Behavior

We define **economics** as the study of the ways in which the choices people make as individuals and as members of societies combine to determine how their society uses its scarce resources to produce and distribute goods and services. The academic discipline of economics developed in a Western market economy, and there has been much debate within anthropology over its applicability to other cultures (Isaac 1993).

The idea of scarcity is a fundamental assumption of Western microeconomic theory. Economists assume that human wants are unlimited but the means for achieving them are not. If this is correct, organizations and individuals must make decisions about the best way to apply their limited means to meet their unlimited desires. Economists assume that individuals and organizations will make such choices in the way they believe will provide them with the greatest benefit. Economists call such choices **economizing behavior.**

Some scholars have equated benefit with material well-being and profit (see Dalton 1961). Will a business firm cut down or expand its production? Will it purchase a new machine or hire more laborers? Where will it locate its plant? Will it manufacture shoes or gloves? How much will be spent on advertising its product? Such decisions are assumed to be motivated by an analysis designed to produce the greatest cash profit and are assumed to be rational—that is, based on the desire to maximize profit.

However, the notion of financial profit does not completely explain economic behavior. Consider a choice you may make this evening. After you finish reading this chapter, you may well be confronted with a series of decisions: Should you reread it for better comprehension? Should you study for another course? Call and get a pizza delivered? Play with your kids? Socialize with your friends? Take care of that project for work? Get some sleep? Of course, there are many other possibilities.

You will make your choice based on some calculation of benefit. However, that benefit is not necessarily reducible to financial profit. It is quite possible for you to believe that you would ultimately make more money if you study and get higher grades. However, your choice is set in a context in which money is unlikely to be the most important element of value; we value our friends, our children, our leisure time, and many other things as well. If you choose to socialize instead of hitting the books, your choice is rational because it is based on some calculation of your needs and goals, but it need not lead to greater profit. If we were to predict your behavior on the assumption that you will always act to increase your material well-being, our predictions would often be wrong. We would do better by asking what motivates you.

Just as you might value an evening spent with friends over an "A" in this class, members of other cultures might value family connections, cultural tradition, social prestige, leisure time, or other things over monetary profit. People everywhere make rational choices based on their needs and their guesses about the future. But culture, values, and institutions provide the framework within which these choices are made. For example, Western culture is dominated by capitalism. As a result,

Decisions these stock traders make on the floor are based almost entirely on profit and loss. However, most of the time, our decisions are motivated by other considerations as well. We may prefer relaxation and free time to financial return.

**economic system** The norms governing production, distribution, and consumption of goods and services within a society.

**economics** The study of the ways in which the choices people make combine to determine how their society uses its scarce resources to produce and distribute goods and services.

**economizing behavior** Choosing a course of action to maximize perceived benefit.

we place an extremely high value on wealth and material prosperity. For us, it seems "natural" to think that these goals are best achieved through earning money and using this to make purchases through the marketplace. Thus, we are easily (although not exclusively) motivated by money.

On the other hand, some other societies appear to be in business for their health (Sahlins 1972). For example, the Hadza live in an area of Tanzania with an abundance of animal and vegetable food. They have considerable leisure time but make no attempt to use it to increase their wealth. Though they know how to farm, they don't do it because it would require too much work (Woodburn 1968).

Leisure time is only one of the ends toward which people expend effort. They may also direct their energies toward increasing social status or respect. In Western society, prestige is primarily tied to increased consumption and display of goods and services, but this is not universal. In many societies, prestige is associated with giving goods away. Conspicuous consumers and stingy people become objects of scorn and may be shunned or accused of witchcraft (see Danfulani 1999, Offiong 1983 for examples). The notion that prestige can be gained through giving is also well established in our own society. Universities have buildings bearing the names of their most generous donors, and Bill Gates is not only the CEO of Microsoft, he is also the head of the world's largest charitable foundation.

To understand the economies of various cultures, anthropologists face two related problems. First, they must analyze the broad institutional and social contexts within which people make decisions, and second, they must determine and evaluate the factors that motivate individual decision making.

One way we can think about any given economic system is to consider a series of fundamental issues that all societies must face. Because all societies must acquire the food and other materials necessary to their lives, all must engage in production. To do so, all societies must acquire resources, such as land and water, and all must have some system through which the rights to use such resources are allocated.

However, resources in and of themselves do nothing. Rather, people must be organized in specific ways to use resources in the production of the goods and services. Thus, each society has some system of organizing their members to use the resources available to them. For example, foragers rely on the plants and animals in their environment. But, foragers never simply gather and eat these randomly. In each group, specific groups of people do specific tasks. Most often, men hunt and women gather. Thus, they are organized to produce. Additionally, people in all societies exchange and consume the products of production. Thus, each society has a system of distribution and in each there are distinct styles and patterns of consumption. In the remainder of this chapter we will explore how different societies tackle the problems of allocating resources, organizing labor, and distributing and consuming the results of production.

## Allocating Resources

The things that members of a society need to participate in the economy are called **productive resources,** and access to them is basic to every culture. People everywhere require access to land and water. Access to the knowledge that allows one to make and use tools plays an important role in all societies. There may be additional important forms of knowledge that can be controlled as well, such as the knowledge of healing, or of religious rituals. Access to knowledge plays a critical role in modern American society. This is shown by the strong relationship between university degrees and income. Universities are not the only place to get knowledge (and one gets a lot more from universities than just knowledge). However, it is clear that possession of a university degree and, hopefully the knowledge it implies, has a direct impact on individuals' economic role in society. According to the U.S. Department of Education, in 2006, Americans between the ages of 25 and 34 with bachelor's degrees earned 28 percent more than those with associate's degree and 50 percent more than those with only a high school diploma (Planty et al. 2008).

An important point of contrast between economic systems is the extent to which individuals and groups have access to productive resources. In general, differential access to resources develops as population and social complexity increase. In some societies, most people have access to the resources necessary to survive and fully participate in society. In others, access to these resources may be exclusively or disproportionately invested in particular social groups. Again, examining access to knowledge in the United States is instructive. Only 3 percent of the students at America's most selective universities come from households in the lowest 25 percent of the income scale; only 10 percent come from the bottom 50 percent (*Economist* 2005). This clearly shows that family wealth plays a critical role in determining access to knowledge and access to such knowledge plays a critical role in future wealth and social position.

Small-scale economies have a limited number of productive resources, and most everyone has access to them. Large-scale societies have a great many more resources, but access to them is limited. This can be seen by com-

**productive resources** Material goods, natural resources, or information used to create other goods or information.

In foraging societies people do not consciously raise the productivity of their land, relying instead upon the animal, plant, and insect foods naturally occurring on the land. Here, Hadza men in Tanzania harvest honey from the hollow of a baobab tree.

paring access to resources among foragers, pastoralists, horticulturalists, and agriculturalists.

## Foragers

Among foragers, weapons used in hunting animals and tools used in gathering plants as well as the knowledge to make and use these are productive resources. The technology is simple, and tools are made by hand. People take great care to ensure that they have access to the tools necessary for their individual survival. Among the Hadza of Tanzania, men spend much time gambling. However, a man's bow, bird arrows, and leather bag are never shared or gambled, because these items are essential to survival (Woodburn 1998).

Besides knowledge and tools, land and water are the most critical resources for foragers, and many forms of land tenure are found among them. The requirements of a foraging lifestyle generally mean that a group of people must spread out over a large area of land. Hunting grounds are not exclusively owned because flexible boundaries have an adaptive value: ranges can be adjusted as the availability of resources changes in a particular area.

The abundance and predictability of resources also affect territorial boundaries. Where resources are scarce and large areas are needed to support the population, territorial boundaries are not defended. Where resources are more abundant and people move less, groups may be more inclined to defend their territory (Cashdan 1989:42).

The Ju/'hoansi of the Kalahari were typical foragers. Although today most Ju/'hoansi are settled, in earlier times their camps were located near water holes, and the area used by a local group was measured by one day's round-trip walk, about 12 miles. Each camp had a core

area best conceived of as a circle with the water hole at the center and a radius of about 6 miles. Points beyond this were rarely used. Although camps were moved five or six times a year, they were not moved far. Sometimes the move was only a few hundred yards; the farthest move was about 10 or 12 miles (R. Lee 1968). Ju/'hoansi territories were associated with long-standing residents who were spoken of as owners. Although they did not have exclusive rights to the land, their permission had to be asked when others wished to use the land's resources. Such permission was rarely refused, although visitors might be made to feel unwelcome (Cashdan 1989:41).

Hunters and gatherers require freedom of movement not only as a condition of success in their search for food but also as a way of dealing with social conflict. Hunting bands are kept small in order to exploit the environment successfully. In such small groups, conflict must be kept to a minimum. When arguments break out, individuals can move to other groups without fear that they are cutting themselves off from access to vital resources. If land were individually or even communally defended against outsiders, the freedom of movement in hunting societies would be severely limited.

## Pastoralists

Among pastoralists, the most critical resources are livestock and land. Access to grassland and water is gained through membership in kin groups. Within pastoralist camps, all members share equal access to pastures. It is this right of access, rather than ownership, that is important.

Animals require a substantial investment in labor. They must be tended and fed. In some cases corals or other structures must be built to house them. When they are ill, they must be cared for. If they are neglected, they do not often survive. Thus, although all members of a pastoral community have access to pasturage, animals themselves are owned by individual families.

In pastoralist societies, animals are kept as wealth in their own right. The prosperity and often the status of a family are determined by the number of animals they own. One result of this is animals are killed only infrequently, often as part of religious celebrations. Instead, pastoralists live off of animal products such as milk and blood. These products as well as the animals themselves may be traded for grain or other goods.

In most places, pastoral tribes are migratory. In mountainous and temperate regions, they spend the summers at high altitude and the winters in lower, warmer pasturage. In highly seasonal tropical climates, they move from dry season pastures to rainy season pastures.

The yearly migrations of pastoral people often traverse the lands of agricultural people. In these cases, accesses to pasturage and migration routes are determined through negotiation with local authorities. Contemporary pastoralists often establish access to land by contracts with the landowners of villages through which the pastoralists move. These contracts, which must be renewed every year, specify the rent for the pasture, the borders of the area, and the date by which the area must be vacated. However, pastoralism and agriculture are very different lifestyles and conflict between pastoralists and sedentary villagers is not uncommon.

The yak-herding Drokba of northwestern Tibet present an interesting historical example of pastoralism. The Drokba were under the control of large Buddhist monasteries that owned all the grassland in the area. Families were granted rights to use pastures in return for tax payments. Allocation of pastureland was reviewed every third year and altered to fit family herd size and composition. The system worked well because the land could be managed to even out grazing (Barfield 1993:188).

© Dorinne Jacobson

## Horticulturalists

In addition to land, tools, and knowledge, horticulturalists often require storage facilities. In such societies, land tends to be communally owned by an extended kin group, although rights to use a piece of land may be given to households or even individuals. For example, among the Ibo, swidden farmers in Nigeria, no individual owns land or has permanent rights to it. Instead, land is vested in kinship groups and allocated to individuals by leaders of these groups (Acheson 1989). But even the group that has rights to use the land may not dispose of it at will; land is "inalienable" and may not be sold. With this type of land ownership, few people are deprived of access to basic resources because almost every person belongs to a land-holding group within the society.

In societies based on horticulture, the work involved in clearing, cultivating, and maintaining the land is a large investment and is more important than exclusive title to the land. The rights to cleared and productive land and to the products of that land are vested in those who work it, most often the domestic group or household. Because the user of the land may die while the land is still productive, some system of inheritance of use rights is usually provided for.

Among the Lacandon Maya in the highlands of Chiapas in Mexico, for example, individuals may farm any unused piece of land. However, clearing virgin land is very difficult, so individuals retain rights to land they have cleared and are likely to reuse, even if it is not currently in production. People who migrate from the area may lose rights to land they have cleared, but their family retains ownership of any fruit trees that have been planted on it. Should a man die after investing time and labor in clearing and planting land, his wife and children retain rights to use the land (McGee 1990).

Where population densities are low or large areas of land are available for cultivation, rights to land use are very loosely held. For example, among the Machiguenga of Peru, a group with extensive lands, there is little sense of exclusive territory (Johnson 1989:58). But when specific geographical conditions limit the amount of land available, or when population pressures increase, land shortages do occur, as among the Enga in the Papua New Guinea highlands. There, the problem is dealt with primarily by warfare. Most Enga warfare is aimed at driving smaller, weaker groups off their land and annexing it (Johnson 1989:62).

## Agriculturalists (Intensive Cultivation)

In more politically and technologically complex societies, agriculture comes to dominate production. In these societies, productive resources take many forms, including complex tools and the technological knowledge required to make them. Ownership of these critical resources may be limited to a small group whose members thereby gain power over others and control their labor.

In some societies, productive resources are continually reinvested in order to generate profit for their owners beyond their subsistence needs. Such resources are referred to as **capital.** Although the use of capital occurs in many different sorts of societies (Berdan 1989), it becomes the principal form of economic organization in capitalist societies (discussed later in this chapter).

**capital** Productive resources that are used with the primary goal of increasing their owner's financial wealth.

In complex societies, enormous amounts of labor often are invested in land. This results in high levels of production, and land ownership becomes an important source of wealth and power. This picture shows rice paddies in Yunnan, China.

© Jialiang Gao www.peace-on-earth.org

Under conditions of intensive cultivation, the material and labor investment in land becomes substantial. However, large quantities of food are generated. This food supports not only those who work the land but a large nonagricultural population as well. In many cases, cities and towns develop. Under these circumstances, land becomes a valuable (and limited) resource and individual ownership or control of the land becomes common.

Individual land ownership may grow out of population pressures that produce land scarcity and lead to intensified methods of agriculture. Under these conditions, communal control of land creates conflict as people begin to grumble about not receiving their fair share. Those who have improved the land are unwilling to see the investment of their labor revert to a kin-based pool. This may be particularly true in the case of cash crops such as coffee, which require long-term care and yield harvests over many years. Individuals thus become tied to particular plots of land. In a study of land use and rights in the New Guinea highlands, Brown and Podelefsky (1976) found that individual ownership of land was correlated with high population density and intensive cultivation.

Private or family ownership of rigidly defined fields does not necessarily mean that landowners work their fields. Instead, fields are usually rented to laborers whose efforts support both themselves and the landowners. For example, a study of a rural village in Bangladesh showed that 48 percent of families were functionally landless. Their members had to rent land from large landowners or work for others (Michael Harris 1991:151–155). Under conditions such as these, a peasantry emerges. Peasants are agriculturalists who are integrated into large state-level societies (see Chapter 6). Part of what peasants produce is taken by a ruling class in the form of rents and taxes. In some cases, peasants may hold land by usufruct right. In this case, an individual or family has the right to use a piece of land and, in most cases, may pass this right to descendants, although the land cannot be sold or traded. However, in most places the peasants' access to land is contingent on payment of rents. Such peasants can be dispossessed if they fail to pay rent or if the landowner finds a more profitable use for their land.

In societies with peasantries, landowners rather than cultivators are able to claim most of the surplus. Landowners enjoy higher levels of consumption and standards of living based on rents and services they receive from the peasants. Landowners use these surpluses to command the services of craft workers, servants, and sometimes armed forces. Agriculture therefore tends to be associated with a political organization characterized by a ruling landowning class and with occupational specialization.

Most current-day societies rely on agriculture but, as we saw in the previous chapter, in many of them only a miniscule percentage of the population are involved in farming. Therefore, access to productive land is not important for most people. In wealthy nations, most people earn their livelihood by working for wages for businesses and other organizations that provide goods and services. These are usually organized as capitalist enterprises.

## Organizing Labor

In small-scale preindustrial and peasant economies, the household or some extended kin group is the basic unit of production and of consumption (B. White 1980). The **household** is an economic unit—a group of people united by kinship or other links who share a residence and organize production, consumption, and distribution of goods among themselves. A household is different from a family because it may include lodgers, servants, and others who are not counted as family members. Household members use most of the goods they produce themselves.

**household** A group of people united by kinship or other links who share a residence and organize production, consumption, and distribution among themselves.

Sex-role specialization in craft activities varies cross-culturally. In Ghana, men do the weaving, but in the Navajo nation, weaving is a woman's task.

Households and kin groups do seek financial gain but this is not their primary purpose. Their goals are often social or religious rather than monetary. Labor is not a commodity bought and sold in the market; rather, it is an important aspect of membership in a social group. The labor that people both perform and receive situates them with respect to others in their family and gives them both a sense of identity and meaning.

The gendered division of labor is a good example of the relationship between work and identity. In all human societies, some tasks are considered appropriate for women and others appropriate for men. At some level, the sexual division of labor is biological because only women can bear and nurse children. Thus, caring for infants is almost always primarily a female role and usually central to female identity (see Nielsen 1990:147 168). Beyond this, there are few jobs that are universally identified as male or female work. However, in almost all societies some sorts of work are considered proper only for men and others proper only for women. And these jobs are important elements of male or female identity. For example, in Aztec Mexico weaving was basic to female identity. Newborn girls were presented with tools for weaving, and weaving equipment was placed with women when they died (Brumfiel 1991, 2006:866). On the other hand, in most West African societies, weaving is considered a male task, part of male identity.

In Western society, work also has very important social implications. Of course people work to put food on their table and a roof over their head. But, as anthropologist Pamela Crespin notes, in our society an individual's self-image and social status is bound up with work. Job-

lessness or the inability to earn a living wage diminishes an adult's identity and status (2005:20). This is a particularly important issue in a nation such as the United States, where, in May 2009, the government reported that 14.5 million people, 9.4 percent of the workforce, were unemployed (Bureau of Labor Statistics 2009).

Economic organization by household can be contrasted with organization by firm. A **firm** is an institution composed of kin and/or non-kin that is organized primarily for financial gain. Individuals are usually tied to firms through the sale of their labor for wages. Labor is thus a commodity, bought and sold on the market. A firm does not produce goods for the use of its members; the items it produces are sold for profit.

In economies where households are the units of production, there can be little economic growth. Households cannot easily expand or contract as the economy fluctuates. They cannot easily fire their members or acquire new ones. Thus, large-scale production and distribution systems tend not to develop under such conditions. Firms, on the other hand, are geared toward economic growth. Their decision making is motivated primarily by financial gain. Their goal is to find the mix of capital and labor that will most increase the firm's financial value to its owners. This usually means that firms wish to increase their size indefinitely.

---

**firm** An institution composed of kin and/or non-kin that is organized primarily for financial gain.

Traditionally, Indian society is organized into occupational castes and these are arranged hierarchically. Here, Dhobi, members of the washerman caste, ply their trade in Mumbai. The dhobi's low rank in the caste hierarchy is linked to their handling of materials contaminated by unclean matter.

ture. Grains are hard, durable, and storable. Landlords and rulers who are able to control them have access to wealth and power in new and important ways and can support many people. Occupational specialization spreads through society as individuals are able to exchange their services or the products they produce for food and wealth. Specialists are likely to include soldiers, government officials, and members of the priesthood as well as artisans, craftsmen, and merchants.

Traditional areas of contemporary India provide an excellent example of occupational specialization. There, only people belonging to particular hereditary kinship groups can perform certain services or produce certain kinds of goods. Literally thousands of specialized activities—washing clothes, drumming at festivals, presiding over religious ceremonies, making pots, painting pictures—are traditionally performed by specific named hereditary groups called castes (see Chapter 12, "Stratification," page 282).

Much of the world's population today lives in industrial or postindustrial societies and almost everyone is a specialist of one kind or another. A quick glance at the Yellow Pages of the phone book of a major American city gives a good indication of the degree of specialization in American society. Each entry represents at least one specialty.

Industrialism and the high degree of specialization it requires have produced unprecedented material wealth. There is no doubt that more people today have more access to more goods and services than ever before in the history of humanity. However, specialization can also take a large physical and emotional toll on members of a society. Since the beginnings of the Industrial Age, many factory jobs involved repetitious and mind-numbing labor often performed under hazardous conditions. In the American automobile plants of the early 20th century, for example, almost all skilled tasks were mechanized. Workers simply inserted pieces into machines, turned a switch, and waited until the machine completed its task. The machinery determined the pace of work and the tasks performed. In the 1920s one worker summed it up simply, saying: "The machine is my boss" (in Meyer, 2004).

Factory labor often led to new notions of identity. For example, in the 19th century, many American workers associated masculinity with skilled labor, independence, and decision-making power at work. On the assembly lines in early 20th century America, labor was boring and monotonous and workers had little decision-making ability. Companies such as Ford Motors, through public speeches, company policies, and employment

Households and firms are not mutually exclusive. In fact, economists often model society in terms of firms and households. Firms, even very large ones, may be controlled by a single family or a small group of families. Further, firms often use the vocabulary of family and team to promote their goals. As Casey (1999:156) notes, firms from supermarket chains to hospitals and airlines promote themselves as communities, inviting employees and customers to "come join our family." Thus economic relationships between employers and employee or firm and customer are partially disguised by ideas about social relationships within a family or household.

## Specialization in Complex Societies

Among hunter-gatherers and most horticulturalists, all adult men and women are actively engaged in the quest for food. Technologies are simple and do not require skills beyond those that can be learned through informal socialization. The few specialists (for example, religious practitioners) are usually also engaged in food and tool production. The characteristic division of labor is not by job but by age and sex.

The division of labor in society becomes more specialized and complex as the population increases and agricultural production intensifies. This is particularly the case where a society is dependent on grain agricul-

practices sought to redefine masculinity, associating it with "working hard—in the company of other men, on a useful product, and being paid well for it" (Lewchuk 1993:852) rather than skill and independence.

# Distribution: Systems of Exchange and Consumption

In all societies, goods and services are exchanged. In fact, some anthropologists have long held that the exchange of goods is one of the fundamental bases of culture. The great French anthropologist Marcel Mauss (1924/1990) theorized that societies were held together by patterns of giving and receiving. He pointed out that because gifts invariably must be repaid, we are obligated to each other through exchange. And in many situations, as with the potlatch and the Kula ring described later in the chapter, it is better to give than to receive.

There are three main patterns of exchange: reciprocity, redistribution, and the market. Although more than one kind of exchange system exists in most societies, each system is predominantly associated with a certain kind of political and social organization (Polyani 1944). Let us look first at reciprocity.

## Reciprocity

The mutual give-and-take of goods and services among people of similar status is known as **reciprocity.** Three types of reciprocity can be distinguished from one another by the degree of social distance between the exchanging partners (Sahlins 1972).

**Generalized Reciprocity** Generalized reciprocity is usually carried out among close kin and is common in foraging bands. In this case, reciprocity carries a high moral obligation. **Generalized reciprocity** involves a distribution of goods in which no overt account is kept of what is given and no immediate or specific return is expected. Such transactions are ideally altruistic—that is, without any thought of economic or other self-interest. In Western society, we are familiar with generalized reciprocity as it exists between parents and children. Parents constantly give things and provide services to their children out of love or a sense of responsibility. What would we think of a parent who kept an account of what a child "cost" and then expected the child to repay this amount? What parents usually expect is some gratitude, love, respect, and the child's happiness.

Generalized reciprocity involving food is an important social mechanism among foraging peoples. In these societies, a hunter or group of hunters distributes meat among the kin group or camp. Each person or family gets either an equal share or a share dependent on its kinship relationship to the hunter. Robert Dentan (1979:48) describes this system among the Semai of Malaysia:

> After several days of fruitless hunting, a Semai man kills a large pig. He lugs it back to the settlement. Everyone gathers around. Two other men meticulously divide the pig into portions sufficient to feed two adults each (children are not supposed to eat pork). As nearly as possible, each portion contains exactly the same amount of meat, fat, liver, and innards as every other portion. The adult men take the leaf-wrapped portions home to redistribute them among the members of the house group.

Similar systems are used by the Ju/'hoansi of the Kalahari and the Inuit (see Figure 7.1). A North American might wonder, What does the hunter get out of it? Aren't some people always in the position of providing and others always receiving? Part of the answer is simply practical. Some of the animals hunted are very large and a single family would most likely be unable to consume or preserve all the meat before it rots. However, hunters have several other motivations for sharing. Hunters gain satisfaction from accomplishing a highly skilled and difficult task (Woodburn 1998). However, they receive other rewards as well. Although not all people in foraging societies give and receive equally, all are obligated to both give and receive. Gifted hunters may give more than they receive, but the gifts they do receive may be critical for their survival. Further, in some cases hunters derive a degree of status from the process of food distribution. For example, among the Pacaa Nova, a horticultural group in Brazil, distributing meat gives a man prestige and an opportunity to display the culture's most valued trait, generosity. At the same time, it builds his credit for future reciprocity (von Graeve 1989:66). In small societies, where the good opinion of others is necessary for survival, the desire not to be thought stingy is a strong motivation to share and to do one's share.

**Balanced Reciprocity** Balanced reciprocity involves a clear obligation to return, within a specified time limit, goods of nearly equal value to those given. **Balanced reciprocity** is often the dominant form of exchange among nonindustrialized peoples without market economies. However, it occurs among individuals and groups characterized by production strategies from pastoralism to industrialism. The goal of balanced reciprocity is not to

---

**reciprocity** A mutual give and take among people of equal status.

**generalized reciprocity** Giving and receiving goods with no immediate or specific return expected.

**balanced reciprocity** The giving and receiving of goods of nearly equal value with a clear obligation of a return gift within a specified time limit.

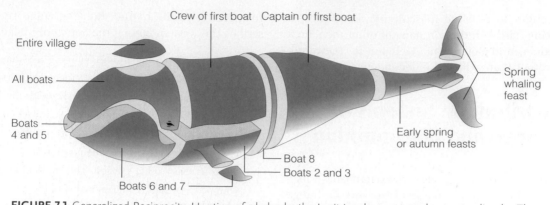

Entire village

All boats

Boats
4 and 5

Boats 6 and 7

Boats 2 and 3

Boat 8

Crew of first boat

Captain of first boat

Spring
whaling
feast

Early spring
or autumn feasts

**FIGURE 7.1** Generalized Reciprocity. Hunting of whales by the Inuit involves 10 to 15 boats standing by. The first eight boats to reach and harpoon the whale receive stipulated portions of the meat. The captain of each boat gets his traditional part of the body, and he shares his meat with his crew. The captain of the first boat gives the shaman a narrow strip cut from the belly between the eighth boat's strip and the genitals. The top of the head is cut up and eaten at once by everyone in the village. Portions of the tail are saved for feasting in the spring and autumn. *Source:* Carleton S. Coon, *The Hunting Peoples* (Boston: Little, Brown, 1971, pp. 124–125). By permission of the estate of Carleton S. Coon.

gain advantage over the gifting partner by giving the least valuable gift possible and trying to receive the most valuable return gift. Rather, partners in balanced reciprocity hope to gain access to valued goods and services while at the same time strengthening social relationships between giver and receiver.

The social obligation to give, accept, and return is at the heart of balanced reciprocity. A refusal to receive or a failure to reciprocate a gift is taken as a withdrawal from a social relationship. A gift that is accepted puts the receiver under an obligation to the giver, and if the social relationship is to continue, a return gift must be given. Sometimes, a return gift may be given immediately. In some marriages, friendship compacts, and peace agreements, people may give each other exactly the same types and quantities of goods (Sahlins 1972:194). For example, 100 yams may be exchanged for 100 yams. More often, the payoff is not immediate. In fact, sometimes an attempt to reciprocate the gift immediately is an indication of unwillingness to be obligated and shows that a trusting social relationship is neither present nor desired (Mauss 1924/1990).

In the United States, we participate in balanced reciprocity when we give gifts at weddings or birthdays, exchange invitations, or buy a round of drinks for friends. The economic aspect of these exchanges is repressed; we say it is the spirit of the gift and the social relationship between the givers that is important. However, we also know that accepting a gift involves the obligation to return a gift of approximately the same value. The individual who fails to return the gift, or returns a gift that is

disproportionately large or small, is unlikely to remain our friend for very long.

Balanced reciprocity is most typical of trading relations among nonindustrialized peoples without market economies. Such trade is frequently carried out over long distances and between different tribes or villages. It is often in the hands of trading partners: men or women who have a long-standing and personalized relationship with each other. Trading partners know each other's personalities, histories, and other aspects of their social lives. Plattner (1989a) notes that the greater the risk of economic loss, betrayal of confidence, or unfair dealing the more important such personalized relations are.

**The Kula Ring** Bronislaw Malinowski's (1984/1922) analysis of the **Kula ring** is one of the most famous anthropological studies of reciprocal trading. The Kula is an extensive system of intertribal trade among a ring of islands off New Guinea (today part of the nation of Papua New Guinea; see Figure 7.2). Among these are the Trobriand Islands where Malinowski did his fieldwork.

Although many kinds of goods are actually traded, Malinowski focused his study on two goods: *mwali* and *soulava*. *Soulava* are long necklaces of red shell, and are always traded in a clockwise direction. *Mwali,* bracelets of white shell, are always traded in the opposite direction. Malinowski wrote that the Trobrianders talked about and thought about the Kula trade in terms of these valuables.

On most islands, all men participate in the Kula and some women are allowed to Kula as well (Macintyre 1983; Scoditti and Leach 1983; Weiner 1976). On the Trobriands, however, only high-ranking men can take part. The exchange of *mwali* and *soulava* is carried out between specific individuals and such partnerships are lifelong affairs, their details fixed by tradition. Although

**Kula ring** A pattern of exchange among trading partners in the South Pacific islands.

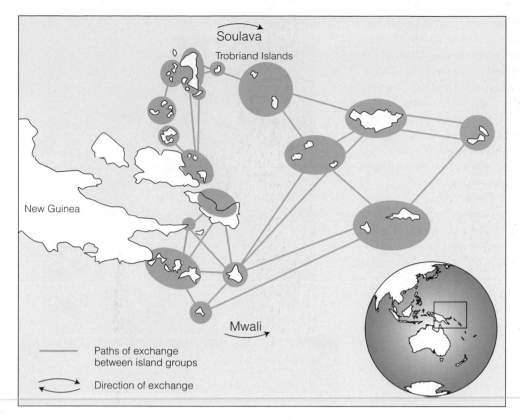

**FIGURE 7.2** The Kula trade is an example of reciprocity. Necklaces *(soulava)* and armbands *(mwali)* are traded among these islands off the coast of Papua New Guinea. Soulava move clockwise while mwali move counterclockwise.

Soulava

Trobriand Islands

New Guinea

Mwali

— Paths of exchange between island groups

⟲ Direction of exchange

Kula items can be permanently owned and may be taken out of circulation (Weiner 1976), people generally hold them for a while and then pass them on.

On one level, the Kula is simply an exchange of goods. However, Malinowski demonstrated that the trade is infused with a great many cultural norms and values related to Trobriand life. It has complex cultural, social, and psychological meanings for its participants. Kinship and political structure, magic, prestige, economy, technology, myth, ritual, feasting, and especially friendship and alliance all come together in the Kula.

Other authors (Damon 1983; Fortune 1932; Munn 1983) emphasize that although *mwali* and *soulava* are the most prestigious items traded, many utilitarian items change hands as well. Canoes, axe blades, pottery, pigs, and other items are exchanged along with armbands and necklaces as part of the Kula. These objects are often unavailable in the district in which they are given. The Kula, like other ritual trading partnership and feasts, allows groups to specialize in different aspects of production. This leads to an increase in both the amount of food and the quantity and quality of craft production within the region (Spielmann 2002).

In addition to promoting economic intensification, both the Kula trade itself and the preparations for it reinforce ties among participants and help ensure that relations among trading partners are relatively friendly. This is important because there is no formal government incorporating the different groups that take active roles in the Kula.

Thus, the system of balanced reciprocity found in the Kula trade contributes to the integration of Trobriand society as well as the maintenance of economic and social relations among all its participants.

**Negative Reciprocity** Negative reciprocity is the unsociable extreme in exchange. **Negative reciprocity** happens when trade is conducted for the purpose of material advantage and is based on the desire to get something for nothing (gambling, theft, cheating) or to get the better of a bargain (haggling). Negative reciprocity is characteristic of both impersonal and unfriendly transactions.

Tribal and peasant societies often distinguish between the insider, whom it is morally wrong to cheat, and the outsider, from whom every advantage may be gained. Anthropologist Clyde Kluckhohn, who studied the Navajo in the 1940s and 1950s, reported that their rules for interaction vary with the situation; to deceive when trading with outsiders is a morally accepted practice. Even witchcraft techniques are considered permissible in trading with members of foreign tribes (1959).

Another good example of negative reciprocity is the historic relationship between traditional dynastic China and the nomadic empires of Mongolia. For more than a thousand years, the nomadic tribes of Mongolia organized

**negative reciprocity** Exchange conducted for the purpose of material advantage and the desire to get something for nothing.

into empires to manage their relationship with China and gain access to its vast resources. The ability of Mongol empires to benefit their constituent tribes was based on their capacity to extract wealth and resources from China. They did this by following a policy of violent raiding and forcing the Chinese government to make tribute payments. Because the nomads were highly mobile, war against them was prohibitively expensive, and the Chinese were repeatedly forced to buy peace from the nomads. The threat of violence lay under the surface of all interactions between the two groups (Barfield 1993:150–155).

Negative reciprocity may be characteristic of certain types of transactions in market economies as well. The e-mail scam artist offering to deposit millions in your bank account, if you will only provide your account number and other personal information, is engaged in negative reciprocity as is the Wall Street manager who offers high returns on investment but who actually steals your money. The issue of honesty in market transactions is further explored later in the chapter within the "Market Exchange" section.

## Redistribution

In **redistribution,** goods are collected from or contributed by members of a group and then given out to the group in a new pattern. Redistribution thus involves a social center to which goods are brought and from which they are distributed. Redistribution occurs in many different contexts. In household food sharing, pooled resources are reallocated among family members. In state societies, redistribution is achieved through taxation.

Redistribution can be especially important in horticultural societies where political organization includes bigmen, self-made leaders who gain power and authority through personal achievement. Such individuals collect goods and food from their supporters. Often these items are redistributed back in communal feasts that the bigman sponsors to sustain his political power and raise his prestige. Redistribution also occurred in some chiefdoms. In these cases, however, a distinct hierarchy was involved. Chiefs collected goods and staple foods from many communities to support their households and attendants as well as finance large public feasts that helped solidify their power (Earle 1987) (see also Chapter 11, page 247).

**The Potlatch** A good example of redistribution is **potlatch** feasting among Native American groups of the Pacific Northwest including the Kwakiutl and Tlingit is. In these

Potlatches are competitive feasts held among Native Americans of the Northwest Pacific Coast. Here Tlingit Chiefs at a potlatch pose for a photo in 1904 in Sitka, Alaska.

Alaska State Library Elbridge W. Merrill Photograph Collection No. P57-021

groups, potlatches were held to honor and to validate the rank of chiefs and other notables, usually in connection with births, deaths, and marriages (Rosman and Rubel 1971). A leader holding a potlatch called on his followers to supply food and other goods to be consumed and distributed during a feast to which he invited group members and rivals. The number of guests present and the amount of goods given away or destroyed revealed the wealth and prestige of the host chief. At a potlatch, the host publicly traced his line of descent and claimed the right to certain titles and privileges. Each of these claims was accompanied by the giving away, and sometimes the destruction, of large quantities of food as well as goods such as blankets and carved wooden boxes. As these were given or destroyed, the individual and his supporters boasted of their wealth and power. In the early 20th century, Franz Boas collected speeches given at potlatches, such as:

> I am Yaqatlentlis. . . . I am Great Inviter. . . . Therefore I feel like laughing at what the lower chiefs say, for they try in vain to down me by talking against my name. Who approaches what was done by my ancestors, the chiefs? Therefore I am known by all the tribes over all the world. Only the chief my ancestor gave away property in a great feast, and all the rest can only try to imitate me. . . . (in Benedict 1934:191).

The feasting and gifts given at a potlatch demonstrated the host's right to the titles and rights he claimed

**redistribution** Exchange in which goods are collected then distributed to members of a group.

**potlatch** A form of redistribution involving competitive feasting practiced among Northwest Coast Native Americans.

and created prestige for him and his followers. Guests either acknowledged the host's claims or refuted them by staging an even larger potlatch. Thus potlatching involved friendship but also competition and rivalry.

From an economic perspective, the drive for prestige engendered by the potlatch encouraged people to produce more than they would otherwise. This increased the amount of work they did but also the amount of food and goods they produced and consumed. Because this wealth was given to people who traveled substantial distances to come to a potlatch, it was distributed to a fairly large population and ecological area.

In the late 19th and early 20th centuries, Canadian government authorities saw the potlatch as a waste of resources and evidence of native irrationality. They believed that investment was the key to economic success and, to them, the potlatch focus on consumption and destruction of goods was both disturbing and wasteful. As a result, potlatching was outlawed between 1884 and 1951 (Bracken 1997). Since then, the potlatch has been revived but primarily as a symbol of tribal identity rather than a major element in tribal economy. Simeone (1995) and Stearns (1975), for example, report that the Tanacross and Haida people consider the potlatch a central symbol of cooperation and respect that separates native from non-native peoples.

Although the term "potlatch" refers specifically to the feasting of Northwest Coast people, Rosman and Rubel (1971:xii) report that rivalrous, competitive feasting is found among many peoples. It is common, for example, throughout the Pacific Islands. We may even see some elements of it in our own society. There may be competition within families or with communities to throw the largest and most elaborate holiday parties, weddings, or coming-of-age celebrations (such as confirmation, bar or bat mitzvah, or quinceañera). In all of these cases, the prestige that accrues to the people who give the party is a critical factor. This reminds us that there is much more to giving a gift than simply trying to determine what another person desires.

**Leveling Mechanisms** Redistribution may either increase or decrease the inequality of wealth within a society. **Leveling mechanisms** are practices, values, or forms of social organization that result in evening out the distribution of wealth.

Leveling mechanisms force accumulated resources or capital to be used in ways that reduce economic differ-

© D. Donne Bryant

**Cargo Leaders in Tenejapa, Mexico. These individuals have taken offices that require them to provide food, alcohol, and other goods during religious celebrations throughout the year.**

ences. They ensure that social goals are considered along with economic ones. Leveling mechanisms take many different forms. For example, if an economy is based around redistribution, and generosity is the basis of prestige, those who desire power and prestige will distribute as much wealth as they receive. We generally associate power and prestige with the accumulation of material wealth. However, in societies based around redistribution, the powerful give much of what they have in exchange for prestige. The potlatch described earlier is a good example of this. The Moka, a type of large feast in Highland Papua New Guinea, is another. There, men who wish to gain prestige prepare for many years for these events, accumulating wealth including pigs, shells, cassowary, and in the modern world, money and manufactured goods. At the feast, all of this wealth is given away, distributed to those who attend.

Manning Nash (1967) describes a number of leveling mechanisms that operate in the village of Amatenango, in the Chiapas district of Mexico. One is the organization of production by households. As mentioned earlier, economic expansion and accumulation of wealth are limited where households, rather than business firms, are the productive units. A second factor in Amatenango is inheritance: all a man's children share equally in his estate. This makes it difficult for large estates to persist over

---

**leveling mechanism** A practice, value, or form of social organization that evens out wealth within a society.

generations. Accusations of witchcraft are a third leveling mechanism. Should anyone in Amatenango manage to accumulate more than his or her neighbors, members of other families are likely to accuse him or her of witchcraft. A man who is thought to be a witch is likely to be killed. Witchcraft accusations are most often leveled at those who are rich but not generous.

Finally, Amatenango and many other villages have cargo systems. In a **cargo system,** every year a number of different cargos, or religious offices, must be assumed by men in the village. Assuming such a cargo is an expensive proposition. The officeholder cannot work full time, and the obligations of the cargo involve substantial purchases and donations, which take up some of a family's extra resources. A man must serve in 12 such cargos before he can retire from public life, so the cost continues throughout adulthood. In addition to these 12 offices, there is the *alferez,* a ritual position filled by a younger man. One of the requirements of this office is sponsoring a community feast, which involves paying for the food and liquor and renting costumes. Men are selected for the cargos and the office of *alferez* by their ability to pay. Thus, the cargo system is a way of forcing the most prosperous households of the village to redistribute some of their wealth.

Community obligations such as a system of expensive religious offices may help to limit the economic gap between the relatively rich and the poor, but they do not eliminate it. In fact, they may help to preserve it. Men who take cargos gain in prestige, differentiating themselves from the poor of the village. Increased prestige often leads to increased wealth. Cancian (1989) showed that in Zinacantan, which has a system of cargos or religious offices similar to that of Amatenango, men who took on cargos remained rich throughout their lives, whereas poor families incapable of filling such offices remained poor. Thus, although it does redistribute some of the wealth in the community, the cargo system in Mexican villages may serve to reinforce economic differences among families rather than equalize them (Cancian 1989:147).

## Market Exchange

Today, **market exchange** is the principal distribution mechanism in most of the world's societies. Goods and services are bought and sold at a money price determined, at least in theory, by impersonal market forces. Unlike reciprocity and redistribution in which the social and political roles of those who exchange are important, in principle a market exchange is impersonal and occurs without regard to the social position of the participants.

The market involves a series of cultural and moral assumptions. For an impersonal market to run smoothly, most participants must believe that they will usually be treated fairly by people they do not know. People who take advantage of anonymity to enrich themselves at others' expense spoil the market and must be punished.

Of course, the ideal of fair and impersonal exchange is just that, an ideal. Real markets are full of conflicts, inequities, and outright cheats. In our own society there are clearly areas of commerce where people anticipate a certain amount of deceit. For example, merchants of used goods, particularly cars and machinery, often have reputations for shady practice. The continued importance of social connections among market participants is well illustrated by electronic marketplaces such as Ebay where buyers and sellers come close to true anonymity. In these cases, a sophisticated system of ratings simulates social connections and knowledge. This gives trading partners a degree of certainty that the terms of trade will be fair. But Ebay participants know that the fewer and worse the ratings of their trading partners, the greater the risk for a hostile exchange. The phrase *caveat emptor,* or "let the buyer beware," neatly captures the notion that the rules of even trade are not always in force.

In principle, the primary factors that set prices and wages in a market are related to supply and demand; also, individuals participate freely in a market, choosing what they buy and sell. However, there are many cases in which these principles do not pertain. In some cases, wealthy and powerful individuals, organizations, and in-

The ideal market is fair and impersonal but the phrase "buyer beware" captures the notion that the rules of fair and even trade are not always in force. Here, Danny DeVito plays a dishonest used car dealer in the 1996 film *Matilda*.

**cargo system** A ritual system common in Central and South America in which wealthy people are required to hold a series of costly ceremonial offices.

**market exchange** An economic system in which goods and services are bought and sold at a money price determined primarily by the forces of supply and demand.

dustries fix prices or wages, forcing people into wage labor or the market at disadvantageous terms. In other cases, cultural ideas about the proper or "just price" of a good or service are more important than supply and demand. Sometimes, governments control or influence the prices of commodities such as grain, setting them either high (to encourage farmers) or low (to feed often rebellious city dwellers cheaply).

Although markets are present in most societies, the goods and services traded in them vary greatly. As we have seen, in many societies people gain access to land, labor, and some goods through ties of kinship or obligations of reciprocity and redistribution. In such places, markets, if they exist at all, are limited to a small number of goods. In theory, in a society dominated by the market everything may be bought and sold. In practice, however, all societies limit what may be purchased legally. We live in a market-dominated society, but for moral, social, and political reasons, governments limit trade in certain goods and regulate trade in others. For example, there are restrictions on the sale of drugs, guns, children, and college degrees.

# Capitalism

In the past 300 years, capitalism has become the world's predominant economic system. Capitalism expanded from northern Europe, North America, and Japan, and has transformed economies worldwide, connecting them in a complex integrated international economy (Wallerstein 1995). In Chapter 15 we describe this historic process, and in Chapter 16 we examine and analyze the problems and promises of the global economy. Here we focus on describing capitalism and pointing out some of its most salient features.

Capitalist economies are based on the principle that consumption must constantly be expanded and that material standards of living must always go up. This pattern contrasts with tribal economies, which put various limits on consumption and thus are able to make lighter demands on their environments.

In noncapitalist societies, most people produce goods to consume them, to trade them for other goods, or to pay rents and taxes. In capitalist societies, firms produce goods as a means to create wealth. For example, General Motors is not really in business to make cars. General Motors is in business to increase the wealth of its shareholders. Manufacturing automobiles is one (but only one) of the ways it tries to achieve that end. GM is also heavily involved in banking and was historically involved in aviation, military contracting, and the production of consumer products such as refrigerators.

General Motors June 2009 bankruptcy filing shows that such attempts to make profit through diversification

Productive resources become capital when they are invested in ways intended to increase their owner's financial wealth, as for this farmer in Bali.

© Judith Pearson

are not always successful. Capitalist firms that fail to make profits are soon dissolved or altered regardless of the products they make.

Productive resources become capital when they are used with the primary goal of increasing their owner's financial wealth. In capitalism, this becomes the most common (though not the only) use of such resources. **Capitalism** is further characterized by three fundamental attributes. First, most productive resources are owned by a small portion of the population. Banks, corporations, and wealthy individuals own the vast majority of farms, factories, and business of all kinds. Although many Americans invest in business through ownership of stocks, mutual funds, and retirement plans, ownership of substantial wealth is highly concentrated. For example, in the United States, in 2002 almost half of all households owned some stocks or mutual funds (and thus owned some share of a business). However, the median value of these investments was $50,000. Fewer than 4 percent of American households had stocks and mutual funds valued at more than half a million dollars (Investment Company Institute 2005). Thus, while a great many people held some ownership of business, the vast majority was held by a comparatively few.

**capitalism** An economic system in which people work for wages, land and capital goods are privately owned, and capital is invested for profit.

# Anthropology Makes a Difference

## Anthropologists in the Corporate World

Sooner or later, most people who decide to study anthropology have to answer questions from friends and family members who say things like "Anthropology? What are you going to do with that?" There are many good answers to this question. Perhaps the best is to remind them that anthropology is a liberal art. It's a way of learning, analyzing, and thinking about actions in the world. These are skills that are applicable to jobs ranging from entrepreneurship to social service. Surveys show that the jobs that anthropology majors actually get are very similar to those for people who study history, philosophy, English, psychology, sociology, and other liberal arts subjects.

Despite this, you may be interested to know that over the past quarter century, professional anthropologists are increasingly in demand by both large and small corporations. Anthropologists have become popular because, while focus groups and opinion surveys explore what people say,

anthropologists using participant-observation focus on what people actually do.

Anthropologist Francisco Aguilera has been consulting with business for more than 25 years. He notes that anthropological research is particularly useful in the modern corporate context. Whereas old-style corporations thought of themselves as fixed organizations with rigid boundaries, the new emphasis is on open production groups and an extension of networks across the organization's boundaries to embrace customers, suppliers, and competitors in partnerships, alliances, and service delivery. In this situation, decision making based on ethnographic description and comparison is essential.

Aguilera says that although other social science disciplines can and do offer consulting to businesses, anthropologists have some unique gifts to bring to the table. First, culture is the mainstay of anthropology, and anthropologists have better ways of talking about it than members of other

disciplines. Second, anthropologists understand that boundaries are artificial, so they seek to understand the entire environment of the business and its employees. Finally, because of the participant-observer methodology of ethnography and the multilevel analysis that makes sense of ethnographic data, anthropologists are more likely to comprehend the fuller meaning of informants' reports than are practitioners of those disciplines that rely heavily on other forms of data collection and analysis.

In addition to consulting for businesses, many anthropologists have gone on to found businesses or work directly for them. Major corporations such as Intel, Motorola, Ford, General Motors, Nissan, Procter & Gamble, Hewlett-Packard, Xerox, and many others hire anthropologists to analyze their own organizations and do market research designed to tailor their products, services, and publicity to the public.

Eleanor Wynn is an anthropologist who works as a principal engineer for informa-

---

The second attribute of capitalism is that most individuals' primary resource is their labor. In order to survive, people sell their labor for a salary or an hourly wage. Most Americans, for example, work for large or small corporations that they do not own, or they are employed by government.

The third attribute is that the value of workers' contribution to production is always intended to be greater than the wages they receive. The difference between these two is the profit that accrues to those who own the productive resources, generally the shareholders of a corporation (Plattner 1989b:382–384). The extremely high wages of some professional athletes and entertainers provide a good illustration of this principle. For example, basketball player Shaquille O'Neal earned more than $27 million playing for the Miami Heat in the 2004–2005 season. For the team owners, his high salary was easily justified. They believed that his presence would enable them to earn substantially more than they paid him. This proved a good guess. Mickey Arison bought The Heat for $65 million in 1995. In December 2008, the team's value was estimated at $393 million (*Forbes* 2008). Since a

good deal of this appreciation was due to O'Neal's skill and popularity, the value of his labor was substantially greater than the wages he received.

In general, workers wish to receive as close to the full value of their labor as possible while owners wish to pay as small a portion of labor's value as possible. This frequently results in conflict between the two groups.

Modern capitalist economies are dominated by market exchange, but this does not mean that people always experience their economy in terms of buying and selling at whatever price the market will bear. Capitalism always occurs within the context of other social relationships and some-

tion technology research at Intel Corporation. She holds a Ph.D. from the University of California at Berkeley. She began her industry career working at Xerox's Palo Alto Research Center as a graduate intern. She has worked for Bell Northern Research, a lab for NorTel, and as a freelance consultant, before moving to Intel. In these positions, she used ethnographic techniques to explore the working lives and decision-making processes of employees and customers who might use new technologies. Her reports helped translate the situated logic and experience of workers and customers into a language that corporate executives and work groups could use to make decisions and better design technology products. Such ethnographic research is essential because it allows the researcher to discover the reasoning of the everyday person at work and to understand the things that are part of the job but not in the job description. In many cases Wynn was able to advocate for workers by giving their voices a legitimacy they otherwise did not possess.

Wynn points out that working for a corporation is a very different task than doing anthropology in an academic setting. Anthropologists working at universities generally do research by themselves and publish their findings under their own names. They generally work on a single project at a time. In a corporate setting, anthropologists work as members of teams. Because of this, the contribution of any single individual to a finished product may be difficult to describe. However, collaborative working allows anthropological input throughout the project process.

Employers often think about work in terms of an individual fulfilling a series of specific discrete tasks. However, one result of thinking about work ethnographically is the realization that this rarely corresponds to an employee's experience. Today, employees in the information industry are likely to be part of multiple working groups and are likely to be working on numerous tasks simultaneously. Additionally, the dividing line between the world of work and the social world, between work and play, becomes thinner as cell phones and social networking utilities such as Facebook come to play ever larger roles in our lives. For Wynn, ethnography exploration can help corporations understand these changes and design workplace environments and products that increase efficiency and improve lives for workers and customers.

In addition to anthropologists such as Wynn, Intel also employs anthropologists in its "People and Practices" research lab. Their goal is to explore phenomena of everyday life and to help Intel think critically about how people, practices, and institutions matter to technological innovation. You can visit them on the web at http://techresearch.intel.com/articles/Exploratory/1752.htm. You can read more about careers in anthropology at the American Anthropological Association, http://www.aaanet.org/profdev/careers.

times these provide a mask behind which it can hide. In other words, capitalist relationships are sometimes camouflaged by family ties or social obligations. When this happens, entrepreneurs may be able to extract extra profits. The production of knitted sweaters in Turkey is a good example of this.

Turkey produces many goods and services used in wealthy capitalist nations. Most of the inhabitants of Istanbul, its largest city, are part of a capitalist economy selling their labor in enterprises aimed at generating a profit. However, as Jenny B. White (1994) reports, many of them, particularly women, understand their work in terms of reciprocity and kin obligations rather than capitalism and the market place.

Turkey is a patrilineal and patriarchal society. Turkish women live in complex social networks that are characterized by social obligations and relations of reciprocity. To a great degree, they measure their worth by the work they do for family members. Married women live with their husband's family and are expected to manage the household and to keep their hands busy with knitting and other skilled tasks. Such tasks are not considered work (in the sense of work outside of the home) but are rather understood as necessary obligations of married life.

Business in Turkey is often patterned on social life and this can be seen clearly in women's piecework. Women produce garments that are sold in the United States and other Western nations. The materials they use are generally supplied to them by an organizer, who also finds a buyer for the finished product. The organizers are often relatives, neighbors, and friends of the women who do the work.

In the Istanbul neighborhood White investigated, almost everyone believed that women should not work for money, yet about two thirds of them are involved in piecework (White 1994:13). How is this contradiction explained? The women who do it see piecework as a way for them to keep their hands busy and thus part of their duty as wives rather than a form of paid labor. Their work forms part of their obligation to their husband's family and to organizers with whom they have social connections, and they consider it a gift of labor. They understand the payments they receive as gifts from someone with whom they have an established social relationship.

# Ethnography

## West African Traders in New York City

Long-distance trade has a deep history in West Africa. For at least 1000 years, groups of traders have traveled vast distances, across the Sahara and into the Sahel and forest regions of West Africa transporting valuables such as gold, salt, kola nut, cattle, and sometimes slaves. Frequently, this trade was in the hands of members of specific ethnic groups such as the Hausa and the Dioula. Some members of these groups spread through West Africa, settling in towns and villages populated by members of other ethnic groups. Thus, they formed a diaspora of minority communities, differentiated from those around them by ethnicity and by religion as well. Until the past century, most West Africans practiced traditional religions. However, most members of these groups, particularly the merchants and those who lived in the diaspora communities, were Muslims. The diaspora communities and the shared practice of Islam gave merchants from these groups a strong competitive advantage. It meant that wherever they went, merchants could be assured of finding members of their own group who shared their values and their language. Local community members could provide lodging and help the merchants trade with members of the groups among whom they had settled. Frequently,

merchants were also connected to diaspora families through ties of kinship as well. Thus, social relationships of ethnic and religious identity, kinship, and friendship were integral to the merchants' success as well as continued ethnic control of trade (Cohen 1969, Warms 1992).

Beginning in 1965, changes in U.S. immigration law ended the quota system that had been in place since the early 1920s and made greatly increased immigration to the United States possible. Economic and educational opportunities in the United States coincided with instability and unrest in Africa and resulted in increased African immigration to the United States. By 2007, there were 1.4 million immigrants born in Africa living in the United States and more than 90 percent of these had arrived since 1980. African immigrants tended to settle in urban areas, and today over one third of them live in four metropolitan areas: New York City, Washington, D.C., Atlanta, and Minneapolis. African immigrants have been successful in many occupations, including construction and transportation. They have been particularly successful in health-care and social service related jobs (Terrazas 2009). Some have become successful as merchants, selling goods on the streets of American cities, in shops, and at ethnic

festivals. Their practice of trade continues the history of African long-distance trade in new geographic and social contexts.

In *Money Has No Smell* (2002) anthropologist Paul Stoller describes the lives of African merchants in New York City. Among them is Issifi Mayaki. Mayaki was born near Maradi, in Niger in West Africa. His father was a successful merchant who spent most of his time in Abidjan, the capital of Côte d'Ivoire. His grandfather was also a merchant. As a young man, Mayaki followed his father to Abidjan, where he learned about trading by watching his father and his father's associates. In Abidjan he learned to value the ability to speak multiple languages and the importance of connections, not only with his own family but with people from different ethnic and cultural groups as well.

When Mayaki's friends in Abidjan began to send some of their products to the United States he saw new opportunities and with their help, arranged to move to New York. Once there, he shared a hotel room with other Hausa merchants and used his connections with his family and friends in Côte d'Ivoire to gain access to the African cloth he sold. However, Mayaki ran into misfortune when a client refused to pay him for a shipment of goods. As a

---

Because the women's work is set within a context of global capitalism, work organizers may be friends and neighbors, but they are also capitalist entrepreneurs hoping to make money. In the end, women produce goods for the capitalist marketplace and their wages ultimately derive from that market. However, these capitalist relationships are masked by social relations of balanced or generalized reciprocity with the labor organizer. Because they understand their work in terms of a social obligation, they rarely think about how much they are earning an hour or how they might use their time and talents to make more money. Thus, they are willing to accept far lower wages than might otherwise be the case.

In some ways, the system serves the women well. They are able to fill their roles as wives and in-laws and their social connections with labor organizers may give them some degree of security from the ravages of the

marketplace. This is important in a country like Turkey where most people are poor and social services are few. However, it is clear that the greatest beneficiaries of this system are firms and consumers in wealthy nations. The fact that reciprocity masks capitalism for poor women in Turkey allows rich consumers in Europe and America to buy hand-knitted sweaters at very low prices and the firms based in these nations to make windfall profits.

Although there are probably some individuals who act as capitalists in most monetized economies, societies organized primarily by capitalism are a late development in the history of humankind. Such societies were not a natural and inevitable outcome of economic evolution. Rather they owed their origin to the specific conditions of the industrial revolution in Europe in the 18th and 19th centuries and have become increasingly prevalent in the world in the past 150 years.

result, he was unable to pay his own debts. In a system based on trust, this was a critical blow. However, Mayaki was able to reestablish himself with the help of other Hausa merchants living in New York, some of whom he had known in Abidjan as well. These provided him with a new place to live, introductions to some Asian businessmen who sold cassettes, and cash loans that enabled him to buy inventory. With their help, Mayaki was able to establish himself as a successful merchant again. As soon as he had sufficient capital, he returned to selling African cloth, which was both more profitable and aesthetically more pleasing to him. With old connections from Abidjan and his new connections from New York, he was able to gain access to a wide range of products, from antique West African cloth to machine-made reproductions of Ghanaian Kente cloth from Tunisia. Mayaki maintains close connections with his family in Africa, sending money to his family in Niger and helping with his father's medical expenses in Côte d'Ivoire.

This description hints at the extensive and varied global connections of West African traders in New York City. Some of these connections between the West African traders and their Asian middlemen are rela-

tively recent, and specific to the street trading milieu of New York City. But many of them repeat the style of historic connections among African merchants in a new context. Like their predecessors, these merchants live as members of minority communities. Their commercial activities are supported by ties of ethnic identity, family, and religion. Such ties favor their success and help them keep control of their markets.

Stoller (2002:178) notes that although Mayaki retains his African identity, he has become a citizen of the world and a player in the global economy. For Mayaki and other African traders, nothing is more important than social relations and mutual trust. Using these, they have negotiated and renegotiated their social lives, mastered the capitalist culture of Abidjan and New York City, and reinforced the traditions of long-distance African trading.

In the 1940s and 1950s, young and adventurous itinerant Hausa traders in Africa and France called themselves "jaguars" after an animal whose power stems as much from its adaptability as from its physical strength. Although the term is no longer in fashion, the global participation of West African traders today is testimony to the

strength of their cultures, the importance of their community and personal relationships, and the qualities of daring and intelligence that serve them so well in Paris and New York, as it did historically in the desert cities of the Arab world and the cities and towns of West Africa.

## CRITICAL THINKING QUESTIONS

1. African traders in New York use ties of ethnicity, kinship, and religion to promote business success. How is this similar to or different from the experience of other immigrants to America?

2. Does the use of ethnic identity in trade act to increase or decrease the degree to which members of these communities are integrated into American culture?

3. The worlds of economics, ethnic identity, kinship, and friendship are often entwined. What experiences have you had that illustrate the ways in which these facets of social life work together?

*Source:* Based on Paul Stoller, *Money Has No Smell: The Africanization of New York City.* Chicago: University of Chicago Press, 2002.

---

As the case of the Turkish women shows, capitalism has outgrown national boundaries. The result has been great movement of resources and capital and migrations of population, as the whole world has gradually been drawn into the global economy, a system we call globalization. For the most part, members of traditional societies enter the market as low-wage laborers. The wealth they produce accrues to elites within poor nations as well as owners and consumers in wealthy nations (E. Wolf 1982).

Capitalism is a powerful economic system. It undoubtedly provides a greater number of goods and services to larger populations than other ways of organizing an economy, but at a cost. When some individuals or groups own or control basic resources, others must inevitably be denied access to them. This results in permanently differentiated economic and social classes. Capi-

talism dictates that there will always be rich and poor. Often, part of the population lives in extreme poverty, without access to basic resources—in American society, this includes the homeless, the landless rural poor, and the permanently unemployed.

Poverty in capitalist societies punishes weakness, failure, or ill fortune in a way that is less true of the other forms of economic organization described in this chapter. Contemporary capitalist societies, characterized by well-coordinated specialized labor forces, increasingly require mobility, skill, and education for success. The creation of complex global systems of exchange between those who supply raw materials and those who use them in manufacturing, as well as between manufacturers and consumers, results in significant economic inequities both within and among nations. Market-oriented agriculture, the predominance of wage labor, and the subse-

Many Turkish women accept knitting as a social obligation. This is one factor that leads them to accept very low wages for their products. However, the goods they produce are sold for high prices in wealthy nations.

quent loss of control over culture and social institutions are some of the constraints within which people in the modern global economy must struggle to make a living.

## Resistance to Capitalism

Not all societies, nor all individuals within a society, are able or willing to accommodate to capitalism. Historically, the expansion of capitalism was accompanied by the wide-scale destruction of traditional societies, a process examined in more detail in Chapter 15. Further, although capitalism has now expanded into every part of the world, there are probably no countries where all of the population is directly involved in it. In many areas, noncapitalist groups remain, although they are often pushed to geographically marginal areas such as the border between Pakistan and Afghanistan or the jungles of Brazil. In other places, issues of race, gender, and ethnicity prevent people from fully participating in the capitalist economy. However, even in these locations mass-produced goods, media, and fashions from capitalist societies are easily found.

Most Americans probably think of themselves as being in favor of capitalism, but many do not wish to actively engage in it. Individuals join the capitalist economy by selling their labor for wages. Alternatively, they might own productive resources and operate these with hired labor, reinvesting any profits to increase the value and size of their operation. However, in the United States there are many individuals and families that resist these options.

Consider the inhabitants of Putnam County, New York (Hansen 1995). Located about 50 miles from New York City, Putnam County has been poor since the time of the American Revolution. Even in the preindustrial era, its farms were unable to compete successfully with surrounding areas. Today, its people follow two fundamentally different strategies for survival and belong to two different but related economic systems.

Many of Putnam's inhabitants are new residents who commute to jobs in New York City. They work for union-scale wages as police officers, firefighters, and schoolteachers, using their wages to buy houses, food, and so on. They are deeply in debt to mortgage and credit card companies but believe that higher future earnings will permit them to accommodate this financial burden. They are committed to economic and social advancement, and many hope eventually to move to more prosperous suburbs closer to the city. Members of this group are deeply committed to capitalism. They own few productive resources, sell their labor for wages, and conduct the economic aspect of their lives almost entirely through the capitalist market.

Putnam County's other residents have lived there for generations. Members of this group very rarely have full-time wage employment. They almost never visit New York City, which to them has become "a metaphor for all the world's evils" (Hansen 1995:146). Instead they follow what Halperin (1990) has called a multiple-livelihood strategy. They acquire their land through inheritance and generally own it outright. Their lands include both forest and gardens that provide almost all of the vegetables they consume. While women work in the gardens, men hunt year-round, taking deer, rabbits, guinea fowl, and pheasants. They fish in ponds and streams and chop wood for fuel. In addition to these subsistence activities,

Garage sales, gardening, raising livestock, and doing odd jobs help many Americans avoid full participation in the capitalist economy.

members of this group do carpentry, electrical repair, masonry, plumbing, and other jobs. They barter these skills among themselves and sell them for cash to the commuters. They may also work temporarily for wages at construction jobs. Although Putnam's traditional residents do depend on markets for goods they cannot produce themselves or get through barter, only a small part of their total subsistence comes from the market.

Through such strategies, these residents avoid participation in the capitalist economy. Their financial goals are not to make money or to move to a higher level of consumption. They are concerned with stability rather than mobility and wish to live as independently as possible. Although they own productive resources such as land and equipment, these do not become capital because they are used to increase the security of their self-sufficiency rather than to accumulate wealth.

The self-sufficient residents of Putnam County remind us that culture counts. For most of us, capitalism seems both natural and inevitable, the way that society must be organized to make sense. However, the ways in which we organize our economy are the result of history, politics, economics, and individual choices; a creation of culture, not natural law.

# The Global and the Local: Product Anthropology

In *Creating Breakthrough Products* Jonathan Cagan and Craig M. Vogel write that the most promising area of research is "new product ethnography." Writing in the jargon of business consulting, they say that new product ethnography uses the techniques of applied anthropology to "turn a descriptive process into a predictive field that helps to determine Value Opportunities." Product ethnographers deliver "actionable insights" into behavior and lifestyle activities and preferences that lead to product attributes (2001:107–108). In plainer English, Cagan and Vogel believe that anthropologists can offer vital services to business. New product ethnography is a way of turning the techniques and theoretical perspectives of anthropology into a resource for the corporate world. Those who promote it argue that anthropologists can and should provide vital information that helps corporations design and market products in ways that maximize their profits.

Paco Underhill's work is an example of the use of anthropological techniques to promote product sales. For more than 20 years, Underhill has used observation, photography, and interviews to study the ways people shop. He is the founder of the consulting firm Envirosell (http://www.envirosell.com), which advises clients such as McDonald's, The Gap, and Microsoft on how best to appeal to consumers. Some of Underhill's discoveries include the "transition zone" and the "butt brush." The transition zone is the area near the entrance to a store. Underhill observed that people need time to slow down and get used to a new environment, so they rarely purchase items from displays of merchandise that are within 12 or 15 steps of the front of the store. He also pointed out that women in particular will avoid purchasing items on low shelves in narrow aisles, because bending to reach such goods exposes them to being "butt brushed," or bumped from behind. Men are much less prone to avoid being jostled in this way. Underhill has summarized many of his findings in a popular book, *Why We Buy: The Science of Shopping* (1999).

In many ways, product anthropology and other uses of anthropology in business and government are promising breakthroughs. Since the founding days of the discipline, anthropologists have wanted their voices heard by people outside the university. Now they are increasingly employed in different capacities in consumer research, product design, and marketing. On one hand, this results in a better fit between products and consumers as well as higher profits for corporations. From the PT Cruiser (partially designed by French anthropologist G. Clotaire Rapaille) to computer software, toothbrushes, cookware, and ethnobanking (developing banking services for ethnic target groups), anthropologists have made products more friendly and businesses more money. As companies design products for markets around the globe, anthropologists have valuable contributions to make to design, production, and marketing. On the other hand, the involvement of anthropologists in these fields raises difficult ethical problems. For example, anthropologists mine information from their informants. If corporations then profit from this information, is payment owed to the informants? Historically, the introduction of mass-produced products has destabilized craft production and destabilized local economies. Should anthropologists sell their services to corporations to promote this process? Should anthropology be a way to help corporations make more money?

## Key Questions

1. Given that the introduction of manufactured goods has undercut traditional economies and drawn people into the capitalist economy (where they often become low-paid workers and consumers of low-quality merchandise), should anthropologists be involved in the

design and marketing of products to groups about which they have expertise?

2. Given that, with the aid of anthropologists, corporations can produce products that meet local needs and are marketed in culturally appropriate ways, and given that the alternative is often inappropriate, poorly designed and poorly marketed products, can anthropologists justifiably refuse to work with corporations?

3. Perhaps the two questions above present a false dichotomy. What are some positions that anthropologists might take between these two?

# Summary

1. **What is economics and what is economic behavior?** Economics is the study of the ways in which the choices people make combine to determine how their societies use their scarce resources to produce and distribute goods and services. Economists assume that people will generally engage in economizing behavior, that they will allocate their scarce goods and resources in ways that maximize their benefit.

2. **What are productive resources? Give some examples.** Productive resources are the things that members of a society need to participate in the economy and access to them is basic to every culture. Such resources generally include land, labor, and knowledge.

3. **How does the allocation of productive resources vary as social complexity increases?** In general, as social complexity increases, access to productive resources becomes more restricted. In foraging societies, all people usually have access to all resources. Among pastoralists, ownership of animals is vested in families and kin groups. Among horticulturalists, people may control land in which they have invested labor. Among agriculturalists, many productive resources are owned by specific individuals.

4. **How is labor organized in most preindustrial and peasant economies?** Labor must be organized in specific ways to produce goods. In most preindustrial and peasant economies, labor is organized by the household or kin group. Work that people both perform and receive locates them with respect in their social network, and is often integral to their identity.

5. **What is the relationship between population, social complexity, and specialization?** As societies become more populous and complex, the number of specialized jobs found in them increases. This is particularly true where societies are dependent on grain agriculture or industrialism. In preindustrial societies, like traditional India, kin groups may have rights or duties to perform particular specializations. Current-day wealthy societies have extremely high degrees of specialization. This creates great efficiency but involves changing notions of identity and often has heavy human costs.

6. **What different systems of distribution are described in this chapter?** In all societies there are systems for distributing and consuming goods and services. Every society uses some combination of reciprocity, redistribution, and the market to redistribute goods and services and to provide patterns and standards for their consumption.

7. **Define reciprocity and describe different types of reciprocity.** Reciprocity is the mutual give and take of goods and services among people. In generalized reciprocity individuals at a close social distance give and take without expecting immediate or specific return. Balanced reciprocity involves individuals at a medium social distance and includes a clear obligation to return goods of nearly equal value to those given. Negative reciprocity is characteristic of impersonal or unfriendly relations and involves attempting to get the better of a trade.

8. **What is redistribution and in what kinds of societies is it commonly found?** In redistribution, goods are collected to a social center from which they are given out to the group in a new pattern. Redistribution occurs in many different contexts but is particularly common in societies that have bigmen and chiefdoms, and in states. Potlatch among Northwest coastal Native Americans provides an example of redistribution. Some forms of redistribution act as leveling mechanisms, forcing wealthier individuals to disburse part of their riches to the rest of the community.

9. **What are the chief characteristics of market exchange and where is it found?** In market exchange, goods and services are bought and sold at a money price determined by market forces. In principle, market exchange is impersonal and occurs without regard to the social position of the participants. Market exchange is the most common mechanism of exchange in the world today and is found in most societies.

10. **What are the defining characteristics of capitalism?** In capitalism, the owners of productive resources use them to increase their financial wealth. In capitalist societies, productive resources are held primarily by a small percentage of the population, most people sell their labor for wages, and the value of people's labor

is always more than the wages they receive. Capitalism can be masked by other relationships such as reciprocity.

11. **Where is resistance to capitalism found and what forms does it take?** Resistance to capitalism is found in almost all capitalist societies. Sometimes such resistance may take the form of movements for social change or violent revolution. However, in many places, people resist capitalism by owning productive resources that they use only for their own subsistence, avoiding wage labor and limiting their participation in the market. Some of the residents of Putnam County, New York, provide an example.

# Key Terms

| | | |
|---|---|---|
| balanced reciprocity | economizing behavior | market exchange |
| capital | firm | negative reciprocity |
| capitalism | generalized reciprocity | potlatch |
| cargo system | household | productive resources |
| economic system | Kula ring | reciprocity |
| economics | leveling mechanism | redistribution |

# Suggested Readings

Halperin, Rhoda. 1990. *The Livelihood of Kin: Making Ends Meet "The Kentucky Way."* Austin: University of Texas Press. An ethnography of communities in Appalachia, this is an outstanding analysis of some of the alternative economic forms in the United States.

Orlove, Ben. 2002. *Lines in the Water: Nature and Culture at Lake Titicaca.* Berkeley: University of California Press. A poetically written description and analysis of the economy and ecology of fishing villages in Peru, this book examines ideas of economy, government intervention, development, history.

Schneider, Jane, and Rayna Rapp (Eds.). 1995. *Articulating Hidden Histories: Exploring the Influence of Eric R. Wolf.* Berkeley: University of California Press. This collection of 21 essays, honoring one of the most influential economic anthropologists, covers topics such as peasants, the market, nationalism, and cultural identity.

Wilk, Richard R., and Lisa C. Cliggett. 2007. *Economies and Cultures: Foundations of Economic Anthropology* (2nd ed.). Boulder, CO: Westview. In this overview of economic anthropology, Wilk and Cliggett focus on what motivates people and what that might say about human nature. They see economic anthropology as a meeting place between materialist and symbolic approaches.

Ties of kinship, through descent and marriage, are important in all societies, even in complex, industrial societies like the United States where they compete with other institutional ties such as citizenship. In the United States, the annual family reunion, like that of the Tracys of Illinois, is an important way of keeping kin ties alive. The importance of the nuclear family is indicated by the different color T-shirts that each family wears.

Courtesy of Tom Curtin

**THINKING POINT:** Americans pride themselves on their self-reliance, making it on their own, basing success on merit rather than on family connections. Yet our political history is filled with family connections: the Adamses, Cabots, Roosevelts, Bushes, and Kennedys, just to name a few. More than 20 members of the present Congress have parents who were also in Congress. Kinship ties help Americans get into elite colleges as "legacy" applicants, provide professional and business contacts, and are an important basis of social networks that maintain wealth and status. Consider the importance of kinship in different societies as you read further in this chapter.

# {chapter 8}

# Kinship

In American society, when you meet someone for the first time, you generally try to find some area of common interest. You may ask where the other person is from, what schools he or she went to, what his or her occupation is, or what hobbies or interests he or she has. Even as kinship is, in fact, an important connection in American society, most people are quite unlikely to ask an acquaintance about his or her grandparents, parents, and siblings. Most of the time Americans understand ourselves and each other as individuals first and family members second. Ideally, Americans deplore **nepotism,** favoritism based on family relationships, especially when it comes to politics. Do you see the examples in our opening statement as an example of nepotism, or just the reality that children of politicians are likely to have a combination of aptitude and exposure that can explain their achievements? Do the close family ties of past and present American politicians "stick in the craw" of Americans as hypocrisy or can we rationalize it as compatible with the values of individuality and self-reliance that are at the core of our culture? As one analyst of political dynasties in the United States points out, "There is none of this squeamishness about kinship in tribal societies, for whom kinship is everything, protection against. . . . all those who are not kin, whether neighbors or strangers" (Murphy 2008). In this chapter we see that in many societies, although kinship may not be everything, it has important functions in all areas of life. <<

The importance of kinship ties in the United States is illustrated in political families, such as the Kennedys, pictured here.

# Kinship: Relationships through Blood and Marriage

**Kinship** refers to those relationships understood in a society as connected through blood and marriage. Although kinship systems are themselves embedded in economic systems, they have an important independent influence on behavior. In almost all societies, kinship is the basis of group formation, and relationships between individuals are governed mainly by kinship norms. The extension of kinship ties is the main way of allying groups to one another and incorporating strangers into a group. In most of the world's cultures, kinship is central in determining people's rights and responsibilities.

**nepotism** The granting of privilege or favoritism on the basis of family relationships.

**kinship** A culturally defined relationship established on the basis of blood ties or through marriage.

**kinship system** The totality of kin relations, kin groups, and terms for classifying kin in a society.

**kinship terminology** The words used to identify different categories of kin in a particular culture.

**genitor** A biological father.

**pater** The socially designated father of a child, who may or may not be the biological father.

**consanguineal relatives** Relatives by blood.

**affinal** Relatives by marriage; in-laws.

In Western societies, other principles of social organization—such as work, citizenship, and common economic and political interests—are also important as bases for group formation and frameworks within which individual rights and obligations are articulated. This does not mean, however, that kinship is insignificant in modern industrialized societies. The nuclear family is a kin group and a core social institution in such societies, and inheritance of property is mainly along kinship lines. Larger groups of relatives also become important on various ritual occasions. For example, in the United States, those who celebrate Thanksgiving generally think of it as a family holiday. A person claiming a kin relation is regarded differently from someone who is not a relative, and there is a strong sentiment that "blood is thicker than water." Although kinship in the United States does not usually determine an individual's choice of occupation, it does play a significant role in some important aspects of American life.

Kinship includes relationships established through blood, described through the idiom of blood, and relationships through marriage. In every society, the formation of groups and the regulation of behavior depend to some extent on socially recognized ties of kinship. Because the different elements of kinship such as behavior, ideology, and terminology are closely related to each other, anthropologists refer to kinship as a system. A **kinship system** includes all relationships based on blood and marriage that link people in a web of rights and obligations, the kinds of groups that may be formed in a society on the basis of kinship, and the system of terms **(kinship terminology)** used to classify different kin.

Kinship systems rest on culturally defined biological relationships; kinship systems are thus cultural phenomena. The ways in which a society classifies kin are cultural; they may or may not reflect a scientifically accurate assessment of biological ties. A classic example demonstrating the cultural element in kinship is that in many societies the term for father as it refers to the child's biological father **(genitor)** is different than the term designating the man who takes on responsibility for the child's upbringing or is socially recognized as the father **(pater).** When fatherhood is established by marriage, the "father" is the mother's husband. In some societies, such as the Toda of India (see page 201 in Chapter 9), biological paternity is irrelevant; fatherhood is established by the performance of a ritual. In this case, social fatherhood is what counts.

Because kinship systems are cultural creations, both **consanguineal relatives** (those related "by blood") and **affinal** relatives (those related by marriage) are classified in dif-

© SV-Bilderdienst/The Image Works

ferent societies in a wide variety of ways. The kinds of social groups formed by kinship and the ways in which kin are expected to behave toward one another also vary widely.

Culturally defined ties of kinship have two basic functions that are necessary for the continuation of society. First, kinship provides continuity between generations. In all societies, children must be cared for and educated so that they can become functioning members of their society. The kinship unit is fundamentally responsible for this task, and kinship structures thus provide the basis for family construction. A society must also provide for the orderly transmission of property and social position between generations. In most human societies, **inheritance** (the transfer of property) and **succession** (the transfer of social position) take place within kin groups according to the specific rules of the kinship system.

Second, kinship defines a universe of others on whom a person can depend for aid. This universe varies widely. In Western societies, the universe of kin on whom one can depend may be smaller than in other societies, where kin groups include a wide range of relations that have significant mutual rights and obligations. The adaptiveness of social groups larger than the nuclear family accounts for the fact that expanded kin groups are found in so many human societies.

## Rules of Descent and the Formation of Descent Groups

In anthropological terminology, **descent** is culturally established affiliation with one or both parents. In many societies, descent is an important basis of social group formation. In one sense, of course, the nuclear family is a **descent group,** but here we use descent group to mean a group of consanguineal kin (kin who are related through blood) who are lineal descendants of a common ancestor extending beyond two generations. Where descent groups are found, they have important functions in the organization of domestic life, the enculturation of children, the use and transfer of property and political and ritual offices, the carrying out of religious ritual, the settlement of disputes, and political organization and warfare.

Two basic types of descent rules, or kinship ideology, operate in society. In a cultural system with a rule of **unilineal descent,** descent group membership is based on links through either the paternal or the maternal line, but not both. Two types of unilineal descent rules are **patrilineal descent** and **matrilineal descent.** In societies with patrilineal descent rules, a person belongs to the descent group of his or her father. In societies with matrilineal descent rules, a person belongs to the descent group of the mother. In societies with a system of **bilateral descent,**

both maternal and paternal lines are used as the basis for reckoning descent and for establishing the rights and obligations of kinship.

A major distinction between systems of unilineal and bilateral descent is that in unilineal kinship systems kin groups do not overlap. In bilateral kin systems, they do. For example, consider your father's brother's children. In the American bilateral kinship system, they are your cousins, and therefore members of your kin. However, they are equally related to their mother's family, but this family is unlikely to be kin to you. If the system was patrilineal, your father's brother's children would be kin to you, but not to their mother's family. Thus, their kinship would not overlap. If all families had the same number of children, more people would be kin in a bilateral system than in a unilineal system. However, because kinship is overlapping in a bilateral system, people in a unilineal system are bound more tightly to each other than those in a bilateral system.

## Unilineal Descent Groups

Most societies throughout the world have unilineal kinship. However, many of the world's people practice bilateral kinship, which is particularly common in Western industrial societies. The frequency of unilineal descent in the world's cultures reflects two major advantages. First, because unilineal descent groups do not overlap, this system provides unambiguous group membership for everyone in the society. Where descent is traced through only one line, group membership is easily and clearly defined. By knowing the descent group to which they belong and the descent group of others, people can be sure of their rights of ownership, social duties, and social roles. They can also easily relate to a large number of known and unknown people in the society.

---

**inheritance** The transfer of property between generations.

**succession** The transfer of office or social position between generations.

**descent** The culturally established affiliation between a child and one or both parents.

**descent group** A group of kin who are descendants of a common ancestor, extending beyond two generations.

**unilineal descent** Descent group membership based on links through either the maternal or the paternal line, but not both.

**patrilineal descent** A rule that affiliates a person to kin of both sexes through males only.

**matrilineal descent** A rule that affiliates a person to kin of both sexes through females only.

**bilateral descent** System of descent under which individuals are equally affiliated with their mothers' and their fathers' descent group.

# Anthropology Makes a Difference

## Kinship Rules and Realities in a Korean Village

The rules of kinship in Asian villages emphasize patrilineality; primogeniture (the eldest son inherits all of his father's property); seniority; Confucian ethics, which stresses filial piety (the obligation of sons to their fathers); and patriarchal authority and control. However, one of the ways in which anthropology makes a difference is that it opens our eyes to the realities of kinship dynamics as they depart from the rules and adapt to changing circumstances.

In Korea, as elsewhere, people manipulate kinship rules for their own advantage. Inheritance and succession to family headship are contested as family members try to ensure that their contributions are acknowledged and rewarded. Times when family property is divided are particularly important occasions for the reckoning of the balance of credits and debts among family members.

According to the local rules of inheritance in Pine Tree, a Korean village studied by anthropologist Soo Ho Choi, the eldest son gets the lion's share of his family's property, including his parents' house and more than half their land. In return, he must care for his elderly parents and worship them as ancestors after their deaths.

However, the realities of contemporary life often lead to conflict and departure from the rules. Most Pine Tree families are

Hundreds of lineage members gather annually to pay their homage to their proto-ancestors who were buried at the same site. The gravesite is the most important symbolic center for lineage activities in rural Korea.

so poor that there is not enough property to divide so that any one child will significantly benefit; in addition, family property has often been acquired through the financial contributions of several family members. When the family property is divided, these people will claim a larger share of the property than the rule of primogeniture would normally allot them. Furthermore, an elder son who does not carry out the important Korean value of "compassionate generosity," by contributing to the mar-

riages, education, and living expenses of his younger siblings, faces strong community disapproval.

The poverty of many Korean villages and the pull of urban industrialization make a city education a highly valued alternative to remaining on the farm. And although a highly educated son is a source of pride to his family, the high cost of education can cause conflict. Money spent on one child's education may be resented by his siblings, who view his success as having taken place

Second, because unilineal group membership is unambiguous, descent groups can perpetuate themselves over time even though their membership changes (as modern corporations can). **Corporate descent groups** are permanent units that have an existence beyond the individuals who are members at any given time. Old members die and new ones are admitted through birth, but the integrity of the corporate group persists. Such groups may own property and manage resources (just as a modern corporation does).

**corporate descent groups** Permanent kinship groups that have an existence beyond the membership at any given time.

Although systems of unilineal descent share certain basic similarities throughout the world, they do not operate exactly the same way in every society. In addition, as the description of the Korean village in the Anthropology Makes a Difference section in this chapter indicates, actual behavior in any society does not correspond exactly to the rules as they are defined in the kinship ideology. Systems of descent and kinship are basically a means by which a society relates to its environment and circumstances. As these conditions change, the rules of kinship, like other cultural ideals, are bent and manipulated so that a group may be successful. The accepted departures from the norm that exist in every society give unilineal systems a flexibility they would otherwise lack—a flexibility necessary for human adaptation.

at their expense and as possibly due to favoritism. Siblings also resent being left with the economically unrewarding burden of farming, as well as the burdens of ancestor worship and other lineage and village responsibilities. On their father's death, therefore, siblings may try to exclude the educated son from inheriting any family property.

Inheritance rules are also complicated by the status of women, who are legally entitled to an equal share of a family's property. In Pine Tree, however, a daughter's right to family property is considered terminated if her family has given her extensive gifts of cash, furniture, cloth, and jewelry on her marriage. A woman who has received such gifts is discouraged from claiming her legal share of family property, but many women do make such claims. Korean village women often assert their importance by participating in the rituals of ancestor worship (formally a male prerogative). This gives them a strong basis for claiming family property and may lead to conflict between brothers and sisters.

In-depth ethnography enables anthropologists to see how the realities of relationships play out to subvert the rules of kinship. In one family studied by Soo Choi, Sungjo, a frail child who had one brother and two sisters, was his mother's favorite. Sungjo's frailty did not bode well for success in farming, and his mother was determined to have him educated in the city. She finally persuaded her husband to sell one-third of their land to finance Sungjo's education. The sale was opposed by his siblings, who now had to work much harder to compensate for the lost income. To earn additional cash, the women family members wove cotton and silk cloth, and Sungjo's elder brother collected and sold natural lacquer extracted from the nearby woods.

After Sungjo's graduation from university, he worked for a big corporation and lived in Seoul in comfort. From his family's perspective, he neglected those left behind in the village. When his elder brother and one sister died young, their children blamed it on the sacrifices they had made for Sungjo's education. The elder brother, Sungman, had no sons. According to the cultural rules, his wife should have adopted Sungjo's oldest son as her heir, entitling this boy to perform the ancestral rites and ultimately inherit Sungman's property. But Sungman's wife refused to do this and performed the ancestor rites herself. When she became senile, her eldest daughter took over the performance of these rites and claimed the heir's right to Sungman's property. Sungjo opposed this claim and, after eight years of wrangling, finally prevailed in having his eldest son adopted by Sungman's family. Two years later,

Sungman's wife died, and his daughter continued to perform the ancestor rites, although her claim to her parents' property was considerably weakened. As a married daughter, she was no longer considered part of her father's lineage, but that of her husband (as is common in patrilineal kinship systems), and she had neither legal nor cultural support for her claims. Sungjo's eldest sister, who stood to gain more from Sungjo's management of the property than that of her niece, allied with Sungjo to wrest the property from Sungman's daughter.

As we noted earlier, a central function of kinship rules is to smooth the transfer of office and property between generations. But, as Sungjo's family history illustrates, cultural rules may be broken to satisfy the demands of changing social circumstances. Cultural institutions like kinship are closely intertwined with economic systems, including access to land, wealth, and property. As economic systems change, people's behavior may depart from the rules. Under rapid economic change, as in Korea, exceptions to the rules become more frequent; ultimately the rules themselves may change, following changes in behavior.

Source: Adapted by permission of the author and publisher from Soo Ho Choi, "The Struggle for Family Succession and Inheritance in a Rural Korean Village," *Journal of Anthropological Research*, 1995, 51:329–346.

Anthropologists have offered a number of explanations for the evolution of unilineal descent groups. The common interests that cause people to join together and define themselves as a collective entity justified by kin relations are very diverse. These interests may be economic, such as land or cattle or gardens; they may be political or religious; or they may involve warfare within the society or with other societies. Kinship ideologies, which grow out of these varied common interests, take on a life of their own. With changing economic and historical circumstances, however, kinship ideologies can be manipulated and negotiated to fit new realities.

A group of kin whose members trace descent from a common ancestor and who can demonstrate those genealogical links among themselves is called a **lineage.** Lineages formed by descent through the male line are called **patrilineages.** Lineages formed by descent through the female line are called **matrilineages.** Lineages may vary in time depth, from three generations upward. Where lineages own land collectively and where the members are held responsible for one another's behavior, the lineage is considered a corporate group.

**lineage** A group of kin whose members trace descent from a known common ancestor.

**patrilineage** A lineage formed by descent in the male line.

**matrilineage** A lineage formed by descent in the female line.

Related lineages may form **clans.** The common clan ancestor may be a mythological figure; sometimes, no specific ancestor is known or named. A **phratry** is a unilineal descent group composed of a number of clans who feel themselves to be closely related. Clans are often named and may have a **totem**—a feature of the natural environment with which they are closely identified and toward which the clan members behave in a special way (see page 297 in Chapter 13).

Clans and lineages have different functions in different societies. The lineage is often a local residential or domestic group whose members cooperate on a daily basis. Clans are generally not residential units but tend to spread out over many villages. Therefore, clans often have political and religious functions rather than primarily domestic and economic ones.

One of the most important functions of a clan is to regulate marriage. In most societies, clans are governed by a rule of **exogamy.** The prohibition against marriage within the clan strengthens its unilineal character. If a person married within the clan, his or her children would find it difficult to make sharp distinctions between maternal and paternal relatives. Robert H. Lowie (1948:237) wrote of the Crow Indians of North America, among whom clans are very important, that in case of marriage within the clan, "a Crow. . . . loses his bearings and perplexes his tribesmen. For he owes specific obligations to his father's relatives and others to his mother's, who are now hopelessly confused. The sons of his father's clan ought to be censors; but now the very same persons are his joking relatives and his clan." Not only would this person not know how to act toward others, but others would not know how to act toward him. Clan exogamy

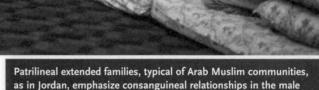

Patrilineal extended families, typical of Arab Muslim communities, as in Jordan, emphasize consanguineal relationships in the male line.

also extends the network of peaceful social relations within a society as different clans are allied through marriage.

## Patrilineal Descent Groups

In societies with patrilineal descent groups, a person (whether male or female) belongs to the descent group of the father, the father's father, and so on (see Figure 8.1).

Thus, a man, his sisters and brothers, his brother's children (but not his sister's children), his own children, and his son's children (but not his daughter's children) all belong to the same group. Inheritance moves from father to son, as does succession to office.

**Nuer Patriliny** The Nuer, a pastoral people who live in the Sudan in East Africa, have a patrilineal society. Among the Nuer, all rights, privileges, obligations, and interpersonal relationships are regulated by kinship; one is either a kinsman or an enemy. Membership in a patrilineal descent group is the most significant fact of life, and the father, his brothers, and their children are considered the closest kin. Membership in the patrilineage confers rights to land, requires participation in certain religious ceremonies, and determines political and judicial obligations, such as making alliances in feuds and warfare.

Nuer patrilineages have important political functions. Lineage membership may spread over several vil-

**clan** A unilineal kinship group whose members believe themselves to be descended from a common ancestor but who cannot trace this link through known relatives.

**phratry** A unilineal descent group composed of a number of clans whose members feel themselves to be closely related.

**totem** An animal, plant, or other aspect of the natural world held to be ancestral or to have other intimate relationships with members of a group.

**exogamy** A rule specifying that a person must marry outside a particular group.

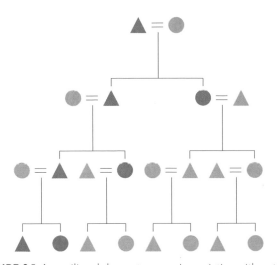

**FIGURE 8.1** A patrilineal descent group. In societies with patrilineal descent groups, membership is based on links through the father only. Sons and daughters are members of their father's descent group (shown in dark green), as are the children of the sons, but not of daughters.

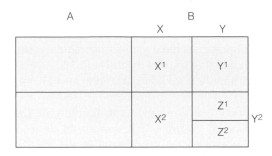

**FIGURE 8.2** A segmentary lineage system with complementary opposition. Complementary opposition functions in the following way: when $Z^1$ fights $Z^2$, no other section gets involved. When $Z^1$ fights $Y^1$, $Z^1$ and $Z^2$ unite as $Y^2$. When $Y^1$ fights $X^1$, $Y^1$ and $Y^2$ unite, and so do $X^1$ and $X^2$. When $X^1$ fights A, $X^1$, $X^2$, $Y^1$, and $Y^2$ all unite as B. When A raids the Dinka (another tribe), A and B may unite. Source: Based on Evans-Pritchard in Marshall Sahlins, "The Segmentary Lineage: An Organization of Predatory Expansion," *American Anthropologist*, 1963:332–345. Reprinted by permission of Oxford University Press.

lages and thus help create alliances between otherwise independent villages. Each Nuer clan, which is viewed as composed of related lineages, not individuals, is also spread over several villages. Because a person cannot marry someone from within his or her own lineage or clan, or from the lineage of the mother, kinship relations extend widely throughout the tribe. In the absence of a centralized system of political control, these kinship-based alliances are an important mechanism of governance. Because the Nuer believe that kin should not fight with one another, disputes within the lineage or clan tend to be kept small and settled rapidly (Evans-Pritchard 1968/1940). However, because all who are not in some way kin are enemies, an attack on one lineage segment may cause all members of a clan to coalesce against a common enemy (Sahlins 1961). This **segmentary lineage system** has important political implications for the Nuer and helps integrate their tribal-level society.

The Nuer are divided into about 20 clans, each of which is further divided into lineages. Below the level of the clan are segments called maximal lineages, which are broken down into major lineages, spread over many villages. Major lineages are subdivided into minor lineages, which in turn are made up of minimal lineages. The minimal lineage contains three to five generations and is the basic descent group that functions in day-to-day activities. Members of a minimal lineage live in the same village and regard one another as close relatives. Minimal lineages are politically independent, and there is no formal or centralized leadership above this level. The higher-order lineages are called upon to function mainly in the context of conflict. They are not corporate groups; as Evans-Pritchard states, neither clans nor lineages have any corporate life, and their members do not live to-

gether. Rather, the coming together of members of clans and lineages occurs when lower-order segments come into conflict. In a serious dispute between members of different lower-order lineages, the higher-order lineage members take the side of their nearest kin. Thus, clans and lineages function as contingent alliance networks, rather than formal parts of the political structure. This kind of political structure, called **complementary opposition,** is illustrated in Figure 8.2.

A segmentary lineage system is particularly functional when stronger tribes want to expand into nearby territories held by weaker tribes. Complementary opposition directs the energies of the society upward, away from competition between kin, to an outside enemy. Lineage segments on the borders of other tribes know that if they attack an enemy, they will be helped by other lineages related to them at these higher levels of organization (Sahlins 1961).

**Gender Relations in Patrilineal Societies** The degree to which a woman is incorporated into the patrilineage of her husband and the degree of autonomy she has vary in different societies. In some cases a woman may retain rights of inheritance in her father's lineage. In general, however, in a patrilineal system great care is taken to guarantee the husband's rights and control over his wife (or wives) and children because the continuity of the descent group depends on this. Patrilineal systems most often have patrilocal rules of residence, so a wife may

**segmentary lineage system** A form of sociopolitical organization in which multiple descent groups (usually patrilineages) form at different levels and function in different contexts.

**complementary opposition** A political structure in which higher-order units form alliances that emerge only when lower-order units come into conflict.

find herself living among strangers, which tends to undermine female solidarity and support.

Anthropologists have had a long-standing interest in understanding the complexity and conflict present within patrilineal families, and in particular on understanding women's roles in kin groups dominated by men. Lila Abu-Lughod's (1993) analysis of families in the Arab world is a good example. The women in these families are often portrayed only in terms of the ideal kinship patterns of patrilineality, polygyny, and patrilateral parallel-cousin marriage. Analyses have focused on issues of honor and shame, with honor revolving around the male's ability to protect the sexuality of women in his family. But like Soo Choi, in his description of the Korean village (see "Anthropology Makes a Difference" in this chapter), Abu-Lughod's ethnography reveals that these generalizations gloss over many of the conflicts, doubts, and arguments of life as it is really lived. They portray life as static and timeless, ignoring changing motivations and historical circumstances. Abu-Lughod challenges these static pictures of authoritarian patriarchy by analyzing the stories Bedouin women tell about themselves: women who refuse their family's choice of a spouse, women who get along (or don't) with their co-wives, women who are sometimes disappointed in their sons, women who assert themselves against their husband's wishes; in short, women who rebel against the norms of their society in small and sometimes effective ways.

Social institutions and cultural ideologies are closely intertwined. Basic to these interrelationships are economic systems, which include access to production, wealth, and property. There are no cultures in which people always behave as they are supposed to, as the rules tell them to behave. However, as economic systems change, people's actual behavior tends to depart more frequently from the rules. When there is rapid economic change, as in Korea, exceptions to the rules become more and more common. Under the pressure of changing economic realities and behavioral adjustments, kinship systems, the rules themselves, may also change, but they tend to change much more slowly than behavior.

## Matrilineal Descent Groups

Two fundamental ties recognized by every society are that between a woman and her children and that between siblings (brothers and sisters). In patrilineal societies, the most important source of male authority and control is the man's position as father and husband; in matrilineal societies, the most important male position is that of the mother's brother. In a matrilineal system, a man gains sexual and economic rights over a woman when he marries her, but he does not gain rights over her children. Children belong to the mother's descent group, not the father's, and many rights and responsibilities belong not to him but to the woman's brother. The mem-

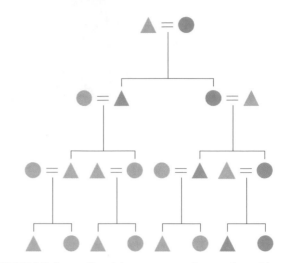

**FIGURE 8.3** A matrilineal descent group. In a society with matrilineal descent groups, membership in the group is defined by links through the mother. Sons and daughters are members of their mother's descent group, as are the children of daughters, but not the children of sons.

bership of a matrilineal descent group (see Figure 8.3) consists of a woman, her brothers and sisters, her sisters' (but not her brothers') children, her own children, and the children of her daughters (but not of her sons).

Matrilineal systems tend to be correlated with a matrilocal rule of residence: a man goes to live with or near his wife's kin after marriage. This means that in the domestic group, the man is among strangers, whereas his wife is surrounded by her kin. The husband plays a far less important role in the household in a matrilineal system than in a patrilineal one, and marriages in matrilineal societies tend to be less stable than those in other systems. In some cases, as among the Nayar of India, described in a classic ethnography (Gough 1961), it is possible for a matrilineally organized group to do away with the presence of husbands and fathers altogether, as long as there are brothers who assume responsibilities. It is important to remember that although women usually have higher status in societies in which there is a matrilineal reckoning of descent, matrilineality is not the same as matriarchy, in which the formal positions of power are held by women. With a few possible exceptions (A. Wallace 1970), the most important resources and highest political positions in matrilineal societies are in the control of males, although the male with the most power and control in these societies is not the husband (father) but the brother (uncle). The role of the mother's brother is an important or special one even in patrilineal societies, but in matrilineal societies it is particularly important. The mother's brother is a figure of authority and respect, and the children of a man's sister, rather than his own, are his heirs and successors.

In a matrilineal society, the relationship between a man and his son is likely to be affectionate and loving because it is free of the problems of authority and control that exist between fathers and sons in a patrilineal society. A man may feel emotionally close to his sons, but he is committed to pass on his knowledge, property, and offices to the sons of his sister. With his nephews he may have less friendly relations or even conflicts because they are subject to his control. Thus, in a matrilineal system a man's loyalties are split between his own sons and the sons of his sister; in a patrilineal system, this tension does not occur as part of the kinship structure.

## Double Descent

When descent is traced through a combination of matrilineal and patrilineal principles, the system is referred to as **double descent.** Double descent systems occur in only 5 percent of the world's cultures. In these societies, a person belongs both to the patrilineal group of the father and to the matrilineal group of the mother, but these descent groups operate in different areas of life.

The Yako of Nigeria have a system of double descent (Forde 1950). Cooperation in daily domestic life is strongest among patrilineally related kinsmen, who live with or near one another and jointly control and farm plots of land. Membership in the patriclan is the source of rights over farmland and forest products. One obligation of the patriclan is to provide food at funerals. Membership in the men's associations and the right to fruit trees are inherited through the male line. The arbitration of disputes is in the hands of senior patriclan members. Cooperation in ritual and succession to some religious offices are also derived from patriclan membership.

Matrilineal bonds and clan membership are also important in Yako society, even though matriclan members do not live near one another and do not cooperate as a group in everyday activities. The rights and duties of matrilineal kinship are different from those of patrilineal kinship. Practical assistance to matrilineal kin, the rights and obligations of the mother's brother and sons, and the authority of the priest of a matrilineal clan are based on mystical ideas regarding the perpetuation and tranquility of the Yako world. The Yako believe that the fertility of crops, beasts, and humans, and peace between individuals and within the community are associated with and passed on through women. Life comes from the mother. The children of one mother are bound to mutual support and peaceful relations. The matrilineage is thus held together by mystical bonds of common fertility, and anger and violence between its members are considered sinful. These sentiments are reinforced in the cult of the matriclan spirits, whose priests are ritually given the qualities of women.

Despite their isolation from one another by the rule of patrilocal residence, matriclan relatives have specific mutual obligations. Rights in the transfer of accumulated wealth, but not land, belong to the matrilineal kinship

group. The members of matriclans supervise funerals and arrange for the disposal of the personal property of the dead. All currency and livestock customarily pass to matrilineal relatives, who also receive the greater share of tools, weapons, and household goods. The movable property of women passes to their daughters. Matriclans are responsible for the debts of their kin, for making loans to one another at reasonable rates, and for providing part of the bridewealth transferred at the marriage of a sister's son.

Thus, for the Yako, paternity and maternity are both important in descent. Each contains different qualities from which flow the rights, obligations, and benefits, both practical and spiritual, that bind people to one another and ensure the continuity of the society.

# Nonunilineal Kinship Systems

About 40 percent of the world's societies are structured around kinship systems that are **nonunilineal,** or **cognatic.** These systems are further divided into bilateral and ambilineal descent. In systems of bilateral descent, an individual is considered to be related equally to other kin through both the mother's and the father's side. In a unilineal kinship system, an individual is formally affiliated with a large number of relations extended lineally through time, but only on one side of the family; in a system of bilateral descent, both maternal and paternal lines are used in reckoning descent, in establishing the rights and obligations of kinship, and in forming social groups. Bilateral kinship systems appear to be particularly adaptive in societies in which mobility and independence are important. They are basic to Western culture, including the United States, and predominate among foraging societies as well.

The people linked by bilateral kin networks are called a **kindred.** A kindred is not a group, but rather a network of relations with a single group of siblings at the center. With the exception of brothers and sisters, every individual's kindred is different from every other individual's. Kindreds are actually overlapping categories of kin, rather than social groups, and are more difficult to organize as cooperative, kin-based collectivities. For example, because a kindred is not a group but rather an ego-centered network, it cannot own land or have continuity over time.

---

**double descent** The tracing of descent through both matrilineal and patrilineal links, each of which is used for different purposes.

**nonunilineal descent** Any system of descent in which both father's and mother's lineages have equal claim to the individual.

**cognatic descent** Any nonunilineal system of descent.

**kindred** A unique kin network made up of all the people related to a specific individual in a bilateral kinship system.

# Ethnography

## The Matrilineal Minangkabau of Sumatra

The Minangkabau, a rice-growing society in Western Sumatra, Indonesia, is one of the few matrilineal Islamic societies in South Asia. In Minangkabau villages, kinship relations and families are organized around mothers and their daughters and sons. Life-cycle ceremonies, a key feature of Minangkabau culture, are organized by women and their brothers and presided over by senior males. The field research of Evelyn Blackwood, a feminist anthropologist, demonstrates that Minangkabau women wield significant informal power in their families and in their matrilineages, based on their ownership of rice land, their significant participation in decisions regarding life-cycle ceremonies, matrilocal residence of daughters after marriage, and matrilineal inheritance in which property and land are transmitted from mothers to daughters.

The "big house," or "matrihouse," is a central site of Minangkabau social relations, and usually contains an extended family of three or four generations, including a senior woman, her daughter(s), their husbands, and children. Compartments at the back of the big house are for the mother and her daughters, and the front half of the house is an open space for public gatherings and ceremonies. The central house post is identified with the senior woman, who is called "the central pillar of the big house."

When a daughter marries, she and her husband move into her big house. Each newly married daughter resides with her husband at the end compartment farthest from the central house post, and elder married sisters move down the line of compartments toward the central post. Sons leave the house at marriage to move in with their wives, but one room next to the kitchen is designated as the men's room, for any di-

vorced or widowed men forced to return home.

Women are not only symbolically identified with the core (pillar) of the house, but also dominate the house in daily life and during ceremonies. A senior woman and

In spite of the pressures of Islam, Christianity, Indonesian national culture, and the global economy, the most important group in Minangkabau society is the three-generational matrilineal descent group.

© Jeremy Hartley/Panos Pictures

her daughters are the core of the house. Because sons marry out, they are not part of the daily life of the house, and even the senior male, or mother's brother, takes center stage only temporarily when he presides over ceremonies. The conjugal unit of husband and wife is a subsidiary unit within the matrilineal extended family, and husbands are peripheral to household affairs, most often away during the day working, returning to the house only in the evenings.

The composition of any particular matrihouse varies: it may be a several-generation extended family, or a two-generation household of adult women, that is, a mother and recently married daughter. Mother-daughter relations are the key to the actual composition of a matrihouse. Matrihouses continue from generation to generation as daughters are born, marry, bear children, and eventually become senior women themselves. Usually only one of a woman's daughters will actually live with her husband and children in the matrihouse, other daughters and their descendants may split and establish their own houses, often close by. Thus, over generations matrihouses may develop into a cluster of houses of related kinswomen.

Matrilineal inheritance of property is key to female power in the household. Women have rights as heirs to and controllers of matrilineal property, and their daughters inherit the right to land and its disposition. Once a daughter is given land by her mother after marriage, it is under her control. The daughter decides how to use it and what to do with its produce, although she cannot pawn it without her mother's permission. No one can interfere with a senior woman's right to use and dispose of her land as she wishes. Sons may be given use rights to land if land is available and their mothers are willing to help them out, but they cannot pass matrilineal land on to their children. The members of a matrihouse share resources in complex ways, guided by the Minangkabau value on mutual cooperation and assistance among kin, as well as the belief that those who earn an income have some rights over how to dispose of it. A family's main income comes from the rice land belonging to the matrihouse, which is controlled by the senior woman, who uses the income to pay for common household needs. In some matrihouses, mother and daughters share the produce of their undivided rice fields; in other cases, daughters also have access to their own income, either from their husbands, through their own labor, or from small-scale businesses, and may use some of this income for joint projects benefiting the matrihouse.

All matrihouse members are expected to contribute some form of unpaid labor or cash to the household. Mothers may leave small children with a variety of adults; both boys and girls watch younger siblings; girls help their mothers clean the house; boys tend to small animals. Young unmarried daughters weed the rice fields; adult daughters plant, weed, and harvest rice on the family land. Unmarried sons help with the harvest and transport unhusked rice to be milled. This expectation of cooperation is buttressed by the "rule" of the senior woman and respect for and deference to elders. As senior women become elderly, the management of the household falls more to their daughters, as do the work and supervision of the rice fields.

Although married sons are not present in the daily life of the matrihouse, they remain kinsmen of the house with certain responsibilities and obligations, contingent on age and rank. Sons maintain a strong interest in and support for their natal kin group, and a son's cooperation with his mother helps ensure her continued support of his interests. A mother displeased with her son may take back some rice land

she has given him, or refuse him return to the house after a divorce, although that is a male right. Apart from practical interests, a man feels emotionally tied to his mother. Young unmarried Minangkabau men who work for wages in other parts of Indonesia usually send home some of their wages to their mothers, or they may work in their mothers' rice fields. These filial obligations last throughout a man's lifetime. Even after marriage, a son remains part of the matrilineal family with a voice in family matters and even substantial influence if he has proven a reliable helper to the matrihouse.

Sons-in-law, unlike sons, are peripheral to the matrihouse; in the past a son-in-law was only a temporary resident in his wife's family house, visiting at night and returning to his mother's house in the morning. Although a husband is now a more permanent part of his wife's house, he is still regarded more as an "honored, but relatively insecure, guest" than as part of the family. As "guest" residents, husbands provide additional labor, land, or income to the household but do not participate in decision making in their wives' lineage affairs. Husbands are expected to have their own source of income, through agricultural or wage labor, which they usually use for expenses associated with raising their children. Men have discretion in spending their income but are subject to strong pressure to be good providers for their wives' families.

A man's duty to provide material assistance to both his own matrilineage and his wife's family creates tensions for men pulled between their responsibilities as husbands and as sons, between financially assisting their wives' families and their own natal family. Mothers and sisters feel they have a right to make claims to a man's income, and there are no set rules for dividing income between the wife's matrihouse and the natal house. Men also maintain enduring ties with their children, even after divorce or remarriage. This, too, may cause

tension as a man is pulled between leaving his assets to his own children or to his sister's children. As husbands, then, men are valued for their labor and income, however supplemental, as well as their reproductive capabilities, but they are subordinate in the household. A senior woman does not control her son-in-law's behavior, but he must show his respect by working hard for the household. If he does not, his marriage and relations with his wife's kin will be negatively affected.

The traditional matrilineal orientation of the Minangkabau conflicts with the patrilineal and patriarchal orientation of other ideologies to which the Minangkabau are subjected. In the last century, the Dutch colonialists, consistent with Western ideals, attempted to put land in men's hands. Both Islam and contemporary Indonesian nationalism emphasize males as household heads, women as dependent caretakers of home and family, and the primacy of patrilineal relations as the basis of family and community life. Participation in the capitalist global economy, which offers more wage work to men than to women, also supports the movement from female to male dominance in families. In spite of these influences, however, a matrilineal ideology and its associated practices continue to hold a predominant place in Minangkabau life.

### CRITICAL THINKING QUESTIONS

1. What are the sources of women's power among the Minangkabau?
2. What are the most important male and female roles in Minangkabau society?
3. Compare the sources of conflict in a matrilineal society like the Minangkabau with those in a patrilineal society.

Source: Evelyn Blackwood, *Webs of Power: Women, Kin, and Community in a Sumatran Village.* New York: Rowman & Littlefield, 2000.

In an ambilineal system, individuals may choose to affiliate with either their mother's or their father's descent group, but not simultaneously with both. **Ambilineal descent** is found in many Pacific Island societies. In these, at marriage, the new couple chooses to live with and identify with either spouse's descent group. Generally, which descent group a couple chooses depends on a variety of factors. The most important of these is probably access to land, a resource in particularly short supply on many Pacific Islands, but friendships and politics also play important roles in such identification. One interesting aspect of ambilineal kinship is that the ancestors of a child might be quite different from the ancestors of his or her parents.

# The Classification of Kin

In all societies, kin are referred to by special terms. The total system of kinship terms and the rules for using these terms make up a kinship classification system. In every system of kinship terminology, some relatives are classed together (referred to by the same kinship term), whereas other relatives are differentiated from each other (called by different terms). Kinship systems vary in the degree to which they have different kinship terms for different relatives. Some kinship systems have only a small number of kinship terms, whereas others have a different term for almost every relative.

The ways in which kin are classified are associated with the roles they play in society. If a person refers to his father and his father's brothers by the same term, the social roles he plays with respect to these individuals will tend to be similar. By the same token, if he uses one term to refer to his father and another to refer to his father's brothers, there will probably be a difference in behavior as well. He will probably behave one way to his father and a different way to his father's brothers. For example, in American society, a mother-in-law and a mother's brother's wife are both relations by marriage. However, only one of them—mother-in-law—is distinguished terminologically; mother's sister and mother's brother's wife are both lumped together under one term—aunt. Given this, an anthropologist would expect that behavior toward the mother would be different than behavior toward the mother-in-law, but behavior toward mother's brother's wife and mother's sister would be about the same. Of course, although kinship terms refer to behavioral expectations, actual behavior is modified by individual personality differences and special circumstances.

Understanding kinship classification systems is not just an interesting anthropological game. Kinship classification is one of the important regulators of behavior in most societies, outlining each person's rights and obligations and specifying the ways in which a person must act toward others and they toward him or her. Kinship classification systems are also related to other aspects of culture: the types of social groups that are formed, the systems of marriage and inheritance, and even deeper and broader cultural values.

## A Comparison of Kinship Classification in North India and the United States

As an American woman married to a North Indian man, I (Nanda, one of this text's authors) was instructed in how to behave with various relatives. My relationship with my husband's brothers and their wives is regulated by the principle of seniority, which is absent in American kinship classification. My husband's elder brother is my *jait* and his wife is my *jaitani*. I must treat both of them with deference, similar to that shown to my father-in-law, by adding the suffix -*ji* to their kinship terms, touching their feet when I meet them, and refraining from using their first names. But my husband's younger brother, who is my *deva,* and his wife, who is my *devrani,* may be treated with the friendly informality more characteristic of sister and brother-in-law relations in the United States. On our trips to India, I can greet my husband's younger brother with an embrace and talk with him in a joking, familiar manner, but I must never embrace my husband's elder brother, even though I feel equally friendly toward him and like him equally well.

A comparison of kinship terms in India and the United States shows that one immediately apparent difference is in the number of kinship terms; 45 in North India but only 22 in the United States. This is because the North Indian system distinguishes several kinds of kin that North Americans group together; this reflects the greater flexibility in behavior toward kin that is acceptable in North America (see Figure 8.4).

Many of the North Indian cultural patterns that underlie its kinship terminology are based on the importance of the patrilineal, patrilocal extended family (the importance of the male principle in inheritance and seniority). These include the lower status of the family of the bride compared to that of the groom; the obligations a male child has toward his parents, including the specific ritual obligations of the eldest son; and the ritual roles played by various kin in life-cycle ceremonies such as marriage and funerals. These patterns are based on two major principles of Indian culture and social organization: hierarchy and the importance of the group. The contrasting Western values of equality, individualism,

**ambilineal descent** A form of bilateral descent in which an individual may choose to affiliate with either the father's or mother's descent group.

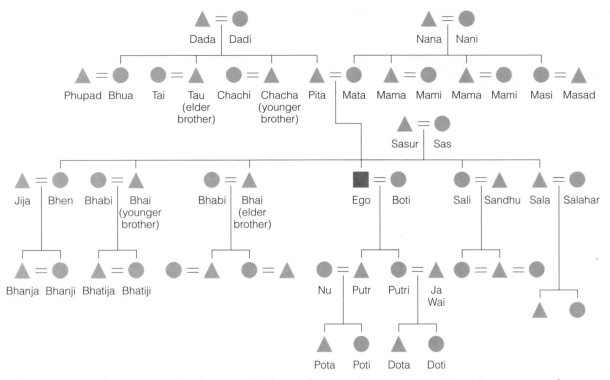

**FIGURE 8.4** Kinship classification in North India: terms of reference from a male's perspective. (*Note:* There is no term for a man's nieces and nephews on his wife's side. They are referred to descriptively as wife's sister's daughters or sons.) Not shown on the diagram are the terms a wife uses for her husband's sister, her husband's sister's husband, her husband's elder brother, his wife, her husband's younger brother, and his wife, which adds 6 terms to the 39 used by a male to describe his kin.

and the nuclear family are expressed in North American kinship terminology.

The principle of relative age, which is an aspect of hierarchy, is critical in the Indian kinship system but absent in North America. Thus, a man uses different terms to refer to his father's elder brother (*tau*) and his father's younger brother (*chacha*), and this carries over to their wives; his father's elder brother's wife is *tai* and his father's younger brother's wife is *chachi*. This terminological difference reflects the respect attached to seniority. Out of respect for the principle of hierarchy, it is still common for many North Indian women to cover their hair, if not their faces, in the presence of both the father-in-law and the husband's elder brother.

A second principle that complicates the Indian kinship system from the point of view of a Westerner is the Indian differentiation of kin according to whether they are from the mother's side or the father's side of the family. This principle (bifurcation) is absent in English kinship terminology. In North India, the father's brothers and the mother's brothers are called by different terms, as are the father's and mother's parents: *Dadi* and *dada* are the grandparents on the father's side, and *nani* and *nana* are the grandparents on the mother's side. These distinctions reflect the Indian principle of respect and formality associated with the male side of the family and the more open show of affection permitted with the maternal side of the family.

The Indian principles of hierarchy and patriarchy turn up again in the higher status accorded the family of the husband's relatives. This status inequality is reflected in a number of ways in Indian kinship terminology and behavior, such as the distinction between a man's wife's brother (*sala*) and his sister's husband (*jija*). Both relations are called *brother-in-law* in the English system, reflecting the general equality in North America of the husband's and wife's sides of the family. In India, a man's sister's husband is in a higher position relative to him than is his wife's brother. Correspondingly, a sister's husband is treated with great respect, whereas a wife's brother may be treated more ambivalently and may be the target of jokes. The behavioral expectations of this unequal relationship between the bride's and groom's families extend even beyond immediate relatives, to relatives of relatives by marriage.

The kinship and other cultural rules that structure relationships between kin in North India, like those in the Korean village, are important. But their functions in guiding behavior, just like their functions in succession and inheritance described for Korea, are resisted and manipulated in response to pragmatic interest, social circumstances, and emotion. Contesting claims over family property may lead to alliances within the family that contrast with cultural rules about seniority and patriarchal power. Illness of some family members also may direct the flow of resources in directions not covered, and even in opposition to, kinship rules governing reciprocity.

In the many rituals involved in an Indian wedding, specific relatives have specific obligations. Here, elder male members of the bride's family perform the ritual of giving sweet food to the groom.

As a close examination of kinship in any society reveals, our understanding of culture and society must be based not just on people's notions about ideal behavior but also the realities of the strategies all people use to negotiate their adaptation to life's contingencies. "The Global and the Local" feature at the end of this chapter indicates some of the ways in which global migration has altered the realities of kinship relations among many immigrant communities.

In addition to informing us about the behavior of people in other societies, the study of kinship systems goes to a fundamental point of anthropology. Most Americans consider it normal and natural to use our kin system. We "automatically" call our parents' brothers and sisters "aunt" and "uncle" and their children "cousin." We feel that this represents an obvious underlying biological reality and find it hard to understand how other people could use different systems. We tend to ignore questions our system raises, such as why we use the same word for our mother's sister, and our mother's brother's wife, or why there are no separate terms for male and female cousins but we do differentiate nieces from nephews. These discrepancies point to a basic fact: kinship systems use the metaphor of biology, but they are social systems, not biological ones. The systems used by other societies feel as natural to their members as ours does to us.

**lineal kin** Blood relations linked through descent, such as Ego, Ego's mother, Ego's grandmother, and Ego's daughter.

**collateral kin** Kin descended from a common ancestor but not in a direct ascendent or descendent line, such as siblings and cousins.

# Principles for Classifying Kin

Kinship can be described using a series of abstract, logical principles. The interesting thing is that the combination of these principles results in kinship systems that are extremely logical, yet very different from our own. Societies differ in the categories of relatives they distinguish and the principles by which kin are classified. To understand the rules by which kin are classified, we must first establish the position of the individual from whose perspective the system is seen. We refer to this person as "Ego." For example, if you were to describe your family from your perspective (I have three siblings, two aunts and uncles on my mother's side. . . .) you would be "Ego." If you were to do the same thing from your cousin's perspective, then he or she would be "Ego." Once we have established Ego, we can examine how different categories of kin are grouped and distinguished according to the following seven principals.

**Generation** The generation principle distinguishes ascending and descending generations from Ego. In American society, you, your brothers and sisters, and the children of your parents' brothers and sisters are members of the same generation. Your parents and their brothers and sisters (as well as the spouses of those brothers and sisters) are members of the ascending generation above you. Your children, as well as those of your siblings and cousins, are members of the descending generation below you. It is important to understand that generation is different from age. It is fairly common for some members of your parents' generation to be the same age as some members of your generation, or even younger.

**Relative Age** A kinship system that uses the relative age principle has different kinship terms for relatives that are older than oneself and relatives that are younger than oneself. English kinship terminology does not recognize this principle.

**Lineality versus Collaterality** Kin related in a single line, such as grandfather–father–son, are called **lineal kin.** **Collateral kin** are descended from a common ancestor with Ego but are not Ego's direct ascendants or descendants. For example, brothers and sisters (siblings) and cousins are collateral kin. They are descended from the same ancestors but are not in a direct ascendant or descendant line. In many societies, collaterality is not distinguished in the kinship terminology. Ego may refer to both his father and father's brother as father. Both the mother and her sisters may similarly be called mother.

**Gender** Kinship systems that use the principle of gender have different kin terms for people of different genders. In English, some kinship terms differentiate by gender, such as aunt, uncle, and brother; the word cousin, however, does not differentiate by gender. In some other cultures, all kinship terms distinguish gender.

**Consanguineal versus Affinal Kin** People related to Ego by blood (**consanguinity**) are distinguished from similar relationships by marriage. For example, English kinship terminology distinguishes sister from sister-in-law, father from father-in-law, and so on. The English word uncle, however, does not distinguish between consanguineal and affinal relationships; it is applied equally to the brother of our father or mother, and to the husband of our father's or mother's sister.

**Side of the Family** Some societies use a kinship system in which kin terms distinguish between relatives from the mother's side of the family and those from the father's side. This principle is called **bifurcation.** An example would be societies in which the mother's brother is referred to differently from the father's brother. This principle is not used in English kinship terminology.

**Sex of Linking Relative** In societies in which distinguishing collateral relatives is an important principle of kinship classification, the sex of the linking relative may be important in the kinship terminology. A linking relative is an individual, related to you consanguineally, that connects you to another relative. For example, if your mother's sister has children, you are linked to those children through your mother's sister. In this case the linking relative is female. If your mother's brother has children, you are linked to those children through him and the sex of the linking relative is male. When the sex of your parent and the linking relative are the same, the children to whom you are linked are known as **parallel cousins** (so, these are the children of your mother's sisters or your father's brothers). If the sex of your parent and the linking relative are different, the children to whom you are linked are known as your **cross cousins** (so, these are the children of your mother's brothers and your father's sisters). In many societies (though not in America) people use different kin terms for parallel and cross cousins. They usually are further distinguished according to whether the linking relative is from the matrilineal or patrilineal line. This is particularly important where Ego is prohibited from marrying a parallel cousin but may, or even must, marry a cross cousin.

# Types of Kinship Terminologies

The seven principles just listed are combined to form seven different systems of kinship. These systems were first described by Lewis Henry Morgan in the 19th century. With one exception, he gave them the names of Native American groups: Hawaiian, Eskimo, Iroquois, Omaha, Crow, and Sudanese. In some cases, these names reflect 19th-century terminology. For example, even though the Eskimo call themselves "Inuit" we still talk about Eskimo kinship terminology. Although the groups that Morgan identified do use the kin terminology he associated with them, Morgan intended for his terminology to be much broader than this. He wanted to classify all the world's kinship systems. So, for example, the Iroquois use the Iroquois kin system but this system is also used by the Yanomamo, a South American group, some villages in rural China, and many other groups around the world.

Systems of kinship terminology reflect the kinds of kin groups that are most important in a society. Each of these systems is described briefly in the following sections. You will find that careful attention to the accompanying diagrams will help you understand the descriptions.

**Hawaiian** As its name suggests, the Hawaiian system is found in Polynesia. It is rather simple in that it uses the fewest kinship terms. The Hawaiian system emphasizes the distinctions between generations and reflects the equality between the mother's and the father's sides of the family in relation to Ego. All relatives of the same generation and sex—for example, father, father's brother, and mother's brother—are referred to by the same kinship term. Male and female kin in Ego's generation are distinguished in the terminology, but the terms for sister and brother are the same as those for the children of one's parents' siblings (see Figure 8.5). This system correlates with ambilineality and ambilocality, which means that depending on circumstances and choice a person may belong to either the mother's or father's descent group. Using the same terms for parents and their siblings establishes closeness with a large number of relatives in the ascending generation, giving Ego a wide choice in deciding which group to affiliate and live with.

**Eskimo** The Eskimo terminology, found among hunting-and-gathering peoples in North America, is correlated with bilateral descent. The Eskimo system emphasizes the nuclear family by using terms for its members (mother, father, sister, brother, daughter, son) that are not used for any other kin. Outside the nuclear family, many kinds of relatives that are distinguished in other systems are lumped together. We have already given the examples of aunt and uncle. Similarly, all children of the kin in the parental generation are

**consanguinity** Blood ties between people.

**bifurcation** A principle of classifying kin under which different kinship terms are used for the mother's side of the family and the father's side of the family.

**parallel cousins** The children of a parent's same-sex siblings (mother's sisters, father's brothers).

**cross cousins** The children of a parent's siblings of the opposite sex (mother's brothers, father's sisters).

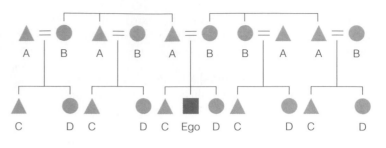

**FIGURE 8.5** Hawaiian kinship. The primary distinctions in Hawaiian kinship are between men and women and between generations. All members of Ego's generation are designated by the same terms Ego uses for brother and sister. All members of Ego's parents' generation are designated by the same terms Ego uses for mother and father.

called cousins, no matter what their sex or who the linking relative is. The Eskimo system singles out the biologically closest group of relations (the nuclear family) and treats more distant kin more or less equally (see Figure 8.6).

**Iroquois** The Iroquois system is associated with matrilineal or double descent and emphasizes the importance of unilineal descent groups. In this system, the same term is used for mother and mother's sister, and a common term also applies to father and father's brother. Parallel cousins are referred to by the same terms as those for brother and sister. Father's sister and mother's brother are distinguished from other kin, as are the children of father's sister and mother's brother (Ego's cross cousins) (see Figure 8.7).

**Omaha** The Omaha system is found among patrilineal peoples, including the Native American group of that name. In this system, the same term is used for father and father's brother and for mother and mother's sister. Parallel cousins are equated with siblings, but cross cousins are referred to by separate terms. A man refers to his brother's children by the same terms he applies to his own children, but he refers to his sister's children by different terms. These terms are extended to all relations who are classified as Ego's brothers and sisters (see Figure 8.8). In this system, there is a merging of generations on the mother's side. All men who are members of Ego's mother's patrilineage will be called "mother's brother" regardless of their age or generational relationship to

Ego. Thus, the term applied to mother's brother is also applied to the son of mother's brother.

This generational merging is not applied to relations on the father's side. Although father and his brothers are referred to by the same term, this does not extend to the descending generation. The different terminology applied to the father's and the mother's patrilineal groups reflects the different position of Ego in relation to these kin. Generational differences are important on the father's side because members of the ascending generation are likely to have some authority over Ego (as his father does) and be treated differently from patrilineage members of Ego's own generation. The mother's patrilineage is unimportant to Ego in this system, and this is reflected by lumping them all together in the terminology.

**Crow** The Crow system, named for the Crow Indians of North America, is the matrilineal equivalent of the Omaha system. This means that the relations on the male side (Ego's father's matrilineage) are lumped together, whereas generational differences are recognized in the mother's matrilineal group (see Figure 8.9). In both the Omaha and Crow systems, the overriding importance of unilineality leads to the subordination of other principles of classifying kin, such as relative age or generation.

**Sudanese** No North American groups used Morgan's final kinship system, so he named it Sudanese, after the African groups, primarily in Ethiopia, who do use it. It's also used

**FIGURE 8.6** Eskimo kinship. A critical distinction in Eskimo kinship is between lineal and collateral relations. Ego uses one set of terms to refer to lineal relations (A, B, C, and D) and a second set to refer to collateral relations (E, F, and G).

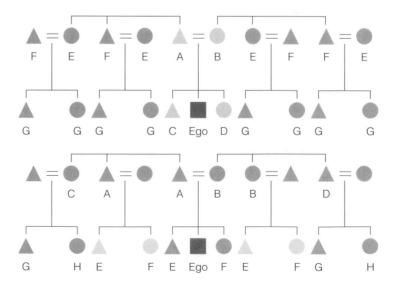

**FIGURE 8.7** Iroquois kinship. The Iroquois system is found in societies with unilineal descent. It distinguishes mother's side of the family (B and D) from father's side of the family (A and C), and cross cousins (in orange) from parallel cousins (in yellow).

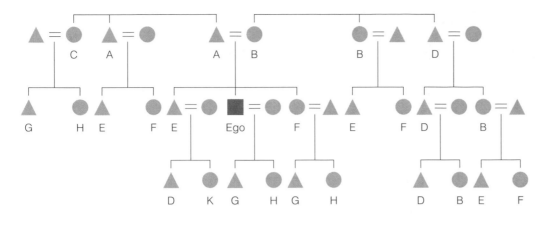

**FIGURE 8.8** Omaha kinship. The Omaha is a bifurcate merging system found among patrilineal people. Like the Iroquois system, it merges father and father's brother and mother and mother's sister. However, in addition, the Omaha system merges generation on the mother's side. So, men who are members of Ego's mother's patrilineage are referred to by the same term as for mother's brother, regardless of age or generation.

in some places in Turkey and was used in Ancient Rome. Sudanese is the most descriptive terminology system. The types included here use different terms for practically every relative: siblings, paternal parallel cousins, maternal parallel cousins, paternal cross cousins, and maternal cross cousins. Ego refers to his or her parents by terms distinct from those for father's brother, father's sister, mother's sister, and mother's brother (see Figure 8.10). The groups using Sudanese kinship tend to be strongly patrilineal and very concerned with issues of wealth, class, and political power.

The great variety of kinship terminologies underscores the fact that kinship systems reflect social relationships and are not based simply on biological relations between people. Kinship classification systems are part of the totality of a kinship system. Each type of classification emphasizes the most important kinship groupings and relationships in the societies that use it. Thus, the Eskimo system emphasizes the importance of the nuclear family, setting it apart from more distant relations on the

maternal and paternal sides. The Iroquois, Omaha, and Crow systems, found in unilineal societies, emphasize the importance of lineage and clan. In the Hawaiian system, the simplicity of terms leaves the way open for flexibility in choosing one's descent group.

In making sense out of kinship systems, anthropologists attempt to understand the relationship of terminologies, rules of descent, and kinship groups to the ecological, economic, and political conditions under which different kinship systems emerge and change. Re-emerging as a topic of central interest in anthropology, studies on the structure and ideologies of kinship become frameworks for examining a range of related subjects: new kinship and family forms (e.g., domestic partnerships), new reproductive technologies, social mobility within family genealogies, gender relations in both colonial and contemporary societies, and new constructions of "blood" relations. We take up some of these topics in the next chapter.

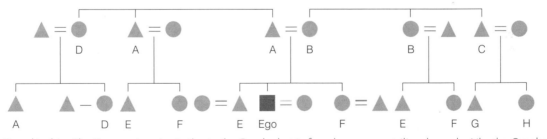

**FIGURE 8.9** Crow kinship. The Crow system is similar to the Omaha but is found among matrilineal people. Like the Omaha and Iroquois, it merges father with father's brother and mother with mother's sister. However, unlike the Omaha, it merges generation on the father's side so that all women who are members of the father's matrilineage are referred to with the term for father's sister, regardless of age or generation.

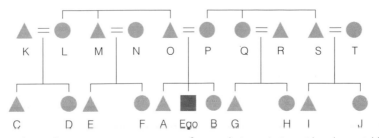

**FIGURE 8.10** Sudanese kinship. The Sudanese system occurs most frequently in societies with substantial hierarchy and distinctions of class. It includes a separate term for each type of relative.

# The Global and the Local: Transmigration and Kinship

Kinship relations are an important context in the migration of people across state borders, itself a significant dimension of globalization. The importance of kinship in this process is apparent in the criteria by which immigration rights and citizenship are granted in most nations of the world. In the United States, the priority of kinship and the cultural importance of bilateral kin relations are basic to contemporary immigration policy. In 1965, 1978, and 1990, new immigration laws abolished the discriminatory national origins quota system of the 1920s and emphasized family reunification. The current preference system, which gives highest priority to members of the nuclear family, indicates American cultural priorities: first preference is given to spouses and married and unmarried sons and daughters and their children. A lower preference is given to brothers and sisters, their spouses, and their children.

Immigration policies that make it easier for kin to immigrate as well as high levels of illegal immigration (often to join family members) have led to a large foreign-born population in the United States. In 1970,

A festive gathering honoring an immigrant from West Africa who worked on the staff of a New York apartment building and sent money home to his family. Now, after many years of transmigration, he will return permanently to take a high official position in his native village.

© Joan Gregg

**transnationalism** The pattern of close ties and frequent visits by immigrants to their home countries.

**transmigrant** Immigrants who maintain close relations with their home countries.

less than 5 percent of the U.S. population was foreign born. By 1994, that number had risen to almost 9 percent and by 2003, almost 12 percent (Larsen 2004).

There are important differences between immigration today and immigration 100 years ago. In the past, most immigrants more or less severed ties with kin who stayed behind. Travel was difficult and very expensive. The only way most kin could keep in contact was by letters. Immigrants today live in a world where communication—by telephone, e-mail, and the Internet—is abundant, relatively simple, and inexpensive, and air travel is within the reach of the middle and working class. Thus, many immigrants, especially those from nearby areas such as the Caribbean, are able to retain much closer social and economic ties with their families and cultures in their homelands than previously (Hamid 1990). This pattern of close ties and frequent visits by immigrants to their home countries is called **transnationalism** (Glick-Schiller, Basch, and Szanton-Blanc 1992).

The term **transmigrant** has been coined to refer to immigrants who maintain close relations with their home countries (Glick-Schiller 1992). Transmigrants move culture, money, and information around the world rapidly, very often through kin networks. The substantial amounts of money migrants send to their families back home are critical in the economies of many nations, and by extension, in the global economy. According to a World Bank report, immigrants in the United States in 2001 sent $18 billion back to individuals in their home countries. Immigrants to Saudi Arabia, Germany, Belgium, and Switzerland also sent very large sums back home. Many national economies depend on these remittances: they account for 15 percent of the economy of Nicaragua, for example, and in Tajikistan, 54 percent of the economy depended on remittances in 2008 (Tavernise 2008a). Money sent home by migrants offers a safety net for those kin left behind both in their domestic lives and in the building of communities. Sadly, the decline in the global economy has its local effects: as employment declines everywhere, the situation of kin left at home also deteriorates.

Kinship ties have also long been an important route for migration, social networking, and earning a living in a new country. Through studying urban migrants, anthropologist Louise Lamphere (2001, in Stone) demonstrates the importance of kin networks in economic survival and success in the United States, and how this may change. Among Chinese immigrants to the United States, for example, pooling resources with kin has been an important factor in their business success. More than 90 percent of new immigrant businesses in the San Francisco Bay area are family firms, initiated and built on family resources and kinship networks. As these firms grow, the family may depend on fictive kinship, incorporating people from the same village or those with the same last name but no known relationship (Wong 1988). Things are changing, however. The newer, successful Chinese immigrant professionals in the high-tech businesses and professions of Silicon Valley have become more like mainstream Americans in their social networks. The traditional importance of Chinese kinship networks—lineage, clan, and regional associations—are giving way in importance to professional organizations, social networks of friends, political organizations, and transnational social networks in their lives and careers (Wong 2006).

Kinship networks continue to be important for many immigrant groups; however, the Chinese in Silicon Valley also indicate that as immigrant situations change, the previous emphasis on kinship networks as a source of support to immigrants may give way, or be balanced by, other relationships.

## Key Questions

1. What are some important connections between kinship and transmigration?
2. Discuss how your own kinship relations (or those of a recent immigrant or child of immigrants whom you know) function in both a global and a local context.

# Summary

1. **What role does kinship play in modern industrial societies like the United States? Is nepotism an American value or is it a contradiction of American values?** Ideally, kinship in the United States should not grant favor or privilege, but nepotism does exist in many areas of life. In many societies, nepotism is expected as part of the almost universal cultural emphasis on kin helping and protecting each other.

2. **What are the functions of kinship systems?** Kinship systems are cultural creations that define and organize relatives by blood and marriage, classify different kinds of kin, provide continuity between generations, and define a group of people who can depend on one another for mutual aid.

3. **What is the most important difference between kinship in traditional societies compared to modern, industrial societies?** In traditional societies, kinship is the most important basis of social organization; in modern industrial societies, citizenship, social class, and common interests become more important than kinship in organizing social relationships.

4. **What is the role of descent in traditional societies?** In many societies, descent is the key factor in the formation of corporate social groups.

5. **What kinds of descent systems are found in different societies?** In societies with a unilineal rule of descent, mainly found among pastoral and horticultural societies, descent group membership is based on *either* the male or female line.

6. **What is the difference between a lineage and a clan and what sort of functions does each have?** A lineage is a group of kin whose members can trace their descent from a common ancestor. A clan is a group whose members believe they have a common ancestor but cannot trace the relationship genealogically. Lineages tend to have domestic functions, clans to have political and religious functions. Both lineages and clans are important in regulating marriage.

7. **What are the central dynamics that characterize patrilineal kinship systems?** In patrilineal systems, a man's children belong to his lineage, as do the children of his sons but not of his daughters. Patrilineality is often associated with patrilocality; husbands have strong control over wives and children, and the common economic interests of brothers is a major feature of the society.

8. **What are the central dynamics that characterize matrilineal kinship systems?** In matrilineal systems, which are normally matrilocal, a woman's children belong to her lineage, not that of their father. The mother's brother has authority over his sister's children, and relations between husband and wife are more fragile than in patrilineal societies.

9. **What is double descent and how does it function?** In systems of double descent, the individual belongs to both the patrilineage of the father and the matrilineage of the mother. Each group functions in different social contexts. The Yako of Nigeria have a system of double descent.

10. **Describe bilateral descent and give examples of the kinds of societies that are most likely to be bilateral.** In bilateral systems an individual is equally related to mother's and father's kin. This rule of descent results in the formation of kindreds, which are overlapping kinship networks, rather than a permanent group of kin. Bilateral kinship is found predominantly among foragers and in modern industrialized states.

11. **What are some of the principles used to categorize relatives in different systems of kinship terminology? Using these principles, give an example of the contrast between the American and North Indian kinship terminology.** Kinship terminologies group together or distinguish relatives according to various principles such as generation, relative age, lineality or collaterality, sex, consanguinity or affinity, bifurcation, and sex of the linking relative. Different societies may use all or some of these principles in classifying kin. For example, the American kinship terminology does not distinguish relative age nor does it distinguish the mother's from the father's side of the family, as is done in North India.

12. **What are the six major types of kinship classification systems and what do such systems reveal about a society?** The six major systems of kinship classification are the Hawaiian, Eskimo, Iroquois, Omaha, Crow, and Sudanese. Because kinship is a principal organizing structure in many societies and because using different kin terms reflects different behaviors expected toward different types of relatives, understanding kin systems helps anthropologists understand important aspects of social organization and behavior in different societies.

13. **What kind of roles does kinship play in immigration and transmigration? How might this change with changing circumstances?** In the past, kinship relationships played a central role in helping immigrants successfully adapt to their new homes. As the social status of immigrants changes, so the importance of kinship in adaptation may also change. For example, among Chinese immigrants in the San Francisco Bay area, kinship was historically very important in social relationships, but among contemporary Chinese professionals, occupational organizations and other non-kin networks play increasingly large roles.

# Key Terms

affinal

ambilineal descent

bifurcation

bilateral descent

clan

cognatic descent

collateral kin

complementary opposition

consanguineal relatives

consanguinity

corporate descent groups

cross cousins

descent

descent group

double descent

exogamy

genitor

inheritance

kindred

kinship

kinship system

kinship terminology

lineage

lineal kin

matrilineage

matrilineal descent

nepotism

nonunilineal descent

parallel cousins

pater

patrilineage

patrilineal descent

phratry

segmentary lineage system

succession

totem

transmigrant

transnationalism

unilineal descent

# Suggested Readings

Abu-Lugod, Lila. 1993. *Writing Women's Worlds: Bedouin Stories*. Berkeley: University of California Press. The author uses women's stories to "write against culture," breathing life and complexity into anthropological categories of polygyny, cousin marriage, patrilineality, and other concepts used in studies of Middle Eastern kinship and family life.

Carsten, Janet. 2004. *After Kinship*. New York: Cambridge University Press. An analysis of the history and role of kinship studies in anthropology. Once central to the field, kinship studies became somewhat marginalized in the mid- and late-20th century, but they have once again become more important. Carsten contemplates the meaning of kinship in an era when individual and state choices as well as technologies shape our families.

Schneider, David M. 1968. *American Kinship: A Cultural Account*. Englewood Cliffs, NJ: Prentice Hall. The classic description of kinship in the United States and what it suggests about American culture.

Stone, Linda (Ed.). 2001. *New Directions in Anthropological Kinship*. Lanham, MD: Rowman and Littlefield. A collection of essays by contemporary anthropologists looking at various dimensions of kinship, such as the role of kinship in the history of anthropology, biology and culture in kinship studies, kinship and new reproductive technologies, kinship and gender, new forms of family, and kinship in the politics of nations.

In almost all societies, marriage is a central structure in the formation of families and forms a critical link in a wide variety of relationships. As in most cultures, the Indian marriage ritual pictured here contains many symbolic elements, such as the color red, which symbolizes fertility, and the bride's hands painted with henna, which not only beautifies but wards off evil on this auspicious occasion.

Courtesy of Chander Dembla

**THINKING POINT:** As suggested by anthropologist Philip Kilbride, polygyny—the marriage of one man to several women—would have many advantages if adopted in the contemporary United States: limiting sex to several wives might halt the epidemic spread of sexually transmitted disease; permit greater autonomy for women who wish to both have a career and provide a loving home for children who would then have access to a co-parent; provide a legal, stable marital relationship for women who might otherwise remain single; and provide a more permanent and happier family situation for the many children of divorced parents. Is Kilbride right? Should Americans consider polygyny "an option for our time?"

—[See page 206 for further discussion.]

{chapter 9}

# Marriage, Family, and Domestic Groups

All human societies face the problem of regulating sexual access between males and females, finding satisfactory ways to organize labor within the family, assigning responsibility for child care, providing a clear framework for organizing an individual's rights and responsibilities, and, in many cases, for transferring property and social position between generations. For most societies marriage and family life offer the best solutions to these challenges, although the specific patterns vary widely in their forms and structures. In studying marriage, the family, and households, anthropologists pay attention to both rules and realities. Residence rules and ideals of family structure are related to cultural values. However, they also grow out of the imperatives of real life, in which individuals make choices that do not always accord with the rules. ≪

# Functions of Marriage and the Family

The need to regulate sexual access is among the foremost requirements of the human animal. This need stems from the fact that human males and females are continuously receptive to sexual activity, rather than only receptive at certain times of the year. Sexual competition could therefore be a source of serious conflict if it were not regulated and channeled into stable relationships that are given social approval. These relationships need not be permanent, and theoretically some system other than marriage could have developed. But in the absence of safe and dependable contraception (as has been the case for most of human history) and with the near certainty that children would be born, a relatively stable union between a male and female that involves responsibility for children as well as economic exchange became the basis for most, though not all, human societies.

Differences in strength and mobility between males and females, as well as women's biological role in infant nurturing, led to a general gendered division of labor in nonindustrial societies. Marriage is the way most societies arrange for the products and services of men and women to be exchanged and for the care of children. An ongoing relationship between an adult male and an adult female provides a structure (a family) in which the male can provide food and protection and the female can nurse and provide the nurturing needed for the healthy development of children. Marriage also extends social alliances by linking different families and kin groups together, leading to cooperation among groups of people larger than the married couple. This expansion of the social group within which people can work together and share resources appears to be of great advantage for the survival of the species.

**Marriage** refers to the customs, rules, and obligations that establish a socially endorsed relationship between adults and children, and between the kin groups of the married partners. Although in most societies marriage and the subsequent formation of families rest on the biological complementarity of male and female and on the biological process of reproduction, both marriage and family are cultural patterns. As such, they differ in form and functions among human societies and also within societies, and change over time with changing political and economic circumstances. Anthropological research documents the conclusion that a vast array of family types, including families built on plural spouses, or same-sex partnerships, fulfill the functions of monogamous heterosexual marriage in satisfactory ways (Lathrop 2004:23). This variation in forms makes it difficult to find any *one* definition of marriage that will fit all cultural situations.

Even the most culturally widespread definition of marriage as establishing the legitimacy or status rights of children, for example, is not universal. Among the Navajo, a woman's children, whether or not she is married, become full legitimate members of her matriclan (Stone 2004:10). Similarly, marriage across cultures most often involves heterosexual unions, but there are important exceptions. Woman–woman marriage is found among the Nuer and some other African groups, in which a barren woman may divorce her husband, take another woman as her wife, and arrange for a surrogate to impregnate this woman. Children born from this arrangement, which did not involve sexual relations between the wives, become members of the barren woman's natal patrilineage and refer to her as their father. A similar cultural pattern, involving two males, is found among the Azande (Kilbride 2004:17), where royal power was importantly sustained by multiple wives. When there was a shortage of marriageable women, men would pay bridewealth for a young man to become their wife. The two men would be socially recognized as a married couple having sexual relations.

A primary function of the family—husband and wife sharing responsibility for children—is illustrated in this yarn painting of the Huichol Indians of Mexico. As the wife struggles to give birth, she pulls on a cord attached to her husband's genitals so that he, too, may share in the birth pains.

*Courtesy of Serena Nanda*

**marriage** The customs, rules, and obligations that establish a socially endorsed relationship between adults and children, and between the kin groups of the married partners.

In the United States, although marriage as a tie between one man and one woman is written into federal and most state laws, beginning in the 1980s, various developments have challenged the culturally based assumption that heterosexuality is a prerequisite for both marriage and parenthood. The growing national and international activism for equal marriage and adoption rights and the normalization of various kinds of reproductive technologies (see below) has put parenting, including biological parenting, within the reach of same-sex couples (Lewin 2009).

Same-sex marriage is only one of the many alternatives to marriage as an exclusively heterosexual, monogamous institution.

Just as any one definition of marriage finds many exceptions, so, too, does the concept of the family. In the United States, the normative idea of family is generally the nuclear family. This includes two marriage partners of different sexes and their offspring. Ties between the marriage partners and between them and their children are assumed to be strong. However, this pattern is not found in all other cultures and may, in fact, account for only a minority of families within the United States. In many societies, the most important family bond is between lineal blood relations (father and children or mother and children), or brothers and sisters, and ties between husband and wife are relatively loose. Within the United States, the high number of single-parent households, the high divorce rate, the increasing number of same-sex commitments and domestic partnerships, surrogacy, the large number of individuals who live in long-term relationships without marriage, as well as those who get married but remain childless challenge the dominance of the nuclear family as the primary cultural model.

Families based on gay relationships are increasingly a part of the American family culture. In the family pictured here, the two fathers of the boy and girl have been together over 20 years. Their mothers have been in a relationship for over 15 years, and together they form a happy and successful family unit, as the children divide their time between their mothers' home and their fathers' home, which are very near each other.

From a cross-cultural perspective, the most basic tie in society appears to be that between mother and child. The provisioning and protective role is generally played by the mother's husband (who is usually a male), but it may be played by the mother's brother, the mother's female husband (see page 192), or even the whole community (Spiro 1958). All societies construct rules about sex, infant care, labor, and rights and obligations between generations, but they do so in very different ways.

## Marriage Rules

Every society has rules concerning mating (sexual relations) and marriage. All societies have an incest taboo. That is, they categorically prohibit certain individuals (and members of certain groups) from having sex with each other. Additionally, societies have rules that encourage marriage between members of certain groups and prohibit it among others, rules determining the number of spouses an individual may have, and rules concerning what happens to a marriage upon the death of one of the partners.

In the United States, marriage is primarily an affair of individuals, and the married couple tends to make a new home apart from the parents. Although choice is not as free in practice as American ideals would lead one to believe, theoretically people choose their own mates. Because sexual compatibility and emotional needs are considered important, mates are chosen on the basis of personal qualities such as physical attractiveness and the complex of feelings Americans call romantic love. Economic considerations are supposed to be subordinated to these. However, in most societies, marriage is less an affair of individual romantic love and more a link that binds two families or kinship groups together. In these societies, the choice of a mate is directly linked to the interests of the family group and most marriages are arranged. In **arranged marriage,** parents and other relatives determine the choice of spouse for their offspring. In most cases, a key purpose of such marriages is to forge or continue an alliance between two families or kin groups. However, depending on the socioeconomic environment and family structure, different qualities are emphasized for the bride and groom. The economic potential of the groom is of great importance almost everywhere; for brides, reproductive potential and health are important. In addition, each culture has its own special emphases. In India, where a woman is expected to live in a joint family, or at least spend much of her time with her husband's

**arranged marriage** The process by which senior family members exercise a great degree of control over the choice of their children's spouses.

## Is Marriage Universal? The Na of China

The Na and some other allied societies of southwest China provide an example of a society whose cultural traditions raise questions about the universality of marriage and "the family" (Blumenfield 2004:15; Cai Hua 2001; Geertz 2001; Harrell 2002; Shih 2001; Walsh 2002). Na society does not have a word for "marriage." The culturally normative and most frequent Na institution that joins men and women in sexual and reproductive partnerships is called *sese*. In this relationship men pass a night in a lover's household and return to their own families in the morning. All sexual (and potentially reproductive) activity takes place at night during this concealed "visit" of a Na male to the household of a woman who has agreed beforehand to "lie" with him. The Na term for this "visit" suggests affection, respect, and intimacy, and the partners are called "lovers." The *sese* relationship does not, however, include notions of fidelity, permanence, paternal responsibility for children, or obligatory economic obliga-

tions (Shih 2001). Both women and men have multiple partners, serially or simultaneously. Ideally, no records are kept of "visits" to ascertain paternity of children, although in reality, knowledge of biological paternity is frequently known (Mattison 2009). There are, however, no Na words for "illegitimate" child, infidelity, or promiscuity; the Na "visit" is culturally treated as a mutually enjoyable but singular occurrence that entails no future conditions.

The *sese* relationship is made—and kept—voluntarily and is largely free of any contractual economic bonds. Although these relationships are generally not made public unless they become stable, *sese* is a culturally regulated custom whose boundaries are clearly understood by all. There is nothing of brute force or coercion in the Na "visits." Either party may offer, accept, or decline an invitation for a "visit." To spare the other's feelings, one may say: "Tonight

is not possible. I already have one for tonight," and a woman may even turn away an invited lover at the door if she chooses. Jealousy is reported not to exist, as any man can choose to visit any woman. But although either the woman or the man may initiate the "visit," it is always the man who comes secretly to the woman's house. Concealment is necessary because of a Na taboo forbidding a household's male members to hear or see any sexual talk or activities involving household females. Males will never answer the door after dark lest they encounter a woman's lover. The lover himself makes every effort to avoid detection, often bringing food to prevent the guard dogs' barking, speaking only in whispers during intercourse, and leaving quietly before daybreak.

The Na are a matrilineal society (see page 176), and as in other matrilineal societies, children stay with the mother's

The matrilineal family, which centers on a core of women, and includes brothers and sons, but not husbands and fathers, is the most important kinship group among the Na and allied ethnic groups in China.

household for their entire lives. This includes children by a variety of fathers, and the blood siblings of two or more generations. Ideas of "motherhood" and "fatherhood" are fluid. When a generation lacks females, a situation that threatens the continuity of the household, a household may "adopt" a relative's child or encourage a son to bring his lover into the household as a wife. Otherwise, the only males in a Na household are boy children born in the various generations, who are "brothers," "uncles," and "granduncles." Unlike some other matrilineal societies (see pages 178 and 209), Na families have no husbands, fathers, nuclear families, or structures of affinal relationships such as in-laws. The Na consider the matrilineal household as the family and both household and family are diverse and flexible.

For some anthropologists, the Na seem to fit neither into "descent" kinship theory, which envisions a universal, "natural" nuclear family of a man, his wife and their children, or the "alliance" theory, which views marriage as an exchange of women that expands into an in-law network (but see Walsh 2002). Anthropologists also seem to disagree on whether marriage is in fact absent among the Na and whether they are indeed unique when set in the context of the many diverse cultural patterns of marriage and family (Harrell 2001). For although the *sese* is the dominant sexual and reproductive relationship in Na culture, marriage has existed as a parallel cultural institution among the elites. In addition, there are two other, though rather infrequent, patterns of sexual encounter: the "conspicuous visit" and "cohabitation." In the conspicuous visit, which always follows a series of furtive visits, the effort to conceal the relationship is abandoned. This usually occurs after a long-term relationship that the community is presumed to know about in any case. Cohabitation, which is even more rare, occurs when a household is short of women by means of which to produce children or short of men to labor in its fields; under these circumstances a woman may bring her lover home as a husband.

Na matrilineal households are very strong and take care of all their members; the *sese* relationship does not undermine the very strong matrilineal household stability, nor the economic position of women or children. Male and female Na describe their society as valuing men and women equally, though almost all agree that women work much harder than men and have many more household responsibilities than their brothers.

In Na culture, (matrilineal) family love is considered more essential and longer lasting than romantic love. Many Na believe that people should not marry because marriage creates conflict within households. On the other hand, some Na say that as they become more wealthy, they will marry and move out of their matrilineal households. Indeed, there are now a variety of family types among the Na (Walsh 2004).

Historically, within the patrilineal, patriarchal, and ancestor-worshipping structure of mainstream Han Chinese culture, the Na are officially identified as a "primitive matriarchy" and the "visit" was condemned as a "barbarous practice." Intermittent government attempts to persuade the Na to marry included distributing land to men who would then set up nuclear families, raising their children together with their wives. The Maoist government also tried to force the Na into "normal" sexual, marriage, and kinship relations, including passing severe laws against unmarried Na "lovers." These laws have not generally been successful in assimilating the Na to mainstream Han Chinese values, although some Na now do marry and for many Na *sese* relationships are more stable than in the past.

It is possible that the recent expansion of China's public school education and state-sponsored movies—imbued with mainstream Han mores and lifestyles—into the formerly isolated Na villages will gradually induce shame among Na children for their cultural deviance, and their inability to name a father on the documents that will come in the wake of the modernization of China will begin to appear as a stigma. In spite of a strong ethnic identity that incorporates the *sese,* as the Na enter the wider world their "walking marriage" may be one more example of human cultural diversity that ultimately faces extinction, leaving us less familiar with the wide variety of cultural patterns of marriage and family that serve as counterpoints to our own.

## CRITICAL THINKING QUESTIONS

1. Can you envision a society without marriage? What do you think that society would look like?

2. Compare the Chinese government's attempt to end Na *sese* relationships and traditional family structure with attempts in the United States to ban same-sex marriage.

3. What are some of the advantages and disadvantages, from the Na point of view, of their system of "walking marriage" and matrilineal families?

Among the Wodaabe of Niger, marriages are based on romantic attachment as well as arranged. To be chosen as the most charming and beautiful dancers and capture the hearts of young women, young men at the annual Gerewol celebration apply makeup, dance, and make facial expressions that display the whiteness of their eyes and teeth.

© Judith Pearson

family, a demeanor of submissiveness and modesty is essential. Also, no one wants to arrange a marriage with a family that has the reputation of being quarrelsome or gossipy (Nanda 1999).

Where marriages are arranged, go-betweens are often used. A go-between, or marriage broker, has more information about a wider network of families than any one family can have. Furthermore, neither the family of the bride nor that of the groom loses face if its offer is rejected by the other party. Although the arranged marriage system tends to become less rigid as societies urbanize and industrialize, in most societies families and larger kin groups have a great deal of control over marriage and the choice of a spouse. Important cultural rules guide the arranging of marriages with, to a variable degree, some leeway for individual variation. Different patterns of choosing a mate are closely related to other social and cultural patterns, such as kinship rules, ideals of family structure, transfer of property at marriage, and core cultural values, all of which are rooted in how people make a living.

## Incest Taboos

The most universal prohibition is that on mating among certain kinds of kin: mother and son, father and daughter, and sister and brother. The taboos on mating between

**incest taboos** Prohibitions on sexual relations between relatives.

kin almost always extend beyond this immediate family group, however. These prohibitions on mating between people classified as relatives are called **incest taboos.** Because sexual access is one of the most important rights conferred by marriage, incest taboos effectively prohibit marriage among certain kin.

There have been some very unusual exceptions to the taboo on mating and marriage among members of the nuclear family. Brother–sister marriage was practiced by Egyptian royalty, in traditional Hawaiian society, and among the Inca in Peru. Although there are numerous explanations for these cases, brother–sister marriage probably served to keep family wealth and power intact and limit rivalries for succession to kingship.

Anthropologists have advanced several major theories to explain the universality and persistence of the incest taboo, particularly as it applies to primary (or nuclear) family relationships. In considering these theories, we should keep in mind that the possible origins of the taboo, its functions in contemporary societies, and the motives of individuals in respecting or violating the taboo are all separate issues.

**Avoiding Inbreeding** The inbreeding avoidance theory holds that mating between close kin produces deficient, weak children and is genetically harmful to the species. According to this theory, proposed in the late 19th century, the incest taboo is adaptive because it limits inbreeding. Work in population genetics appears to support the view that inbreeding is usually harmful to a human population. Moreover, these disadvantages are far more likely to appear as a result of the mating of primary relatives (mother–son, father–daughter, sister–brother) than of other relatives, even first cousins. However, it is not clear whether or not this effect would be observable in premodern societies with very high infant mortality rates or how prescientific peoples could understand the connection between close inbreeding and the biological disadvantages that result.

**Preventing Family Disruption** Bronislaw Malinowski and Sigmund Freud believed that the desire for sexual relations within the family is very strong. They suggested that the most important function of the incest taboo is preventing disruption within the nuclear family. Malinowski argued that as children grow into adolescence, it would be natural for them to attempt to satisfy their developing sexual urges within the group of people emotionally close to them—that is, within the family. Were this to happen, the role relationships within the family would be disrupted as fathers and sons, and mothers and daughters, would be competing for sexual partners. These conflicts would hinder the family in carrying out its activities in a harmonious and effective way. According to this theory, the incest taboo arose to repress the attempt to satisfy sexual desires within the family and to direct such desires outward.

Although unregulated sexual competition within the family would undoubtedly be disruptive, it is not clear that the incest taboo is the only way this problem could be solved. An alternative to the incest taboo could be the regulation of sexual competition among family members. Furthermore, although Malinowski's theory suggests why the incest taboo exists between parents and children, it does not explain the prohibition of sexual relations between brothers and sisters or why the taboo should be extended beyond the nuclear family.

**Forming Wider Alliances** Another theory (Lévi-Strauss 1969/1949) stresses the adaptive value of cooperation among groups larger than the nuclear family. The incest taboo forces people to marry outside the family, thus joining families together into a larger social community. This has surely contributed to the success of the human species. However, the alliance theory really concerns marriage rather than sexual relations. It is possible to imagine a society where individuals had to marry outside of their family groups but were permitted to have sex within those groups, but no such society exists.

Thus, the familial incest taboo appears to have a number of advantages for the human species. In other animal species, incest is often prevented by expelling junior members from family groups as they reach sexual maturity. Because humans take so long to mature, the familial incest taboo seems to be the most efficient and effective means of promoting genetic variability, familial harmony, and community cooperation. These advantages can explain the spread and persistence of the taboo, if not its origins (Aberle et al. 1963).

## Exogamy

Two types of marriage rules, exogamy and endogamy, together work to define the acceptable range of marriage partners. **Exogamy** specifies that a person must marry outside particular groups; **endogamy** requires people to marry within certain groups. Because of the association of sex and marriage, prohibitions on incest produce an almost universal rule of exogamy within the primary family group of parents and children and between brothers and sisters. Exogamous rules also apply to groups larger than the nuclear family. Most often, descent groups based on a blood relationship (such as lineages and clans) are exogamous.

The advantages of exogamy include the reduction of conflict over sex within the cooperating group, such as the hunting band, and the alliances between groups larger than the primary family, which are of great adaptive significance for humans. Such alliances may have economic,

political, or religious components; indeed, these intergroup rights and obligations are among the most important kinds of relationships established by marriage.

Early humans living in hunting-and-gathering bands exchanged women in order to live in peace with one another and to extend the social ties of cooperation. One outstanding feature of marriage arrangements among contemporary foragers is a system of exchange and alliance between groups that exchange wives. These alliances are important among peoples who must move frequently to find food. Different groups take turns visiting and playing host to one another, and this intergroup sociability is made easier by exogamy. One consequence of exchanging women is that each foraging camp becomes dependent on others for a supply of wives and is allied with others through the bonds that result from marriage. This system contributes to the maintenance of peaceful relations among groups that move around, camp with one another, and exploit overlapping territories. It does not entirely eliminate intergroup aggression, but it probably helps keep it down to a manageable level.

The Arapesh, a horticultural society in Papua New Guinea studied by Margaret Mead, were very clear and explicit that keeping one's own women for oneself is not advantageous. In these societies, not exchanging women between families would be just as unthinkable as not sharing food. In many societies, the very mention of incest is often accompanied by protestations of horror. For the Arapesh, incest simply does not make sense (Mead 1963:92/1935). When Margaret Mead asked about a man marrying his sisters, her Arapesh informant responded, "What, you would like to marry your sister? What is the matter with you? Don't you want a brother-in-law? Don't you realize that if you marry another man's sister and another man marries your sister, you will have at least two brothers-in-law, while if you marry your own sister you will have none? With whom will you hunt, with whom will you garden, with whom will you visit?" (Mead 1963:97/1935).

In peasant societies, rules of exogamy may apply to the village as well. In northern India, a man must take a wife from outside his village. Through exogamy, the Indian village becomes a center in a kinship network that spreads over hundreds of villages. Because the wives will come from many different villages, the typical Indian village has a cosmopolitan character. Village exogamy also affects the quality of Indian village family life. In a household where brothers' wives are strangers to one another, peace at any price is an important value. The

---

**exogamy** A rule specifying that a person must marry outside a particular group.

**endogamy** A rule prescribing that a person must marry within a particular group.

All societies have rules of endogamy. In the United States, endogamy within so-called racial groups was at one time prescribed by law. This law against interracial marriage, which continued in some states until 1967, no longer exists but most, though not all, marriages continue to be within so-called racial groups.

potential for conflict among sisters-in-law shapes child rearing and personality and helps explain many rules of conduct in the northern Indian family, such as the repression of aggression.

## Endogamy

Endogamy is a rule that requires marriage within one's own group, however that group is defined. In order to keep the privileges and wealth of the group intact, blood relations may be encouraged or required to marry. This helps explain endogamy among royalty. In India, the caste is an endogamous group. A person must marry someone within the caste or within the specific section of the caste to which he or she belongs. In the United States, although there are currently no named groups within which one must marry, so-called racial groups and social classes tend to be endogamous. In the past, racial endogamy was enforced by law in many states. In the case of social classes, opportunity, cultural norms, and similar-

**cross cousins** The children of a parent's siblings of the opposite sex (mother's brothers, father's sisters).

**parallel cousins** The children of a parent's same-sex siblings (mother's sisters, father's brothers).

**exogamous group** A group within which one is not permitted to marry.

ity of lifestyle all contribute to maintaining endogamy. It may be as easy to love a rich person as a poor one, but it is a lot harder to meet one unless you are rich yourself. Endogamy is also an important rule for some religious groups in the United States, such as the Amish.

## Preferential Marriages

In all societies, relatives are classified according to the rules of kinship that are part of culture. These classifications of kin are an important basis for choosing marriage partners. In addition to rules about whom one may not marry and the group within which one must marry, some societies have rules about the preferred categories of relatives from which marriage partners are drawn. Preferred marriage partners are often "cousins," that is, children of siblings at the parental generation, who are in fact biologically related, but who may not culturally be defined as such.

A common form of preferential marriage rules is cross-cousin marriage. **Cross cousins** are the children of one's parents' siblings of the opposite sex (mother's brother or father's sister) (see Figure 9.1). These statuses actually extend beyond first cousins, and would include, for example, a mother's mother's brother's daughter's daughter. Got that? **Parallel cousins,** children of the parents' same-sex siblings (mother's sister or father's brother), are rarely preferred marriage partners. In fact, marriage to them is often forbidden. In the differentiation between cross cousins and parallel cousins in many cultures we see clearly how kinship is not literally based on blood relations but rather culturally constructed.

Preferential cross-cousin marriage is related to the organization of kinship units larger than the nuclear family. Where descent groups are unilineal (formed by either the mother's or the father's side exclusively)—parallel cousins are members of one's own kinship group but cross cousins are not. Because unilineal kinship groups are usually **exogamous,** a person is prohibited from marrying a parallel cousin (who is often considered a brother or sister) but is allowed, or even required, to marry a cross cousin, who is culturally defined as outside the kinship group. Preferred cross-cousin marriage reinforces ties between kin groups established in the preceding generation. In this sense, the adaptive value of preferential cross-cousin marriage is that it establishes alliances between groups and intensifies relationships among a limited number of kin groups generation after generation.

There are a few societies that prefer parallel-cousin marriage, but even in these societies, such marriages are, in fact, not universally contracted (Webber 2007). For Muslim Arabs of North Africa, the parallel-cousin marriage preference is for the son or daughter of the father's brother. Muslim Arab culture has a rule of patrilineal descent; that is, descent and inheritance are in the male

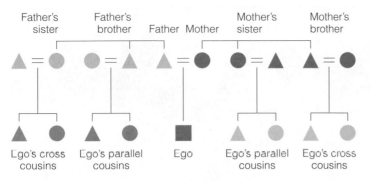

Father's sister    Father's brother    Father    Mother    Mother's sister    Mother's brother

Ego's cross cousins    Ego's parallel cousins    Ego    Ego's parallel cousins    Ego's cross cousins

**FIGURE 9.1** This diagram indicates the relationships of cross cousins and parallel cousins. In many cultures these relationships are important for determining who can and cannot marry, and for designating preferred marriage partners. Western cultures distinguish cousins by degree of biological closeness but do not distinguish between cross cousins and parallel cousins for purposes of marriage.

line. Parallel cousin marriage within this system helps prevent the fragmentation of family property because economic resources can be kept within the family. Another result of parallel-cousin marriage is to reinforce the solidarity of brothers. But, by socially isolating groups of brothers, parallel-cousin marriage adds to factional disputes and disunity within larger social systems. Thus, each system of marriage and family has elements that contribute to solidarity and stability at one level but may be disruptive at another level.

**The Levirate and the Sororate** The **levirate** is a custom whereby a man marries the widow of his dead brother. In some cases, the children born to this union are considered children of the deceased man. Among the Nuer, a pastoral people of Africa, a form called ghost marriage exists: A man can marry a woman "to the name of" a brother who has died childless. The offspring of this union are designated as children of the deceased. Thus, the levirate enables the children to remain within the dead husband's descent group and also keeps them from being separated from their mother. The **sororate** is a custom whereby, when a woman dies, her kin group supplies a sister as a wife for the widower. Also, where the sororate exists, the husband of a barren woman marries her sister, and at least some of these children are considered those of the first wife.

The levirate and sororate attest to the importance of marriage as an alliance between two groups rather than between individuals. Through such customs, group alliances are maintained and the marriage contract can be fulfilled even in the event of death. Because marriage involves an exchange of rights and obligations, the family of the wife can be assured that she will be cared for even if her husband dies. This is only fair if she has fulfilled her part of the marriage contract by providing domestic services and bearing children.

Where there are no available marriage partners in the right relationship for a preferential marriage, other kin may be substituted. For example, if a man is supposed to marry his father's sister's daughter, the daughters of all women classified as his father's sisters (whether or not they are biologically in this relationship) are eligible as marriage partners. Sometimes, if no brother, sister,

or other qualifying relative is available, or if the brother or sister is undesirable, the levirate or sororate will not take place. A point to note here is that the levirate and the sororate are ideals; they refer to what people say should happen in their society, not to what necessarily does happen.

## Number of Spouses

All societies have rules about how many spouses a person may have at one time. **Monogamy** permits only one man to be married to one woman at any given time. Monogamy is the rule in Euro-American cultures, but not in most of the world's societies. Given the high divorce rate and subsequent remarriage in the United States, perhaps the term *serial monogamy* is more accurate. In this pattern, a man or woman has one marriage partner at a time but, because of the ease of divorce, does not necessarily remain with that partner for life.

**Polygamy** is plural marriage. It includes **polygyny,** the marriage of one man to several women, and **polyandry,** the marriage of one woman to several men. Most societies permit (and prefer) plural marriage. In a world sample of 554 societies, polygyny was favored in 415, monogamy in 135, and polyandry in only 4 (Murdock 1949:28). Thus, about 75 percent of the world's societies prefer plural marriage. However, this does not mean that most people in these societies actually have more than one spouse.

**levirate** The custom whereby a man marries the widow of a deceased brother.

**sororate** The custom whereby, when a man's wife dies, her sister is given to him as a wife.

**monogamy** A rule that permits a person to be married to only one spouse at a time.

**polygamy** A rule allowing more than one spouse.

**polygyny** A rule permitting a man to have more than one wife at a time.

**polyandry** A rule permitting a woman to have more than one husband at a time.

**Polygyny** Polygyny is related to different factors in different societies. Where women are economically important, polygyny can increase a man's wealth and therefore his social position. Also, because one of the most important functions of marriage is to ally different groups with one another, having several wives from different groups within the society extends a man's alliances. Thus, chiefs, headmen, or leaders of states may have wives from many different clans or villages. This provides leaders with increased economic resources that may then be redistributed among the people, and it also binds the different groups to the leader through marriage. Polygyny thus has important economic and political functions in some societies.

Although the Mormon Church officially outlawed polygyny in 1890, as many as 30,000 people who call themselves Mormon fundamentalists live in polygynous families in the western United States today.

© Evan Hurd/Sygma/Corbis

Polygyny is found most typically in horticultural societies that have a high level of productivity. Although the most obvious advantages in polygynous societies seem to go to men—additional women in the household increase the labor supply and the productive yield, as well as the number of children—the status of females in such societies is not uniformly low. In some societies, women welcome the addition of a cowife because it eases their own workload and provides daily companionship. Although polygyny combined with patrilineality may mean that women are restricted by patriarchal authority, polygyny can also be combined with a high degree of sexual and economic freedom for women. Even in cultures in which polygyny is preferred, the ratio of males to females is usually such that few men can have more than one wife. Furthermore, where men must exchange wealth for wives, most men cannot afford more than one wife.

People from cultures where sexual fidelity in marriage is considered essential (particularly in the context of romantic love) may expect to find sexual jealousy in polygynous societies. This is not necessarily the case. Jealousy may occur in polygynous households, but relations between cowives may also be friendly and helpful. Some polygynous societies have mechanisms to minimize conflict between cowives. One is **sororal polygyny,** in which a man marries sisters, who may be more willing to cooperate and can get along better than women who are strangers to each other. Also, cowives usually live in separate dwellings. A husband who wants to avoid conflict

will attempt to distribute his economic resources and sexual attentions evenly among his wives so there will be no accusations of favoritism. Where women's work is hard and monotonous, cowives may also provide welcome company for one another.

**Polygyny among the Tiwi** Although polygyny is mainly found in horticultural societies, the foraging Tiwi of Australia (Martin and Voorhies 1975) also have polygyny. Within the constraints of the marriage rules, a Tiwi father betroths his infant daughter to a friend or potential ally that he thinks will bring him the most economic and social advantage, or to a man who has bestowed a daughter to him (Hart and Pilling 1960:15). If he is looking for "old-age insurance," a father might choose a man much younger than himself who shows signs of being a good hunter and fighter and who seems likely to rise in influence. When the older man can no longer hunt, his son-in-law will still be young enough to provide him with food. Because the girl is an infant when her future marriage is decided, husbands are a great deal older than their wives.

As a young man who looks good to one girl's father is usually attractive to other fathers, some men rapidly acquire several wives. As these wives begin to have children, he will betroth his own daughters to other men, while still acquiring more wives for himself. Young men who do not seem particularly promising to potential fathers-in-law have difficulty getting wives and will marry widows (and because men are much older than women in marriage, there are many widows).

---

**sororal polygyny**  A form of polygyny in which a man marries sisters.

The large, multiple-wife Tiwi household is an adaptation to their ecological conditions. The more wives a man has, the more food they can collect, and old wives are particularly useful in this respect because they know the environment well and are experienced in finding food. Younger wives serve as apprentices and reinforcements for older wives. For this reason, every man tries to marry an older woman first. Households with only one or two wives have a much lower standard of living than those with many wives, especially if both wives are young.

Because girls are betrothed when they are infants, their mothers are introduced to the men who will become their sons-in-law long before the marriage takes place. The relationship between a woman and her prospective son-in-law is very important. The son-in-law must immediately begin to provide food and favors to his mother-in-law, and he often joins her camp at this time. This strong relationship continues for the remainder of the mother-in-law's life.

From a Western perspective Tiwi women may appear to be pawns in a marriage game over which they have little control, but Tiwi women see themselves not simply as wives but as women who have a fluctuating inventory of husbands (Goodale 1971). Until their first pregnancy, Tiwi wives enjoy both sexual and social freedom. Young Tiwi women traditionally engage in several extramarital sexual unions with lovers of their own age, a practice that is tolerated although not officially approved. As a Tiwi woman gets older, her respect and power increase. As a senior wife, she has power in the domestic group and considerable influence over her sons. Cowives and their daughters form a cohesive economic and social unit, and Tiwi women have prestige, power, and independence based on solidarity with other women and economic complementarity with men.

Polyandry Polyandry (the marriage of one woman to more than one man) is found in parts of Tibet and Nepal and among the Toda and Pahari Hindus of India. Polyandry may be an adaptation to a shortage of females, but such a shortage is created among the Toda and Tibetans by female infanticide. In a society where men must be away from home for long periods of time, polyandry provides a woman with more than one husband to take care of her. In Tibet, polyandry appears to be related to the shortage of land. If several men marry one woman, this limits the number of children a man has to support. If brothers marry the same woman, land can be kept within the family rather than fragmented over the generations.

The Toda of southern India were a classic case of **fraternal polyandry.** Toda women married one man and at the same time become the wife of his brothers. If other brothers were born after the original marriage, they also shared in the marital rights. Sexual access to the wife rotated rather equally, and there is little reported friction or jealousy. When all the brothers lived with their wife in one hut, a brother who was with the wife placed his cloak and staff outside as a warning to others. When a wife became pregnant, determining the biological father is not considered necessary. Rather, a ceremony called "giving the bow," held in the seventh month of pregnancy, assigned the child a legal or social father. In this ritual, a man presented a ceremonial bow and arrow made from twigs and grass to the wife in front of his relatives. Usually the eldest brother performed this ceremony first, and subsequent children are considered his. After two or three children were born, another brother usually gave the bow. Occasionally a woman married several men who were not biological brothers. When these men lived in different villages the wife lived in the village of each husband for a month. The men arranged among themselves who gave the bow when she became pregnant. Because the practice of female infanticide has largely ceased among the Toda, the male-female ratio has evened out. For this reason, as well as the influence of Christian missionaries, the Toda today are largely monogamous (Queen and Haberstein 1974).

# Exchange of Goods and Rights in Marriage

The essence of marriage is that it is a publicly accepted relationship involving the transfer of certain rights and obligations. These rights primarily involve sexual access of husband and wife to each other, rights over any children born to the wife, obligations by one or both parents to care for children born to the union, and rights of husband and wife to the economic services of each other.

In many cultures, marriage is also an important means of making alliances between families. Thus, marriage may also give the families or kin groups of the bride and groom certain rights to goods or services from each other. Sometimes this exchange is simply of gifts—items customarily given as a way of winning the goodwill of those with the power to transfer marital rights, though not necessary to complete the transfer. In other cases, the exchange of goods and services is an essential part of the transfer of marital rights (although the exchanges may still be called gifts). If these exchanges are not completed, the rights in marriage can be forfeited. Three kinds of exchanges made in connection with marriage are bride service, bridewealth, and dowry.

**fraternal polyandry** A custom whereby a woman marries a man and his brothers.

## Bride Service and Bridewealth

In **bride service,** the husband must work for a specified period of time for his wife's family in exchange for his marital rights. Bride service occurs mainly in foraging societies, where accumulating material goods for an exchange at marriage is difficult. Among the Ju/'hoansi, for example, a man may work for his wife's family for as long as 15 years or until the birth of the third child.

The most common form of marriage exchange is **bridewealth,** in which cash or goods are given by the groom's kin to the bride's kin to seal a marriage. (Bridewealth was formerly called bride price, an inaccurate term conveying the misleading perception that marriage was merely an economic exchange [Ogbu 1978a]). A major function of bridewealth is legitimating the new reproductive and socioeconomic unit created by the marriage. In societies where bridewealth is customary, a person can claim compensation for a violation of conjugal rights only if the bridewealth has been paid. Furthermore, bridewealth paid at marriage is returned (subject to specified conditions) if a marriage is terminated.

Although most studies of bridewealth emphasize its role in entitling the husband to domestic, economic, sexual, and reproductive rights in his wife, bridewealth also confers rights on the wife. By establishing the marriage as legal—that is, recognized and supported by public sanctions—bridewealth allows wives to hold their husbands accountable for violations of conjugal rights. In sanctioning the proper exchanges of rights and obligations of both husbands and wives, bridewealth serves to stabilize marriage by giving both families a vested interest in keeping the couple together. However, that does not mean that divorce does not occur in societies with bridewealth.

Bridewealth transactions, although globally widespread, are particularly characteristic of Africa. They are especially common among East African pastoralists such as the Gusii, Turkana, and Kipsigis. Cattle, which dominate these societies culturally and economically, traditionally make up the greater part of bridewealth. Bridewealth payments are embedded in the economic strategies of households; they are related to the ways in which men and women engage in labor, distribute property, and maintain or enhance status. Thus, the amount of bridewealth paid varies as people adapt to changing economic, demographic, and social conditions.

**bride service** The cultural rule that a man must work for his bride's family for a variable length of time either before or after the marriage.

**bridewealth** Goods presented by the groom's kin to the bride's kin to legitimize a marriage (formerly called "bride price").

**Bridewealth among the Kipsigis** This adaptation to changing conditions is illustrated by bridewealth practices among the Kipsigis, a pastoral/horticultural society in East Africa. Although in some societies bridewealth payments extend over many years, the Kipsigis make a single bridewealth payment, traditionally consisting of livestock but now including some cash, at the time of marriage. The Kipsigis distribute the bridewealth within the immediate families of the bride and the groom. First marriages are paid for by the groom's father and subsequent marriages by the groom himself, although grooms working for wages may also help with the first payment. The bride's parents are primarily responsible for the negotiation and final acceptance of the bridewealth offer (Borgerhoff Mulder 1995:576). Although young people occasionally pick their own spouses, both young people and their parents are expected to be satisfied by the marriage arrangement, and sometimes the young are brought into line by threats of disinheritance. Personality differences and individual circumstances play a role in bridewealth payments, but certain patterns are also observable.

Kipsigis bridewealth amounts have fluctuated over time. In the past, when agricultural land was available and prices for crops were high, bridewealth was high because of the importance of women's labor in cultivation. As population increased in the 20th century and land became scarce, the value of women's labor in agriculture declined and therefore bridewealth payments have declined as well. Additionally, increased urbanization and participation in the national and global economy have opened numerous other opportunities for men to invest their wealth, making less available for bridewealth payments.

The bride's family must balance its desire for higher bridewealth payments with their concern for their daughter's happiness, the need to attract a good son-in-law, and the desire to avoid impoverishing the daughter in her new household. However, Kipsigis parents of girls educated beyond elementary school often demand high bridewealth, both as compensation for the high school fees they have spent on their daughters and because her increased earning potential will benefit her marital home.

Many Westerners who encountered bridewealth practices assumed that it was both a cause and a symbol of a very low status for women. This is not necessarily the case. John Ogbu (1978a) argued that such payments enhance rather than diminish the status of women by enabling both husband and wife to acquire reciprocal rights in each other. Indeed, as the Kipsigis illustrate, it is the families of higher-status, more educated women who demand higher bridewealth. The low status of women in some parts of Africa has nothing to do with the role of bridewealth in the legitimization of marriage. Despite the general persistence of bridewealth, women's status has declined with increasing modernization, urbanization,

Bridewealth is the most common form of gift exchange at marriage. Among the Medlpa of New Guinea, a marriage is formalized by the family of the groom giving gifts to the family of the bride. The bride's family comes to the groom's village to receive the gifts. The bigman of the groom's family (left) praises the quality of the gifts, while the bigman of the bride's family denigrates their value. Traditionally, pigs and various kinds of shells were part of the bridewealth. Pigs are still given, but these days cash and pig grease (rendered fat from the pig), which is in the can in the center, have replaced shell money.

and participation in wage labor economies (Borgerhoff Mulder 1995).

## Dowry

Dowry—a presentation of goods by the bride's kin to the groom's family—is less common than other forms of exchange at marriage. **Dowry** has somewhat different meanings and functions in different societies. In some cases, this transfer of wealth represents a woman's share of her family inheritance. It may be used by her and her husband to set up a new household, kept by her as insurance in case her husband dies, or spent on her children's future. In other cases, dowry is a payment transferred from the bride's family to the groom's family.

In Indian culture, the use of dowry was typical. However, in 1961 it became illegal to demand dowry as a precondition for marriage. Dowry was outlawed because it was often misused as a way of extorting payments from families eager to marry off their daughters. Marriage gifts given without precondition remain legal in India. Because the difference between gifts given with preconditions and those given without is often difficult to deter-

mine, gift exchange at marriage remains very common. The functions of dowry in India are debated. One view is that dowry is a voluntary gift, symbolizing affection for a beloved daughter leaving home and compensating her for the fact that traditionally she could not inherit land or property. Dowry may also be viewed as a source of security for a woman because the jewelry given as part of her dowry is theoretically hers to keep. However, theories that view dowry as a source of economic security for a woman are challenged in the Indian context on several grounds. First, in reality, most women have no control over their dowries, which remain in the custody of their mothers-in-law or their husbands. Second, if the purpose of dowries really was economic security, they would be of a more productive nature, such as land or a shop, rather than the personal and household goods that constitute the main portion of Indian dowries today.

---

**dowry** Presentation of goods by the bride's kin to the family of the groom or to the couple.

Another theory holds that dowry in India is a transfer of resources to the groom's family as a recognition of their generosity in taking on an economic burden because upper-class and upper-caste women in India are not supposed to work. Dowry from this standpoint is a compensatory payment from the bride's family, which is losing an economic liability, to the groom's family, which is taking one on. Even as demanding dowry has been outlawed in India, a new emphasis on consumerism has increased its importance, especially among members of the middle classes striving for upward social mobility.

Globalization is beginning to have an effect on the dowry system in parts of India where lower class women have begun to work in expanding factory production. In South India, the increase of garment factories now allows these women to earn salaries that, while generally lower than those of men, are nevertheless becoming essential for family subsistence. Traditionally, the families of these women amassed dowries for their daughters (even if they had to borrow much of it), but now many of these women are saving their salaries for their own dowries. Even though the knowledge that a family's daughters and even wives are working brings lowered prestige, the material benefits are often essential. This somewhat greater independence for young, unmarried women is leading to more "love marriages," disrupting the kin support networks that traditionally accompany arranged marriages (Lessinger 2008).

Whatever the exact nature of exchanges of goods or services in marriage, they are part of the process of the public transfer of rights that legitimizes the new alliances formed. The public nature of marriage is also demonstrated by the ritual and ceremony that surround it in almost every society. The presence of members of the community at these ceremonies is a way of bearing witness to the lawfulness of the transaction. It is these publicly witnessed and acknowledged ceremonies that distinguish marriage from other kinds of unions that resemble it.

**nuclear family** A family organized around the conjugal tie (the relationship between husband and wife) and consisting of a husband, a wife, and their children.

**conjugal tie** The relationship between a husband and wife formed by marriage.

**extended family** Family based on blood relations extending over three or more generations.

**consanguineal** Related by blood.

**domestic group (household)** Persons living in the same house, usually, but not always members of a family.

**neolocal residence** System under which a couple establishes an independent household after marriage.

# Families, Domestic Groups, and Rules of Residence

Three basic types of families identified by anthropologists are the elementary, or nuclear, family, the composite family, and the extended family. **Nuclear families** are organized around the **conjugal tie,** or the relationship between husband and wife. Composite (compound) families are aggregates of nuclear families linked by a common spouse, most often the husband. **Extended families** are based on **consanguineal,** or blood, relations extending over three or more generations.

A **domestic group,** or household, is not the same as a family. Although households most often contain related people, non-kin may also be part of a household. In addition, members of a family may be spread out over several households. The composition of a household is affected by the cultural rules about where a newly married couple will live.

## The Nuclear Family

A nuclear family consists of a married couple and their children. It is most often associated with **neolocal residence,** where the married couple establishes an independent household. This type of family may exist as an isolated and independent unit, as it does in the United States, or it may be embedded within larger kinship units. Only 5 percent of the world's societies are neolocal.

The nuclear family is adapted in many ways to the requirements of industrial society. Where jobs do not depend on family connections, and where mobility may be required for obtaining employment and career success, a small, flexible unit such as the independent nuclear family has its advantages. Independence and flexibility are also requirements of foraging lifestyles, and more than three-quarters of all foraging groups live in nuclear family groups. In such societies, however, the nuclear family is not nearly as independent or isolated as it is in U.S. society. The family unit almost always camps together with the kin of the husband or the wife.

## The Changing American Family

In the United States, in contrast to most other cultures, the monogamous, independent, neolocal nuclear family is the ideal for most people. It is related to the high degree of mobility required in an industrial system and to a culture that places emphasis on romantic love, the emotional bond between husband and wife, privacy, and personal independence. In nuclear family societies, a newly married couple is expected to occupy its own residence and to function as an independent domestic and economic unit. Larger kin groups are not involved in any substantial way in mate selection or the transfer of goods, and the nuclear family's dissolution (whether from death or divorce) primarily affects only the nuclear family members.

The American nuclear family is ideally regarded as egalitarian, although for many families this is not the case. Although roles in the American nuclear family are less rigidly defined than in other societies, research indicates that even where mothers work full time, they are also responsible for most of the housework and child care (Lamphere 1997).

The idealistic picture of the independent nuclear family as typical of the United States must be modified to reflect some new (and some not so new) realities. One of these is the high rates of divorce and remarriage that enmesh nuclear families in ever larger and more complicated kinship networks. Sometimes called **blended families,** these networks include previously divorced spouses and their new marriage partners, and sometimes children from previous marriages, as well as multiple sets of grandparents and other similar relations. Although blended families do sometimes provide the kind of support provided in two-parent families, the facts are that only one child in six averages a weekly visit with a divorced father, and only one in four sees him once a month. Almost half of the children of divorced parents have not seen their biological fathers for more than a year and 10 years later more than two-thirds have lost contact with him (Hacker 2002:22).

Another factor in the changing American family is the availability of new technologies, particularly those involving the possibility of **surrogate motherhood,** in which a third party assists a couple to have a child. Surrogate motherhood also involves, of course, the willingness of some women to conceive, gestate, and part with a child. As anthropologist Helena Ragoné illustrates in her ethnography *Surrogate Motherhood: Conception in the Heart* (1994), surrogacy is both in opposition to, and also consistent with, American cultural assumptions and ideals about the importance of family, motherhood, fatherhood, and kinship. American laws surround surrogacy with many restrictions, reflecting fears of abuse of this technology for commercial purposes, and surrogacy has received much negative representation in the media. In some surrogacy programs, the surrogates and the couples are introduced to each other and interact closely throughout the process, beginning with insemination, through pregnancy and delivery. In other programs, the couple sees only the biography and photograph of the surrogate and they meet her only for finalizing the stepparent adoption and the pro forma court suit for paternity brought after the child is born.

Many anthropologists predicted that the increase in surrogate births would change the pattern of American kinship. In fact, Ragoné found the opposite to be true,

One of the important changes in the family in the United States over the past 50 years is the increasing number of women who work outside the home. In most families, women's domestic responsibilities have not decreased, but in some two-career families there is a movement toward more equal sharing of domestic work and child care.

illustrating once again the powerful hold of culture. The participants in surrogacy programs universally used reinterpreted traditional American kinship ideology and definitions of motherhood to recreate the conventional cultural norms that surround American parental roles, reproduction, birth, ideas about the importance of the family, and the biogenetic essence of kinship. Ragoné found that because the women who employ surrogates are not biologically related to their children, they tended to redefine motherhood as consisting of two parts: biological motherhood and social motherhood (a view held by many cultures with regard to fathers, see page 170). Regardless of the mechanics of surrogacy, the couples involved all emphasized the biological relationship of the child to the father, demonstrating the continued importance of the blood tie at the core of traditional Euro-American kinship ideology. The determination of childless couples to pursue surrogacy, in spite of the many difficulties, is also a testimony to the American cultural

**blended family** Kinship networks occasioned by divorce and remarriage in the United States that include the previously divorced spouses and their new marriage partners.

**surrogate motherhood** A variety of reproductive technologies in which a woman helps a couple to have a child by acting as a biological surrogate, carrying an embryo to term.

## Culture, Power, and Violence within Families

Although ideally families and households are tranquil and benign, too often this is not the reality. All over the globe, violence often occurs within families. Women and children, often the most vulnerable family members, are often its victims. (Eller 2006:115–145). As human rights activist Cesar Chelala points out, domestic violence—physical as well as psychological—occurs more frequently in societies where male power is embedded in cultural and religious patterns (2008; 2007). Thus, domestic violence is found more often in patrilineal, patrilocal societies than in matrilineal, matrilocal societies. It is the relative powerlessness of women within families; women's physical vulnerability; women's isolation from potential sources of support; concepts of sexual honor tied to female chastity; and the lack of alternative economic opportunities to marriage that often provide the context for domestic violence.

Domestic violence against women occurs in Western and non-Western societies, and in some cases, increases with urbanization, upward social mobility, or other factors associated with modernization. Dowry, for example, though outlawed as a prerequisite for marriage in India, is becoming more important among India's urbanized, increasingly modern, and upwardly mobile families. Sometimes, where a groom's family is dissatisfied with a bride's dowry, they may harass her to get her family to give more, or even murder her so that her son can marry again and receive another, and larger, dowry (Nanda and Gregg 2009; Sanghavi et al. 2009; Stone and James 2005).

Domestic violence is a major problem in the United States, where it often involves relative female powerlessness and economic dependence as well as a still strong ideology of male dominance. Though many women are vulnerable to domestic violence, immigrant women are particularly vulnerable. Many come from cultures with strong patriarchal values; they also often lack the language, cultural, and economically valuable skills that would provide alternatives to violent treatment within their families or access to social services. In addition, their U.S. visas are often dependent on their husbands, an added source of leverage against wives taking legal action (Sokoloff and Pratt 2005).

Anthropological understanding has been useful in providing social service and law enforcement agencies with a better knowledge of immigrant cultures, enabling culturally sensitive responses to domestic violence; but, in an ironic twist, this knowl-

---

ideology that a "family is two adults with a child or children" (Ragoné 1994:115), despite the expansion of alternative family structures we described earlier.

The many changes affecting the American family led anthropologist Philip Kilbride, in his book *Plural Marriages for our Times: A Reinvented Option* (1994), to suggest that the current problems of many American families might well be addressed by accepting polygyny as an alternative form of marriage. Kilbride notes, as we have, that many societies allow or even prefer polygyny. It is disparaged and illegal in the United States, he suggests, because of our particular cultural values rooted in religious beliefs that regard sexuality as sinful and identify polygyny with promiscuity and the valuing of sexual pleasure for its own sake. He points out the contradiction in the fact that the American ideal of monogamous marital fidelity is often transgressed by sexual relations outside marriage. As suggested in our chapter opening, polygyny might have many possible advantages in the United States, and we might be advised to rethink our resistance to it.

Another important trend in the United States is the increasing number of single-parent households. Single-mother families now account for almost 22 percent of all households with children—more than double the proportion of a generation ago. According to one study (Luker 1996), about half the children in the United States will spend at least some of their childhood in a single-parent family. Half of these will do so as the result of divorce or separation; the other half are mainly children of mothers who have never married, a figure about 5 times higher today than it was in the 1960s. Although there have always been many teenage pregnancies in the United States, until the 1970s, such pregnancies were quite likely to result in marriage. However, in the last several decades, there has been less pressure for pregnant teens to marry, and perhaps less advantage in doing so. In 1970, 30 percent of teenage mothers were unmarried at the time they gave birth; by 1995, this figure was 70 percent. To some extent, this mirrors the overall rise in the number of single mothers of every age. Just after World War II, almost every single mother was either a widow or a divorcee; fewer than one in 100 was an unmarried mother. Today unmarried mothers make up more than a third of the households headed by single women. And, though the focus of media attention is often on teenage single mothers, the rise in single motherhood is largely accounted for more by women in their 20s (*New York Times* 2006; Hacker 2002:22). Although woman-headed households are three times more common among African Americans than among European Americans (Andrews 1992:241), two-parent black fami-

edge has sometimes been used in the "cultural defense" to justify the abuse of women (Renteln 2004). In the cultural defense, attorneys argue that the mores concerning the treatment of women in a defendant's culture are so different from those of the United States, that they should be considered a mitigating factor in a defendant's violent behavior. This defense most frequently is used for males who have killed their wives, daughters, or other female relatives whom they view as having sullied their honor or family's reputation.

In an infamous 1988 New York City case, a Chinese man who beat his wife to death because he thought she was being unfaithful was acquitted when the defendant's lawyers, backed by anthropological testimony, argued that the intense shame and dishonor a Chinese man experiences when his wife is unfaithful meant that the husband could not be held fully accountable for his actions (Cardillo 1997). Women's groups, Asian Americans, and legal scholars strongly protested that "there should be only one standard of justice," which should not depend on a defendant's cultural background, and that the court's decision sent out the dangerous message that Asian women cannot be protected by American law (Norgren and Nanda 2006: 177).

In another case, *People v. Metallides* (1974) (Winkelman 1996), Metallides, a Greek immigrant, killed his best friend after this friend raped his daughter. Metallides's lawyers, supported by anthropological evidence, argued successfully that in Greek culture maintaining the family honor demanded that Metallides attempt to kill his friend. Similar cases have involved Hmong (Vietnamese) and Laotian refugees where anthropological testimony about a Hmong husband's culturally sanctioned control over his wife was used to mitigate homicide charges (Norgren and Nanda 1996: 272).

Anthropological testimony in cases using the cultural defense involving violence against women has been the subject of debate within the discipline. The cultural defense raises issues about the degree to which culture can compel individual actions as well as the role anthropologists should play in our legal system (Demian 2008). Anthropology makes a difference: Not by reinforcing the idea that "culture made me do it" is a valid excuse for domestic violence, but in raising awareness of the need for culturally and linguistically sensitive interventions that more effectively serve victims of domestic violence who come from other cultures.

lies are showing gains (Roberts 2008). At the same time, the rates of female-headed single-parent families and unmarried teenage mothers are increasing among both groups, and the differences between the two groups are shrinking.

Also changing is the number of single-father families, which now make up almost 6 percent of all households with children and approximately 20 percent of all single-parent households. Single-mother families and single-father families are different in important ways, however. A 2000 census study found that single fathers were 72 percent more likely to have a woman residing with them than a single mother was to have a man residing with her. And perhaps more important, the median income for custodial fathers is approximately $35,000 whereas that for single mothers is $21,000, including child-support payments (Hacker 2002:22).

The increase in single parenting has a number of causes: one is new forms of contraception that make it easier for couples to have an active sex life without being married, bringing with it a new cultural climate in which marriage can be disconnected from having and rearing children. As moral disapproval of out-of-wedlock births loses cultural force, the number of unmarried mothers can be expected to grow. Although much of the concern over single-parent female-headed households is expressed as political rhetoric about "family values," the real problem is that female-headed households and teenage pregnancy are correlated with poverty. Although single mothering is often cited as a cause of poverty, it has also been suggested as a symptom, because many unmarried teenage mothers are already disadvantaged by the poverty of their parents (Luker 1996).

## Composite Families

**Composite (compound) families** are aggregates of nuclear families linked by a common spouse, most often the husband. Composite families are thus mainly **patrilocal,** structured by rules that require a woman to live in her husband's home after marriage. A polygynous household, consisting of one man with several wives and their respective children, constitutes a composite family. In this case, each wife and her children normally occupy a separate residence.

**composite (compound) family** An aggregate of nuclear families linked by a common spouse.

**patrilocal residence** System under which a bride lives with her husband's family after marriage.

In much of Asia, the family is an extended group of kin connected through patrilineal descent. Although this extended kinship group involves an individual in obligations to others, it is also, ideally, a source of lifetime security, social connectedness, and help when needed.

The dynamics of composite families are different from those of a family that consists of one husband, one wife, and their children, all of whom occupy a common residence. In the composite family, for example, the tie between a mother and her children is particularly strong. The relations between the children of different mothers by the same father is different in a number of ways from the relationship between full siblings in the typical European-American nuclear family. In analyzing the dynamics of the composite family, the interaction between co-wives must be taken into account, as well as the different behavior patterns that emerge when a man is husband to several women rather than just one, and where competition over inheritance and succession are likely.

## Extended Families

The extended (consanguineal) family consists of two or more lineally related kinfolk of the same sex and their spouses and offspring, occupying a single household or homestead and under the authority of a household head.

**stem family** A nuclear family with a dependent adult added on.

**patrilineal** A lineage formed by descent in the male line.

**matrilineal** A lineage formed by descent in the female line.

**matrilocal residence** System under which a husband lives with his wife's family after marriage.

**avunculocal residence** System under which a married couple lives with the husband's mother's brother.

**bilocal residence** System under which a married couple has the choice of living with the husband's or the wife's family.

An extended family is not just a collection of nuclear families. In the extended family system, lineal ties—the blood ties between generations—are more important than ties of marriage. The extended family is the ideal in more than half of the world's societies. However, in stratified societies, even if it is ideal, it is found most often among the landlord and prosperous merchant classes; the nuclear or **stem family** (a nuclear family with a dependent adult added on) is more characteristic of the less prosperous peasants.

Extended families may be patrilineal or matrilineal. A **patrilineal** extended family is organized around a man, his sons, and the sons' wives and children. Societies with patrilineal extended families also tend to have patrilocal residence rules; that is, a woman lives with her husband's family after marriage. A **matrilineal** family is organized around a woman and her daughters and the daughters' husbands and children. Matrilineal families may have **matrilocal residence** rules (a man lives in the household of his wife's family) or **avunculocal residence** rules (a married couple is expected to live with the husband's mother's brother). If a couple can choose between living with either the wife's or the husband's family, the pattern is called **bilocal residence.**

**Patrilineal, Patrilocal Extended Families** In premodern China, the patrilineal, patrilocal extended family was the ideal. Lineal descendants—father, son, and grandson—were the backbone of family organization. The family continued through time as a permanent social entity. As older members were lost through death, new ones were added through birth. As in India, marriage in China was viewed more as acquiring a daughter-in-law than as taking a wife. It was arranged by the parents, and the new couple lived with the husband's family. The obedient relationship of the son to his father and the loyalty and solidarity of brothers were given more importance than the ties between husband and wife. In both India and China, the public demonstration of affection between a married couple was severely criticized. In both systems, it was feared that a man's feeling for his wife would interfere with his carrying out responsibilities to his own blood kin.

In these cultures, a good wife was one who was a good daughter-in-law. She had to work hard, under the eyes of her mother-in-law and her husband's elder brothers' wives. With the birth of a son, a woman gained more acceptance in the household. As the years went by, if she had been patient and played her role well, the relationship between husband and wife developed into one of companionship and a more equal division of power. As her sons grew up, the wife achieved even more power as she began to arrange for their marriages. When several sons were married, a woman might be the dominant person in the household, even ordering her husband about, as his economic power, and consequently his authority, waned.

**Matrilineal, Matrilocal Extended Families** In the matrilineal extended family, which is also generally matrilocal, the most important ties are between a woman and her mother and her siblings. In a patrilineal society, a child's father is responsible for providing for and protecting the mother-child unit. He has control over women and their children, and owns property with other males in his family. In a matrilineal society, these rights and responsibilities fall to a woman's brother rather than her husband. In matrilineal societies, a man gains sexual and economic rights over a woman when he marries her, but he does not gain rights over her children. The children belong to the mother's descent group, not the father's.

In matrilineal systems, a man usually goes to live with or near his wife's kin after marriage. This means that the man is the stranger in the household, whereas his wife is surrounded by her kin. Because a husband's role in the matrilineal household is less important than in the patrilineal one, marriages in matrilineal societies tend to be less stable.

**The Hopi: A Matrilineal Society** The Hopi, a Pueblo group in the American Southwest, are a matrilineal society. The matrilineage is conceived of as timeless, stretching backward to the beginnings of the Hopi people and continuing into the future. Both male and female members of the lineage consider their mother's house their

The Hopi family is matrilineal and revolves around a core of women. A husband moves to his wife's household, in which he has important economic responsibilities but few ritual obligations. The most important male role in Hopi society, as in other matrilineal societies, is a man's relation to his sister's son, and a man retains authority and leadership in his natal household even after he marries.

home, but men move out to live with their wives after marriage. They return to this home for many ritual and ceremonial occasions, however, and also in the case of separation or divorce. The relationship of a man with his father's lineage and household is affectionate, involving some economic and ritual obligations but little direct cooperation or authority.

The Hopi household revolves around a central and continuing core of women. The mother-daughter relationship is an exceedingly close one, based on blood ties, common activities, and lifelong residence together. A mother is responsible for the economic and ritual training of her daughters. The daughter behaves with respect, obedience, and affection to her mother and normally lives with her mother and mother's sisters after marriage. A mother also has a close relationship with her sons, although a son moves to his wife's home after marriage.

A son belongs to his mother's lineage and keeps much of his personal and ritual property in her home. A son shows respect for his mother as head of the household and consults her on all important decisions.

The strongest and most permanent tie in Hopi society is between sisters. The foundation of the household group is the relation of sisters to one another and to their mother. The children of sisters are raised together; if one sister dies, another looks after her children. Sisters cooperate in all domestic tasks. There are usually few quarrels, and when they occur, they are settled by the mother's brother or their own brothers.

As in all matrilineal societies, a man's relationship to his sister's sons is very important. As head of his sister's lineage and household, a Hopi man is in a position of authority and control. He is the chief disciplinarian and has the primary responsibility for the important task of transmitting the ritual heritage of the lineage and clan. He is consulted in the choice of a spouse, instructs his nephews in the proper behavior toward his new relatives, and formally welcomes his niece's husband into the household. A man usually selects his most capable nephew as his successor and trains him in the duties of whatever ceremonial position he may hold. Boys may fear their maternal uncles as sources of power and authority.

Hopi husbands have important economic functions but do not participate in the matrilineage ritual. They may be peripheral in their wives' households, having not only divided residences but divided loyalties. A Hopi father's obligations to his sons are primarily economic. He prepares them to make a living by teaching them to farm and herd sheep. At a son's marriage, a father often presents him with a portion of the flock and a small piece of land. The economic support a son receives from his father is returned in the father's old age, when he is supported by his sons.

Whereas a boy's relationship with his maternal uncle is characterized by reserve, respect, and even fear, his relationship with his father is more affectionate and involves little discipline. A Hopi man's relationship with his daughter is also generally affectionate but not close, and he has few specific duties in regard to her upbringing.

In addition to matrilineages, the Hopi also have matrilineal clans that extend over many different villages. A Hopi man must not marry within his own clan or the clan of his father or his mother's father. Through marriage a Hopi man acquires a wide range of relatives in addition to those resulting from his membership in his mother's clan. Kinship terms are extended to all these people, leading to a vast number of potential sibling relationships and the lateral integration of a great number of separate lineages and clans. This extension of kinship relates a Hopi in some way to almost everyone in the village, to people in other villages, and even to people in other Pueblo groups who have similar clans. In the clans, men play important political and religious roles, in contrast to the marginal positions they have in domestic life (Eggan 1950).

**Advantages of Extended Families** Societies such as the United States that extol the benefits of individualism and material success are structured around the relatively isolated nuclear family unit. Other kinds of families, however, whether extended families or nuclear families embedded in small communities, are clearly adaptive under certain economic and social conditions, and have advantages for members of those societies. The extended family system prevails in all types of cultivating societies, where its main adaptive advantages are economic. One advantage of the extended family is that it provides more workers than the nuclear family. This is useful both for food and crafts production and marketing. Furthermore, in stable agricultural societies, ownership of land becomes important as a source of pride, prestige, and power. The family becomes attached to the land, knows how to work it, and becomes reluctant to divide it. A system in which land is divided into small parcels through inheritance becomes unproductive. The extended family is a way of keeping land intact, providing additional security for individuals in times of crisis.

Although the nuclear family appears well adapted to industrialized society, the extended family is not necessarily a liability in some urban settings. The principles of mutual obligation of extended kin, joint ownership of property, and an authority structure in which the male household head makes decisions after consulting with junior members have proved useful among the upper classes of urban India in their successful management of modern corporations (Milton Singer 1968).

Like family types, residence rules are usually adaptive to food-producing strategies and other economic factors. Patrilocality, for example, is functional in societies practicing hunting and in agricultural societies, where men must work cooperatively. Matrilocality appears to be adaptive in horticultural societies, where women have an important role in the economy. Nevertheless, many horticultural societies are patrilocal.

Patrilocal residence rules may also be adaptive in societies where males must cooperate in warfare (Ember and Ember 1971). Where fighting between lineages or villages is common, it is useful for men who will fight together to live together. Otherwise, they might wind up having to choose between defending their wife's local group, the one with whom they live, against the families with whom they grew up. Where warfare takes place between societies, rather than within them, and where men must leave their homes to fight, cooperation among women is very important. Because common residence promotes cooperation, matrilocal residence is a functional norm when males engage in warfare that extends beyond local groups.

# The Global and the Local: A Cross-Cultural View of Aging

Individuals learn to understand and adjust to aging, a universal biological aspect of being human, within a matrix of cultural meanings and social institutions. Americans tend to associate old age with death; this is not universal. In many nonindustrial and economically underdeveloped societies, where the human life span is short, death is associated with infant mortality, childhood diseases, as well as accidents and sickness in adulthood, rather than with old age. Ironically, the association of old age and death in the United States is partly a result of scientific advances that have lengthened the life span. Under these conditions, old age becomes associated with the long dying process and such diseases as hypertension, cancer, coronary heart disease, and Alzheimer's, that are almost absent in some nonindustrial societies. But even with the physical problems associated with increased longevity, almost 40 percent of Americans over 65 say they are very happy, compared to 30 percent of people between 18 and 29.

Students sometimes romanticize age in more traditional societies. It is true that when age brings control over resources and knowledge, accomplishments, and the accumulation of descendants the elderly may be deeply respected. However, in many cases elderly individuals who do not have wealth, power, or descendents are not likely to be particularly respected (Counts and Counts 1985:261). In most cases the experience of growing old and treatment of the elderly are significantly dependent on the ability of elderly individuals to be productive and the availability of resources to care for them. Even in societies with extended family systems, aging may be difficult. When sons begin to raise families of their own, patrilineal extended families often split apart, and as the father loses productive abilities, he is slowly divested of his status and power. In Fiji, for example, although ideally an old father should be properly cared for by his brothers and sons, he may just as likely be barely kept alive, his counsel is never sought, and he is more often considered silly rather than wise (Sahlins 1957:451).

Where aging is linked to physical decline, decreasing productive participation in society and scarce material

Among the Ju/'hoansi, elderly people remain surrounded by kin and continue to make important contributions to community life.

resources, it is experienced negatively both by the elderly themselves and by the families, kin, or communities who care for them. Thus, the concept of caring for the elderly as a burden is culturally widespread, occurring even in societies like Japan, where integration and group harmony are valued over competitive independence. The Japanese elderly are frequently anxious about becoming a burden because they fear incurring obligations that cannot be paid back (Traphagan 1998).

In societies where family care of the aged at home is embedded in traditional cultural values, current economic changes are leading to changing practices. In China, for example, as the young migrate to cities, old people are left in the villages and the traditional Confucian obligations for a son to provide for his parents in their old age are breaking down (French 2006). Some urban communities, in an effort to shame people who neglect their elderly parents, post their names on public bulletin boards; in others, local homes for the elderly fine children who miss weekend parental visits.

American Muslims, also, are finding that the realities of modern life may conflict with the Koranic interpretation to care for one's elderly relatives at home. Many American Muslims find the idea of nursing homes unthinkable, but for some working families there are no other options. In response to this problem, some Muslims are designing assisted living and nursing home facilities that will make this option more acceptable: adjoining the homes to mosques or providing communal prayer rooms; serving halal food; providing same-sex medical and nursing care; and adding multilingual staff (Clemetson 2006).

One society well known for its positive treatment of the elderly is the Ju/'hoansi of Botswana (Rosenberg 2003). Formerly foragers, the Ju/'hoansi are now mainly sedentary pastoralists and agriculturalists, but their traditional values, particularly their ideology of sharing, remain largely intact. Elder caregiving is an important Ju/'hoansi value and the responsibility of all adult children. Ju/'hoansi elders are independent and autonomous. The able-bodied continue to forage or participate in other economic activities; they fetch water, visit, trade gifts, make crafts, dance, and exercise their valuable healing powers. Ju/'hoansi elders are not considered a burden, even those who cannot care for themselves. The difficulties of old age, including the decline of sexual prowess and interest among both men and women, are a source of Ju/'hoansi humor, and even the very old and helpless do not experience a sharp decline of social status. Elders are associated with generative and life giving activities in the community, are felt to have special powers, and may occupy strong leadership roles. The Ju/'hoansi elders do not have fears of pauperization or anxieties about personal security, interpersonal violence or abuse, loneliness, or abandonment by their families.

The Ju/'hoansi illustrate that even in a society with very limited material resources, the situation of the elderly might well be envied by those in societies with a much richer material base. This is particularly impressive because, as foragers without property to pass on, Ju/'hoansi elders lack the leverage of inheritance to exact compliance from their children. Things may be changing, however: as the Ju/'hoansi become pastoralists, livestock becomes an important asset and inheritance of property may become increasingly significant in the status and treatment of the elderly.

## Key Questions

1. What are some of the factors that influence the experience of aging in different cultures?
2. What do you see as your responsibilities in relation to (the future) care of your elderly relations?

# Summary

1. **What are some of the major functions of marriage and the family?** Three major functions of marriage and the family are regulating sexual access between males and females, arranging for the exchange of services between males and females, and assigning responsibility for child care.

2. **How do the Na of China and other cross-cultural examples raise questions about the universality of marriage as grounded in the biological differences between male and female?** Although marriage and family are grounded in the biological complementarity of male and female and the biological process of reproduction, there is great variety in the forms and functions of families. The Na of China do not traditionally practice marriage, and children remain throughout their life in their mother's household. The Na raise the question of whether marriage is universal and whether procreation is a universal function of the family. Same-sex marriages in some African cultures and in the United States raise similar questions.

3. **What is an incest taboo? What are some theories of why incest taboos are universal?** Incest taboos are prohibitions on mating between people classified as relatives. Some theories that attempt to account for the universality of such taboos are that they limit inbreeding, prevent disruption within the family, and force people to marry out of their immediate families, thus joining people into a larger social community.

4. **What is the difference between exogamy and endogamy? How do these rules function in different cultural contexts?** Exogamy requires that people marry outside a particular group. This rule is adaptive in forging alliances between families within a society. Endogamy requires marriage within a specified group. Its function may be to keep wealth within the group or to maintain the so-called purity of the bloodline.

5. **What are some preferential marriage rules and what functions do they have?** Preferential marriage rules include the preference for cross cousins or parallel cousins to marry. Cross-cousin marriage reinforces ties between kin groups established in the preceding generation, strengthening group alliances. Parallel-cousin marriage helps prevent the fragmentation of family property and strengthens solidarity between brothers. The levirate and the sororate attest to marriage as an alliance between groups and allow the fulfillment of the marriage contract even if one partner dies.

6. **What are the two forms of polygamy? How do these function in different societies?** All societies have rules about the number of spouses one may have. Whereas the United States has a rule of monogamy (one spouse only), most of the world's societies allow some form of plural marriage (polygyny or polyandry). Polygyny is found mainly in horticultural societies but also in foraging societies, such as the Tiwi of Australia, where women make important contributions to the food supply, which benefits men but which is also a source of power for women, who become the center of a cohesive economic and social unit of cowives and daughters. Polyandry (one woman with several husbands) is much rarer than polygyny and occurs in societies where men must be away from home for long periods of time.

7. **Why, in most societies, does marriage emphasize the relationship between groups rather than between individuals? How does this affect the ways in which marriages are formed?** Because of the substantial economic investment of kin groups in marriage in most societies, family elders have substantial or even total control over

choosing their children's spouses. In addition, marriage is frequently legitimated by an exchange of goods between the bride's kin and the groom's kin. The most common form of exchange is bridewealth, in which the groom's kin gives various goods to the bride's kin. Dowry is an exchange in which the bride's kin must give various goods to the family of the groom.

8. **What is the relationship between power and domestic violence? How has culture been used to explain the widespread occurrence of domestic violence?** Because in most societies males have culturally sanctioned power over females, domestic violence occurs in many societies, including the United States. Where cases of domestic violence involve immigrant women in Western societies, cultural practices may be raised as a legal defense, an intervention deplored by many feminist groups.

9. **What are the differences between nuclear and extended families? How is each type of family structure related to economic factors?** There are two basic types of families: nuclear and extended. The nuclear family is organized around the tie between husband and wife (the conjugal tie) and is found predominantly in contemporary industrial societies and foraging societies. It appears to be adaptive where geographical mobility is important. The extended family predominates among cultivators. It provides a larger number of workers than does the nuclear family, and it allows land holdings to be kept intact over generations.

10. **What are the three most common rules of residence and how do they differ from each other?** The most widespread rule of residence is patrilocality, which requires a wife to live with her husband's family. Matrilocality, which requires the husband to live with his wife's family, is found primarily in horticultural societies. Neolocality, in which the married couple lives independently, is particularly well adapted to industrialized societies where the mobility of labor is important.

11. **What is the ideal concept of the American family and how is this changing?** American ideology often stresses the importance of the neolocal, independent, nuclear, monogamous family. However, this form is challenged by the high divorce rate, increasing number of single-parent (especially single-mother) families, the increasing presence of women in the labor market, as well as the increase of same-sex couple families and in the increasing acceptance of surrogate motherhood.

12. **What accounts for cross-cultural variability in the treatment of the aged?** Aging is a universal, biologically based human characteristic, but it is treated differently in different societies. In many societies the aged remain within their families or communities; in others, independence is valued, even among the aged. Important local variations in treatment of the aged include factors such as the cultural value on independence, the economic situation of families and individuals, the advances of medical technology, and the availability of facilities of care.

# Key Terms

| | | |
|---|---|---|
| arranged marriage | endogamy | neolocal residence |
| avunculocal residence | exogamous group | nuclear family |
| bilocal residence | exogamy | parallel cousins |
| blended family | extended family | patrilineal |
| bride service | fraternal polyandry | patrilocal residence |
| bridewealth | incest taboos | polyandry |
| composite (compound) family | levirate | polygamy |
| conjugal tie | marriage | polygyny |
| consanguineal | matrilineal | sororal polygyny |
| cross cousins | matrilocal residence | sororate |
| domestic group (household) | monogamy | stem family |
| dowry | | surrogate motherhood |

# Suggested Readings

Nanda, Serena, and Joan Gregg. 2009. *The Gift of a Bride. A Tale of Anthropology, Matrimony and Murder.* New York: Altamira/Rowman and Littlefield. An ethnographically based novel about family violence in an Indian immigrant community in New York City.

Therborn, Goran. 2003. *Between Sex and Power. Family in the World, 1900–2000.* London: Routledge. A majesterial work of history and imagination, this powerful book combines theory with a wealth of fascinating evidence on changes in family structures in every corner of the planet. Differences both within and between cultural areas highlight the complexity of the subject.

Rites of passage ceremonially and symbolically highlight a passage from one social status to another. Here, a young girl from the Samburu group of East Africa, is adorned with a beaded mask as part of her engagement ritual.

© Judith Pearson

**THINKING POINT:** Among the Tchambuli, women had the major economic role and showed common sense and business shrewdness. Men were more interested in esthetics. They spent much time decorating themselves and gossiping. Their feelings were easily hurt, and they sulked a lot.

—From Margaret Mead, *Sex and Temperament in Three Primitive Societies*
[See next paragraph for more details.]

# {chapter 10}

# Gender

In the 1930s, Margaret Mead (1963/1935) began to question the biologically determined nature of gender. Mead organized her ethnographic research around the question of whether the characteristics defined as masculine and feminine in Western culture, specifically the United States, were universal. In one of her many field research projects, she examined masculine and feminine traits among three groups in New Guinea—the Arapesh, the Mundugamor, and the Tchambuli (1963/1935). She reported that among the Arapesh, men and women both were expected to act in ways that Americans considered "naturally" feminine. Both sexes were concerned with taking care of children and nurturing. Neither sex was expected to be aggressive. In Mundugamor society, both sexes were what American culture would call "masculine": aggressive, violent, and with little interest in children. And, as we saw in the "Thinking Point", among the Tchambuli, traditional American notions of masculine and feminine were, to some degree, reversed. Women had the major economic role and were noted for common sense and business shrewdness. Men were more interested in esthetics. They spent much time decorating themselves and gossiping. Their feelings were easily hurt, and they sulked a lot. Thus, Mead found that many of the behaviors, emotions, and roles that go into being masculine and feminine are patterned by culture.

In addition to its importance in gender studies, Mead's work is significant because it reinforces a central anthropological thesis: in order to grasp the potential and limits of diversity in human life, we must look at the full range of human societies—particularly those outside Western historical, cultural, and economic traditions. In nonindustrial, small-scale, kinship-based, more egalitarian societies, gender relationships clearly differ from those of the West. Indeed, research on gender diversity indicates that the very construction of sex and gender is extraordinarily diverse, as are the relationships between sex, gender, and other aspects of culture. **>>**

Ethnographic evidence for this diversity is legion. Among some subarctic Indian peoples, for example, where a son was depended on to feed the family through big game hunting, a family that had daughters and no sons would simply select a daughter to "be like a man." When the youngest daughter was about 5 years old, the parents performed a transformation ceremony in which they tied the dried ovaries of a bear to a belt the child always wore. This was believed to prevent menstruation, protect her from pregnancy, and give her luck on the hunt. From then on, she dressed like a male, trained like a male, and often developed great strength and became an outstanding hunter (W. Williams 1996:202). For these Indians, being male or female included both biological elements, such as menstruation, and cultural features, such as the ability to hunt. «

Anthropologist Margaret Mead was a key figure in emphasizing the cultural element in gender roles. She was also important in introducing these anthropological ideas to the general public.

# Sex and Gender

In contemporary social science, the distinctions between biological and cultural aspects of being male or female are very important. **Sex** is the term used to describe the biological differences between male and female, particularly the visible differences in external genitalia and the related difference in the role each sex plays in the reproductive process. **Gender** is the term for the cultural and social classification of masculine and feminine. Thus,

**sex** The biological difference between male and female.

**gender** A cultural construction that makes biological and physical differences between male and female into socially meaningful categories.

**cultural construction of gender** The idea that gender characteristics are the result of historical, economic, and political forces acting within each culture.

gender is the social, cultural, and psychological constructs that different societies superimpose on the biological differences of sex (Worthman 1995:598). Every culture recognizes distinctions between male and female, but cultures differ in the meanings attached to these categories, the supposed sources of the differences between them, and the relationship of these categories to other cultural and social facts. Furthermore, all cultures recognize at least two sexes (male and female) and two genders (masculine and feminine), but some cultures recognize additional sexes and genders.

The current anthropological approach to gender emphasizes the central role of gender relations as a basic building block of culture and society (Yanagisako and Collier 1994:190–203). Gender is central to social relations of power, individual and group identities, the formation of kinship and other groups, and meaning and value. As was noted in Chapter 3, until the 1970s the central role of gender in society and culture was largely overlooked, and both ethnography and anthropological theory were skewed as a result.

## The Cultural Construction of Gender

The central assumption of an earlier, androcentric (male centered) anthropology was that gender, like sex, was "natural" or biologically determined. The different roles, behaviors, personality characteristics, emotions, and development of men and women were viewed as a function of sex differences, and thus universal. An assumed biological determinism meant that many important questions about the role of gender in culture and society were never asked. The emergence of feminist anthropology in the 1970s focused attention on cross-cultural variability in the meaning of gender. Biological determinism began to give way to the view that gender is culturally constructed (Ortner and Whitehead 1981). The **cultural construction of gender** is the idea that gender is established by social norms and values rather than by biology. Work focusing on the cultural construction of gender emphasizes the different ways cultures think about, distinguish, and symbolize gender.

This revised understanding of gender raised new questions about the culturally patterned nature of women's and men's lives in all cultures. It focused attention on historical changes in gender relations (Lancaster 1989; Spector and Whelan 1989; Zihlman 1989), the role of gender in human development (Chodorow 1974, 1978), the constructions of feminine and masculine in different cultures, and the connections between gender systems and other sociocultural patterns (Ortner and Whitehead 1981). It also raised questions about the effect of European expansion on gender relations in non-European societies (Nash and Safa 1986) and the changes in gender relations within Europe and North America as a result of industrialism, capitalism, and expansion of the global economy (Andersen and Collins 1995; Warren and Bourque 1989).

## Alternative Sexes, Alternative Genders

Since the late 1970s, anthropological research and reinterpretation of older ethnography added weight to the view of gender as culturally constructed. Particularly important were cultures that recognized more than two sexes and more than two genders (Costa and Matzner 2007; Herdt 1996; Matzner 2001; Nanda 1999; W. Roscoe 1991; W. Williams 1986; Winter 2009) or where heterosexuality and homosexuality were defined differently than they were in the United States (Herdt 1981).

The division of humans into two sexes and two genders, characteristic of most cultures, appears to be natural and inevitable. Sex assignment, which takes place at birth, is assumed to be permanent over a person's lifetime. The view of sex and gender as a system of two opposing and unchangeable categories is taken for granted by most social science. It is difficult for most of us even to think about any alternative to this view.

However, a cross-cultural perspective indicates that sex and gender are not necessarily or universally viewed as identical and limited to a system of male/female opposites. Among the Igbo of Nigeria, for example, Amadiume (1987) notes that members of either sex can fill male gender roles. Daughters can fill sons' roles and women can be husbands, without being considered "masculine" or losing their femininity. Before the influence of Christianity among the Igbo, both women and men could use wealth to take titles (achieve rank) and acquire wives. Although Christian missionaries attempted to eliminate woman–woman marriage in Africa, the practice continues today. In some African societies that practice woman–woman marriages, such as the Nandi of Kenya, the female husband is considered to be a man and adopts many aspects of the male gender role, such as participating in male initiation and public political discussions (Oboler 1980). The presence of female husbands has been reported for more than 30 African groups (D. O'Brien 1977). Although there are important variations among the different groups' woman–woman marriages, the literature specifically notes that the relationship between the female husband and wife is not sexual.

Alternative gender roles—neither man nor woman—have been described for many societies. The **xanith** of Oman on the Saudi Arabian peninsula (Wikan 1977), the **two-spirit role** in many Native American tribes (W. Roscoe 1991; 1995; Whitehead 1981; W. Williams 1986), the **mahu** of Tahiti (Besnier 1996; Levy 1973), the *muxe* of Mexico (Lacey 2008), and the **hijra** of India (Nanda 1999; Reddy

2005) are among the gender roles in which men take on some of the attributes of women and are classified as an in-between gender.

The Native American two-spirit role has long been a subject of anthropological interest. Two spirit roles took different forms in different Native American cultures, but most often the two-spirit person was a man who dressed in women's clothing, engaged in women's work, and was often considered to have special supernatural powers and privileges in society (Whitehead 1981). There were also female two-spirit people (Blackwood 1984). Although alternative-gendered people were not equally valued in all Native American cultures, they were very highly valued in some, such as the Zuni (W. Roscoe 1991).

The form, frequency, and cultural specificity of alternative sex/gender roles are not random occurrences, but appear to be woven into cultural patterns. Sex/gender diversity varies cross-culturally: cultures differ on their criteria for constructing sex/gender variation, the extent to which this variation is recognized and/or ritualized, the degree to which sex/gender transformations are considered to be complete and/or irrevocable, the association of sex/gender transformations with males or females, the special functions of alternative sexes and genders (such as healing or acting as go-betweens in marriages), and the value or stigma placed on such variations (Nanda 2000b).

Anthropologists attempt to explain the occurrence and form of sex/gender alternatives, though no one explanation covers all the ethnographic variation. In some cases, for example among some Native American groups or in Polynesia, sex/gender diversity is associated with an ideology that recognizes all individuals as having their own special characteristics, including sex/gender variation. In cultures such as those in Thailand, there is less concern for an individual's private life as long as he or she observes social obligations in public, so that sex/gender diversity is not severely stigmatized. In India, the sex/gender alternative of the hijra is related to the Hindu philosophy of dharma, where each person is expected to follow his or her own life path, no matter how different or even painful that may be. In addition, Hinduism in general has the ability to incorporate cultural contradictions and ambiguities to a larger extent than, for example, Western religions, and this too is congenial to the

---

**xanith** An alternative gender role in Oman on the Saudi Arabian peninsula.

**two-spirit role** An alternative gender role in native North America (formerly called berdache).

**mahu** An alternative gender role in Tahiti.

**hijra** An alternative gender role in India conceptualized as neither man nor woman.

## The Hijras: An Alternative Gender Role in India

The hijra of India is a gender role that is neither masculine nor feminine. Hijras are born as men, but they dress and live as women. The hijras undergo an operation in which their genitals are surgically removed, but unlike transsexuals in the West, this operation turns men into hijras, not into women. Hijras are followers of a Hindu goddess, Bahuchara Mata, and the hijra subculture is partly a religious group centered on the worship of this goddess. By dressing as women, and especially through emasculation as a ritual expression of their religious devotion, the hijras attempt to completely identify with the goddess. Through this operation, the hijras believe that the procreative powers of the goddess are transferred to them.

Traditionally, the hijras earn their living by performing at life-cycle ceremonies, such as the birth of a child (formerly only for male children, who are much desired in India, but sometimes for female children today) and at marriages. Because the hijras are vehicles of the goddess's powers of procreation, their presence is necessary on these occasions. They ask the goddess to bless the newborn or the married couple with prosperity and fertility. Hijras also serve the goddess in her temple.

The word hijra may be translated as either eunuch or hermaphrodite; in both cases, male sexual impotence is emphasized. Few hijras are born hermaphrodite, almost all are born biologically male. Because there are many causes for male impotence, there are many reasons that men may choose to join the hijras. In some parts of India, it is believed that an impotent man who does not become a hijra, in deference to the wishes of the hijra goddess, will be reborn impotent for seven future lives.

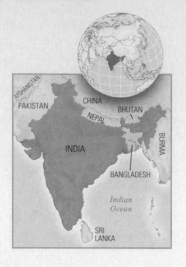

The concept of the hijra as neither man nor woman emphasizes that they are not men because they cannot function sexually as men, though they were assigned to the male sex at birth. Hijras also claim that they do not have sexual feelings for women, and a real hijra is not supposed to have ever had sexual relations with women. But if hijras, as a third gender, are "man minus man," they are also "man plus woman." The most obvious aspect of hijras as women is in their dress. Wearing female attire is a defining characteristic of hijras. They are required to dress as women when they perform their traditional roles of singing and dancing at births and weddings, and whenever they are in the temple of their goddess. Hijras enjoy dressing as women, and their feminine dress is accompanied by traditionally feminine jewelry and body decoration. Hijras must also wear their hair long like women.

Hijras also adopt female behavior. They imitate a woman's walk, they sit and stand like women, and they carry pots on their hips as women do. Hijras adopt female names when they join the community, and they use female kinship terms for each other such as aunt or sister. They also have a special linguistic dialect, which includes feminine expressions and intonations. In public accommodations, such as the movies, or in buses and trains, hijras often request "ladies only" seating. They also request that they be counted as females in the census.

Although hijras are like women in many ways, they are clearly not women. Their female dress and mannerisms are often exaggerations almost to the point of caricature, especially when they act in a sexually suggestive manner. Their sexual aggressiveness is considered outrageous and very much in opposition to the expected demure behavior of ordinary Indian women in their roles of wives, mothers, and daughters. Hijra performances are essentially burlesques of women; the entertainment value comes from the difference between themselves, acting as women, and the real women they imitate. Hijras often use obscene and abusive language, which again is considered contrary to acceptable feminine behavior. In some parts of India, hijras smoke the hookah (water pipe) and cigarettes, which are normally done only by men.

The major reason hijras are not considered women, however, is that they cannot give birth. Many hijras wish to be women so that they can give birth, and there are many stories within the community that express this wish. But all hijras acknowledge that this can never be. As neither man nor woman, the hijras identify themselves with many third-gender figures in Hindu mythology and Indian culture: male deities who change into or disguise themselves as females temporarily, deities who have both male and female characteristics, male reli-

emergence of sex/gender diversity. In some cases, sex/gender alternatives appear related to cultural systems with relatively low gender differentiation (the distinctions between male and female gender roles), though sex/gender alternatives also appear in cultures, such as in Brazil, where gender differentiation is high. Sex/gender alternatives also are found in cultures where transformations of all kinds—of humans into animals or vice versa, for example—are common, such as in some African cultures and in African diasporic religions. Where androg-

Courtesy of Serena Nanda

These hijras, celebrating a marriage, exhibit exaggerated female gestures and clap their hands in the unique style of this subculture.

gious devotees who dress and act as women in religious ceremonies, and the eunuchs who served in the Muslim courts. Indian culture thus not only accommodates such androgynous figures but views them as meaningful and even powerful.

The emphasis in this ethnography is on the cultural conception of the hijra role. The realities of hijra life do not always match the ideal, and, as in other societies, there are some tensions between the ways in which hijras understand themselves and the realities of their lives. A significant source of conflict among hijras is their widespread practice of prostitution. Hijras serve as sexual partners for men, which contradicts their identity as ascetics. Hijras see prostitution as deviant within their community, and many deny that it occurs. Others justify it by reference to their declining incomes from traditional performances.

Unlike many societies throughout the world with alternative gender roles that were suppressed by colonial authorities and Christian missionaries, hijras continue to function as an integral part of Indian culture, both in traditional roles and in changing roles that reflect new adaptations. One new role for hijras is in contemporary Indian politics, in which hijras have achieved some notable success. In recent years hijras have stood for and even won election to local, state, and even national office (Reddy and Nanda 2005). Significantly, hijra success in politics has been achieved not by denying, but by emphasizing their ambiguous gender. (However, the election of one hijra has been overturned by a lower state court on the grounds that hijras are men masquerading as women and therefore cannot stand for election to seats reserved for women. What we seem to see here is a

clash between traditional concepts that admit of in-between or alternative genders and Western concepts that recognize two genders only—man and woman.)

When they enter politics, hijras explicitly construct themselves as individuals without the obligations of family, gender, or caste, and emphasize that they are therefore free from the corrupting influence of nepotism, which plagues Indian politics. They also emphasize their identity as ascetics, Hindu religious figures who renounce sexual relations, claiming historical continuities with many Hindu political reformers. Many Indians believe that hijras are more empathetic to issues of poverty and social stigma because of their own low social status, and this has enabled hijras to defeat traditionally powerful upper caste opponents.

The continued recognition of hijras in Indian society is a strong testimony to the cultural construction of genders. Unlike many other traditional alternative genders among indigenous peoples that have been stamped out or repressed by the powerful states in which they now live, the hijras continue both in their traditional roles and in new roles, contributing to the cultural variation that characterizes the human species.

### CRITICAL THINKING QUESTIONS

1. How does a study of the hijras contribute to an understanding of gender as culturally constructed?
2. Discuss some of the similarities and differences between the hijras and similar gender roles in other societies.
3. In what ways do elements of Indian culture relate to the maintenance of the hijra role?

Source: Serena Nanda, *Neither Man nor Woman: The Hijras of India* (2nd ed.). Belmont, CA: Wadsworth, 1999.

yny (the mixture of male and female) is considered sacred and powerful, as in southeast Asian island cultures, sex/gender alternatives also frequently appear. And where continuation of a patrilineage is central to a society's kinship structure, such as in the Balkans, or among

the Ibo of Nigeria, one way of making sure there are people to fill all important kin positions is to permit women to take on not only male roles, but also other male gender characteristics. As in all things, from the seemingly most ordinary to the seemingly most exotic, anthropology not only documents human diversity, but also tries to explain that diversity by drawing on the ethnographic record and the related aspects of culture and society.

## Cultural Variation in Sexual Behavior

In addition to varying in the number of sexes and genders they recognize, cultures also vary in their definitions of appropriate sexual behaviors. The cultural component of sexual behavior is not easily understood. Of all the kinds of human behavior, sexual activity is most likely to be viewed as "doing what comes naturally." But a cross-cultural perspective on sexual behavior demonstrates that every aspect of human sexual activity is patterned by culture and influenced by learning, sometimes in contradictory or paradoxical ways.

Culture patterns the habitual responses of different peoples to different parts of the body. What is considered erotic in some cultures evokes indifference or disgust in others. For example, kissing is not practiced in many societies. The Samoans learned to kiss from the Europeans, but before this cultural contact, they began sexual intimacy by sniffing. The patterns of social and sexual preliminaries also differ among cultures. The Trobriand Islanders, as described by Malinowski, "inspect each other's hair for lice and eat them. . . . to the natives a natural and pleasant occupation between two who are fond of each other" (1929b:327). This may seem disgusting to people from the West, but to the Trobrianders, "the idea of European boys and girls going out for a picnic with a knapsack full of eatables is. . . . disgusting and indecent" (1929b:327) although it is a perfectly acceptable custom for a Trobriand boy and girl to gather wild foods together as a prelude to sexual activity.

Who is considered an appropriate sexual partner also differs in different cultures. In some societies, for example, same-sex sexual activity is considered shameful and abnormal, but in other societies it is a matter of indifference, approval, or even required in some cases. Among the Sambia of Papua New Guinea, the rite of passage for every adolescent male incorporates same-sex activity in the form of fellatio, where it is believed that only men can create men through this transfer of semen. During their initiation boys live away from their parents in a men's cult house and this same-sex activity is considered essential as part of their training to become vigorous, strong warriors. Those participating in these relationships are not considered homosexual, and as adults, the boys are expected to enter heterosexual marriages (Herdt 1981). The assumptions of Sambia culture contrast strongly with the dominant cultural ideology in the United States, where consistent heterosexuality is considered essential to masculine identity and same-sex sexual activity defines one as "homosexual."

Among other cultural variations in beliefs about sexuality are the ages at which sexual response is believed to begin and end, the ways in which people make themselves attractive, the importance of sexual activity in human life, and its variation according to gender—all these are patterned and regulated by culture and affect sexual response and behavior. A comparison of two cultures, the Irish of "Inis Beag," a community on one of the Aran Islands in the Bay of Galway, and the Polynesians of Mangaia, makes clear the role of culture in sexuality.

John Messenger describes Inis Beag as "one of the most sexually naive of the world's societies" (1971:15). Sex is never discussed at home when children are near, and parents provide practically no sexual instruction to children. Adults express the belief that "after marriage nature takes its course." (As we shall see, "nature" takes a very different course in Inis Beag than it does in Polynesia!) Women are expected to endure but not enjoy sexual relations; to refuse to have intercourse is considered a mortal sin among this Roman Catholic people. There appears to be widespread ignorance in Inis Beag of the female capacity for orgasm, which in any case is considered deviant behavior. Nudity is abhorred, and there is no tradition of "dirty jokes." The main style of dancing allows little bodily contact among the participants; even so, some girls refuse to dance because it means touching a boy. The separation of the sexes begins very early in Inis Beag and lasts into adulthood. Other cultural patterns related to sexual repression here are the virtual absence of sexual foreplay, the belief that sexual activity weakens a man, the absence of premarital sex, the high percentage of celibate males, and the extraordinarily late age of marriage. According to a female informant, "Men can wait a long time before wanting 'it' but we [women] can wait a lot longer" (1971:16).

Although the idea of total sexual freedom in the South Sea Islands is a Western myth, Mangaia, as described by Donald Marshall (1971), presents a strong contrast to Inis Beag. In this Polynesian culture, sexual intercourse is one of the major interests of life. Although sex is not discussed at home, sexual information is taught to boys and girls at puberty by the elders of the group. For adolescent boys, a 2-week period of formal instruction about the techniques of intercourse is followed by a culturally approved experience with a mature woman in the village. After this, the boy is considered a man. This contrasts with Inis Beag, where a man is considered a "lad" until he is about 40.

Sexual relations in Mangaia take place in private, but there is continual public reference to sexual activity. Sexual jokes, expressions, and references are expected as part of the preliminaries to public meetings. This pattern of public verbal references to sex contrasts with the public separation of the sexes. Boys and girls should not be seen together in public, but practically every girl and boy has had intercourse before marriage. The act of sexual intercourse itself is the focus of sexual activity. What Westerners call sexual foreplay generally follows intercourse in Mangaia. Both men and women are expected to take pleasure in the sexual act and to have an orgasm. Female frigidity, male celibacy, and homosexual identity are practically unknown. The contrast between Inis Beag and Mangaia indicates clearly that societies' different attitudes pattern the sexual responsiveness of males and females in each society.

## Sexuality and the Cultural Construction of Gender

A culture's construction of gender always includes reference to sexuality and the differences between men and women. Cultural views of gender-related sexuality have often been used to support various sexual ideologies, which also intersect with the construction of race, class, and colonialist relationships. European constructions of masculine and feminine sexuality have been an important part of European images of their own society and of others.

Not all societies so strongly differentiate male and female sexuality. When gender ideologies do make these distinctions, however, they are also likely to use this distinction as the basis of gender hierarchy, in which social control of women's sexuality is central. These controls may take such forms as the seclusion of women (S. Hale 1989); a cultural emphasis on honor and shame as related to female sexuality (Brandes 1981); and control by men, or by the state and organized religion, over marriage, divorce, adultery, and abortion. Controls are also imposed on women through medical/scientific definitions of what constitutes the normal or the pathological in female bodily processes (Martin 1987) and sexuality (Groneman 2000). Society's control of female sexuality is often inscribed on female bodies: female circumcision in some African societies (Barnes-Dean 1989), Chinese footbinding (Anagnost 1989), gang rape in the United States (Sanday 1992), sati (the Hindu practice of a woman burning herself on her husband's funeral pyre) (Narasimhan 1990), and eating disorders in the United States (Brumberg 1989).

## Coming of Age in Cross-Cultural Perspective: Male and Female Rites of Passage

All cultures have changing expectations of an individual at different points in life, as new capacities unfold or old ones diminish. At each of these points, individuals learn what is necessary for the new roles associated with these changing expectations. The cultural learning that takes place in childhood is particularly important, but the teaching and learning of culture continues throughout life.

In the United States, adolescence is understood as a distinct stage of life associated with the physiological changes of puberty as well as emotional changes. In some other societies, adolescence may not be viewed as a stage of life at all. One important contribution of Margaret Mead's classic study *Coming of Age in Samoa* (1971/1928), was her finding that the idealism, psychic conflict, and rebellion against authority that Americans view as an inevitable part of adolescence did not occur in Samoa. Rather, in Samoa, as in many societies, an individual's transition from childhood to adulthood involved a gradually increasing participation in society, with little psychological trauma.

In many societies, although the stage of adolescence is not recognized, children's passage into adulthood is marked by rituals, which are called **rites of passage** (see Chapter 13). Arnold Van Gennep (1960/1909) viewed rites of passage as a way of publicly and ceremonially acknowledging a change of social roles, or a passage from one social group to another. These rites were performed at important life events, such as puberty, marriage, and death. Their function was to reduce the potentially traumatic effects of such transitions both on the society and on the individual by formalizing and ritualizing them. Subsequent to Van Gennep's discussion, most anthropological studies focused on the very widespread pattern of male initiations—the rituals surrounding the transition from childhood to the adult male status.

### Male Initiation

The importance of male initiation in many societies led anthropologists to focus attention on their possible psychological and sociological functions, along with the cultural symbols and rituals that embodied the society's concept of masculinity or referred back to these functions (see the description of female envy later in this section). Sociological theories held that male initiation rites primarily expressed and affirmed the enduring order of male relationships and male solidarity. In some societies, they also served to culturally validate male dominance. The most obvious purpose of the rites appeared to be the legitimization of a change of status from child to adult. They often involved an extended period of separation, during which the initiates learned the beliefs,

**rite of passage** A ritual that moves an individual from one social status to another.

Among the Maasai, initiation signals a break between childhood and adulthood. A young man's ability to repress any emotional reaction to the pain of circumcision, a key ritual of male initiation, indicates whether he is worthy of the warrior role that is central to Maasai adulthood.

Other psychological theories of male initiation rites, particularly those involving bloodletting, explain the rites as symbolic reactions by males to their envy of female procreative ability and the mother-son bond (see, for example, Bettelheim 1996/1962). Margaret Mead noted that male initiation rites frequently involved men ritualizing birth and taking over, as a collective group, the functions women perform naturally. Gilbert Herdt (1981) described the male initiation rites of the Sambia of Papua New Guinea in terms of men's symbolic control over the rebirth of boys, making them into men. Viewed from this perspective, male initiation is a type of fertility cult in which men celebrate and ritually reproduce their control over the fertility of crops, animals, and humans.

Whatever the underlying psychodynamics, male initiation rituals clearly have an important sociological role in moving young people from childhood to adulthood. Radcliffe-Brown (1956), for example, viewed the ordeals, taboos, and solemnity of these rites as essential to communicating the seriousness of life and its duties to the initiates. The sociological and psychological features of initiation rites complement each other.

## Female Initiation

Historically, there was a general ethnographic neglect of female initiation rites in comparison to male initiation rites even though such rites, which are generally performed for individuals at their **menarche** (first menstruation), actually occur in more societies than male initiation rites. This anthropological neglect resulted partly from an androcentric bias and partly from the definition of initiation rites as group activities. Recent research on girls' coming-of-age rituals indicates much cross-cultural variability (Lutkehaus and Roscoe 1995). Sometimes the initiate is isolated from society; sometimes she is the center of attention. Some rituals are elaborate and take years to perform; others are performed with little ceremony.

Several interpretations have been offered for girls' initiation rites. Judith Brown (1965) found that such rites are more likely to occur in societies in which the young girl continues to live in her mother's home after marriage. This suggests that the rites are a way of publicly announcing a girl's status change, because she will spend her adult life in the same place that she spent her childhood. Although the girl may continue to do the same kinds of tasks she did as a child, she now has to do them as a responsible adult. The rites are thus the means by which the girl publicly accepts her new legal role. As with boys, girls' initiation rites also teach them what they will need to know as adults. Bemba women explain their elaborate girls' initiation rite, called Chisungu (Richards 1956:125), by saying that they "make the girls clever." The word they use means "to be intelligent and socially competent and to have a knowledge of etiquette."

skills, and knowledge necessary to participate as a functioning adult in society. Thus, another function of the rites was the transmission of culture. The social order was reinforced by dramatizing its values in a public context. By taking the child out of the home, initiation rites emphasized the importance of citizenship. An individual was responsible to the whole society, and society as well as the family had an interest in him (Hart 1967).

There are several different psychological theories of male initiation. The Freudian view is based on the Oedipus complex. Initiation rituals are seen as a symbolic means of mastering universal conflicts that are generated by boys' identification with their mothers, from whom they must be separated in order to carry out their male adult responsibilities. Evidence for this theory can be found in the work of John Whiting, who showed that male initiation rites are more likely to occur in cultures where boys have strong identification with their mothers and hostility toward their fathers (Whiting, Kluckhohn, and Anthony, 1967). This may grow out of sleeping arrangements in which children sleep with their mothers apart from their fathers. In these cases, says Whiting, male initiation rites are necessary to ensure the development of an adequate male role.

**menarche** A woman's first menstruation.

Many of the analytical frameworks of male initiation—transmission of cultural skills and traditions, the social importance of publicly moving individuals from one social status to another, and the channeling of sexuality into adult reproduction—are also relevant to female initiation. Female rites, however, are most productively analyzed on their own terms. **Feminist anthropology,** along with the current anthropological interest in women's bodies and reproductive experiences as sources of power as well as subordination, has given girls' initiation rites a new ethnographic and theoretical prominence.

Ethnography in Papua New Guinea suggests that although girls' initiation rites are individual, they are connected to the larger social whole. These connections are seen in the ritual's sponsors, public observation of the rituals, and the meanings the rituals have as metaphors for other cultural patterns. In addition to making cultural statements about what it means to move from girlhood to womanhood, female initiation rites may also make more general cultural statements about gender and gender relations. Many female initiation rites in Papua New Guinea suggest the complementarity of male and female, rather than male dominance and antagonism between the sexes. Among the Yangoru Boiken of Papua New Guinea, for example, (Roscoe 1995:58–59), where achievement of success in the political and ritual fields depends on the complementarity of husbands and wives, female initiation rites emphasize those qualities that will help women to be strong wives who can help their husbands. The various elements of the rites motivate girls to bear and rear children, strengthen their fortitude, and provide them with the capacity for the hard work necessary to assist their husbands in gathering wealth.

In acknowledging gender difference, initiation rites for males and females may convey the message that both male and female powers and potentials are necessary for social reproduction—that each sex is dependent on the other to complete its personhood and make its contribution, as a father or a mother, to society. Thus, the sexual symbolism of girls' initiation rites may refer not only to male–female sexual relations and biological reproduction, but also to the reproduction of society.

The Papua New Guinea studies also emphasize that initiation rites—for females as well as males—are processual; that is, they move individuals through successive stages of life. Among the Murik, a girl's transition to adulthood does not end with a puberty rite. Rather, the puberty rite is just one ritual step in a series of rites celebrating reproduction, culminating in marriage and the birth of the first child.

Analysis of female initiation provides new insights into the ritual manipulation of the body that is often central to these ceremonies. The ceremonies may include ordeals, scarification, circumcision, and infibulation (the stitching together of the vulva, leaving a small opening for the passage of urine and menstrual blood). The usual

During female initiation, elders impart important information to girls that allows them to participate as responsible adults in their society. Where female initiation involves circumcision, as among the Kikuyu of Kenya, elder women give girls the necessary emotional support to help them get through this very painful ritual.

explanation of the emotional and symbolic significance of these often painful and traumatic transformations is that they are a test of the initiate's preparation for adulthood, and the permanent signs of the initiate's change of status. This emphasis, derived mainly from male initiation, overlooks the importance in body manipulation of the association among sexuality, beauty, and power. In some cultures, like those in Papua New Guinea, this is a prominent theme in both female and male initiation.

This bodily attractiveness is one form of female power, manifest in procreation. Female initiation rites display other forms of power as well. Among the Manam of Papua New Guinea, the exchange of valuables plays an important role in female initiation. In the Manam girl's initiation rite, the initiate displays the wealth her parents and clan have contributed for the event, which significantly influences later bridewealth negotiations. The wealth displayed in the initiation rite also affects the social reputation of the kin group who sponsors it. The attention to girls' initiation not only deepens our understanding of cultural worldviews and symbolic meanings within cultures, but also suggests new directions for theorizing about an old topic of cross-cultural interest.

**feminist anthropology** A theoretical perspective that focuses on describing and explaining the social roles of women.

## The Construction of Masculinity in Spain

With the contemporary interest in feminist anthropology and the construction of femininity in different cultures, there has been a parallel increase in exploring more explicitly the construction of masculinity, and how these constructions are supported by society beyond what is taught in the passage from childhood. Like many cultures in the Mediterranean area, Andalusia, in southern Spain, includes a construction of masculinity in which control of female sexuality is central (Gilmore 1996). "Women are the Devil," a butcher in San Blas, Andalusia, explained to anthropologist Stanley Brandes, "because when Eve fell to the temptation of the serpent in the Garden of Eden, she then went on to tempt Adam to eat the apple of the tree of knowledge. . . . [Woman] was that way from the beginning, and she has been trying to tempt and dominate man ever since."

For San Blas men, this biblical story justifies their view that men are more virtuous than women, more pure (because man sinned only after he was tempted by woman), and closer to God. Consistent with this religiously based view, men in San Blas assert that all women are "seductresses and whores," possessed of insatiable, lustful appetites, who can break down a man's control over his passions and lead him into temptation. Women possess goodness only in their role as mothers, an idealized, pure version of womanhood. Otherwise they are devils who threaten family unity and honor. The ability of women to bring down the reputation of their whole family and kin group through their lustful sexuality underlies the male ambivalence toward women that permeates San Blas social life.

One significant source of this view is early and medieval Christianity, in which Eve's temptation was explicitly interpreted as sexual, and sexual passion was viewed as the mainspring of female nature. The particular suspicion with which medieval Christianity viewed single or widowed women is echoed in the mistrust with which widows are viewed in San Blas. Although wives devote themselves to their husbands, husbands fear that women drive them to a premature death by sapping their strength through demands for frequent sexual activity and heavy physical labor. The women do this, men explain, in order to live off their husbands' social security payments without having to share them and to satisfy their voracious sexual appetites without the constraints of marriage (Brandes 1981:225).

The cultural construction of manhood in San Blas explicitly opposes the cultural construction of women. Space is constructed in gender terms: women belong to the home, men to the streets, bars, and other public spaces. Most men fear that their wives, driven by insatiable sexuality, will be unfaithful, emasculate them, and ruin the honor of their families. They counter this fear by adhering to an image of manliness that centers on aggressive sexuality, a willingness to confront and compete with other men in public, and the demonstrated drive and ability to be successful, whatever the risks, in their marital and economic lives. Even language reflects the sexual inequality of Andalusian culture: terms from the sexual arena, in which men are supposed to be "on top," are reflected in the language of social stratification in which the rich and powerful not only occupy the higher spaces in Andalusian towns but are considered to be "on top" of the poorer classes, dominating them the way men dominate women (Gilmore 1996).

## Proving Manhood: A Cultural Universal?

The concept of a "real man" as one who proves himself to be virile, controls women, is successful in competition with other men, and is daring, heroic, and aggressive (whether on the streets, in bars, or in warfare) is an almost universal cultural pattern (Gilmore 1990). On the island of Truk, a U.S. trust territory in Micronesia, young Trukese men, who in the past were fierce warriors, are now known as hard drinkers and violent brawlers (M. Marshall 1979). Most young men in Truk go through a turbulent adolescent period of heavy drinking, which generally results in violent fights and serious injuries, particularly on weekends. Through the ethnography of anthropologist Mac Marshall, they have become known as the Weekend Warriors. Masculinity in Truk is defined in terms of competitiveness, assertiveness, risk-taking in the face of danger, physical strength, and, during adolescence, hard drinking, smoking, and physical violence. There is no initiation ritual that turns a boy into a man, and Trukese males must continually demonstrate their manhood in the public arena by cultural competence and

Throughout the Mediterranean and in Muslim dominated societies, as in the tribal areas of Pakistan, there is a strong bond among men and almost all social activities are sex segregated, except between close family members.

© Joan Gregg

effectiveness in everyday affairs (Gilmore 1990:66). This includes being successful at an occupation, acquiring consumer goods, and defending one's relatives, particularly women, against danger and dishonor.

As we saw earlier in this chapter, in many societies, becoming a man is tested by initiation ceremonies in which boys are expected to bear much physical pain without showing any emotion. Among the Sambia of Papua New Guinea, boys were required to undergo a very long and painful process of initiation, which included whipping and beatings, before they were regarded as men (Herdt 1981). In the United States, similar patterns exist in the oppositional cultures of urban streets and schools (see page 274) and in the great attraction of occupations such as firefighting, where the heroic ideal of sacrifice in the face of physical danger is played out on a regular basis (Kaprow 1991).

The near universality of the need to test and prove one's manhood has been called the **manhood puzzle.** Why, in so many different cultures, is the state of manhood regarded as uncertain or precarious, a prize to be won or wrested through struggle? Why does the transformation of a male into a "real man" require trials of skill or endurance, or special rituals? Various attempts to solve this puzzle, particularly in terms of the need for the young boy to separate himself from his mother, are suggested in our earlier discussion of male initiation.

Some psychological anthropologists offer orthodox Freudian explanations. Thomas Gregor, for example, has described patterns of manhood among the Mehinaku Indians of Brazil (1985). Gregor ascribes the Mehinaku male's preoccupation with the public display of manhood to a culturally conditioned defense against castration anxiety. In order to compensate for their fears about castration, he suggests, Mehinaku men feel compelled to demonstrate their masculinity at every opportunity.

Anthropologist David Gilmore acknowledges the importance of **machismo** in resolving male ambivalence, but suggests that these "real man" concepts have important social as well as psychological functions. According to Gilmore (1990), such cultural patterns help ensure that men will fulfill their roles as procreators, providers, and protectors of their families. This essential contribution to society, he argues, is at the heart of the "macho" role and accounts for its intensity, near universality, and persistence.

The anthropological emphasis on the cultural construction of masculinity, as represented by David Gilmore, is a welcome and important addition to the literature of sex and gender, but also raises important questions. One problem with this universalist view of masculinity is that it does not recognize the plurality of masculinities within a culture, as well as possible differences among cultures (Conway-Long 1991). Although individual differences among men may be noted, this is usually ascribed to "deviance," and little work has yet been done on alternative masculine ideologies as cultural patterns. A second issue that needs to be addressed is that of the power differences between men and women in society: why is it that the important contributions of women in reproduction and food production, and their potential for group protection, are not culturally recognized and elaborated in ideologies and rituals similar to those of men, and why (as Margaret Mead noted more than 70 years ago) is whatever men do in a society more culturally valued and publicly elaborated than what women do? As Don Conway-Long points out, as masculinity becomes more central to gender research, these theoretical questions will undoubtedly become a more important part of the ethnographic research agenda.

# Gender Relations: Complex and Variable

Fueled by European and American concerns about male dominance and women's subordination, much of the gendered anthropology in the last three decades has focused on the status of women and gender hierarchy. Studies have examined the significance of women's roles as mothers, sisters, wives, and daughters; women's economic contributions; women's perceptions of their cultures; women's roles in creating symbolic and collective worlds within the context of ideologies of male superiority; the sources of women's power and influence; the development of women's identities; and the ways in which violence against women is related in various ways to gender hierarchy. As noted in the previous chapter, one dimension of the imbalance between the power of men and the power of women is gender violence, which takes a variety of forms, including but not limited to violence within families.

**Gender roles** are the cultural expectations of men and women in a particular society. Gender roles include expectations about the "natural" abilities of men and women, the occupations considered suitable for each sex, differences in temperament and personality, the kinds of behavior that are most appropriate for men and women, and their attitudes toward themselves and others—in short, almost the entire range of the inner and outer life

---

**manhood puzzle** The question of why in almost all cultures masculinity is viewed not as a natural state but as a problematic status to be won through overcoming obstacles.

**machismo** A cultural construction of hypermasculinity as essential to the male gender role.

**gender role** The cultural expectations of men and women in a particular society, including the division of labor.

that characterizes human nature and society. **Gender hierarchy** is the ways in which these attributes are differentially valued and related to the distribution of resources, prestige, and power. Gender roles and gender hierarchy are clearly related to each other because access to material resources, prestige, power, and autonomy depend significantly on what one does, or is allowed to do, in society.

The question of whether (and if so, why) male dominance is universal emerged as an early debate in the anthropology of gender. One theoretical position held that women's subordination to men is universal, based on women's universal role as mothers and homemakers (Rosaldo and Lamphere 1974). In this view, all societies are divided into a less prestigious domestic (private) world, inhabited by women, and a more prestigious public world, dominated by men. This **private/public dichotomy** emerged most sharply in highly stratified 19th-century capitalist societies, such as those of Victorian Europe and the United States, as productive relationships moved out of the household and middle-class women (but not working-class women) retreated into the home. There they were supposed to concern themselves solely with domestic affairs, repress their sexuality, bear children, and accept a subordinate and dependent role (E. Martin 1987). It became apparent, however, that the private/public dichotomy was not applicable in many non-Western societies, where home and family and economics and politics were not easily separated. Indeed, the dichotomy also obscured the relationships among power, workplace, and family structures critical to understanding much of gender stratification in contemporary Western societies, particularly the United States.

Anthropologist Ernestine Friedl was an early critic of the notion that the private/public dichotomy was the key to women's status. She attributed widespread male dominance to economic factors. In her comparative examination of foraging and horticultural societies, Friedl (1975) noted that one key factor in women's status was the degree to which they controlled the distribution and exchange of goods and services outside the domestic unit. She argued that in foraging societies the fact that men exercised control over the distribution of meat within the larger community gave them more power and status in society than women. In horticultural societies men cleared the forest for new gardens, and thus were in a position to exercise control over the allocation of land,

An emphasis on male dominance and aggression in horticultural societies overlooks the elements of affection and nurturance that males play as fathers, as in the Iban society of Indonesia.

© Judith Pearson

which put them in a position of power. On the other hand, in societies where women had control over resources beyond distribution within the domestic unit (such as some West African societies, where women sold produce in the market), their status increased. Friedl also suggested that because the care of small children can be shared by older children, neighbors, relatives, and others, women's low status cannot be explained by their obligations in child rearing. Thus cultural norms regarding family size and systems of child care are arranged to conform with women's productive work, rather than the norms of work being an adaptation to pregnancy and child care.

Marxist-oriented feminist anthropologists added another dimension to the importance of economic factors, emphasizing the cultural and historical variation in women's status, particularly the effects of the expansion of capitalism and European colonialism. Eleanor Leacock's (1981) work on the Montaignais of eastern North America, for example, was persuasive in documenting that they were egalitarian before European contact, demonstrating in detail how European expansion led to gender inequalities in some non-Western societies. Leacock's work led to a greater focus on changes in gender relations wrought by the European encounter.

In yet another approach to understanding the cultural variability in male dominance, Peggy Sanday (1981)

**gender hierarchy** The ways in which gendered activities and attributes are differentially valued and related to the distribution of resources, prestige, and power in a society.

**private/public dichotomy** A gender system in which women's status is lowered by their almost exclusive cultural identification with the home and children, whereas men are identified with public, prestigious, economic, and political roles.

used a controlled cross-cultural comparison to ascertain whether male dominance was universal and, if not, under what conditions it emerged. Sanday concluded that male dominance was not universal, but it was correlated with ecological stress and warfare. She showed that where the survival of the group rests more on male actions, such as warfare, women accept male dominance for the sake of social and cultural survival.

Regardless of their position on the universality or variability of gender hierarchy, all sides in this debate agree that gender hierarchies are culturally, not biologically, determined. Both the division of labor by sex and the meanings attached to gendered patterns of activity show great cultural variability and historical specificity. In fact, the debate over the universality of male dominance has been not so much resolved as transcended. As one anthropologist put it, a gendered anthropology has moved from an interest in "woman" to an interest in "women" (Mukhopadhyay and Higgins 1988:486). This move poses new challenges to old assumptions.

Because each cultural situation is complex and unique, it is difficult to generalize about the ways in which gender affects the distribution of prestige and power in different kinds of societies. Generally speaking, egalitarian foraging societies, such as those in native North America (Klein and Ackerman 1995), some tribal populations in Southeast Asia (Ong 1989), some hunters and gatherers in Africa (Shostak 1983), and the Mbuti of the Ituri forest in Africa (Turnbull 1961), do offer women more autonomy and power than do horticultural or agricultural societies, although there is great variety among these also. Even generalizing about women's status by region becomes risky; it has been demonstrated that within such regions as aboriginal Australia (Burbank 1989) and sub-Saharan Africa (Potash 1989) there are great variations in women's roles and status.

## Gender Relations in Foraging Societies

The interest in the cross-cultural variability of women's roles has led to a reexamination of the sexual division of labor in foraging societies, in which men were previously seen as the sole hunters and male hunting was seen as the basis of male dominance. This issue was a subject of much anthropological debate in the 1960s, largely based on a new look at earlier ethnographies of foraging societies, which gave evidence that women significantly contributed to the food supply by gathering vegetable foods and also by hunting.

Among the Tiwi of Australia, for example, women made important contributions to the food supply by gathering vegetable foods and hunting small animals (Goodale 1971; see page 200), whereas among the largely foraging Agta of the Sierra Madre in the Philippines, women make an important economic contribution to their households through hunting. Agta men tend to hunt alone, stalking pigs, deer, and monkeys with their bows and arrows. Women hunt in groups, with men or with other women, using dogs to drive the animals and killing them with long knives or bows and arrows (Estioko-Griffin 1986).

The Agta illustrate Ernestine Friedl's contention that in foraging societies, which rely heavily on women's economic contributions, child rearing is adapted to economic needs. Agta women carry nursing infants on their backs on their forest trips for hunting and gathering. Older children are left with older sisters or grandmothers. Fathers also spend significant amounts of time caring for their children. Although women's economic contributions appear to be an important factor in their social power, other factors are also important. For example, even in foraging societies where women make important economic contributions, men may have greater prestige and power through their (exclusive) participation in hunting large animals (as among the Inuit) or through male-dominated ritual activities, as in native Australian groups (Bell 1981; Kaberry 1939; Merlan 1988).

In the many non-Western societies where the private/public dichotomy cannot be applied, women's power cannot be judged solely on the basis of formal political status. In addition to their important roles within households, women in many of these societies make alliances and participate in networks outside the household, which are important arenas for prestige, influence, and self-esteem.

Native foraging groups in North America were among the most gender egalitarian societies (Albers 1989). Even in those few groups, such as the Tlingit of the Northwest coast, whose society did involve social hierarchy, men and women both had a high degree of individual autonomy (Klein 1995). Both women and men could achieve prestige through their own efforts and their kin relationships. Kinship relations and wealth obtained through extensive trade with other coastal societies were the keys to social status for both men and women. The Tlingit sexual division of labor was clear but not rigid, and economic roles had little bearing on the power and influence of women. The abundant food supply of the Tlingit depended primarily on salmon, which were generally caught by men and smoked and dried by women. The plentiful products of sea and land provided the basis for long-distance trade in luxury items such as furs and copper, wood carvings, and woven blankets, which were distributed at festive giveaways (potlatches) as indicators of wealth.

Although long-distance trade was centered on men, women often accompanied men, acting as negotiators and handling the money—a fact commented on by early European traders, missionaries, and anthropologists. Tlingit women regarded men as "being foolish with money," and both girls and boys were expected to "work, save, get wealth and goods" (Klein 1995:35). Becoming a shaman was one route to wealth outside the kinship system, and this role was equally open to men and women.

The private/public dichotomy was not relevant to gender status among the Tlingit. Power and influence were embedded in kinship and rank, which applied equally to men and women. Although Europeans generally recognized only men as chiefs, some women were heads of clans or tribes, and Tlingit aristocrats were both male and female. In any case, wealth, kinship connections, and personality were more important sources of status than formal political roles. Titles of high rank were used for both men and women, and the ideal marriage was between a man and woman of equal rank.

The assertive competitiveness that appears to have characterized both women and men in traditional Tlingit society—noticed, not always favorably, by European observers—remains part of Tlingit life (Klein 1995). Tlingit women are found in the highest offices of the native corporations administering Tlingit land and in government, social action groups, and business and cultural organizations. Traditional female roles in accumulating wealth and handling money have served Tlingit women well in their contemporary communities, where they hold political positions and sit on the boards of the influential voluntary associations. With no traditional inhibitions about women appearing in public roles, Tlingit women have taken advantage of opportunities for education and easily enter modern professions. Unlike many societies in which the impact of Europeans resulted in a diminishing of women's economic roles and influence, modernization has led to a broadening of women's roles among the Tlingit.

Anthropologist Laura Klein, who has studied the Tlingit, warns against a Eurocentric reading of women's status as one that diminishes men. Tlingit men and women both take pride in the accomplishments of prominent Tlingit women. Husbands proudly describe the achievements of their wives and daughters, encouraging them to go into public life. Klein concludes that the Tlingit are best described not as a matriarchy, or even as a society where exceptional women can occupy important masculine roles, but rather as a society in which roles are structured more on the basis of individual ability, training, and personality than on the basis of gender (1976:179).

## Gender Relations in Horticultural Societies

Horticultural societies encompass a very wide range of gender relationships, from the highly egalitarian Iroquois of eastern North America (J. Brown 1975) to the highly sex-segregated and male-dominated Yanomamo of South

© Judith Pearson

Most horticultural societies have culturally patterned ideas about men's work and women's work. Men most often do the clearing and planting, and women, the food processing. Among the Dani of New Guinea, tending pigs and barbecuing them is women's work, though men accrue the prestige for their use in ritual and in exchange networks.

America (Chagnon 1997) and most societies in highland Papua New Guinea (Strathern 1995). There is a correspondingly wide variety in the sexual division of labor in horticultural societies, although some general similarities can be noted.

A high degree of segregation between the sexes, paralleled by the importance of males in ritual, is associated with male dominance in some horticultural societies. For example, among the Mundurucu of South America, adolescent boys are initiated into the men's cult and thereafter spend most of their lives in the men's house, only visiting their wives, who live with the children in their own huts in the village. These men's cults are closed to women and surrounded by great secrecy. The men's house itself is usually the most imposing structure in the village and the sacred musical instruments and paraphernalia of the cult are kept in or near it. The musical instruments, which are often flutelike (shaped like the male genitals), are the symbolic expressions of male dominance and solidarity (Murphy and Murphy 1974). Often, especially in Australia, such men's cults are associated with circumcision rites for newly initiated boys, after which the initiates are considered men and introduced to the secrets of the cult. Sometimes these cults include a religious explanation of why women are not allowed in them. These myths may also explain from a religious perspective why women are considered socially inferior to men and why men and women have different roles in these societies.

The solidarity of women in horticultural societies is usually not formalized in cults or associations, but is based on the cooperation found in domestic life and strong interpersonal bonds among female kin. In sub-Saharan Africa, for example, the most important economic and emotional ties for both men and women are not between a married couple (conjugal ties) but between generations (consanguineal ties). Women's most important ties are with their children, particularly their sons, on whom women depend for emotional support and security in old age (Potash 1989:199). The importance of kinship ties for African men has long been noted. Ethnographies focusing on the lives of women show how they, too, use kinship ties with their natal groups to gain access to land, gain support in marital disputes, or participate in ritual activities (Sacks 1982).

The impact of European expansion on women in horticultural societies varied. Generally, women's role declined as indigenous economies shifted from subsistence horticulture to cash crops to be sold in a world market. This process of change is illustrated by the Polynesian atoll of Nukumanu, a fishing and horticultural society studied by anthropologist Richard Feinberg (1986). Before European contact, Nukumanu depended for its food on the abundant marine life and a few indigenous plants, such as the coconut, pandanus (a type of fruit), and taro (a starchy root). Women's primary responsibilities were domestic, whereas men contributed food acquired some distance from the home through fishing, collecting shellfish, and collecting and husking coconuts. Men also made canoes and constructed new buildings, and women cooked food and collected and prepared leaves for thatch.

Both women's and men's roles were highly valued in Nukumanu society. Women exclusively controlled and cultivated swamp taro lands, which were inherited matrilineally. Matrilocality added to women's status, whereas men's power came from their economic contribution and the fact that only they could occupy formal positions of power in the chiefly hierarchy. In the 1880s, under German colonialism, most of Nukumanu was turned over to production of copra (dried coconut meat). Wage laborers were brought in from nearby islands. This resulted in irreversible cultural and economic changes, most of which lowered women's status. Commercial foods such as wheat flour and rice supplanted taro, and men's wages were needed to buy coffee, tea, and sugar (once luxury items). As a result, women's traditional sphere of influence declined, and men's sphere expanded.

In addition, the traditional segregation of men's and women's activities has intensified. With the introduction of kareve (sap of the coconut tree fermented to make a potent alcoholic beverage) in the 1950s, men's economic activities, such as canoe building, took on a social aspect involving drinking. Because the production and consumption of kareve takes up a great deal of men's leisure time and excludes women, sexual segregation has increased.

With the declining importance of taro, women's collective activities have become more individualized, leaving women more isolated and dependent on their husbands and brothers than they were in the past. Male–female tensions have also increased, partly as a result of kareve drinking, which many women vehemently oppose. The traditional tendency for men to travel off the island more than women also lowered women's status, and this pattern has continued because it is mainly men who go overseas for wage labor and higher education. But by the 1980s, as a result of Western influence, more opportunities were made available for women to attend school and pursue careers off the atoll. These changes may enable Nukumanu women to return their culture to its tradition of sexual egalitarianism.

## Gender Relations in Pastoral Societies

Pastoral and agricultural societies tend to be male dominated, though some variation exists. In pastoral societies women's status depends on the degree to which the society combines herding with cultivation, its specific historical situation, and the diffusion of cultural ideas, such as Islam. Generally speaking, women's contribution to the food supply in pastoral societies is small (Martin and Voorhies 1975). Men do almost all the herding and most of the dairy work as well. Male dominance in pastoral society is partly based on the required strength to handle large animals, but females sometimes do handle smaller animals, engage in dairy work, carry water, and process animal by-products such as milk, wool, and hides (O'Kelly and Carney 1986). Pastoral societies generally to not have the rigid distinction between public and domestic roles of agricultural societies: herders' camps are typically divided into male and female spaces, but both men and women work in public, somewhat blurring the private/public dichotomy.

In pastoral societies men predominantly own and have control over the disposition of livestock, which is an important source of power and prestige. However, the disposition of herds is always subject to kinship rules and responsibilities and animals also may be jointly held by men and women. Still, the male economic dominance in pastoral societies seems to give rise to general social and cultural male dominance, reinforced by patricentric kinship systems and the need for defense through warfare (Sanday 1981).

This generalization again, however, is subject to variation. Among the Tuareg of the Central Sahara, for example, women generally had high prestige and sub-

# Anthropology Makes a Difference

## Advocating for Female Factory Workers in China

The importance of women's work to meet the demand for cheaper goods in the national and the global economy is clear in the People's Republic of China. Global capitalism is expanding, and sweatshop working conditions in factories that produce goods for a global market particularly affect women.

Pun Ngai, a Hong Kong anthropologist, spent 6 months tightening screws in computer hardware at an electronics factory in Shenzhen, People's Republic of China, as part of her ethnographic study of how *dagongmei*, or "working girls," are responding to the pressure of China's increasing participation in the global economy (Tsui 2000). The factory directors were interested in Dr. Pun's work because they hoped to learn more about what the workers want so they would know better how to deal with the workers. At first, the factory directors assumed that Pun would focus on the factory's operations and inundated her with personnel and administrative documents. They were astounded when she told them she wanted to work on the line and live with the workers, in the participant-observation mode of anthropology.

Although the dagongmei were initially suspicious of Pun, when they saw she was really interested in their lives, they were so eager to talk with her she didn't have enough time to listen to them all. As an outsider, Pun quickly became a confidante, dealing with workers' complaints, offering academic guidance, and giving advice on love and other personal relationships.

Pun found the factory work interesting for the first week, but it soon became a monotonous routine. Dagongmei, most of whom are in their late teens or early 20s, spend 15 hours a day in the factory. They sleep in dormitory-type accommodations called cagehouses. In addition to boredom on the job, dagongmei also suffer from many physical ailments. Long working hours cause menstrual pain and anemia. Those who weld microchips suffer eyesight problems, and those who wash plates with acids are constantly at risk for chemical poisoning. Accommodation and other expenses are deducted from their already low wages. The dagongmei also work and live under very strict rules. They have to wait their turn to go to the restroom. They are thoroughly searched before they are allowed to leave the factory premises. Security guards wielding electric batons guard the locked quarters at night.

Dr. Pun has followed up her field study with a continuing commitment to improving conditions for dagongmei in China. She represents the interests of dagongmei at labor conferences, fighting for their rights. In China, a residence permit is required to live in a particular city; dagongmei are denied residential rights even if they have been working in the same city for more than 10 years. They are also overcharged for medical and other services and consumer goods. Urban factories recruit dagongmei as cheap labor but then do not want to take proper care of them. When unemployment hits, the first thing people want to do is send the dagongmei back to their rural villages. After years of urban living and participation in a consumer-oriented global lifestyle, dagongmei find it difficult to readapt to village life.

Dagongmei receive little sympathy in China, especially from men who say they are taking away their jobs. In fact, times are getting harder for dagongmei. With China's admission to the World Trade Organization and the opening up of its agricultural market, more people are rushing to the cities. Urban unemployment is high, and getting higher, thousands of workers have been downsized as a result of the privatization of factories, and factories themselves are now

---

stantial influence (Rasmussan 2005). The Tuareg, who are Muslims of Berber origin, herd camels, sheep, goats, and donkeys. Because the Tuareg are matrilineal, Tuareg women enjoy considerable rights and privileges: they do not veil their faces, and they have minimal social and economic separation from men. Women are singers and musicians and organize many social events. They traditionally enjoyed freedom of choice in sexual involvements, though this has been somewhat modified among those Tuareg who are more devout Muslims. The traditionally high status of Tuareg women, and matrilineality itself, are also undermined today by the migration of men to cities, where they work for wages, and the incorporation of the Tuareg into larger nation-states, with their patrilineal cultures. Cities, however, may also provide increasing opportunities and freedom for Tuareg women. The Tuareg appear to be an unusual exception to the generally patriarchal nature of pastoral—and

While Tuareg engage in the traditionally domestic occupation of processing food, in contrast to the male role of herding animals, Tuareg women have considerable prestige, influence, and privileges in their societies.

Courtesy of waterishope.org

closing by the thousands as part of the worldwide recession and steep decline in the global demand for Chinese-made goods

In spite of all these hardships, dagongmei see advantages in their factory work. It exposes them to a wider view of the world and permits some escape from the rigid patriarchal structure of the village. Dagongmei enjoy having boyfriends, keep up with the latest fashions, and search for the secrets of success, especially in the form of making money (toward which goal many are determinedly studying English) and maybe finding a husband (Chang 2008). Some dagongmei, by pooling their earnings, have managed to open small factories. Others have ambitions for a business career, or to improve their education. Urban migration offers the opportunity to take a computer class or learn a little English, which can lead to switching jobs and earning more money. Indeed, it may be that dagongmei are at the cutting edge of a changing Chinese culture: moving from traditional commitments and filial loyalty to the cultural values of upward social mobility, individualism, and the pursuit of a more prosperous future, though Pun cautions that out of 70 million dagongmei, few succeed.

Multinational corporations' desire for cheap labor will lead to more women working in the global factory. Anthropologists such as Pun Ngai are trying to make sure their rights are protected when they do.

An important part of the multinational factory worker workforce, and particularly of the Asian economic "miracle," consists of young woman workers.

© Mike Yamashita/Woodfin Camp & Associates

Muslim—societies, but they are also an essential reminder that gender roles vary greatly, even within similar economic types of societies and within religious traditions.

## Gender Relations in Agricultural Societies

With the transition to agriculture, the direct female contribution in food production generally drops drastically, though this also varies. Agricultural work by women declines with the introduction of plow agriculture but women have an important productive contribution in wet rice agriculture. Generally, agricultural societies are a good example of the principle that women lose status in society as the importance of their economic contribution declines. The decline of women's participation in agriculture is also generally accompanied by their increasing isolation in domestic work in the home and increasing numbers of children (Ember 1983). The transformation of agricultural production through machine technology reduces the overall labor force, and because most machinery is operated by men, this change particularly affects women, who are disproportionately excluded from the productive process. The inequality between the sexes is also apparent in the lower wages paid to women as agricultural laborers and in the concentration of women in the labor-intensive aspects of agriculture such as weeding, transplanting, and harvesting. This situation is exacerbated as societies increasingly rely on cash economies and the marketplace. It is relatively easy for men to enter the cash economy by selling their crops or animals to buy goods and services. Entering the cash economy is far more difficult for women, who thus become more depen-

In Guatemala, as in many agricultural societies, the income from women's craftwork, which they sell in local markets and to tourists, is an important source of family income

## Gender Relations in a Global Economy

Women's status in modern, stratified societies varies greatly and is affected in multiple ways by economic development, political ideology, and globalization. In the past 25 years, industrial production by multinational corporations in Latin America, Asia, and Africa has exploded. For example, in China (as described in this chapter's "Anthropology Makes a Difference" section), in the search for cheap labor, clothing manufacturing, food processing, pharmaceuticals, and electronics assembly factories have recruited women—particularly young women. These jobs give women a chance to earn money on their own, and they offer women an important opportunity to act in their own interests. But there are also social costs to the involvement of women in the workforce, especially in more traditional cultures, such as those of Taiwan for example. In these cultures, women's efforts to act in new ways disrupt the conventional organization of power within families, in which men, by virtue of their economic dominance, have power over women, and parents have power over children. This widening of alternative roles, for young women particularly, is becoming intensified in the global economy (Lee 1996).

As rural lifestyles and agriculture are replaced by urban lifestyles and industrial production, women may benefit relative to men. For example, in Mata Chico, Peru, in the 1930s, access to land was critical, and the only way for women to get land was to marry. By the 1980s, Peru was increasingly urbanized, and many occupations were available to both men and women. Because women could support themselves and their children through employment in urban areas, they began to remain single longer and in some cases chose not to marry at all (Vincent 1998). But although women may benefit financially from these new opportunities, particularly as factory labor, these benefits often come at a high price. As illustrated by the work of Pun Ngai (see "Anthropology Makes a Difference"), women are often exploited as cheap labor and work under sweatshop conditions in factories producing for the global market. And even in societies in Europe, Japan, and the United States—nations that are much further along on the scale of economic development—women's status is not equal to that of men; women still earn less pay for similar work, for example.

Gender stratification is a complex issue in a global economy. It consists of social, economic, and political dimensions; it is embedded in culture; and it affects both men and women and the relationships between them.

dent on men. For example, in Zinacantecan, Mexico, men control cash crops and participate in the market. As a result, they are now able to purchase many of the goods and services that women used to contribute to the household. Zinacantecan women are increasingly dependent on men, but men are less and less dependent on women (Flood 1994).

The lower status for women in agricultural societies is often exacerbated by foreign aid and development programs, which, while increasing production in the man's sphere of work, tend to be more restrictive for women. Economic development is intended to improve people's lives but such projects often fail to take women's economic contributions into account. Frequently they increase gender inequality, worsening women's position in their societies (Moser 1993; Warren and Bourque 1989). Some development projects have resulted in more prestige, income, and autonomy for women. These include projects promoting the global marketing of women's textiles and pottery in Mexico and Guatemala. However, in some cases this has led to greater tension and even violence between men and women (J. Nash 1993, 1994:15). As anthropologists increasingly point out, the impact of development projects on women is a result of the interplay of specific material and cultural conditions in a particular society (Lockwood 2005).

# The Global and the Local: Islam and Female Modesty

Islam is a global religion, having expanded from its origin in Saudi Arabia to all parts of the world, including Europe and the United States. Muslim gender ideologies and practices regarding women are much debated, among both Muslims and non-Muslims. As with other global religions, there are many local differences in ideology and practice, shaped by varying interpretations of the Qur'an and by local histories, politics, and cultures. Much of the debate on the correct roles and attire for Muslim women centers on the **hijab,** or head covering. For some Muslims as well as non-Muslims, the hijab is a sign of oppression of women; these people think the hijab makes women invisible and restricts their freedom of choice. Others, however, especially young Muslim women, may view the hijab as a liberating garment that forces the world to see them as more than sexual objects and establishes their identity as a Muslim.

Muslims base their commitment to modest dress for women on the Qur'an (24:30–31), which says, "And say to the believing women that they should lower their gaze and guard their modesty; . . . [and] that they should draw their veils over their bosoms and not display their beauty except to their husbands."

The Qur'an also speaks of the need to erect a "curtain" (hijab, which means to hide from view or conceal) between women and men. Some Muslims interpret this as requiring separation of men and women within a house, others that it requires that women wear clothes that conceal their bodies (Bowen 2007). Although the Qur'an specifically requires face covering only for Muhammad's wife, some Muslims interpret this command as requiring all women to cover their head, hair, neck, and bosom (see Center for Muslim-Jewish Engagement 2008). Thus, although Islam requires female modesty, it does not command any specific styles, nor specifically mention hijab, making room for much local variation.

Local interpretation of female modesty is shaped by different historical and cultural contexts, particularly the

The hijab, or headscarf, worn by these Malaysian girls is one means by which some Muslims accommodate the Islamic requirement for women to dress modestly. Wearing the headscarf has become a political issue in Turkey and in many European countries, which have large numbers of Muslim immigrants.

degree of male dominance in a society and the commitment to secularism of governments in largely Muslim societies. In some societies, most Muslim women wear a hijab that loosely covers only their hair and neck; in others, such as in Yemen, women wear full head and body coverings as well as a face veil. In the airlines of the United Arab Emirates, a compromise is reached between fashion and religion—air hostesses wear "jaunty little caps with attached gauzy scarves that hint at hijab" (Zoepf 2008).

The specific practices of modest female dress vary among different societies, sects, social classes, rural and urban populations, generations, and to some extent depend on whether Muslims are a dominant or minority group. In Saudi Arabia, women must wear a face veil, whereas in Afghanistan, under Taliban rule, women were required to wear a burka, or full body and face covering. In all of these countries, these laws and customs are resisted by some women (Ali 2006; Manji 2003; Revolutionary Association of the Women of Afghanistan (Revolutionary Association of the Women of Afghanistan 2009). Wearing the veil is discouraged in Tunisia, and neither veil nor hijab are generally worn by Muslim Bedouin women (see page 230). In Egypt, conflict over what constitutes women's modest dress is an important political issue between religious parties and the government. Today, almost 90 percent of Egyptian women wear a headscarf and many Egyptians believe it is explicitly required by the Qur'an. At the same time some government officials publicly oppose the Egyptian Islamist call for women to cover themselves entirely, including their faces. One official called the hijab "a step backward for Egyptian women" (Slackman 2007), and some Egyptian authorities are also concerned about the small but growing number of women wearing the niqab, the black flowing garment that covers the entire body and the face. In

---

**hijab** A widespread term used for the head covering worn by some Muslim women as part of modest dress.

Turkey, women commonly wear the headscarf in public, though previously they were not permitted to wear it in government offices or universities. Today the hijab is part of a contentious public debate about the secular versus the religious character of this largely Muslim state (Tavernise 2008a).

In Europe and the United States, the headscarf has also become a source of conflict. In France, the growing number of Muslim immigrants led to a law banning headscarves (and other religious symbols) in public institutions, specifically public schools. Those supporting the law claimed headscarves are a symbol of female oppression, though many Muslim young women want to wear the headscarf as a proud display of their Muslim identity. In the United States, some discrimination cases have been filed by Muslim women denied the right to wear the headscarf, for example, while teaching in public schools. However, the American commitment to individual freedom of religious practice has made Islamic dress less of an issue here (Moore 1998).

In the Islamic Republic of Iran, women are required to wear hijab and wearing a burka is increasingly common, because of government and some public pressure. At the same time, however, anthropologist Pardis Mahdavi, in her new ethnography of sexuality in Iran (2009), describes the widespread breach among upper class, educated Iranian families of many Muslim sexual restrictions, such as premarital chastity, marital fidelity, and the wearing of modest dress. Dating, nail polish, and immodest dress are outlawed in Iran, and although these restrictions are policed in public spaces, in private girls wear layers of makeup and women's headscarves are often so transparent and fashionable that they actually look sexy. In sum, a cross-cultural study of Islamic practices illustrates that despite the global reach of Islam, as in other religions, local patterns emerge that resist attempts at global uniformity.

## Key Questions

1. Why do Muslim women wear the hijab? What are some of the factors that explain its local variations within the global context of Islam?

2. Using ethnographic evidence, outline an argument either that Islamic "modest dress" oppresses women or that it liberates them.

# Summary

1. **What is some of the anthropological evidence that gender is culturally rather than biologically determined?** Margaret Mead's early studies, as well as subsequent studies of variation in gender roles across cultures, support the prevailing view in anthropology today that gender is culturally constructed, rather than biologically determined.

2. **What is the difference between sex and gender?** Sex refers to biological differences between male and female; gender refers to the social classification of masculine and feminine.

3. **How does cross-cultural evidence raise questions about the Western view that sex and gender are universally divided into male and female, man and woman?** Although all cultures distinguish between masculine and feminine, some cultures also include alternative, in-between, or third-gender roles. These include woman–woman marriage in parts of Africa, the two-spirit role among Native Americans, and the hijras of India.

4. **How do you define the hijras and how is their position in Indian society different from sex/gender roles in American culture?** Hijras are men who dress and act like women, are regarded as ritually powerful devotees of the Mother Goddess, and perform ritually at weddings and childbirths. As an "in-between" gender the hijra role contrasts with the sex/gender dichotomy symbolized in American society by transsexuality, in which a male or female becomes a member of the opposite sex.

5. **Are sexual behavior and sexuality "doing what comes naturally"?** Views about the nature of male and female sexuality are part of gender ideologies. Sexuality and sexual behavior, though rooted in biology, are patterned by culture.

6. **What are initiation rituals and how do they function socially and psychologically in different societies?** Initiation rituals, or rites of passage, transform boys and girls into adult men and women. Both male and female initiations transmit cultural values and emphasize the importance of citizenship in a society. Male initiations also reinforce the solidarity of men, culturally validate male dominance, and from a psychological perspective symbolically enable men to master the conflicts generated by boys' early identification with their mothers. In matrilineal societies, female initiations publicly emphasize the status change from child to adult, make statements about gender relations, and enhance a girl's beauty and her attractiveness to men, in preparation for marriage.

7. **Is male dominance culturally universal? How do you explain male dominance in any particular society?** A male-dominated gender hierarchy is a sociocultural system in which men are dominant, reap most of the social and material rewards of society, and control the autonomy of women. One explanation for gender hierarchy in some societies (mainly more complex ones) is the private/public dichotomy, in which men are associated

with public political and economic activities and women are identified with the home and children. Gender hierarchy is also related to men's control of economic processes and warfare.

8. **Are foraging societies gender equalitarian? What is the evidence for or against this theory?** The classical anthropological view that hunting is exclusively a male occupation in foraging societies is contradicted by a closer look at forager ethnographies which indicates that in some foraging societies, women also hunt (although not as much as men, who often exclusively hunt large animals) and make important contributions to the food supply, giving them autonomy and influence. Also, as among the Tlingit, a matrilineal society of the Northwest coast of North America, women were actively involved in economic exchanges and had important positions in kinship and political networks.

9. **How has the impact of Western economy and culture influenced gender relations in different horticultural societies?** Gender relations in horticultural societies vary considerably. Often, the impact of Western economies has led to a decline in the economic status and prestige of women, as illustrated in the Nukumanu atoll in the Pacific.

10. **What appears to be the effect of the rise of agriculture on gender relations? How do globalization and industrialization affect gender roles in different societies?** In agricultural societies, women's role tends to decrease and the private/public dichotomy becomes more relevant. De-velopment projects, particularly those involving the use of heavy technology, such as tractors, also tend to marginalize women and reduce their autonomy and status. And, as illustrated in our ethnography on China, even when women benefit by working in factories, they are also subject to severe restraints and difficult working conditions.

11. **What is the relationship between pastoralism and gender hierarchy? In what ways are the Tuareg an exception to most pastoralist societies in this regard?** In pastoral societies men gain dominance through their control over large herd animals and male dominance is also supported by patrilineality, although the public/private dichotomy is weaker than in agricultural societies. The Tuareg, a matrilineal society of North Africa, are an exception, and women have substantial freedom, which, however, varies with the commitment to Islam and is both strengthened and weakened by male migration to cities for employment.

12. **What is the hijab and its relation to female modesty as required in Islam? What are some of the local variations of this practice?** The hijab is a head covering adopted by many women in Islamic cultures as an expression of the universal Muslim injunction for female modesty. In fact, Islamic dress for women varies locally, ranging from a full head, face, and body covering, to the rejection of full covering of women and even headscarves by some politicians in places like Turkey and Egypt.

# Key Terms

cultural construction of gender
feminist anthropology
gender
gender hierarchy
gender role
hijab

hijra
machismo
mahu
manhood puzzle
menarche

private/public dichotomy
rite of passage
sex
two-spirit role
xanith

# Suggested Readings

Gutmann, Matthew C. 1996. *The Meanings of Macho: Being a Man in Mexico City*. Berkeley: University of California Press. An original look at the construction of masculinity in Mexico City, with implications for the rest of Mexico, this ethnography undermines stereotyped views of machismo as the sole basis of Mexican manhood as it reveals the complexities and contradictions of Mexican gender.

Mascia-Lees, Frances E. 2009. *Gender and Difference in a Globalizing World: Twenty-First-Century Anthropology*. Prospect Heights, IL: Waveland. The right book for the student who wants to explore how globalization shapes gender identities, gender behavior, and gender inequalities, including an incisive examination of different anthropological theories and perspectives on the relationship between gender and power.

Merry, Sally Engle. 2008. *Gender Violence: A Cultural Perspective.* New York: Wiley-Blackwell. Through personal accounts and ethnographic case studies, an outstanding legal and cultural anthropologist examines the social and cultural contexts of gender violence and its history as a public issue.

Nanda, Serena. 2000. *Gender Diversity: Cross-Cultural Variations.* Prospect Heights, IL: Waveland. Aimed at introductory students, this short book presents a cross-cultural look at alternative gender roles for both males and females among Native American societies and in India, Brazil, Thailand, the Philippines, Polynesia, Europe, and North America.

As societies become more complex, specialized positions develop as centers of power and control. Among the Yoruba of Nigeria, the king is surrounded by symbols of his office as he presides over public events.

© Mark & Evelyn Bernheim/Woodfin Camp & Associates

**THINKING POINT:** In the Asante Kingdom of West Africa the accumulation of wealth in the hands of an elite was considered a benefit to the whole society. Wealthy individuals who squandered their wealth were held in contempt and individual bankruptcy was considered antisocial, a theft from the future well-being of the whole society. How do Asante values compare to those in the contemporary United States?

—[See pages 250–251 for details.]

# Political Organization

All societies must address the problem of how to maintain themselves over time with a minimum of social disorder and social discontent. This means that every society must provide a means of managing conflicts, dissent, and deviance and generally regulate behavior so that it is consistent with social order. **Political organization** refers to the patterned ways in which power and authority are legitimately used in a society to regulate behavior. Societies vary in their systems of political organization, and this diversity is a primary interest of anthropology.

A society's specific type of political organization is related to many factors, particularly the ways in which the society produces and distributes valued goods, that is, the degree of access individuals and groups have to basic material resources, power, and prestige. This structure is called a system of **social differentiation.** Social differentiation is also related to **social complexity,** the number of different kinds of groups there are in a society and the ways in which they are connected to one another. Although political organization, social differentiation, and social complexity are sometimes studied separately for analytical purposes, in reality they are intimately connected.

This chapter describes the ideal types of societies that anthropologists have developed in examining systems of social differentiation, social complexity, and related forms of political organization. Please remember that although these typologies are useful analytically, they hide a much more complex reality and every ideal type includes many variations. <<

# Social Differentiation

Inequalities exist in all societies: individuals differ in talents, physical attractiveness, mental abilities, and skills. But not all societies formally recognize these inequalities, nor do individual inequalities always affect access to important resources. Anthropologists commonly distinguish three types of systems of social differentiation: egalitarian societies, rank societies, and stratified societies.

## Egalitarian Societies

In an **egalitarian society,** individual differences in skills and personality qualities are recognized but no individual or group is denied the right to a livelihood or is subject to the control of others. Age and sex/gender differences are a basis for social respect, but these statuses are not the basis for differences in the accumulation of wealth. In egalitarian societies there is no inheritance of prestige or material goods over generations. Egalitarian societies have no fixed number of social positions for which individuals must compete. The status of "good hunter" or "wise elder" can be filled by as many people as meet the cultural criteria. Egalitarian societies usually operate on the principle of generalized or balanced reciprocity in the exchange of goods and services and are associated with the forms of political organization called bands or tribes (Fried 1967).

## Rank Societies

In **rank societies** there are formal differences among individuals and groups in prestige and symbolic resources, and these social attributes may be inherited, but all members of society have access to basic resources through their membership in kinship groups. Although some rank societies had slaves, their status was not hereditary. They were individuals attached to wealthier families and did not form an exploited class, as was true in state societies.

Rank societies are normally based on highly productive horticulture or pastoralism, which permit sufficient accumulation of food so that a surplus can be appropriated by leaders and redistributed throughout the society. Both redistribution and balanced reciprocity are characteristic modes of exchange in rank societies (see pages 156–157). Social ranking is associated with the form of political organization called a chiefdom.

## Stratified Societies

**Stratified societies** have formal and permanent social and economic inequalities. Wealth, prestige, and office are frequently inherited, and some individuals and groups are denied access to the basic material resources needed to survive. Stratified societies are characterized by permanent and wide differences among groups and individuals in their standard of living, security, prestige, political power, and the opportunity to fulfill one's potential. These differences may be based on birth or result from individual accomplishments (see pages 158–159). Most stratified societies are economically organized by market exchange and are generally based on agriculture and industrialism. Stratified societies are the most socially complex kinds of societies and are associated with a form of political organization called the state.

# Power and Social Control

The ability to cause individuals or groups to take actions that, of their own accord, they might prefer not to take is called **power.** Power ultimately derives from the control of resources that people need or desire. For example, professors hold a degree of power in classrooms. They control grades, and because students need and desire good grades, they do things they would probably prefer not to do, such as take quizzes and exams or write papers.

**Authority** is the ability to cause others to act based on a person's characteristics such as honor, status, knowledge, ability, lineage, and/or the holding of formal public office. Authority is only one important source of power. For example, you may listen to your professors because of their knowledge, their ability to engage students, and the position they hold, as well as because they control your grade. Similarly, the power of a political office holder may derive from the respect accorded him or her, but also from the coercive ability that comes from control of resources. And, indeed, power can be held by people without authority. An armed robber certainly has

---

**political organization** The patterned ways in which power is used in a society.

**social differentiation** The relative access individuals and groups have to basic material resources, wealth, power, and prestige.

**social complexity** The number of groups and their interrelationships in a society.

**egalitarian society** A society in which no individual or group has more privileged access to resources than any other.

**rank society** A society characterized by institutionalized differences in prestige but no important restrictions on access to basic resources.

**stratified society** A society characterized by formal, permanent social and economic inequality in which some people are denied access to basic resources.

**power** The ability to compel other individuals to do things that they would not choose to do of their own accord.

**authority** The ability to cause others to act based on characteristics such as honor, status, knowledge, ability, respect, or the holding of formal public office.

power, but most people do not obey his commands because of their respect for him or because of the high social position he holds.

The shared values and beliefs that legitimize the distribution and uses of power and authority in a particular society make up its **political ideology.** Not everyone in a society may agree with a dominant political ideology, and it is often accepted to a greater extent by those who benefit the most from it and to a lesser extent by those who benefit less. When fewer people in a society accept its reigning political ideology, the society may rely on a greater use of coercion, and even perhaps violence, to maintain itself. Although political systems differ in how much they rely on coercion, both coercion and consensus contribute to maintaining order in almost all societies.

People conform to the political ideology of their society for complex and wide-ranging reasons. They may have a deep and abiding belief in the values the ideology represents. They may expect a short- or long-term benefit from the exercise of power and authority. They may fear the consequences of resistance to power. They may see no practical alternative. They may believe in the worth of their political system despite its failure to return benefits to them.

Contemporary anthropologists are very interested in **political processes,** the ways in which groups and individuals use power and authority to achieve various public goals. These goals may include changing the relationships between groups in society, for example, between labor unions and corporations; changing the relationship of a group to its environment, for example, building a road or clearing public land; waging **war;** making peace; or changing a group's position in the social hierarchy. Political goals have many motivations. Although, by definition, all political behavior *affects* the public interest, it is not always *in* the public interest. Groups and individuals may be motivated by personal profit or prestige or by altruism and idealism, although these are not necessarily mutually exclusive. In politically complex societies, those in power use various means to establish **hegemony,** that is, a close identification between their own goals and those of the larger society (see the Ethnography section on page 250 for a description of hegemony in the Asante state).

## Formal and Informal Sources of Power and Authority

Formal political institutions are a source of power and authority, but power and authority may also have more informal bases. **Leadership,** or the ability to direct an enterprise or action, may be a function of political office, but it can also be wielded through more informal means such as the manipulation of kinship networks, control

Political processes are the ways in which different, often conflicting interest groups mobilize to achieve their goals. This protest is directed against the American invasion of Iraq under President George W. Bush.

over the distribution of wealth, or through movements based on personal charisma, as with Mahatma Gandhi or Martin Luther King, Jr.

In many small-scale societies the use of power, authority, decision making, and the coordination and regulation of human behavior are not formally separated from other aspects of culture, but are embedded in other social institutions such as kinship, economics, and religion. Leadership may be based on an individual's position as the head of a family, lineage, or clan. Where supernatural intervention is an important aspect of decision making (where to hunt, when to move camp, how to find a thief), individuals with perceived access to supernatural power have important political roles in society. Where politics involves control over the distribution of goods and services, as it most often does, power and authority are embedded in economic roles and modes of exchange,

**political ideology** The shared beliefs and values that legitimize the distribution and use of power in a particular society.

**political process** The ways in which individuals and groups use power to achieve public goals.

**war** A formally organized and culturally recognized pattern of collective violence directed toward other societies, or between segments within a larger society.

**hegemony** The dominance of a political elite based on a close identification between their own goals and those of the larger society.

**leadership** The ability to direct an enterprise or action.

Mahatma Gandhi, who led India's fight for freedom from British colonial rule, and Martin Luther King, Jr., who led the African-American civil rights movement in the United States, were leaders with great authority who did not hold political office. Both men depended on persuasion and nonviolent methods of civil disobedience to achieve their political goals.

© Hulton Archive/Getty Images

© Bettmann/Corbis

as with the chiefs on the Northwest Coast of North America or the "bigmen" of Papua New Guinea. These interconnections also exist in complex societies, like our own, even though the connections may be intentionally obscured, as when people with great wealth exert their dominance through lobbying and campaign contributions rather than holding political office.

In the small-scale societies studied by anthropologists, women did not hold formal political office. However, there are some important exceptions, particularly in Africa (Matory 1994; Potash 1989:205). Among the Yoruba of Nigeria, certain offices were reserved to represent women's interests. Also in Nigeria, some Igbo groups had a female ruler and council that paralleled that of the king and his council but were concerned with women's affairs. The Mende in Sierra Leone had women paramount chiefs, who were seen as "mothers writ large"; that is, they derived their authority and power from the reproductive and supportive roles of women as mothers. The Mende women's secret society, called Sande, was very powerful, reflecting the important economic roles of wives, who were authority figures and who might even succeed a chief in office. One of the most famous Mende women of power was Madam Yoko. Taking advantage of the opportunities offered by the changing political status of Sierra Leone in the 19th century, she succeeded her husband in office and was recognized as a paramount chief in 1884 (Hoffer 1974).

Women also have informal sources of power. In West Africa, for example, women derive power from their control over marketing agricultural and other products (Potash 1989). In matrilineal societies, as we have seen among the Minangkabau of Indonesia, or the Hopi, women's power is interwoven with their roles in the kinship, ceremonial, and economic systems (see Chapter 8, page 178, and Chapter 9, page 209).

The study of political processes emphasizes how power changes hands and how new kinds of political organization and ideologies develop. Political processes are never static. The use of power and authority may stabilize a social order, avoid or resolve conflicts, and promote the general welfare. However, power and authority may also be used to contest prevailing political ideologies and to change or even destroy existing political systems. Groups or **factions** within a society, as well as governments themselves, use legitimate and sometimes illegitimate means (terrorism or torture, for example) to gain their ends, but illegitimate means are no less political than legitimate ones.

Conflict and violence do not necessarily destroy social order. In some societies, violence is a legitimate means of dealing with conflict and solving disputes, for example, blood feuds or legally sanctioned death penalties. Conflict may even support the social order, as competition for legitimate goals makes those goals seem worth fighting over. Even violent conflict for political office does not necessarily destroy the power or authority of the office being sought, as the struggle itself emphasizes that the conflicting groups view the office as politically important. **Rebellion** is the attempt of one group to

**factions** Informal alliances within well-defined political units such as lineages, villages, or organizations.

**rebellion** The attempt of a group within society to force a redistribution of resources and power.

reallocate resources within an existing political structure, while **revolution** is an attempt to overthrow the existing political structure and put another type of political structure in its place.

## Law: Social Control and Conflict Management

No human society has eternal peace and harmony. Individuals do not always conform to the rules and they often act in ways that cause conflict and disrupt the social order. For a society to function satisfactorily, however, there must be some conformity among its members.

In societies organized through kinship and face-to-face social relations, conformity is largely achieved through the internalization of norms and values. This process begins in childhood (see Chapter 4, pages 77–78), but most often lasts a lifetime. In complex societies behavior is also regulated by the internalization of norms, but in addition, behavior is also regulated by the government's control of social institutions and regulatory processes and its capability and willingness to use force.

Every society has some social mechanisms to deal with non-normative behavior and conflict. In face-to-face communities and informal groups within complex societies, informal mechanisms such as gossip and ridicule can be effective ways to ensure conformity (Merry 1981). Fear of witchcraft accusations is another informal control mechanism (Evans-Pritchard 1958; Lemert 1997; Seitlyn 1993). In societies with witchcraft beliefs, when something goes wrong, witchcraft accusations are directed at people who stand above the group, are malicious, have a nasty temper, or refuse to share according to group norms. The fear of being accused of witchcraft exerts pressure on people to conform.

Small-scale communities also use avoidance to sanction social deviants, and a person shunned by others is at a great psychological and economic disadvantage. In complex societies, avoidance is effective in smaller groups within larger institutions, such as the workplace in an industrial society.

Supernatural sanctions regulate human behavior in almost all societies. A sin is a violation of an important social norm that calls forth punishment by supernatural forces. In the Trobriand Islands, incest is a sin, which brings a divinely imposed skin affliction caused by an insect spontaneously generated by the sexual act that breaches the incest taboo (Malinowski 1929b:504).

In every society, some offenses are considered so disruptive that force or the threat of force is applied to those who commit them. **Law** refers to a situation where the whole community, or some part of it, is *authorized* to punish an offender against a society's most important norms. Law may also be used to resolve a conflict or redress a wrong. In more complex societies, these functions of law belong to separate legal institutions, such as courts. In other societies, law, like power, is often embedded in other social institutions, for example, religion. Law is distinguished from the more general reciprocal rights and obligations that underlie conformity in all societies.

Law addresses conflicts that would otherwise disrupt community life. In politically complex societies such as contemporary nation-states, law addresses both crimes against the state and conflicts between individuals. In structurally simpler societies, disputes between individuals are treated as potential threats to society because they have ripple effects throughout the community. Unlike Western law, however, conflict management in egalitarian societies is more often directed at maintaining existing social relationships than defining winners and losers.

## Types of Political Organization

As noted above, all cultures have political organization. Anthropologists have identified four ideal types of political organization: bands, tribes, chiefdoms, and states. Typically, bands and tribes are egalitarian societies, chiefdoms are rank societies, and states are stratified societies (Service 1962).

### Band Societies

Band organization is characteristic of foragers. A **band** is a small group of people (20 to 50) belonging to nuclear families who live together and are loosely associated with their foraging territory. Generalized or balanced reciprocity dominates economic exchanges in band societies, which tend to be egalitarian. Band societies have minimal role specialization and few differences of wealth, prestige, or power. Bands are fairly independent of one another, with few higher levels of social integration or centralized mechanisms of leadership. Bands tend to be exogamous, with ties between them established mainly by marriage. Bilateral kinship systems link individuals to many different bands through ties of blood and marriage. Trading relations also link individuals to other band members. Membership in bands is flexible, and people may change their residence from one band to another fairly easily. The flexibility of band organization is particularly adaptive for a foraging way of life and low population density.

---

**revolution** An attempt to overthrow an existing form of political organization and put another type of political structure in its place.

**law** A means of social control and dispute management through the systematic application of force by a politically constituted authority.

**band** A small group of people related by blood or marriage, who live together and are loosely associated with a territory in which they forage.

**Leadership** Band societies have no formal leadership; decision making is by consensus. Leaders in foraging bands are usually older men and women whose experience, traditional knowledge, and special skills or success in foraging are a source of prestige. Leaders cannot enforce their decisions; they can only persuade, and attract others to their leadership, on the basis of past performance. Thus, among some Inuit, the local leader is called "The One to Whom All Listen," "He Who Thinks," or "He Who Knows Everything Best."

In foraging bands, sharing and generosity are important values and an important source of respect. Among some whaling Inuit, for example, successful whaling captains who do not generously distribute their accumulated wealth are merely called "rich men." They are distinguished from those whose superior ability *and* generosity make them respected leaders in the village.

**Social Control and Conflict Resolution** Social order in band societies is maintained informally by gossip, ridicule, and avoidance. In extreme cases, a person may be killed or driven out of the community. Among the Inuit, supernatural sanctions are an important means of social control (Balikci 1970). Violations of norms are considered sins, and offenders may be controlled through ritual means such as public confessions, which are directed by a shaman. The offender is defined as a patient rather than a criminal and is led to confess all the taboos he or she has violated. The local villagers form the audience and participate as a background chorus. These confessions are mainly voluntary, although a forceful shaman may denounce a member of the community he feels has engaged in acts repulsive to the spirits and therefore dangerous to the whole group.

The romanticized view of band societies as nonviolent is based on a confusion between collective violence and personal violence (Knauft 1987). The Ju/'hoansi, for example, do not engage in collective violence, but men frequently fight, mostly over women, and these fights often result in death (R. Lee 2003). Thus, although the need for cooperation and norms of reciprocity in band societies minimize conflict, it does occur. Because quarrels and conflicts between individuals may disrupt the group, band societies have developed social mechanisms to inhibit conflict from spreading. Flexible band membership is one such mechanism. Among the Mbuti of the Ituri Forest, for example, a process called flux operates: bands regularly break up into smaller units and reform into larger ones throughout the year. Breaking the band down into smaller units separates people who have been in conflict with one another, thus preventing prolonged hostilities (Turnbull 1968).

**tribe** A culturally distinct population whose members consider themselves descended from the same ancestor.

In Inuit bands, disputes are sometimes resolved through public contests that involve physical action, such as head butting or boxing, or verbal contests, like the famous song duels. Here the weapons are words—"little, sharp words like the wooden splinters which I hack off with my ax" (Hoebel 1974:93). Although murder is normally resolved by killing the murderer, a man may choose to avenge his kin in a song duel if he feels too weak to kill his opponent or if he is confident he will win the song contest. Each contestant in a song duel tries to deliver the traditional compositions with the greatest skill. The one for whom the audience claps the loudest is the winner. Although winning a song duel is not based on the facts of the conflict, it does resolve the quarrel and restore normal relations between the hostile parties. The judgment of the community is accepted by the contestants, and the original complaint is laid to rest.

Because of the low level of technology, lack of formal leadership, and other ecological factors, warfare is largely absent in band societies. They have no formal organization for war, no position of warrior, little or no production for war, and no cultural or social support for sustained armed conflict. When there is violence, its primary objectives are personal, and fighting takes place in short skirmishes.

When band societies encounter technologically and culturally dominant groups, bands tend to retreat and isolate themselves in marginal areas rather than fight. Alternatively, they may form peaceful relations with their neighbors. Part of the debate over whether band societies have warfare is due to the way in which war is defined. If warfare is defined as formally organized and culturally recognized patterns of collective violence against another society, or between segments within a larger society, band societies do not have warfare. An important contribution of anthropology is to document societies where warfare is absent, as a counterexample to a prevalent belief in the contemporary United States and elsewhere, that "warfare is in our genes" (Wallman 2000).

## Tribal Societies

A **tribe** is a culturally distinct population whose members think of themselves as descended from the same ancestor or as part of the same "people." Tribes are found primarily among pastoralists and horticulturists. Their characteristic economic institutions are reciprocity and redistribution, although as part of larger states, they may also participate in market systems. Like bands, tribes are basically egalitarian, with no important differences among members in wealth, status, and power. Also like bands, most tribes do not have distinct or centralized political institutions or roles. Power and social control are embedded in kinship, religion, or other cultural institutions.

Tribes are usually organized into unilineal kin groups, which are the units of political activity and the "owners" of basic economic resources. The emergence of local kin groups larger than the nuclear family is consistent with the larger populations of horticultural and pastoral societies. The effective political unit in tribal societies is a shifting one. Most of the time, the local units of a tribe operate independently; in some societies, such as the Yanomamo (see later discussion in this chapter), the local units may be in a state of ongoing violent conflict among themselves. A higher-level unity among tribal segments most often occurs in response to the threat of attack from another society or the opportunity to attack another society.

**Political Integration in Tribes** The local segments of a tribal society are integrated in various ways. Age and sex may be the basis of organized groups who move through life's stages together. Cross-cultural comparison of societies in which age is an important basis of organization—in Africa, Melanesia, South America, and the Great Plains of North America—suggests that they are associated with frequent warfare and unstable local groups. Where men cannot rely on their kin as allies in warfare because their kin may not be nearby, **age sets** provide a more dependable source of allies (Ritter 1980).

**Age grades** among the Maasai are one example of this type of tribal integration. In this herding society of Kenya and Tanzania, males follow a well-ordered progression through a series of age grades. Entry into each grade requires a formalized rite of passage. A new age grade is opened for recruitment for groups of boys every 14 years. After childhood, boys are initiated into the warrior stage, which lasts about 15 years. Warriorhood is a period of training in social, political, and military skills, and is traditionally geared to warfare and cattle raiding. The warriors then ceremonially graduate to a less active status, during which they can marry. Finally, about 20 years after the formation of the age grade, when another age grade has become established, the original age grade retires to elderhood in another great ceremony.

Maasai age-mates are a cohesive group. They provide reciprocal hospitality when they visit each other's villages, expressing a warm and intimate relationship. Age grade ceremonies periodically bring together Maasai from different sections of the tribe. These gatherings renew their shared identity and sense of unity and cooperation, and confirm a system of leadership under age grade spokesmen. This lends political coherence to a people who live dispersed from one another and have no centralized government (Saitoti 1986).

Other associations that cut across and thus integrate the local segments of a tribe are the military societies among some Plains Indian tribes in North America, the **secret societies** (such as Poro society for males and Sande society for females) that are found in West Africa, and the segmentary lineage system described for the Nuer (see page 175 in Chapter 8, "Kinship").

**Leadership** Tribal societies have leaders but no centralized government and few positions of authority. Many Native American societies had different kinds of leaders for different kinds of activities. The Cheyenne had war leaders and peace leaders. The Ojibwa of Canada had different leaders for war, hunting, ceremonies, and clans. Europeans who first came in contact with the Ojibwa often misinterpreted their political system and imposed the Western concept of a supreme leader or chief on the Ojibwa. When the Canadian government insisted that the Ojibwa must have a chief, the Ojibwa coined a native word, *okimakkan,* which is best translated as "fake chief."

Another kind of tribal leader, found throughout Melanesia and Papua New Guinea, is the **bigman**—a self-made leader who gains power and authority through

In most Native American societies, there was no role of chief. Instead, there were different leaders for different activities, such as war leaders, peace leaders, and dance leaders.

---

**age set** A group of people of similar age and sex who move through some or all of life's stages together.

**age grades** Specialized associations based on age that stratify a society by seniority.

**secret societies** West African societies whose membership and rituals are known only to society members. Their most significant function is the initiation of boys and girls into adulthood.

**bigman** A self-made leader who gains power through personal achievements rather than through political office.

him. Bigmen command obedience from their followers through this personal relationship of gratitude and obligation.

A bigman's activities provide leadership above the local level, but it is a fragile mechanism of tribal integration. It does not involve the creation of permanent office, but depends on the personality and constant striving of an individual. Bigmen rise and fall, and with their deaths, their followings may dissolve. Most important, however, the bigman must spur his local group on to ever greater production if he is to hold his own against other tribal bigmen. To maintain prestige, he must give his competitors more than they can give him. Excessive giving to competitors means the bigman must begin to withhold gifts to his followers. The resulting discontent may lead to defection among his followers, or even murder of the bigman. A bigman cannot pass on his status to others; each person must begin anew to amass the wealth and forge the internal and external social relationships on which bigman status depends (Sahlins 1971). Under certain ecological and social conditions, permanent political leadership may emerge in some tribal societies, which then develop into chiefdoms (see page 246).

### Social Control and Conflict Resolution

Tribes, like bands, depend mainly on informal mechanisms for controlling deviant behavior and settling conflicts, but they also have more formal mechanisms of control. Among the Cheyenne, for example, formal social control mechanisms came into play during the summer season when the Cheyenne bands came together for communal buffalo hunts and tribal ceremonies. On the buffalo hunt strict discipline was required because an individual hunter could ruin the hunt for others by alarming and scattering the buffalo. The tribal gatherings and communal hunts were policed by members of military associations. These associations not only punished offenders but also tried to rehabilitate them, bringing them back within the tribal structure. The function of these tribal "police" was to get the deviant to conform to tribal law in the interest of the welfare of the tribe. People were punished in various ways: their tepees might be ripped to shreds, or the ears of their horses cut off, a mark of shame; offenders might also be whipped and if they resisted punishment, they might be killed on the spot. However, if they accepted the punishment and appeared to have learned a lesson, they were accepted back into the group, and their belongings were often replaced. The Cheyenne military societies operated only during the hunt period. At other times, more informal sanctions and leadership operated at the band level (Hoebel 1960).

In many tribal societies, conflicts between parties with ongoing relationships are resolved by **mediation.**

The bigman is an informal leader in many Melanesian cultures. Much of his influence is based on his ability to distribute resources, among which pigs are the most important.

personal achievements rather than through holding office. A bigman begins his career as the leader of a small, localized kin group. Through a series of public actions, such as generous loans, the bigman attracts followers within the community. He skillfully builds up his capital and increases his number of wives. Because women take care of pigs, a polygynous bigman can increase the size of his pig herds. He distributes his wealth in ways that build his reputation as a rich and generous man: sponsoring feasts, paying subsidies to military allies, purchasing high ranks in secret societies, and paying the bridewealth of young men seeking wives. By giving generously, the bigman places many other people under obligation to

**mediation** A form of managing disputes that uses the offices of a third party to achieve voluntary agreement between the disputing parties.

Mediation resolves disputes so that the social relationship between the disputants is maintained and harmony is restored to the social order. Among the Kpelle of Liberia, conflict between individuals is addressed by a moot, a form of mediation which takes place before an assembled group of kinsmen and neighbors (Gibbs 1988). After an opening ritual, the mediator reminds the audience of its common interests and unity. The two disputing parties may question each other directly, but the mediator or others may interrupt with questions. After everyone has been heard, the mediator proposes a solution to the conflict that expresses the consensus of the disputing parties and the audience. The party found to be at fault apologizes to the other party and a ritual distribution of food and drink again unites the group. In conclusion, the mediator again stresses the importance of the restoration of community harmony. Through the moot, reconciliation is achieved with a minimum of resentment, so that conflicts do not continue and disrupt the social order (Gibbs 1988).

The kava-drinking circle in the Pacific Island Kingdom of Tonga is another example of a community-oriented mechanism for dispute resolution. Kava is an indigenous alcoholic drink often consumed in ritual contexts throughout Oceania. In Tonga, drinking kava is a semi-ritualized male activity that serves as a nonviolent alternative to alcohol-drinking events. The kava circle is an informal social context in which the status distinctions, otherwise so important in Tonga, are dissolved and men air their grievances and reconcile their differences in an atmosphere of social camaraderie.

The principles of the West African moot, the kava circle in Tonga, and other nonadversarial conflict man-

agement systems have been widely incorporated into the U.S. legal system, which normally depends on adversarial confrontations between disputants. The adversarial system, which operates through formal courts, is costly and time consuming, and frequently leaves the disputants feeling dissatisfied with the outcome. As courts become overburdened and litigation becomes more expensive, mediation is increasingly used to resolve many kinds of disputes, especially when the disputants are in long-term relationships. These include divorce proceedings, minor civil disputes, and conflicts in schools, housing projects, neighborhoods, and the workplace, and even in international disputes between nations.

**Warfare in Tribal Societies** Compared to band societies, tribal societies have a high degree of warfare, a fact for which anthropologists have suggested various explanations. In the absence of strong mechanisms for tribal integration through peaceful means and the absence of strong motivations to produce food beyond immediate needs, an ecological explanation suggests that warfare helps regulate the balance between population and resources in tribal societies. With slash and burn horticulture, for example, it is much harder to clear forest for cultivation than to work land that has already been used. Thus, a local group may prefer to take land from other groups, by force if necessary, rather than expand into virgin forest. Warfare is then one way for societies to expand when they are experiencing a population increase or have reached the limits of expansion into unoccupied land (Vayda 1976). Where there are effective ways other than war for distributing population within the tribe's total territory, tribes may not engage in war.

Tribal warfare may also be linked to patrilineality and patrilocality, which promote male solidarity. This makes the use of force in resolving local conflicts more feasible than in matrilineal, matrilocal societies, which emphasize solidarity among women, although matrilineal societies such as the Iroquois did carry out warfare over long distances (Ember and Ember 1971). Although anthropologists may not agree about the specific causes of warfare, one area of wide agreement is that war is grounded in historical, material, cultural, and ecological conditions, and not in any biologically based human instinct for aggression.

The Yanomamo of the Amazon areas of Venezuela and Brazil, sometimes called "the fierce people," are well known for their high level of personal violence and frequent warfare. Anthropologist Napoleon Chagnon views Yanomamo violence—by men against women, violence among men in the same village, and warfare between villages—as central to Yanomamo culture (Chagnon 1997), a view challenged by other anthropologists (Ferguson 1992; Good and Chanoff 1996).

Chagnon explains ongoing Yanomamo warfare and violence as a way of preserving village autonomy. The

© Andrew Arno

In Fiji and other Pacific Islands, conflicts are often addressed through community participation in informal kava drinking circles where disputants reconcile their differences.

The Yanamamo of the Amazon, sometimes called "the fierce" people, are a tribe that experiences both endemic warfare and a high degree of personal violence both within and between villages.

high degree of violent conflict between men within villages leads to the division of villages into hostile camps. In order to survive as an independent unit in an environment of constant warfare, a village adopts a hostile and aggressive stance toward other villages, perpetuating inter-village warfare in an endless cycle.

Another view of Yanomamo violence and warfare is that it helps control population, not by causing deaths in battles, but indirectly through female infanticide (Divale and Harris 1976). In societies with constant warfare, there is a cultural preference for male children who can become fierce and aggressive warriors. Because male children are preferred over females, female infants are often killed. The shortage of women that results from female infanticide among the Yanomamo provides a strong conscious motivation for warfare—when asked, the Yanomamo say they fight for women, not for land—and a continuing "reason" to keep fighting among themselves. In a Yanomamo raid on another village, as many women as possible are captured.

European contact may also explain Yanomamo warfare. Anthropologist Brian Ferguson (1992) notes that the extreme Yanomamo violence documented by Napoleon Chagnon in the 1960s was precipitated in the 1940s by severe depopulation, which was caused by European disease epidemics, fatal malnutrition, and intensified competition over European goods. The high death rate led to disruption of Yanomamo family life, and negotiating marriages became particularly difficult because of the deaths of adult males. In addition, the Yanomamo desire for European manufactured goods—particularly the metal machetes, axes, and knives so useful in horticul-

ture—increased competition among Yanomamo males, and firearms substantially increased the number of fatalities in warfare. Whereas previously such goods were traded into even remote Yanomamo villages, by the 1960s the desire to acquire these goods led to the increasing settlement of Yanomamo around European outposts such as missionary stations. This led to the depletion of game, a highly desired food for Yanomamo cultivators, who were also hunters. With the depletion of game, cultural norms of reciprocity broke down, meat was less likely to be shared, and conflict within villages increased. This, in turn, led to enmity between villages. The increasing inter-village warfare reinforced the low status of Yanomamo women and helped further male violence against them, perpetuating the cycle of female infanticide, shortage of women, and raids for women. Thus, historical factors must be considered along with other explanations of Yanomamo "fierceness."

## Chiefdoms

Although the chiefdom is a classic anthropological "type," the term has been a subject of anthropological debate. Some anthropologists argued that chiefdoms encompass such a diverse group of societies that lumping them together as a separate category obscures more than it clarifies (Earle 1987). Nevertheless, the term chiefdom is sufficiently useful if we keep in mind that ideal types are theoretical devices and reality is much more diverse.

**Political Integration** Two main characteristics distinguish chiefdoms from tribes. Whereas tribes consist of structurally and functionally similar segments (lineages and villages for example), a **chiefdom** is made up of parts that are structurally and functionally different from one another. Chiefdoms have been called the first step in integrating villages as units within a multicommunity political organization. Robert Carneiro (1981:45) defines the chiefdom as "an autonomous political unit comprising a number of villages or communities under the permanent control of a paramount chief." Carneiro holds that chiefdoms are an important human cultural "invention" because it is in this type of society that villagers first surrendered their political autonomy to leaders from other villages, thereby creating a second level of political authority in society.

Chiefdoms vary greatly in their social complexity (Peoples 1990). Some ancient chiefdoms had monumental architecture, distinct ceremonial centers, elaborate grave goods reflecting high social status, and larger settlements, or administrative centers, surrounded by smaller villages. Each geographical unit within a chiefdom may also have had its own chief or council.

Chiefdoms are found mainly among cultivators and pastoralists (and the few foraging societies where food resources are plentifully available, such as the groups of the Northwest Coast of North America). The abundance

**chiefdom** A society with social ranking in which political integration is achieved through an office of centralized leadership called the chief.

of food means that chiefs do not need to put excessive burdens on commoners to extract surpluses (Peoples 1990).

**Leadership** Although chiefdoms, like tribes, are organized through kinship, an important difference is that whereas tribes are **acephalous,** that is, they have no centralized government, chiefdoms have centralized leadership—the political office of the chief. Chiefly office is inherited and often sustained by religious authority. Chiefdoms keep lengthy genealogical records of the names and acts of specific chiefs, which are used to verify claims to rank and chiefly title.

Anthropologists generally argue that the rise of a centralized governing center (a chief) is related to an exchange pattern of redistribution, in which goods move into the center (the chief) and are redistributed through the chief, who sponsors feasts and rituals. Ideally, the economic surplus appropriated by a chief is dispersed throughout the whole society and his "generosity" is a primary support of the chief's power and prestige. In fact, these redistributions may occur relatively infrequently and chiefs may well control their populations by coercion or despotism (Earle 1987). The chief also deploys labor as well as redistributing food, making for a higher level of economic productivity. Compared to tribes, the centralized authority of the chief helps prevent violent conflict between segments of the society, and gives a chiefdom more military cohesion than acephalous tribes.

Chiefdoms may also be based on a **tributary mode of exchange,** in which the primary producers, whether pastoralists or agriculturalists, are allowed access to the means of production and tribute is exacted from them by political or military means by the ruler or chief (Wolf 1982:80).

Chiefdoms are ranked societies. Some lineages, and some people in them, have higher social status than others, and these statuses are inherited. For example, among the Nootka, who live on the northwest coast of North America, rights to manage all economic resources, such as fishing, hunting, and gathering grounds, were held by individuals, although relatives could not be prevented from using them. Inheritance of these rights passed only through the line of the eldest son.

This was also true for the office of chief. The line that went through lesser sons was ranked lower than that of eldest sons, and these differences in rank were typically expressed in terms of wealth. Although such wealth consisted partly of important economic resources, it was also symbolic, as in the right to use special names, perform certain ceremonial functions, sponsor potlatches, and wear certain items of clothing and decoration. For example, only chiefs were allowed to wear abalone shell jewelry and sea otter fur on their robes. The right to direct the use of economic resources supported the symbolic ranking system. As manager, a chief of a kin group

received resources that formally acknowledged his rank: the first of the salmon catch, the best parts of sea mammals that had been killed, blankets, and furs. It was with these resources that a chief could sponsor a potlatch, at which most of these goods were given away.

Some of the most complex chiefdoms were found in Polynesia. In Tahiti, society was divided into the Ari'i, who were the immediate families of the chiefs of the most important lineages in the larger districts; the Ra'atira, who were the heads of less important lineages and their families; and the Manahune, which included the remainder of the population. Social rank in Tahiti had economic, political, and religious aspects. Mana, a spiritual power, was possessed by all people, but in different degrees depending on rank. The Ari'i had the most mana because they were closest to the ancestral gods from which mana comes. An elaborate body of taboos separated those with more mana from those with less and also regulated social relations among the three ranks. Higher-ranked people could not eat with those of lower rank, and because men had higher rank than women and children, they could not eat with them. The highest-ranking Ari'i was so sacred that anything he touched became poison for those below him. In some Polynesian islands, the highest chief was kept completely away from other

Chiefdoms are characteristic of Pacific Island cultures. Here, Paramount Chief Daniel Polayasi of Kiriwina, the Trobriand Islands, Papua New Guinea, is seated on his throne.

© Caroline Penn/Panos Pictures

**acephalous** Lacking a government head or chief.

**tributary mode of exchange** Primary producers are allowed access to the means of production, and tribute is exacted from them by coercion.

people and even used a special vocabulary that no one else was allowed to use.

Chiefdoms are also frequently found among pastoral nomads, such as the Basseri of Iran. To avoid exhaustive grazing of an area, famine of the flocks, and intertribal fighting, nomads such as the Basseri must stick to their migration schedules and fixed routes. Thus, an important role of the chief is to coordinate movements of the tribe and conduct relations with outsiders through whose territories nomadic pastoralists must move (Barth 1964).

Social Control and Conflict Resolution Internal violence within chiefdoms is lower than in tribes because the chief has authority to make judgments, punish deviant individuals, and resolve disputes, although the stability of chiefly societies, for example, the Basseri, rests on mainly decisions backed up by popular consensus (Salzman 2000). In the Trobriand Islands, the power of a chief to punish people is achieved partly by hiring sorcerers to kill the offender by magic. The greatest power of the Trobriand chief lies in his control of garden magic. As garden magician, he not only organizes the efforts of the villagers under his control but also performs the rituals considered necessary for success at every step of gardening. The ultimate power of the Trobriand chief is his magical control of rain: he is believed to be able to produce a prolonged drought, which will cause many people to starve. This power is used when the chief is angry as a means of collective punishment and enforcement of his will (Malinowski 1935).

Social order in chiefdoms is maintained through both fear and genuine respect for and loyalty to the chief. The chief's authority is backed by his control of symbolic, supernatural, administrative, economic, and military power, which offers a source of stability absent in acephalous tribes, although violent competition for the office of chief does sometimes occur. Chiefdoms may also be rendered unstable if the burdens the chief imposes on the people greatly exceed the services they receive from him. Chiefs generally suppress any attempt at rebellion or threats from competitors and deal harshly with those who try to take their power. To emphasize the importance of this office for the society, offenses against a chief are often punished by death.

## State Societies

The most complex form of political organization is the state. A **state** is a hierarchical form of political organization in which a central government has a legal monopoly over the use of force. Unlike chiefdoms, where ranking is based on kinship, in state societies kinship ties do not extend throughout the whole society and kinship does not regulate relations between the different social classes.

The legitimacy of the state rests on ties of **citizenship,** which supplant those of blood and marriage for many purposes. The concept of citizenship enables the state to expand without splitting, through the incorporation of a variety of political units, classes, and ethnic groups (some of which may also be excluded from full citizenship, as was true of African Americans before emancipation). Thus, states can become much more populous, heterogeneous, and powerful than any other kind of political organization.

The Rise of State Societies State societies are associated with the ability to organize large populations for collective and coordinated action, to suppress internal disorder through monopoly over the legitimate use of force, and to defend against external threats. More than any other form of political organization, the state can carry out military action for both defensive and offensive purposes.

States are formed as a result of various interrelated events feeding back on one another in complex ways, and the origin of the state, one of humankind's most significant cultural achievements, cannot be explained by any one theory of cause and effect. Some states emerged as cultural solutions to various kinds of problems that demanded highly centralized coordination and regulation of human populations (Cohen and Service 1978; Fried 1967). Other states emerged as a result of particular historical or ecological conditions, and still others, like the Asante (see this chapter's "Ethnography" section), emerged out of military triumph. Prestate societies in various situations respond to different selective pressures by changing some of their internal structures, by subduing a competing group, or by establishing themselves as dominant in a region. This initial shift sets off a chain reaction that may lead to state formation.

Anthropologist Robert Carneiro (1970) emphasizes the importance of ecology in his theory that a limit on agricultural land available to expanding populations may result in the emergence of a state. This seems to have occurred in pre-Columbian Peru, where independent, dispersed farming villages were confined to narrow valleys bounded by the sea, the desert, or mountains. As the population grew, villages split and populations dispersed until all the available land was used up. At this point, more intensive methods of agriculture were applied to land already being farmed, and previously unusable land was brought under cultivation by terracing and irrigation. As population continued to increase, pressure for land intensified, resulting in war. Because of the constraints of the environment, villages that lost wars had

---

**state** A hierarchical, centralized form of political organization in which a central government has a legal monopoly over the use of force.

**citizenship** Membership in a state.

This photograph illustrates the view of the Sun Gate in the great city of Machu Picchu, which was the center of the Inca empire. The empire emerged as a result of specific ecological conditions and was destroyed by the Spanish conquistadors.

In state societies, the government emerges as a social institution specifically concerned with making and enforcing public policy and engages in other functions that keep the society going. The state, for example, intervenes in every aspect of the economic process. Through taxation, it stimulates the agricultural production of households. It also controls labor; it can order people to work on roads and buildings and to serve in armies, thus affecting the workforce available for agriculture. The state also intervenes in the exchange and distribution of goods and services through complex market networks. It protects the distribution of goods by making travel safe for traders as they move their goods from one place to another and by keeping peace in the marketplace. The state may also intervene in the consumption process by passing laws regarding which people are allowed to use which goods—for example, by reserving for the elite such items as gold, silk, or other costly symbols of high status.

# The State and the Control of Force

The many economic, coordinating, and controlling functions of states, in peace and war, require extensive record keeping, giving rise to writing and systems of weights and measures. In some states, cities arose as administrative, religious, and economic centers. These centers then stimulated important cultural achievements in science, art, architecture, and philosophy, which are characteristic of states. But the major defining characteristic of state societies is the government's monopoly over the use of force. A state uses a code of law to make clear how and when it will use force and forbids individuals or groups to use force except under the state's authorization. Laws (usually written) are passed by authorized legislative bodies and enforced by formal and specialized institutions of law enforcement. Courts and police forces, for example, have the authority to impose all kinds of punishments: fines, confiscation of property, imprisonment, and even death.

The state also has important military functions. Engaging in warfare strengthens the power of the state. At the same time, it leads to increased political centralization because of a greater need (from the state's perspective) to regulate daily life and to suppress internal conflicts. Because waging war is costly, it often leads to more centralized control over production. Unlike warfare in

nowhere to go. In order to remain on their land, they had to accept a politically subordinate role. As more villages were defeated, the political organization of the area became more complex and chiefdoms developed. The warring units were now larger, and as conquest of larger areas continued, centralization of authority increased. Finally, the entire area was brought under the control of one chief. The next step was the conquest of weaker valley chiefdoms by stronger ones until powerful empires emerged, most notably that of the Inca.

Anthropological theories of state formation tend to emphasize either conflict (Fried 1967) or integration and functionalism (Service 1971). Functionalist theories emphasize the benefits of the state to its members: its ability to provide the stability needed for growth and technological development, protection of the rights of its citizens, effective mechanisms for the peaceful settlement of disputes, protection of trade and financial arrangements, defense against external enemies, and the ability to expand. Conflict theories tend to emphasize the emergence of the state as directly connected with the emergence of an elite class that protects its power and privileges through coercive power and management of political ideology.

States are characterized by centralized **government:** an interrelated set of status roles that become separate from other aspects of social organization, such as kinship. In state societies, groups based on territory become central and an individual belongs to a state through citizenship. The administrative divisions of a state are territorial units, cities, districts, and so on. Each unit has its own government, although these governments are not independent of the central government.

---

**government** An interrelated set of status roles that become separate from other aspects of social organization, such as kinship, in exercising control over a population.

## The Connection between Wealth and Power in the Precolonial Asante State

The Asante, a Twi-speaking Akan people, have long occupied the tropical forest area of what is now south-central Ghana in West Africa. The Asante state emerged in 1701, when the Asante decisively defeated a rival Akan power, and state expansion and elaboration occurred throughout the 18th century.

The resource bases of the Asante state were intensive cultivation; substantial, accessible deposits of alluvial and shallow-reef gold; and participation, in the 17th and 18th centuries, in the European slave trade (Wilks 1993). Asante agricultural productivity rested on a simple, labor-intensive technology, producing staple crops of yam, plantain, cocoyam, cassava, Indian corn, sweet potato, millet, rice, sugar cane, ginger, tomato, onion, groundnut, orange, lime, banana, custard apple, and pineapple. Oil palm fruits, palm wine, fungi, and wild yams provided additional dietary support, as did wild game, freshwater fish, and on a lesser scale, domestic sheep, fowl, goats, and pigs, which were used as food mainly on ritual occasions. This economy was coordinated and controlled by a systematic rationalization and concentration of labor, organized, overseen, and given direction by the state. The economic productivity supported the rural population and a surplus was appropriated by the state to support a nonproducing urban elite, centered in the state capital of Kumasi.

The highly productive Asante economy was the basis of a complex social hierarchy ruled by the Asantehene, or king. The urban elite was mainly involved in transacting government business, performing elaborate state ceremonies, or producing luxury artifacts for the wealthy. The prodigious food requirements of Kumasi reflected the association of high social status with material well-being characteristic of state societ-

ies. The Asantehene's household alone— his royal wives and children—daily consumed large quantities of locally grown food, along with imported delicacies such as mutton, turkey, duck, wild game, rice, European biscuits, tea, sugar, and wine. Some of these were gifts from foreign visitors, which were reciprocated with local food supplies.

Asante society was composed of several social classes: unfree, alien slaves; peasant commoners living in outlying villages; urban specialists offering their services to the elite; government officials of various classes and positions; and the Asantehene himself, with his royal family, at the top of the hierarchy. It was a dynamic social system, based on achievement, competition, and accumulation of wealth, with widely different levels of material well-being and many opportunities for social competition and social mobility.

The precolonial Asante state lacked the social infrastructure and technology to command society by coercive force alone, although it did use espionage, detention, fines, confiscation of property, exile, and execution to keep its people in line. In addition to coercion, a key factor in the state's ability to maintain itself for more than 150 years was the government's regulation of social hierarchy and its success in promoting a core Asante value: that wealth and power went hand in hand, and that the accumulation of wealth by an individual was of benefit to the whole society. Thus, wise investment and accumulating wealth resulted in high office, and holding high office had to be justified by the accumulation and display of wealth. This Asante ideology legitimized the state, which maintained its power by redistributing wealth; regulating the wealth any individual could accumulate through discretionary use of law and cus-

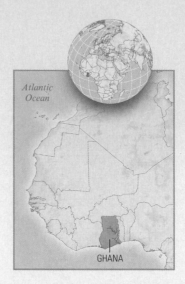

tom; and controlling and managing the rituals in which wealth was displayed.

Social status in Asante society was based on control of human labor, ownership of land, and holding of high office, but most importantly, on the accumulation of wealth, especially gold, which was the currency of the state's taxes and fines and was internationally negotiable. The state controlled both access to and distribution of all wealth, including gold. With the ending of the transatlantic slave trade, desired European goods such as guns, gunpowder, cloth, and luxury articles could only be paid for in gold. Gold ornaments were also necessary for display of social status. Thus, gold became a scarce commodity, increasing the Asante tendency to accumulate, hoard, and hide it. This led to high interest rates for loans of gold.

The state accepted only gold for payment of fines, tributes, taxes, and levies. Those who could not pay had to provide land and laborers instead, enriching the state coffers. The state also accrued wealth by using discretion in applying legal sanctions. For example, an individual could buy

The paramount chiefs surround the sixth Ashanti king (Asantehene) of his dynasty, Osei Tutu II, for his enthronement ceremonies in Kumasi, the capital of Ghana.

himself out of a mandatory death sentence with a payment of gold to the state. The state also imposed a "death tax," on self-acquired movable property, and might also impose inheritance taxes on land, before the residue of the deceased person's wealth was restored to the heirs or successors. These death assessments were made on a case-by-case basis, allowing the state to fine-tune its control over the elite and prevent the emergence of a class of hereditary property owners that might be a threat to its own power. The state also controlled the opportunities to accumulate wealth on the largest scale: commanding the state's armies, conducting the state's trade, holding state office, or being a favored beneficiary of the state's law—all of these were gifts of the state. Thus did the Asante state maintain its power.

The state also controlled "symbolic capital." Only the state could bestow titles or other symbols of high status, such as the right to the elephant tail insignia, on individuals in recognition of their success in accumulating wealth. Complex rituals and ceremonies, which combined public display with public acclamation, included symbolic and historical references aimed at glorifying the state and recalling the role of public officials as providers and protectors of the people. The Asantehene possessed the "Golden Elephant Tail," which took precedence over all other symbolic achievements. The Golden Elephant Tail symbolized the commitment of each successive Asantehene to uphold and transmit the inheritance of Asante culture. The Golden Tail, symbolizing wealth, was intimately connected to the Golden Stool, symbolizing political authority and legitimate power. The elephant tail was the "helper" of the stool—wealth helps power. This symbolic conjunction, reinforced in ritual, promoted the political ideology that Asante culture and society were "helped" into being by the processes of accumulation, activated by the state.

Understanding that foreign practices and ideas, particularly as they related to the accumulation and distribution of wealth, might undermine the control of the Asante state, the government tried to control the entry of foreign culture into the Asante kingdom. However, as European contact increased in the mid-19th century, the Asante state suffered from both internal and external pressures, and by the late 19th century it became a British colony. Upon independence from Britain in 1957, the Asante became an ethnic group within the Republic of Ghana, but the Asantehene today retains his high position as a ritual, spiritual, and cultural leader of the Asante people.

## CRITICAL THINKING QUESTIONS

1. What were some of the local economic factors that enabled the Asante state to maintain its power?
2. What were some important global factors that both supported and undermined the power of the Asante state?
3. Compare the ideology of the relation between wealth and power in the Asante state with that of the United States.

Source: Adapted from T. C. McCaskie, *State and Society in Pre-Colonial Asante*. Cambridge: Cambridge University Press, 1995.

tribal societies, which is conducted mainly through the voluntary (though sometimes under pressure) contribution of adult males, in a state society coercion replaces voluntary recruitment, where necessary. Because going to war in state societies benefits some economic and political groups more than others, states also take increasing control over information and channels of communication, using propaganda to mask the unequal benefits of war. This strengthens not only the war effort but also the power of the state.

## The State and Social Stratification

The Asante state (as described in the "Ethnography" box) illustrates many typical qualities of early or preindustrial state societies, which generally rest on agriculture. It is the productivity of intensive cultivation that enables the central ruling authority or government to appropriate an economic surplus. Unlike in chiefdoms, in states, only part of this surplus goes directly back to the people. The rest is used to support the activities of the state itself, such as maintaining administrative bureaucracies, standing armies, artists and craftworkers, and a priesthood. This in turn, permits the development of cities, economic and occupational specialization, and extensive trade. Through the power of taxation, states appropriate food surpluses to support an elite or ruling class in a luxurious lifestyle that differs substantially from that of ordinary people. Thus social stratification is a key factor in the rise and maintenance of state societies.

The elite classes in state societies are jealous of their control and wealth and strive at every turn to keep what they have. In addition to controlling the integration of power and wealth, states maintain their power in two ways. First, they maintain control over the centralized government and its institutions, particularly its institutions of coercion. Second, they establish hegemony. Hegemony, as we noted earlier, is the establishment of elite power in socially stratified societies through identifying the interests of the elite with those of the society at large through encoding it in culture and law. As illustrated by the Asante, the elite's hegemony in culturally legitimating the connection between wealth and power was essential in maintaining state stability.

Even with their great coercive and hegemonic power, however, states are not necessarily peaceful and stable. They persistently experience rebellion, directed at overthrowing those who control the government, and sometimes revolutionary attempts to overthrow the entire structure of government. The state is constantly on the alert to ward off threats to depose the government, outbreaks of violence that might result in civil war, or the disruption of the privileges of vested interests. To the extent that a state wins the loyalty of its people, through its ability to shape political ideology and to implement effective protection of their economic and political rights, the constant use of force is not necessary. It is always there in the background, however, as a potential instrument of social control (Nagengast 1994:116).

# The Emergence of the Nation-State

The **nation-state** is a government or territory that is identified with a (relatively) culturally homogeneous population and a national history. A nation is popularly felt by its members to be a natural entity based on bonds of common descent, language, culture, history, and territory. In fact, however, all modern nation-states are composed of many ethnic (and other kinds of) groups. Benedict Anderson (1991) calls nation-states "imagined communities," because it takes an act of imagination to weld the many disparate groups that actually make up the state into a coherent national community. Anthropologists are particularly interested in the historical circumstances under which nation-states evolve, the processes by which they are constructed and maintained, and the circumstances under which they are challenged and destabilized (Stolcke 1995).

One way nation-states construct national identities is to draw boundaries between spatially defined insiders and outsiders (Bornstein 2002; Handler 1988). Regardless of some cultural differences, people who live within these boundaries are viewed as having an essential identity based on a common language, history, and culture. People outside the national boundary are viewed as essentially different or "other." The importance of the spatial dimension of the nation-state is continually impressed on us by colorful world maps, which visually represent the world of nation-states as a discrete spatial partitioning of territory (Alonso 1994:382). See Figure 11.1 for an example.

Nation-states are constructed by attaching people to time as well as space. A common interpretation of the past is essential in creating national identities. This is problematic because different groups within the nation are likely to have different interpretations of its history. Because of this, the creation of national histories is often marked by struggles over which version of history will prevail (J. Friedman 1992). "Tradition," "the past," "history," or "social memory" are all actively invented and reinvented to accord with contemporary national interests and reproduced through rituals, symbols, ceremonies, memorials, and representations in museums and other cultural institutions (Hobsbawm and Ranger 1983;

**nation-state** A sovereign, geographically based state that identifies itself as having a distinctive national culture and historical experience.

**FIGURE 11.1** World maps reinforce the importance of the nation-state as a territorial unit.

Nanda 2004; White 1997). Coronations, inaugurations, a daily pledging of allegiance to the flag, the singing of national anthems, history museums, parades, ceremonies linking the nation's dead to its living—and thus the past to the present—are all essential in maintaining the nation-state.

## Ethnicity and the Nation-State

Ethnicity, like the nation, is a social construction. **Ethnicity** refers to *perceived* differences—such as culture, religion, language, national origin—by which groups of people distinguish themselves and are distinguished from others in the same social environment. Unlike the concept of race, which always involves perceived *physical* differences, ethnicity refers to perceived *cultural* differences, though it may incorporate physical differences as well. **Ethnic groups** are categories of people who view themselves as sharing an ethnic identity that differentiates them from other groups or from the larger society as a whole. **Ethnic boundaries** are the perceived cultural attributes by which ethnic groups distinguish themselves from others. The perception that one belongs to a particular ethnic group, and the emergence of particular ethnic groups and identities, evolves from the interaction of a group with other groups and with the larger society, significantly shaped by competition and conflict over resources.

Ethnicity, like the nation, is popularly viewed as based on a "bedrock" of "natural" ties based on "common blood, religion, language, attachment to a place, or customs" and passed down largely unchanged from generation to generation (Geertz 1973b:277; Meier and Ribera 1993). But ethnicity is no more natural than the nation: ethnic groups, ethnic identities, and ethnic conflicts are shaped by politics, economics, and history. Ethnicity thus becomes more or less important, and takes its particular shape, under specific historical, demographic, and economic conditions (De Vos and Romanucci-Ross 1995).

Constructing national identities has been particularly problematic for postcolonial states, whose artificial colonial boundaries encompassed many different ethnic groups, but it is also problematic in older nations. After World War II, for example, the ethnic homogeneity of many nation-states had to be achieved by the coerced migration of ethnic minorities (Judt 2005). In Canada, also, because of the dual influence of English and French culture, the search for Canadian national identity is ongoing, occasionally flaring up in demands for French-

**ethnicity** Perceived differences in culture, national origin, and historical experience by which groups of people are distinguished from others in the same social environment.

**ethnic groups** Categories of people who see themselves as sharing an ethnic identity that differentiates them from other groups or the larger society.

**ethnic boundaries** The perceived cultural attributes by which ethnic groups distinguish themselves from others.

## Refugees and Political Asylum

One of the by-products of the many wars and racial, religious, ethnic, political conflicts, human rights violations, and genocides of the 20th and 21st centuries has been the creation of millions of **refugees** throughout the world. Refugees are people who have been uprooted from their native lands and forced to cross national boundaries into countries or regions that do not necessarily want them or who cannot provide for them. Since World War II there have been approximately 16 million refugees worldwide.

The wealthier industrialized nations have been traditional havens for refugees and the United States continues to be a beacon for millions. The film *Well-Founded Fear,* made by anthropological filmmakers Michael Camerini and Shari Robertson, highlights the process by which refugees are granted political asylum in the United States. In order to be granted political asylum, a refugee must prove a "well-founded fear of persecution based on race, religion, nationality, membership in a particular social group, or political opinion." Any foreigner who finds a way into the United States may apply for refugee protection in the form of political asylum.

This widely acclaimed film, whose aim is to "get Americans to think about the world," is unique in penetrating, with the consent of officers and applicants, the normally closed and confidential hearings of the Immigration and Naturalization Service (INS), whose officers make the decisions to approve or deny applications for political asylum. In 1998, these officers heard 41,000 asylum cases and approved 13,000 applications.

Among those documented in the film are applicants claiming asylum from the one-child policy in China, the rule that women must be veiled in Algeria, the suppression of political dissent in Romania and Nigeria, and the persecution of Jews in the former Soviet Union. Other issues involve refugees fleeing from violence in Haiti and West African women seeking asylum based on their fear of forced genital mutilation if they remain in their home countries (Lee 2008; Norgren and Nanda 2006:178–179). Iraqis are one of the newest refugee populations in the United States, driven here by the violence resulting from the U.S. invasion of Iraq in March 2003 (Sturm 2008). Unlike the 900,000 Vietnamese refugees accepted in the United States after the Vietnam War, under President Bush, acceptance of Iraqi refugees has been very limited; so far only 463 have been accepted, although 12,000 Iraqi refugees are slated for U.S. resettlement (compared to the almost 4 million who have become refugees in countries in the Middle East) (Jones 2009). Many of these refugees have settled in Detroit and an organization there, called RefugeeWorks, has been launched by anthropologists, and is designed to improve the refugees' chances for employment. Another refugee group accepted into the United States, in flight from the civil war in Sudan, are the Nuer, the subject of a classic ethnography by E. E. Evans-Pritchard (Shandy 2007).

The current economic downturn and the increasing ultra-nationalistic rhetoric in many European countries has led to a decline in the willingness of many European countries to accept refugees. Since 1999, the United States has also reduced the number of people who can apply for refugee status, jailing people who arrive at U.S. borders applying for asylum, and limiting their rights of appeal. Hearing the stories of well-founded fear in Camerini and Robertson's film is a moving reminder of the ways in which the United States is part of a global community, and how anthropology, by reminding people of this reality, can make a difference.

---

speaking Quebecois separatism (Handler 1988) (see also discussion of U.S. immigration policies in Chapter 12, pages 278–279).

The nation-state has many resources available as it seeks to repress the invented or imagined nature of national unity (Foster 1991:238) and foster nationalism as opposed to loyalties to smaller cultural groups. States use education, law, and the media to create a national culture and identity that becomes the only authorized representation of society. Through law, the state can suppress certain aspects of minority cultures, particularly their languages, thus undermining their cultural cohesion. The state may also promote nationalism by incorporating, for its own purposes, elements of subcultures into the national culture. In many nations of Central and South America, indigenous Indian ethnicity, where not totally repressed, is defined in ways that serve nationalistic purposes. Even where indigenous peoples are not identified as backward cultures standing in the way of national development, their cultures may be incorporated into national identity only as a fossilized past or an artistic expression that encourages the increase of foreign tourism (Alonso 1994:398).

## The Nation-State and Ethnic Conflict

Popular media often attribute intranational conflict and violence—including **genocide**—between the Irish and the English in Northern Ireland, between Hutu and Tutsi in

**refugees** People who have been uprooted from their native lands and forced to cross national boundaries.

**genocide** The deliberate and systematic extermination of a national, racial, political, or cultural (ethnic) group.

Although it is true that Shi'a and Sunni Muslims differentiated themselves very soon after Muhammad's death in the 7th century, the characterization of *ancient* struggles omits the impact of British colonial intervention and creation of the Iraqi state in the 1920s, pan-Arab nationalism, authoritarianism, the oil boom, the Iran-Iraq War, the 1991 Gulf War, and the 1990-2003 United Nations sanctions: all of these are modern historical phenomena that have little to do with religion per se (Saleh 2009; Toensing, 2008). And indeed, the 2008 provincial elections in Iraq witnessed the decline of ethnic and sectarian conflicts and the rise of Iraqi nationalism. This points to the hopeful, though by no means assured, future of Iraq as a nation in which different ethnic and religious groups can more or less overcome some of the violent ethnically based conflict of its recent past, a conflict heightened by the U.S. invasion and the involvement of Iran (Dreyfuss 2009).

It is certainly true that ambitious politicians often promote ethnic identity and ethnic conflict by building constituencies from ethnic groups that hope to gain increased access to economic and po-

Courtesy of Serena Nanda

Nation-states intensify national identities by presenting history in emotionally intense ways, such as this sculpture of the capture of Iwo Jima in World War II by the U.S. Marines.

Central Africa, between Hindus and Muslims in India, between Tamils and Sinhalese in Sri Lanka, between French-speakers and English-speakers in Canada, between Bosnians and Serbs, Croatians and Albanians in the former nation of Yugoslavia, between Kurds, Shi'a, and Sunni Muslims in Iraq, between Basques and Spanish in Spain, between Georgians and Russians, among many others, to ethnicity.

These contemporary ethnic conflicts are often presented as natural eruptions of age-old ethnic hatreds and culture clashes between different ethnic groups within nation-states. In fact, many of these conflicts are rooted not in some distant past, but in relatively recent circumstances, shaped by contemporary political events and conflicts over economic resources. For example, much of the mainstream American media projects the oversimplification that violence in Iraq today is a result of an "ancient power struggle" between different Muslim sects.

© Joan Gregg

These indigenous men from Chichicastenango, Guatemala, are instantly recognizable by their distinctly ethnic clothing. While Guatemala capitalizes on its many indigenous ethnic groups as a tourist attraction, Mayans and other indigenous peoples have been the victims of violent attacks by the repressive Guatemalan government.

Ethnic violence in the former Yugoslavia began as a result of the political exploitation of relatively small cultural differences between Croats and Serbs.

litical power. These politicians mobilize a rhetoric of historical abuses and inequities, arousing fears of victimization among members of different groups who, in the past, lived fairly amicably together.

Ethnic conflict in the former state of Yugoslavia illustrates this point well. The former state of Yugoslavia was part of the Ottoman Empire, ruled by Muslim Turks, which contained a large population of Serbs, among other ethnic groups. Conflict between the Turks and Christian Europeans was a central force generating Serb nationalism in the 19th and 20th centuries. After World War II the multiethnic state of Yugoslavia was created, held together by a powerful central government, supported by the Soviet Union (also Serbs). However, after the death of Yugoslav dictator Josip Tito and the collapse of the Soviet Union, Yugoslavia disintegrated into ethnic violence. Throughout the 1990s bitter conflicts among different ethnic and religious groups—Serbs, Croats, Bosnians (many of them Muslim), Macedonians, and Albanians—led to deaths numbered in the hundreds of thousands. By the early 2000s, six new nations, divided largely along ethnic lines, had emerged from the former Yugoslavia.

But the ethnic conflict of the 1990s was not "caused" by the cultural distinctions and past conflicts among Yugoslavia's ethnic groups (Gilliland 1995; Judt 2005:665–684; Maybury-Lewis 1997; Ramet 1996). Rather, a selectively remembered past of cultural differences was mobilized in contemporary struggles over economic and political power, which began in the 1980s, illustrated by the emergence of the new nation of Croatia.

In 1981, after Tito's death, the new political leadership of Yugoslavia introduced an economic austerity program in an attempt to shore up the nation's import/export imbalance. The resulting shortages of consumer goods undermined faith in the government, and people depended even more than usual on kinship and friendship networks within their ethnic groups in order to survive. Hostility was mainly directed toward the national government, which exploited long-standing cultural differences among the main ethnic groups to secure its own political power. A Croat nationalist leader, Franjo Tudjman, gained supporters for Croat nationalism by urging Croats to claim their national rights against Serbs, Muslims, and others. These moves reignited the bitter divisions between the Croats, who supported Hitler in World War II, and the resistance to Hitler primarily carried out by the Serbs. In 1990, after the breakup of the Yugoslav Communist Party, Tudjman led his own nationalist party to victory in Croatian elections and declared an independent state in Croatia, resulting in a bloody war with the Serbs that ended with Croatian independence.

Within this context, old attributes of cultural similarity were transformed into markers of difference. Croats and Serbs, for example, are both Christian but belong to different sects: the Croats are Catholic and the Serbs Eastern Orthodox. They speak the same language but use different writing systems. Croatians now call their language Croatian rather than Serbo-Croatian, as it was formerly called (Gilliland 1995:202). The actual cultural differences between Serbs and Croats are very small, and the conflict is not one of "culture clash," but rather the vehicle of cultural differences, however small, became the framework of a conflict over power and material resources. Once given free rein, however, the framework of "culture clash" becomes difficult to demolish.

## The Nation-State and Indigenous Peoples

All over the world, but particularly in North and South America, Africa, and parts of Asia, indigenous peoples are an important part of the ethnic landscape. **Indigenous peoples** are those small-scale societies designated as bands, tribes, and chiefdoms that occupied their land prior to European contact. Generally, indigenous people are closely identified with their land, are relatively egalitarian, manage resources at the community level, and (previously) had high levels of economic self-sufficiency. They consider themselves distinct from other sectors of society now living in their territories and are incorpo-

**indigenous people** Small-scale societies designated as bands, tribes, or chiefdoms that occupied their land prior to European contact.

Courtesy of Cultural Survival

rated as nondominant groups in the larger nation-states where they live. The determination of many indigenous peoples to maintain their autonomy, their lands, and their culture in a world dominated by nation-states and a global capitalist economy often brings them into conflict with the nation-states of which they are a part (Bodley 1999; R. Lee 2000).

The assault against indigenous peoples began with European expansion and conquest in the 15th century, after which many indigenous societies completely disappeared as a result of epidemics, frontier violence, and military conquest; others survived as remnants in marginal geographic areas. The destruction of indigenous peoples intensified rapidly by the mid-19th century as new frontiers opened up in nations like the United States, Australia, and Brazil. Indigenous people resisted but were no match for the military and economic power of nation-states. After World War II, many indigenous peoples were incorporated into new postcolonial states such as Indonesia, Malaysia, and India, and few independent, self-sufficient indigenous societies remain (Maybury-Lewis 1997).

Because indigenous peoples require control over their land base and subsistence resources in order to remain self-sufficient and politically autonomous, their political defeat was usually accompanied by their economic marginalization. Europeans appropriated their land, pushed indigenous peoples into participation in the global market economy, and forced them to give up their traditional livelihoods. Although indigenous peoples were also pulled into the global economy by their desire for Western goods, where this pull was not sufficiently strong, colonial powers fell back on threatened or actual coercion and military conquest. In the name of social reform and the European "civilizing" mission, colonial

powers also helped destroy indigenous cultures by enforcing Western law, with severe sanctions for nonconformity (Merry 1991, 2000), and enabling missionary activity. These strong assimilationist pressures on indigenous peoples continue right up to the present by nation-states.

After World War II, the United Nations provided an international framework within which the concept of human rights was steadily expanded to include indigenous peoples as cultural groups and to legitimize their struggle for self-determination. But because the United Nations policy worked within the framework of the nation-state, there was little of substance implemented to support indigenous rights. With the passage, on September 13, 2007, of the Declaration on the Rights of Indigenous Peoples, this may change, although some world powers, such as the United States and Canada, among others, refused to sign the declaration (Keating 2007).

National policies reflecting neglect or hostility toward indigenous peoples were frequently based on the expectation that indigenous peoples would eventually disappear, as they assimilated into national cultures and participated in national and global economic programs. International financial organizations, such as the World Bank and the International Monetary Fund, also based their policies on this assumption, initiating lending practices that supported economic "development" programs adversely affecting the subsistence economies of indigenous peoples (Bodley 2000:378).

### Saami Reindeer Herders and the Nation-State

The Saami reindeer herders of Scandinavia are an indigenous people attempting to retain their traditional livelihood and culture in the face of opposition by the modern nation-state of Norway. More than 100,000 Saami have lived in Scandinavia for more than 2000 years. For most of that time they hunted wild reindeer, though over the past 400 years they have become reindeer herders. The Saami primarily consume reindeer dairy products rather than the meat, and reindeer are slaughtered only reluctantly, even for ritual occasions. Today, many Saami do not herd reindeer, but make their living through fishing, small-scale agriculture, crafts, logging, road building, and some government welfare payments; even for these Saami, however, reindeer herding has important historical and symbolic meanings.

The Norwegian government considers the 60,000 Saami a culturally distinct ethnic group and is *officially* committed to furthering the Saami reindeer-herding way of life. At the same time, however, Norway is committed to national economic development and environmental conservation, both of which, the government says, are impeded by unregulated Saami reindeer herding (Paine 1994). In attempting to achieve its goals as a progressive, modern, egalitarian, multicultural nation, Norway regulates Saami reindeer herding in ways that impinge on Saami cultural values and practices and bring them into conflict with the government.

Saami reindeer are individually owned and inherited by men, women, and children, but are herded collectively by a few families who make up a work unit. Reindeer herding is physically exacting. It demands access to the lichen-rich subarctic tundra areas of northern Norway and Sweden, which provide winter pasture for their reindeer, and extensive knowledge of the animals' terrain,

seasonal weather patterns, and ecology, all of which involve uncertainty and risk (Stephens 1987). Although the Saami now participate in a global economy where reindeer products are valuable commodities, reindeer also have intrinsic value to the Saami, both as a form of wealth and a source of Saami cultural distinctiveness.

The Norwegian government regards many traditional Saami herd-management practices as "unproductive," "irrational," and detrimental to the environment. The government's aims are to reduce the overall number of Saami reindeer, to equalize the number of reindeer in each family's herd, and to rationalize reindeer-marketing practices. To this end, the government restricts reindeer pastureland and restricts the number of herders, permitting herding only in a limited number of officially designated "reindeer districts." This regulation directly conflicts with—and overrides—Saami cultural knowledge about the importance of pasture flexibility.

Like many indigenous peoples, through their own desire to selectively "modernize," as well as through government efforts, the Saami have become fully engaged in the cash-based global economy. At one time, reindeer herding supplied the Saami with their basic needs—food, clothing, transportation, and hides for tents—but now Saami need money to buy many things: houses, furniture, radios, televisions, video recorders, clothes, food, cars, and snowmobiles (and the gasoline to run them), the latter essential to compete in herding large numbers of animals. Since World War II, a luxury market for reindeer meat has emerged in northern Europe. Reindeer hides are a popular tourist souvenir item, and even reindeer antlers have a market in the Far East, where antler powder is believed to have aphrodisiac powers (Stephens 1987:37).

As part of its incorporation into the global economy, the Norwegian government insists on more efficient, productive, and profitable herding, slaughtering, and marketing of reindeer. As part of its marketing efforts, the Norwegian government pays a minimum price for slaughtered reindeer and has set up regional slaughtering and marketing centers, where the reindeer are slaughtered in sanitary conditions and the meat grade certified. This requires Saami herders to bring their reindeer to these centers to be slaughtered, which many Saami are reluctant to do. The Saami also resent the "experts" provided by the government for their lack of experience-based knowledge of reindeer herding and their lack of interest in the Saami way of life (Paine 1994).

Today more Saami lead a settled way of life, and many Saami children go further in school, leading them away from their traditionally based livelihood. The sur-

Saami reindeer herders are involved in the global economy through which they earn cash to buy food, clothing, snowmobiles, and the gas to run them. Although recognized as a cultural minority, the Saami are subject to many restraints on their traditional herding practices by the Norwegian government.

© Nik Wheeler/Corbis

vival of the unique Saami culture now must compete with other national needs, such as tourism, mining, and hydroelectric development, and military bases. Although Norwegian government policy protects some Saami reindeer herding, it gives priority to its own goals of social egalitarianism and economic development. The Norwegian state views pastoralism as productively inferior to agriculture, and considers the traditional Saami pastoral way of life as a gift from the state that will continue only so long as it does not interfere with other state objectives, including economic progress in the form of agricultural and industrial development. Government intervention is now transforming Saami pastoralism, whose aim is to *keep* all animals except those slaughtered for domestic needs, into Norwegian reindeer ranching, whose aim is to *sell* all animals except those needed to feed the family. The conflict between the Saami and the Norwegian state illustrates that even a benevolent state, based on universalism, bureaucracy, and economic rationalism, can negatively impact indigenous peoples, and offers little reassurance of a secure future for other indigenous peoples.

# The Global and the Local: Crossing National Borders

A fixed and secure geographical border is an essential characteristic of contemporary states and the vulnerability of state borders is a central concern for all governments. Labor migration, which plays an increasingly important role in economic globalization, as well as fears of terrorist attacks on the state, give the protection of state borders a new political as well as economic urgency.

Anthropologist Avram Bornstein (2002) describes the many ways that the "Green Line," the border between Israel and the West Bank, impacts Palestinian politics, culture, and economics. Because of the unequal economic development between Israel and the West Bank, tens of thousands of Palestinians must cross the border each day to seek work. Although Israeli work permits allow thousands of Palestinians to cross the border legally, thousands of other workers, without permits, cross the border as well, responding to the availability of mainly unskilled jobs such as agricultural work or construction. This heavy human traffic in both legal and undocumented workers results in increased Israeli militarization and law enforcement at the border. This is a source of increasingly hostile encounters between Israel and Palestinians, exacerbating political mistrust and violence on both sides.

Protecting borders is an urgent concern for nation-states as they try to hold back refugees, illegal immigrants, and terrorists, who increasingly cross borders for economic or political reasons.

© Jackie Mercandetti Photography

Bornstein's ethnographic analysis of the economic inequalities generated by the construction of a wall along the Green Line raises obvious comparisons with the border between the United States and Mexico, illustrating how global processes play out in local settings. Like the Israeli border, the American border has become increasingly militarized in an effort to keep out undocumented workers (as well as to interdict drug traffic and prevent terrorism). In a study of undocumented Mexican immigrants in the United States, anthropologist Leo Chavez refers to the border as "political theater," a place in which the American debate over immigration is dramatically played out.

In the United States, the most passionate debate over immigration concerns the border with Mexico. The latest policy of the United States government to control undocumented migration is the erection of a double-layered 700-mile-long border fence, which crosses the back yards of modest homes but skips over the property of wealthy landowners. The fence also crosses Native American tribal lands and highlights the clash of interests and cultures in the American Southwest (Speed 2008). Seventy-five miles of the border, at one of its most vulnerable points, is located on the Tohono O'odham (Native American) Reservation, near Tucson, Arizona.

The Tohono O'odham oppose the wall, claiming a need to freely cross the border to visit friends and relatives in Mexico, take their children to school, gather traditional foods, and visit religious sites to perform rituals, all of which they have been doing for years. Their cultural concerns also focus on the wall's restricting the free range of deer, wild horses, coyotes, jackrabbits, and other animals they revere and regard as kin.

The Tohono O'odham cooperate extensively with the U.S. border patrol and the Department of Homeland Security in patroling the border. As the federal government is the trustee of all Indian lands, it could build the fence through the reservation without tribal permission, but that would jeopardize the valuable help the Tohono O'odham now gives the government (Archibold 2006).

In the debates over controlling the flow of undocumented Mexican immigrants, those who call for open borders claim that these immigrants are needed in the U.S. economy, that this immigration is in any case, wall or no wall, unstoppable, and that measures such as the border fence only direct undocumented immigration to more difficult and dangerous terrain, making the immigrants even more vulnerable to exploitation (Chavez 1998:196; Holthouse 2007; Johnson 2007). They empathize with the words of the American poet Robert Frost, who wrote, "Something there is that doesn't love a wall."

## Key Questions

1. What effects do you think the border wall will have on undocumented immigration at the U.S.–Mexican border?

2. What alternative policies would you suggest to address the issue of undocumented immigrants entering the United States?

3. How much weight should the American government give to the cultural values of the Tohono O'odham in opposing a wall along the border?

# Summary

1. **How does political organization relate to social differentiation? What are the major types of systems of social differentiation?** Social differentiation is a key feature of political organization. Anthropologists have identified three major systems of social differentiation: egalitarian, rank, and stratified societies. Each of these are typically associated with different economic, social, and political features.

2. **What are the main characteristics of the different systems of social differentiation within egalitarian and rank societies?** Egalitarian and rank societies are both nonstratified systems of social differentiation. Egalitarian societies, mainly found among foragers and in some horticultural societies, give every individual and group in society equal access to basic resources, power, and prestige. Rank societies, or chiefdoms, recognize differences in prestige among individuals and groups, but no one is denied access to the resources necessary for survival. Rank societies are organized through kinship and chiefly position maintained largely through redistribution of goods.

3. **What are stratified societies and what kinds of social systems are they identified with?** Stratified societies are associated with the state. Social, political, and economic inequality are institutionalized and maintained through a combination of internalized controls, political power, and force. Kinship ties between the upper and lower classes no longer integrate the society, there are wide gaps in standards of living, and some people have no access to basic resources.

4. **What are some of the functions of political organization and law? What are some of the means for achieving these aims?** Political organization and law address the universal human problems of coordinating and regulating human behavior through making and enforcing decisions affecting the common good and resolving conflicts, through both formal and informal means. Informal social control is achieved through gossip, ridicule, and ostracism; formal sanctions include exile, death, and punishments meted out by courts, judges, police, and other institutionalized forms of regulation.

5. **What are the four major types of political organization identified by anthropologists and what is the basis of this typology? What are the differentiating characteristics of the two least specialized forms of political organization?** Political organization varies according to the degree of specialization of political functions, the extent to which authority is centralized, and the number of groups found in the society (social complexity). Four major forms of political organization are bands, tribes, chiefdoms, and states. Band societies, found mainly among foragers, have little integration of groups beyond the level of the band, with no central leadership or formal means of social control. Tribal organization, found mainly among horticulturists and pastoralists, is based on localized kin groups who act independently, but under certain conditions may also act collectively.

6. **How do chiefdoms and states differ from each other and also differ from bands and tribes?** In chiefdoms, kinship is the most important principle of social organization. Unlike tribes, however, chiefdoms concentrate power in the office of the chief, which heavily depends on his control over the redistribution of food and other goods. A state is a hierarchical, centralized form of political organization in which a central government has a legal monopoly over the use of force. States are characterized by social stratification and, unlike chiefdoms, are not organized through kinship.

7. **How is the connection between social stratification and the state illustrated in the ethnography of the Asante kingdom?** The Asante state consisted of political elites and peasants, with the King at the top of the social system. The centralized government controlled the sources, distribution, and ritual display of wealth, maintaining itself through an ideology which held that accumulated wealth in the hands of the elite benefitted the whole society.

8. **What are some of the economic, social, political, and cultural features of state societies?** State societies, which usually rest on agriculture, provide economic surpluses that permit the development of centralized government, cities, occupational specialization, trade, taxation, social stratification, and bureaucracy. In state societies the government controls the legitimate use of force, which it may use against its citizens and other peoples, but states also maintain themselves by developing ideologies that justify the elite's control of the population (hegemony).

9. **What is a nation-state? How do national governments attempt to maintain their grip on power and control?** The nation-state is a government or territory identified with a (relatively) culturally homogenous population and a national history. It maintains power by drawing cultural boundaries between its members and outsiders; by promoting historical narratives that support nationalism; by creating laws that suppress minority cultures; and by sponsoring celebrations that highlight the national identity.

10. **What are some dimensions of ethnicity? Why do some anthropologists argue that ethnic conflicts are not *about* ethnicity?** Ethnicity refers to *perceived* differences in culture, language, and religion between groups of people who experience themselves as sharing an ethnic identity. Anthropologists emphasize that ethnic conflicts are not about these cultural differences but rather are differences exploited in situations of conflict over political power and economic resources.

11. **What is the relationship between contemporary indigenous groups and the states in which they live? How do the Saami of Norway illustrate some of the conflicts between indigenous peoples and their national governments?** Indigenous peoples, in the past, have been exterminated or marginalized by populations who appropriated their land, repressed their culture, and transformed them into minority populations, often struggling to survive. The Norwegian government, like many states, views the Saami, an indigenous reindeer-herding people, as standing in the way of modern economic development and profitable participation in the global economy. Through various restrictions on reindeer herding, the government is viewed by the Saami as interfering in its traditional subsistence economy and demeaning its culture, transforming the Saami from reindeer herders into reindeer ranchers.

12. **How are national borders implicated in problematic contemporary political issues?** Migration from one country to another involves millions of people worldwide. Some of these people are refugees, seeking asylum from oppressive governments or oppressive cultural practices, such as genital mutilation or coerced abortion. Others are migrants, fleeing poverty and seeking work in bordering nations. Because of terrorism and illegal immigration, many borders (for example, in Israel and the United States), are now militantly policed and guarded by walls or fences, both of which promote protests and often violent conflict.

# Key Terms

| | | |
|---|---|---|
| acephalous | ethnic boundaries | leadership |
| age grades | ethnic groups | mediation |
| age set | ethnicity | nation-state |
| authority | factions | political ideology |
| band | genocide | political organization |
| bigman | government | political process |
| chiefdom | hegemony | power |
| citizenship | indigenous people | rank society |
| egalitarian society | law | rebellion |

refugee

revolution

secret societies

social complexity

social differentiation

state

stratified society

tribe

tributary mode of exchange

war

# Suggested Readings

Kaplan, Flora E. S. (Ed.). 1997. *Queens, Queen Mothers, Priestesses, and Power: Case Studies in African Gender.* New York: New York Academy of Sciences. Eighteen case studies of elite women from a variety of ethnic groups in southern Africa and West Africa focus on their political and ritual roles in both the public and the private domain.

Norgren, Jill, and Serena Nanda. 2006. *American Cultural Pluralism and Law* (3rd ed). Westport, CN: Praeger/Greenwood. An examination of the intersection of many ethnic, racial, religious, and gender groups with American law. Important legal cases include Latino immigration, post-9/11 security measures affecting American Muslims, Mormon polygyny, and the Native Hawaiian sovereignty movement.

Waterston, Alisse (Ed.). 2009. *An Anthropology of War: Views from the Frontline.* New York: Berghahn. A very readable, provocative look at war from an anthropological and ethnographic perspective, with articles on such diverse locations as Colombia, Guatemala, Israel and Palestine, Iraq, Afghanistan, and Haiti. Through this anthropological lens students will gain a deeper understanding of the causes, patterns, and practices of war, one of the greatest issues of our time.

Wolf, Eric R. 1998. *Envisioning Power: Ideologies of Dominance and Crisis.* Berkeley: University of California Press. In his typically insightful and original style, Wolf examines three uses of power in extreme cultural situations: Nazi Germany, the ancient Aztec, and the Kwakiutl.

The first African-American president, Barack Obama, and his appointment of the first Hispanic Supreme Court Justice, Sonia Sotomayor, represent an historic moment in the intersection of race, class, and ethnicity in the United States.

© AFP/Getty Images

**THINKING POINT:** While traveling in Malaysia I (Nanda) asked a friend to explain this exceptionally diverse society. He began by saying, "The Indians are the black people," referring to the dark skin color of the Indians in Malaysia who are mainly from South India. Joking with him a little, I asked, "If the Indians are the black people, who are the white people?" "Oh," he answered, without missing a beat, "the Portuguese used to be the white people but now the Chinese are the white people."

—[To learn more about how different societies construct race, see page 271.]

# {chapter 12}

# Stratification

In this chapter we look at how class, race, ethnicity, and caste are constructed and intersect in our own and other socially stratified societies. As our opening story makes clear, social stratification involves the intersection of culturally constructed categories that change over time within specific economic and historical contexts. **Social stratification** is the structure that results from unequal access to and distribution of goods and services in a society, and is related to the organization of production and cultural values. <<

# Explaining Social Stratification

As we noted in Chapter 11, social stratification is related to social complexity and is one of the criteria by which states, the most socially complex type of society, are defined. No society has ever successfully organized a large and diverse population without stratification and inequalities.

Two basic perspectives on social stratification are functionalism and conflict theory. **Functionalism** holds that social stratification generally benefits the whole society, by rewarding people socially and economically for working harder, taking risks, doing difficult jobs, or spending more time in school or occupational training. For example, the rewards of prestige and high income motivate some people to become medical doctors, a profession that requires more than 10 years of higher education and is difficult to achieve but necessary for the well-being of the whole society.

But the inequality characteristic of social stratification does not always serve the general good. Not all of society's most difficult jobs are well rewarded. In the United States, for example, schoolteachers, nurses, and many others do difficult jobs that may require substantial training, yet are not that well compensated financially. Nor are many of the low-prestige "dirty jobs" that are nevertheless essential to the functioning of society well paid. Furthermore, social stratification does not necessarily result in recruiting the most able people to the most demanding positions, as those of us who have ever had an incompetent boss can attest!

A functionalist perspective emphasizes the functions of inequality in a stable social order, but this theory makes some faulty assumptions. For example, though it is obvious that in many contemporary societies wealth is a powerful motivating force, money's ability to motivate a person may have limits. A person making $25,000 a year would work harder for a salary of $50,000 a year, but would a person making $400,000 a year be motivated to work harder for $450,000 a year? Yet $50,000 is still a great deal of money.

Furthermore, beyond financial considerations is an issue of the human spirit. Although inequality seems inevitable in large-scale social systems, resentment, however repressed, always seems to accompany substantial inequalities (Scott 1992), especially when the inequalities are based on such ascribed factors as race, gender, caste, or other attributes an individual is born with and cannot

change (Berreman 1988). And no society, even the most theoretically open class system, actually offers everyone the same opportunities to achieve economic and social success. In all stratified societies, family background and social connections, gender, ethnicity, race, accumulated wealth, and other factors play important roles in determining the sorts of opportunities available to individuals. Resentment between people of different levels of wealth and power is particularly likely when inequalities between groups are large and are perceived to be unfair. Anthropologist Gerald Berreman attributes much of the conflict in modern societies—crime, terrorism, ethnic conflict, civil and international wars—to organized and systemic inequality (1981:4–5).

In **conflict theory,** social stratification results from the constant struggle for scarce goods and services. Inequalities exist because those individuals and groups who have acquired power, wealth, and prestige use their assets and their power to maintain control over the system of production and the apparatus of the state, as was described for the Asante kingdom (see the "Ethnography" section in Chapter 11). When these attempts to establish dominance falter or are challenged, elites may fall back on the threat of force or its actual use to maintain the status quo. This emphasis on conflict and change provides an essential dimension in the understanding of social stratification.

Conflict theory is central to the work of Karl Marx. For Karl Marx and those who follow his thinking, the economic system is the critical factor in explaining social stratification. Marx differentiated two main social classes in capitalist society on the basis of wealth: the capitalists, who own the means of production, and the workers, who must sell their labor in order to survive. According to Marx, the relationship of individuals to the means of production is critical in determining their wealth, power, and prestige. Marx viewed the conflict between the workers and the owners of the means of production as central to capitalism, and predicted this would eventually lead to capitalism's downfall. By asking, "cui bono," or who benefits economically, conflict theory enables us to understand some of the hidden motivations of social actors and to assess institutions by their economic and social consequences as well as by their articulated intentions. However, just as the functional view of inequality may lead theorists to ignore the possibility of structural conflict, conflict theorists may sometimes ignore the social mechanisms that promote solidarity across class, racial, ethnic, and caste lines.

**social stratification** A social hierarchy resulting from the relatively permanent unequal distribution of goods and services in a society.

**functionalism (functionalist perspective)** The anthropological theory that specific cultural institutions function to support the structure of a society or serve the needs of its people.

**conflict theory** A perspective on social stratification that focuses on economic inequality as a source of conflict and change.

# Criteria of Stratification: Power, Wealth, and Prestige

The social stratification system of any society depends on the complex interaction of the three main dimensions of stratification: power, wealth, and prestige. Anthropologists analyze **power** (the ability to control resources in one's own interest) by examining its sources, the channels through which it is exercised, and the goals it is deployed to achieve (see Chapter 11). For example, in the United States, we might analyze the different sources, uses, and goals of power among corporate presidents, elected public officials, entertainment celebrities, or heads of organized crime families. From a cross-cultural perspective, we might compare the sources and uses of power of an American president, the prime minister of France, the chairman of the Communist party in the People's Republic of China, or the Ayatollah who is the supreme leader in an Islamic Republic like Iran.

**Wealth** is the accumulation of material resources or access to the means of producing these resources. Although wealth is not the sole criterion of social status even in capitalist societies, it can eventually translate into high social position and power. Wealth enables people to send their children to the most prestigious schools, buy homes in the best neighborhoods, and join the right social clubs. It enables people to gain access to important politicians by giving large campaign contributions. It may also allow them to run for political office themselves. Wealth can also translate into symbolic power, which in turn reinforces political power, as we described earlier for the Asante.

**Prestige,** or social honor, is the third dimension of social stratification. The cultural bases of prestige are different in different societies: they may be related to race and ethnicity, income, accumulated wealth, power, personal characteristics such as integrity, family history, and the display of material goods. Not all wealth, in and of itself, is a source of prestige. For example, people who earn their incomes illegally have less prestige than do those whose incomes are legally earned. The head of an illegal gambling syndicate, a drug czar, or a Somali pirate may make hundreds of millions of dollars but have little prestige. On the other hand, few winners of the Nobel Peace Prize make much money but they surely have great prestige. And committing oneself to poverty, as India's great leader Mahatma Gandhi did, may paradoxically be a source of greater prestige than the display of wealth.

A key source of prestige in all societies is occupation, both for its relation to income and the cultural values attached to it, though different societies rank occupations differently. In the Hindu caste system (see page 282), occupations are ranked according to their level of spiritual purity or pollution, a concept formally absent from occupational rankings in the United States. Americans do, however, make some connections between prestige—or lack of it—and the "dirt" involved in various occupations, though this is not always voiced aloud. Dirty jobs are generally not prestigious jobs.

As socioeconomic conditions change, the value system that supports a particular system of ranking occupa-

© Joan Gregg

Repairing train lines is physically demanding and hazardous. A functional theory of social stratification holds that differential financial rewards are needed to attract people to dirty, dangerous, and difficult jobs.

tional prestige may also change. In 18th-century Europe, surgery was performed by barbers and was a lower-class occupation; in contemporary North America, surgeons rank very high in prestige, not only because they make a great deal of money but also because surgery requires great skill and training. In the People's Republic of China, the prestige and power associated with different occupations has almost completely reversed itself from traditional Chinese society. Before the Communist Revolution, China followed a Confucian value system, in which scholars had the highest honor. After the revolution, workers were honored and scholars often explicitly ridiculed and despised. Today, with China's growing free-market practices and increasing economic role in globalization, businesspeople, previously a target of socialist contempt and even violence, are highly regarded, though this has also changed with the 2008 global economic downturn.

Social scientists have long debated whether prestige or economic factors are more important in explaining the behavior of people in complex, stratified societies. Karl

**power** The ability to compel other individuals to do things that they would not choose to do of their own accord.

**wealth** The accumulation of material resources or access to the means of producing these resources.

**prestige** Social honor or respect.

Marx argued for the primacy of economic or class interests while Max Weber, a German sociologist of the late 19th century, argued for the importance of status rather than economic interests. Whereas Marx thought that people were (or should be) most conscious of their class membership (their economic status), Weber believed that people may value prestige and the symbolic aspects of status even more than their economic position. Weber further argued that political action can be motivated by a group's desire to defend its social position as well as, or even in opposition to, its economic self-interest, a position Marx called "false consciousness." In the American South, for example, poor whites did not join poor blacks in working to improve their common economic position because they were more committed to maintaining the prestige value based on color or race.

## Ascription and Achievement

In comparing social stratification systems, anthropologists differentiate between systems where social position is based on **ascribed status,** or birth, with systems based on **achieved status,** that is, a person's individual efforts. Race, ethnicity, family of origin, and biological sex are ascribed statuses. Wife, college professor, criminal, and artist are achieved statuses. In open stratification systems, social position is primarily based on achievement; in closed stratification systems, social position is based on ascription. In fact, in most modern complex societies both achievement and ascription play a role in the social stratification system.

## Class Systems

A **class** is a category of persons who all have about the same opportunity to obtain economic resources, power, and prestige and who are ranked high and low in relation to other class categories. In a **class system** there are possibilities for **social mobility,** or movement between the classes or social strata, which are (ideally) based on individual achievement rather than ascribed status. Even in the most open class systems, however, ascribed statuses always play a role in moving from one class to another. Closed stratification systems, in which there is little or no possibility of social mobility, are called caste systems and are discussed later in the chapter.

In class systems, the different strata (classes) are not sharply separated from one another but form a continuum. Social status is dependent on both achievement and ascription. Social mobility (upward) from one class to another—through various means such as education, marriage, good luck, hard work, taking risks—is a central cultural value and theoretically possible for all society's members. In the United States we call this opportunity for upward social mobility for all "the American Dream." Although belief in the American Dream and an open society is strong among all the diverse racial and ethnic groups in the United States (*New York Times* 2005), social science evidence demonstrates that educational achievement, levels of indebtedness, income, and wealth accumulation, including home ownership and home foreclosures, are significantly correlated not just with race, ethnicity, and gender, but also to an individual's class status (Haskins, Isaacs, and Sawhill 2008). Evidence is clear, for example, that (even before the recession of 2008), class-based differences are very significant in achievements in higher education: high school seniors who come from homes where neither parent attended college are less likely to get admitted to college, less likely to have a high grade point average, less likely to complete an undergraduate or graduate degree, and less represented on college faculties than those with at least one college-educated parent (Bialostok 2009).

## The American Class System

In 2006, Gloria Castillo, 22, a child of undocumented immigrants, was married, with two children, and lived in a tough neighborhood in Dallas, Texas. She worked the night shift at the drive-through window at a highway Burger King, from 10:30 p.m. to 6:30 a.m., for $252 a week before taxes, and received no health care benefits. To help make ends meet, she worked a second job, earning $150 a night for the 1½ hours it took her to clean three bathrooms in a local bar. Her husband worked at an auto parts place during the day, so Gloria took the children, ages 7 and 8, for a fast food breakfast before dropping them at school, returned home, slept until 2, picked up the kids, prepared their frozen food dinners, put them to bed at 7, spent a few hours with her husband, and left for work. On Saturdays she attended a community college, working toward a degree as a paralegal. "I got dreams," she said (LeDuff 2006).

The American Dream, as expressed in the life of Gloria Castillo, is closely tied to other core American values such as individualism, meritocracy, the work ethic,

---

**ascribed status**  A social position that a person is born into.

**achieved status**  A social position that a person chooses or achieves on his or her own.

**class**  A category of persons who all have about the same opportunity to obtain economic resources, power, and prestige and who are ranked relative to other categories.

**class system**  A form of social stratification in which the different strata form a continuum and social mobility is possible.

**social mobility**  Movement from one social strata to another.

optimism, pragmatism, progress, and a belief in the ability of individuals to control the circumstances of their lives. One corollary of the American Dream is that economic failure and downward social mobility is largely viewed as a result of the individual failings as well as the behaviors, attitudes, and cultures of members of the lower classes, rather than as a systemic aspect of social structure.

Two decades ago, anthropologist Katherine Newman was prescient in revealing the significance and meaning of downward mobility in the American class system. In her book *Falling from Grace: Downward Mobility in the Age of Affluence* (1999), Newman defines downwardly mobile middle-class people as those who had secure jobs, comfortable homes, and reason to believe that the future would be one of continued prosperity for themselves and their children. Newman noted that downward mobility was almost institutionally invisible in the United States. The media most often focused on the lives of the rich and famous and those in the business world who made fantastic salaries, or on people like Gloria Castillo, who are inspired by the American Dream. American culture provides many rituals and symbols of upward mobility and success in the form of displays of wealth and status, but there are no such occasions to mark status deterioration. As Newman observes, "Downward mobility is a hidden dimension of our society's experience because it. . . . does not fit into our cultural universe."

Yet even prior to the 2008 financial crisis, downward mobility affected many Americans. Newman emphasizes that job loss entails not only economic decline but also a decline in prestige: individuals who lost their jobs lost their place in society and with it, their sense of honor and self-esteem. Many types of workers—factory employees, retail clerks, truck drivers, store managers, computer technicians, middle managers, engineers, architects, CEOs, and many others, have lost their place in what was once a secure middle, or even upper middle, class (Greenhouse 2008).With the 2008 recession, downward mobility has become a highly visible dimension of the American class system, increasingly making media headlines. It has now become clearer to many Americans that systemic aspects of our economic system outweigh individual factors in explaining failure and class inequality. Instead of reading stories like those about Gloria Castillo, we read about people like Mark Cooper, who lost his $70,000-a-year job as a security manager for a Fortune 500 company and is now working as a janitor for $12 an hour and feels lucky to have the job (Luo 2009).

The cultural emphasis on individualism central to the American Dream also represses the important role of government programs and policies—the G.I. Bill, Social Security, unemployment insurance, a progressive income tax, and federal mortgage assistance programs—that resulted in a growing middle class since World War II. After the Great Depression, from the 1930s until the 1970s, social mobility was significantly based on a cultural vi-

This rally is aimed at protesting the increasingly inequitable aspects of the economic system of the United States, in which job loss and declining income have most affected the working and middle classes.

sion that held that government should provide a safety net and enable upward mobility for all Americans. By the 1980s, however, a new cultural ideology emerged as dominant: that government should be kept small, its spending restricted, and that success depended on individual achievement free of government help or interference. These two contrasting cultural visions have been central to the political differences between the two main political parties and again became a central issue with the 2008 economic crisis.

**The Material Basis of Class in the United States** There is no complete cultural consensus in the United States on the social class structure, how the social classes are defined, or even whether there are social classes at all (Durrenberger 2001). American optimism and the economic growth since the early 1980s enhanced the perception that the American stratification system was not one of deep divides but rather that it was like a ladder with lots of rungs, which could be climbed with ingenuity and hard work.

Recent—and growing—statistical and ethnographic evidence in several areas, however, makes the ladder image of class more problematic. If one defines the middle class as people who have a roof over their heads, television sets, computers, cell phones, air conditioners, and cars (even if all financed by debt, much of it beyond their current means to pay off), then one could say that America is indeed a "middle class" society. Others, however, cite the current decline in the economic position of much of the American middle class as people struggle with growing unemployment, loss of wealth in the form of stocks, lack of access to medical care that often accompanies unemployment, inability to pay one's mortgage and home foreclosures, the rising cost of college tuition and the high cost of student loans, and particularly the huge inequalities in wages and wealth between the rich and others, to raise questions about the American class system and, specifically, the reality of realizing the American Dream.

Central to questioning previous images of America as a middle-class society is the growing income and wealth inequality between the very rich and the rest. Despite ambiguities about the definitions of the American class system, most Americans would agree that the rungs on the ladder of social mobility are most significantly defined by income. Income is the gateway to a middle-class lifestyle and serves as the basis for family economic security. Over the long term, sufficient and steady income is essential toward saving and accumulating assets, especially home ownership.

The view that America is a middle-class society, and for many, even a classless society, is largely based on the perception that most Americans were in, or could reach, a middle-class income level. This was justified by many statistics, though it also willfully ignored the many Americans mired in poverty. This culturally engineered perception about class equality in America has become unhinged from reality over the past 30 years, which has seen an extraordinary jump in income inequality. During this period, the after-tax income of the top 1 percent of American households jumped 139 percent to more than $700,000; the income of the middle fifth of households rose only 17 percent, to $43,700; and the income of the poorest fifth rose only 9 percent. In 2004, the chief executives at the 100 largest companies in California took home a collective $1.1 billion, an increase of nearly 20 percent over the previous year. For most workers, only during the speculative bubble of the 1990s did income rise above inflation. Reductions in pensions have also increased the prospect of financial insecurity in retirement. Tax cuts for the wealthy under President George W. Bush greatly exacerbated this inequality: the 400 taxpayers with the highest incomes—over $87 million a year each—now pay income tax, and Medicare and Social Security taxes, amounting to the same percentage of their incomes as people making $50,000 to $75,000 a year. As Warren Buffett, one of the richest men in the world, has repeatedly emphasized, his 2006 tax rate on his $46 million income was 17.7 percent, while his secretary's tax rate was 30 percent (Brown 2009).

Income and accumulated wealth have a tremendous impact on people's lives: they are correlated with health, quality health care in illness, and the life span itself (J. Scott 2005). The high and rising cost of pharmaceuticals and medical care is merely one aspect of the different life chances available to the poor, the middle class, and the wealthy. People with higher education and income are less likely to have and die of heart disease, strokes, diabetes, and many types of cancer (Scott 2005). They are also more likely to benefit from advances in medicine, have more useful information about medicine, and be covered by health insurance. In addition, they are less likely to smoke, are less overweight, exercise more, and eat healthier food than people in the lower classes.

**Life chances** are the opportunities that people have to fulfill their potential in society. Sufficient and steady family income is the essential gateway to increasing life chances and social mobility: it is the basis of a decent standard of living including access to food, clothing, shelter, health care, a quality education, and the accumulation of some resources or equity as a safety net for emergencies. Conversely, insufficient and irregular income negatively affects not only one's own life chances but also those of one's children.

Social mobility itself is a life chance that depends on where one already is in the class system. People born into positions of wealth, high status, and power use these resources to maintain their high class positions and often have the means to keep others from achieving upward mobility. Rich and powerful people have a better chance of maintaining their position over generations than people born into the middle class have of reaching these positions, and middle class people have a better chance of improving their own and their children's life chances than do those of working or poorer classes (Bowles et al. 2005; Corak 2004; Frank and Cook 1996; Lareau 2003; Neckerman 2004).

**Social Classes as Subcultures** In addition to material differences, and partly based on material differences, social classes have also been found to differ in attitudes, behavior, consumption patterns, lifestyle, values, and social connections. The members of a social class tend to share similar life experiences, occupational roles, values, educational backgrounds, affiliations, leisure activities, buying habits, religious affiliation, and political views. Not merely income, but how that income is spent, is an important dimension of class status (*New York Times* 2005).

On the surface, some cultural aspects of social class seemed to be blurring; even while income and wealth inequalities rose over the past 30 years, consumer-related lifestyles seemed to grow more similar. This was partly because, thanks to globalization, cheaper consumer goods

**life chances** The opportunities that people have to fulfill their potential in society.

The consumer culture of the American middle class has largely been built on credit card debt. As this system has collapsed in the current recession, realizing the American Dream is no longer possible for many working-class and middle-class Americans.

were more easily available; partly because credit was easy to get (this has now turned out to have a very high price); partly because more people within a household work, contributing to slightly increasing median household incomes; and partly because a "culture of consumption" meant spending on consumer goods rather than saving (*New York Times* 2005:135). For example, a middle-class family earning about $50,000 a year may own a flat screen TV, drive a BMW, buy expensive chocolates, take a Caribbean cruise, and will almost certainly have a cell phone.

But this accumulation of consumer goods that seems to blur class lines is only a small part of the story of class-differentiated lifestyles. Money does make a lifestyle. As luxury has gone down-market, the market produces ever more expensive luxury goods that are affordable only for those with great incomes and wealth: $4,000 handbags, $130,000 Hummer automobiles, and $12,000 mother/baby diamond bracelet sets. Even more than material goods, class differences are expressed in personal services and exclusive experiences: personal chefs and personal trainers, face lifts and other cosmetic surgery, $400-an-hour tutors for the children, who in any case will be attending private schools. And while the middle class may have taken group tours to Europe or Caribbean cruises, the rich are shelling out $50,000 for a 10-day, private jet tour of the seven most wonderful sights in the world sponsored by National Geographic (Newman and Chen 2007). But perhaps the most important lifestyle difference related to income is the ability of the wealthy to buy homes in residential areas restricted to those with a great deal of money; where people live reflects the American class structure in one of its most permanent aspects

and impacts on many other dimensions of life, such as safety, availability of high-quality schools, and, as we see later in the chapter, the chances of being affected by environmental pollution and disasters. The high standard of material comfort so widely spread across America clouds the importance of class divisions compared to the rest of the world, even if much of this material comfort was based on growing debt obligations, and even as, in the wake of growing unemployment and underemployment, many Americans are now restricting many of those purchases such as home improvements, new clothes, eating out, and taking vacations, which once seemed essential to their middle-class identities but now seem like nonessentials.

Although American class differences are less reliable in predicting political choice or religious affiliation than they once were, class status is still very significant in such things as family structure and educational achievement. The upper classes are more likely to be married before they have children, they have fewer children, and they have them later in life. All these factors are related to the possibilities of upward social mobility (*New York Times* 2005:125). As Katherine Newman notes, family circumstances are among the most important factors determining whether those in the category she calls the "near poor," who have household incomes between $20,000 and $40,000 a year for a family of four, can make it into the middle class (Newman and Chen 2006). "Women with children and no one to help them with those kids [are] much more likely to get trapped—they [can't] get more education which limit[s] their job options [and] their contact with the labor market [is] more fragile and episodic." (Newman quoted in Press 2007:23).

Beyond participating in shared patterns of spending, family structure, and educational achievement, members of a social class also tend to associate more with one another than with people in other classes. Thus, the cultural and interactional dimensions of social class reinforce one another. Through interaction based on common residence and schooling, religious participation, voluntary associations, and other social institutions, people learn the lifestyle of their social class. Because lifestyle is an important part of sociability, informal and intimate social relationships, such as friendship and marriage, also tend to bring together people from the same social class. This partly explains why social classes tend to be largely endogamous.

## Race: A Cultural Construction

As noted in the chapter opening story about Malaysian diversity, "race" is a cultural construction, based on specific histories and social structures. To make sense of the conversation between Nanda and her friend, we need to understand Malaysia's history. Malaysia has three primary ethnic groups—Chinese, Indian, and Malay—as well as a small population of Portuguese descended from 16th-century traders who politically dominated Malay society for 100 years. The Portuguese were later defeated by the British, who colonized Malaysia (then called Malaya), and replaced the Portuguese in the most important political and economic positions. When the British left, after Malaysia's independence, the Chinese moved into many commercial and professional positions and now dominate the Malaysian economy. Having taken over the economic position formerly occupied by the Portuguese and then the British, the Chinese are now defined as having taken over their racial category as well.

The term **race** is used to define people based on *perceived* physical differences that imply hereditary differences. The conversation on Malaysia illustrates, however, that race is not a natural category, but one constructed by humans in specific cultural and historical contexts. But although race is a culturally constructed category, it becomes a significant social fact: it is used to justify differential treatment and discrimination and affects the lives of both the racial majority and racial minorities.

Even when there are no objective physical differences, such as skin color, between groups of people, other differences, such as class, ethnicity, and caste, are often conceptualized in racial terms. For example, the 19th-century English theologian Charles Kingsley described the Irish as "human chimpanzees. . . . a race of utter savages, truly barbarous and brutish. . .," noting unhappily, that "[their] skins are as white as ours" (in Curtis 1968:84). The idea of a "degenerate Irish race," differing also from the British by class and religion, was used by the British to justify their control over Ireland. As the Irish migrated to the United States, the notion of their cultural and biological inferiority was also commonly expressed in the language of race (Shanklin 1994:3–7).

Similarly, in Japan, the concept of race is applied to the Burakumin, a stigmatized and oppressed group perceived by the Japanese as innately physically and morally distinct from other Japanese, although there are in fact no physical differences between them. The Burakumin are thus an "invisible race," distinguished by differences in family name, occupation, and place of residence. Despite their official emancipation in 1871 and no cultural differences from other Japanese, however, the hereditary

---

**race** A culturally constructed category based on *perceived* physical differences.

**apartheid** The South African system of exclusive racial groups—black, white, colored, and Asian—that were formally recognized, segregated, treated differently in law and life, and occupied different and almost exclusive statuses within the society.

---

stigma against the Burakumin lives on (De Vos and Wagatsuma 1966; Onishi 2009).

As in many systems of inherited stratification, even where physical differences do not define groups, ethnicity, class, caste, or other social distinctions are symbolized in biological or racial terms. These differences are then associated with traits of culture, character, morality, intelligence, personality, and purity that are seen as natural, inherited, and unalterable, in a word, ascribed. Although it is socially easier to distinguish a race when individuals differ in obvious physical characteristics, the Japanese-Burakumin relationship, the English perceptions of the Irish, and, as we see later in the chapter, the racial designation of many European immigrants demonstrate that a lack of observable physical differences does not prohibit the invention of racial categories or the emergence of racial stratification.

# A Comparison of Race and Racial Stratification in the United States and Brazil

Racial stratification occurs in societies with different culturally constructed views of race. For example, in Brazil, race is viewed as a continuum. In the United States, race is largely defined as a binary opposition between black and white. In South Africa, under **apartheid,** multiple exclusive racial classifications—black, white, Coloured, and Asian—were formally recognized, treated differently in law and life, and occupied different and almost exclusive statuses within the society (Frederickson 2009; A. Marx 1998).

## The Cultural Construction of Race and Racial Stratification in the United States

In the United States, race is culturally constructed largely on the basis of a few observable traits such as skin color and hair texture and presumed ancestry. Apart from a few regional variations on race—for example, the Anglo-Hispanic distinction in the American Southwest, the complex racial/ethnic system in Hawaii, and the place of Native Americans—historically, the North American system of racial stratification primarily divides people into blacks and whites. This dichotomy ignores two realities: first, that skin color actually forms a continuum; and second, that widespread racial mixing occurred historically and continues in the present (Basson 2008). Recent trends show, however, that a cultural view of race that includes a mixed racial identity is increasing. For the first time, the 2000 U.S. Census permitted people to self-identify as more than one race and 7 million people, almost half of whom were under 18, chose to do so

(Boynton 2006; Nobles 2000). Indeed, some scholars suggest that the United States and Brazil may be converging in their racial formations, as multiraciality undermines the American "binary race project" (Daniel 2006), though other scholars find this unlikely, and indeed, hope for a post-racial American society rather than a "hyper-racial" one similar to Brazil.

The culturally constructed nature of the American binary of race is revealed in antebellum Southern court decisions. For the purposes of school segregation, courts held that the Chinese were white but that individuals with at least 1/32nd "Negro blood" were black, even if their skin color was indistinguishable from whites (Dominguez 1986:3; Loewen 1988). In an ironic comment on the American construction of race, Haitian dictator "Papa Doc" Duvalier once told an American reporter that 96 percent of Haitians were white. Surprised and puzzled, the reporter asked on what grounds he arrived at this percentage. Duvalier explained that Haiti used the same procedure for counting whites—a "drop" of white blood—that Americans used for counting blacks (Hirschfeld 1996).

In the United States, we think of race mainly in terms of African-, Hispanic/Latino, Asian-, or Native Americans—that is, minority races. But white is also a racial identity. Because white is a cultural norm in the United States, however, the privileges and advantages that go with it are unconsciously assumed and largely invisible (T. Allen 1997; Frankenburg 1993; Hartigan 1997; J. Hill 1998). For whites, ordinary experiences such as shopping, buying or renting a place to live, finding a hairdresser, or using a credit card, do not generally involve a reflection on their racial identity. But for Hispanic/Latino Americans, Asian Americans, Native Americans, and particularly African Americans, these everyday activities cannot be taken for granted (McIntosh 1999).

The binary form of American racial classification grew out of historical conditions of slavery. The racial stereotypes that were used to justify slavery and later segregation were, shamefully, supported by the then emerging biological and social sciences, which legitimized races as hierarchically arranged natural categories characterized by physical, cultural, intellectual, and moral differences (Smedley 1998), though such hypotheses today are roundly criticized by anthropologists (Nisbett 2009).

There is much academic debate over whether social class or race is more important in explaining the American stratification system. In fact, the two factors, along with ethnicity, interact in complex ways to produce the particular social stratification system of the United States. Race is misguided as a scientific concept, but race as a social fact is centrally implicated in the American social stratification system. Race, particularly as it intersects with class, impacts every aspect of life, indeed, it impacts the potential of life itself. This is demonstrated by statistics on the higher mortality rate for both infants and mothers among African Americans (Chelala 2006; Stolberg 1999): a black male baby born in the United States today will live 7 years less than a white male baby (Calman et al. 2005:8). Racial disparities are also revealed in access to health care and health care outcomes. Cancer survival rates, death rates for heart disease and HIV/AIDS, and complications from diseases like diabetes, such as loss of a limb or kidney disease, are all substantially higher for African Americans than for whites. The causes of these and many other health disparities are clearly linked to unequal treatment and health care. And these are linked significantly to medical insurance. In New York City, for example, 30 percent of African Americans, Latinos, and members of other minority groups, are uninsured, compared to 17 percent of whites. Where people are covered by Medicaid, they are also treated differently by health care institutions, more likely, for example, to be seen by rotating medical students and interns, and thus less likely to receive coordinated medical care (Calman 2005:25).

Not only are race and racism highly correlated with industrial pollution (Akom 2008), as we see in this chapter's "Ethnography" section, but race compounded by class also affects the traumas caused and experienced in environmental disasters, as tragically demonstrated by Hurricane Katrina. In New Orleans, death came most often for the poor: those who had no private transportation, no credit cards, no wealthy relatives to rely on, no home insurance, and no resources to evacuate the young and the aged. As anthropologist Neil Smith notes, not just the effect of the hurricane, but the government's response to it, deepened the social grooves—of class and race—already built into New Orleans society (Paredes 2006; Smith 2005:9). In a sad confirmation of this view, a white vigilante caught shooting African Americans during the Katrina aftermath justified his action as a defender of his property and neighborhood, saying, "I'm not a racist. . . . I'm a classist. I want to live around people who want the same things as me" (Thompson 2009). Thus do race and class intersect!

Racial stratification also affects job and educational opportunities open to racial minorities; access to fair credit, salary levels, and accumulation of wealth, all of which affect social mobility; home ownership, mortgage rates, and housing foreclosures; use of public spaces; levels and types of violence; and interactions with law enforcement and the criminal justice system (Bajaj and Nixon 2006; New York Times 2005; Reed, Jr. 2006). As anthropologist Faye Harrison points out (2009), in spite of the election of the first African-American U.S. president, racism as a system is still embedded in American society, particularly in the forms of mass unemployment, mass incarceration, and mass disenfranchisement. Although African Americans and Latinos comprise only 25 percent of the national population, they are more than 60 percent

# Anthropology Makes a Difference

## The RACE Project

**RACE**
**Are We So Different?®**
A Project of American Anthropological Association

*Am. Anthropological Assn.*

This logo from the RACE: Are We So Different project emphasizes that race is not a sound biological concept but rather a social construction.

"Racism is not about how you look, it is about how people assign meaning to how you look." This idea underlies the *RACE: Are We So Different?* Project, an exhibit developed by the American Anthropological Association (AAA) aimed at educating the public about the reality—and the unreality—of race. The project was initiated by a group of anthropologists during the AAA presidency of Yolanda Moses and under the project leadership of Mary Margaret Overbey, an AAA senior staff member. Over 6 years in the making, the RACE Project is organized as a traveling museum exhibit, website, and program of educational materials, whose aim is to convey a comprehensive and understandable narrative about race and human variation.

The three main messages of the exhibit and its associated materials are that race is a recent human invention, that race is about culture, not biology, and that, despite the election of America's first African-American president, race and racism continue to be embedded in American culture, social institutions, and everyday life. The RACE Project uses the lens of history, science, and lived experience to explore the everyday experience of race, the contemporary science that is challenging commonly held ideas about race, and the history of the idea of race in the United States.

As Mary Margaret Overbey notes, "we like to think that America has moved beyond race but race remains a powerful, if unspoken, idea in the United States"

---

of those in prison. Black women, too, are overrepresented in prison, convicted at rates 10 to 35 times higher than white women. The effect of these disparities on minority communities are also reflected in many state laws that disqualify ex-felons from employment, public housing, welfare benefits, college student loans, and voting.

The importance of the intersection of race with class is indicated by long-standing inequalities in income and wealth between blacks and whites: in 2005, the median per capita income for blacks was $16,629; for whites it was $28,946. This economic gap is even more obvious in asset accumulation: in 2004, African-American families' median net worth was $20,600, and that of Latinos $18,600, only 14.6 percent and 13.2 percent, respectively, of the $140,700 median net worth for whites (Muhammad 2008). And the current recession has made this gap even wider: the meltdown in Detroit particularly impacted African Americans because the auto industry was one of their most important routes to upward mobility into the middle class, and the chances for new employment among African Americans is reduced by their lack of college education compared to other groups (Chapman 2008).

Educational achievement is only one among the many social institutions that reflect the stratified nature of class, race, ethnicity, and indigenous status in the United States. Anthropologists differ in explaining the variation in educational achievements among different American minority groups. Anthropologist John Ogbu argued for the importance of culture: he believed that "voluntary minorities," those who came to the United

States voluntarily in order to better their lives, are higher educational achievers than "involuntary minorities." Involuntary minorities include Native Americans; African Americans, who were brought here as slaves; and Mexican-Americans, who were incorporated through military policies of expansion (though their present population consists substantially of voluntary migrants and it is unclear how, or if, this has affected their educational achievement). Ogbu wrote that voluntary minorities believe in the possibilities for social mobility and thus emphasize education as a route to getting ahead (Gibson and Ogbu 1991:211–218), whereas involuntary minorities view the social hierarchy of the United States as unfair, permanent, and systemically discriminatory. They are less likely to believe that educational achievement will lead to success in life.

Ogbu (and others, see Patterson 2006) hold that many students from involuntary minorities cope with their subordinated social status by creating a secondary culture in which peer group values of cool behavior are more important than academic achievement. This "oppositional culture," characteristic of inner-city Latino and African-American ghettos, makes academic failure likely (see Smedley 1998a:697). Indeed, as anthropologist Philippe Bourgois (1996), in his study of East Harlem, New York, points out, the school itself is a significant place for learning this oppositional culture, which includes the necessary skills for surviving on the streets of inner cities—fist fighting, verbal jousting, and strategic cruelty at the expense of weaker classmates—all of which undermine effective learning.

(2007). Through videos, oral histories, visuals, and provocative interactive computer exercises, the RACE Project exhibit demonstrates that race is embedded in almost all areas of American life: home and neighborhood, health and medicine, and education and schools. Race and racism are not just inside our heads, but are built into American laws, culture, and social institutions.

The RACE Project has an historical perspective, underlining that racial and ethnic categories are made by humans and change over time. The exhibit draws on contemporary science to demonstrate that human beings are more genetically alike than they are different and that no one gene, or any set of genes, supports the idea of race. Race—or sorting people by physical differences—is a recent invention, not more than a few hundred years old. In the United States it is closely linked to the growth of the plantation economy, and in other countries is also linked to a specific set of political and economic histories.

The RACE Project is informed by extensive research interviews with high school students, community groups, museum visitors, and focus groups, as a way of discovering what people think about race and how they talk about it; the Project also involved collaboration with many scientific institutions and scholars from different disciplines. The interactive website (http://www.understandingrace.org) includes a virtual tour of the RACE exhibit, videos, historical timelines, and quizzes, as well as scholarly papers and a bibliography, and a family guide that helps parents talk to children about race. With its four-field holistic approach, anthropology was a natural to tackle this longstanding issue in American life. Check out the website: We know you'll agree that the RACE Project is an important contribution anthropology makes in its role of addressing significant issues in today's world.

---

Other anthropologists, while acknowledging the negative effect of the inner city oppositional culture, emphasize that these cultural patterns have their source in the poverty of inner-city neighborhoods; discriminatory educational policies such as low expectations of minority students; overcrowded and underfunded schools; and less-qualified teachers (Gibson 1997; Mateu-Gelabert and Lune 2003, 2007). They note that much social science research shows that most inner-city residents support mainstream cultural norms and behaviors, especially educational achievement (Anderson 1999; Mateu-Gelabert and Lune 2007).

Thus, where an oppositional cultural model puts the burden on inner-city students to change their culture, the model's critics emphasize that educational achievement among minorities depends on a fairer distribution of resources, more equitable educational policies, and the transformation of schools into safer, more disciplined environments. This approach emphasizes political economy, race, and class as more important than culture in explaining and maintaining the American system of racial, ethnic, and class stratification.

## The Cultural Construction of Race and Racial Stratification in Brazil

As in the United States, Brazil had a plantation economy whose core labor force consisted of African slaves. After 1888, when Brazil abolished slavery, the Brazilian government followed a policy of "whitening" by encouraging immigration of Europeans. Brazil, however, did not translate racial distinctions into law and interracial marriage and sexual relations were not illegal (Goldstein 1999; Sheriff 2001). This is in contrast to the United States, where such laws, affecting not only the marriage of whites with African Americans, but also with Japanese, Filipinos, and Native Americans, became central ideological tools for constituting and reproducing white supremacy (Pascoe 2008).

Interracial sex and marriage was not uncommon in Brazil, which is reflected in Brazilian racial self-identity. Today, individuals of African descent account for about 45 percent of Brazil's population, yet only about 15 percent of these people identify themselves as *preta* (black) on the census forms. The rest self-identify as *parda* (brown, of partially African ancestry). This self-identification is tied to social stratification: Brazilian understandings of race may be flexible, but the distribution of wealth and education in Brazil is profoundly unequal and racially based: whites at the top, blacks at the bottom, and *parda* somewhere between the two.

Brazilian racial classification is extremely complex, particularly among those who self-identify as African descended. In a community studied by anthropologist Conrad Kottak (1992:67), almost everyone had slave ancestry and most would have been considered black in the United States. However, almost half identified themselves as mulatto, an intermediate category between black and white. Again in contrast to the American racial determination by ancestry, in this village brothers and sisters were often classified as belonging to different races, using multiple physical criteria such as skin color,

## Polluted Promises: Race, Health, and the Environment

The relationship between pollution and health and racial and class stratification in the United States is well documented. A new ethnography of a small Southern community, by anthropologist Melissa Checker, documents the vulnerability of African Americans to industrial pollution and the ways in which a community response is shaped by racial stratification in both its successes and its failures. Checker's study of environmental injustice in Hyde Park, a black community on the outskirts of Augusta, Georgia, explores how racism shapes the very notion of "the environment." For middle-class and upper-middle-class professionally oriented environmentalists, the environment is defined as wild spaces and their conservationist movement is aimed at protecting these spaces from human intervention. The African Americans of Hyde Park, on the other hand, see the environment as something poisonous that they need to be protected from and as another example of racial discrimination. Checker's ethnography demonstrated that, when it comes to the environment, race trumps class. She found that middle-class Hispanics and African Americans suffered greater exposure to lead, dioxin, and mercury poisoning than lower-class whites (Checker 2005:14). Race is particularly potent in predicting where hazardous waste facilities are located. Environmental pollution is 500 percent higher in African-American communities than in white communities, and in the Environmental Protection Agency southeastern region, three-quarters of the largest hazardous waste landfills sit in majority black areas.

Checker calls the environmentalist movement that grew out of Hyde Park's attempts to deal with contamination an environmental justice movement. It aims to redress the disproportionate incidence of environmental contamination in communities of color and communities of the poor and enable them to live unthreatened by the risks posed by environmental degradation and contamination. She demonstrates that mainstream American culture, which views black urban communities as isolated, apathetic enclaves of violence and crime, engenders public policies that dismiss the voices of these communities and leads to the proliferation of toxic waste sites in their midst.

People flee their homes with their belongings after Hurricane Katrina struck New Orleans. The African-American community was hit particularly hard by this disaster, demonstrating how environmental issues are affected by racial stratification.

© MAI/Landov

nose length and shape, eye color and shape, hair type and color, and shape of the lips. The village used more than 10 different racial categories to describe people; these included mulatto, *mulatto claro* (light mulatto), or *sarara*, meaning a person with reddish skin and light curly hair. The terms were applied inconsistently, and there was wide disagreement among the villagers in placing themselves and others in racially defined categories. These placements were frequently mediated by social and economic class standings.

Although Brazilian culture has in the past emphasized its Euro-Brazilian history, Brazil, like many nations throughout Latin America today, promotes its mixed racial/ethnic heritage as a central aspect of its national identity and progressive ideology. In the 1940s, the influential Brazilian anthropologist and politician Gilberto Freyre promoted the idea that Brazilian national identity resulted from mixing people of European, African, and indigenous ancestry (Bailey and Telles 2006; Freyre 1946). Freyre, a student of Franz Boas at Columbia, adopted many of Boas's understandings of race and racial equality (Sánchez-Eppler 1992). His influence gave race mixing in Brazil a positive connotation, compared to the United States, where it has been generally repressed among both whites and blacks.

Freyre's work was used to promote the notion among politicians, academics, and in the culture at large, that Brazil was a racial democracy. The 1970 census, for ex-

The residents of Hyde Park were mainly sharecroppers from rural Georgia who used their savings to buy plots of land in a swampy area on the outskirts of Augusta after World War II. Beginning around 1970, Hyde Park residents began noticing the environmental and health problems besetting the community: T cell lymphoma, children fainting in school, children with asthma, fruit trees and vegetables rotting in previously healthy gardens. Their growing awareness that local people were getting sick and dying at an alarming rate paralleled the growth of industrial plants. A power plant, a ceramics factory, a junkyard, a wood treatment plant, and more than 35 chemical plants were all built near middle- and low-income black subdivisions, including Hyde Park, under low environmental standards and ineffective enforcement of environmental laws. "This positioned Hyde Park residents [and the residents of other African-American communities] on the front line of toxic hazards. . . . [the] ceramic factory left white dust on cars; its smokestack penetrated the skyline, pyramids of tires from the junkyards were higher than the houses; odiferous water filled the ditches in heavy rains; and the chemical companies contaminated the air, water, and soil." (Checker 2005:64). By 1990, the community noticed residents falling ill with mysterious or uncommon forms of cancer and skin diseases, and discovered one possible reason, a nearby wood-preserving factory. The factory had been sued by a nearby white community, but the black community was not informed either about the findings of contamination or the lawsuit. They were thus not eligible for compensation, so they decided to investigate on their own and found many other sources of pollution.

In 1991 the University of Georgia analyzed produce and soil from Hyde Park gardens and found elevated levels of arsenic and chromium; there were also well-founded fears that the groundwater serving Hyde Park was contaminated. In the absence of gas lines, which were not installed until 1970, community residents cooked on leftover creosote-treated wood chips from the wood factory, not knowing at that time that creosote was a cancer-causing agent. The noise pollution in the community was also an unbearable source of stress: release sirens from the ceramics plant sometimes blared for 8 hours straight. As information about the poisoned land in Hyde Park spread, it became impossible for residents to sell their property. The Hyde Park inhabitants were caught in a deadly bind: too poor to move, they were tied to an environment dangerous to their health and for many their poverty made health care unavailable.

As Hyde Park now became identified with decline and destruction, many residents ceased investing in their homes and the neighborhood became rundown, leading to a vicious downward cycle from which they had tried to escape in search of the American Dream. Checker's ethnography documented not only the racism of environmental injustice but also the ways in which the environmental movement in Hyde Park was shaped by the past history of racism and its continuation into the present. Ultimately, the movement achieved some successes, both by joining with mainstream environmentalists and by continuing its own culturally unique processes of political and civil rights activism. In her ethnographic study of one small community, Checker illustrates the many issues at stake in the fight for environmental justice.

## CRITICAL THINKING QUESTIONS

1. How does racism impact the health and life chances of African Americans?
2. How does the intersection of race and class impact environmental pollution?
3. What are some of the official and informal factors that have become built into America's racial stratification system?

Source: Melissa Checker, 2005. *Polluted Promises: Environmental Racism and the Search for Justice in a Southern Town.* New York: New York University Press.

ample, did not ask people's race; the government argued that because there was no race issue in Brazil, there was no need to ask the question (Bailey and Telles 2006:77). The public denial of race in Brazil has had both positive and negative effects. On the one hand, the linkage between Brazilian identity and mixed ancestry has probably made it easier for many Brazilians to negotiate their identity. It has also led to a society where, at least in theory, opportunity is open to people of diverse physical characteristics and ancestry. On the other hand, the persistent denial that race is a social issue has led to a widespread refusal to take discrimination and racial stratification seriously (Reichman 1995), in spite of the many studies that show that racial inequality exacts a high toll.

On every measure of social and economic well-being, Brazilians who self-identify as having African ancestry are far worse off than those who self-identify as white. Their illiteracy rates are far higher and their wages are far lower. Higher education is almost exclusively the domain of white Brazilians. In the United Nations Human Development Index (HDI) for all nations in 2000, which measures national quality of life, Brazil ranked 74th in the world. However, by the same criteria ranking white and African-descended populations separately, the white population would rank 48th and the African-descended population 108th (Roland 2001).

In Brazil, the educational disparities between whites and nonwhites are much greater than in the United

Unlike the American system of two races, white and black, in Brazil, the construction of race allows for a wide spectrum of physical characteristics. However, both cultures are characterized by racially based stratification.

States, a difference based partly on different traditions of public education (Andrews 1992:243). In the United States, providing education is a major obligation of the state and local government, but in Brazil, governments have assumed that responsibility only since World War II. Thus the general level of education in Brazil for both whites and nonwhites is much lower than in the United States; Brazil has a high rate of illiteracy, and higher education is almost entirely the province of white elites (Danaher and Shellenberger 1995:91). In contrast, most Americans, white and black, are literate, and most are high-school graduates, though black education levels lag far behind whites.

The comparison of Brazil and the United States clearly shows that racial stratification can occur in societies with very different cultural constructions of race.

# Ethnicity and Ethnic Stratification in the United States

In Chapter 11, "Political Organization," we emphasized the dominant anthropological perspective that ethnicity, like race, is a cultural construction that changes over time (page 253). As anthropologist Fredrik Barth (1998/1969) argued, ethnicity has important cultural content, but ethnic identity is constructed by groups to differentiate themselves from other similar groups. Barth further argued that ethnicity must be viewed as an aspect of rela-

tionships among groups in a society which may be competitive, conflictual, cooperative, or a combination of these. Barth's approach led anthropologists to ask new questions about how ethnicity works as a vehicle for association, collective action, and personal identity; and how ethnic groups and ethnic identities emerge, change, and disappear in responses to economic and social environments. Especially important for these processes are the contexts of political or economic inequality, competition between groups for resources, and more recently, globalization.

The continuous process of constructing ethnicity in the United States, and the many debates over ethnic diversity, largely focuses on the narrative of America as a nation of immigrants, who come to this country to pursue freedom from fear and the vision of the American Dream. This narrative takes place simultaneously with the ongoing project of creating an American national identity—a process that began with the American Revolution (A. Wallace 1999). From the beginning, ethnicity has been implicated in America's system of social stratification: the early, idealistic visions of America as a land of economic opportunity, upward mobility, and political freedom were largely restricted to immigrants from northern and western Europe. The American Constitution limited citizenship to those who were "free and white (and male)," which early on excluded Native Americans, Mexican Americans, and African Americans, and later excluded Asians and others from Latin America, southern and eastern Europe, and the Middle East.

Immigrants to America were identified by their national origins—the countries they came from and the cultures they brought with them—what today we call their ethnicity. But between 1880 and 1920, the era of the largest and most varied immigration to the United States, immigrants also came to be defined in racial terms. Southern and eastern Europeans, such as Greeks and Poles, were racially distinguished from the "Nordic" races of northern and western Europe. By the 1920s restrictive immigration laws effectively limited immigration to these Nordic groups, who were viewed as culturally, physically, and politically similar to members of the groups who held political power in the United States. Proponents of restrictive immigration claimed that members of the southern and eastern European "races" could never become good American citizens and that the United States would degenerate if it tried to incorporate them. Immigration of people from Asia, the Middle East, Africa, and Latin America was all but completely halted. The nexus between national origin and race in this period led to several legal cases in which the Supreme Court grappled with the definition of "white" as immigrants from India, Lebanon, and other places appealed

Multiculturalism highlights the cultural contributions different immigrant groups make to the American nation. One element of highlighting ethnic diversity is through ethnically focused parades, as in this St. Patrick's Day parade in New York City.

emerged, with competition for jobs and political power again at the heart of the conflicts, though the rhetoric of "culture clash" persists.

## Models of Immigrant Adaptation

Until the mid-20th century, the dominant American ideology regarding immigrants was **assimilation,** a process through which immigrants were expected to abandon their distinctive cultures and become "mainstream" Americans. Settlement houses, public schools, and citizenship classes were formed to teach immigrants "American" ways and motivate them to assimilate. The famous "melting pot" analogy compared American society to a stew in which all ethnicities were blended to produce an American identity (see Glazer and Moynihan 1970). To some extent this was true and by the 1950s much of the cultural distinctiveness of many ethnic groups had been lost in the so-called melting pot. However, the melting pot analogy referred primarily to ethnic groups descended from European populations. The pot excluded the racially defined minorities—Mexican, African American, and Native American—as well as the very small numbers of Asians or people from the Middle East. Additionally, although European ethnic groups lost much of their identity, they persisted and tended to organize around political goals and mobilize to gain access to economic resources (Glazer and Moynihan 1970).

their denial of entry into the United States based on their "nonwhite" racial status (Lopez 2006; Moore 2002).

Race remains a salient category in the definition of Native Americans and African Americans, whereas Latinos, including Mexican Americans, are less likely to identify themselves—and be identified by others—in racial terms now than they were 50 years ago (Strum and Selee 2004). Latinos are now more likely to figure importantly in the American narrative of ethnic diversity. For many ethnic groups of European ancestry the most obvious cultural differences, particularly language, have faded, but more subtle ethnic patterns, such as food preferences; verbal and nonverbal means of communication; the experience of health, illness, and pain; occupational choices; and voting patterns continue to exist (Cerroni Long 1993; Schensul 1997).

Although the dominant American national narrative is that it is "a nation of immigrants," in fact, debates over immigration have a very long history in this country. These debates were often couched in cultural terms: whether or not a particular group of immigrants brought with them cultural values and practices—republicanism, individualism, hard work, thrift, a commitment to freedom, and reason—that were consistent with or in opposition to American culture. But economic and political considerations were always present. At the height of immigration during the mid to late 19th century, for example, some widely expressed concerns were that an influx of immigrants would result in lower urban wages, or that immigrants would flood and then dominate the western part of the country, or that they would form voting blocs subject to political manipulation. Passionate debate over immigration—both legal and illegal—has currently re-

A policy of assimilation was also imposed on Native Americans, though even those such as the Cherokee, who had adopted many "American" cultural patterns, were subject to removal from and appropriation of their land by whites (Norgren 1996; Wallace 1999), indicating the importance of economic motivations by the majority population. By the mid-19th century, Native Americans had been largely forced onto reservations and become a captive audience for the teaching of the American values of individualism, Christianity, privately owned land, and the English language by missionaries and Indian agents of the U.S. government. Native Americans were also forced to send their children to American boarding schools, often hundreds of miles from their local communities. Such schooling was intended to permanently alienate native children from their cultures and languages.

---

**assimilation** The view that immigrants should abandon their cultural distinctiveness and become mainstream Americans.

Although these assimilationist policies largely failed to persuade Native Americans to adopt mainstream culture, the policies did result in loss of culture and land, and an increase in social problems such as alcoholism and poverty. By the 1930s, under the directorship of John Collier, an anthropologist who headed the Bureau of Indian Affairs, these government policies were reversed to support the strengthening of Indian cultures and societies (Norgren and Nanda 2006). In the 1960s, with the emergence of the civil rights movement, Native Americans again mounted a struggle, which continues, to reclaim their cultures and their land. These were only partially successful, however, and their position on the lower rungs of the social stratification system has hardly changed (Perry 2008).

After the civil rights movement of the 1960s, concepts of ethnicity and its relation to American nationhood changed again. **Multiculturalism,** which embraces cultural diversity as a positive value that adds richness to the whole society, emerged to contest older, assimilationist views and to challenge the theory of the melting pot. Most important, a new Immigration and Nationality Act, passed in 1965, explicitly aimed at reversing the discriminatory basis of earlier immigration laws. This act greatly expanded the number of people permitted to immigrate from previously discriminated against nations; abolished immigration quotas; gave high priority to the social goal of family unification; and put refugee immigration on a more structured basis (Fix and Passel 1994; Lamphere 1992: Introduction). As a significant result of this law, immigration increased substantially, particularly from China and Korea, the Middle East, the Indian subcontinent, the Caribbean, parts of Central and South America, including Mexico, and Africa, groups that were previously restricted by earlier immigration laws.

As anthropologists study these new immigrants, they take into account the variety of changing contexts of immigration as these are shaped by changes in local, national, and global economies and political conditions (Brettell 2003; di Leonardo 1984; Foner 2003; Lamphere 1992). Such conditions include the rise of international terrorism; the cyclical nature of global, national, and regional economies; the increase of illegal immigration; transnationalism (see page 186); and the events of 9/11.

## Muslim Immigrants after 9/11 in the United States and Europe

For more than 200 years, Muslims lived in almost near invisibility in the United States, blending into an ethnically diverse landscape. From 1870 to World War I, there was an increase in Christian immigration from Muslim-dominated countries such as Syria and Lebanon. In the effort to establish national organizations to facilitate their integration into American society, however, these immigrants constructed a common ethnic identity as Arab (Ewing 2008).

The 1965 immigration laws opened the United States to skilled, highly educated Muslim immigrants, from South Asia as well as from the Middle East. As the numbers and diverse origins of Muslims increased, the new immigrants began organizing as Muslims, focusing on maintaining Islamic religious practices rather than identifying themselves with their distinctive nationally based ethnicities. In the United States this is reflected in a more public presence for Islam, with expanded construction of mosques and Islamic schools (Abdo 2006), the expansion of a Koranically acceptable banking system that rejects charging interest on loans (*New York Times* 2009), and particularly after 9/11, the emergence of Muslim institutions providing information about Islam to the American public.

This new emphasis on Muslim religious identity is particularly strong among the younger generation, who frequently adopt public expressions of Islam, for example, young men wearing beards and young women wear-

American Muslims are generally well educated and are found in all walks of American economic life. Ethnically, they are a very diverse community, but today outward expressions of Islamic identity, such as modest dress for women, are becoming more widely adopted, especially among young people.

ing head scarves. This generation also expresses a greater interest in an intellectual understanding of Islam than their parents, along with a greater commitment to Islamic practice (Goodstein 2009). The religious orientation of younger Muslims has resulted in closer ties between Muslim immigrants with the many African Americans who have converted to Islam (Strum 2005).

Previous to 9/11, there was little ethnography or social science research on immigrant Muslim communities, but this is changing (Abdo 2006; Ewing 2008; see also Strum 2005, 2006; Strum and Tarantolo 2003). Particularly since 9/11, Muslims, like many other groups of immigrants, have faced considerable hostility in the United States (Nguyen 2005). The historically widespread American concerns about the incompatibility of various immigrant cultures—for example, Catholics; Japanese and other Asian Americans; Latinos; German anarchists; Mormons; among others (Norgren and Nanda 2006)—provide a broader context in which to analyze Muslim immigration (Moore 2002; Shryock 2002). However, recent surveys indicate that although Americans have both little knowledge of and a strong hostility toward Islam, American Muslims express almost as much satisfaction with their lives as other Americans, and on many socioeconomic indicators, such as annual income, compare favorably with non-Muslims (Pew Research 2007). Fifty percent of American foreign-born Muslims have attended college and most believe that with hard work they can fulfill their American Dream; this is a higher percentage than among African-American Muslims. Sixty-three percent of American foreign-born Muslims see no conflict between being a devout Muslim and living in a modern society, although some younger Muslims do identify with extreme fundamentalism. The title of a Pew Research Report, "Muslims: Middle Class and Mostly Mainstream," reflects the report's conclusion that American Muslims are highly assimilated and believe in adopting American customs (2007).

This picture contrasts in many ways with the experiences of Muslims in European countries (Goodstein 2009). Although after 9/11 young American Muslims increasingly express feelings of alienation from other Americans, the Muslim presence in America has engendered little of the extreme conflict and violence that has occurred in Europe. This is partly because European nations tend to be far more culturally homogenous than the United States and their Muslim populations make up a far greater percentage of their populations; in France, for example, Muslims are 10 percent of the population. European Muslims are also far less economically integrated into their societies. In France, for example, their widespread poverty, discrimination in employment, and spatial segregation in huge housing projects at the margins of big cities has been a cause of much conflict and frequent violent interaction with the police (Ireland 2005).

Many European Muslims, like the Turks in Germany, or the North Africans and West Africans in France, were recruited into the economy under conditions of economic growth. With economic contractions, they are now not only viewed as an economic burden, but often as a social problem and a source of cultural disturbance as well (Ireland 2005). Flashpoints between Muslims and Europeans include issues such as the building of mosques or the wearing of head scarves by Muslim women (Bowen 2007; Buruma 2006). So far, attempts to address these conflicts with the larger society by various European governments have been only partly successful (Laurence and Strum 2008).

## Latino Immigrants and Social Stratification in the United States

Latinos in the United States are a large and diverse ethnic group, sharing a common cultural heritage of the Spanish language (see page 115). The approximately 21 million Latino immigrants and their descendants include approximately 13 million Mexican Americans; 3 million Puerto Ricans; 1 million Cuban Americans; and 4 million other Latin Americans, mostly from Central America. Legal immigration of Latinos sharply increased subsequent to the 1965 immigration law, so a larger proportion

Latinos, who make up the largest number of immigrants in the United States, are often economically exploited by employers. In recent years they have become active in immigrant associations aimed at immigration reform and ensuring fair labor practices for their workers.

of Latinos, particularly Mexican Americans, are first-generation immigrants. As of 2002, Mexicans accounted for about 20 percent of the total legal immigration to the United States. It is also estimated that they constitute approximately three-fifths of the almost 12 million undocumented immigrant population (*New York Times* 2009; Strum and Selee 2004).

Much of the Mexican-American population of the United States originated in the populations of the southwest and California, whose settlement predated the 1846–1848 Mexican–American War. Originally rural agricultural workers, since the 1950s, Mexican Americans have become about 90 percent urban, concentrated in California, Texas, New Mexico, and Arizona. Puerto Ricans and Cubans, in contrast, initially migrated to urban areas, especially East Coast cities, whereas Cubans are mainly concentrated in South Florida. Political upheavals in Central America led to increasing numbers of both documented and undocumented immigrants from Guatemala, Nicaragua, and El Salvador, and since the 1960s there has been large-scale immigration from the Dominican Republic.

Although Mexican immigrants are still largely concentrated in the Southwest, since 1990, they have been drawn, primarily by low-wage meatpacking factory and construction employment, to other parts of the country that had not previously experienced Latino immigration, such as Arkansas, Georgia, Colorado, and North Carolina. Much of the work performed by Latino immigrants, as we noted for the meat-processing plants in the Midwest, is difficult, dirty, and hazardous, with no vacation pay or health benefits (Preston 2009). With the current downturn in the economy and a crackdown on undocumented immigrants through raids on their places of employment, stricter scrutiny of Social Security cards, the withdrawal of social services, local laws prohibiting driving licenses, and greater cooperation between local police forces and federal immigration agents, the already low economic position of Latinos is under increasing threat. And whereas many Americans losing their jobs can turn to the government for a safety net of unemployment insurance and job assistance, this is not available to undocumented immigrants, who are working longer hours for less pay, at any job they can get. As one sociologist pointed out, many factories in rural parts of the country are only able to hang on because of immigrant workers taking jobs other Americans will not take. As wages fall, employers tend to move from white employees, to black employees, to Latino employees and, in many cases, ultimately to closing their doors (Preston 2009).

**caste system** Social stratification based on birth or ascribed status in which social mobility between castes is not possible.

# Caste

In contrast to open class systems, characterized, at least theoretically, by individual social mobility, a **caste system** is based on birth, or ascribed status, and movement of an individual from one caste to another is not possible. Also, in class systems, people may marry outside their class. Castes, on the other hand, are hereditary and endogamous. Because caste membership is determined by birth and cannot be changed, caste systems are called closed stratification systems. Castes are ranked in relation to one another and characteristically associated with traditional occupations. A caste system, then, consists of ranked, culturally distinct, interdependent, endogamous groups, with rigidly maintained boundaries between the castes.

Caste systems exist in various cultures; in many West African societies blacksmiths, praise-singers, and leather workers function as endogamous castes. In traditional European society peasants and nobility were endogamous castes and in Japan the Burakumin people, who were set apart based on their participation in "unclean" occupations, represented a caste, although they were defined in racial terms. Indeed, before the 1950s era of expanding civil rights, black/white relations in the American South also incorporated many elements of a caste system. The ascribed status of race prohibited people from intermarrying, eating together, and interacting with each other in ways very similar to those of a caste system (Dollard 1937). Most frequently however, caste is identified with India, where it is deeply and historically embedded in culture and plays a central role in social stratification.

## The Caste System in India

The unique elements of the Indian caste system are its complexity, its relation to Hindu religious beliefs and rituals, and the degree to which the castes (or, more accurately, subcastes) are cohesive and self-regulating groups. The Hindu caste system contains four main categories, called *varna,* ranked according to their ritual purity, which is largely based on traditional occupations. The highest ranked varna, the Brahmins, are priests and scholars; next highest is the Kshatriyas, the ruling and warrior caste; third ranked are the Vaisyas, or merchants; and fourth are the Shudras, or menial workers and artisans. Below these four varnas is a fifth group, previously called untouchables, now called Dalits, who perform spiritually polluting work such as cleaning latrines or tanning leather. They are considered so ritually impure that their mere touch, or even shadow, contaminates the purity of the higher castes. A person's birth into any one of these caste categories is believed to be a reward or punishment for his or her actions in a previous life. Strict social rules maintain caste boundaries: inter-caste marriage and eating together is prohibited and a higher-caste person will not accept most kinds of food or drink from a lower-caste person. In Indian villages, the lowest castes are spatially and socially segregated, and prohibited from using high caste wells and temples.

In its rural setting, the Indian caste system involved traditional exchanges of goods and services between higher and lower castes. Families of various artisan and serving castes—such as carpenters, potters, blacksmiths, water carriers, and leather workers—perform their services for high-caste landowning families and in return receive food, grain, clothing, fodder for animals, butter, milk, small amounts of cash, and many other things. These relationships, which may continue over several generations, are viewed by the higher castes as of social benefit to all: landowners have a steady supply of available workers while the serving castes gain a relatively reliable source of subsistence. The lower castes, however, emphasize their exploitation in the system rather than its mutual benefits.

Although Indian castes are ranked on the basis of prestige rather than wealth, the gains of high caste position are not merely symbolic. The higher castes benefit materially as well as symbolically from their higher status; they use their considerable political power to maintain these material benefits and resist any efforts by lower castes to attempt to change the system. Although, on the surface, the lower castes appear to accept their low position, their conformity largely hinges on their awareness that economic sanctions and physical force will be used against them if they try to resist the system or rise above it. And indeed, in both local and regional arenas, violent conflict between castes has been frequent in rural India.

The traditional Hindu religious belief that individuals occupy a social position based on the virtue of their actions in a previous life is used to justify elite caste hegemony: the upper castes benefit from the widely shared Hindu belief that social position reflects an individual's spiritual achievement. Just as in the American class system, political and economic power furthers the interests of some social strata over others, a conflict obscured by widespread cultural consensus.

## Changes in the Caste System

The caste system in India, like any social stratification system, is not static. An important change occurred at Indian independence when "Untouchability" was outlawed by the new constitution and affirmative action programs for lower castes and untouchables were initiated. In addition to government action, groups may try to change their own caste status. Unlike a class system, change in

the Indian caste system relies primarily on group rather than individual mobility. A caste that has been economically successful in some new occupation may try to raise its prestige by adopting the customs of a higher caste, claiming a new rank for itself. These new behavior patterns are formulated by caste councils, and nonconforming members will be publicly censured or even cast out of the group, a serious sanction where caste membership controls so much of a person's life. As part of its attempt to increase its caste ranking, a lower caste may also invent a new origin myth, claiming it originally belonged to a higher-ranked varna than it is presently assigned.

These dynamics are illustrated by the Camars of Agra, a previously untouchable caste of leather workers and shoemakers, who became fairly wealthy due to an increased domestic and global demand for leather shoes. As their wealth increased, the Camars claimed they were actually Kshatriyas (the warrior caste), outlawed the eating of beef and buffalo among their members, and adopted some high-caste rituals. This attempt to raise their caste status was rejected by the high castes, however, who maintained the traditional caste boundaries limiting social interaction, including marriage. Subsequently, the Camars tried a different strategy, that of conversion to Buddhism, which put them outside the Hindu caste system altogether (Lynch 1969).

In addition to legal changes regarding caste in the past 50 years, other changes have also occurred (Fuller 1995). In rural as well as urban India, caste ranking appears to be less sharply defined than formerly, at least within the higher caste categories. This is partly the result of the increasing differentiation of wealth, prestige, and power *within* each caste. A very significant change is a weakening in the traditional connection between caste

In India, the upper-caste view that the lowest castes are content in their socioeconomic position is contradicted by the many protests of Dalits against the unfairness of the caste system.

and occupation. New occupations, such as factory work, government service, information technology, and the professions, which are not caste related, have opened opportunities, especially for the middle and lower level castes. At the same time, many low-caste occupations, such as potter and drummer, have declined as sources of income. Still, a connection between caste status and economic success continues, as the higher castes have primarily benefited by new economic opportunities through their previous accumulation of capital, their higher education, their business and social contacts, and their ability to speak English (Beteille 1998).

There is also a significant change in public discourse about castes, which are now commonly referred to in public as culturally differentiated communities or associations, rather than *jatis* (which literally means species) (Fuller 1995). In public, the strict maintenance of caste boundaries such as inter-dining, has weakened, particularly in cities. However, in private and in rural areas, many caste-related boundaries remain, particularly regarding arranged marriages. Affirmative action in education and employment, based on (low) caste status, which is incorporated into the Indian constitution, keeps caste

alive for more pragmatic reasons. Even with the rise of a new Indian class system, caste remains an important structural element in Indian society and is unlikely to disappear in the near future.

Both India's caste and class systems are changing under the impact of the global economy. India's current economic growth has greatly expanded the urban middle class while its newly expanded free-market ideology has meant cutbacks in government-supported education and medical care. This has disproportionately affected the poor: millions of cotton farmers are impoverished by a global system of trade in which the agricultural products of heavily subsidized farmers in the United States and Europe depress international prices. Because the Indian government does not provide much of a social support network and financial aid for farmers, they are forced to rely on the informal sector moneylenders, which often leads them into extreme and permanent debt. These conditions have contributed to the suicide of thousands of cotton farmers (Mishra 2006:50). India's new economic growth has meant that class, with its expression in luxury consumerism, as well as caste, is now a significant factor in the Indian system of social stratification (Luce 2007).

# The Global and the Local: The Global Economy and the Changing Class System in China

Globalization, neoliberal economic policies, and the rise of multinational corporations have led to increasing prosperity for some nations but also increasing economic inequality between and within nations (Schneider 2002). China is a good example of how the global economy impacts local systems of social stratification. In the Maoist period, people lived very harsh lives and certain social classes, such as rich peasants and merchants, were targets of harassment and violence, although the reigning ideology was one of egalitarianism and significant attempts were made to reduce inequalities in wealth and provide supports for poor farmers and workers. Today, many in China live more prosperous lives but this has come at the expense of increasing social differentiation, contrary to the Maoist ideology.

In just one generation China's exploding participation in the global economy has produced a rising inequality of social classes. As capitalism has moved forward those who have made it in the new society live side by side with the have-nots, and particularly large inequalities exist between rural and urban areas. This widening income gap is potentially subversive to China's official socialist ideology and the antigovernment protests arising from this inequality are a source of great concern to the government. The Chinese motto of the new economy,

"to get rich is glorious," has not fulfilled its promise to all sectors of society equally.

The People's Republic of China is ideologically committed to a society in which opportunity and wealth are widespread. Traditionally, China's social stratification system contained rigidly defined social classes: peasants, a small trading and artisan class, a legal and governing bureaucracy appointed through rigorous written examinations, and an emperor, his court, and his relatives. Intellectuals and administrators were highly regarded; merchants and soldiers were disrespected, and peasants had no status beyond the produce they contributed to the state.

In 1947, with the success of Mao Zedong's Communist revolution, the new state, the People's Republic of China (PRC), attempted to create a "classless" Marxist society. But after Mao's death in 1976, the PRC adopted a program of rapid liberalization and has since steadily moved toward capitalist relations of production, with its attendant increase in economic inequality. Millions of villagers migrated to urban areas in order to find wage-earning jobs to help support their families in the countryside. Because peasants must now pay for schooling, health care, and other basic services, agriculture alone frequently provides inadequate income. In many fami-

This skyline and grand avenue of the Pudong New Area in Shanghai was built on the recent economic prosperity of China, which led to growing inequalities between urban and rural areas. Currently hit by the closing of thousands of urban factories resulting from the global recession, millions of unemployed rural migrants are returning to their villages.

Although some rural migrants have succeeded in the cities, few of the rural poor have the skills to meet the demands of urban living. They are cut off from the privileges of urban life, such as universal education, high-quality health care, and individual family housing, and often do not know how to negotiate for proper wages or how to redress grievances when they are cheated. Although some farmers have benefitted by selling their produce under new free-market prices and some villages formed farming cooperatives that were more economically viable than individual farming, rural/urban economic inequality remains large.

With the global economic meltdown of 2008, however, urban as well as rural populations are now suffering. As exports dropped, thousands of factories closed, sending the millions of rural migrants who worked in them heading back to their villages with their dreams unfulfilled (Wong 2008). Whole villages and industries that depended on American consumerism are now finding themselves out of business and the Chinese government is under pressure, similar to that in the United States, to invest in infrastructure spending in order to put people back to work.

Social stratification systems, whether in the United States or in China, may be justified by cultural norms, but the global economy has local effects that may undermine the cultural bases of social stratification and eventually lead to significant changes in a stratification system.

### Key Questions

1.  How has the traditional Chinese social stratification system changed over time?
2.  What are some impacts of the global economy on China's social stratification system?

lies, both parents migrated to send money back home to their household, which typically consists of their child and the grandparents, and rural families are split up for years at a time. One peasant mourned, "... where rich city people call their one child 'little sun,' we call ours 'left behind, growing up without their parents'" (Yardley 2004).

# Summary

1.  **What are the differences between functionalist and conflict theories of social stratification?** Functionalist theory holds that social stratification benefits the whole society because it motivates people to undertake all the jobs necessary for the society to survive. Conflict theory emphasizes the conflicts that occur within stratified societies as different social strata, with opposing interests, clash with one another over goals and resources.

2.  **What are the major dimensions of social stratification and how do they relate to other aspects of culture and society?** The major dimensions of social stratification are power, wealth, and prestige, which are closely tied to occupation. The particular value system of a culture determines how these factors interact to determine where a person is placed in the stratification system.

3.  **What are the core elements of a social class system?** In a class system, social position is ideally achieved, rather than ascribed, although in reality class status is also ascribed. People can move between the social classes. Classes are largely based on differences of income and wealth, but also characterized by different lifestyles and cultural differences.

4.  **Is there a class system in the United States? What are its main features?** The culture of the United States emphasizes "the American Dream," the idea that one can and should improve one's life chances and material wealth. Although many Americans dismiss the importance of class in the United States, there are important material and life change differences in the different social classes. Inequality between social classes is increasing, as is downward social mobility.

5. **What is the purpose of the RACE Project? How is it based on an anthropological definition of race?** Anthropologists define race as a culturally constructed category that refers to groups of people *perceived* as sharing similar physical and other characteristics transmitted by heredity. The RACE Project, a traveling museum exhibit, demonstrates that although race is a scientifically invalid concept, racial categories are important in many systems of social stratification.

6. **What are the differences between the racial systems and racial stratification system of the United States and Brazil?** The United States racial system divides people primarily into two races: black and white. Brazil has a multiracial system that divides people into many different categories. However, both systems incorporate racism and racial inequalities, as evidenced by racial differences in wealth, education, health status, and occupation.

7. **What is the major narrative of America's story of cultural diversity? How has this changed over time?** The cultural diversity of the United States has largely been framed in terms of ethnicity based on the national origins of immigrants, largely ignoring the presence of African Americans, Native Americans, and Mexican Americans. Previously committed to the assimilation of cultural minorities, multiculturalism has now supplanted the concept of the melting pot and cultural differences among immigrants and other minorities are now viewed in a more positive light.

8. **What are some important characteristics of Muslim immigrants in the United States?** After the new immigration laws of 1965, Muslim immigration both increased and diversified. Their ethnic differences have become less important than their religious identity as Muslims, which is expressed in the expansion of Muslim institutions and practices, particularly among the younger generation. American Muslims are mostly middle class, in contrast to European Muslims, who are largely economically disenfranchised.

9. **What is the position of Latino immigrants in the American social stratification system?** The majority of Latino immigrants are from Mexico and half of these immigrants are undocumented. Latino immigrants are mainly engaged in low-wage agricultural and factory work and both legal and undocumented immigrants are vulnerable to the current hostility toward immigrants in the larger society, which centers on language issues and the strain on social services.

10. **What are the main characteristics of the Indian caste system and how is it changing?** In the Indian caste system, based on Hindu ideas of ritual purity, social position (caste) is largely ascribed (based on birth). Caste boundaries are sharply defined by prohibitions on inter-caste marriage and inter-caste sharing of food, as well as by some cultural differences. Although caste boundaries may weaken, especially in cities, a caste-based social system is partly maintained by low-caste benefits of affirmative action. As economic and occupational opportunities expand, the relationship between caste and class becomes less strong, especially in urban India.

11. **What has been the effect of globalization and the new economy on the social stratification system in China?** The People's Republic of China has moved from its official ideology of a classless socialist society under Mao Zedong to one in which the pursuit of wealth is encouraged and business entrepreneurs are honored. This has resulted in steep and increasing inequalities, particularly between rural and urban populations. Such inequalities were intensified by the 2008 global recession.

# Key Terms

| | | |
|---|---|---|
| achieved status | class system | prestige |
| apartheid | conflict theory | race |
| ascribed status | functionalism | social mobility |
| assimilation | life chances | social stratification |
| caste system | multiculturalism | wealth |
| class | power | |

# Suggested Readings

Davila, Arlene. 2008. *Latino Spin: Public Image and the White-washing of Race.* New York: New York University Press. An anthropologist with previous works on Latino culture and identities examines the shifting place Latinos have in the popular and political culture of the United States and their impact on U.S. national identity. A provocative look at the diversity of the Hispanic/Latino population in America and their integration into the nation, based on exposing the realities in contrast to the stereotypes of this substantial ethnic group.

Fredrickson, George M. 2009. *Diverse Nations: Explorations in the History of Racial and Ethnic Pluralism.* New York: Paradigm. A collection of essays written by one of America's foremost historians of race and ethnicity from a comparative perspective. Fredrickson's jargon-free writing style, deep research, insightful understandings of American history, and meaningful cross-cultural comparisons make his work of great interest to scholars from many disciplines as well as to the general public.

Jadhav, Narendra. 2005. *Untouchables: My Family's Triumphant Escape from India's Caste System.* Berkeley: University of California Press. A moving story about a Dalit and his family that introduces Western readers to this relatively unknown segment of Indian society.

Nguyen, Tram. 2005. *We Are All Suspect Now: Untold Stories from Immigrant Communities after 9/11.* Boston: Beacon Press. A highly readable account of the many ways different immigrant groups in different places in the United States were affected by the increased, and often misdirected, security operations by the government after 9/11, resulting in a climate of fear and growing intolerance.

Sharman, Russell, and Cheryl Harris Sharman. 2008. *Nightshift, NYC.* Berkeley: University of California Press. This ethnography is set in the context of the shift from manufacturing to the service sector of New York City after the 1980s, a sector that employs large numbers of immigrants. Using a storytelling ethnographic style, the Sharmans movingly reveal the commitment of these immigrants to the education of their children as the route to achieving the American dream.

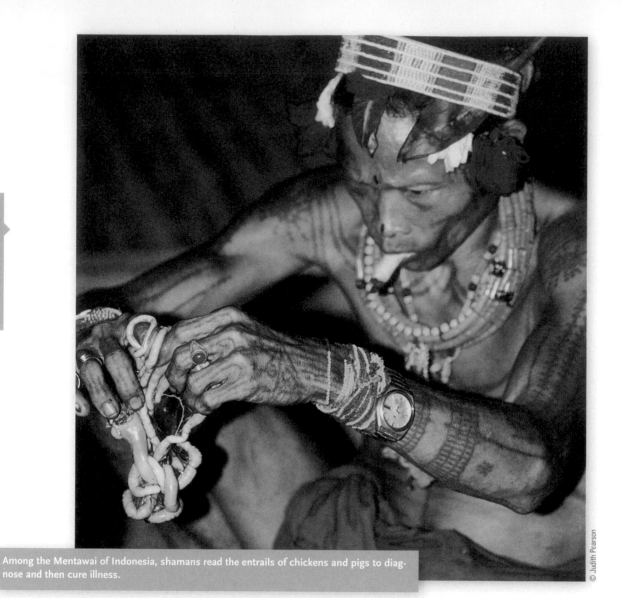

Among the Mentawai of Indonesia, shamans read the entrails of chickens and pigs to diagnose and then cure illness.

© Judith Pearson

**THINKING POINT:** In 1932, Leonard Howell returned to his native Jamaica from a time spent working for the U.S. Army. Once there, he had a prophetic revelation. He declared that the 1930 coronation of Ras (Duke) Tafari as Emperor Haile Selassie I of Ethiopia fulfilled biblical prophecies. Haile Selassie was the messiah and the hope of freedom for all black people.

—[See pages 308–309 for details.]

{chapter 13}

# Religion

In Trinidad, before harvesting, farmers make sacrifices to the *di,* the spirits of the first owners of their fields. They believe that failure to do so will result in a poor harvest. Because many fields are owned by absentee landlords, they also set aside a portion of the harvest to pay rent. Most people from industrialized societies would say that sacrifices to the *di* are supernatural and rent payments are part of the natural world. But is it really so simple? After all, as anthropologist Morton Klass (1995) points out, the farmer may have never seen a *di* or the landlord. He knows of people who have been evicted because they failed to pay the rent, but he also knows people whose crops have failed when they did not sacrifice to the *di.* Some people say that the *di* do not really exist, but others say that landlords really do not exist and everyone has a right to the land they live on and work. If we assume that the payments the farmer makes to the *di* are part of religion and those he makes to the landlord have nothing to do with religion, we seem to miss something essential.

All societies have spiritual beliefs and practices and anthropologists generally refer to these as religion; yet as Klass's example of the *di* and the landlord suggests, because not all societies distinguish between the natural and supernatural the way most Americans do, defining religion is surprisingly difficult. It is unlikely that any single belief is shared by all the world's people. Differences vary from issues as grand as the nature of life itself (whether we live once, as the Judeo-Christian-Islamic tradition teaches, or repeatedly, as the Hindu and Buddhist traditions teach) to issues as specific as sexual relations between men (discouraged by the Judeo-Christian-Islamic tradition but compulsory among the Sambia of Papua New Guinea [Herdt 1987]).

Despite the bewildering variety of religious beliefs and practices, in every society there is something that anthropologists (though not necessarily the members of the society) ≫

identify as **religion.** It is very difficult to formulate a concise definition of religion, but all religions share at least six common characteristics. First, religions are composed of stories that members believe are important. Second, religions make extensive use of symbols and symbolism. Third, religions propose the existence of beings, powers, states, places, and qualities that cannot be measured by any agreed upon scientific means—they are nonempirical. Fourth, religions include rituals and specific means of addressing the supernatural. Fifth, in all societies there are individuals who are particularly expert in the practice of religion. And, lastly, like other aspects of culture, all religions are subject to change.

In the 19th and early 20th centuries, many anthropologists were concerned with trying to find the origin of religion and trace its development. E. B. Tylor, one of the founders of anthropology, saw religion as beginning with **animism,** the notion that all objects (living and nonliving) are imbued with spirit, and evolving through polytheism to monotheism. Tylor and many of his contemporaries believed the evolution of religion was part of the more general human progression toward logic and rationality. This view of religion has long been discredited; no religion is any more or less logical than any other and none is more evolved than another. Although some anthropologists today still puzzle over the origins of religion, most are more concerned with the ways in which it operates in societies and ways in which it creates meaning in human life. In this chapter, we will briefly discuss some of the things that religion does in society and then turn to a more thorough examination of each of the six points enumerated above. <<

# What Religion Does in Society

Religion has many functions in a society. It may provide meaning and order in people's lives. It may reduce social anxiety and give people a sense of control over their destinies. It may promote and reinforce the status quo. But it does not always do these things. In some cases religion may make people profoundly disquiet or fearful. It may be an important force resisting the status quo and it may catalyze radical politics and, on occasion, murderous violence.

## Searching for Order and Meaning

From a purely materialist, objective point of view, the world appears to lack any purpose or meaning. However, human beings seem ill suited to live in such a world.

Even in desperate situations, in which all hope and reason seem gone, humans strive to find meaning and survive better when they do find it.

For example, psychologist Victor Frankl, a survivor of the Nazi death camps, found that those whose lives retained meaning, even in those camps, were more likely to retain their sanity and to survive than those whose lives lose meaning. Frankl came to believe that taking responsibility for finding meaning under all circumstances was a central task of life (1962:113).

Although there are many possible ways to give one's life meaning, historically and cross-culturally, religion is the principal means that people have used. In a sense, religions are symbolic images of reality that serve as a framework for interpreting events and experiences. Through religion, humans impose order and meaning on their world and often gain the feeling that they have some measure of control over it.

Although there is no single question answered by every religion, belief systems all provide responses to some of the central concerns of their believers. A key way they do so is by explaining aspects of the physical and social environment. Religions provide **cosmologies**—sets of principles or beliefs about the nature of life and death, the creation of the universe, the origin of society, the relationship of individuals and groups to one another, and the relation of humankind to nature. Such cosmologies give meaning to the lives of believers.

Religions provide a sense of order and meaning in a world that often seems chaotic. In hectic Bangkok, ethnic Chinese Thais offer prayer at Chi Se Ma Chinese temple.

**religion** A social institution characterized by sacred stories; symbols and symbolism; the proposed existence of immeasurable beings, powers, states, places, and qualities; rituals and means of addressing the supernatural; specific practitioners; and change.

**animism** The notion that all objects, living and nonliving, are imbued with spirits.

**cosmology** A system of beliefs that deals with fundamental questions in the religious and social order.

By defining the place of the individual in society and through the establishment of moral codes, religions provide people with a sense of personal identity, belonging, and meaning. When people suffer a profound personal loss or when life loses meaning because of radically changed circumstances, religion can supply a new identity and become the basis for personal and cultural survival.

All of the above may sound like religion is a force for peace and tranquility, and indeed, often it is. However, this is clearly not always the case. Beliefs give meaning to people's lives in a wide variety of ways. Sometimes these involve denying the physical reality or importance of the material world, even to the point of suicidal individual or group action (as in the cases of Jonestown, Heaven's Gate, the Branch Davidians, and many other groups). Sometimes models of meaning include unspeakable violence practiced on other peoples. Sometimes meaning is found in oppressing others or murdering them. The meanings that religion creates can be a chaotic wilderness of violence and destruction.

## Reducing Anxiety and Increasing Control

Many religious practices are aimed at ensuring success in human activities. Prayers, sacrifice, and magic are used in the hope that they will aid a particular person or community. Rituals are performed to call on supernatural beings and to control forces that appear to be unpredictable. Although such practices are widespread, their presence is usually related to risk. The less predictable an outcome is, the greater likelihood prayer, magic, and sacrifice will be used. For example, if you have studied for a test and know the material well, you are unlikely to spend much time praying for success. You are more likely to pray if you have not studied, and you may even bring your lucky pencil or another charm to the test.

Prayer and magic are prevalent in sports and games of chance. Anthropologist and former minor league ball player George Gmelch (2000) notes that professional baseball players are likely to use magic for the least predictable aspects of the game, hitting and pitching. Fielding has little uncertainty, and few magical practices are connected with it.

The efficacy of prayer and magic has never been demonstrated by convincing scientific experiments (see Flamm 2002, Tessman and Tessman 2000). Despite this, prayer and magic can be effective in achieving results indirectly. They may alter the emotional state of those who practice them (or whom they are practiced upon), reducing or increasing their anxiety and perhaps creating other psychological states as well. In many cultures worldwide, much of prayer and magic concerns curing disease or creating it in others. There is surely a strong connection between our psychological and physiological states but it is poorly understood.

## Reinforcing or Modifying the Social Order

Religion is closely connected with the survival of society and generally works to preserve the social order. Through religion, beliefs about good and evil are reinforced by supernatural means of social control. Sacred stories and rituals provide a rationale for the present social order and give social values sacred authority. Religious ritual also intensifies social solidarity by creating an atmosphere in which people experience their common identity in emotionally moving ways. Finally, religion is an important educational institution, inculcating the values and understandings central to the culture. Initiation rites, for example, almost always include transmission of information about cultural practices and tradition.

In reinforcing the social order, religion generally serves the interests of the powerful. However, religion may serve the powerless as well. At times, religion provides an escape from a grim political reality. Through the religious belief in a glorious future or the coming of a savior, powerless people who live in harsh and deprived circumstances can create an illusion of power. Under such conditions, religion provides an outlet for frustration, resentment, and anger. It can serve to drain off energy that might otherwise be turned against the social system. In this way, religion contributes indirectly to maintaining the social order.

Although in most times, religion is a conservative force, validating and reinforcing the historical conditions and beliefs of society, it can, under some circumstances, be a catalyst for social change. When the image of the social order that a religion presents fails to correspond to the daily experience of its followers, prophets may emerge who create new religious ideas or call for a purification of existing practices. Sometimes prophecies encourage people to invest themselves in purely magical practices that have little real effect on the social order. At other times, however, prophets call on their followers to pursue their goals through political or military means, which may result in rapid social change. The American civil rights movement, the Iranian revolution, the rise of the Taliban government in Afghanistan, and the conflict between Pakistan and India over the state of Kashmir are all examples of social movements in which religion has played a critical role.

## Characteristics of Religion

Anthropologists may attempt to analyze what religion does in a society. However, members of the society do not experience religion in these terms. They experience it through their beliefs and practices.

## Religion and Fertility

Most preindustrial and industrializing societies have very high rates of population growth. For example, in many African nations, women have, on the average, between six and seven children each.

In wealthier countries such as Canada, Italy, and Spain, the rate is between one and two children per woman. This shift from high to low rates of fertility is known as the "demographic transition." Because high levels of population growth are often linked to poverty, land scarcity, migration, and the loss of culture, anthropologists, economists, and experts on international poverty have been extremely concerned with the demographic transition.

Some experts believe that a basic understanding of mathematics is part of the demographic transition. They argue that in many societies, people simply do not think about numbers and therefore have few notions about the size of their families, how many children the average woman has, or how many children they desire. Because they do not count, they do not believe they have any control over these factors. If these beliefs are correct, the first step to limiting population growth is to teach people to count their children and understand that they can decide on the number of children they want. For example, Etienne van de Walle, a past president of the Population Association of America, has argued that numeracy about children is central to population control and that "A fertility decline is not very far away when people start conceptualizing their family size, and it cannot take place without such conceptualizing" (1992:501).

Anthropologist Sarah Castle, on the other hand, argues that the idea that people do not count their children is often based on a failure to understand that statements people make about fertility and family size are often based on religious ideas. Castle found that among the Fulani, a herding and farming society in Mali, West Africa, women rarely give numeric answers when asked how many children they want, frequently answering that it is "up to God." They do not count their children, or even point at them to confirm that they are theirs. Not only that, but they seem to show a lack of regard for their children, describing them as "not at all nice," "ugly," or "useless." Children are sometimes dressed in rags and straw; bits of broken gourd are woven into their hair. Mothers often appear indifferent to their fate, seeming not to care when their children are sick and grieving little if they die. Given these observations, it is easy for outsiders to conclude that Fulani do not care deeply for their children and take an extremely fatalistic view of them, believing that whether or not they have children, the number of their children and their survival rate are matters strictly in God's hands.

## Stories, Sacred Narratives, and Myths

At a fundamental level, all religions consist of a series of stories told by members of a group. **Sacred narratives** are powerful ways of communicating religious ideas. These narratives are not merely explanatory stories of the cosmos, but sometimes have a sacred power in themselves. This power is evoked when they are told or acted out. Sacred narratives may recall historic events, although these are often clothed in poetic and sometimes esoteric language. Anthropologists study the meanings and structure of these narratives.

Sacred stories or narratives are often called **myths,** but this is problematic. In some ways it is appropriate to use the term myth. When we think of myth, we think of stories of great deeds, explanations of origins of people, the world, or particular practices in it; stories of heroes such as Athena or Hercules; stories where time is compressed or expanded and reality is composed of many levels. These are indeed characteristics of religious stories. However, it is also true we use the word myth to denote a false belief, or a religious belief we do not share. Thus, we are likely to claim that our own religion is composed of history and sacred story, but other people have myths. For example, we may say that Christians, Jews, and Muslims have Bible stories, but Native Americans have myths. Clearly, we should apply the same terminology to others' religious beliefs that we apply to our own.

By explaining that things came to be the way they are through the activities of sacred beings, sacred narratives validate or legitimize beliefs, values, and customs, particularly those having to do with ethical relations. As Bronislaw Malinowski pointed out, there is an intimate connection between the sacred tales of a society and its ritual acts, moral deeds, and social organization. These stories are not merely idle tales, wrote Malinowski, "but a hard-worked active force; the function of myth, briefly, is to strengthen tradition and endow it with a greater

**sacred narratives** Stories held to be holy and true by members of a religious tradition.

**myths** Sacred stories or narratives.

Castle argues, however, that understanding the statements and actions of Fulani parents requires knowledge of their belief system. Fulani actions do not indicate an inability to count children or a lack of caring for them, but their reverse. Understanding Fulani beliefs about the supernatural world and beliefs about proper conduct is critical to analyzing their behavior.

The Fulani believe many aspects of the supernatural world are dangerous. There are sorcerers who inhabit human forms and those who are invisible or take animal shape. There are other spirits that are hostile to humankind. Critically, these sorcerers and spirits attack anything present in excess. As a result, it is very important that children (and other things as well) not be counted. For counting may show excess and draw the attention of spirits and sorcerers. Counting one's children or saying that one wants a certain number may cause the spirit world to reclaim them or prevent their births (Castle 2001:1836). It is critical that children not be praised as beautiful, smart, or helpful because that too is likely to draw the attention of spirits who might then make them ill or kill them. Castle found that families keep careful track of the average number of children women have in their communities. When communities experience more child deaths than expected, people become particularly cautious, taking measures to make sure their children do not draw the attention of spirits. Calling children ugly or worthless, dressing them in rags, or in some cases, hobbling them at night as one would a donkey are, in fact, measures to keep children from the attention of sorcerers and spirits and make sure they survive.

Similarly, parents' show of indifference might camouflage their feelings rather than demonstrating them. Fulani believe in a code of honor they call *pulaaku*. One aspect of this is to appear self-controlled and stoic at all occasions, including the sickness and death of a child. Thus, parents who appear extremely indifferent to a sick child will be understood by members of their community to be telegraphing their concern, demonstrating that they are deeply worried about the risks their child runs (Castle 2001:1836).

Castle's findings, and others like them, are critically important. If the high birth rate among the Fulani is not based on an inability to count and plan for children but is intended to counter the frequent deaths of children, programs to educate them about family planning, fertility, and conception will fail. Among the Fulani, and perhaps the vast majority of people in poor nations, reducing family size is linked to reducing the high rate of child mortality and improving economic conditions. This will lead to a short-term rise in family size but a long-term decline.

Religions narratives legitimize beliefs and social arrangements. In this image from the Temple of Osiris at Abydos, the Pharaoh Seti I (ruled 1294–1279 BCE) is confirmed in kingship by the Horus, the god of order (right) and Seth, the god of chaos (left). Egyptians believed that the spirit of Horus entered the Pharaoh and acted as his guide.

value and prestige by tracing it back to a higher, better, more supernatural reality of initial events" (1992:146).

A clear example of what Malinowski meant is provided by a portion of the origin narrative of the Hopi, an agricultural people who live in Arizona and New Mexico. Traditionally, blue corn was the staple of their diet. Blue corn is more difficult to grow than most other varieties, but it is a strong, resistant strain. Hopi life is difficult; the Hopi say "it is hard to be a Hopi but good to be a Hopi" (Loftin 1991:5). Through the growing of blue corn, the Hopi re-experience the creation of their world.

According to Hopi belief, in earlier, imperfect creations they lived underground. Just before the Hopi appeared on the Earth's surface, they were given their choice of subsistence activities. They chose blue corn and were given the *sooya*, or digging stick, to plant it. The techniques for the farming of blue corn were established by the god Maasaw, who taught the Hopi to treat the earth respectfully, as a relative. The Hopi believe that doing so recreates the feelings of humility and harmony that the ancestors chose when they selected the blue corn. Before the 20th century, the Hopi farmed their fields in work groups made up of clan members. Because their tradition holds that clans were given land to farm together as they became members of the tribe, Hopi reexperience the settlement of their land by various clans as they farm (Loftin 1991:5–9). It is easy to see how the Hopi creation story serves as a charter for society. The Hopi live their religious understanding of their world as they grow blue corn. The telling of such stories, as well as the actions that accompany them or are implied in them, reinforce social tradition and enhance solidarity.

## Symbols and Symbolism

As the story recounted in the previous section shows, religious stories make critical use of symbolism. Religious symbolism may also be expressed in material objects such as the cross, the Star of David, and the crescent moon and star of Islam. Masks, statues, paintings, costumes, body decorations, or objects in the physical environment may also be used as symbols. In addition, religions frequently use verbal symbols. The names for gods and spirits, and certain words, phrases, or songs themselves are often believed to be powerful.

Religious symbols are intrinsically **multivalent.** That is to say, they pack many different and sometimes contradictory meanings into a single word, idea, or object. Consider the Christian cross. Christians have been pondering the meaning of the cross for most of the last 2000 years. Among its meanings are death, love, sacrifice, identity, history, power, weakness, wealth, poverty, and many more. It means all these things simultaneously.

Because it carries so many meanings, the cross has enormous emotional and intellectual power for Christians. As a result it can be used in leadership. For example, the cross has been a critical military symbol from 312 CE when the Roman Emperor Constantine ordered his soldiers to paint it on their shields (Nicholson 2000:158), until the 20th century when it was a frequent feature of military insignia and propaganda in World Wars I and II. Desecration of the cross may inflame passions and provoke very strong reactions as well.

Symbolic representation allows people to grasp the often complex and abstract ideas of religion without much concern for the specifics of the theology that underlie them. The Christian ritual of the communion service, for example, symbolizes the New Testament story of the Last Supper, which communicates the abstract idea of communion with god. This idea is present in other religions but is represented by different symbolism. In Hinduism, for example, one of the most popular representations of communion with god is the love between the divine Krishna, in the form of a cowherd, and the *gopis,* or milkmaids, who are devoted to him. In the dramatic enactment of the stories of Krishna and in the singing of songs to him, the Hindu religion offers a path to communion with god that ordinary people can understand.

## Supernatural Beings, Powers, States, and Qualities

A great many important religious narratives and symbols concern the world of spirits and sacred powers. Although many religions do not separate the natural from the supernatural, all propose that there are important beings, powers, states, or qualities that exist apart from human beings. These beings, powers, states, and qualities are nonempirical. That is to say that there is no scientifically agreed upon way to measure their presence. Consider the god of Christian, Jewish, and Islamic tradition. Many religious people claim to see proof of god's existence everywhere. However, there is nothing that members of all religious traditions as well as those who do not believe could agree upon to measure to demonstrate the presence of god. Thus, science, which depends on such empirical measurement, can neither prove nor disprove the existence of god. God is nonempirical.

Most religions populate the world with nonempirical beings or spirits. Such spirits may be anthropomorphic, or human in form; zoomorphic, with the form of an animal; or naturalistic, associated with features of the natural environment. They are generally anthropopsychic; that is, they have features of personality similar to those of human beings.

Spirits can act in the material world. They can be happy or unhappy, stingy or generous, or can experience any other human emotion. The understanding of the spirits and souls of animals in hunting societies provides a good illustration. Among the Netsilik Inuit, the souls of bear, caribou, and seal were particularly important. The Netsilik believed that if the soul of an animal they killed received the proper religious attention, it would be pleased. Such an animal would reincarnate in another animal body and let itself be killed again by the same hunter. In this sense, a hunter who treated the spirits of the animals he killed properly would always hunt and kill the same animals. An animal soul that did not receive proper attention, however, would be angered and would not let itself be killed a second time. As a result, the hunt would fail. Particularly offended animal souls might become bloodthirsty monsters and terrorize people (Balikci 1970:200–201).

The term **god** is generally used for a named spirit who is believed to have created or to control some aspect

---

**multivalent** Containing many different and sometimes contradictory meanings in a single word, idea, or object.

**god** A named spirit who is believed to have created or to control some aspect of the world.

In religious ceremonies, humans may be transformed into supernatural beings. This masked dancer from the Côte d'Ivoire is not simply a person wearing a mask, but a person who has become a supernatural being.

there is God the Father, God the Son, and God the Holy Spirit; yet these are all part of a single, unitary god.

One class of spirit that may be singled out for special treatment is the **trickster**. Trickster spirits come in many guises, but their key characteristic is that they are interested in their own benefit, not that of human beings. Some tricksters, such as the Christian Devil, are personifications of evil. Others are much more sympathetic. They often combine attributes such as greed, lust, and envy with humor and wisdom. Tricksters are powerful, but they themselves are often fooled. In African religions, monkey and hyena spirits are often tricksters. In many Native American cultures, the key trickster spirit is Coyote.

In addition to nonempirical or supernatural beings, religions also posit the existence of states, qualities, or powers whose existence cannot be scientifically measured. Enlightenment, in the Buddhist tradition, is a state of being that is not subject to measurement and verification. Similarly, groups such as the Society for Ethical Humanism search for Truth, a quality whose objective description has eluded philosophers for millennia.

Religious beliefs often include the notion of an impersonal spiritual force that infuses the universe. In the early 20th century, R. R. Marett coined the term **animatism** to refer to this force. Today, it is probably best known as **mana.** Mana may be concentrated in individuals or in objects. For example, as noted in Chapter 11, chiefs in Tahiti had a much higher degree of mana than ordinary people. Mana gives one spiritual power, but it can also be dangerous and therefore mana is often associated with an elaborate system of taboos, or prohibitions. Mana is like electricity; it is a powerful force, but it can be dangerous when not approached with the proper caution.

Mana is most often found in areas (spatial, temporal, verbal, or physical) that are the boundaries between clear-cut categories. Hair, for example, is believed to contain supernatural power in many different cultures (as in the Old Testament story of Samson and Delilah). Hair is a symbol of the boundary between the self and the not-

of the world. In some religions, gods are of central importance, but this is not always the case. High gods—that is, gods understood as the creator of the world and as the ultimate power in it—are present in only about half of all societies (Levinson 1996:229). In about one-third of these societies, such gods are distant and withdrawn, having little interest in people, and prayer to them is unnecessary. An example is the creator god of the Igbo of Nigeria. Like other remote gods, he is accessible only through prayer to lesser spirits (Uchendu 1965:94).

A religion may be **polytheistic** (having many gods) or **monotheistic** (having only one god). However, the difference between them is not always clear-cut. In polytheistic religions, the many gods may really be different aspects of one god. In India, for example, it is said that there are literally millions of gods; yet all Indians understand that in some way they are all aspects of one divine essence. Conversely, in monotheistic religions, the one god may have several aspects. In Roman Catholicism, for example,

**polytheism**  Belief in many gods.

**monotheism**  Belief in a single god.

**trickster**  A supernatural entity that does not act in the best interests of humans.

**animatism**  Belief in an impersonal spiritual force that infuses the universe.

**mana**  Religious power or energy that is concentrated in individuals or objects.

self, both part of a person and separable from the person. Doorways and gates—which separate the inside from the outside and can thus serve as symbols of moral categories such as good and evil, pure and impure—are also widespread symbols of power. Because these boundary symbols contain supernatural power, they are often used in religious ritual and surrounded by taboos.

# Rituals and Ways of Addressing the Supernatural

Sacred narratives, symbols, spirits, and sacred power all find their place in religious ritual. A **ritual** is a ceremonial act or a repeated stylized gesture used for specific occasions (Cunningham et al. 1995). A religious ritual is one that involves the use of religious symbols. Through ritual, people enact their religion. Rituals may involve the telling or acting out of sacred stories as well as the use of music, dance, drugs, or pain to move worshippers to an ecstatic state of trance.

The specific content of religious rituals—the stories and symbols they use, and the spirits and powers they address—varies enormously from culture to culture. However, certain patterns of religious behavior are extremely widespread, if not universal. Most religious rituals involve a combination of prayer, sacrifices, and magic to contact and control supernatural spirits and powers. In addition, rites of passage and rites of intensification are found in almost all cultures.

## The Power of the Liminal

The word **"liminal"** refers to those objects, places, people, and statuses that are understood as existing in an indeterminate state, between clear-cut categories. Objects that are liminal, such as the hair and doorways described earlier, often play important roles in religious ritual.

Anthropologist Victor Turner (1969) wrote that rituals frequently generate liminal states and statuses in which the structured and hierarchical classifications that normally separate people into groups such as caste, class, or kinship categories are dissolved. Because of this, in ritual, people can behave in ways that would be clearly unacceptable under other circumstances. In some cases this includes role reversals. For example, many Japanese festivals included ritual transvestism, where community members dance in the clothing of the opposite sex (Norbeck 1974:51). In the Wubwang'u ritual among the Ndembu of Zambia, men and women publicly insult each other's sexual abilities and extol their own, but no one is allowed to take offense (V. Turner 1969:78–79). Ritual role reversals include class as well as gender. In Holi, the Hindu harvest festival, members of the lower class and castes throw colored powder (and in the old days, excrement and urine) at males of the middle and upper classes.

More controversially, Turner argued that in liminal states people experienced a state of equality and oneness he called **communitas.** In communitas, the wealthy and the poor, the powerful and the powerless are, for a short time, all equals. In the United States one example of communitas is the incredibly diverse crowd of over a million people who gather on New Year's Eve to watch the falling of the illuminated ball in the center of Times Square.

In state-level societies, institutionalized liminal statuses sometimes emerge. Organizations such as monasteries and convents where people live permanently as members of a religious community embody liminality.

Anthropologists often refer to rituals and statuses involving liminality as **antistructure.** Although all societies must be structured to provide order and meaning, according to Turner (1969:131) antistructure—the temporary ritual dissolution of the established order—is also important, helping people to more fully realize the oneness of the self and the other.

Though Turner's ideas are provocative, in reality people in higher statuses may experience the unity of communitas more than the powerless. The powerless may use liminal symbols and rituals of reversal to subvert the social order (even if temporarily), expressing feelings not of oneness, but of conflict with the powerful. Further, where liminal groups exist, either temporarily, during rituals or religious festivals, or permanently, associated with certain occupations, they frequently have low status and an ambiguous nature. This, paradoxically, is the source of their supernatural power and their perceived subversion of the social order, as illustrated by the hijras of India (see the "Ethnography" section in Chapter 10), whose sexual ambiguity contains the power both to bless and to curse.

## Rites of Passage

Public events that mark the transition of a person from one social status to another are known as **rites of passage.** Rites of passage almost always mark birth, puberty, mar-

---

**ritual** A patterned act that involves the manipulation of religious symbols.

**liminal** Objects, places, people, and statuses that are understood as existing in an indeterminate state, between clear-cut categories.

**communitas** A state of perceived solidarity, equality, and unity among people sharing a religious ritual, often characterized by intense emotion.

**antistructure** The socially sanctioned use of behavior that radically violates social norms. Antistructure is frequently found in religious ritual.

**rite of passage** A ritual that marks a person's transition from one status to another.

At the Hindu festival of Holi, some social rules are relaxed. Members of the lower class and castes throw colored powder (and in the old days, excrement and urine) at males of the middle and upper classes.

ends with a large ceremony that reintegrates the recruits—now soldiers—into society with a new identity.

## Rites of Intensification

In addition to rites of passage, most societies have **rites of intensification.** These are rituals directed toward the welfare of the group or community rather than the individual. These rituals are structured to reinforce the values and norms of the community and to strengthen group identity. Through rites of intensification, the community maintains continuity with the past, enhances the feeling of social unity in the present, and renews the sentiments on which cohesion depends (Elkin 1967).

In some groups, rites of intensification are connected with totems. A **totem** is an object, an animal species, or a feature of the natural world that is associated with a particular descent group. **Totemism** is a prominent feature of the religious of the Australian aborigines. In Aboriginal society, people are grouped into societies or lodges, each of which is linked with some species in their natural environment that is its totem. Under most circumstances, members of a groups are prohibited from eating the group's totem and in religious rituals, members of societies or lodges come together to celebrate their totems. The ceremonies explain the origin of the totem (and hence, of the group) and reenact the time of the ancestors. Through singing and dancing, both performers and onlookers are transported to an ecstatic state. In a classic description, French sociologist Émile Durkheim wrote:

> When they are once come together, a sort of electricity is formed by their collecting which quickly transports them to an extraordinary degree of exaltation. . . . [O]n every side one sees nothing but violent gestures, cries, veritable howls, and deafening noises of every sort. . . . One can readily conceive how, when arrived at this state. . . . a man does not recognize himself any longer. . . . [and feels] himself dominated and carried away by some sort of external power. . . .[E]verything is just as though he really were transported into a special world (1961:247–251/1915).

riage, and death and may include many other transitions as well. Rites of passage involve three phases (van Gennep 1960/1909). The first phase is separation, in which the person or group is detached from a former status. The second phase is transition and is often characterized by liminality. The individuals in this phase have been detached from their old statuses but not yet attached to a new one. The third stage is reincorporation, in which the passage from one status to another is symbolically completed. After reincorporation, the person takes on the rights and obligations of his or her new social status.

The rites of initiation for boys and girls described in Chapter 10 are good examples of rites of passage. Before these rituals, the boys and girls have the public status of children. Afterward, they have the public status of grown men and women. Other rites of passage effect similar changes of status. Baptisms and other ceremonies around birth move the new child from the status of not-a-community-member to membership in the community. Quinceañeras mediate between the status of childhood and that of young womanhood, eligible for dating. Marriages mediate between single and couple status. Funerals mediate between the living and the dead.

Basic training for military service is an example of a rite of passage with which many Americans are familiar. In basic training, recruits are separated from their friends and families and places of origin. They are taken to a military post, where they are given identical haircuts and identical uniforms. All signs of differences among them are minimized. No matter their position in life before joining the military, ideally they are treated identically during training. Training itself involves a wide variety of rigorous exercises and tasks designed to impart knowledge and build trust and camaraderie. In this state, they experience communitas, a shared identity along with the breaking down of barriers between individuals. Training

**rite of intensification** A ritual structured to reinforce the values and norms of a community and to strengthen group identity.

**totem** An animal, plant, or other aspect of the natural world held to be ancestral or to have other intimate relationships with members of a group.

**totemism** Religious practices centered around animals, plants, or other aspects of the natural world held to be ancestral or to have other intimate relationships with members of a group.

Rites of intensification create and reinforce group identity. They can be used for religious, political, or economic purposes. the Nazi Nuremberg rally, held annually from 1933 to 1938, was designed to reinforce enthusiasm for the Nazi party and showcase its power.

Thus, in dance and worship, the aborigines achieved an ecstatic religious experience of their shared identity. Durkheim argued that such experiences helped to bind the members of their society together. For Durkheim, totems were symbols of common social identity. When people worshipped them, they were, at the same time, worshipping the moral and social order of their society.

The religious rituals of the Australian aborigines may seem exotic, but Americans participate in similar observances all the time—and to the same effect. Some American rites of intensification are religious, but many are secular. One with which most students are familiar is the college football game and the rallies associated with it. If the game is "good" or the school has "spirit," these gatherings produce enormous excitement among their fans and transport them to "a special world," as Durkheim called it. They also increase collective identity. If you are a fan, you will probably feel intense identification with your school and your team at such an event. Identification with your team and the excitement of sporting events will help to keep you "loyal" to your school (and

hopefully encourage you to donate to it as an alumnus/a). Schools have totems (animal mascots) as well.

## Prayer

Any conversation held with spirits and gods is **prayer.** In prayer, people petition, invoke, praise, give thanks, dedicate, supplicate, intercede, confess, repent, and bless (Levinson 1996). A critical feature of prayer is that people believe that its results depend on the will of the spirit world rather than on actions humans perform. Prayer may be done without any expectation of a particular response from the beings or forces prayed to. When prayer involves requests, the failure of a spirit to respond to a request is understood as resulting from its disinclination rather than from improper human action.

When Westerners think of prayer, most probably think of words that are recited aloud or silently. However, there are many forms of prayer. For example, in Buddhist tradition, people may pray by hoisting flags or spinning wheels with prayers written inside them. Words addressed to gods and spirits are not always humble compliments either. For example, Benedict (1961:221/1934) reported that among the Northwest Coast tribes of North America when calamities fell or their prayers were not answered, people vented their anger against the gods by saying, "You are a great slave."

**prayer** Any communication between people and spirits or gods in which people praise, plead, or request without assurance of results.

## Sacrifice

Sacrifice occurs when people make offerings to gods or spirits to increase their spiritual purity or the efficacy of their prayers. People may **sacrifice** the first fruits of a harvest, animal lives or, on occasion, human lives. Changes in behavior are often offered as sacrifices. Many Americans are familiar with the practice of giving up something for the Christian holiday of Lent, a form of sacrifice intended to help the worshipper identify with Jesus, show devotion, and increase purity. In many religions, including Christianity, it is common to make a vow to carry out a certain kind of behavior, such as going on a pilgrimage or building a place of worship, if a request for divine assistance is answered.

Some sacrifices may have important material functions. For example, the essence of the East African cattle complex as practiced by groups such as the Nuer and the Pokot is that cattle are killed and eaten only in a ritual context. This is clearly adaptive. In the absence of refrigeration, animals must be consumed rapidly after they are slaughtered. One family could not consume a whole steer by itself, but this problem is solved by offering it to the community in a ceremonial setting. Cattle sacrifices happen in community feasts that occur about once a week. Because the portions are distributed according to age and sex by a rigid formula, meat can be shared without quarreling over the supply (Schneider 1973). Furthermore, the religious taboo that a person who eats ritually slaughtered meat may not take milk on the same day has the effect of making milk more available to those who have no meat.

## Magic

Magic is an attempt to mechanistically control supernatural forces. When people do **magic,** they believe that their words and actions compel the spirit world to behave in certain ways. Failure of a magical request is understood as resulting from incorrect performance of the ritual rather than the refusal of spirits to act.

Two of the most common magical practices are imitation and contagion. In **imitative magic,** the procedure performed resembles the result desired. A voudou doll is a form of imitative magic with which many people are familiar. The principle is that mistreatment of a doll-like image of a person will cause injury to that person. The Christian practice of baptism can also be seen as a form of imitative magic. Most Christians believe that in baptism, original sin, often ritually compared with dirt or a stain, is washed away with holy water. Christians generally do not see themselves as compelling God in the baptism ritual, but they do believe that if the ceremony is done properly by duly constituted authority, God will not fail to remove original sin from the child.

With **contagious magic,** the idea is that an object that has been in contact with a person retains a magical connection with that person. For example, a person might attempt to increase the effectiveness of a voudou doll by attaching a piece of clothing, hair, or other object belonging to the person they wish to injure. People in the United States often attribute special power and meaning to objects that have come in contact with famous or notorious people. Signed baseballs, bits of costumes worn by movie stars, and pens used to sign famous documents all become collectors' items and are imbued with special power and importance.

In many cultures, magical practices accompany most human activities. Among the people who live along the upper Asaro River in Papua New Guinea, when a child is born, its umbilical cord is buried so that it cannot later be used by a sorcerer to cause harm. To prevent the infant's crying at night, a bundle of sweet-smelling grass is placed on the mother's head, and her wish for uninterrupted sleep is blown into the grass. The grass is then crushed over the head of the child who, in breathing its aroma, also breathes in the mother's command not to cry. When a young boy kills his first animal, his hand is magically "locked" into the position of the successful kill. When he later tries to court a girl, he will use love magic, which in a particularly powerful form will make him appear in front of her with the face of another man to whom she is

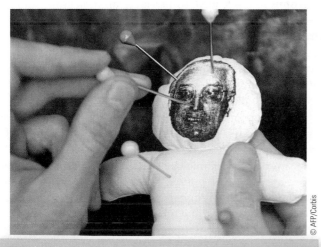

A voudou doll is an example of both imitative and contagious magic.

© AFP/Corbis

---

**sacrifice** An offering made to increase the efficacy of a prayer or the religious purity of an individual.

**magic** An attempt to mechanistically control supernatural forces. The belief that certain words, actions, and states of mind compel the supernatural to behave in predictable ways.

**imitative magic** The belief that imitating an action in a religious ritual will cause the action to happen in the material world.

**contagious magic** The belief that things once in contact with a person or object retain an invisible connection with that person or object.

known to be attracted. Both magical and technical skills are used to make gardens and pigs grow. One technique is to blow smoke into the ear of a wild pig to tame it. This is based on the belief that the smoke cools and dries the pig's "hot" disposition. Magical techniques are used to treat serious illness: blowing smoke over the patient to cool a fever (which is hot) or administering sweet smelling leaves with a command for the illness to depart (Newman 1977:413).

**Cargo Cults, Colonialism, and Magic** Cargo cults are religions known for their focus on rituals that involve the use of magic to acquire consumer goods. They were originally described on the islands of Melanesia, including the Solomon Islands and Papua New Guinea where Western culture has been spreading for the past several hundred years. Initially, Melanesians were receptive to Western culture, which reached them primarily through trade goods, called "cargo" in pidgin English. Islanders believed that welcoming missionaries and colonial governments would bring them cargo and riches. However, not only did Melanesians fail to gain wealth and power but, in many cases, they grew poorer and were more deeply oppressed.

In Melanesian society, secret knowledge and ritual action were major sources of power. Unsurprisingly, many Melanesians concluded that these were the source of the wealth and power of the whites as well. Melanesians observed that whites did not seem to work (at least as Melanesians understood work) but instead made "secret signs" on scraps of paper, built strange structures, and behaved in seemingly unusual ways. For example, they built airports and seaports with towers and wires and they drilled soldiers to march in formation. When the whites

On Vanatu, John Frum worshippers celebrate by marching in military formation. The letters USA are painted in red on their chests.

did these things, planes and ships arrived, disgorging a seemingly endless supply of material goods. Melanesians, who did so much hard physical labor, got nothing. Plainly, the whites' actions were a kind of secret knowledge and if Melanesians could learn it they could rid their societies of oppressive colonial governments and gain access to immense wealth.

So-called cargo cults appeared all over Melanesia. Though there was some variety, the cults shared certain common features. A local prophet announced that the world was about to end in a terrible catastrophe, after which God (or the ancestors, or a local culture hero) would appear, and a paradise on earth would begin. The end of the world could be caused or hastened by the performance of ritual that copied what they had observed the whites to do. In some places the faithful sat around tables dressed in European clothes, making signs on paper. In others they drilled with wooden rifles and built wharves, storehouses, airfields, and lookout towers in the hopes that such ritual would cause planes to land or ships to dock and disgorge cargo.

The first Europeans to write about cargo cults were colonial administrators, who saw them as the irrational beliefs and activities of primitive people who had succumbed to a kind of "madness." This view explicitly opposed Melanesian irrationality to European rationality and justified the Australian colonial administration's control over New Guinea (Buck 1989; Lindstrom 1993).

Anthropologists, who began describing cargo cults in the 1950s, attempted to understand their logic from the Melanesian perspective. They pointed out that cargo cults were based in the experience of Melanesians, particularly during World War II, when they witnessed Americans, Japanese, and others arrive and engage in seemingly odd ritualistic behavior. Such behavior was followed by planes and ships bearing an apparently endless supply of goods and by cataclysmic battles. Thus, Melanesians were not irrational, but rather working with the objective knowledge derived from their limited experiences. Furthermore, anthropologists pointed out that these observations and practices dovetailed neatly with central themes in Melanesian culture: the importance of wealth, the seeking of economic advantage through ritual activities, and the role of ritual leader as supernaturally inspired prophet.

Anthropologists also interpreted the movements as symbolic of the Melanesian desire for social equality with Europeans. Cargo cults were seen as a form of religious resistance against colonial rule (Worsley 1959). The repressive colonial regime made it necessary to clothe resistance in the religious form, as political rebellion would have been immediately suppressed. Anthropologists argued that when colonial rule ended, cargo cults would as well. Although they have not entirely disappeared, cargo cults have certainly declined in importance since independence.

Numerous aspects of American society have similarities to cargo cults. One good example is prosperity theology, or the Word-Faith Movement. The central tenet of prosperity theology is that God wants Christians to be wealthy. If they give money to churches (the more the better) and pray with enough sincerity, devotion, and frequency, God will reward them with material wealth in the form of cash or objects such as cars and houses. In other words, if they perform the correct rituals, they will receive cargo. Conversely, if they are poor, it is because they have failed to properly ask God for wealth.

Prosperity theology has become extremely popular in the United States and in Latin America. Oral Roberts was one of its best-known earlier promoters. Prosperity theology preachers such as Jan and Paul Crouch, Creflo Dollar, Benny Hinn, and Kenneth Copeland appear on hundreds of television stations in the United States and abroad. The prosperity theology–based Universal Church of God's Kingdom, headquartered in Brazil, claims 3 million followers in that country and another 3 million worldwide. Officials of Copeland's ministry estimate its annual revenue at about $70 million. The Crouches own TBN, the Trinity Broadcast Network, with an annual income greater than $100 million.

Some scholars have also wondered if the American economic system itself is a bit like a cargo cult. Lamont Lindstrom (1993) argues that Westerners are obsessed with cargo, with desire for wealth and material goods, and that they increasingly turn to ritual strategies to obtain them. The endless desire for consumer goods and beliefs that purchases of specific brands of cars, drinks, or clothing will make us forever young, sexy, and powerful may not create happiness or give us the lifestyles featured in advertisements, but they do serve the market well.

## Divination

A ritual practice directed toward obtaining useful information from a supernatural authority, **divination** is found in many societies. Divination discovers the unknown or the hidden. It may be used to predict the future, diagnose disease, find hidden objects, or discover something about the past. In many cultures, divination is used to discover who committed a crime.

The Naskapi, who hunt caribou on the Labrador Peninsula, use a form of divination called scapulomancy. In this divination ritual, a shoulder blade (scapula) of a caribou or other animal is scorched by fire. The scorched bone is used as a map of the hunting area, and the cracks in the bone are read as giving information about the best place to hunt (O. Moore 1969). This technique was also used in ancient China and Japan (de Waal Malefijt 1968:220). Scapulomancy may be adaptive because it randomizes the choices of hunting sites, a strategy that modern game theorists know results in the least chance of repeated failures.

Most Americans are familiar with a wide variety of divination techniques. Tarot cards, palmistry, flipping coins, and reading auras are all forms of divination. Some farmers use a divination technique called water witching or dowsing to find sources of well water. In one technique, the dowser holds a forked willow branch (a willow is a tree found by river banks and is "sympathetic" to water) in his hands as he walks over a property. When he stands above water, the wand is supposed to bend downward. Although dousing has a wide following in the United States, when subject to scientific testing, dousing does no better than chance (Vogt and Hyman 2000:xvii).

The practice of divination makes people more confident in their choices when they do not have all the information they need or when several alternative courses of action appear equal. Divination may also be practiced when a group decision has to be made and there is disagreement. If the choice is made by divination, no member of the group feels rejected.

Prayer, sacrifice, and magic can be found in most religious traditions, and the distinctions between them are more a matter of degree than of exclusive classification. For example, a great many prayers contain elements of sacrifice, and most magical practitioners agree that, in theory, it is possible that the spirit world will not honor their request, although they argue that in practice it does not happen.

# Religious Practitioners

Every society has people who are considered to have a special relationship with the religious world. These religious practitioners are charged with organizing and leading major ritual events. There are many different kinds of religious practitioners, but anthropologists generally organize them into two broad categories: shamans and priests.

## Shamans

Shamans are part-time practitioners. In many respects, **shamans** are average members of the community; they must hunt, gather, garden, or get up and go to work like anyone else. Their shamanic activities are reserved for specific ceremonies, times of illness, or crisis.

---

**divination** A religious ritual performed to find hidden objects or information.

**shaman** An individual who is socially recognized as having the ability to mediate between the world of humanity and the world of gods or spirits but who is not a recognized official of any religious organization.

Although learning to be a shaman may involve arduous training, such study is never sufficient. To be a shaman, one must have direct personal experiences of the supernatural that other members of the community accept as authentic. Shamans believe they are chosen by the spirit world and able to enter into it. They use prayer, meditation, song, dance, pain, drugs, or any combination of techniques to achieve trance states in which they understand themselves (and are understood by their followers) as able to enter into the supernatural world. They may use such contact to bring guidance to themselves or their group, heal sick people, or divine the future. Almost all societies have some shamans, but they are likely to be the only religious practitioners in band and tribal societies.

### Vision Quest

In some cultures, almost every adult may be expected to achieve direct contact with the supernatural. The **vision quest,** common among many Native American groups, was an example of this. In these cultures, a person was expected to develop a special relationship with a particular spirit that would give the person power and knowledge. The spirit acted as a personal protector or guardian. People seeking visions had very strong expectations of success and used fasting, isolation in a lonely spot, or self-mutilation to move themselves to an ecstatic religious state in which such a vision was possible.

For example, among the Thompson Indians of western Canada a boy would begin to search for guardian spirits between the ages of 12 and 16. He would prepare himself with ordeals such as running until exhausted and diving into ice-cold water. He would paint his face and wear special clothing. The nights before the quest were spent in dancing, singing, and praying around a fire on a nearby mountain peak.

The boy then went on lonely pilgrimages into the mountains, eating nothing for several days on end. He intensified his physical suffering by sweating himself with heated rocks over which he threw water and by whipping his body with nettles. This strenuous regimen continued until the boy had a religious experience. In an ecstatic state, he would experience meeting with his guardian spirit, usually an animal or bird, and receiving various forms of instruction. The guardian spirit would teach the boy a spirit song by which he could be called. He would learn how to prepare a medicine bundle of powerful magical objects (Pettitt 1972).

Although the vision quest was an intensely individual experience, it was shaped by culture. Among the Crow Indians, for example, several informants related the same vision and interpretation to the anthropologist Robert Lowie (1963). They told Lowie that they saw a spirit or several spirits riding along and how the rocks and trees around the riders turned into enemies who attacked them but were unable to do any harm. They interpreted this to mean that the spirits were making them invulnerable. This motif is common in Crow religious narratives, and the vision seekers worked it unconsciously into their experience. Another cultural influence is that most Crow Indians obtained their spiritual blessing on the fourth night of their seclusion, and four is considered a mystical number among the Crow.

### Shamanic Curing

Before the advent of modern technological medicine, illness was treated by means that we would today consider spiritual. Shamans frequently played important roles in curing. Illnesses were often thought to be caused by broken taboos, sorcery, witchcraft, or actions that caused the ill person to fall out of spiritual balance. In shamanic curing, the shaman, usually in a trance, travels into the supernatural world to discover the source of illness and what might be done to cure it. The following description of a Netsilik Inuit curing performance shows the shaman battling with evil spirits:

> The shaman, adorned with his paraphernalia, crouched in a corner of the igloo. . . . and covered himself with a caribou skin. The lamps were extinguished. A protective spirit called by the shaman entered his body and, through his mouth, started to speak very rapidly. . . . While the shaman was in trance, the tupiliq [an evil spirit believed to be round in shape and filled with blood] left the patient's body and hid outside the igloo. The shaman then dispatched his protective spirits after the tupiliqs; they. . . . drove the tupiliqs back into the igloo through the entrance; the audience encouraged the evil spirits, shouting: "Come in, come in, somebody is here waiting for you." No sooner had the tupiliqs entered the igloo than the shaman, with his snow knife, attacked them and killed as many as he could; his successful fight was evidenced by the evil spirits' blood on his hands (Balikci 1970:226–227).

If the patient died, it was said that the tupiliqs were too numerous for the shaman to kill or that after the performance evil spirits again attacked the patient.

In the modern world, shamanic curing often exists alongside modern technological medicine. People go to shamans for healing when they have diseases that are not recognized by technological medicine, they lack money to pay for modern medical treatment, or they have tried such treatment and it has failed.

Shamanistic curing does have important therapeutic effects. First, shamans generally do treat their patients

---

**vision quest** A practice common among many Native American groups in which individuals seek to achieve direct contact with the supernatural.

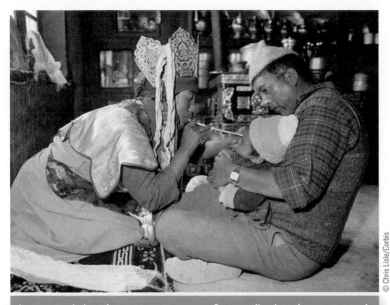

In many societies, shamans act as curers, often traveling into the supernatural to discover the source and treatment of a disease. In this picture, a shaman treats a child in Ladakh, India.

with drugs. All traditional cultures have a **pharmacopoeia,** or collection of preparations used as medication. Scientific testing has shown that some (though not all) traditional medicines are effective (Fábrega 1997:144). Second, shamanic curing ritual uses story, symbolism, and dramatic action to bring together cultural beliefs and religious practices in a way that enables patients to understand the source of their illness. In other words, such rituals present a coherent model of sickness and health, explaining how the patient got ill and how he or she may become well again. These models can exert a powerful curative force (Roberts et al. 1993). Curing rituals express and reinforce the values of a culture and the solidarity of a society. They often involve participation by the audience, whose members may experience various degrees of ecstasy themselves. Shamanic curing ceremonies work by cultivating an awareness that "one's body is located at a central intersection within a system of relations. Illness ruptures this pattern, and healing restores the perception of harmony" (Glucklich 1997:95). The ceremonies are cathartic in the sense that they release the anxiety caused by various disturbing events. The natural and supernatural forces that have the power to do evil in a society are brought under control, and seemingly inexplicable misfortunes are given meaning within the traditional cultural pattern.

## Priests

In most state societies, religion is bureaucratized; that is, it is an established institution consisting of a series of ranked offices that exist independently of the people who fill them. Anthropologists use the term **priest** to refer to a person who is formally elected, appointed, or hired to a full-time religious office. Priests are responsible for performing certain rituals on behalf of individuals, groups, or the entire community.

Priests are most often associated with gods who are believed to have great power. They may be members of a religion that worships several high gods, as in the religions of the ancient Greeks, Egyptians, and Romans, or only one high god, as in the Judeo-Christian-Islamic tradition. Where priests exist, there is a division between the lay and priestly roles. Laypeople participate in ritual largely as passive respondents or audience rather than as managers or performers.

People generally become priests through training and apprenticeship. For example, to become a cleric in any mainstream American religion, you would enter the training program (usually a seminary) of the appropriate religion. If you were successful, at graduation you would be certified by the religious body (or church) and generally given an assignment. However, priestly authority derives from certification by the religious institution the priest represents and this may sometimes be given with little or no training. For example, in Europe in the medieval and renaissance church, men often attained high positions because of their family and political connections rather than their piety or training.

In most mainstream religions in the United States, it is not considered essential for priests to have ecstatic religious experiences. However, this is not the case in all priestly religions. Although ultimately the priests' authority derives from certification, such status may give a person the right to seek direct contact with gods and spirits. For example, in ancient Maya states, priests were members of a ranked bureaucracy. In many cases, they were also political leaders and as such exercised both priestly and political authority. Their religious and political positions gave them the right to use ecstatic techniques to travel in the spiritual world. At the dedication of buildings consecrated to the royal lineage, priests, including the king and other nobles, take hallucinogenic drugs and let blood by perforating their penises and other body parts with special lancets. These methods created ecstatic states in which they would travel to the supernatural underworld to inform their ancestors of the new building and invite the souls of these former rulers

**pharmacopoeia** A collection of preparations used as medications.

**priest** One who is formally elected or appointed to a full-time religious office.

to inhabit it. A Mayan ritual might have looked like this:

> Against a backdrop of terraced architecture, elaborately costumed dancers, musicians, warriors, and nobles entered the courts in long processions. . . . A crowd of participants wearing bloodletting paper or cloth tied in triple knots sat on platforms and terraces around the plaza. . . . [T]these people would have prepared themselves with days of fasting, abstinence and ritual steam baths. Well into the ceremony, the ruler and his wife would emerge from within a building high above the court, and in full public view, he would lacerate his penis, she her tongue. Ropes drawn through their wounds carried the flowing blood to paper strips. The saturated paper. . . . [was] placed in large plates, then carried to braziers and burned, creating columns of black smoke. The participants, already dazed through deprivation, public hysteria and massive blood loss, were culturally conditioned to expect a hallucinatory experience (Schele and Miller 1986:178).

As among the Maya, priests in state societies may pursue ecstatic religious experience. However, states generally attempt to suppress independent shamans or bring them under bureaucratic control. Shamans claim the ability to directly contact the supernatural without certification by any institutionalized religion, and this challenges the authority of church and state.

## Witches and Sorcerers

Although not universal, belief in the existence of witches and sorcerers is a common element of many of the world's cultures.

**What Are Witchcraft and Sorcery?** In some societies, **witchcraft** is understood as a physical aspect of a person. People are witches because their bodies contain a magical witchcraft substance. They generally acquire this substance through inheritance and may not even be conscious that they possess it. If a person's body contains the witchcraft substance, his or her malevolent thoughts will cause ill to befall those around him or her. For example, the Azande, an East African group, believe that witches' bodies contain a substance called *mangu,* which allows them to cause misfortune and death to others (Evans-

Mayan temples were elaborate stages for rituals during which priests and rulers used dramatic techniques to travel into the supernatural world.

Courtesy of Serena Nanda

Pritchard 1958/1937). This sort of witchcraft is always understood as causing evil to others. It is only thoughts such as jealousy, envy, and rage that cause disease and ill fortune. A witch's positive thoughts do not help others. People are suspected of having the witchcraft substance when evil befalls those around them, particularly family members. Such witches are generally believed to be unable to prevent themselves from causing evil.

The conscious manipulation of words and ritual objects with the intent of magically causing either harm or good is **sorcery.** Bone pointing, a magical technique of sorcerers in Melanesia, is a good example of the use of sorcery to cause illness. The sorcerer first makes a magical arrow of a pointed object. Then he catches sight of his victim and viciously stabs the air as if to wound his victim and twist the point in the wound. Malinowski (1984/1922:75) reports that "This, if carried out properly and not counteracted by a still more powerful magician, will never fail to kill a man."

Cases of death from sorcery have been observed by anthropologists in many parts of the world. In a study of such reports, Walter Cannon (1942) argued that an individual who was psychologically vulnerable to begin with and aware that he or she was being attacked by sorcery would exhibit an extreme stress reaction that would have profound physiological effects. Such an individual may despair, lose his or her appetite, and slowly starve to death, unable to overcome the inertia caused by the belief that he or she is a victim. Persistent terror and the weakening effects of hunger may make the victim vulnerable to infectious agents as well as stroke and heart attack. Much work in biomedicine in the past 60 years confirms

---

**witchcraft** The ability to harm others by harboring malevolent thoughts about them; the practice of sorcery.

**sorcery** The conscious and intentional use of magic.

Cannon's ideas and details the specific biochemical pathways through which such reactions may occur (Sternberg 2002).

### Accusations of Witchcraft or Sorcery
Although people do actually practice witchcraft and sorcery, their main effects on society are probably through accusations. Leveling witchcraft or sorcery accusations against friends and neighbors is common in many cultures and serves various purposes.

The most frequent form of witchcraft accusation serves to stigmatize differences. People who do not fit into conventional social categories are often suspected of witchcraft. The European and American image of the witch as an evil old hag dressed in black is a good example. In traditional Western European society, social norms dictated that women should have husbands and children (or alternatively, they might become nuns). Impoverished women who remained in the community yet were unmarried or widowed without children violated this social convention and might be subject to witchcraft accusations. It is they who would have appeared as old hags dressed in black (Brain 1989; Horsley 1979). Those accused of witchcraft because they fail to conform may be ostracized and harassed but are unlikely to be killed or driven out of the community. They are valuable as negative role models, examples of what not to be. The lesson that a young girl might derive from the witch is: get married and have children or you might end up a witch.

Witchcraft and sorcery accusations may also be used to scapegoat. In times of great social change, when war, disease, calamity, or technological change undermines the social order, people's lives lose meaning. Under such circumstances, they may well turn to accusations of witchcraft. They may conclude that witches and sorcerers are responsible for their misfortunes and must be found and destroyed for their own lives to be improved.

Although we often think of witch-hunting as belonging to the Middle Ages, during that era the social order remained stable and accusations of witchcraft were fairly rare. The witch craze belongs to the 1500s and 1600s, a time of great artistic and technological achievement but social disaster. Plague swept repeatedly through Europe, and the medieval social and religious order collapsed in war and chaos. Where governments and religious institutions remained strong, witchcraft accusations were relatively scarce. However, in areas where these institutions collapsed, accusations were frequent (Behringer 2004). Under conditions of instability, people were willing to believe that witches were the cause of their misery and pursue reprisals against people they suspected of witchcraft. The accused witch who is a social deviant may be scorned and ostracized, but witches who are believed responsible for wide-scale social disaster are more likely to

Modern-day Wiccans are members of a religion of nature worship. In this picture, Gypsy Ravish, of Salem, Mass., a high priestess of Wicca, holds a ritual drum. The drum is used to raise energy during Wiccan ceremonies.

© Associated Press

be killed or banished. Current scholarship estimates that about 50,000 Europeans were murdered as witches, half of these within the borders of current-day Germany (Behringer 2004:149–150).

### Modern Witches, Wiccans, and Neopagans
Recent times in Europe and the United States have seen the emergence of religious worshippers who call themselves witches, **Wiccans,** or neopagans. A basic principle of most Wiccan belief is the threefold law, which proclaims that whatever good or ill people do in the world returns to them three times. Wiccans are no more likely to commit evil acts than are members of more mainstream religions.

Many Wiccan beliefs are derived from the work of 19th and 20th-century authors, particularly Gerald Gardner. Gardner claimed to have rediscovered the ancient beliefs of an aboriginal fairy race, and many Wiccans today say that they practice an ancient pre-Christian religion of nature worship. However, most scholars believe that Gardner composed his religion from a variety of modern sources (Hutton 1999; A. Kelly 1991; Orion 1995). This doesn't matter much to most Wiccans. For example, Diotima Mantincia, associate editor of the Witch's Voice website (http://www.witchvox.com), says: "It doesn't matter to me how old Wicca is because when I connect with Deity as Lady and Lord I know I am connecting with something much larger and vaster than I can fully comprehend" (in Allen, 2001).

**Wiccan (or neopagan)** A member of a new religion that claims descent from pre-Christian nature worship. A modern-day witch.

It is not clear how many Wiccans and neopagans there are. Many current estimates put the figure at somewhere between 100,000 and 200,000. The majority of Wiccans and neopagans live in the wealthy countries of North America and Europe. The majority, perhaps about two-thirds, are female and they have a higher than average level of education (Orion 1995:66).

# Religion and Change

As we have seen, religion is generally a force that preserves the social order. This may be particularly evident in stratified societies where the elite invoke religious authority to control the poor. In such situations, religion acts as a way of maintaining social, economic, and political inequality. However, even when religion does not support oppression, it is usually a conservative force, promoting the idea that the way that society has historically been ordered is right and proper.

Most religions contain implicit or explicit visions of the ideal society—images of the way a correct, just social order should look. No society actually achieves its vision; people never live exactly the way they are supposed to. However, most of the time religion validates society. The image of society as it should be is not so different from life in society as it is. As a result, most people feel that the society they live in is reasonably good (or the best available). If it hasn't achieved the perfection their beliefs tell them to strive for, it is at least on the right path.

However, if societies change very rapidly (as a result of colonization, disease, or technological change) or if groups are systematically enslaved and oppressed, the vision of the ideal world painted by people's religious beliefs may move far from their daily experience. People may feel that they are lost, that their vision of the ideal cannot be attained, or that, in light of new developments, it is simply wrong. Under these conditions, prophets may emerge, and new religions may be created. Religious movements vary in the effectiveness with which they bring social and political change. Even those that fail in these respects may create powerful new identities among their members.

In the United States, rapid cultural and economic change, economic oppression, powerlessness, and anomie experienced by different social groups have frequently led to new religious movements, sometimes with dire results. The prophecies of People's Temple leader Jim Jones or the Branch Davidian David Koresh provided new lives for their followers, giving them consistent and meaningful (if, in others' view, misguided) ways of understanding the world. However, these prophecies also led to the deaths of Jones, Koresh, and most of their followers.

Religion offers a series of principles, encapsulated in story, symbol, and interpretation. Believers organize their lives around these, with varying results. Religion can be a powerful force for social change, providing people with the rationale and motivation for political involvement and personal renewal. From the Iranian Revolution and the Taliban to the Christian Coalition and the 700 Club, religious leaders can have a powerful political impact. However, prophets may also give their followers convincing models that cannot exist in our material, social, and political world. When that happens, the results may be explosive.

## Varieties of Religious Prophesy

To begin a new religion or create a substantial modification in an existing religion, prophets must have a code that consists of at least three elements: they must identify what is wrong with the world, present a vision of what a better world to come might look like, and describe a method of transition from the existing world to the better world. Religious movements can, to some degree, be characterized by the nature of their understanding of the world to come and the methods for achieving that world.

Many religious movements are either nativistic or vitalistic. A **nativistic** movement aims to restore what its followers believe is a golden age of the past. The nativistic message is generally that things in the past were far better than at present. The reason things have degenerated is because the people have fallen away from the ways of the ancestors. The glorious past may be regained if certain practices are followed. The Ghost Dance, described in the next section, is a good example of a nativistic prophesy.

A **vitalistic** prophesy looks to the future rather than the past. For the vitalist, the past is seen as either evil or neutral. The golden age is in the future and can be achieved following the teachings of the prophet. The Rastafarian religion described in the "Ethnography" section in this chapter is a good example of a vitalist religion. Though it is not specifically religious, another example of a vitalism with which most Americans are familiar is Martin Luther King's "I Have a Dream" speech. In that speech, King describes a future where "the sons of former slaves and the sons of former slave owners will be able to sit down together at the table of brotherhood" and where children "will not be judged by the color of their skin but by the content of their character." King thus looks ahead to a then unprecedented chapter in American history.

---

**nativism** Focusing on the return of society to an earlier time that believers understand as better, more holy, than the current era.

**vitalism** Looking toward the creation of a utopian future that does not resemble a past golden age.

Often, the poor and powerless in a society create religions that challenge those of the mainstream. Such religions may rationalize their lower social position and emphasize an afterlife in which their suffering will be rewarded. In some cases, these religions have a **messianic** outlook; they focus on the coming of a special individual who will usher in a utopian world. Other religions are **millenarian;** they look to a future cataclysm or disaster that will destroy the current world and establish in its wake a world characterized by their version of justice. In many messianic and millenarian religions, members participate in rituals that give individuals direct access to supernatural power. They experience states of ecstasy heightened by singing, dancing, handling dangerous objects such as snakes, or using drugs.

The holiness churches common in Appalachia among coal miners and other rural poor who lead difficult and dangerous lives are a good example of a religion that has emerged in response to poverty and hardship. In church services, loud music, singing, and dancing cause some members to experience "being filled with the Holy Spirit." In this ecstatic state, they handle poisonous snakes, frequently throwing them at each other. Snake handlers are frequently bit and sometimes die. However, for members, snake handling proves that "Jesus has the power to deliver them from death here and now" (Daugherty 1993:344). For holiness congregation members, practices such as snake handling, faith healing, and glossolalia (speaking in tongues) are daily demonstrations of their ability to gain access to God's power. The fact that social elites are rarely members of such groups is proof that holiness members have access to forms of power that social elites lack (T. Burton 1993; Covington 1995).

Religious **syncretism** is often found among deeply oppressed people. In syncretism, people merge two or more religious traditions, hiding the beliefs, symbols, and practices of one behind similar attributes of the other. Santeria, an African-based religion originating in Cuba, is a good example (J. Murphy 1989). Santeria emerged from slave society. Europeans attempted to suppress African religions, but the slaves resisted by combining African religion, Catholicism, and French spiritualism to create a new religion (Lefever 1996). They identified African deities, called **orichas,** with Catholic saints and used them for traditional purposes: curing, casting spells, and influencing other aspects of the worshipper's life. In this way, they could appear to practice Catholicism to their masters as they continued to practice their own religions as well. Each *oricha*-saint has distinct attributes and is believed to control a specific aspect of human life. For example, Orunmila, identified with Saint Francis of Assisi, is believed to know each person's destiny and can therefore give guidance about how to improve one's fate. Santeria has spread through the Spanish Caribbean, Brazil, and North America, taking different forms in different locations.

Santeria is a syncretic religion that combines elements of the Yoruba religion from Africa with elements of Catholicism. In Santeria, Yoruba *orichas* are combined with Catholic saints. In this picture from Cuba, a Santeria devotee hods a saint's image during a ceremony.

## Religious Change in Native North America

The history of native North America provides a particularly good example of religious innovation. The European and (involuntary) African invasion brought disaster to Native American societies. Disease, warfare, and technological change undermined traditional native lifeways and belief systems. In this situation, a series of prophets and religious movements emerged. These included the prophetic movements of Handsome Lake, the Delaware Prophet, the Shawnee Prophet, and the Ghost Dance movement. As with the Rastafarian movement described in the "Ethnography" box, the timing and particular beliefs of these movements were closely tied to the social and political positions of their followers.

The visions of the **Ghost Dance** prophets of the second half of the 19th century were directly related to the expansion of Euro-American power. In the late 1860s, Wodziwab, a Northern Paiute Indian living in the Sierra Nevada, became the first Ghost Dance prophet. Wovoka,

**messianic** Focusing on the coming of an individual who will usher in a utopian world.

**millenarian** Focusing on a coming catastrophe will signal the beginning of a new age and the eventual establishment of paradise.

**syncretism** The merging of elements of two or more religious traditions to produce a new religion.

*oricha* An African deity identified with a Catholic saint in Voudou and Santeria.

**Ghost Dance** A Native American religious movement of the late 19th century.

# Ethnography

## The Rastafari: Religion and Resistance to Domination

The Rastafari religion began on the Caribbean island of Jamaica in the 1930s, a time when much of the Jamaican peasantry was being incorporated into the emerging capitalist economy as wage labor. Since that time, the Rastafari have spread throughout the Caribbean, into parts of the African states of Kenya and Ethiopia, and to the urban centers of the United States, England, and Canada. The Rastafari are an example of the successful emergence of a new religion that resists the culture that surrounds it.

In the 19th century, after slavery had ended in Jamaica, a peasant economy developed, organized around a system of localized, small-scale exchanges involving interpersonal networks of extended kin. But by the 1920s, capitalism, primarily in the form of the American United Fruit Company, had considerably undermined the peasant economy. Some Jamaicans benefited, but there was substantial racial stratification. Whites and mulattos accumulated wealth at the expense of black peasants. Lacking land or wages, these peasants soon found themselves penniless. As Jamaica became increasingly tied to the capital provided by the international economy, the pool of landless unemployed grew. By the mid-1930s, they numbered in the hundreds of thousands.

It was out of this milieu that the Rastafarians emerged. In 1930, Ras (Duke) Tafari was crowned emperor Haile Selassie I of Ethiopia. In Jamaica, the splendid coronation ceremonies, during which Ras Tafari was proclaimed "King of Kings" and "Lion of Judah," included a retinue of European dignitaries paying homage to the emperor and drew enormous publicity. Shortly after this event, Leonard Howell, a former cook in the U.S. Army (Lewis 1998), had a prophetic revelation. Born in 1898, Howell lived in the

JAMAICA
Kingston

United States from 1918 to 1932. Probably influenced by Trinidadian black nationalist George Padmore (Chevannes 1994), on his return to Jamaica in 1932 Howell declared that the coronation of Haile Selassie fulfilled biblical prophecies: Haile Selassie was the messiah and the hope of freedom for all black people. Howell proclaimed:

> People, you are poor but you are rich, because God planted mines of diamonds and gold for you in Africa, your homeland. Our King has come to redeem you home to your motherland, Africa. (W. Lewis 1993)

Although Howell is generally credited with being the first preacher of Rastafari, others had similar visions—among them, Robert Hinds, Joseph (Teacher) Hibbert, and Archibald Dunkley.

The Rasta leaders founded communities in and around Kingston, Jamaica, that emphasized what they understood as traditional African values. Haile Selassie became their central symbol, embodying the value of cooperative work efforts, respect for life, and the unity of all peoples of African descent. Through their belief that he is the messiah (a faith that his overthrow and

assassination in 1974 did nothing to diminish), the Rastas affirm blackness and their African roots. Through him, they proclaim their rejection of the values of capitalist society and the competitive marketplace.

A central theme in Rasta philosophy is return to Africa. The concept of return has several meanings. It may mean a literal passage to Africa, and some Rastas did actually move to Africa (though with little economic or social success). Alternatively, return may be interpreted as a call to live what Rastafarians believe are African lifestyles in whichever country they find themselves.

Two other important symbols of Rastafarian culture are the use of marijuana and a special vocabulary. The use of ganja (marijuana) has been common on Jamaican agricultural estates since the turn of the century and is considered a legitimate part of Jamaican working-class life. Although it was illegal, the upper classes approved of ganja use because it acted as a stimulant and an incentive to work. Rastafari, however, have reversed these meanings. To them, ganja is a tool of illumination. They use it to stimulate discussion at "reasoning sessions," where they gather to interpret biblical passages and to share beliefs about freedom, slavery, colonialism, and racism. Ganja, they believe, allows them to see through the evils of the bourgeois world, understand the roots of their oppression, and verify the authenticity of the Rasta lifestyle. Thus, whereas traditional use of ganja in Jamaica supported the dominant society, Rasta use subverts it.

In addition, the illegal sale of marijuana is part of the underground economy of many Rasta groups. The networks for growing it, preparing it for sale, and distributing

the second Ghost Dance prophet, was the son of an early follower of Wodziwab and had probably seen the Ghost Dance and heard its prophecies as a boy. Both prophets foresaw that the ancestors would return on an immense train. Following this event, a cataclysm would swallow up all the whites but leave their goods behind for the Native Americans who became his followers. Heaven on earth would follow, and the Great Spirit would return to live with the people (de Waal Malefijt 1968:344; Mooney 1973:771/1896). Wodziwab and Wovoka taught that the

**Rastafarians are members of a religion of resistance that started in the 1930s.**

suffixes, such as *ital* for *vital;* and the replacement of such diminutive prefixes as *under-* and *sub-* by their opposites. For example, *understand* is rendered *overstand.* For Rastas, the use of *I*-centered words focuses attention on the radical equality of all people and their identity with God. As one said:

Who is you? There is no you. There is only I, I and I. I is you, I is God, I is I. . . . We are all each other and one with God because it is the same life energy that flows within all of us (in Homiak 1998:167).

Rejecting aspirations of social mobility and participation in wage labor, the Rastas fashion a livelihood by forming networks of cooperation. In Jamaica, they engage in fishing, handicrafts, and hustling in the cities and, in the rural areas, in family-based subsistence agriculture with minimal involvement in the market economy. The small group of Rastas living in Shashemane, Ethiopia, rely on their agricultural produce and financial donations from abroad. In urban England, Canada, and the United States, Rasta economic activities tend to be small-scale cooperative businesses such as eateries, craft shops, small clothing stores, and the illegal sale of marijuana. All of these enterprises are based on the productivity of extended family networks, and Rastafari circulate their wealth through the community in the form of gifts, loans, parties, and many other personalized relationships.

The Rastas draw boundaries around themselves to exclude the outside world from participation in their economic and social relationships. There is strong solidarity against outsiders, particularly those in positions of authority. Rastas have rejected much of the social and psychological orientation of modern society, which they call Babylon. Although much of Rastafarian culture reflects the milieu out of which it emerged, including sources in the Hebrew and Christian testaments, Rastas have created a new religion and culture that allow them to survive in a manner consistent with their own worldview.

## CRITICAL THINKING QUESTIONS

1. The Rasta movement arose in Jamaica but has gained enormous popularity worldwide. What sorts of people are likely to be attracted to the Rasta message, and what elements of that message are likely to be particularly appealing to them?

2. Rastafarians are probably better known worldwide for their association with reggae music than with specific religious beliefs. Consider a reggae song by a major artist such as Bob Marley, Burning Spear, or Peter Tosh (do some research if you are not familiar with any of these artists). How do the lyrics reflect Rasta religious belief?

3. There are many new religions in the United States. Are any of them similar to the Rasta movement? In what ways are they similar?

Source: Adapted with permission from William F. Lewis, *Soul Rebels: The Rastafari.* Prospect Heights, IL: Waveland, 1993.

it are all based on friendship, alliances, and reciprocity. Although the Rastas have encountered difficulties with law enforcement in connection with their use and sale of marijuana, ganja has provided the Rastas with a livelihood that allows them independence and freedom from the capitalist system, a position they value highly. Ultimately, many Rastafarians hope that their world will become more and more based on reciprocity and redistribution and that money as a medium of exchange will disappear from their community.

Rastafarian linguistic usages include the invention of *I*-centered words, phrases, and

---

arrival of paradise could be hastened by specific rituals, including a series of dances, songs, and, in the case of Wovoka, the wearing of special clothing painted with designs he saw in his visions. Some of Wovoka's followers believed that these shirts had the power to protect them from bullets. Although Wovoka called for peace with the whites, he also taught that the whites would either be carried away by high winds or become Indians (Lesser 1933), and he urged Indians to return to their traditional practices.

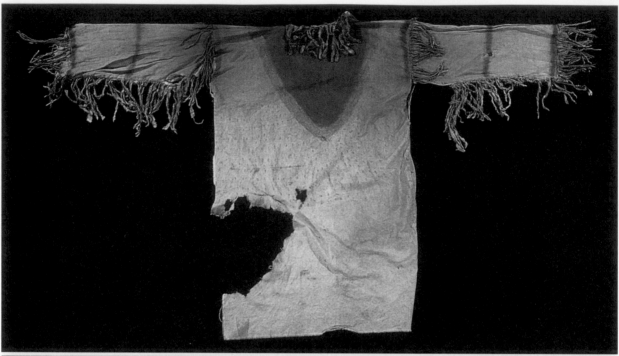

Some followers of the ghost dance prophet Wovoka believed that special ghost shirts would protect them from gunfire, but 350 Indian men, women, and children died at the massacre at Wounded Knee on December 29, 1890, including the individual who wore this ghost shirt.

The Ghost Dance prophecy was welcomed by many Native Americans who sent representatives to speak with Wovoka and learn the rituals of the Ghost Dance. The tribes heard the Ghost Dance vision in diverse ways, but it received its most radical interpretation among the Sioux, for whom the conditions of conquest and reservation life were particularly oppressive. Although the Sioux had defeated Custer at the Little Big Horn in 1876, they were eventually forced into submission. Starved and expected to survive by agriculture on nonproductive lands, they found a vision that promised the disappearance of their oppressors and the return of traditional ways extremely appealing.

During the fall of 1890, Ghost Dancing spread among the Sioux. Government agents were frightened by the popularity of the dance and the Sioux belief that the whites would shortly disappear. They ordered the Sioux to stop the dance; some but not all Sioux groups obeyed. The government tried to suppress the remaining dancers, but they fled into the badlands to perform the Ghost Dance ceremonies and await the cataclysm that would sweep the oppressors from the plains. A complex series of moves followed as the government tried to force an end to the Ghost Dance. The final act of the drama oc-

curred on December 28 and 29, 1890, when the Seventh Cavalry, the same unit that had been destroyed by the Sioux at the Little Bighorn, captured the last remaining band of Ghost Dancers. In the battle that ensued at Wounded Knee, about 350 Sioux Ghost Dancers, including many women and children, were killed, and the notion that doing Ghost Dance rituals would hasten the disappearance of the whites or protect Native Americans from them lost credibility.

The Ghost Dance religion did not end with the battle at Wounded Knee. Especially in Oklahoma, people continued to do the Ghost Dance into the 1930s, and one group of adherents continued to practice until the 1960s (Kehoe 1989). However, after Wounded Knee, the Ghost Dance declined, and by the first years of the 20th century, few people practiced it.

Another religion that appeared at about the same time as the Ghost Dance, however, prospered and has become a major force in Native American communities. The **Native American Church,** sometimes known as the peyote religion, now has between 250,000 and 500,000 members in the United States and Canada ("For Indian Church" 1995; "Field Full of Buttons" 1999).

A small, hallucinogenic cactus, peyote grows only in south Texas and northern Mexico. Although peyote has long been used in religious rituals by indigenous peoples in Mexico and South Texas, until the late 19th century it did not spread from this area. The spread of the modern peyote ceremony was due largely to the ef-

**Native American Church** A religious revitalization movement among Native Americans, also known as the peyote religion.

forts of Comanche, Kiowa, and Caddo leaders, including Quannah Parker, Apiaton (Wooden Lance), and John Wilson. Some of them had visited Wovoka, the Ghost Dance prophet, but all had rejected his teachings (Stewart 1987:80). Peyote leaders (called Roadmen) taught that God was accessible to Indians through the sacrament of peyote. In all-night meetings, members of the Native American Church chew peyote, pray and sing, and experience the presence of God. Quannah Parker said, "When an Indian Peyotist goes to [a peyote ceremonial meeting] he talks to God, and not about what man has written in the scriptures about what God said" (quoted in Brito 1989:14).

Although the use of a hallucinogen to achieve communion with the supernatural may seem an affront to mainstream American society, church leaders preached a vision they called the **Peyote Road.** The elements of the Peyote Road include abstinence from alcohol, attentiveness to family obligations, marital fidelity, self-support, helpfulness among members of the group, and attempting to live at peace with all peoples (Brito 1989; Stewart 1987). These are all values that are likely to be supported by Americans of any ethnic origin. The teachings of the Native American Church provide a pathway through which Native Americans can operate successfully in mainstream American society. At the same time, the notion that, for Native Americans, communion with God is possible through the use of peyote and the rituals surrounding it separates them from other Americans and allows them to affirm their identity. Thus, the church has been successful because it simultaneously allows its members to reinforce their identity and adapt to the demands of the larger society.

## Fundamentalism and Religious Change

In the past two decades, there has been an increase in religious fundamentalism. Islamic fundamentalism is implicated in the attacks of 9/11, the war in Afghanistan, attacks in London and Madrid, the continuing violence in Israel, Gaza, and the West Bank, as well as numerous other conflicts around the world. Membership in American Christian denominations that describe themselves as fundamentalist has ballooned. For example, between 1960 and 2000, membership in various Pentecostal churches rose from about 2 million to about 12 million. At the same time membership in less conservative churches fell. The Episcopal Church, for example, had about 3.5 million members in 1960 but had fallen to about 2 million by 2000. Jewish ultraorthodox groups such as the Lubavitch Hassidim have also been growing. Christian fundamentalism and Islamic fundamentalism are most in the news in the United States, but other fundamentalisms have been growing in importance as well. For example, in India, there are numerous Hindu fundamentalist organizations including the Bharatiya Janata Party (BJP), which plays a very important role in national politics.

Although members of fundamentalist groups sometimes see their religious beliefs as unchanging, the rise of fundamentalism is an important religious change. Further, fundamentalist movements tend to have specific original leaders and points of origin. For example, much of the American fundamentalist movement began with the publication of *The Fundamentals: A Testimony to the Truth,* a series of books published between 1910 and 1915. More than 3 million copies of these books were given to American Christian religious leaders. Modern Islamic fundamentalism is associated with the work of Sayyid Qutb (born in the Egyptian village of Musha described in Chapter 6) and the Muslim Brotherhood.

The rise of fundamentalism raises important questions for anthropologists. Three questions seem particularly critical. First, it is clear that the people we call fundamentalist have greatly varying beliefs. Hindu and Christian fundamentalists will find little to agree upon. Despite differences in belief, do fundamentalist groups have commonalities? Second, have these groups emerged in response to purely local forces or are there global forces at work that have encouraged the development of fundamentalism in so many different locations? Finally, is fundamentalism a problem and if so, what should be done about it? None of these questions can be answered easily or definitively, but we can propose some partial explanations.

Scholars have shown that fundamentalisms throughout the world have similar properties. Fundamentalists tend to see religion as the basis for both personal and communal identity. They tend to believe that there is a single unified truth and that they can possess and understand it. They tend to envision themselves as fighting in a cosmic struggle of good against evil. In this battle, demonizing the opposition is a perfectly appropriate tactic. Fundamentalists tend to perceive themselves as a persecuted minority even when this is not the case. They are selective about which parts of their tradition they emphasize and which parts of modernity they accept and reject (Almond, Sivan, and Appleby 1995; Haddon and Shupe 1989).

Determining the reasons for the surge in the popularity of fundamentalism is enormously difficult. To some degree, the pattern of emergence fits the model described in this chapter. In the past 50 years, the world has faced truly revolutionary changes. The forces of technology and global capitalism have permeated societies and brought people of disparate cultures together in a vast global network. However, this process has not been peaceful and has not produced equity. Traditional livelihoods, from cloth dying in West Africa to family farming

**Peyote Road** The moral principles followed by members of the Native American Church.

in the Midwestern United States, have been undermined. The gap between the wealthy and the poor, both within societies and between them, has grown. Governments that seemed to offer the possibility of peace and prosperity have been discredited. Faced with profound change, people look for stability and certainty. For some, fundamentalism of various kinds seems to hold this promise. Much (but not all) fundamentalism is nativistic; it presents a call to purification, to a return to the society and values of an earlier time, a time that believers understand as better, more holy, than the current era. However, it is also true that specific local histories play an extremely important role in the emergence of fundamentalisms. It would be impossible, for example, to explain the appearance of the fundamentalist radical group Hamas without reference to specific aspects of the long Israeli–Palestinian conflict. Similarly, the development of the Taliban is directly related to the events surrounding the Russian invasion of Afghanistan.

The forces that create rich ground for fundamentalism do not seem likely to abate any time soon. In fact, continual political and technological change seems likely to create even more extreme dislocations in the future.

The various fundamentalisms will probably continue to experience strong growth. This poses an extraordinarily difficult problem. On the one hand, people are surely entitled to their religious beliefs. The vast majority of people who might be classified as fundamentalist are innocent of any wrongdoing; they neither promote nor condone violence. They live peacefully with neighbors of different religious beliefs. On the other hand, fundamentalist beliefs have been repeatedly implicated in murderous violence: from the bombings of abortion clinics and the Olympic Games in Atlanta to the 9/11 attacks on the United States to the repeated anti-Muslim and anti-Sikh violence perpetrated by Hindu fundamentalists in India.

There is no doubt that much violence is enflamed by the harsh political and economic conditions of life and by the subversion of long-standing cultural practices. Promoting prosperity, more equitable distribution of resources, greater cultural sensitivity, and more responsive and honest government will certainly reduce popular support for violence. However, a small percentage of believers in all fundamentalist traditions understand the world in absolutist terms and see violence as a divinely ordained response.

## The Global and the Local: The Globalization of Religion in America

Although many people think of the United States as having an extremely secular culture, it is actually one of the world's most religious industrialized nations. When the French traveler and political philosopher Alexis de Tocqueville visited America in 1831, the religious aspect of the country was the first thing that struck his attention (1956: 319/1835–1840). Additionally, America has a long history of religious diversity. In that same era, the French diplomat Talleyrand is reported to have complained that the United States had 32 religions but only one sauce (Smith 2002).

Today, 96 percent of Americans say they believe in God. Church attendance has risen steadily in recent years (Warner 2005). In 1940, only about 37 percent of

The Most Rev. Francisco González, Rabbi Haskel Lookstein, and Dr. Ingrid Mattson, president of the Islamic Society of North America, join others including Dr. Uma Mysorekar, president of the Hindu Temple Society of North America, and Archbishop Demetrios, Primate of the Greek Orthodox Church in America, at the Presidential Inaugural prayer service in January 2009.

© Donovan Marks

Americans attended church regularly; today, according to the world values survey (Morin 1998), 44 percent do. This compares with 27 percent in Great Britain, 21 percent in France, and 4 percent in Sweden.

Not only are more Americans participating in religion, but religious diversity is increasing. There have been Muslim, Hindu, and Buddhist communities in America for more than a century, but these groups have grown enormously over the past several decades. In *A New Religious America* (2001) Diana Eck of Harvard University's Pluralism Project reports that the changes in U.S. immigration policies that have drawn new immigrants from India, Pakistan, China, Korea, Vietnam, and elsewhere have resulted in large increases in minority religions. These religions have drawn new American converts as well.

In the 1970s, members of non–Judeo-Christian religions accounted for less than 1 percent of the U.S. population. By the early 2000s, that number had grown to about 2.5 percent. Estimates of the membership of many religions are highly controversial, but in rough numbers, the Buddhist population is currently about 2.3 million and the Hindu population about 1.1 million (Smith 2002). According to Eck (2003:38), Los Angeles, home to many Asian immigrants, is "the most complex Buddhist city on Earth." Estimates of the Muslim population range from about 2 million (Smith 2001) to more than twice that number.

One result of the growth of these religions has been an explosion in the construction of places of worship. There are Buddhist and Hindu temples, mosques, and Islamic learning centers in most large American cities. Although these celebrate their respective traditions, they have in many cases become quite Americanized, offering classes, youth programs, and scout troops, programs similar to those often offered by churches and synagogues.

Eck points out that as religions expand they often meet with hostility. Thus, Muslims, Hindus, and Buddhists have frequently faced opposition from local groups and corporations. Zoning boards have sometimes denied them permission to build places of worship, and corporations sometimes tried to prohibit traditional garb such as head scarves. The conservative Christian Family Research Council attacked the U.S. House of Representatives for allowing a Hindu to offer the daily prayer. Pat Robertson, founder of the Christian Coalition, has repeatedly attacked Islam, calling it a religion that seeks to control, dominate, or, if need be, destroy others.

Despite some incidents of bigotry, most Americans have responded with tolerance. A good indication of this was the public reaction to the terrorist attacks of 9/11. Although in the month that followed the attack there were about 700 hate crimes committed against Muslims and Hindus, the overwhelming majority of Americans rejected hatred and reacted with support. In one incident, an attack on a mosque in Toledo, a Christian radio station called for people to come to the mosque and pray in solidarity with its members. More than 1500 individuals of all faiths came to join hands around the mosque. Around the nation, political and religious leaders from all groups and parties called for tolerance and support for the American Muslim community.

Mosques and temples are increasingly joining churches and synagogues on the American landscape. But if the acceptance of religious diversity holds a promise for members of minority religions, it hides a danger as well. Pressures for assimilation are strong, and it is difficult for members of minority religions to preserve their beliefs, practices, and identity. For example, the 2008 American Religious Identification Survey showed that Asian Americans are substantially more likely to indicate no religious identity than other racial or ethnic groups (Kosmin and Keysar 2009).

## Key Questions

1. Do you believe the increasing diversity of religion in America will result in meaningful changes in American politics?

2. In many countries, religious groups have fought each other. Thus far, this has not happened in the United States. Why do you think this is the case? Will there be religious violence in the American future?

3. How have religions in America influenced each other? Have you incorporated beliefs and practices from various religions in your own beliefs? Will you?

---

# Summary

1. **What characteristics do all religions have in common?** The enormous variety in people's beliefs and practices worldwide makes religion difficult to define. However, all religions are composed of stories, make extensive use of symbols, have immeasurable beings, powers, and states, have rituals, have specific practitioners, and undergo change.

2. **Describe several functions of religion.** Through religion, people create meaning and order in their world. Religion has many functions. Some of the most significant are explaining aspects of the physical and social environment, reducing anxiety in risky situations, increasing social solidarity, educating, ensuring conformity, maintaining social inequalities, and regulating the relationship of a group of people to their natural environment.

3. **What are sacred narratives and what roles do they play in religion?** Sacred narratives, sometimes called myths, are stories that express religious ideas. Sacred narratives explain and validate or legitimize beliefs, values, and customs.

4. **What is the importance of symbols in religion?** Religious symbols are a means by which abstract ideas can be expressed in terms that most people can grasp.

5. **What roles do supernatural beings and powers play in religion?** Most religions assume the world to be populated with nonempirical beings. Religions teach that such

beings have life, personality, and power. Some common forms are gods, spirits, and tricksters. Additionally, religions usually postulate that people, objects, or places may be imbued with spiritual power, or mana.

6. **What is liminality and what is its importance in religion?** Many rituals involve liminality, or "betweeness." In states of liminality normal social rules may be overturned and people may experience temporary states of equality and oneness, or communitas.

7. **What is a rite of passage?** A rite of passage is a public ritual that marks a person's transition from one status to another. Examples of rites of passage include initiation rituals, marriages, and funerals.

8. **What is a rite of intensification?** A rite of intensification is a ritual that strengthens group identity and reinforces the values and norms of the community. Rites of intensification often involve the use of totems, animals, plants, or other aspects of the natural world that are held to be ancestral to a group or have a strong relationship with it.

9. **What are prayer, sacrifice, and magic? What are critical differences among them?** Prayer, sacrifice, and magic are rituals used by individuals and groups to interact with the world of the supernatural. Most religions include examples of all three. The key difference between the three is the degree to which people believe their own actions determine outcomes. Also common is the use of divination, a religious technique to discover the hidden.

10. **What are shamans and where are they found?** Shamans are religious practitioners whose legitimacy depends on their ability to achieve direct contact with the supernatural world. They are not members of bureaucracies and often mediate between their communities and the supernatural world. Shamans are found in most societies.

11. **What are priests and where are they found?** Priests are professional religious specialists who hold offices in bureaucracies. Although priests' authority depends on their official positions, they may also use ecstatic techniques to contact the supernatural. Priests are typical of socially stratified societies.

12. **What is the difference between witchcraft and sorcery?** Witchcraft and sorcery are common elements of belief in many societies. Some anthropologists differentiate between witches and sorcerers. Witches are people who unconsciously use their evil thoughts to harm people. Sorcerers use magic for both good and evil purposes.

13. **What are the critical functions of accusations of witchcraft and sorcery?** Although people do perform magic, accusations that others are sorcerers or witches probably have a greater effect on society. Such accusations may function to promote conformity and explain catastrophic events.

14. **What are the varieties of religious prophecy and under what conditions are they most likely to occur?** Prophecies can be described as looking back to a previous time (nativistic), looking forward to a utopian future (vitalistic), or merging elements of two or more religious systems (syncretic). Prophecies are most likely to be successful under conditions of oppression, radical change, and loss of identity.

15. **What was the Ghost Dance and what is the Native American Church?** The Ghost Dance was a Native American religious movement of the late 19th century. Ghost Dance prophets envisioned the restoration of Native American power in the western United States. The Native American Church is a religious movement originating in the 19th century and teaching that God is accessible to Native Americans through the use of peyote.

16. **Under what conditions does fundamentalism occur and what are its characteristics?** Fundamentalism tends to occur in times of rapid change. Fundamentalists view religion as the basis for both personal and communal identity and believe that there is a single truth that they can know. They understand the world as a battle between good and evil and believe they are a persecuted minority even when this is not the case. Fundamentalists are selective about the parts of their tradition they emphasize and the parts of modernity they reject.

# Key Terms

animatism

animism

antistructure

communitas

contagious magic

cosmology

divination

Ghost Dance

god

imitative magic

liminal

magic

mana

messianic

millenarian

monotheism

multivalent

myths

Native American Church

nativism

*oricha*

Peyote Road

pharmacopoeia

polytheism

prayer

priest

religion

rite of intensification

rite of passage

ritual

sacred narratives

sacrifice

shaman

sorcery

syncretism

totem

totemism

trickster

vision quest

vitalism

Wiccan (or neopagan)

witchcraft

# Suggested Readings

Brown, Karen McCarthy. 2001. *Mama Lola: A Vodou Priestess in Brooklyn.* Berkeley: University of California Press. This outstanding person-centered account illustrates that ethnography is a human relationship and introduces a fascinating religion to the reader.

Covington, Dennis. 1995. *Salvation on Sand Mountain: Snake Handling and Redemption in Southern Appalachia.* Reading, MA: Addison-Wesley. This powerful account of a snake-handling church in Alabama gives readers a sense of the meaning of holiness worship and raises important questions.

Fadiman, Anne. 1998. *The Spirit Catches You and You Fall Down.* New York: Farrar, Straus, & Giroux. In this engrossing and tragic book Fadiman explores the conflicts between spiritual and scientific understandings of disease. Lia Lee, an infant Hmong immigrant, has seizures. Western doctors diagnosed the problem as epilepsy, but her parents understood her illness as caused by her soul wandering.

Warms, Richard L. James Garber, and R. Jon McGee. 2009 *Sacred Realms: Readings in the Anthropology of Religion* (2nd ed.). New York: Oxford University Press. A comprehensive reader on the anthropology of religion including essays on religion and society, altered state experiences, healing and bewitching, and new religious movements.

These Huli dancers from Papua New Guinea, reenacting their warrior tradition in a cultural festival, formerly used naturally colored clay for their body and face painting. Today, they often use manufactured tempera.

© Judith Pearson

**THINKING POINT:** The anthropological view of art is well expressed by Marshall Sahlins, who quipped, "There is no such thing as an immaculate perception," and by Franz Boas, who called "the seeing eye. . . . an organ of tradition."

—[For more about how anthropology changes Western perceptions of world art, see page 320.]

# {chapter 14}

# Creative Expression: Anthropology and the Arts

Art is a universal aspect of human experience; there is no known culture without art. In every society, people express themselves in ways that go beyond the need for physical survival with characteristic forms of creative expression that are guided by aesthetic principles involving imagination, beauty, skill, and style. These expressive activities are sometimes called the **arts.** In this chapter we use the broadest definition of that term to include the graphic and plastic arts, such as painting, architecture, sculpture, carving, pottery, and weaving; **crafts,** or the application of aesthetic principles to the production of utilitarian objects and activities; the structured use of sound in music, song, poetry, folklore, and myth; the movements of the human body in dance, sports, games, and play; and combined forms of these in dramatic and ritual performance. From the very broad anthropological perspective used in this chapter, tea drinking is an art form in Japan, bullfighting is an art form in Spain, and calligraphy is an art form in China and the Islamic Middle East.

Evidence of human artistic expression goes back to the very dawn of the modern human species, indicating that artistic expression is a fundamental dimension of our species. Tools manufactured according to aesthetic principles, the embellishment of burial sites beyond the merely practical, and the sophisticated and complex cave paintings and sculptures of prehistoric peoples all indicate the inherent connection between the arts and being human. Evidence suggests that Neanderthals, who lived between 70,000 and 35,000 years ago, were the earliest groups to artistically embellish their world. They had ritual burials with flowers, and made simple pendants of animal teeth and bones and even shaped various ritual objects. No culture today, no matter how simple its technology or how difficult its environment, lacks art. In fact, cultures in which making a living is difficult and in which social structure is relatively simple, such as Inuit and aboriginal Australian groups, often exhibit sophisticated artistic skills, and their artworks are much prized in the international market (Myers 2002). ≪

# Art in Its Cultural Context

Because art has different forms and functions in different societies, and because an important characteristic of all art is the expression—whether conscious or unconscious—of cultural themes, art must be understood in relation to the culture whose themes it is expressing.

For example, although artistic expression is universal, in different cultures, creative expression attaches to different aspects of culture. Furthermore, the high value the modern West places on art for art's sake is by no means universal. In fact, the opposite is true. In most societies, art is not produced or performed solely for the purpose of giving pleasure but is inseparable from other activities. The separation of art from other social behaviors, and the separation of a class of objects or acts labeled art is a dimension of the generally more fragmented nature of modern society. In nonindustrial societies, art is embedded in almost all aspects of culture. Few separate classes of material products, movements, or sounds are created solely to express aesthetic values.

The Inuit, for example, who have a highly developed artistic skill, do not have a separate word for art. Rather, all artificial objects are lumped together as "that which has been made," regardless of the purpose of the object. This does not mean that the Inuit do not have aesthetic values, but that their plastic art was traditionally applied to the manufacture of objects that have primarily instrumental value, such as tools, amulets, and weapons. The Inuit, like most other nonindustrial societies, do not make a distinction between artist and craftworker, a distinction that does exist in Western societies, though here, too, in the case of mosaics, for example, this distinction is often blurred. Similarly, many creative acts (such as dancing, weaving, singing, and playing a musical instrument) that in the West are performed as a special category of behavior called the arts are used in other societies in connection with other cultural activities such as religion, exchange, or storytelling. In all societies, some people are recognized as more competent in these skills than others, but this competence does not necessarily translate into the specialized role of artist.

The Western emphasis on originality has also led to underestimating the role of the artist in societies where art conforms more to cultural tradition. The Western emphasis on innovation and difference has led to conceptualizing the artist as a special person, often a deviant, working alone, and more likely to be in opposition to

**arts** Forms of creative expression that are guided by aesthetic principles and involve imagination, skill, and style.

**crafts** The application of aesthetic principles to the production of utilitarian objects and activities.

than in harmony with society. This perception is usually absent in art production in non-Western cultures (and historically not always true in the West itself). In much of the art in Africa, for example, interaction with the audience is of central importance because much art is aimed at conveying a message through its content, an important function in community life that may contrast with the Western emphasis on the individual aspect of artistic expression and the more private nature of its content, collection, and display.

The contemporary Western identification of art with originality, when imposed on other cultures, is also ethnocentric. Although anthropologists, and particularly art historians, have not generally investigated aesthetics in non-Western, nonindustrial societies, evidence indicates that the making of art in all cultures is recognized as a creative process, though not necessarily an innovative one (Price 1989). Many cultures do not prize originality—the creation of something entirely new—in their arts. In many societies in Africa, for example, improvisation is more highly valued than artistic originality and in these cultures creativity is expressed in creating interesting and endless variations on an already established artistic theme (Vogel 1991:20). Indifference to or even inhibition of originality in art occurs particularly when the arts are connected with religion. Among the Navajo, for example, there is believed to be only one right way to sing a song. Improvisation is not valued in Navajo singing, which has ritual connections, and the Navajo believe that "foreign music is dangerous and not for Navajo" (McAllester 1954). In other Navajo arts, such as weaving, styles remain stable but innovation is permitted; indeed, where marketing is the motive, traders may encourage innovation to increase sales.

# Some Characteristics of Art

The arts are a means of interpreting the world through images and marking the real world symbolically. Art expresses the basic themes, values, and perceptions of reality in ways that are culturally meaningful. Art is thus a reflection of cultural values and patterns at the same time that it intensifies the experience of these cultural values. Much of the power of the arts comes from their symbolic nature, which leaves their production and performance open to a variety of interpretations. An artistic product or performance may convey a basic cultural theme, or it may combine several themes, some of which may even be in opposition to one another. An important anthropological perspective on the arts is to understand both the surface and the deep symbolic structures through which the arts communicate and elicit responses from their participants and audiences.

But in some cultures, art is not only symbolic, that is, an image that stands for something else, but rather art products or performances—whether paintings, masks, sculptures, sounds, or movements—are believed not merely to represent but to be—to partake of the spirit of—the thing visualized. In these cultures, under specific ritual conditions, the spirit travels into the mask, painting, or dancer, which itself becomes powerful. Taking these forms, the spirits can be more easily manipulated and controlled by humans.

When objects, dances, songs, or other artistic forms are believed to be powerful in themselves, they are often created in ways that are strictly guided by traditional processes and resistant to variation or change. One important cultural factor that may limit the range of variation an artist displays is the relationship between art and religion. Where art and religion are entwined, there tends to be more stability in the creation of images, than where art and religion are independent of each other. This was true in earlier periods of Western history and is true for many contemporary non-Western cultures. Where religion and art have become separated, as in much of the contemporary world, experimentation, innovation, and real change in artistic style are more likely to occur, though even here, religious groups may attempt, sometimes successfully, to impose limits on art they consider sacrilegious. In 1999, for example, Rudolph Giuliani, then mayor of New York, with the backing of the Catholic Church, attempted unsuccessfully to close down an art exhibit featuring a painting of a Black Madonna that incorporated elephant dung, by African artist Chris Ofili. The protestors claimed the painting was "disgusting" (Steiner 2002). In another example, religious leaders in the United States successfully put pressure on a television studio to exclude showing the portion of Madonna's 2000 concert in Rome incorporating a mock crucifixion (Nanda and Warms 2009:282–283). More recently, a series of cartoons of the Prophet Muhammad in a Danish newspaper led to outrage by Muslims the world over (Nickerson 2006) and a representation by a Muslim artist of a Hindu goddess was subject to wide protests in India (Jain 2008).

Even in cultures where artistic forms are not themselves viewed as containing spiritual power, the arts are always powerful means of symbolic communication. They convey knowledge and provoke interpretations and emotions that have both individual and cultural dimensions. Each culture has specific traditional artistic symbols that stand for things or events in nature and human society or are associated with particular emotions. Because these symbolic elements are culturally specific, one needs to know the particular cultural meanings assigned to a particular artistic element to understand it. Conveying these meanings to cultural outsiders is one of the important contributions of an anthropological perspective on art.

In Western music, for example, the use of the minor scale conveys the emotion of sadness; various other musi-

The all-powerful hand is a highly symbolic image. Dating from the colonial period, it is still popular in Mexico today. Several layers of meaning are referenced in the image. The Eucharist is symbolized in the bleeding hand; the nail wound at the center is meant to recall the wounds Christ received on the cross. The seven lambs drinking the blood recall Revelations. The extended family of Christ is represented by the individual figures on each of the five fingers.

cal forms are traditionally associated with other emotions. The traditional element is important in evoking the emotion because people in that culture have been taught the association. In the United States, for example, a story that begins with the phrase "Once upon a time" is a signal that this is not going to be a story about real events and people. This knowledge sets the stage for the audience to respond to the story emotionally in certain ways.

Each artistic endeavor embodies an artistic style, which refers to a characteristic manner of expression, and different cultures (as well as different artists) have different artistic styles. Although all cultures experience stylistic changes in their arts, aesthetic principles are often very stable. Archaeological evidence indicates that the artistic styles of many cultures changed very slowly over very long periods. That is why artistic styles are often used by archaeologists to characterize different chronological periods in a culture; to differentiate different cultures in a

## Anthropology, Museums, and the Representation of Culture

Art historians, the traditional gatekeepers of Western concepts of art, generally claim that great art is measured and responded to in terms of universal intrinsic artistic qualities. Anthropologists, in contrast, as Marshall Sahlins and Franz Boas note in this chapter's "Thinking Point," emphasize the culturally mediated perspective through which art is not only produced but viewed. The cultural factors that a viewer brings to art—one's education, social status, knowledge about the reputation of the artist, the commercial value of the art, and in the case of the art from nonindustrial cultures, the Western perceptions of those cultures—are highly significant in shaping the response of audiences to the arts. These anthropological perspectives have made an important difference in changing the attitudes of art historians—and the museum-going public—toward non-Western art and the cultures that produce it.

Museum exhibits were—and are—a major point of contact between Western viewers and the art of indigenous cultures. Museums originated as national treasure houses, scientific institutions, preservers of disappearing cultures, and ethnographic collections. Today museums operate within still other cultural contexts, including fluctuating international art markets; politically charged funding policies; competition with commercial ventures such as theme parks; anthropological theorizing; and the identity politics involved in reconstructing national histories.

The impact of anthropological perspectives on museum exhibits really began in the early 20th century when Western art underwent a modernist revolution, in which

This sculpture of a female from the Luba of Africa is an example of the so-called "primitive" art that made such an important impact on European modernist artists.

European artists like Pablo Picasso began to incorporate features of African and Oceanic art into their own artistic creations. These artists and the art historians of the time had almost no interest in understanding this art, then called "primitive art," in its original cultural context.

Anthropologists had a very different perspective. While the European modernists were incorporating features of indigenous art into their own works, anthropologists were looking at this art from a functionalist view, trying to understand what the art, like other cultural institutions, contributed to the functioning of society. They were particularly interested in the social or symbolic worlds in which indigenous art was originally seen or used, such as religious ritual or social relationships. This anthropological approach, which informs this chapter, made a real difference in enriching Western understandings of indigenous art; it is now included in many contemporary indigenous art exhibits in both ethnographic and art museums (Cotter 2009; Nanda 2005).

In addition to emphasizing the importance of cultural context in understanding indigenous arts, anthropology influenced contemporary museum exhibits in another important way. In its early functional emphasis, anthropology had largely ignored the diverse paths through which the arts of indigenous societies had "migrated" from their original cultures into the world of Western museums and art collections, a path that anthropologist Sally Price called an examination of "primitive art in civilized places" (Adams 2006; Jones 1993; Price 1989; Steiner 1994, 2002; Venbrux 2006).

This anthropological interest gained particular intensity in the mid-1980s, partly in response to a very controversial 1984 exhibit at the Museum of Modern Art (MOMA) in New York, called *Primitivism in*

*Photo credit: © Jerry L. Thompson/Courtesy of the Museum for African Art, New York*

region from each other; to trace out the connections between different prehistoric cultures; and to speculate about life and social structures in ancient cultures who either had no writing or whose writing systems are not entirely understood by contemporary scientists.

Cultures also differ in their artistic emphases. In some cultures, masks and painting are the most important media for the expression of aesthetic values and technical skill. In other cultures, verbal skills are more important, reflected in a wealth of myths, folktales, and word games. Calligraphy (writing) is an important art form in both China and the Islamic Middle East, but is associated with quite different meanings in each of these cultures. In China, written language is considered one of the defining attributes of Chinese civilization and is a key source of Chinese cultural identity and unity. Writing

*Twentieth-Century Art: Affinity of the Tribal and the Modern.* The exhibit included a wide selection of modernist European masterpieces by Picasso, Klee, Brancusi, and others placed alongside the "primitive" objects that inspired them. Anthropologists now focused on the "life histories" of indigenous art objects; in addition to exploring their original cultural contexts, they investigated how these objects were originally taken from these contexts and found their way into Western museums and art collections (Jones 1993).

Anthropologists now also focused on how museum exhibits of indigenous art affected Western perceptions of the people who created it. Some anthropological critics noted that the very construction of a category called "primitive art" by art historians was itself an example of cultural imperialism, noting that this category indicated the ethnocentric limitations of the Western world view. These anthropological critiques were particularly concerned that the repression of ethnographic context, meaning, and intention in the exhibition of indigenous art made "primitives" seem less than human and "consolidate[d] Western feelings of superiority" (see Jones 1993).

James Clifford, a well-known postmodern anthropologist, claimed that art museum exhibits of decontextualized non-Western art, which emphasized the antique, the pure, and the authentic, ignored the actual values of those who made the art, and instead placed this art within the Western capitalist culture, viewing the objects as commodities to be circulated, bought, and sold in ways similar to European art

(1988:220–221). Furthermore, as postmodernism grew in influence, a general consensus was emerging in anthropology that the representation of cultures—whether in written ethnographies or in museum exhibits—was a political act, reflecting particular choices set in particular relationships of power and having significant political implications.

These anthropological perspectives slowly gained influence, and today, many art museums, as well as ethnographic museums, do consider both cultural context and political dimensions of their exhibits of indigenous art. Today, Western museum collections and exhibits of indigenous arts are critically examined for what they say about these arts, about the cultures the art represents, and also about their own colonial history (Hochschild 2005). Indeed, museum exhibits themselves have become the subject of ethnographic inquiry, as in anthropologist Sally Price's critical study of the new Branly Ethnographic Art Museum in Paris (2007). Price critically describes how this museum, which grew out of a relationship between "two old white men"—a former president of France and an art dealer—ignores the cultural context of the art it exhibits, "reinvigorating museum colonialism."

Most contemporary museum exhibits of indigenous art, however, have moved in the opposite direction. Not only is this art now mainly exhibited within an ethnographic context, but frequently, members of the communities involved collaborate with the museum professionals in designing the exhibits themselves. For many years, for example, Native Americans have contested museum exhibits of their material culture,

claiming that such exhibits have misleadingly represented their societies as timeless rather than dynamic; excluded Native American voices, consultation, or collaboration; neglected contemporary Native American artists; displayed sacred objects that should not be seen by the non-Native public; and ignored any representation of contemporary political issues involving Native Americans. The efforts of Native Americans to change these traditional museum approaches have been largely successful. Museum exhibits of Native American cultures now almost always include stories of Native American cultural revitalization, remembrance, and political struggle. Furthermore, consultation and collaboration with Native Americans is now practically standard procedure in both ethnographic museums and art museums, for example, in the outstanding exhibit, "The Enduring Potlatch" at the American Museum of Natural History in New York (Jonaitis 1991). This new approach is also the basis of the Smithsonian Museum of the American Indian, opened in 2004 on the National Mall in Washington, D.C (though some Native Americans feel strongly that the Museum has not gone far enough in presenting the full scope of Native American history. See, for example, Rand 2007).

Museums, like other cultural institutions, both reflect and influence our perceptions of other cultures, as well as our own. And it is anthropology that has made the difference in deepening our understandings of indigenous art, the diverse cultures in which that art is created, and the various implications of the exhibits in which it is presented to the public.

---

was the ruler's instrument of legitimacy, and it appeared on state monuments and documents. Gradually, it became revered as an art form. In Islam, calligraphy is the most respected of the graphic arts because it is the visual representation of the Koran. Islam forbids the worship, or even the creation, of graven human images, a prohibition often extended to the depiction of animals. In the Islamic cultures influenced by Persia (Iran), such as

Mughal India and Ottoman Turkey, animals and even humans are portrayed in paintings and carpets, but the religious prohibition has led to an emphasis on abstract geometric designs and calligraphy in much Islamic Arabic art (Schuyler 1995). These two examples indicate that even where cultures seem to have a similar emphasis on artistic form, the cultural meanings may be very different.

# Some Functions of Art

Art has many functions in society, such as expressing the symbolic elements in ritual; displaying cultural themes; confirming social hierarchies by making visible the power of the state or a governmental elite; resisting authority by giving expression to voices from the margins; and expressing personal and social identities. Both early and modern states use art to symbolize their own power, as we saw in the Asante state (see the "Ethnography" section in Chapter 11). Indeed, sometimes the very rules for the creation and display of artistic endeavor are determined by elites in a way that confirms and extends the domination of those elites, as, for example, in sumptuary laws, which allow only people in certain social statuses to wear certain materials, such as gold, fur, or other precious jewels. Art may also be used to resist the domination of the state and elites. Graffiti is sometimes an example of this. Art is also used to intensify ideas of nationhood, to express ethnic identities and record ethnic histories, and to make political statements. Art is used to express personal identity, or social status, or identification with a particular group in society, as illustrated in art as varied as the painting of their trucks by Pakistani truck drivers and the use of tattoos by American college students.

Art is often central to ritual, whether in artifact, movement, or sound. In many cultures, artistic expression using ritual acts and ritual objects is a powerful way of communicating with and attempting to control the natural and supernatural worlds. In hunting and gathering cultures, for example, dance movements that imitate the movements of animals are believed to exert control over those animals. In these foraging societies, dependence on nature leads to a perception of it as an active and personal force to which people must appeal in order to survive. Artistic expressions in contemporary hunting societies may represent the ritual restoration to nature of the animals that are killed. Whenever an animal is killed, its essence may be restored to nature by a ritual performance imitating the animal, or by a representation of the animal's image at a sacred spot, as we often see in rock paintings (Levine 1957).

## Art as Ritual: Paleolithic Cave Art

Our understanding of the very early cultural connections between art and ritual owes much to the collaboration of archaeologists and cultural anthropologists studying Paleolithic cave art. Cave paintings are among the most spectacular cultural remains left by early *Homo sapiens*. The earliest cave paintings are about 32,000 years old and the most recent about 10,000 years old. The best-known sites are caves in Europe, particularly in the protected valleys in eastern France and northern Spain, an area that supported abundant and varied animal and plant species.

The Altamira caves in Spain, and the Lascaux and Grotte Chauvet caves in France, are sites of the most elaborate cave paintings, made during the last Ice Age, about 32,000 years ago. These hunters of reindeer, mammoth, bison, and horses, put images on rock faces deep in caves and decorated themselves and their dead. The artists used naturally occurring bulges and dips in the rock to make their animal portrayals more realistic or partially sculpted the rock in low relief, to make their work more dramatic. They also made costume pieces and jewelry, carved and engraved human figures and ritual and ceremonial objects, placed elaborate grave goods in burial sites, made patterned notations that may indicate some form of record keeping, and made systems of signs and symbols, in addition to their paintings. This art supplies modern anthropologists one of the most useful tools with which to explore the inner and outer worlds of Paleolithic hunting societies.

The hills and river valleys of France and Northern Spain contained many diverse species of plants and animals, which were depicted by these Ice Age artists. These hunters clearly knew every detail of the anatomy and behavior of the animals in their territory. Deep in the caves with no animal models to copy, their animal paintings are rendered with magnificent realism. Many of the

The spots and handprints seen in this 15,000-year-old painting of a horse, found in Pech Merle Cave in France, support the argument that such prehistoric paintings had ritual significance for their creators.

© President and Fellows of Harvard College, Peabody Museum, Alexander Marshack # 2005.16.351.2

images indicate the sexual and seasonal characteristics or behavior of various animal species, for example, stags baying in the autumn rut, a bellowing bison bull and butting mammoth bulls in the autumn, a bison licking a summer insect bite and a bison with molting fur in the summer, and a bull and cow seal together in the early spring of the salmon run.

These images were not simply illustrations, but were symbols that stood for processes in nature. Archeologists speculate that these images played a role in ritual, religion, and storytelling, and were possibly used in different kinds of ceremonies—perhaps in curing ceremonies, or to mark changes in life stages or the seasons. The caves may have been visited seasonally or only for rare and special occasions. In addition to animal paintings, the caves also contain frequent markings of human hands; one appears to be that of an adult holding an infant's hand to the wall by the child's wrist, interpreted as an act of ritual participation performed by the adult for the infant (Marshack 1978). In caves used as living sites, entirely different images, such as signs and symbols in different shapes—a key, a badge, a hut, a grid, or a series of dots and lines—were engraved on stones and bones, and sometimes on broken ivory. These symbols may have been part of ritual marking systems.

This sophisticated art made by a people living many thousands of years ago raises many questions about their meaning. Archaeologists differ in their interpretations of cave art. Because many of the images are of animals that were commonly eaten, some anthropologists argue that they were drawn as part of ceremonies intended to magically increase the chances of a successful hunt; one weakness in this theory is that the bone remains indicate that few of the many species depicted were eaten. A more commonly accepted theory is that many of the images were made for ritual use. The association of animals with varying signs and symbols reinforces this view: some animals are marked with handprints, or abstract signs, whereas others are pictured with plant forms. Infrared photography indicates that many of the animals were over-painted with other animals or reused by repainting and adding symbols. This ritual function of these animal images is supported by other evidence. Lions, for example, were not intended as a food source, nor would the hunter have sought their increase, so that the paintings of lions—and, similarly, bears—apparently had symbolic functions in these Paleolithic cultures. It may also be that these prehistoric hunters drew an image of an animal they had killed in a sacred spot in order to restore its essence to nature, an interpretation that draws upon analogous rituals among contemporary foragers (Levine 1957). Still another interpretation argues that the cave paintings contain encoded information about hunting techniques and other information useful for survival in the harsh conditions of the Ice Age (Strauss 1991). Another, more controversial interpretation is that these paintings depict things seen by shamans in altered states of consciousness and that the caves were painted as part of religious rituals (Lewis-Williams and Dowson 1988). Because cave paintings were made by many different artists over a 20,000-year period, show many different subjects, and are painted in different kinds of space, it is unlikely that any single theory can explain them all, and each of the theories mentioned above may hold true for some cases.

# Art and the Expression of Cultural Themes

Because artistic performances and products emerge from widely shared cultural themes, the arts can heighten the feeling of belonging to a particular group by generating intense emotions. Thus art forms are not merely a mirror of culture—though they may be that as well—but art also heightens cultural and social integration by displaying and confirming the values that members of a society hold in common. The powerful artistic symbols of a society express universal themes—death, pride, gender relations—in ways that are culturally particular and therefore culturally compelling, even when (some might say particularly when) their content is not consciously articulated. The arts make dominant cultural themes visible, tangible, and thus more emotionally compelling.

These cultural themes, cultural values, and psychological underpinnings of a culture may be explicitly or openly expressed in art, but art also expresses the unconscious, repressed aspects of a culture. The phenomenon we call pop culture has often been analyzed in terms of how it provides a particularly direct view of the repressed unconscious of a culture, including the creators of pop art, the consumers of pop art, and the broader culture and society itself. In Japanese popular culture, the cockfight in Bali, and the bullfight in Spain, discussed below, we see examples of how diverse arts function in the display and confirmation of cultural themes; later in the chapter we show that art may often subvert rather than support culture as well.

**Cultural Themes and Popular Culture in Japan** Among the most important aspects of post–World War II popular culture in Japan are **anime** (animation) and **manga** (comic book art). Anime, the animation of manga, is very familiar in the West and, indeed, throughout the world,

---

**anime** Animation, as in the popular culture of Japan; usually refers to animation of manga, or comic book graphic art.

**manga** Japanese comic book art.

displayed in animation films, video games, children's toys, the Internet, and commercial products. These popular art forms have also been taken up by a pop art movement, whose work is displayed in museums and art galleries in Japan and abroad. They have also spawned a subculture in Japan, called *otaku* (the closest translation is "nerd" or "geek"), whose darker side includes an obsession with themes of war and violence, including nuclear catastrophes, mutant monsters, robots, and science-fiction, sometimes joined with another major pop culture theme, *kawaii,* or "cuteness." Cuteness is particularly displayed in images of Lolita-like preadolescent, seemingly innocent, schoolgirls, who nevertheless also convey a sexual knowingness that belies their innocence. Another major cuteness image is Hello Kitty, a big-eyed, beribboned, expressionless pussycat character (without a mouth to express emotion), whose images—on clocks, stuffed toys, purses, music boxes, and wallpaper—fuel more than a billion dollars a year in domestic and international sales.

On the apocalyptic side of this popular culture are monsters like Godzilla, who was awakened from eons of submarine sleep by a hydrogen bomb explosion. Godzilla exhibits radiation-induced physical deformities and engages in nightly attacks on Tokyo, which reduce the city and its screaming population to ashes.

One of the leaders of this Japanese contemporary pop-art culture is Takashi Murakami, a very successful designer for Louis Vuitton, who, in 2005, curated a museum show in the United States that included manga and anime art. He called the exhibit "Little Boy: The Arts of Japan's Exploding Subculture," after the name given to the atomic bomb dropped by the United States on Hiroshima, to end World War II. Murakami interprets the contemporary pop culture of anime and manga, and its *otaku* subculture, as growing out of the repercussions of the Japanese defeat by the United States, the dropping of the atomic bomb, and the postwar Japanese society, dominated by the American-imposed democratization and demilitarization.

Murakami, like other analysts of Japanese culture, emphasizes that Japan has not really examined its responsibility for the trauma of its militarism, its role in World War II, the atomic-bombing of Hiroshima and Nagasaki, and the prolonged American occupation that followed the Japanese defeat. In his analysis, Murakami holds that denying these traumas created displaced emotions such as anxiety, shame, and a pervasive sense of impotence, which find their outlets in popular culture (Smith 2005). In calling his museum show Little Boy, Murakami reinforces his view that Japan's postwar dependence on the United States has kept it from growing up. This infantilism is reflected in the popular fascination in Japan with fantasies of violence and power, such as the Godzilla-like monsters and mushroom-cloud explosions that are so frequently used in Japanese animation. In a seeming contradiction, this infantilism and sense of powerlessness also shows up in the opposite obsession with "cuteness."

But even as the popular culture of anime and manga display cultural and psychological themes that are particularly Japanese, this popular culture has also become widespread throughout the world, particularly in the United States, which has, in fact, produced some of its own Japanese-style anime (Condry 2005; Solomon 2005). There has also been some cross-cultural fertilization, as Japanese anime now also includes elements of African-American culture. In the teenage martial arts series *Tenjho Tenge,* for example, an athletic black teenager break-dances across the titles, demonstrating the new combination of hip-hop and Japanese anime. A hip-hop sound track now accompanies a new anime series, *Infinite Ryvius,* and in *Samurai Champloo* one of the main characters uses break-dance spins and flips in place of martial arts moves; for fashion-conscious Japanese teenagers, the height of fashion now is "cool, black, and American." In this expanding cross-cultural fertilization, a new phenomenon, called "fansubbing" has emerged, whereby small groups of Japanese and American anime fans digitally record Japanese animated TV shows, translate the dialogue, add subtitles, and make them available (for free) online (Condry 2005). Anthropologist Ian Condry emphasizes the great potential for anthropological and ethnographic research not only in exploring the cultural context of this Japanese popular culture, but in exploring the global interactions of its participants.

© AFP/Getty Images

A customer in Tokyo checks out computer game software, much of it based on 'manga' comics, which are not only a very widespread form of popular culture in Japan but also has spread throughout the world.

## The Display of Cultural Themes: Deep Play

There are many kinds of cultural performances, such as games and sports, in which participants and spectators are joined together in experiences that have functions similar to those of the arts (Geertz 1973a). Clifford Geertz calls these performances **deep play.** Examples of deep play include cockfighting in Bali, falcon hunting in Pakistan and other parts of Muslim Asia, football in the United States (see Chapter 4), and bullfighting in Spain. All of these are expressive forms of culture that heighten emotions, display compelling aspects of social structure and culture, and reinforce cultural identities.

**The Balinese Cockfight** Cockfights are a consuming passion of the Balinese that reveal much of Balinese culture, particularly the competition for prestige among men. Balinese men have an intense identification with their fighting animals and spend much time caring for them, discussing them, and looking at them. The cocks embody two opposing Balinese cultural themes. They are both a magnification of the owner's masculine self and an expression of animality, which in Bali is the direct inversion of what it means to be human. Thus, in identifying with his animal, the Balinese man is identifying with his ideal masculine self but also with what he most fears, hates, and is fascinated by: the powers of darkness that the animals represent. The cockfight embodies the opposition of man and beast, good and evil, the creative power of aroused masculinity, and the destructive power of loosened animality, fused in a bloody drama of violence as cocks with razor sharp, 5-inch-long steel spurs on their feet fight to the death.

Gambling is central to Balinese cockfighting and bets on the cockfight are a basic part of the competition for prestige that forms its deep play aspect. The money at stake in the cockfight gambling is very important, but for the Balinese, esteem, honor, and dignity are even more important. The two are tied together: it is because so much money is involved that risking it publicly is also risking one's status, especially one's masculinity. This belief increases the meaning of the cockfight for the Balinese.

The Balinese cockfight is a symbolic contest between male egos, but it is also a symbolic expression of Balinese social hierarchy. Prestige is the driving force in Balinese society and the central driving force of the cockfight, transforming the fight into a "status bloodbath." The more nearly a match involves men of equal status, especially high-status men or men who are personal enemies, the deeper and more emotional the match is felt to be.

The Balinese are aware of the deep status concerns involved in cockfighting, which they refer to as "playing with fire without getting burned." Cockfighting activates

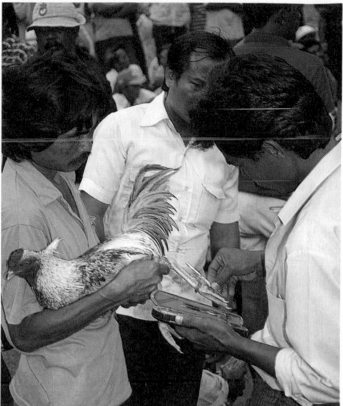

Cockfighting among the Balinese is a form of deep play that embodies important cultural themes such as masculinity and social status. In this picture, men attach steel spurs to a cock's leg, preparing it to fight.

© Wendy Bass/Viesti Associates Inc.

village and kin group rivalries and hostilities in "play" form. It comes dangerously and entrancingly close to the expression of open interpersonal and intergroup aggression, something that almost never actually happens in the course of ordinary Balinese life. But then, the Balinese say, cockfights are not quite the same as real aggression because, after all, it is only a cockfight.

**Bullfighting in Spain** For many Americans, bullfighting is simply a violent, cruel assault on animals; however, for anyone who has watched a bullfight or analyzed its patterns and meaning to the cultures within which it occurs, bullfighting is clearly an aesthetic ritual. To outsiders, the bullfight looks like an engagement in which a man tries to hurt or kill an animal in front of an approving audience (Eller 2006:104). But in Spanish culture, the bullfight is not viewed as violence or cruelty. In spite of the violent acts of the bullfighter, he is culturally compelled not to show any sign of anger or aggression; indeed, such signs

**deep play** Performances (like sports) that are expressive forms of culture with functions similar to the other arts.

would be considered a negation of the essence of the ritual of running the bulls. Bullfights involve a complex and elaborate process of ritualized violence that makes it, for Spaniards, not only acceptable, but beautiful.

Within the Spanish cultural context, the point of a bullfight is not simply to kill a bull: that would be easy and would lack any cultural meaning. Rather, it is the skill, grace, and courage of the bullfighter that is critical. In some ways similar to cockfighting, the bullfight embodies the values of male competition in defense of the male self-image of honor (see Chapter 10, page 224). For the audience, the maximum vindication of honor is in the physical showdown, in public, between two men. The matador symbolizes the role of the honorable male; he is not a fighter or a man with a reputation for violence, nor is he an athlete, nor personally aggressive, nor necessarily big or muscular. In a bullfight the matador does not initiate violence, nor does he act against the bull in self-defense. It is the bull that is angry and ferocious while the matador is skilled, self-controlled, and calm—he is able to master the violent situation without becoming violent himself.

For the matador and the spectators, it is not the suffering of the bull but the style and aesthetic performance of the matador that is the central element in this aesthetic ritual. At the kill, the most dangerous part of the performance for the matador, the matador cannot use his sword to weaken the bull or defend himself. Any prolonged suffering of the bull is vociferously disapproved of by the spectators and a matador who performs a "sloppy" kill is called a "murderer." For the Spanish, a bullfight is not an example of indulging in man's animal nature (which is how they view a North American boxing match), but a performance that allows man to transcend his animal nature of violence and aggression and to display all of the elegance, poise, and self-control that distinguishes a man of honor from a man of anger.

## Art and Politics

Another important function of the arts is the expression of social structure, particularly the social hierarchy and its relation to power (see the "Ethnography" section on page 332). In politically complex and hierarchical societies, the power embodied in the ruler or the state is represented through the graphic, oral, architectural, or performing arts. These artistic displays reiterate and legitimate the divine or other source of the ruler's power and the political structure through which the society is governed. The totem poles of the Native American groups on the northwest coast of North America are an example of the arts that reflect and send powerful messages about the importance of social hierarchy in these societies, as are the many artistic products and performances associated with the potlatch (Jonaitis 1991) (see page 156 in Chapter 7).

Another example of how the arts legitimate social hierarchy and power, contributing to stability, especially in transitional times, are the paintings of colonial Peru. After the Spanish conquest, Inca royalty commissioned indigenous artists to paint portraits of the Inca kings in order to keep alive the memory of Inca rulers for those claiming royal descent and noble status. Upper-class natives of Peru thus asserted their claims to high status and power in the colonial hierarchy by depicting their own illustrious forebears in paintings, the visual language of European culture. In imperial China, also, the arts were central in legitimizing the ruling class, especially the emperor (Hearn 1996). The Chinese believed that only those with knowledge of the past could have a vision of the future. Thus, it was essential for the imperial courts to possess historical writings and paintings to display that knowledge. Throughout Chinese imperial history, figure painting was directed toward commemorating the emperor. Life-size portraits of the emperor had to incorporate the two main Chinese ideals of imperial rule: moral authority and the power of the emperor's central role in

This widespread graphic art photograph of the Argentinean revolutionary, Che Guevara, has become an icon for the political left throughout the world and is particularly popular on T-shirts.

© Kevin Foy/Alamy

a controlled bureaucratic administration. Thus, paintings of the emperor had to show him with individualized features representing the humanistic Confucian values of compassion and virtue while conveying the imposing demeanor of the absolute ruler, the Son of Heaven. Another artistic representation that conveyed imperial power was a series of almost life-size portraits of Chinese cultural heroes, commissioned by some emperors in the 12th century. By displaying these paintings in the court, the emperor demonstrated his identification with a mythologized past and his rightful place in the lineage of Confucian rulers.

At the same time that the arts can help stabilize a society by validating its social hierarchy and expressing its common cultural elements, they also provide powerful ways to express disunity and conflict within a society, to resist state authority, and to give voice to members of oppressed or marginalized classes or social groups. Resistance to prevailing social structure is often an important dimension in folktales and other oral traditions. These oral traditions may reverse, ridicule, or question the social order and, in doing so, may provide satisfactory solutions to the conflicts that arise out of domination and control.

African-American oral traditions, for example, commonly contain the figure of the trickster, or clever hero, who is smaller and weaker than his opponent but triumphs through his wits rather than through force. The trickster tales, popular in one form as the Br'er Rabbit stories, have an obvious relation to slavery in the pre–Civil Rights South. At the same time that they conveyed a representation of the social structure based on race, these stories convey a message about how to overcome the system and provided an outlet for anger (Friedheim and Jackson 1996:24). The Br'er rabbit stories are the direct descendent of the Anansi stories from West Africa and were also possibly responses to those local hierarchies.

As the American social structure changed, however, and as possibilities of open protest against the racial caste system increased, African-American oral traditions also changed. The "badman," who openly displays his arrogance and virility, came to supplant the trickster as hero (Abrahams 1970), an image diffused into the blaxploitation films of the 1970s and into the gangsta figure in hip-hop and gangsta rap.

## Art and the Recording of Cultural History

Another important function of the arts is to express a people's sense of their cultural identity through depictions of the past. The use of art to link the present with the past is widespread. In many cultures, the most important artistic efforts and performances are those representing ancestors and the continuity of group identity; this is true for both literate and nonliterate societies, but is particularly important in the latter. Because they display cultural identity and history in ways that are visible, tangible, and emotionally compelling, the arts are an important way of interpreting and remembering both an actual and a legendary past.

The **ledger drawings** of some Native American groups are an example of the use of art to record history and preserve cultural identity (Berlo 1996; Greene 2001; Powers 2005). Native Americans recorded their histories in various ways. Some of these involved material artifacts, such as the Iroquois practice of carving a record of their chiefs into canes; others were stories more in the nature of the Bible, that is, stories about events, origins, and values that can be imagined but not proved. These records, whether material or oral, embody the effort of a people to define, explain, and amuse themselves and to keep alive their cultural identity. Many of the old stories told by Native American groups incorporate jokes (see page 105 in Chapter 5) and demonstrate the resilience of people who have experienced great hardship. Native American ledger drawings also provide a readable historical record, a way for the people to anchor themselves in the real world and locate themselves in history beyond myths and legends.

Ledger art got its name from the ledger books obtained from trading posts in which the Native Americans drew their records. The ledger drawings were made only

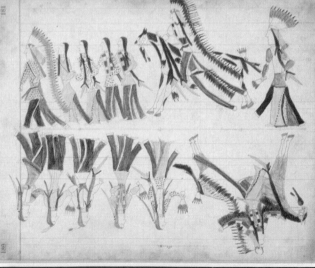

The Bridgeman Art Library

Entitled "Pawnee chased by Cheyenne and a white man killed by Crooked Lance" is an illustration from the "Black Horse Ledger." Ledger drawings, such as this one, made in 1877, are an important record of Native American histories.

**ledger drawings** Drawings, in ledger books, made by some Native American peoples to record personal and historical events.

by men, and initially served mainly to record the lost life of warfare, hunting, and tribal identity. At the turn of the 19th century, Native Americans were already using drawings, on skin shirts, robes, and teepee covers, to record personal histories. By the 1860s, these drawings had become more elaborate, colored, and carefully composed, and the original material of war deeds had expanded to include social customs and communal history. Ledger drawing flourished as an art form from about the 1870s to about the 1920s, during the early reservation period, a time of profound cultural change. It expanded when about 70 Native Americans, mostly southern Cheyenne, were imprisoned for a time at Fort Marion, in St. Augustine, Florida. They produced scores of ledger drawings, for personal pleasure, for sale to tourists, and as gifts for the whites with whom they interacted. This period was a time of profound cultural trauma as Native Americans left the old free life of the buffalo-hunting days for a new life as semi-prisoners living on government rations, under official pressure to abandon their religion, traditional ceremonies, and the old ways of communal living. Ledger drawings serve not only as an important expression of Native American arts, but also as important documents in the recording of actual events that can be used to expand knowledge about the past.

# Art and the Expression of Identities

## Body Art and Cultural Identity

For thousands of years, people all over the world have been marking and adorning their bodies. One of the ways people use **body art,** and other bodily adornment, is to announce their identification with a particular group or to mark their social position in a society. In some societies, such as those of Polynesia, body tattooing indicates high social status; in Japan, however, body tattoos developed as a form of decoration that identifies men on the margins of society, such as criminals. In Western societies, people who tattooed their skin were often from the military; other groups known for their tattooing, such as motorcycle groups, were considered social deviants. Today, in North America and Europe, however, the increasing popularity of piercing and tattooing seems to indicate that these forms of body decoration are now part of the mainstream (Burton 2001).

In many cultures, body art is associated with enhancing beauty, and thus related to gender. In India and the

**body art** Marking and adorning the body as an expression of cultural and personal identity, or which serves other functions.

Middle East, henna, an orange-red dye made from the leaves of a small shrub, is used to dye fingernails and other parts of the hands and feet to enhance a woman's beauty, especially on ceremonial occasions such as religious holidays or marriage (Messina 1988). In Morocco, where anthropologist Maria Messina studied the body art of henna application, a young girl is first decorated with henna at age 3 or 4, in preparation for the important Muslim holiday of Ramadan. But the cultural importance of henna is primarily related to marriage, and marks the transition of a girl to a woman. The "night of henna" is the first night in the 3-day marriage celebration; a girl is also decorated with henna at a "henna party" toward the end of her pregnancy. The month of Muharram, which marks the Muslim New Year, is another occasion for decorating married women with henna.

Henna parties are also viewed as a way of preventing illness or misfortune by placating malevolent spirits, called *jinn*. Sometimes women hire a specialist in applying henna designs on the skin, but this may also be done by a member of the woman's family. Although certain designs are traditional in certain regions, henna specialists also innovate in styles, and designs change according to the occasion and also according to fashion. Most of the designs have no explicit meaning, as representational art (art depicting any figures or forms found in nature or culture) is forbidden in Islam.

In addition to the cosmetic function of henna, and the prevention of illness, henna parties are celebrations during which friends visit and singing and dancing may take place. They also provide occasions where women are the center of attention. The application of henna designs has diffused from its original home (probably in India), and is now common also among non-Indians in the United States, functioning less as a display of a group identity than as an expression of an individual's assertion of choice and personal preference.

## Art and Personal Identity

For people in European-based cultures, one of the more obvious functions of the arts is the expression of personal identity. Indeed, in these cultures, personal identity is assumed to be deeply connected to an artist's body of work, and art critics and historians often try to link the artist's personal identity with his or her art.

The work of Frida Kahlo, a 20th-century Mexican painter, illustrates particularly well how artworks combine elements of the artist's personality, life experiences, political ideology, and national identity. Frida Kahlo was born in 1907, three years before the Mexican Revolution of 1910, to an ethnically mixed middle-class family. Her father was a German Jew and her mother half Mexican and half Native American. In her childhood she caught polio and a subsequent bus accident left her leg deformed and her body in great pain. Her marriage to the great

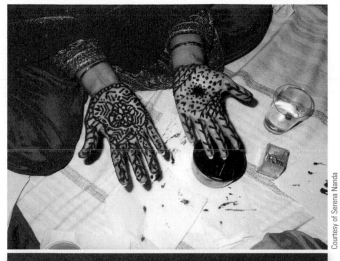

Body art has symbolic meanings and is often used in important life cycle ceremonies. In North Africa, India, and the Middle East, henna painting is an essential ritual for women getting married. It not only beautifies but serves to ward off evil on this auspicious occasion.

Mexican muralist Diego Rivera was filled with conflict, and her attempts to have a child ended in a miscarriage. All of these cultural and personal issues are reflected in her painting, the subjects of which deal with issues of illness and health, female sexuality and gender identity, marginality, cultural identity, power, and pain.

Frida Kahlo was profoundly influenced by the Mexican Revolution; to demonstrate her identification with the poor and the peasants, in whose name the Revolution was carried out, she claimed that she was born in 1910 (actually it was 1907). The Mexican Revolution ushered in a time of political freedom that led to a new pride in Mexico, fostering the incorporation of indigenous Mexican art, craft, and native traditions; these artists looked to pre-Columbian Mexico for their artistic roots while at the same time embracing European-trained or European-influenced painters such as Frida Kahlo and her husband Diego Rivera.

In her paintings Frida Kahlo drew on many elements of Mexican culture, such as *retablos* (votive paintings of Christian saints and martyrs); the Mexican folklore image of La Llorona, the archetypical, sexually voracious predator and evil woman who stands in contrast to the saintly wife and mother; and the indigenous Mexican Tehuana costume, with its long embroidered skirts and blouses, which expressed her solidarity with the peasants and poor of Mexico. She also wore this Mexican dress herself to demonstrate the cultural independence of Mexico (the dress had the added benefit of hiding her deformed leg). Kahlo's paintings, especially her self-portraits, also evidenced dualistic principles, like contrasts of dark and light and night and day, which have their origin in pre-Columbian myth. Kahlo's paintings

also examine the imbalance of power between Mexico and the United States, and the images of her broken body reflect the shattered dreams of the Mexican Revolution.

Although Frida Kahlo was well known in her own country, it was most recently in the 1990s that she emerged as an artist of great interest beyond Mexico, and she has now become an international cult figure. Her art particularly speaks to women, especially women's experiences of physical pain, of childbirth, and of the emotional pain of love, which is symbolized by the many broken hearts in her self-portraits. In Frida Kahlo's art, we clearly see the important role of art in expressing the many strands—cultural, political, physical, and familial—that make up an artist's personal identity—and through their expression in art, speak to a world wider than the artist's own.

**Fritz Scholder: Indian not Indian** Another very interesting and controversial artist who explores his self and cultural identity through his paintings is Fritz Scholder, in his "Indian not Indian" works. Scholder's father was half Indian and half German and his family did not live on an Indian reservation. Although enrolled in his

An important function of art is the expression of personal and national identification. Frida Kahlo incorporated Mexican cultural elements in her self-portraits to assert her personal identification and her identification with the Mexican peasantry and their revolutionary ideals.

father's tribe (the Luiseno), he often said he was not Indian. Until Scholder's work in the 1960s, much American Indian painting, both by Native and non-Native artists, romanticized Native life and the natural world, reflecting popular clichés about the lives of Native peoples. In contrast, Scholder's more realistic works, which combined historical images with abstract expressionism and pop art, presented a provocative challenge to these clichés. He addressed directly some uncomfortable truths about contemporary Native American life, such as alcoholism, poverty, and injustice. Scholder's painting *Indian with Beer Can* generated especially outraged responses among both Native and non-Native viewers, because it broke the taboo on talking about the ways that alcoholism devastated so many Indian lives. Scholder also pictured Indians wrapped in the American flag, his ironic response to the 200 years of unjust government policies toward Native peoples. Another of his powerful and controversial paintings is that of a Buffalo Dancer with an ice cream cone. Whereas many viewers found this image disrespectful, for Scholder it cast a realistic look at the contact between the traditional and the modern in contemporary Native life.

Scholder's ambivalence about his Indian identity, reflected in his art, and his frequent statements that he was not Indian, led other Native artists to criticize what they saw as his denial of the very source of his artistic success. Scholder's powerful art, recently exhibited at the National Museum of the American Indian, illustrates both his own shifting identities and new perspectives on his culture and how the two are intertwined (Ringlero 2008).

# The Arts: Representing the Other

We have seen so far in this chapter some of the important functions of art as they relate to cultural identities and personal identities that may be constructed in terms of kinship, geography, culture, ethnicity, gender, nationality, political alliance, or several of these criteria intersecting in different ways. But in representing cultural identities, art depicts not only the "we"—that is, the cultural in-group—but also the "other"—the alien, the foreigner, the outsider. Indeed, artistic forms are important aspects of cultural ideologies of difference, communicating in subtle but significant ways the nature of we/they distinctions in any society. As we noted earlier (see "Anthropology Makes a Difference"), the differences in museum exhibits of Western and non-Western art implicitly distinguished between the "civilized" us of the West and the non-Western "primitive" other.

One result of the encounters between Europeans and other peoples was a profound rethinking of European cultural identity (S. Schwartz 1994). Although these encounters were experienced differently in different times and places, Europeans most often responded by creating opposite categories of "them" and "us" (Bitterli 1986). These dichotomies take many forms: East and West; primitive, or barbarian, and civilized; traditional and modern; developed and undeveloped.

## Orientalism in European Art: Picturing the Middle East

The rendering of the other appears in many aspects of European (or Western) art. Artistic products may reflect the subjects of the art, but they are also a source of insight into the mind-set of the artist, reflecting, perhaps, the cultural fantasies one group of people entertains about another (Bassani and Fagg 1988). Artistic images of outsiders may be useful as historical documents, portraying details of behavior and costume, but the unknown aspects of foreigners also act as an invitation to the imagination in which the reality of the observed becomes subordinate to the fantasies of the observers (Tsuruta 1989).

In the 19th century, Europeans explored, conquered, and excavated, and then wrote about and painted, North Africa, Arabia, the Levant, and the Ottoman Empire. This region, today called the Middle East, was then called the Orient. European artists of the 19th and 20th centuries offered armchair travelers a vividly graphic image of the Islamic, largely Arabic cultures inhabiting this world. One important impetus for these representations, particularly in France, was the Napoleonic campaigns in Egypt (1798–1799). By the mid-19th century, the Egyptian experience had become part of the French cultural spirit and was found in a wide range of artistic representations in a style called **Orientalism** (Hauptman 1985:48).

Europeans saw the Oriental other as threatening because they perceived it as the opposite of European civilization. The Orient was viewed as despotic, static, and irrational, whereas Europe was viewed as democratic, dynamic, and rational. But the Orient was also enchanting: a land of mystery, fairy tales, and exotic beauty. This perception of the Orient was reflected in and reinforced by its depiction in European paintings. Orientalist paintings emphasized the exoticism and glamour of Oriental markets, camel caravans, and snake charmers. Islam was captured not in its religious experience (to which Europeans were generally hostile) but in the architecture of its mosques and its practice of prayer, all portrayed in lavish, opulent detail. Although many Europeans traveled to the Orient, painters generally worked from secondhand sources or, in some cases, purely from imagination. How-

**Orientalism** Scholarship and art generated by Europeans, representing their views of the Middle East.

The enigma of the Middle Eastern woman, whether hidden behind her veil or revealed in the harem, was a core image of Oriental painting. In many cases, the artist was not painting from life. This scene by Juan Gimenez-Martin, called "In the Harem," was actually painted in the artist's studio in Rome.

ever, their works were rendered in exquisite detail, which gave the viewer a sense of historical accuracy.

Gender roles and relationships were a central theme in Orientalist painting. Men were perceived as clearly dominant and pictured in public places, where women were mostly absent. The Arab warrior was the most common symbol of Oriental masculinity, but men were also painted in more relaxed poses, drinking coffee or smoking the hookah. But it was Oriental women who were central to European fantasies of the period (Thornton 1994). The difficulty of finding women to pose in no way inhibited their depiction; indeed, this difficulty gave free rein to artists' imaginations. Women were portrayed as the Orient's greatest temptation, whether hidden behind the veil or revealed in the harem.

Harems and slave markets, painted for male patrons by male artists, offered a convenient way of feeding European lust by displaying the dominant men and vulnerable women of another culture, far removed from home. Pornographic scenes disguised as either documentation or art were integral to the European market for Orientalist painting (Thubron 2009). These images were not confined to fine art but found frequent expression in other elements of culture such as the picture postcard, a genre that Alloula (1986) calls the "comic strip of colonial morality." The postcards reveal the preoccupation of Europeans with the veiled female body. The native models for these postcards were photographed in studios reenacting exotic rituals in costumes provided by photographers. The models represent the French fantasy of the inaccessible Oriental female, more tempting because she is behind the veil in the forbidden harem.

Alloula connects these Orientalist fantasies to colonial reality, noting that the raiding of women has always

been the dream and the obsession of the total victor: "These raided bodies are the spoils of victory, the warrior's reward." The postcards are an "enterprise in seduction directed to the troops, the leering wink in the encampment" (1986:122).

Orientalist representations of women also reflected the long-standing conflict between Christian Europeans and Middle Eastern Muslims. Since the Middle Ages, Europeans had criticized Muslims for their practice of polygyny, which Europeans associate with promiscuity. Thus, popular images of slave girls, harems, and concubines provided a continual source of horror and titillation for Western critics of the Muslim world. Even today, much Western thinking about the contemporary Middle East is concerned with the veiling, segregation, and oppression of women (S. Hale 1989).

# Marketing World Art

Anthropologists are now particularly interested in the role of the arts in the global economic and cultural system (Mullin 1995; Venbrux et al. 2006), including as we have seen, the presentation of indigenous arts in Western museums. As a result of this global context, the boundaries between "high" and "low" arts and stereotyped concepts of "primitive" or "tribal" art are increasingly contested (Bright and Bakewell 1995), now incorporated into the new anthropological concept of **world art.** The concept of world art incorporates an examination of the Western and international art worlds, in which the arts of indigenous peoples are increasingly circulated (Marcus and Myers 1995; Price 1989; Venbrux et al. 2006).

Part of the contemporary anthropological interest in world art is a new look at the role of the artist in society, as this becomes part of the international market. The ethnocentric perception of tribal societies as an exotic world apart, and the distinction made between the high art of modern Western societies and the "primitive" or folk art of tribal societies, meant that an important (and commercially valuable) dimension of the Western notion of primitive or tribal art was that of the anonymous artist. Thus, even when an individual artist can be tracked down, dealers and collectors are generally not interested

**world art** The contemporary visual arts and cultural performances of non-Western peoples, as they are increasingly part of a capitalistic global art world that includes international collections, museum exhibits, and tourism.

## The Arts, Tourism, and Identity in Tana Toraja, Indonesia

The connection between the arts, tourism, and the construction of cultural identity is well illustrated by the Toraja who live in the highlands of South Sulawesi, Indonesia. The Toraja are mainly subsistence cultivators who also raise water buffalo, pigs, and chickens, which are eaten mainly on ritual occasions. Two artistic Toraja products that are particularly important in their society, and for which they are known throughout the world, are *tongkonan,* or ancestral houses, and the *tau-tau,* wooden effigies of nobles carved in connection with mortuary ritual.

Kathleen Adams, an ethnographer of the Toraja for more than 15 years, describes how the *tongkonan* and the *tau-tau* are key elements in the cultural, political, and economic struggle of the Toraja to define their many cultural identities: in their local social hierarchy; in relation to a regional multiethnic social hierarchy; in the larger Indonesian state; and in the wider world (2006).

Torajan art plays an important role in Toraja social structure; because of the emotional power of material objects, and particularly art, these become an important arena for embodying and challenging, social hierarchy. Although social class, as a category denoting differences in wealth, education, and occupation, has not yet become salient in Torajan society, social rank, a descent-based identity (see page 247), is central to their social structure. The emphasis on rank, which is mainly articulated by nobles, or "big people," in contrast to "ordinary people," is prominently embodied in the *tongkonan* and the *tau-tau.*

The *tongkonan* is especially closely linked to family prestige because it is the visual symbol of one's descent group, as well as the seat of the extended family. Each *tongkonan* has a unique history and they are ranked in terms of prestige, accorded both according to their age and also to the illustriousness of their founding families. The visual aspect of the *tongkonan* also communicates the status of its members: the *tongkonan* of the nobility are fully carved and adorned with intricate patterns, whereas commoners were traditionally restricted to carving only small portions of their houses, and slaves were prohibited from decorating their houses at all. The relationship between the *tongkonan,* family prestige, and power is reinforced by consecrating *tongkonan* in public rituals. These invoke glorious memories of one's ancestral kin and, by implication, boost one's own prestige.

The Indonesian government's use of *tongkonan* imagery on its currency and stamps give the Toraja an important identity as part of the Indonesian state. Indonesia's tourist development program, aimed at increasing the inflow of Western capital, focused on Tana Toraja, and particularly on the spectacularly carved *tongkonan.* In fact, because of the tourist interest in the *tongkonan,* the Toraja were forbidden by Indonesian officials to alter them. Some officials even questioned whether the Toraja should be permitted to live in their houses because human occupancy could damage these valuable tourist objects (Adams 1990:33).

Torajan art also defines the Toraja in the context of regional ethnic politics, in which they contrast themselves, as nominally Christian, with two important Muslim ethnic groups, the Bugis and the Makassarese, who live in the adjacent lowlands. In the past, the Toraja elite occasionally intermarried and traded with the elites in both these groups, but Toraja narratives of this ethnic

interaction focus more on themselves as victims of slave raids and exploited workers in the coffee fields. Also, in the past the Bugis, who dominate the lowland coastal area of South Sulawesi, controlled Toraja access to the outside world. But the rise of tourism to Tana Toraja raised Toraja status in the competition for ethnic superiority and has become another source of regional ethnic conflict.

The *tau-tau* is another unique artistic element in Torajan cultural identity. Because they are carved only for the wealthiest Toraja nobility, *tau-taus* are also an important symbol of aristocratic status. *Tau-taus* are commissioned by the family of the deceased and the carving is surrounded at every step by religious ritual. When the funeral begins, the *tau-tau* is adorned with finely woven clothing, a betel nut bag filled with silver and bamboo utensils, a head dressing, gold jewelry, and a sacred knife— all heirlooms associated with nobility or deities. The *tau-tau* is supposed to resemble the dead person; it makes his or her

in doing so (Price 1989). Art middlemen in West Africa learned that an object was worth more to Westerners "if it [was] perceived by the buyer to have been created by a long-departed and unknown artist and to have come directly out of a remote village community." The middlemen are quite willing to manipulate both the art objects and the information about their production to meet these demands of Western buyers (Steiner 1995:157). This is changing, however, not only for Africa but also in the case of many indigenous societies. Indeed, the identification of tribal artists has now become an important factor in both understanding and marketing their arts.

soul visible. During the funeral, the *tau-tau* is placed near the body of the deceased, from where it observes the mortuary ritual. When the mortuary rites are completed, the *tau-tau* is placed with its relatives on platforms chiseled into limestone cliffs, where it becomes a visual link between the community of the living and the community of the dead.

The Toraja today are predominantly Christian, but the *tau-tau* remains an important element of their traditional cultural identity. In order to reconcile the "way of the ancestors" with Christianity, the Toraja have made some changes in both the form and the concept of the *tau-tau*. Today the *tau-tau* are viewed less as a "vessel of the Torajan soul" (Adams 1993) than as a realistic portrait of the dead person. *Tau-tau* have lost some of their traditional spiritual identity, while at the same time incorporating such Christian elements as Bibles and crosses.

In the 1960s, tourism began to expand in the Toraja area, almost all of it oriented toward viewing the Toraja mortuary rituals of animal sacrifice, the spectacularly carved *tongkonan*, and the eerie *tau-tau*. Through some early tourist-oriented films, and later, through the Internet, the Toraja became known throughout Europe in connection with their rituals and their art, specifically the *tongkonan* and the *tau-tau*.

Both these artistic elements, reflecting the tourist demand for portable art, are now carved in miniature for sale in tourist shops. Thus, tourism began a process by which ritually significant objects have been transformed into art objects of economic significance. As the *tau-taus* became known as art objects in the Western world, hundreds of them were stolen and sold to

© Judith Pearson

Tau-taus, effigies of the spirit of a recently deceased noble person, have taken on new identities, both for the Toraja and for outsiders, as they have become transformed into artistic commodities for tourists and international collectors.

American, European, and Asian art collectors; *tau-taus* today are openly sold for thousands of dollars in international art galleries. Redesignated by Western curators and collectors as archaic Indonesian art, some effigies have also found a home in Western museums. For the Toraja, the theft of a *tau-tau* is tantamount to the abduction of an ancestor, and the loss must be redressed by ritual propitiation. Additionally, the Toraja realize that without the *tau-taus*, tourism will decline, depriving them of an important source of income and prestige. Paradox and pathos thus attend the *tau-tau* today: its meaning has changed from ritual object to art object, and where once the *tau-tau* served as a protection for the family of the deceased, today the family of the deceased must protect the *tau-tau*.

## CRITICAL THINKING QUESTIONS

1. One of the effects of tourism is to make people more self-conscious about their culture. This can have both positive and negative effects. What effects has tourism had on Toraja cultural identity?

2. What forms of artistic expression are particularly important in relation to your own cultural identity?

3. What does it mean to say that culture has become a commodity? How does the buying and selling of cultural symbols affect the identities of those who sell them and those who buy them?

Source: Adapted from Kathleen M. Adams, *Art as Politics: Re-Crafting Identities, Tourism, and Power in Tana Toraja, Indonesia*. 2006. Honolulu, HI: University of Hawaii Press.

The importance of the artist in native North American societies contrasted with the more general emphasis on the anonymous artist in indigenous societies. Anglo-American interest in developing and marketing indigenous arts in the United States helped create the status of artist where it did not previously exist. One of the best-known examples is in the life and work of the renowned Pueblo Indian potter Maria Martinez of San Ildefonso (Babcock 1995). In the early 1920s, as part of this Anglo interest in reviving Native American arts, a number of wealthy Easterners and museum directors who had moved to the Southwest "reinvented" Native American pottery as

Outside interest in Native American art created the status of artist and led to prominence for some individuals. Here, Maria Martinez, a major figure in the development of an art market for Native American pottery, makes one of her signature black-on-blackware pieces.

© George Haling/Photo Researchers, Inc.

a fine art. The pottery was sold to wealthy Americans in the newly established Santa Fe Native American market, and exhibited in museums (Mullin 1995). Maria Martinez and her husband, Julian, produced a matte-and-polish black-on-blackware that was an almost instant success in the Anglo market. To award Maria Martinez status as an artist within the Western meaning of that term, she was encouraged to sign her pots as a way of increasing their value for collectors. When other San Ildefonso potters asked her to sign their pots too, she willingly did so, expressing the egalitarian quality of Native American pueblo life—but causing havoc among her sponsors (Babcock 1995:137).

Maria and Julian Martinez shared their techniques with other members of their pueblo, and several members of her family actually participated in the various stages of making her pots. As a result, San Ildefonso as a community became identified with fine pottery. It was Maria Martinez, however, who became the star in the Pueblo pottery revival. Maria Martinez's image was reproduced in photographs, videotapes, books, and other media, and she became identified with a romanticized image of the Native American woman potter.

## Tourism and World Art

The arts have always been important in marking cultural boundaries. They retain that importance in the contemporary world, particularly with regard to the construction of ethnic identities of indigenous peoples and their relation to tourism (Graburn 1976). The linking of the arts to cultural identity is promoted by popular television shows about non-Western, "exotic" cultures, the worldwide sale of ethnic arts (including on the Internet), traveling museum shows in which indigenous peoples are represented through their arts, the circulation of tribal arts among Western art collectors, and particularly, tourism. As we see in the ethnography of the Toraja of Indonesia, artistic objects and performances that have their origin in the ritual and social life may become, through tourism, a core around which modern cultural identities are constructed and an important source of income as well.

Tourism often debases indigenous, culturally authentic, and creative art into mass-produced souvenirs of low quality, lacking any cultural meaning, but its effects on art and cultural identity have actually been mixed. Tourism can also support and reaffirm cultural identities by reviving respect for traditional art forms, as has occurred to some extent in the American Southwest (Mullin 1995). In Bali, also, for example, the interest of tourists in cultural performances has given such events an economic boost and allowed local troupes to buy new instruments for their gamelan orchestras and new costumes. It also has encouraged the opening of schools and institutes throughout Indonesia for training people in creating traditional art forms. An expert and professional group of Indonesian artists has maintained tight control over performances in order to conserve the quality of the arts. Similarly, interest in the Inuit arts and their sale to tourists has been an extremely important alternative source of income for them, especially as their traditional hunting declines. The connection between art, tourism, and the strengthening of cultural identity is also seen in the weaving of Native American women in Guatemala and Mexico (J. Nash 1986).

Ritually and socially significant cultural elements change meaning as they become part of staged performances for tourists or move from their original cultural contexts into the world art market. This is part of a larger process in which culture itself has become a marketable commodity, reshaped and packaged in part in response to the demands of a world market. Among the more recent anthropological interests in art are the ways in which the artworks of nonindustrial societies have become commodities in the process of globalization and the ways in which they have been reconceptualized functionally and stylistically to meet a worldwide demand.

Will this marketing of culture move the world inevitably toward cultural homogenization? Or will the global economy and the global village always leave room for the emergence of meaningful local artistic expressions of cultural identity?

Many traditional arts have been given new life by the tourist industry. Here an artist in Bali paints traditional designs on a cloth hanging designed for sale to tourists.

© Joan Gregg

# The Global and the Local: World Music

Despite the close connection between the arts and particular cultural themes, the arts today have a global reach. One of the fastest growing global phenomena is the emergence of **world music.** World music incorporates different musical styles from cultures throughout the world. It includes Caribbean sounds such as reggae and salsa but also Celtic folk songs, Louisiana blues and Cajun songs, and African, Middle Eastern, and Asian songs. World Beat concerts are common in most large cities, and there are World Beat festivals in many countries.

World music is based on local musical traditions, produced for local occasions, in local languages. Communications technology and the movement of people have spread these musical traditions around the world and often made them very popular. Reggae songs, originally a Jamaican musical style linked to religion and resistance, and widely popularized by Bob Marley (Jelly-Schapiro 2009), today are written and performed by Africans, Asians, and Europeans as well as Jamaicans. Traditional musicians have frequently adopted Western instruments and styles. For example, Mory Kanté is an African musician who plays traditional African instruments: the balafon and the kora. However, he is backed by a band of Western drums, guitars, basses, and keyboards. Western

musicians, for their part, have adopted many of the styles and instruments of traditional music and modern world music. Paul Simon, Sting, and David Byrne have all recorded albums very heavily influenced by indigenous musical traditions.

Many cultures are contributing to musical fusion, but the influence of Africa and African-derived music stands out. For centuries, African and New World music have traded ideas, creating endless variations from shared foundations in call-and-response and polyrhythm. The music of African religious ceremonies was preserved by slaves and adapted into the sacred and secular music of the New World (Pareles 1996). From the polyrhythmic basis of North American ragtime and early New Orleans jazz, through the African-Cuban percussionist influence of Mongo Santamaria, to the performance combination of Youssou N'Dour of Senegal, to the contemporary albums of griots from West Africa such as Salif Keita, Africa has influenced world music. The music of African Americans also has worldwide popularity: hip-hop music of urban

**world music** World music incorporates different musical styles from cultures throughout the world.

African-American culture is found in places as distant from its origin as Cambodia (Mydans 2008) and China (Wang 2009), in addition to Europe. In a multicultural city like Marseille, which includes Muslims, Jews from North Africa, and Armenians, among other immigrant groups, the widespread popularity of hip-hop music is given the credit for transcending narrow cultural identities and helping to prevent the kind of violence that has characterized other French cities (Kimmelman 2007).

Bhangra is another musical style that has been widely diffused from its place of origin, and that has changed in the process. **Bhangra** originated in the folk music of Punjab, a region that includes parts of northern India and eastern Pakistan. Originally performed to celebrate harvest festivals, by the 1970s, the large South Asian population of Britain began mixing bhangra beats and lyrics with British pop music and reggae. This trend has continued, and today bhangra is an amalgam of Punjabi, rock, pop, reggae, and hip-hop styles. It has spread from London and other large British cities to large cities in the United States, Canada, and many other nations where there are substantial South Asian populations and has become popular in India and Pakistan.

Bhangra is a music of identity but means different things to different communities (and to different elements within those communities). To the young, urban, British-born South Asians who created it, bhangra was often a music of resistance. It united South Asians of many different backgrounds—Indians and Pakistanis, and Bangladeshis, Sikhs, Muslims, and Jains—in a common community. Its lyrics, often in Punjabi but sometimes in English, articulated the problems of South Asians living in Britain—especially racism and the balancing of tradition and modernity. Bhangra was thus a distinctly new musical form, a music of and by South Asians in Britain, giving identity and shape to that ethnic community, differentiating it and supporting it in contrast to both the white British majority and South Asians who had not immigrated (Lipsitz 1994).

A popular component of world music and dance, hip-hop originating among African Americans has become wildly popular in Europe and Asia. Here, Jero, an African-American who has a Japanese grandmother wows audiences of all ages as he sings soul music in perfect Japanese combined with hip-hop style.

© AFP/Getty Images

Bhangra was looked at differently in smaller British towns with small South Asian populations. Here, South Asians understood bhangra as a more traditional art form, and used bhangra parties as occasions to dress in traditional Indian clothing (Bennett 1997). As one participant in bhangra parties said, "It's good to go to a bhangra gig because. . . . it brings back memories. . . . it's like tradition. . . . it gives you a buzz to be doing something a bit traditional." But even here, bhangra was viewed as a mainstream musical style, and it was locally mixed with rock, pop, and other ethnic musics to make it attractive to a broader audience.

In the United States, bhangra is increasingly popular, particularly in large urban centers, like New York, where artists such as DJ Rekah mix the lives of South Asian immigrants, community politics, bhangra, reggae, and hip-hop. However, in American communities, although bhangra may bring people together, it also often divides them. Though both older and younger people identify bhangra with tradition, for youth, bhangra represents a connection to South Asian traditions, whereas their elders often object to its modern elements, which they consider a Western pollution of their tradition. Resistance to the styles of dance associated with bhangra and the close contact between men and women they encourage may be behind these objections (Katrak 2002).

Thus, although bhangra is an art form linked tightly to South Asian ethnic identity, it has different, and even inconsistent, meanings and messages. Some listeners hear the music of resistance, separating South Asians from the larger communities they live in; others hear the sounds of assimilation, of a popular music drawing on multicultural traditions, dealing with current problems, and increasingly attractive to non-Asian audiences. Still others hear the sounds and traditions of the lands they or their parents left. Like all world music, bhangra retains its links with its local identities but has also changed as it has diffused around the world.

## Key Questions

1. Discuss how world music incorporates both the local and the global elements of song, dance, music, and performance.
2. How may musical forms and meanings be transformed as they diffuse from their original locations to other parts of the world? You might give the example of bhangra or any other musical form you are familiar with.

> **bhangra** A musical form originating in the folk music of Punjab in Northern India and Eastern Pakistan that is mixing with British pop music and reggae to become a popular form of world music.

# Summary

1. **What is the core approach to an anthropology of art, and how does this differ from the approach of art history?** For anthropologists a key perspective on art is to examine it in its cultural and functional contexts. Unlike art historians, who focus on what they call the intrinsic aesthetic value of an art object, anthropologists examine the wide range of activities and material products in which creative expression is guided by standards of beauty in a particular culture. They also ask how these artistic products and performances function in ritual and social relationships.

2. **What are some of the ways in which the arts of various cultures differ from each other?** The arts in different societies take different forms: depending on the culture, writing or tea drinking may be art forms. Cultures also differ in the rules by which art is created, the importance of originality in art forms, the expected interactions of the artist with his or her audience, and the concept of art for art's sake. Whereas in the West, the artist occupies a specialized status, in many indigenous societies, the artist and art making are not separated out from other social activities, but rather may be embedded in crafts, economics, or ritual.

3. **What are some of the ways in which art can be powerful?** In some cases the power of an art piece or performance is its emotional power, because it draws upon cultural themes meaningful in a particular society. Sometimes, however, an artistic piece or performance itself may be regarded as inherently powerful. This may be the case when art is performed as part of a ritual, as among prehistoric hunters who painted pictures of animals in order to achieve control over hunting.

4. **What is the relationship between art and cultural themes? Discuss one example described in the text.** Art is always symbolic, and artistic creations most often have multilayered levels of meaning, communicating several cultural themes. One important function of art is the display of cultural themes. In Japan, one significant interpretation of the content of anime and manga is that they display the repressed themes of Japanese militarism in World War II, the trauma suffered by the atomic bombing of Hiroshima and Nagasaki, and the postwar dependence of the Japanese on the United States and resulting feelings of powerlessness.

5. **What is deep play? Give examples of art forms that are deep play.** Deep play is the idea that certain activities and art forms manipulate profound cultural themes. Such activities are texts that both culture members and anthropologists might use to interpret cultural values. Examples of deep play include cockfighting in Bali, bullfighting in Spain, and football in the United States.

6. **What are some of the relationships between art and history, art and social structure, or art and power?** An important function of the arts is the validation of a social or political structure, as in memorials to ruling powers, and art forms that are limited to the aristocracy. But art can also challenge existing social and political structures by mocking those in power or questioning society's rules. The arts may also be used to record history and remember important past events, as illustrated by Native American ledger drawings.

7. **What are some of the connections between the arts and personal identities?** Body art can express a cultural identity, a social status, or a personal identity. In Morocco, for example, henna painting of women's hands is intimately related to celebrating a marriage. For artists like Frida Kahlo, the elements and subjects of her art emphasized her personal development and her great identification with the peasants of Mexico. Native American artist Fritz Scholder uses his paintings to question his own Indian/not Indian identity.

8. **How does art express boundaries between the cultural in-group and the cultural other?** Art can be used to express the cultural identity of an in-group, but also to reinforce that identity by depicting the other—those felt to be different in basic ways from oneself. In Europe, Orientalism was an art style that represented European fantasies of the Middle East, particularly through paintings and photographs of women in the harem.

9. **How does art become an important factor in the cultural identities of indigenous peoples as they interact with others in a globalized context?** Today, many indigenous societies, such as the Toraja of Indonesia, are known throughout the world because of their art forms. The global context for indigenous art around the world includes the Internet, international art collections, museum exhibits, and particularly, tourism. Although tourism may confer economic benefits, it also sometimes results in artistic objects, performances, and rituals that had spiritual meanings becoming transformed into staged displays or commodities in international art markets.

# Key Terms

anime

arts

bhangra

body art

crafts

deep play

ledger drawings

manga

Orientalism

world art

world music

# Suggested Readings

Adams, Kathleen M. 2006. *Art as Politics: Re-Crafting Identities, Tourism, and Power in Tana Toraja, Indonesia.* Honolulu, HI: University of Hawaii Press. An exciting and highly readable ethnography demonstrating the importance of art forms in the culture and social structure of the Toraja. Adams puts herself in the story, and we learn about classic anthropological method, contemporary theories of art, and a fascinating culture as it interacts with the forces of globalization.

Dubin, Lois Sherr. 1999. *North American Indian Jewelry and Adornment: From Prehistory to the Present.* New York: Harry N. Abrams Inc. An astonishingly beautiful book that interweaves anthropological and Native American perspectives. Dubin undermines stereotypes of Native Americans through her emphasis on the connections between past and contemporary artistic creativity and by highlighting the voices of Native Americans as they explain the meaning of their art.

Shohat, Ella, and Robert Stam. 1994. *Unthinking Eurocentrism: Multiculturalism and the Media.* London: Routledge. A spectacular, encyclopedic, and essential resource on the ways in which European films have represented non-Europeans and the contemporary ways non-Europeans are representing themselves.

Venbrux, Eric, Pamela Sheffield Rosi, and Robert L. Welsch. 2006. *Exploring World Art.* Long Grove, IL: Waveland Press. A cutting-edge collection of essays about art and anthropology covering a wide range of cultures. The essays are particularly valuable in exploring the ways in which "world art" (previously labeled "primitive" or "tribal" art) alters local cultural identities as it becomes absorbed into global processes of collecting, museum exhibits, and tourism.

Man with a painting of his father, a veteran of the *Tirailleurs Sénégalais*. The *Tirailleurs Sénégalais* was an army the French drafted and recruited from their colonial possessions in West Africa between 1857 and 1960.

**THINKING POINT:** Bernal Díaz del Castillo, a chronicler of the Spanish conquest of the Americas and swordsman under the command of Cortés, perhaps put it best: "We came here to serve God, and the King, and also to get rich."

# Power, Conquest, and a World System

Even though we are all aware that things change, most of the time, most people tend to treat the world as static. We assume that the social arrangements we see today, the distribution of wealth and poverty, of power and powerlessness, are of great historical depth. When we think of history at all, we tend to think of the histories of individual nations. But thinking about the world this way fails to account for change and limits our understanding. Our world is the current result of large-scale historic processes that involved the ebb and flow of wealth and power, not only among nations but among different areas of the world. These processes have had a particularly important impact on the kinds of small-scale, seemingly isolated societies that anthropologists often study.

The pace of change over the past several centuries has been enormous. Consider that the earliest writing probably appeared about 5500 years ago. The first movable type printing press was invented in China about 1000 years ago. Gutenberg was the first European to use movable type about 570 years ago. The telegraph was invented about 165 years ago; the telephone about 135 years ago; radio, 90 years ago; TV, 70 years ago; satellite communications, 50 years ago; Internet access, about 25 years ago; and cell phones have become ubiquitous within the last 10 to 15 years. Although there are no reliable statistics for such things, the amount of information in the form of text and pictures that flows around the world in a single 24-hour period in the present probably exceeds the total worldwide text and image production of the 11th century.

Although we are aware that the world has changed profoundly, we know less about the patterns of change and their effects on cultures around the world. The story of these patterns is complex and diverse; it is a story of contact between cultures. State-level societies have always expanded and contracted; however, our world today was substantially created by a specific instance of this. Although the empires of Asia, Africa, and Latin ≫

# Anthropology Makes a Difference

## Recovering Hidden Histories

The 19th-century French political philosopher Ernest Renan once said that getting one's history wrong is part of being a nation. He was arguing that nations come to exist partly by constructing a common past, a series of stories that show the people who make up the nation that they are united by great past deeds, common values, and ideas of future destiny. However, such stories can be maintained only if critical aspects of history were forgotten. Renan points out, for example, that the union of northern and southern France was achieved only at the expense of a century of massacres and terror but that for the French to feel themselves part of a modern nation, such events must be ignored.

Although anthropologists understand the point that Renan was making, part of their job is to fight against this tendency. Anthropologists want to tell the stories of the people whose history is ignored and remind nations that their unity is more a product of selective memory than a reflection of actual lived history. Anthropologists have been engaged in this task since the early days of the discipline. For example, in the 1930s Hortense Powdermaker and Zora Neale Hurston wrote extensively about the experiences of African Americans in the south.

Shackel and Palus's (2006) work on the workers of Virginius Island in the late 19th century is a more recent example. Virginius Island is part of Harpers Ferry National Park in West Virginia. There, in the 19th century, a series of entrepreneurs estab-lished cotton mills, flour mills, and finally paper and pulp mills. Shackel and Palus note that almost all of the historical inter-pretation at the National Park discusses the mills themselves and their owners. Very little explores the lives of the workers. Us-ing archaeology and oral history, Shackel and Palus traced the changes in the lives of workers at Virginius between the 1850s and the early 20th century. They found that early mill owners took a partially paternalistic approach to their workers, living on the is-land and building housing and other facili-ties for their workers. Paternalism created a system of mutual responsibilities and even rights between owners and workers. How-ever, it was based on the premise that work-ers would not demand too much from mill

---

America play important roles in history and have their own stories of expansion and retreat, the expansion of the affluence and power of places that are now wealthy, principally the nations of northern Europe and the colonies settled by their English-speaking (and sometimes French-speaking) subjects and citizens, has been the most important factor determining the political and economic condition of the world in the past several hundred years.

The expansion of European power occurred in thousands of locations and had many different effects. Sometimes cultural con-tact was accidentally genocidal, sometimes intentionally so. Many traditional cultures were destroyed, but others have prospered, although in altered forms. Members of different cultures often confronted each other through a veil of ignorance, suspicion, and accusations of savagery. But sometimes common interests, com-mon enemies, mutual curiosity, and occasionally friendship among people overrode their differences.

In this chapter, we describe the overall pattern of change dur-ing the past several hundred years. In the broadest sense, this in-volved the incorporation of relatively separate cultures and econo-mies into a vast, chaotic, yet integrated world economic system. The formation of this system resulted in enormous inequality both within and among nations as wealth and labor flowed from one area of the world to another. It created the financial accumulation necessary for the Industrial Revolution and the development of capitalism. In this era, empires rose and fell as powers competed for dominance within their own borders and with each other. The Ottoman Empire as well as the growth of Russia and of Japan played critical roles in the story. However, it was the expanding in-fluence and power of western European states that probably had the greatest impact worldwide. For that reason, we begin with a bird's-eye view of Europe and the rest of the world as it might have appeared in 1400.

As surprising as it may seem now, a visitor touring the world on the eve of European expansion in 1400 might well have been amused by the notion that European societies would soon become enormously wealthy and powerful. Other areas of the globe would have seemed much more likely prospects for power. Europeans had devised oceangoing vessels, but Arab and Chinese ships regularly made much longer voyages. The cities of India and China made those of Europe look like mere villages. Almost no European states could effectively administer more than a few hundred square kilo-meters. Certainly there was nothing that could compare to China's vast wealth and centralized bureaucracy. Europeans were masters of cathedral and castle construction, but other than that, their technol-ogy was backward. War, plague, and economic depression were the order of the day (Scammell 1989). Moreover, other areas of the world

owners. This, in turn, both reinforced and was reinforced by racism and segregation. The manufacturing workforce was entirely white. Owners limited workers' demands through the threat of hiring lower paid African-American workers.

As time went on and the profitability of 19th-century manufacturing techniques declined, owners increasingly became absentees and living conditions on the island deteriorated. Workers' communities became increasingly homogenized, and work became more and more simple. Skilled craftsmen were replaced by machine tenders. Contact between owners and workers declined and workers were increasingly subject to arbitrary decisions of absentee landlords. Finally, the community's infrastructure decayed. As these processes took place, there were changes in the material lives of the workers. On the one hand the promotion of consumer goods as well as their declining price of manufacture resulted in increasing consumerism and the contents of houses became more and more uniform. On the other hand, workers clearly rejected some aspects of consumerism, choosing only the aspects of dominant social behavior that had meaning for them (Shackel and Palus 2006:835). Their use of medicines and various other health and beauty products may have helped them create a greater sense of self and individuality. The remains of wild foods and plants as well as market gardens show that they resisted firm connection to the market economy.

National narratives show history as a march of progress. They celebrate the founding and development of corporations rather than the violence that often accompanied such events. They focus on the lives of the wealthy and powerful or, sometimes, the infamous. The lives, experiences, and struggles of families, of members of ethnic and religious minorities, of women, and of children are often omitted from the record. Their voices are silenced. One job of anthropology is to recover these voices and experiences. Listening to them gives us a deeper and broader understanding of the forces that make a nation and the tensions that underlie its existence.

seemed to be growing in wealth and power. Despite occasional setbacks, the Islamic powers had expanded steadily in the five centuries leading up to 1400, and Muslim societies stretched from Spain to Indonesia. Not only had these empires preserved the scholarship of India and the ancient Mediterranean civilizations, but they had greatly improved on ancient scholarship, making important discoveries in astronomy, mathematics, medicine, chemistry, zoology, mineralogy, and meteorology (Lapidus 1988:96, 241–252).

China's ancient civilization was extraordinarily powerful. As late as 1793, Emperor Ch'ien Lung, believing China to be the most powerful state in the world (or perhaps showing bravado in the face of foreign traders), responded to a British delegation's attempt to open trade by writing to King George II: "Our dynasty's majestic virtue has penetrated into every country under heaven and kings of all nations have offered their costly tribute by land and sea. As your Ambassador can see for himself, we possess all things. . . . we have never valued ingenious articles, nor do we have the slightest need of your country's manufacturers" (Peyrefitte 1992:288–292). Unfortunately for the Chinese, by the time the emperor wrote this letter, advances in military technology as well as the Industrial Revolution were giving Europeans decisive advantages. Within a half century, at the end of the First Opium War, Britain and other European powers virtually controlled China. <<

*L'Empereur Kien-Long.*

Ch'ien Lung, the Quianlung Emperor of China, rejected trade with the West in the 1790s. But within half a century, Britain and other European powers virtually controlled China.

# European Expansion: Motives and Methods

From slow beginnings in the 15th century, European power grew rapidly from the 16th to the 19th centuries. Many theories have been suggested to account for the causes and motives of European expansion. Although it was often a cover for more worldly aims, the desire of the pious to Christianize the world was certainly a motivating factor. The archives of the Jesuit order include more than 15,000 letters, written between 1550 and 1771, from people who wanted to be missionaries (Scammell 1989:60). The desire to find a wide variety of wonders, both real and imagined, was also important. Europeans searched for the mythical kingdom of Prester John, a powerful but hidden Christian monarch, the fountain of youth, and the seven cities of Cibola.

Beyond this, there was always the desire for wealth. Nations and nobles quickly lost their aversion to exploration as gold and diamonds were discovered. Bernal Díaz del Castillo, a chronicler of the Spanish conquest of the Americas and swordsman under the command of Cortés, perhaps put it best: "We came here to serve God, and the King, and also to get rich" (Simmons 1991:40). The wealthy and powerful looked for easy trade routes to the wealth of Eastern empires, such as China and Japan. The poor and oppressed of Europe saw opportunities for wealth and respect in the colonies. There, they sometimes fulfilled their dreams of wealth by re-creating the very social order they had fled.

Europeans were aided in their pursuit of expansion by various social and technological developments. These included the rise of a banking and merchant class, a growing population, and the development of the caravel, a new ship that was better at sailing into the wind. Two other developments, the monoculture plantation and the joint stock company, were to have critical impacts on the world's people.

In many cases, however, the key advantage Europeans had over other people was the diseases they carried. Almost every time Europeans met others who had been isolated from the European, African, and Asian land masses, they brought death and cultural destruction in the form of microbes. In many instances, virtually the entire native population perished of imported diseases within 20 years. Although Europeans too died of diseases, they did so in far smaller numbers (Karlen 1995; Newson 1999; Palkovich 1994; Wolf 1982).

**pillage** To strip an area of money, goods, or raw materials through the threat or use of physical violence.

The European search for wealth depended on tactics that, in their basic form, were ancient. Two of the quickest ways to accumulate wealth are to steal it from others and to get other people to work for you for free. State societies have always practiced these methods. War, slavery, exploitation, and inequality were present in most of the world before European contact, so there was nothing fundamentally new about their use by Europeans. However, no earlier empire had been able to practice these tactics on the scale of the European nations. All previous empires, however large, were regional affairs. European expansion, for the first time in history, linked the entire world into an economic system. For example, in the late 18th and early 19th centuries, the British consumed an average of 1.5 pounds of tea (grown almost entirely in India) and 11 pounds of sugar (mostly produced on Caribbean islands using African slave labor) per capita each year (Johnstone 1976:60; Mathias 1976:92). Although these had previously been luxury products consumed only by the wealthy, falling prices made these commodities available to the vast majority of the British population. Thus Britons of almost all social classes expressed the economic unification of the world in their daily patterns of consumption. This system, linking regions of the world at great distance from one another, created much of the wealth of Europe and ultimately that of many of today's industrialized nations. At the same time, it systematically impoverished much of the rest of the world.

## Pillage

One of the most important means of wealth transfer was **pillage.** In the early years of expansion, Europeans were driven by the search for precious metals, particularly gold and silver. When they found such valuables, they moved quickly to seize them. Metals belonging to indigenous peoples were soon dispatched back to Europe, and mines were placed under European control. The profits of these enterprises were enormous. For example, in 1531, Pizarro captured the Inca emperor Atahuallpa and received $88.5 million in gold and $2.5 million in silver (current value) as his ransom. A gang of Indian smiths worked nine forges day and night to melt down this treasure, which was then shipped back to Spain (Duncan 1995:158). In the early 17th century, 58,000 Indian workers were forced into silver mining in the town of Potosi in the Peruvian Andes (Wolf 1982:136). Between 1500 and 1660, Spanish colonies in the Americas exported 300 tons of gold and 25,000 tons of silver (Scammell 1989:133). At current prices, this would be worth about $23.5 billion. Such looting was not limited to the New World. After the British East India Company came to power in India, it plundered the treasury of Bengal, sending wealth back to investors in England (Wolf 1982:244). In 1860, during the Second Opium War, the Summer Palace northwest of Beijing was looted and

European expansion was often accompanied by violence and slaughter. Here, Bartolomeo, the brother of Christopher Columbus and founder of Santa Domingo (present-day capital of the Dominican Republic), destroys a village that resisted his rule.

its contents auctioned off to the looters for 26,000 pounds (Hevia 2007). Art, artifacts, curiosities, and occasionally human bodies were stolen around the world and sent to museums and private collections in Europe. Some Europeans became known for the scale and daring of their plundering. Giovanni Belzoni, sometimes known as The Great Belzoni, plundered the 7-ton head of Ramesses from the mortuary temple of Pharaoh Ramesses II. The head was sent to the British Museum, where it remains today. Later, with the help of a battering ram, Belzoni plundered four tombs in the Valley of the Kings, including that of Seti I (Aufderheide 2003:520). Belzoni went on to great fame in Europe. A small town in Mississippi is named after him.

## Forced Labor

Forced labor was another key element of European expansion. The most notorious example was African slavery, but impressing local inhabitants for labor, debt servitude, and other forms of peonage was common. Europeans forced both the peoples whose lands they conquered and their own lower classes into vassalage. Europeans did not invent slavery in general or African slavery in particular.

For example, non-Europeans probably exported more than 7 million African slaves to the Islamic world between 650 and 1600 (Lovejoy 1983). However, Europeans did practice African slavery on a larger scale than any people before them. Between the end of the 15th century and the end of the 19th century, approximately 11.7 million slaves were exported from Africa to the Americas. More than 6 million left Africa in the 19th century alone (Coquery-Vidrovitch 1988). No one really knows how many died during the capturing and transferring of slaves within Africa. However, scholars estimate that for each African slave successfully landed in the Americas, anywhere from one to five other Africans died in the process of slave capture, holding, and transportation.

The massive transport of people had two important economic effects. First, the use of slave labor was extremely profitable for both slave shippers and plantation owners. Second, slave labor created continuous warfare and impoverishment in the areas from which slaves were drawn. Although some undoubtedly grew rich on the profits of slavery, the loss of so many people and the violence and political instability resulting from the capture and transport of slaves radically altered African societies (Coquery-Vidrovitch 1988).

Forced labor was critical to extracting wealth from newly acquired lands. Growing sugar in the West Indies was extremely profitable but demanded huge amounts of human labor. This demand for labor led to the importation of millions of African slaves. This 1855 woodcut shows men and women making holes for planting sugarcane, a process known as "cane-holing."

The demand for slaves was created by **monoculture plantations**—farms devoted to the production of a single crop for sale to distant consumers. Sugar and cotton produced in the Americas and spices produced in Asia were sold to consumers located primarily in Europe. Through the 19th century, sugar was the most important monoculture crop. British consumption of sugar increased some 2500 percent between 1650 and 1800. Between 1800 and 1890, sugar production grew another 2500 percent, from 245,000 tons to more than 6 million tons per year (Mintz 1985:73). The massive amount of labor required for the growing and processing of sugar was largely provided by slaves. Between 1701 and 1810, for example, Barbados, a small island given over almost entirely to sugar production, imported 252,500 slaves, almost all of whom were involved in growing and processing sugar (Mintz 1985:53).

## Joint Stock Companies

The joint stock company was another innovation that allowed extremely rapid European expansion and led to enormous abuses of power. Most early European exploration was financed and supported by aristocratic governments or small private firms. By the turn of the 17th century, however, the British and Dutch had established joint stock companies. The French, Swedes, Danes, Germans, and Portuguese followed by midcentury. The best known of these companies include the Dutch East India Company (founded 1629), the British East India Company (founded 1600), the Massachusetts Bay Company (founded 1629), and the Hudson's Bay Company (founded in 1670).

**Joint stock companies** were the predecessors of today's publicly held corporations. The idea was simple. In order to raise the capital necessary for large-scale ventures, companies would sell shares. Each share entitled its purchaser to a portion of the profits (or losses) from the company's business. Exploration and trade by joint stock companies had critical advantages over earlier forms. First, a great deal of capital could be raised rapidly, so business ventures could be much larger than previously possible. Second, joint stock companies existed simply to provide profits to their shareholders. This differentiated them from the aristocratic governments that had previously dominated European exploration. Such governments wanted to make money, but they were also motivated by missionary zeal and the desire for prestige. Thus, joint stock companies pursued wealth with a single-mindedness and efficiency that governments often lacked. Because they frequently were empowered to monopolize trade, raise armies and conduct wars, and engage in diplomatic negotiations, they could have devastating effects on the societies they penetrated.

**monoculture plantation** An agricultural plantation specializing in the large-scale production of a single crop to be sold on the market.

**joint stock company** A firm that is managed by a centralized board of directors but is owned by its shareholders.

The **Dutch East India Company** (VOC, after its initials in Dutch) is a model example of a joint stock company. Based on money raised from the sale of shares, the VOC was chartered by the Dutch government to hold the monopoly on all Dutch trade with the societies of the Indian and Pacific Oceans. Shares in the VOC were available on reasonable terms and were held by a wide cross-section of Dutch society (Scammell 1989:101). In many ways, the company functioned as a government. Led by a board of directors called the **Heeren XVII** (the Lords Seventeen), it was empowered to make treaties with local rulers in the name of the Dutch Republic, occupy lands, levy taxes, raise armies, and declare war. The fundamental difference between a government and the VOC was that governments were to some degree beholden to those they governed, whereas the East India Company was interested solely in returning dividends to its shareholders. Through the 17th and early 18th centuries, the VOC distributed annual dividends of 15.5 to 50 percent. It returned dividends of 40 percent per year for six consecutive years from 1715 to 1720 (Boxer 1965:46). By comparison, the average annual dividend paid by a Standard and Poor's 500 stock index company between 1960 and 2007 was between 2 and 5 percent.

Through the 17th century, the VOC used its powers to seize control of many of the Indian Ocean islands. Among these were Java, including the port of Jakarta (which became their headquarters, renamed Batavia), Sri Lanka (Ceylon), and Malacca. In addition, the VOC acquired the right to control the production and trade of the most valuable spices of the area (cloves, nutmeg, and mace) and took brutal steps to maintain this monopoly. For example, during the 1620s, virtually the entire population of the nutmeg-producing island of Banda was deported, driven away, starved to death, or massacred. They were replaced with Dutch colonists who then used slave labor to operate the plantations (Ricklefs 1993:30). By the 1670s, the Dutch had gained complete control of all spice production in what is now Indonesia (Wolf 1982). The VOC acquired slaves through warfare, purchase, and levy from China, India, Indonesia, Madagascar, and East Africa.

Natives of this region did not submit passively to VOC control, and the company did not have a clear-cut military advantage. Instead, the VOC rapidly (and ultimately disastrously) became embroiled in the area's wars. For example, in the 17th century, the Maratram Dynasty controlled most of central Java. In 1677, when the dynasty faced rebellion, the VOC intervened on its behalf in hopes of cash payments and trade concessions. In a bloody campaign, the combined VOC and dynasty forces crushed the rebellion and established Emperor Amangkurat II on the throne. Trouble ensued when the VOC received neither payments nor concessions. In 1686, the company sent an armed force to make its demands but was defeated by Amangkurat II. The company was unable to recoup its losses or to claim its trading privileges (Ricklefs 1990). This was just the be-

Because the Dutch colonial period had such an important impact in Indonesia, figures of the Dutch rulers are incorporated into the centuries-old Indonesian shadow puppet play tradition.

ginning of a series of extremely brutal wars pitting different factions of Javanese kingdoms against each other and against the VOC. Kingdoms alternately allied with and fought against the VOC as their interests dictated. These conflicts lasted until 1757.

The company often acted with extraordinary brutality. The treatment of the Chinese in Batavia is a good example. The Chinese had come to Batavia as traders, skilled artisans, sugar millers, and shopkeepers. Despite harsh measures against them, by 1740 roughly 15,000 lived there. VOC officials believed they were plotting rebellion, and after an incident in which several Europeans were killed, VOC governor general Adriaan Valckenier hinted that a massacre would not be unwelcome. In the melee that followed, Europeans and their slaves killed 10,000 Chinese. The Chinese quarter of the city burned for several days, and the VOC was able to stop the looting only by paying its soldiers a premium to return to duty (Ricklefs 1993:90).

The burden of continual warfare, as well as corruption and inefficiency, forced the VOC into serious financial difficulties. By the last quarter of the 18th century, large areas of coastal Java had been depopulated by years

**Dutch East India Company** A joint stock company chartered by the Dutch government to control all Dutch trade in the Indian and Pacific Oceans. Also known by its Dutch initials VOC, for Verenigde Ostendische Compagnie.

**Heeren XVII** The Lords Seventeen, members of the board of directors of the Dutch East India Company.

of warfare, but the VOC had not succeeded in controlling the principal kingdoms of the island. The Heeren XVII were dismissed by the Netherlands government in 1796 after an investigation revealed corruption and mismanagement in all quarters. On December 31, 1799, the VOC was formally dissolved, and its possessions were turned over to the Batavian Republic, a Dutch client state of France.

The story of the VOC was, in large measure, repeated by other mercantilist trading firms organized by the British, French, Germans, Portuguese, Danes, and Swedes. In each case, companies generated enormous profits but eventually fell into disarray and either were dissolved or were taken over by their national governments. Despite their eventual failure, the trading companies placed fantastic riches in the hands of European elites. Europeans invested this wealth in many different ways: in the arts, in luxury goods, in architecture, but also in science and industry. This supply of wealth became one of the sources for the Industrial Revolution and the rise of capitalism itself.

The effects were far less pleasant for the regions in which the trading companies operated. The VOC and other trading companies left poverty and chaos in their wakes. In every case, Europeans fundamentally altered the communities with which they came into contact. Frequently, brutal policies and disease destroyed entire cultures. However, in most cases, societies were not simply overrun. Before the 19th century, Europeans did not have a truly decisive technological advantage over others. As a result, when unaided by disease, they were unable to simply defeat and dominate other cultures. Instead, Europeans had to collaborate with local elites who were often able to use their contact with the foreigners to increase their own wealth and power. However, as a whole, their societies suffered. For example, the British in India came to power through alliances with local elites. They were the subjects of the Mughal emperor in Delhi until 1857, although by that time, the relationship existed in name only. In that year, a savage war broke out between the British and their supporters and the supporters of the Mughal emperor. The British won this war a year later and formally abolished the Mughal Empire. The British referred to the war as "The Great Mutiny" and understood it as an uprising against British rule. However, technically, it was the British who mutinied, overthrowing the Mughal emperor, their nominal ruler (Dalrymple 2007).

**colonialism** The active possession of a foreign territory and the maintenance of political domination over that territory.

**colony** A territory under the immediate political control of a nation state.

# The Era of Colonialism

Colonialism differs in important ways from the earlier expansion of European power. Whereas much of the initial phase of European expansion was carried out by private companies and often took the form of raid and pillage, **colonialism** involved the active possession of foreign territory by European governments. **Colonies** were created when nations established and maintained political domination over geographically separate areas and political units (Kohn 1958).

There were several different types of European colonies. Some, such as the Belgian Congo in Africa, existed primarily to exploit native people and resources. In other areas, such as North America and Australia, the key goal was the settlement of surplus European population. Still other locales, such as Yemen, which borders on the Red Sea and thus controlled shipping through the Suez Canal, were seized because they occupied key strategic locations.

At one time or another, much of the world came under direct European colonization, but the timing of colonialism varied from place to place. The Americas were colonized in the 1500s and 1600s, but most other areas of the world did not come under colonial control until the 19th century. As long as Europeans confronted others with broadly similar weaponry and military tactics, the result was indecisive, and local governments were able to retain autonomy and power. By the 19th century, however, the Industrial Revolution gave Europeans (and their North American descendants) decisive advantage in both technological sophistication and quantity of arms. Although European colonizers faced frequent rebellions and proved unable to entirely subdue guerrilla activity in all places, no other government or army could offer effective resistance to them.

## Colonization 1500 to 1800

As we have seen, before the 1800s, very little of Africa or Asia was colonized. In these places, Europeans were able to establish small coastal settlements, but these existed largely because they were profitable for Europeans and at least some local elites. In most cases, local powers had the ability to expel Europeans or to strictly limit their activities. Relatively few Europeans settled permanently in such colonies.

In the Americas, the situation was radically different. There, Europeans quickly established colonies and immigrated in large numbers. For example, between 1492 and 1600, more than 55,000 Spaniards immigrated to the New World. In the 50 years that followed, another quarter million joined them (Boyd-Bowman 1975). By comparison, in the first half of the 19th century, the total Dutch population of Indonesia, Holland's most important colonial possession, was about 2,100 (Zeegers et al. 2004).

Although there was stiff resistance to European expansion in the Americas and Indian wars continued until the late 19th century, Europeans were quickly victorious almost everywhere they wanted to expand. The main reason for rapid European success was disease. Europeans, Africans, and Asians shared similar diseases and immunities. New World natives did not. In the wake of contact, up to 95 percent of the total population of the New World died (Karlen 1995; Palkovich 1994; Wolf 1982).

Although occasionally epidemics may have been caused intentionally, neither Europeans nor natives had any knowledge of contagion or germs. The vast majority of deaths were not premeditated. However, Europeans came to see the handiwork of God in the disappearance of native populations. In their view, God clearly intended them to populate the Americas and was removing the native population to make that possible.

New World natives lacked immunity to European diseases for two principal reasons. First, the key diseases that killed indigenous populations, such as smallpox, influenza, and tuberculosis, require large reservoirs of population, in some cases up to a half million individuals (Diamond 1992). Many North American groups were too small to sustain such crowd diseases and therefore lacked immunity to them. Second, although some Central and South American groups did have large populations, most crowd diseases originate in domesticated animals, which were largely absent from the Americas.

Cortes's conquest of Mexico is a good example of the effects of disease. When Cortes first appeared in 1519, the Aztec leader Montezuma, following his tradition, gave Cortes gifts and opened the city of Tenochtitlan to the Spanish. When it became clear that the Spanish were their enemies, the Aztecs expelled them from the city in a fierce battle that cost the Spanish and their allies perhaps two-thirds of their total army. By the time Cortes returned in 1521, a smallpox epidemic had killed up to half the Aztecs. Even after such crushing losses to disease, the Spanish conquest of Tenochtitlan took more than 4 months to accomplish (Berdan 1982; Clendinnen 1991; Karlen 1995). Had the Aztecs not been devastated by disease, they might have again defeated Cortes. Disease played an even bigger part in the conquest of the Incas in Peru. It swept across Central and South America well in advance of the Europeans themselves. By the time Spanish conquistador Francisco Pizarro reached Peru, the Inca Empire had already been decimated.

The die-off of Native Americans had dire effects throughout the Americas. The increasing population of Europeans and the diminishing population of natives ensured that resistance could not be very effective. When Winthrop, the first governor of Massachusetts, declared that the settlers had fair title to the land because it was

By the time Spanish conquistador Francisco Pizarro reached Peru, Inca society had been devastated by disease. In this condition, they were unable to resist Spanish conquest. This picture shows Atahuallpa, the last Inca, being executed before Pizarro.

*vacuum domicilium* (empty land), he was creating a legal fiction (he was well aware of the natives and their need for agricultural and hunting land) (Kiernan 2007:218). But he also knew that the native population was declining sharply.

If not for disease, the European experience in the Americas would probably have been very similar to its experience in Asia and Africa. Rather than establishing control over vast amounts of territory, Europeans probably would have been confined to small coastal settlements and involved in protracted battles with powerful local kingdoms.

## Colonizing in the 19th Century

By the beginning of the 19th century, industrialization was under way in Europe and North America. This had two immediate consequences. First, it enabled Europeans and Americans to produce weapons in greater quantity and quality than any other people. Second, it created an enormous demand for raw materials that could not be satisfied in Europe. In addition, discoveries in medicine, particularly vaccines and antimalarial drugs, improved the odds of survival for Europeans in places previously considered pestilential. Thus, Europeans had both motives and means to colonize.

By 1900, most nations in the Americas had achieved independence. However, much of the rest of the world was under colonial rule (see Figure 15.1). Many areas not for-mally colonized, such as China, were dominated by European powers. Acting in their own self-interest, Europeans and Americans generally did not move rapidly to place other areas under their colonial control. The primary goal of European expansion continued to be the pursuit of wealth and plunder. Mercantilist firms were rapid, cost-effective ways to get them. The financial burden of establishing companies such as the VOC was borne by their shareholders. However, colonizing an area required some level of government expenditure. At the very least this included government officials and the troops to back them, all of whom had to be equipped and paid out of government funds. In most cases, infrastructure such as roads, bridges, and railways had to be built. These were expensive undertakings, and European taxpayers and governments were generally not enthusiastic about funding them.

Most often, European governments felt forced to assume colonial control either because of the scandals surrounding the collapse of mercantile companies (as in the case of the VOC and the British East India Company) or out of fear that their national commercial interests were threatened, generally by other European nations. For example, it was this fear that led to the Berlin Conference partitioning Africa among European powers in the late 19th century.

Europeans used a combination of diplomacy and military conquest to force colonization on subject populations. In most cases, they created military forces of native troops led by European officers and used these forces to conquer the areas they wished to colonize. The *Tirail-*

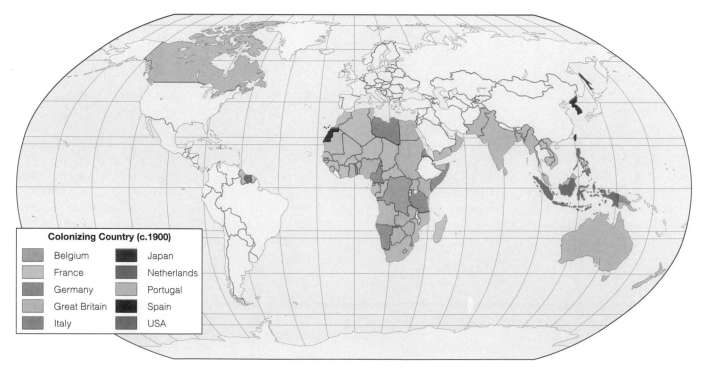

**FIGURE 15.1** As the European powers and Japan expanded, much of the world fell under their colonial rule. The Americas were colonized in the 16th and 17th centuries, but by 1900 most American nations had gained their independence. By 1900, the key areas under colonial rule were in Africa and Asia. Most of these nations gained their independence by the mid-1960s. Today, very few colonies remain, but many modern nations remain deeply affected by their colonial past.

*leurs Sénégalais* described in the "Ethnography" section accompanying this chapter is one such force.

European politicians and military leaders often created colonies without the full backing of the citizens of their nations (and sometimes without the support of their own legislatures). Thus, after colonies were established, European governments had to convince both their own populations and their colonial subjects that colonization was beneficial. They attempted to do this by cloaking their actions in the ideology of social betterment. In Britain, citizens were encouraged, in the words of the poet Rudyard Kipling, to take up "the white man's burden" of bringing civilization to the "savage." In France, the population was told that it had a *"mission civilisatrice,"* a **civilizing mission** that would both help the "savages" in the colonized areas and increase French political and cultural power throughout the world. The government portrayed its colonial practices as *"rayonnement,"* lighting the way for others (Cole and Raymond 2006:158–159). In the colonies, as we will see next, subjects were taught that they were colonized for their own good and that their societies would advance as a result.

## Making Colonialism Pay

Once colonies were seized, they had to be administered and they had to be made profitable. Colonizing powers hoped that tax revenues from colonial subjects would support the cost of colonial government as well as the construction of various public works. However, in many cases taxes were insufficient, and taxpayers in the colonizing country were required to make up the difference between colonial income and expenses. Despite this situation, colonies were extremely profitable.

Colonies gave businesses based in the colonizing country places in which they could operate free of competition. This was particularly important for Britain and France, two of the most important colonial powers. In the late 1700s, the Industrial Revolution began in Britain, but by the end of the 19th century, its factories were aging. New, more efficient industrial processes developed in the United States and Germany enabled these countries to produce cheaper manufactured goods (Allitt 2002). France came to industrialization relatively late and had a relatively weak road and rail network. As a result, France too had difficulty competing with the United States, Germany, and Britain. Colonies created zones of protection for older British industries and newer French manufacturers, thus enabling high profits for firms in these nations.

The costs of the colonies were born (unequally) by subject colonial populations and by colonizing-country taxpayers. The windfall profits from colonialism went to shareholders of companies operating in the colonies.

Finding ways to extract taxes and create the conditions in which corporations could make money often meant the systematic undermining of indigenous ways of life. Although the newly colonized communities had traded with other communities and frequently with Europeans for centuries, trading generally accounted for only a small percentage of their economy. For the most part, their economic relations were drawn along kinship lines, and most of their production was for their own consumption. For colonialism to be profitable, these patterns had to change. Colonial subjects had to be made to produce the goods that colonizing societies wanted and to labor in ways that would be profitable to the colonizers. From the colonizers' perspective, the key problem was finding ways to cause these changes. Some of the methods they used were control of local leaders, forced labor, forced production of particular commodities, taxation, and direct propaganda through education.

Sometimes colonial powers seized direct control of the political leadership, but this was expensive, and foreign colonial leaders often lacked sufficient knowledge of local language and culture. More often colonialists ruled indirectly through native leaders. Promises of power and wealth as well as the realization that colonial governments held the reins of power and were unlikely to lose them any time soon drew colonial subjects to support them. In some cases, colonial powers offered education, employment, and improved status to people who were oppressed or outcast in precolonial society; and these individuals were particularly drawn to support the colonizers.

A well-organized chain of command was needed for colonial powers to rule effectively. In hierarchical societies where kings or chiefs already existed, this did not pose a difficult problem. Most often, local elites sympathetic to the colonizers were able to retain a degree of power, although they became answerable to the colonial authorities. Those unsympathetic to colonial rule were rapidly replaced. Regions where precolonial relationships were largely egalitarian posed a more difficult problem. If there was no chief or there were many co-reigning chiefs, establishing colonial authority was far more difficult. Colonizers tried to solve this problem by creating new chiefly offices. Sometimes colonialists and missionaries forged entire new ethnic groups, lumping together people with different traditions and even different languages (Harries 1987). For example, the Bete, an ethnic group of the central Ivory Coast in Africa, did not exist before the era of colonialism but was created by the actions of colonial and postcolonial governments (Dozon 1985). In the long run, these policies of indirect rule created the preconditions for instability and violence. Politi-

---

**civilizing mission** The notion that colonialism was a duty for Europeans and a benefit for the colonized.

## African Soldiers of Misfortune

When I (Rich Warms) was young, I served as a Peace Corps Volunteer and lived in a town called Ouahigouya in the country then called Upper Volta (now Burkina Faso) in West Africa. I spent most of my time working in small villages, but I'd also wander around the town. Frequently on my wanderings I'd be stopped by a grizzled-looking old man who would start yelling at me in German. Then in French (the language of government and education in Upper Volta) he'd inform me that he'd been a prisoner of the Germans in World War II. At first I took him to be a drunk and a crazy person (where he stopped me was always near a bar). But, as I got to know him and other residents of the town better, I learned he had indeed been a German prisoner. That left me wondering how it was possible. After all, I didn't think he could have been visiting Europe when the war broke out. As I spoke to him and, over the 15 years that followed, to many others like him, I learned a story that had been left out of my high school and college history lessons.

Europeans saw in their colonies not only opportunities for the extraction of mineral and agricultural wealth, but also reservoirs of manpower. This was particularly true in Africa, which had traditionally served Europeans as a source of labor. Both the British and the French saw the military potential of African labor, and both formed armies composed of Africans. The British unit was known as the King's African Rifles, and the French as the **Tirailleurs Sénégalais** (Senegalese Riflemen). The *Tirailleurs Sénégalais* was officially created in 1857. Most of its soldiers were slaves, bought by the French for army service. Armed with French weaponry and led by French officers, their first task was the capture and control of colonies in sub-Saharan Africa.

The French completed their empire in Africa by the turn of the century, but the *Tirailleurs Sénégalais* was not disbanded. Instead, powerful interests in France argued that Africans had an obligation to serve the French state and could revitalize its army. The first practical trial of this idea was in 1912, when Africans were used to quell a rebellion in Morocco, but the real test came in World War I. More than 135,000 African troops, mostly drafted conscripts, served for the French in the trenches of Europe and almost 30,000 of these died there (Page 1987). Those who made their way back to Africa in 1918–1919, like many other veterans of World War I, had witnessed horrors incomprehensible to most of their countrymen. Like European and American soldiers suffering from "shell shock," members of this group were often considered deranged.

Though manpower needs slackened after World War I, France continued to draft African men into the *Tirailleurs Sénégalais*. Historian Myron Echenberg writes that French conscription in West Africa was "indeed a tax in sweat and blood" (1991:47). Between World Wars I and II, hundreds of thousands of Africans were conscripted into the army, and by 1939, on the eve of World War II, about 9 percent of the French army in France was composed of Africans. By the end of that war, France had recruited (most often drafted) more than 200,000 Africans and of these as many as 25,000 perished. In addition, France's African possessions were also taxed heavily to provide food and raw materials for the war effort (Lawler 1992).

The role played by African troops was critical for France in World War II. Most

*Courtesy of Richard Warms*

Veterans of *Tirailleurs Sénégalais*, Bougouni, Mali, 1995.

cal leaders were compromised by their close connections with colonial authorities, losing the confidence and respect of those they purported to lead. Ethnic groups created for the purposes of colonial rule tended to fragment when that rule diminished.

**Tirailleurs Sénégalais** Senegalese Riflemen. An army that existed from 1857 to 1960 composed largely of soldiers from French West African colonies led by officers from Metropolitan France.

people have heard of de Gaulle's Free French, but few realize that between the fall of France in 1940 and the summer of 1944, most of the members of the Free French Army were Africans. Even in late 1944, sub-Saharan Africans constituted as much as one-fifth of the total French army. For political reasons, both during and after the war, de Gaulle concealed the importance of African contributions, but it is clear that events in France might have taken a very different course without African soldiers (Echenberg 1991:104).

After the war, the returned soldiers occupied an important place in African society. Frequently veterans were respected by their peers because they understood modernity, foreigners, and in particular, the French (Lawler 1992:212). In addition, the sacrifices they had made, as well as the sacrifices of their countrymen, gave veterans a degree of moral suasion over the French colonialists. Veterans emerged as leaders, organizers, and agitators in the fight for African independence. The French, meanwhile, continued to enlist Africans in the *Tirailleurs Sénégalais* and used them against natives fighting wars of independence in Indochina (Vietnam) and Algeria in the 1950s.

Most of the French colonies in Africa received their independence in the early 1960s. The years since then have not been kind to the veterans of the *Tirailleurs Sénégalais*. The military service that gave them moral power as subjects of France was something of an embarrassment after independence. Members of radical governments and younger people saw them as men who had wasted their time in the service of a discredited authority. They were considered promoters of colonialism rather than, more accurately, its victims. Today, the veterans of the *Tirailleurs Sénégalais* are all but forgotten. Rapidly aging, their struggles and trials seem irrelevant to the young. Most rarely talk about their experiences except with those who shared them.

I was privileged to interview veterans of the *Tirailleurs Sénégalais* in the 1980s and 1990s. Some veterans had used pensions they received to marry several wives and raise large families. These often became prosperous and well-respected members of their community. Such veterans sometimes look back on their military careers with pride and some fondness. One said, "Well, [my military career was] the work of God. It's the way God made it to be. . . . I had love for the army, and because of my love for the army, I was able to continue serving" (Warms 1996).

Most veterans, however, received no pension. When they returned home, they often faced hostility or isolation. Fellow villagers couldn't understand their experiences and often thought poorly of them because they had returned with nothing to show for their labors. For these veterans, military service was best forgotten. One said, "When you come back, you have to follow the ideas of the people in the village. If not, if you try to tell them all about the army and what you have seen, they are never going to understand you. You can explain things and there are those who will just say you are lying. You just let them alone, at least that's the way I've gotten along" (Warms 1996).

Even those veterans who received pensions were given far less than French veterans and receive few services. Though they are proud of their accomplishments, they often feel like forgotten men, and many are profoundly disillusioned. In 1991, Mory Samake, a veteran of World War II, told me:

> When we were there fighting the war, no one said "this one is white, this one is black". . . . We gave our blood and our bodies so that France could be liberated. But now, since they have their freedom, they have thrown us away, forgotten us. If you eat the meat, you throw away the bone. France has done just that to us.

The story of the *Tirailleurs Sénégalais* and Mory Samake's anger with the French remind us of several extremely important points. A cliché has it that history is written by the winners. It might be more accurate to say that history is written by the powerful and often presented as a narrative of their inevitable triumph. But such a history ignores inconvenient truths or relegates them to footnotes and appendices. The relation between wealth and poverty and between the powerful and the powerless, or, in this case, between the colonized and the colonizer, are among the most important of these.

### CRITICAL THINKING QUESTIONS

1. Although the *Tirailleurs Sénégalais* played an important role in World War II, most readers of this book probably haven't heard of them. Why do you think that is so?
2. Most West African veterans live in conditions that would, in France, be considered deep poverty. What obligations, if any, does France have to these men and their families?
3. Veterans of the *Tirailleurs Sénégalais* fought for the French, sometimes against other colonized people. How do you think they justified their participation in these colonial wars?

## Forced Labor

One of the most direct ways that European governments tried to make their colonies profitable was by requiring **corvée labor**—unpaid work demanded of native populations. Until World War II, most colonial governments insisted on substantial labor from their subjects. The British often compelled subjects to work for up to 1 month per year, the Dutch 2 months. In 1926, the French enacted a law that permitted an annual draft of labor for their

**corvée labor** Unpaid labor required by a governing authority.

West African colonies. Conscripts were compelled to work for 3 years on bridge and road building, irrigation projects, and other public works. Mortality rates during the 3 years of forced labor often were very high, making this one of the most hated institutions of colonialism. Natives resisted colonial demands by concealing workers or by fleeing from authorities when such work was demanded (Evans 2000; Ishemo 1995).

Even when subject populations were not forced into labor gangs, economic and social policies of colonial regimes required them to radically alter their cultures. For example, Portuguese colonial policy in Mozambique forced almost 1 million peasants to grow cotton. The colonial government controlled what these growers produced, where they lived, with whom they traded, and how they organized their labor. Although a few growers prospered, the great majority became impoverished and struggled to survive against famine and hardship (Isaacman 1996). By the 1960s, the brutality and terror used by the colonial regime resulted in a civil war that continued into the 1990s.

At the turn of the century, conditions were perhaps worst in the Congo, ruled between 1885 and 1908 as the personal property of King Leopold of Belgium. There, each native owed the government 40 hours of labor per month in exchange for a token wage (Bodley 1999:116). Failure to work sufficiently or to produce the proper quantities of goods (particularly rubber) were met with extreme measures. Leopold's subjects were held hostage, were beaten or whipped, had their hands cut off, and, in many cases, were killed outright. By the time the Belgian

government stripped Leopold of his control of Congo, between 4 million and 8 million Congolese had been killed or had starved to death (Hochschild 1998).

In addition to forced labor and forced production, the British and French both drafted natives into their armed forces. They used these armies to capture and control their colonies, fight colonial wars, and augment their regular armies wherever needed. The *Tirailleurs Sénégalais* are described in this chapter's "Ethnography." Additional *Tirailleurs* units included groups from Algeria, Morocco, Madagascar, Vietnam, Cambodia, and other French colonial possessions. In East Africa, the British drafted and recruited the King's African Rifles. In India, the British created an entire army led by British officers but consisting almost entirely of colonial subjects drawn primarily from ethnic groups the British considered particularly warlike. About 1.3 million members of the Indian Army served in World War I, primarily on the Western Front but also in the Middle East (according to the U.K. National Archives).

## Taxation

Although particular projects might use forced labor, to make a colony truly profitable colonial masters also used other methods to encourage the population to work for them voluntarily or to produce the goods they desired. Taxation was a key mechanism for accomplishing this goal. Taxation was needed to support the colonial government, but because colonizers knew that colonial economies were small and their tax receipts low, they rarely expected taxes to provide the full cost of governing. However, taxing colonial subjects had another purpose: to force them into the market system. Taxes generally had to be paid in colonial money, which native subjects could obtain only by working for a colonist or by producing something that the colonists wanted to buy. This participation in the market and wage labor was viewed as the essential precondition for "civilizing" the natives.

Taxation often forced colonial subjects into a vicious cycle of dependency on the market system. To raise money for taxes, subjects had to work directly for the colonizers or produce things that colonizers desired. But spending time on these tasks meant that less time could be spent making goods or raising crops for one's own consumption. This in turn meant that increasingly food and goods had to be purchased from the market, which was dominated by companies owned by colonialists. This process meant that colonial subjects were increasingly enmeshed in a global capitalist economy. They entered this economy as producers of raw materials and consumers of manufactured goods. Thus, they received relatively low prices for the goods they produced but paid relatively high prices for those they purchased. Both the manufacturing processes and ownership of the corporations were located in the colonizing countries. Thus, it was there that profits were made and wealth created.

From 1885 to 1908, Congo was the property of King Leopold II of Belgium. Atrocities committed during that era cost the lives of 4 million to 8 million Congolese. Punishments for disobedience or failure to meet payment quotas included chopping off children's hands.

Anti-Slavery International Reg Charity 1039160

## Education

In addition to policies aimed at forcing subjects to take part in an economy centered in the industrial world, colonial governments took more direct aim at cultures through educational policies. Colonial education was often designed to convince subjects that they were the cultural, moral, and intellectual inferiors of those who ruled them. For example, education in 19th-century India encouraged children to aspire to be like the ideal Englishman (Viswanathan 1988). In France's African colonies, children were directly taught to obey their colonial masters, as illustrated in this passage from a turn-of-the-century reader designed to teach French to schoolchildren and used in the colonies:

> It is. . . . an advantage for a native to work for a white man, because the Whites are better educated, more advanced in civilization than the natives, and because, thanks to them, the natives will make more rapid progress. . . . and become one day really useful men. . . . You who are intelligent and industrious, my children, always help the Whites in their task (cited in Bodley 1999:104).

Education was often aimed at the children of elites. For example, in the 1860s, Faidherbe, the Governor General of the French West African colony of Senegal, established a "school for hostages" (*école des otages*) and "requested" that newly conquered chiefs send their sons to be educated. Although the name of the school was eventually changed to the "school for chiefs" (*école des chefs*), many of the students really were hostages. Chiefs and other notables often sent the sons of slaves and prisoners rather than their own children (Bouche 1966:234). At such schools, colonizing powers tried to create a class of literate subjects who would serve as junior grade civil servants. The children were taught skills that would be useful to them in such occupations. They were also taught that, although they might never reach the level of the colonists, they were considerably more advanced than their uneducated countrymen. In France's African colonies, individuals who were educated and assimilated to French culture were known both by the French and by themselves as *evolues,* or evolved people. This increased the perception of the uneducated and unassimilated as being backward and primitive. Thus, schooling both reinforced the colonizers' position and created a subservient educated class convinced of its superiority (Kelly 1986).

# Colonialism and Anthropology

The origins and practice of modern anthropology are bound up with the colonial era. Both anthropology and 19th-century colonialism are products of the 18th century age of European enlightenment, the romantic retrenchment of the 19th century, the Industrial Revolution, the birth of modern science, and other historical and philosophical forces. For example, the evolutionary theories of 19th-century anthropologists described a world in which all societies were evolving toward perfection. This idea shows elements of enlightenment rationality (the anthropologists were systematizing knowledge and trying to discover laws of social development) and 19th-century romanticism (the idea that nations were moving toward perfection) and was very clearly influenced by the scientific theories of Charles Darwin and the social theories of Herbert Spencer. It was also a convenient philosophy that could be pressed into service as a rationale for colonization (Ghosh 1991; Godelier 1993).

One of the most important impacts colonialism had on anthropology was in determining the locations of fieldwork. British Commonwealth anthropologists tended to work in British colonies, French anthropologists in their colonies, and Americans within U.S. borders, in areas "protected" by the Monroe Doctrine or in areas of American influence and control in the Pacific. In some cases, colonialism may have played a role in determining the topics of anthropological research. Studies of indigenous political systems or law were of particular interest to colonial governments. For example, Evans-Pritchard's classic exploration of the segmentary lineage system of the Nuer discussed in Chapter 8 was done at a time when the British rulers of Sudan were particularly interested in learning how to rule groups that lacked unified political leadership such as the Nuer (Johnson 1982). Colonialism and, more importantly, the discourse of rationalism and science also tended to promote a kind of anthropology where the anthropologist speaks as an active authority claiming to objectively describe essentially passive subjects.

In the first half of the 20th century, colonial governments faced with the practical problems of governing their possessions sometimes relied on information provided by anthropologists. Anthropologists, anxious to find funding for their research, argued that their studies had practical value to colonial administrators (Malinowski 1929a, for example). However, anthropology did not come into being to promote or enable colonialism, which would have gone on with or without it (Burton 1992).

Anthropologists did not generally question the political reality of colonialism, but they often self-consciously tried to advance the interests of the people they studied. The result was that colonial officials generally mistrusted anthropologists, believing they were much too sympathetic to colonial subjects (Prah 1990). Evans-Pritchard, for example, hoped that some of his work would humanize British colonialism. However, British colonial officials found him arrogant and skeptical, sometimes claiming that he was a "wild anthropologist," and "one of those denationalized scientists who take pride in advertising their freedom from the simpler loyalties" (Johnson 1982:244, 244f). Most anthropological research was financed by private charitable organizations with reformist agendas and not by governments (Goody 1995). Sometimes anthropologists financed their own research. The great French ethnographer Marcel Griaule, for example, put on a circus and promoted boxing matches to finance his ethnographic expeditions.

# Decolonization

The eras of Western expansion and colonization radically and permanently changed the world. By the time of World War II, all peoples had been affected by Western expansion and their cultures altered by this experience. Some, attempting to resist foreign influences and protect their ways of life, had moved as far away from outsiders as possible (for example, see Breusers 1999). However, most people lived in societies where the presence and influence of outsiders, their demands for goods and labor, and their attempts to change culture were fundamental facts of life.

Most of the nations of the Americas had gained their independence in the 18th and 19th centuries. In Africa and Asia, independence from European colonialism was not achieved until after World War II. Many nations that were part of the Soviet Union only received their independence in the late 1980s and early 1990s. Some colonies persist today, although usually with the consent of the majority of their residents. For example, Britain has some 14 "overseas territories," including Bermuda, Gibraltar, and the Pitcairn Islands. French "overseas departments" include Martinique and French Guiana. U.S. "organized unincorporated territories" include American Samoa and Guam. Many consider the U.S. relationship with Puerto Rico colonial as well (Grosfoguel 2003; Melendez 1993).

There were as many reasons for the granting of independence as there were for exploration and colonialism, but three are of particular importance: civil disobedience, changing political structures, and changing economic structures.

Governing colonies was never a simple affair, and from the beginning there was rebellion against colonial rule. Strikes, acts of terrorism, and in some places guerrilla warfare were common throughout the colonial era. However, for several reasons there was a substantial upsurge in these following the Second World War. One reason was the return of combat veterans. Veterans knew how to fight European-style warfare. Moreover, they and their supporters felt that colonizing countries owed them a deep debt for their service, a debt to be paid partially by increased political liberties.

In some places, resistance took the form of agitation and demonstrations. For example, in Côte d'Ivoire (West Africa), French attempts to rig elections in the late 1940s were answered with hunger strikes, mass demonstrations, acts of civil disobedience, as well as street fighting which resulted in scores of deaths, hundreds of injuries, and thousands of arrests (Smith 1978:87). In other places, bitter anticolonial wars broke out. In Madagascar, for example, almost 90,000 died in a rebellion in 1947 and 1948. In Algeria, between 1954 and 1962 France fought a protracted war that left at least one-quarter of a million dead (Kepel 2005). Anticolonial wars also broke out in Vietnam, Mozambique, Angola, and numerous other places.

The end of World War II also created a fundamentally different balance of world power. European nations, which held the largest number of colonies, were greatly weakened, which left the United States and the Soviet Union as the dominant superpowers. They quickly engaged each other in a Cold War that was to last for more than 4 decades. However, neither the United States nor the Soviet Union had a strong interest in preserving the colonial status quo. Based on the belief that they could bring former colonies into their own economic and political orbit, both nations promoted rapid independence for colonial possessions and both supplied money and weaponry to their supporters within the colonies.

Finally, international economics was also changing. In many cases colonies had been created to allow European corporations access to areas where they could operate free of competition from those based in other nations. However, in the wake of World War II, corporate ownership began to become multinational, and corporations were less tied to their nations of origin, a move that continues today. This process undercut an important economic rationale of colonialism.

Kwame Nkrumah, Ghana's first president, proclaims independence on March 6, 1957.

National Archives Photo No. 306-RNT-57-18116

By December 1960, when the United Nations declared that "all peoples have the right to self determination" and that "immediate steps shall be taken. . . . to transfer all powers to the peoples of [countries that have not yet achieved independence]" (UN Resolution 1514), the process of decolonization was already well under way. At that time, recently decolonized nations included India and Pakistan (1947), Cambodia (1953), Vietnam (1954), Ghana (1957), Guinea (1958), and many others.

By the late 1970s, almost all colonies held by western European nations had achieved independence. With the formal end of the Soviet Union in 1991 and the collapse of South African apartheid in 1994, almost all areas of the world had some form of home rule. Colonized areas became independent under a variety of circumstances and with many different levels of preparedness. In some, like Ghana, the transition to independence was reasonably orderly, and there were a sizable (though still inadequate) number of individuals trained as administrators. In others, like Congo, the transition was profoundly violent, and very few colonial subjects had any experience with running government. But although there were great differences among colonies, all came to independence as relatively poor nations in a world that was increasingly divided into the wealthy and the poor rather than the independent and the colonized.

Formal independence was critical for former colonies. However, compelling connections between newly independent nations and their former colonial powers remained. In most cases, diplomatic and cultural ties between nations and their former colonies continued to be strong. In many cases, economic ties persisted as well. European and American corporations continued their operations, albeit frequently with new names, and in many places countries continued to supply the raw materials for European, American, and increasingly Asian industries. For example, in Côte d'Ivoire, the number of French expatriates actually increased after independence: from 30,000 in 1960 to almost 60,000 by 1980 (Handloff and Roberts 1991:93). In the 1960s, the word "neocolonialism" came to express the idea that although nations were no longer colonized, many of the institutions of colonialism remained intact.

The European expansion and the era of colonization were historic processes that changed the world from a collection of relatively independent economies and societies to a complex world system. Technological and political processes since the end of colonialism have only accelerated this process. In Chapter 16 we explore some of the problems faced by independent but poor nations as well as the forces of technology, finance, and politics that are weaving an increasingly dense fabric of globalization.

## The Global and the Local: Who Owns History?

In February 2009 there was a controversy in the art world. Two Chinese bronzes depicting signs of the Chinese Zodiac had been held in the collection of Pierre Bergé and Yves Saint Laurent. Despite the protests of the Chinese government, they were to be auctioned by Christie's. Similar pieces had fetched very high prices in 2007, so multimillion dollar bids were expected. The auction was won by a Chinese art dealer with a bid of about $40 million. However, the story took a strange turn when the art dealer announced that he had no intention of paying the bid and demanded that the bronzes be voluntarily returned to China. He argued that the bronzes had been looted from China in the 19th century and formed part of that country's patrimony. The owner of the objects rejected all Chinese legal claims but said that he would be glad to return the bronzes if the Chinese government "gives in return human rights, the liberation of Tibet, and a welcome for the Dali Lama" (Eakin 2009:19).

The Chinese bronze incident highlights a persistent controversy over the ownership of historical objects. Nations in which such objects were found have long attempted to claim ownership of them and demand their repatriation. For example, in the early 19th century,

Thomas Bruce, the 7th Earl of Elgin, removed much of the Parthenon's marble sculpture and sold it to the British government, which displayed it at the British Museum in London. Controversy erupted almost immediately. Today, close to 200 years later, the Elgin Marbles remain on display in London and the Greek government continues to demand their return. However, some governments have been far more successful demanding the return of other objects and, since 1970, when UNESCO adopted a convention on preventing the illicit import, export, and transfer of ownership of cultural property, thousands of items have been repatriated from museums to their countries of origin. In the United States, the Native American Graves Protection and Repatriation Act (NAGPRA), passed in 1990, requires the return of certain artifacts.

The ownership and repatriation of historical objects is deeply controversial and raises both practical and philosophical questions. On the practical side, many claims of ownership are problematic. For example, much of the ancient Byzantine Empire was located in what is now the modern nation of Turkey. The Byzantines often looted art from ancient Greece. A substantial amount of this art is now in Western museums. Does it belong to Turkey, from which it was taken in modern times, or to Greece, from which it was taken in ancient times?

Beyond this, there are important concerns about the uses to which such objects are put. Major museums are more than simply research institutions and holding places for antiquities. They are building blocks in creating national identity. For example, the British Museum, founded in the mid-18th century, collected art from around the world. It promoted the idea of Britain as national and imperial power. Through the display of objects such as the Elgin Marbles, Britain laid claim to status as the modern heir of ancient empires. National museums today often have similar functions. James Cuno argues that such museums frequently use artifacts found within their borders to bolster national mythologies that are, to a great degree, fictional, so "Etruscan pots (more often than not manufactured in Athens) are used to define Italianness; Sumerian sculptures to define Iraqiness. . . . and so on (Eakin 2009:18). Cuno argues that the connections between the modern populations of these nations and the ancient cultures are dubious and that museums press such objects into the service of a spurious nationalism that denies evidence of cultural diversity and promotes ethnic chauvinism. On the other hand, the large modern museums in wealthy nations, such as the Metropolitan Museum of Art in New York City, the Getty in Los Angeles, and the modern British Museum in London, where many such objects reside today, often "direct attention to distant cultures, asking visitors to respect the values of others and seek connections between cultures" (quoted in Eakin 2009:17). Cuno

Museum de Rouen, France

Drawing of a mummified Maori head. This head has been in the collection of the Museum of Natural History at Rouen, France. In 2007, the mayor of Rouen offered to return the head to New Zealand in "atonement" for the trafficking of human remains that occurred in the colonial era. However, the French government prevented the return of the head.

offers the example of an ivory box on display at the Art Institute of Chicago that was used for Christian devotion in 13th-century Sicily, but was made from East African elephant tusk and included Arabic inscriptions.

Anthropologists often find themselves caught in the middle of debates about the repatriation of historical objects. On the one hand, in most cases, anthropologists identify with the aspirations and interests of the people they study. Thus, they support what they often view as people's legitimate desire to have their objects (and in some cases, the bodies of their relatives and ancestors) returned to them. For example, in 2006, anthropologist Monica L. Udvardy played an important role in securing the return of statues stolen from Kenya and displayed at American museums (Lacey 2006). On the other hand, anthropologists are also aware that the return of such objects sometimes makes them more difficult to study. Indeed, returned objects may be reburied or destroyed, making further study impossible. Further, most large museums promote understandings of cultural diversity and the interrelations among cultures, goals that anthropologists support.

## Key Questions

1. How should the ownership of historical objects be determined and who should get to make such a determination? Are geographical origins or claims of historical relationship sufficient?
2. Should the fact that the current possessors of objects may not like the uses to which nations put repatriated objects play any role in determining whether or not they should be returned?

# Summary

1. To what degree is the current distribution of wealth and power in the world similar to what it was 1000 years ago? Although we are aware of history, we tend to think of current world conditions as similar to past conditions. This is incorrect. The world as we see it is the result of historical processes that have moved wealth and power from one area to another. Places that are impoverished today were in many cases wealthy 1000 years ago. The rise of today's wealthy nations was connected with the emergence of modern poverty.

2. What was the condition of Europe in the 15th century? In the 15th century, Europe was neither wealthy nor technologically advanced. The centers of world power lay primarily in the Middle East and Asia. However, Europe was poised on the brink of a great expansion.

3. What were the primary motivations for European expansion? A combination of religious faith, greed, new social arrangements, and new technologies drove European expansion.

4.  **In what parts of the world were Europeans most successful at capturing and controlling new lands and why?** Europeans were most successful in controlling lands in the Americas. This was because Native Americans lacked resistance to European diseases. As a result, native societies were depopulated and succumbed to European military pressure.

5.  **What were the key mechanisms used by Europeans to make their control of foreign territory pay?** Plunder of precious metals, the use of slave labor on monocultural plantations, and the joint stock company were all instrumental in creating wealth for Europeans. Additionally, military and diplomatic maneuvering helped draw wealth from around the world into Europe.

6.  **What was colonialism and when did it happen?** Colonialism is the active possession of a foreign territory and the maintenance of political dominance over that territory. The Americas were first colonized in the 16th century. However, elsewhere in the world, colonization did not happen until the 19th century.

7.  **Why did Europeans colonize in the 19th century and how did they justify their taking of colonial possessions?** Europeans colonized because of the collapse of earlier mercantilist firms or to protect their national companies from competition from other Europeans. They wished to increase their wealth and protect their trade. They justified colonialism by calling it a civilizing mission.

8.  **What methods did Europeans use to try to make colonialism pay?** Europeans pressed colonial subjects into forced labor on roads and other projects. They used taxation in colonial money to fund the government and force natives to participate in the European-dominated cash economy. They used education programs to discredit local culture and create a class of people who could help with colonial administration.

9.  **What was the role of anthropology in colonialism?** Anthropological knowledge was sometimes used in the process of colonialism, and some anthropologists wished to make themselves useful to colonial governments. However, anthropology did not come into being to promote colonialism, which would have gone on without it.

10. **When did the colonies taken in the 19th century gain their independence and what key factors were responsible for this?** Most colonies gained their independence between the end of World War II and 1965. Civil unrest in the colonies, the emergence of the United States and the Soviet Union as superpowers, and changes in the structure of international economics played critical roles in the timing of independence.

# Key Terms

civilizing mission
colonialism
colony
corvée labor

Dutch East India Company
Heeren XVII
joint stock company

monoculture plantation
pillage
*Tirailleurs Sénégalais*

# Suggested Readings

Bodley, John H. 2008. *Victims of Progress* (5th ed.). Lanham, MD: Altamira. A comprehensive review of the effects of Western expansion on tribal and indigenous people. Bodley has written several books detailing the relationship of the industrialized powers to native peoples.

Mintz, Sidney W. 1985. *Sweetness and Power: The Place of Sugar in Modern History.* New York: Penguin. A fascinating account of the ways in which sugar has changed the world economy. Mintz explores how sugar production and consumption changed both Europe and the Americas and altered our eating habits and diet.

Scammell, G. V. 1989. *The First Imperial Age: European Overseas Expansion c. 1400-1715.* London: HarperCollins Academic. This work explores Europe's rise to world power, focusing on the precapitalist period. It is a particularly good source for understanding European involvement in Asia.

Wolf, Eric R. 1982. *Europe and the People without History.* Berkeley: University of California Press. A classic introduction to the history of Western expansion. Wolf's book underscores the relationship between wealth and poverty and highlights the importance of history to understanding current societies.

We live in a world of sharp contrasts. Individuals and cultures worldwide are affected by changes in communication, technology, and the flow of wealth among nations.

© Time & Life Pictures/Getty Images

**THINKING POINT:** In the face of economic and political change, some indigenous groups have simply disappeared. Many groups have managed to adapt, preserve some of their ways of life, and maintain a degree of cultural integrity. New identities have been forged as people and cultures have responded to change.

{chapter 16}

# Culture, Change, and the Modern World

Consider an average family in North America. There probably are four family members with a combined income of more than $50,000. They live in a comfortable house or apartment and have one or two cars. Each child has a separate bedroom. They have numerous consumer goods, mostly manufactured outside North America. There are three meals a day and plenty of snacks. Much of their food is imported. The children are healthy and attend school. They can expect to complete their secondary education, probably go to college, choose among a variety of careers, and live to an average age of 77 years.

On the surface life seems good for this family, but there are problems as well. The competitive pressures are strong and take their toll on the health of both parents. Rising medical costs, high costs for college education, job insecurity, and debt threaten their way of life. But on the whole, theirs is an economic status and lifestyle toward which many millions of people throughout the world seem to be aspiring.

Now consider a typical "extended" family in rural Asia. The household likely comprises 10 or more people, including parents, children, and other relatives. They have a combined annual income of less than $500. They live in a one-room house as tenant farmers on a large agricultural estate owned by an absentee landlord. The adults and older children work all day on the land. None of the adults can read or write. Of the five school-age children, only two attend school regularly, and they will get only a basic primary education. There is often only one meal a day; it rarely changes and rarely is sufficient to alleviate the children's hunger pains. The house has no electricity or fresh water supply. There is much sickness but very few medical practitioners. The work is hard, the sun is hot, and the aspirations for a better life are continually being snuffed out. ≫

Shifting to a large city along the coast of South America, we would immediately be struck by the sharp contrast in living conditions among neighborhoods. There is a modern stretch of tall buildings, wide boulevards, and gleaming beaches, but just a few hundred yards away there are squalid shanties. It is a typical Saturday evening at an hour when families should be preparing dinner. In the apartment of a wealthy family, a servant sets the table with imported china, high-quality silverware, and fine linen. The family's eldest son is home from his university in North America, and the other two children are on vacation from their boarding schools in France and Switzerland. The father is a medical doctor with a wealthy clientele. Annual vacations abroad, imported luxuries, and fine food and clothing are commonplace amenities for this fortunate family.

And what of a poor family? They live in a dirt-floor hillside shack. The stench of open sewers fills the air. There is no dinner table being set; in fact, there is no dinner—only a few scraps of stale bread. The four children spend most of their time on the streets begging, shining shoes, or even trying to steal. They are recent immigrants to the city. The father has had part-time jobs but nothing permanent, and the family income is less than $1000 a year. The children have been in and out of school many times because they have to help out financially in any way they can. Occasionally the eldest teenage daughter seems to have some extra money, but no one asks where it comes from or how it is obtained.

The contrast between these two South American families is disturbing, but had we looked at almost any other major city in the world, we would have seen similar things (although the extent of inequality might have been less pronounced).

Finally, imagine that you are in eastern Africa, where many small clusters of tiny huts dot a dry and barren land. Each cluster contains a group of extended families, all participating in and sharing the work. There is very little money because most food, shelter, and other goods are made and consumed by the people themselves. There are few roads and no schools, hospitals, electricity, or water supply. In many respects life is as difficult as for the poor family in Latin America. Yet, because it is shared by all, it is probably less psychologically troubling.

Soon a road will pass near this village. It will bring more information about the outside world, more gadgets of modern civilization. Before long, exportable tropical fruits will be grown in this region. They may even end up on the dinner table of the rich South American family. Meanwhile, radios made in southeast Asia playing music performed by African bands recorded in northern Europe will become prized possessions. Throughout the world remote villages are being linked with the rest of the world in an increasing number of ways. This process will only intensify in the coming years.

The scenarios you've just read, adapted from Todaro and Smith's (2003) classic textbook *Economic Development,* is simplis-

tic but dramatically captures some important truths. The historical processes we described in Chapter 15 have transformed the world, creating a global economic network. However, it is not a global village. The global village is a pastoral metaphor. Thinking of the world as a global village suggests a relatively small place, a place where anyone can easily visit any part, a place where differences are minimized, a world of screen doors, broad porches, and friendly neighbors. But we live in a world of privilege and exclusion, a world of rapid change and of shocking inequality. In our world, some areas are centers: easy to get to, wealthy, powerful, and in constant communication with each other. Other places are more difficult to reach, less in contact with the rest of the world. Still others can be entered and exited only with real difficulty. In our world, the distances created by inequality often dwarf those of mere distance. For example, a technology or financial specialist working in Manhattan is likely to have close ties to colleagues, relatives, and friends living and working thousands of miles away and to communicate frequently with these people. They may have almost no social connections with members of the urban poor living within sight of their office and may almost never communicate with these people.

As the opening passages of this chapter show, our world is an enormously contradictory place. All around us, we see increasing cultural homogeneity; you can find a bottle of soda, a radio, or a CD player almost anywhere. Cell phones connect people in remote African villages to relatives in industrialized urban metropolises. The Internet lets teenagers in Houston bid on products in Hong Kong. At the same time, it is in many ways an increasingly divided world. The disparities in both quality and quantity of life are enormous. More than 1.2 billion of the world's population live on less than $1 a day. At the same time, a meal for two at a good restaurant in any American city can easily top $100. Someone born in the late 1990s in Japan had a life expectancy of 81 years. People born in those same years in Malawi or Mozambique had life expectancies of only 37 years. Moreover, although many forces at work in the world favor cultural homogeneity, in many places people are insisting, sometimes violently, on their right to preserve their cultural identity or to create new identities intentionally separating themselves from the dominant global culture (for examples see Friedman 2003; Hefner 2002).

The end of colonial rule brought numerous challenges to the newly independent nations. They were beset by issues of poverty, the presence of multinational corporations, urbanization, population growth, problems of immigration and emigration, ecological disaster, war, and instability. A few nations, such as Singapore (formerly a British colony) and Korea (a Japanese colony from 1905 to 1945), have done extremely well. In 1981 almost 64 percent of Chinese were living on less than $1 a day. By 2001, that number had dropped to 16.6 percent and today is believed to be close to

8 percent (in constant dollars). Despite these successes, most nations remain poor.

The **gross national income (GNI)** of a nation is the total value of all its production and provides a rough estimate of national prosperity. Adjusting the GNI for price differences between nations (a method called purchasing power parity) allows us to compare countries. In the United States, in 2007 the GNI per capita, adjusted for purchasing power, was $45,840, but 73 of the 208 nations listed by the **World Bank** had a per capita GNI of less than $5000. For 50 of these nations, the figure was less than $2500. In 2004, about 1 billion people were living on less than $1 a day.

No culture has been left unchanged by history. However, the burden of history has fallen with particular force on the world's indigenous people. Their cultures have had to adjust to extraordinary circumstances. In the face of economic and political change, some indigenous groups have simply disappeared. Many groups have managed to adapt, preserve some of their ways of life, and maintain a degree of cultural integrity. New identities have been forged as people and cultures have responded to change. In this chapter we examine some of the principal challenges resulting from globalization and consider what anthropology teaches us about the effects of global forces on cultures worldwide. <<

# Development

The decline of colonialism after World War II did not mean the end of forced cultural change, foreign intervention, or foreign influence. Nations were brought into ever closer contact, the pace of change increased as communications improved, and both individuals and groups, attracted by new opportunities or compelled to flee from violence, moved to new locations. Virtually all nations were drawn into the long conflict between the Western powers and the Soviet bloc. In wealthy nations, the Cold War was fought with military construction programs, diplomacy, and espionage. In poor nations such as Nicaragua, Congo, and Vietnam, it was fought with bullets and aircraft as well.

Under colonialism, economic plans focused on making colonies productive for their owners, but independent nations needed to be prosperous in their own right. Both Eastern and Western blocs saw this as an opportunity to spread their ideology and advance their economic systems. Both provided financial and military aid to poor nations. Their goals were to create political allies and stable trading partners as well as to secure sources of raw materials. Additionally, some international agencies, wealthy nation governments, and thousands of private organizations truly hoped to bring a better life to the world's poor.

© Associated Press

**The Bretton Woods conference in 1944 established the World Bank and International Monetary Fund. Here, the chairmen of the delegations of the 44 countries represented pose for an official picture.**

The Bretton Woods agreement of 1944 was a key instrument inaugurating the era of development. In that agreement, 44 Allied nations of World War II established the International Monetary Fund and the International Bank for Reconstruction and Development, also known as the World Bank. The goal of these institutions was to stabilize the international financial system and to provide loans and credits, first for the reconstruction of war-ravaged Europe, and then for economic **development** in poor nations.

## Modernization Theory

The model of progress promoted by Western nations from the end of World War II until the 1970s was called modernization theory. The clearest statement of the theory was W. W. Rostow's 1960 work *The Stages of Growth: A Non-Communist Manifesto.* The title of Rostow's book emphasizes the Cold-War context of much of this work. **Modernization theory** started with the presumption that former

**gross national income (GNI)** The total value of all goods and services produced in a country.

**World Bank** Officially called the International Bank for Reconstruction and Development, an international agency that provides technical assistance and loans to promote international trade and economic development, especially to poor nations. The World Bank has often been criticized for interfering in the affairs of these nations.

**development** The notion that some countries are poor because they have small industrial plants and few lines of communication and that they should pursue wealth by acquiring these and other things.

**modernization theory** A model of development that predicts that non-industrial societies will move in the social and technological direction of industrialized nations.

colonies were poor because they had underdeveloped, backward economies. They had such economies because their cultures and ways of thinking were dominated by traditions that opposed the rational style of thinking demanded by modern society. Modernization theorists assumed that, several hundred years ago, all areas of the world were economically undeveloped and culturally dominated by tradition. Through a historical series of political, economic, and cultural choices, some areas of the world had been able to develop and were today wealthy, modern, and rational. Given this understanding of history, the pathway to wealth was clear: analyze the historical experience of today's wealthy nations and design policies so that today's poor nations could repeat that experience. . . . hopefully at an accelerated rate. To this end, foreign advice and financial aid were designed to alter the structural, cultural, and psychological features the theorists believed stood in the way of modernization. New roads and factories would bring industrialization to the countryside. New farming techniques would allow peasants to cultivate cash crops. The market would replace the old mechanisms of obligation and reciprocity. Education would dispel the irrationality of tradition. The result would be increased wealth and higher standards of living as well as the disappearance of irrational superstition. Poor nations were the recipients of substantial cash gifts from the wealthy nations. However, they were also encouraged to take large loans from governments and banks in wealthy nations. The ability of poor nations to repay these loans was predicated on expectations of reasonable success for the development programs they funded.

This kind of development served the interests of both donors in wealthy nations and elites in poor nations. It spread the influence of wealthy nations and made new markets for their products. In poor nations, money from development aid was often used to support an elite lifestyle and opened many possibilities for political patronage, not to mention bribery, graft, and other forms of corruption. However, it did little to improve conditions for most people in the recipient nations. In most cases, the economic gains made were small; in some cases, nations' economic output actually declined. For example, the GNI per capita for Ghana declined about 13 percent between 1960 and 1980. In some places the fall was far worse (UC Atlas of Global Inequality n.d.). There were many reasons for this failure, but surely a critical reason was a problem with the theory itself. The proponents of modernization theory believed that poor nations could become wealthy by repeating the historical experience of wealthy nations. They assumed that poor nations were traditional and timeless, ignoring the roles that colonialism and exploitation

had played in the history of both the rich and the poor. Poor nations could not repeat the historical experiences of the wealthy because they were products of that history. In many cases, their cultures were not "traditional" but had been shaped by the experiences of exploitation, colonization, and warfare with Europe.

## Human Needs Approaches

The failure of economic development plans in the 1960s led to the emergence of new ideas. Some argued that development had failed because it had focused on large-scale projects and technological change. However, conditions in many places in poor nations were so bad that hunger, sickness, and illiteracy prevented people from participating in development programs or taking advantage of their benefits. They proposed a different style of development called the basic human needs approach. In 1972 and 1973, the World Bank and other development agencies began to focus on filling the basic needs of the rural poor. Speaking in Nairobi in 1973, Robert McNamara, then World Bank president, identified the elimination of absolute poverty as a principal goal of development aid. McNamara described absolute poverty as:

> a condition of life so degraded by disease, illiteracy, malnutrition and squalor as to deny its victims basic human necessities and a condition of life so common as to be the lot of some 40 percent of the peoples of the developing countries (World Bank Group Archives 2003).

**Basic human needs** projects focused on improving the lives of the very poor and increasing their capacity to

Basic human needs approaches to development focused on providing education, health care, and clean water as in this well-digging project for a hospital in Wajir, Kenya.

**basic human needs approach** Projects aimed at providing access to clean water, education, and health care for the poorest of the world's people.

contribute effectively to the economy. Such projects attempted to ensure poor people access to land and improved but simple farming techniques. They funded basic education, access to pure water, and basic health and sanitation facilities. The focus was on involving members of rural communities in managing and promoting these goals. Because anthropologists often had expertise in studying such communities, they came to play increasingly important roles in development aid. In 1974, the United States Agency for International Development (USAID) employed one full-time anthropologist. By 1980 this number had risen to more than 50 (Escobar 1997).

Basic human needs projects are very popular with many donors in wealthy countries and continue to play an important role in foreign aid, particularly aid given by smaller nongovernmental agencies. However, by the end of the 1980s they had lost their prominent role in development. There were several reasons for this. First, although the projects did provide benefits to some communities, they failed to provide the economic growth that planners hoped for. Beyond this, donor governments did not like these projects because they had high overhead expenses and did not generate very much publicity. Recipient governments disliked them because the amount of money disbursed for them was lower than for more traditional modernization projects, and often the groups that the projects tried to help had relatively little political power. Perhaps most importantly, beginning in the 1980s, political changes in developing countries resulted again in changes in the philosophy of development.

## Structural Adjustment

Many development programs had been financed by loans from governments and banks in wealthy nations. Because the wealth that was envisioned by program planners failed to materialize, by the late 1970s, poor nations found themselves with insufficient funds to operate their governments and repay their loans. This coincided with the rise of neoliberalism in the United States and Europe. **Neoliberalism** is a series of political and economic policies promoting free trade, individual initiative, and minimal government regulation of the economy. Neoliberals have opposed state control of industries or government subsidies to them as well as all but minimal aid to impoverished individuals. They argued that their policies would unleash capitalist economic forces that would result in improved standards of living for all people. This political philosophy led to a new approach to development called **structural adjustment.** Following neoliberal policies, before making any additional loans or grants, wealthy nations demanded that poor nations restructure their economies. They required poor nations to sell off state-owned enterprises; reduce subsidies to local businesses and industries; reduce spending on education, health, and social programs; and open their markets to free trade. Most

poor nations protested vociferously against these policies but, because they were unable to repay their debts and needed new money to operate their governments, they were forced to accept them.

In most places, the results of structural adjustment policies have been equivocal at best. Critics charge that these policies have created a spiral of deepening impoverishment that particularly affects the poorest and most vulnerable populations. Supporters argue that although such policies do cause pain, earlier policies were unsustainable and, in the long run, structural adjustment will lead to a better standard of living for all. However, the results of structural adjustment have been equivocal at best. For example, a World Bank study of the economic growth in Africa showed that early adopters of structural adjustment did perform somewhat better than late adopters and countries that did not adopt such reforms. However, such differences were relatively small and no country showed the dramatic improvement planners had hoped for. Further, the better performance of early adopters might have been more closely related to ending of wars and the removal of certain dictatorial and corrupt governments than to any purely economic factors (World Bank 2005:277). Although there certainly are two sides to this argument, it is clear that, thus far, structural adjustment policies have increased inequality within nations and that poverty remains an intractable problem (Greenberg 1997; Kim et al. 2000; SAPRIN 2004).

Despite many failures and the persistence of global poverty, development efforts of both governments and private organizations have led to some notable successes. For example, in poor nations, life expectancy has increased 20 percent and literacy 25 percent in the past generation. Children are only half as likely to die before the age of 5 as they were a generation ago. The Grameen Bank is an important success story. The bank, a grassroots organization that offers small loans to poor women, has reached over a million families around the world and has been effective in raising the standard of living among some of the world's poorest people. The Grameen Bank and its founder, the Bangladeshi economist Muhammad Yunus, won the Noble Peace Prize in 2006. However, the overall record of development projects around the world continues to be poor. Projects have been plagued by poor design, inappropriate technologies, and deleterious effects on environment, culture, and political stability. For

**neoliberalism** Political and economic policies that promote free trade, individual initiative, and minimal government regulation of the economy, and oppose state control or subsidy to industries and all but minimal aid to impoverished individuals.

**structural adjustment** A development policy promoted by Western nations, particularly the United States, that requires poor nations to pursue free-market reforms in order to get new loans from the International Monetary Fund and World Bank.

# Anthropology Makes a Difference

## Development Anthropology and the Anthropology of Development

In the second half of the 20th century, wealthy nations and newly independent poor nations turned their attention to the eradication of poverty. Early efforts based on modernization theory concentrated on large-scale projects that focused on infrastructure: the building of roads, dams, and power plants. However, by the 1970s, it was clear that such construction projects were having little effect on the deeply entrenched problems of poverty. In response, major development organizations such as the World Bank and the United Nations moved toward a basic human needs approach to development. This meant turning their focus to projects aimed more directly at improving the welfare of the poor, particularly in rural areas.

Few anthropologists had been involved in modernization approaches to development. However, the basic human needs approach required providing services to the sorts of small rural communities that anthropologists often studied. Governmental aid agencies did not know how to operate in such communities and looked to anthropologists for expertise. Anthropologists were often deeply sympathetic to the people who were the targets of basic human needs projects and saw such projects as beneficial. Thus, anthropologists were drawn into development both by the needs of governments and their own desire to help. This conjuncture of interests gave birth to a new specialty: development anthropology. Anthropologists drawn to development anthropology viewed economic development as both desirable and, in the long run, inevitable.

Development anthropologists are trained to act as culture brokers—intermediaries between development organizations and the recipients of aid. With their specialized knowledge and ability to provide cogent analysis and assessment, they hope to make development projects work and directly benefit the world's impoverished people.

Two good examples of development anthropology are Gerald R. Murray's work on deforestation in Haiti and Margaret Clarke's work with midwives in Kenya, Egypt, Turkey, and other places. Murray used his knowledge of Haitian peasant agriculture to design successful forestry projects that treated fast-growing trees as a cash crop. His efforts resulted in projects that led to greater prosperity for the villages in which he worked (Murray 1986). Clark designed instructional materials for midwives and training materials for Peace Corps volunteers; she also examined household economics in Greece, worked in strategic planning for the U.S. Agency for International Development, and worked on education programs in Egypt.

Clarke says that anthropology makes a major contribution to international development. Because anthropologists take a holistic approach, they tend to look for links between different facets of society that others may miss. They think in terms of understanding the entire system rather than single elements. Whereas economists and development planners often assume that all people think alike and respond to the same incentives, anthropologists use their skills in listening and observing to under-

example, aid projects helped Honduras to increase its export of shrimp by more than 1500 percent, but the price of this growth was pollution, environmental destruction, and the impoverishment of people who lived near the shrimp farms (Stonich, Murray, and Rossart 1994).

Although the track record of development projects is mixed and the politics behind them controversial, they still have strong support and are likely to continue. Anthropologists play increasingly important roles in the planning of development. For example, Margaret Clarke has worked in projects in health care and education in Kenya, Egypt, Greece, and Turkey as well as other places. She has designed instruction for midwives and training materials for Peace Corps volunteers. She notes that economists and development planners often err because they assume that all people think alike and that they respond to the same incentives. Anthropologists, on the other hand, take a holistic approach, looking for links between different facets of society that others may miss. They think in terms of understanding the entire system rather than single elements. Anthropologists use their skills in listening and observing to understand local people's perceptions of the world and to access their knowledge, a process that makes for better, more effective project designs (Clarke 2000). Anthropologist Jim Igoe's work with wildlife conservation, national parks, and indigenous communities in East Africa provides a good example. Igoe's work explores the difficulties in communication, perspective, and goals between donors and the local organizations and indigenous peoples they work with. He reports that development in general and conservation in particular are never as simple as they may seem. In working with the Maasai, Igoe found that the ideas and plans of Westernbased conservation agencies were oversimplified and ignored local history. They were based primarily on long-standing Western ideas about the place of human beings in nature and the ways in which society and economy should be organized. Igoe (2004:133) writes that because such ideas resonate with Western ideas and Western history, "these simple solutions seem plausible to Westerners, but usually less plausible to the non-Western people who they target."

stand local people's perceptions of the world and to access their knowledge (Clarke 2000).

However, development anthropology has also been controversial. In the past two decades a field we might call the anthropology of development has emerged. Specialists in the anthropology of development do not understand development as either inevitable or inevitably desirable. Instead they take a perspective derived from postmodern thought and examine the historical, political, and economic grounds on which the ideas and practices of development emerged (Escobar 1997). Such anthropologists argue that in order to do development anthropology, people must buy into the basic ideas and practices of the governments and other agencies behind development programs. In most cases, either by design or practice, this results in projects that reinforce and validate the structures of inequality that create poverty in the first place. They call for a new model that validates local forms of knowledge and empowers the oppressed (see Crush 1995).

Development anthropologists often respond that this is romantic and does little to help the immediate problems of people who are poor and often hungry. There are, however, many anthropologists working on projects that help people without validating oppressive power structures. Anthropologist Stacy Pigg, for example, explores the Nepalese understanding of sex and its relation to language. One of her particular concerns is AIDS prevention. She notes that the medical community "assumes that 'sex' exists out there in the world as a self-evident natural domain of experience and that the kind of information that would constitute sex education is an equally transparent truth about the body" (2001:523). However, attempts to teach sex education or talk about AIDS immediately confront deeply entrenched cultural attitudes. Pigg found that even though many Nepalese do not speak English well, conveying information in a combination of Nepalese and English was effective because English had different cultural referents than Nepalese

and thus opened a space for public discussion of sexuality.

Regardless of whether you favor development anthropology or the anthropology of development, many informative websites provide information about the subject. Websites of large governmental development organizations such as the World Bank (http://www.worldbank.org), the U.S. Agency for International Development (http://www.usaid.gov), and the United Nations (http://www.un.org) contain an enormous wealth of information. Volunteer opportunities abound on the web. The Peace Corps (http://www.peacecorps.gov) maintains an extensive and highly informative website, including information on volunteering as well as stories from former volunteers. Other volunteer associations with interesting websites are WorldTeach (http://www.worldteach.org) and Global Citizens Network (http://www.globalcitizens.org).

Sometimes anthropological interventions are aimed at mitigating the worst effects of development projects. Several good examples of this concern the construction of large hydroelectric dams. Such construction projects often involve the forced resettlement of entire communities. In 2008, anthropologists served on panels reviewing resettlement programs necessitated by dam construction in Laos, Turkey, and Uganda. In all three cases anthropologists documented significant failures in the environmental and social programs that accompanied these large-scale construction projects. In two of the three cases, anthropological contributions resulted in substantial changes to the programs (Checker 2009:165).

## Multinational Corporations

Businesses that own enterprises in more than one nation or that seek the most profitable places to produce and market their goods and services regardless of national boundaries are known as **multinational corporations (MNCs).**

MNCs bring employment opportunities as well as goods and services to people who otherwise would not have them. At the same time they create major and controversial changes in the natural, economic, social, and cultural environments.

Because MNCs control vast amounts of wealth, they are significant political forces throughout the world. Multinationals can be problematic for both wealthy and poor nations. In 2008 and 2009, the problems of multinational financial corporations threatened the global economy. Wealthy nations found that some MNCs might be too big to fail and were forced to provide public funding for them. Poor nations are particularly vulnerable to MNCs. No corporation controls more than a small percentage of the economy of any rich nation. But many MNCs may have yearly budgets that are greater than those of poor-nation governments. For example, in 2005, each of the

**multinational corporation (MNC)** A corporation that owns business enterprises or plants in more than one nation.

Multinational corporations such as McDonald's have profound economic and cultural impacts on the societies in which they produce and sell their products.

world's 20 largest MNCs had gross revenues of more than $100 billion, larger than all but 47 of the 208 countries tracked by the World Bank. ExxonMobil's 2006 *profit* of $39.1 billion was larger than the 2005 total economy of 147 of these countries (*Fortune* 2006; World Bank 2008). The financial power of these corporations enables them to exert enormous influence on poor nations and makes it extremely difficult for these nations to set and enforce policies that effectively regulate them.

Multinationals are also problematic because, like all capitalist corporations, their fundamental goal is to return wealth to their shareholders, the vast majority of whom live in wealthy nations. Thus, most of the profits earned by MNCs in poor nations contribute to the economy of wealthy nations. Although few poor nations remain colonies, MNCs contribute to the persistence of colonial-style relationships. Through them wealth continues to move from the poor to the rich.

An important debate over the impact of multinationals involves sweatshops. **Sweatshops** are factories where workers, particularly women and children, are employed for long hours under difficult conditions and at low pay (see Chapter 10, pages 230–231 for another example).

> **sweatshop** Generally a pejorative term for a factory with working conditions that may include low wages, long hours, inadequate ventilation, and physical, mental, or sexual abuse.

Large areas of South and East Asia including China, South Korea, Indonesia, Malaysia, India, and Bangladesh might be considered a sweatshop belt. Kristoff and WuDunn (2000) estimate that this area accounts for about one-quarter of the global economy. Much of the production of sweatshops is funneled into the United States in the form of cheap consumer goods. For example, in 2004 more than 3000 factories in 50 nations made the clothing sold at The Gap, Old Navy, and Banana Republic. All three chains are owned by a single company. The company's own study found that between 10 percent and 25 percent of its factories in China, Taiwan, and Saipan use psychological coercion or verbal abuse and more than 50 percent of the factories in sub-Saharan Africa had inadequate safety practices (Merrick 2004).

In spite of the terrible conditions in sweatshops, for many of the people who work there, the alternatives are worse. Many workers are drawn from the ranks of the landless poor, and the money they earn, however small, often marks the difference between food and a roof over their head and hunger on the streets. Furthermore, historically, both conditions and wages tend to improve (although the economic recession of 2008 and 2009 might change this tendency). Finally, public protests and import restrictions aimed at sweatshops tend to backfire, causing drops in sales, throwing people out of work, and harming the very workers these actions are designed to help (Bhagwati 1996; Brown, Deardorff, and Stern 2003; Maskus 1997).

Although working conditions in Chinese factories are often difficult by United States standards, most cannot be considered sweatshops. However, an examination of Chinese migrant workers demonstrates the appeal of factory labor, even under difficult conditions. As international economic conditions deteriorated in 2008 and 2009, many factories closed and by early 2009, about 20 million rural migrants had lost their jobs. Although some of these have returned to the countryside, most opted to stay in cities searching for new jobs, even though the chances of finding such jobs were slim. The Chinese government, considering unemployed migrants a dangerous political force, has offered them incentives to return to the countryside, including funds and training to start their own businesses. However, thus far, such incentives have not worked. For example, in Henan province, home to one-sixth of China's migrants, about 80 percent have chosen to remain in the cities (Rabinovitch 2009).

Still, those who favor taking action against sweatshops argue that conditions in sweatshops are fundamentally dehumanizing and insist that governments should apply global standards to labor conditions. They point out that sweatshops were once common in the United States and other wealthy nations. It took strong government intervention to improve factory conditions, limit child labor, and impose minimum wages. Today's poor nations are often discouraged from taking the ac-

In sweatshops, workers, often women and children, are employed for long hours under difficult conditions at low pay. Here boys press tin in Mumbai.

$10.7 billion. In its early years, most of Nike's manufacturing took place in New England. However, by the late 1970s it had begun shifting production off shore and by the mid-1980s no longer had any manufacturing plants of its own. Instead, it contracted with other companies to make shoes under the Nike brand. Today, Nike uses manufacturing facilities in more than 50 countries (Nike 2005).

In the late 1980s and early 1990s, a series of political reforms in countries where Nike operated, particularly Indonesia and China, enabled workers to speak about conditions in Nike manufacturing facilities. Dire reports from these workers led to a series of investigations by academic, labor, religious, and human rights organizations. Although the accuracy and methodology of these reports varied, a grim picture of Nike's employment practices began to emerge. More than 75 percent of Nike workers were women who put in 10- to 13-hour days 6 days a week. Frequently forced to work overtime, their wages were less than the subsistence level for a single adult. In some cases, workers were subject to harsh corporal punishment, including having their mouths taped shut for disobedience (Sage 1999:209).

As these reports became public, opposition to Nike's practices began to build. Nike responded by blaming its subcontractors and denying it had any direct role in the oppression of workers. These reactions showed the company as naïve or willfully ignorant and callous. The result was the formation of a loose coalition of organizations located in wealthy nations and concerned with labor rights, called the Anti-Nike Transnational Advocacy Network. Network members shared information, coordinated efforts to monitor working conditions at Nike factories, and pressured the company to change its policies. They lobbied U.S. congressmen and senators, held protests at shopping malls, and organized three Nike International Mobilization days that included protests in multiple cities and nations in 1997, 1998, and 1999 (Rothenberg-Aalami 2004; Sage 1999). Hackenberg (2000) reports that university students and campus organizations played a major role in this mobilization effort.

At first Nike met these protests with small policy changes and advertising campaigns. However, when these methods proved ineffective, the company was forced to move toward real reform. It increased the minimum age for workers, adopted some U.S. occupational safety standards, offered its employees expanded educational and loan programs, and began to implement effective monitoring of the workplace. Although many problems remain, the company has made significant strides toward eliminating the worst of the abuses.

The Nike campaign shows that a well-orchestrated grassroots campaign can help to improve conditions for low-wage workers. However, it also suggests some of the limits of such a campaign. The Anti-Nike Transnational Advocacy Network was successful because Nike was extremely vulnerable to its tactics. The market for athletic

tions that enabled wealthy nations to restrict sweatshop labor and create a strong middle class (Rothstein 2005).

Sweatshop labor is not entirely a problem of poor nations. Sweatshops had an important place in early 20th-century America. In that era, hundreds of thousands of Americans worked long hours in dangerous and often unsanitary conditions. Debilitating and sometimes fatal accidents were common. Perhaps the most tragic of these was the fire at the Triangle Shirtwaist factory in 1911 in New York City. In that incident, 146 people, mostly young immigrant women, died. Sweatshops are not just a thing of our past. As many as 175,000 people, most of them immigrant women, currently work in sweatshop conditions in the United States (Malveaux 2005), and there are hundreds of sweatshop garment factories in New York City alone (Port 2001). In many cases, sweatshop workers are the victims of labor law violations. Some of them are held against their will, victims of human trafficking as well.

## The Nike Boycott

The 1990s campaign against labor abuses by footwear corporation Nike, studied by anthropologist Robert Hackenberg, provides a good example of globalization, sweatshop labor, and both the influence and limits of public opinion.

Nike was founded in 1964 as Blue Ribbon Sports and by the 1980s had become the world leader in sports shoes. In fiscal year 2003, it reported revenues of

# Ethnography

## Child Labor in Brazil

Movie audiences in America and Europe were struck and in many cases shocked by the portrayal of childhood in Mumbai in the 2008 film *Slumdog Millionaire*. The childhoods of Jamal, Salim, and Latika, the film's principal characters, seem the very opposite of what childhood should be. For the middle and upper classes in both wealthy and poor countries, childhood is understood as a period of life distinct and separate from adulthood. Relationships between parents and children should be permanent and characterized by love. The proper place for children is in school. Certain types of labor, including schoolwork, household chores, and working alongside of related adults, are considered appropriate for children. However, work that occupies most of a child's life and is directly remunerated in cash, such as employment in manufacturing or begging, is considered inappropriate. Many of these values are, at least theoretically, enshrined in law in the United Nations Convention on the Rights of the Child, which declares that children should "grow up in a family environment, in an atmosphere of happiness, love and understanding." The convention further states that "children should be protected from economic exploitation and from performing any work that is likely to be hazardous or to interfere with the child's education, or to be harmful to. . . . [their] development." However, millions of children worldwide live in conditions similar to those portrayed in *Slumdog Millionaire*. Although numbers are controversial, the United Nations reports that around the world 1 billion children live in poverty and as many as 100 million of these live on the streets.

Anthropologist Mary Kenny studied child workers in Olinda, a town of about 400,000 in northeastern Brazil. Because Olinda was an important town in the 17th century and preserves some of its colonial heritage, it is a destination for tourists. However, it is an impoverished town in a deeply impoverished part of Brazil. Kenny reports that, during her study, about 60 percent of Olinda's population lived in *favelas* (shantytowns) or other poor neighborhoods. She describes the *favelas* as mazes of small pathways leading to two- and three-room homes made of brick, wood, paper, and tin. Each building was home to an average of 10 people. Throughout the *favela* are "open cement drains filled with a grey liquid with bubbles on top, emitting a wretched stench that never quits" (Kenny 1997:90). Kenny reports that relations among residents of the *favelas* are neither friendly nor cooperative. Although solidarity, pooling of resources, borrowing, and sharing do occur, they are obliterated by suspicion and scarcity (2007:59).

For adult residents of the *favela* regular paid work is very difficult to find. Some men are day laborers, others wash cars, or

sell peanuts and ice pops. Women sometimes work as laundresses, hairdressers, or seamstresses. However, none of these jobs earns enough money to support even a small family. In these circumstances, the labor of even very young children becomes essential. Children under the age of 12 sell small items, guard cars, carry goods, wash dishes, and clean. Garbage picking and begging are also key occupations for them. Conditions for garbage pickers are harsh and Kenny reports that the health of children and adults is jeopardized by a wide range of diseases, infections, parasites, and rodents. Horrors abound at the dumps, for example; at least two human bodies are

---

footwear is highly competitive, and Nike's success is based primarily on its image. Nike commercials focus not on the quality of its product but on the feelings and associations it is supposed to inspire. The campaign against Nike dealt a severe blow to these, substituting images of oppressed workers for those of sports heroes. Other companies are far less vulnerable. For example, a supplier of electronic or mechanical components to other manufacturers may be virtually unknown to the public, unconcerned with its image, and face little competition. Such companies account for a high percentage of the economy, but actions against them are very difficult to organize and not likely to be effective.

Anthropologists are deeply concerned about labor abuses by MNCs (Gill 2005; Hackenberg 2000; Jamali 2007) but also are interested in the ways MNCs are changing social structures and cultural ideals. Gender relations is a field of particular interest. In some places, MNCs and close links with the world economy have given new economic power to men. In Papua New Guinea, for example, oil revenues paid to male groups have enabled them to expand their social networks but have alienated them from earlier exchange networks and from women as well (Gilberthorpe 2007). In other places, MNCs employ large numbers of female workers because they are perceived as more easily controllable than males. Indeed, women are victims of some of the worst labor abuses. However, money earned working may give women economic power that can improve their position and in society and that of their families (Freeman 2007). Reeves (2006:8) reports that the young female Indonesian immigrant workers he

found there each week (1997:105). However, with the labor of children, a family of garbage pickers can earn enough to survive. Additionally, children and adults find food that is still edible in the dumps. Children under 12 can also make money as beggars. Dalva is a 12-year-old who organizes the four younger children in her family to beg from tourists in the old colonial district of town. Because Dalva's parents produce very little income, Dalva's family is able to survive only because of her abilities to beg. She says: "If I don't work, my family will go hungry. . . . I can take it. It's my fate" (1997:108). Although Dalva gives her parents most of the money she and the younger children receive, she does retain some for herself. Additionally, she begs and buys a variety of food and small items during her work day. Although Dalva lives with her mother and her father is sometimes present, Kenny reports that Dalva's income-generating abilities effectively make her a household head. Beggars, trash pickers, and other working children do sometimes go to school. However, school is expensive. Even though there is no tuition, students require proper clothes and school supplies that families cannot afford.

Stories of children such as Dalva are disturbing to us not only because of the horrific conditions under which they live but also because they challenge our notion of childhood. However, although at some level, childhood is a biological state, it is clear that the roles and behaviors appropriate to young children vary enormously from culture to culture. In today's wealthy nations, child labor was the rule rather than the exception until the late 19th century. Then, as industrial and agricultural processes changed, increased emphasis was placed on childhood as a time of schooling rather than work. Universal compulsory education in the United States dates only to the early years of the 20th century. In places such as Olinda, families are able to survive only because of the income-generating activities of their children. In fact, in many cases, children have higher earning abilities than adults.

Kenny notes that for the children of Olinda's *favelas* the efforts of well-intentioned reformers are often ineffective, or worse yet, work against the interests of those they are intended to help. Such efforts are based around the norms of the middle and upper classes, which are assumed to be universal. Reformers promote policies intended to keep families together but the families of Olinda's poor are often brutally exploitative of children. Reformers promote education, but education is not only expensive, it reduces the time children can spend earning money and thus threatens their families' survival. Further, education is only economically valuable when it provides access to higher paying jobs. In the *favelas* this simply is not the case.

Kenny's study of Brazilian child workers makes it clear that the exploitation of children is not the problem. Rather it is a symptom of poverty. She notes that while child advocates drawn from the middle and wealthy classes advocate for the elimination of child labor, child laborers themselves advocate for better wages and more secure jobs. These demands are the same as those made by adults from the same areas "who work in conditions as damaging to health and as exploitative as those faced by their children" (Kenny 1997:216).

### CRITICAL THINKING QUESTIONS

1. The ethnography suggests that our notions about childhood are often culturally bound. Do you believe there are any aspects of childhood that are or should be universal?

2. Many studies of the poor have documented their use of networks of cooperation to survive. According to Kenny, these are not characteristic of life in the *favelas*. What forces do you think prevent such networks from forming?

3. Anthropologists have often favored a human needs approach to economic development. Would that approach benefit the children of Olinda?

---

studied were drawn to wage labor for many disparate reasons including "a desire for financial independence from family. . . . a commitment to improve one's family's economic outcomes. . . . personal development goals, [and] a long-term hope of saving enough seed capital to open small businesses upon return to Indonesia."

Multinationals raise critical questions that must be faced by people in wealthy and in poor nations alike. Can low-wage jobs lead to prosperity? Can groups maintain cultural distinctiveness in the face of an increasingly uniform society? What are the consequences of a system that makes people wealthier and increases their access to consumer goods but, at the same time, both increases the disparity between the rich and the poor and makes people increasingly aware of that disparity?

# Urbanization

Although many preindustrial societies had cities, their size and importance have increased dramatically in the contemporary world. In 1950, only about 16 percent of the total population of nonindustrialized nations lived in large cities. By 2000 this figure had reached 40 percent, and by 2008, more than half of the world's population lived in cities. The number of people living in cities is expected to double in the next four decades. This means that by 2050, the world's urban population will be about 6.4 billion. That is equal to the world's total population in 2004 (United Nations 2008:3). In 1950, seven of the world's ten largest cities were located in Europe, Russia,

Japan, and the United States. The average population of these cities was about 6.5 million. By 2015, eight of the world's ten largest cities are expected to be located in poor nations, and the average population of these cities will be more than 20 million (Population Reference Bureau 2005). In fact, almost all the urban population growth between now and 2050 is expected to occur in the world's poor nations (United Nations 2008:4). Some of the cities that will result will be truly enormous. For example, in 2025, the population of Kinshasa in the Democratic Republic of the Congo will be 16.8 million, Mumbai (Bombay) will be more than 26 million, and São Paulo in Brazil more than 21 million. They truly will be megacities. Providing basic services to such large populations in nations that are not wealthy will be an extraordinary challenge.

Rural people come to cities seeking jobs and the social, material, and cultural advantages they believe are available in urban areas. They are forced out of the countryside by high population levels, inability to acquire land, environmental degradation, and, sometimes, violence. When new migrants arrive in urban areas, they often find dismal living conditions. In places such as Bogota, Casablanca, Cairo, Calcutta, and Caracas, more than half of the urban population lives in slums and squatter settlements (Todaro and Smith 2003). However, in many cases they have access to more amenities in these places than in the rural communities they left.

Migration changes both the migrants themselves and the communities they leave. Links between urban migrants and those that remain at home in the countryside allow new ideas and values as well as consumer goods to enter rural areas. Radio, television, and websites operated primarily by people located in urban areas broadcast their messages and their advertisements to the countryside.

With urbanization comes the development of a great variety of social groups based on voluntary membership. Such associations may serve as mutual aid societies, lending money to members, providing scholarships for students, arranging funerals, and taking care of marriage arrangements for urban migrants. Some develop along kinship or ethnic lines that were relevant in the traditional culture; others, such as labor unions, are based on relationships deriving from new economic contexts and have no parallel in rural society.

Urban life can be extremely difficult. Many of the urban poor are unemployed and face hunger, unsafe drinking water, inadequate sanitation facilities, and substandard shelter. Disease and early death are rampant in the slums of the world's large cities. Many of those who do have employment fare little better, and most migrants to cities live in poverty for many years. In one study, Ariella Friedman and Judith Todd (1994) used a storytelling technique to study Kenyan rural women in a traditional village, poor urban women, and middle-class urban

More than half of the world's largest cities are in poor nations. These pictures of Rio de Janeiro, Brazil, show the enormous contrasts present in such cities. While Rio de Janeiro has an extremely prosperous elite, most of its residents live in abject poverty. Modern office and apartment buildings, as well as luxury resorts (left), exist alongside shantytowns with only minimal access to safe drinking water or sanitation.

women. They showed each woman a picture and asked her to tell a story about it. The stories provided information on the ways the women perceived their lives. The researchers found that the traditional women almost always told very positive stories that usually had a happy ending. Middle-class, nontraditional urban women told stories that emphasized their own power and competence. Poor urban women told stories that generally were tragic and focused on powerlessness and vulnerability. The researchers note that many poor urban women have "lost the security and protection of the old [traditional] system without gaining the power or rewards of the new system."

The fact that urban centers continue to grow is indicative both of their appeal and of the desperate poverty of the countryside. Any solution to the problems caused by urbanization must focus on both rural and urban areas. Nations must provide adequate services, including water, sewage, education, and health care to their urban populations. However, unless life chances and opportunities also are greatly improved for rural populations, better services in the cities will only draw more migrants who will quickly overwhelm any advances made.

portant cultural changes. Among the Waluguru in Tanzania, population increase resulted in land shortage, which increasingly resulted in the privatization of land. In the first half of the 20th century and before, people gained access to land through their lineage, and the lineage head was a powerful figure. Now land must be purchased, and not only has the institution of the lineage head completely disappeared, it is hardly even remembered (van Donge 1992). Van Donge (1992) reports that, as land has become scarce, women in this matrilineal society have tightened their hold over it. This has weakened the position of men in marriage to the point where many prefer to migrate to the cities to marry. More than 37 percent of women over 20 are now unmarried compared with 15 percent of men.

In other cases, the population explosion and the search for land and wealth have pushed people onto land previously occupied only by indigenous groups. For example, between 1955 and 1993, the Agta, a foraging group in the Philippines mentioned in Chapter 10, was increasingly encroached upon by loggers and migrant farmers. By 1993, the Agta had become landless migrant workers living at the lowest rung of Philippine society (Early and Headland 1998).

# Population Pressure

The rate of population growth provides a dramatic index of the increasing speed of social change. About 2 million years ago, our remote ancestors numbered perhaps 100,000. By the time the first agricultural societies were developing 10,000 years ago, world population had reached 5 to 10 million. Two thousand years ago there were about 250 million people in the world. By 1750, this number had tripled to 750 million. Then population growth really began to accelerate. Fifty years later, in 1800, there were 1 billion people; by 1930, there were 2 billion. Since then, world population has tripled, surpassing the 6 billion mark in the summer of 1999 (Erickson 1995; Fetto 1999). In Spring 2009, the world population stands at 6.78 billion. World population continues to increase and is expected to rise to more than 10 billion by 2050. In the past 50 years, much of the world's population growth has taken place in poor nations. For example, between 1950 and 2000 the population of poor nations rose by some 3 billion (*Geographical* 2005). This trend is expected to continue (see Figure 16.1).

In some cases, high population levels mean that traditional subsistence strategies can no longer provide enough food. In parts of East Africa, for example, the amount of arable land per person declined 40 percent between 1965 and 1987 (World Bank 1992), and this has resulted in im-

## China's One-Child Policy

Programs to control population growth are often extremely controversial. They both affect and are affected by culture. China's attempt to control its population is a good example. In 1979, the Chinese government introduced a radical population policy limiting families to a single child (although parents were allowed to keep twins or triplets). Families faced stiff financial penalties for additional children. This policy was a key factor in reducing fertility in

IT IS BETTER TO HAVE ONE CHILD ONLY

© Joan Gregg

Population growth is a critical problem in many nations. Some, such as China, have taken strong and often controversial measures to limit family size.

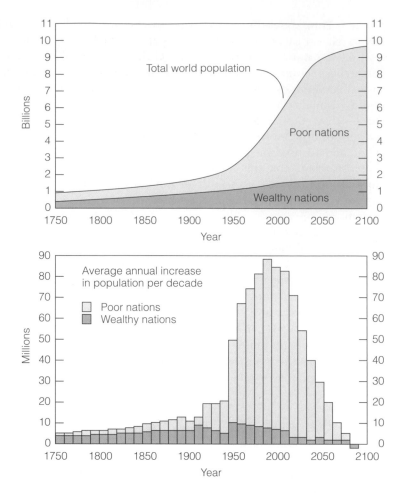

**FIGURE 16.1** If current trends continue, world population will increase to about 10 billion by the middle of the 21st century before leveling off. The great majority of this increase will occur in poor nations.

China from about five births per women 30 years ago to fewer than two today (Baochang et al. 2007). However, the cultural effects of the policy have been dramatic.

The most evident effect has been a skewing of births in favor of males. In 2000, for every 100 girls born, 120 boys were born, and in some poor regions of the country, there were twice as many male births as female births. By 2005, there were believed to be about 32 million more males than females under the age of 20 (LaFraniere 2009). The reason for the imbalance is a cultural preference for boys. Boys have been preferred because historically they were expected to live with their parents and provide support for them as they aged. Daughters, on the other hand, lived with their husbands and took care of his parents. However, in some places, particularly cities, this is changing. According to anthropologist Susan Greenhalgh (2005, 2007a), among the newly prosperous urban Chinese, girls now are considered as good as or even preferable to boys because girls are believed to be emotionally closer to their parents and more willing to provide support in their parents' old age. However, girls fare less well in poorer rural areas, where population control policies are less rigid and second children more common. The continued strong preference for boys is shown by the fact that, in some areas, up to 90 percent of second pregnancies are aborted if the fetus is female.

The extreme sex imbalance resulting from China's policy is creating fundamental changes in society. Wealthy men have no trouble finding mates, but it is much more difficult for the rural poor. Greenhalgh reports that 27 percent of rural men with little schooling were unmarried at age 40. The difficulty of marriage has led to the importation of women from poorer countries such as Vietnam and Myanmar, informal polyandry, the sale of young women, and a trade in kidnapped girls. Because such women are essentially captives in their husband's home, physical and emotional abuse are rife.

China's limits on family size and the emphasis it places on creating "quality children" have produced a generation of single children, the most prosperous and best educated children in the nation's history. However, they also are the subjects of intense family affection and pressure to succeed. Greenhalgh (2007b) describes them as little emperors and empresses, "talented and savvy, but also spoiled and self-centered." She wonders if, when such children grow up, they will be the sort of decisive and culturally sophisticated leaders who are able to make wise decisions on behalf of their nation.

Although China's population issues are unique to its historical and cultural circumstances, population control is problematic in other societies as well. In many places, a woman's value is measured to some degree by the number of children she bears. Religious and political authorities often take active stands against the use of birth control. Furthermore, intellectuals and governments in many poor nations are deeply suspicious of population control programs coming from wealthy nations. They note that the economies of wealthy nations have often prospered in times of population growth and suspect that the wealthy nations are promoting their own interests when they attempt to limit population in other countries. Sometimes, they accuse the promoters of population control programs of racist intentions, observing that such programs usually consist of efforts by wealthy white people to limit the population growth of poor nonwhite people (Lichtenberg 1994).

Behind these accusations lies a series of difficult political and economic issues. It is often asserted that there is a maximum population the earth can support (its "carrying capacity"), and some analysts worry that the total population is approaching that number. They argue that we must control population or face wide-scale starvation. They see population growth as a "bomb" that will destroy Western society (see Ross 1998 for a historical review of this literature). This position ignores several important factors. First, the number of people who can be supported by any given environment is critically dependent on the technologies used to support them. Because technological change is unpredictable, estimates of future carrying capacity are inaccurate. But, more importantly, populations cannot be considered apart from their levels of consumption. One way of comparing consumption levels is through the use of an ecological footprint. An ecological footprint provides a rough estimate of the numbers of acres of land it takes to support different lifestyles. The world average is about 2.7 hectares for each individual, but supporting an average American requires 9.5 hectares (Bodley 2007; Pearce 2009). Clearly the number of people who can be supported living this lifestyle is far different than the number of people who could be supported if wealthy populations consumed at a lower level. Finally, the number of people who could be supported is critically dependent on assumptions we make about the value of the natural world. If we desire to preserve forest land, tropical rain forest, or other environments, we diminish the amount of land that is available for human population growth. Thus, the issues central to problems of population growth are primarily cultural, social, political, and moral, not scientific.

The high level of population growth and the low level of wealth and consumption in poor nations are closely related. When life expectancy at birth is low and poverty is rampant, it makes good economic sense for families to have large numbers of children. Having many children helps to ensure that at least some will survive to adulthood. It increases the labor pool available to the family and improves the odds that one or more child will prosper and increase the family wealth.

As the wealth and consumption level of a population increases, the benefits of large families decline. When health conditions improve, children are more likely to survive. When jobs that pay livable salaries are available, fewer children are necessary to support a family. Additionally, increasing wealth and consumption makes raising children far more expensive, which makes large families less desirable. Clearly the best way, indeed perhaps the only way, to control population growth is to improve the life chances and increase the wealth of people in poor countries.

# Environmental Challenges

## Pollution

Ironically, even though the world's poor consume only a small fraction of the earth's resources, they also face some of the world's worst problems of pollution and environmental deterioration. The energy consumption of the United States alone is more than 14 times the energy consumption of the entire African continent (excluding the nation of South Africa) (Harrison and Pearce 2000). Given that consumption creates pollution, one might expect that people in the United States would live in a far dirtier environment than those in Africa. But this is not the case. Consider the city of Bamako, the capital of Mali, on any late afternoon in the dry season. Most streets are unpaved, and automobiles, trucks, carts, bicycles, and foot traffic have been stirring up dust all day. Because most of the city lacks regular trash pickup or sewage, waste from humans and animals has been churned into the air. People are beginning to cook their evening meal. Many, perhaps the majority, of the city's 1.6 million residents cook either on charcoal or wood fires that consume about 1 million tons of wood a year (Cisse 2007), and the smoke from cook fires joins the dust in the air. The combined effect of smoke and dust is like a thick, hot, dry fog. Because most houses are relatively open, lacking glass windows or doors that seal, the dust permeates the indoors as well as the outdoors. And Bamako's population suffers. Pollution contributes to respiratory ailments, malaria, many diseases borne by sewage-contaminated water and air, and high childhood mortality.

Compare this with a similarly sized American city, say San Antonio, Texas, a city of about 1.4 million. In San Antonio, most streets are paved, and almost all homes have access to safe, publicly maintained water and sewage systems. Meals are cooked on appliances powered by electricity or gas. There is a huge amount of vehicular traffic, but cars and trucks are equipped with pollution-controlling devices. Although San Antonio is not one of America's wealthier cities, its population consumes many times the resources than does the population of Bamako. But almost all of San Antonio's population lives in envi-

Although people in poor nations use only a small fraction of the world's resources, they face some of the world's worst pollution. Here, dust, car exhaust, and smoke fill a typical afternoon sky in Bamako, Mali.

ronments that are healthier and far less polluted than Bamako.

Pollution is closely related to industrialization and globalization. Poor nations often are desperate to provide some degree of prosperity to their citizens. They have limited amounts of capital to invest and limited means of attracting investment from abroad. Less expensive production technologies are generally more polluting than more expensive, higher-technology processes. Therefore, industry in poor nations tends to be dirtier and more polluting than similar industries in wealthy nations. For example, China has experienced enormous economic growth but has relied extensively on lower-cost, more highly polluting industries. A Chinese government study estimated that at least 20 percent of the Chinese population lives in severely polluted areas. Ameliorating this problem by installing adequate pollution control in existing Chinese industries would cost $135 billion (Bremner 2006).

Multinational corporations may play an important role in pollution because their financial power allows them to circumvent national laws designed to control pollution. A good example is oil production in the Niger delta in Nigeria, where gas flaring (the burning off of the natural gas that is a by-product of oil production) releases toxins into the air as well as more carbon dioxide than is released by automobiles and other industry in the rest of Africa combined. Gas flaring has been illegal in Nigeria since the 1980s but continues today because strong and wealthy corporations, using techniques that include bribery and intimidation, are able to ignore or circumvent

regulations enacted by the relatively weak government (Adetunji 2006; Walker 2009). Gas flaring, oil spills, and other ecological problems have created an environmental disaster that has been instrumental in fomenting violence and civil unrest in the region.

## Global Warming

Global warming is another important aspect of ecological change. Human activity substantially contributes to the warming of the planet (Intergovernmental Panel on Climate Change 2007; Oreskes 2004), and it is unclear what the long-term effects of this warming trend will be. For example, there are some possible benefits to global warming, particularly in northern Europe and Russia, where it may extend the growing season through increased rainfall and reduce fuel consumption for heating. However, the impacts of warming are expected to be largely negative and to fall disproportionately on the poor. Many of the world's poor live in the tropics, where the effects of climate change are expected to be particularly severe. Warming in these climates may cut the growing season and reduce crop yields. The intensity of tropical storms is also expected to increase, which could have devastating effects on areas affected by them. Wealthy nations have the resources to respond to climate change. They can build levees to control flooding, move their populations and their industries, and open new land to cultivation. Poor nations simply do not have the means at their disposal to do such things. Where survival is precarious today, climate change is likely to precipitate disaster (Intergovernmental Panel on Climate Change 2007; see pages 126–127 in Chapter 6).

# Political Instability

Political instability has had dire consequences for cultures worldwide. Violent confrontation is nothing new. Traditional societies often fought with one another, and Western expansion was accompanied by great loss of life and culture. However, in the past hundred years people have unleashed more brutality on each other than at any time in earlier human history. Industrialized and wealthy societies are primarily responsible for this savagery, having created the trenches of World War I, the death camps of World War II, nuclear weapons, the purge, and the Gulag.

Violence and disaster often seem overwhelming. In 1994, in Rwanda, in a matter of weeks, more than 800,000 Tutsis and their Hutu friends and supporters were slaughtered by Hutu troops and citizens acting with encouragement from the government. This photograph shows a memorial at the Ntarama church, south of the capital, Kigali, where up to 5000 people were murdered in the church where they sought refuge

© Associated Press

Although poor nations were deeply affected by Europe's wars, the era since the end of World War II has been devastating for them. In some, such as French Indochina (later Vietnam), World War II faded into wars of independence that persisted until the 1970s. In many cases, traditional people became involved in networks of warfare that drew them into competition between the great powers. Both the United States and the Soviet Union furnished guerrilla movements, impoverished governments, and rebel armies with vast amounts of weaponry.

Most anthropology students are familiar with the !Kung or Ju/'hoansi foragers of southern Africa. They were featured in many films by John Marshall, and anthropological work done on their lifestyle in the 1950s and 1960s contributed heavily to our understanding of foragers. Most students are unaware that many of the Ju/'hoansi became soldiers in South Africa's war against guerrillas fighting for the independence of Namibia. In 1974, the South African Defense Forces (SADF) began to recruit foraging peoples to act as trackers, and by 1981 virtually the entire foraging population of the Caprivi area in Namibia was supported by the military. When South Africa lost its war in 1990, almost 4000 foragers were resettled in South Africa (Gordon 1992:185–192). Today little remains of the hunting-and-gathering lifestyles documented by anthropologists in the 1950s and 1960s (Lee 2003; Marshall 2002).

The end of the Cold War brought relief to some poor nations. Wars that were fueled by great power rivalries, such as those in Namibia and El Salvador, came to a rapid end. However, in other nations, rivalries that had been muted by the Cold War reemerged in new violent forms. In many places strong, centralized, and frequently repressive governments had been supported by aid from the United States, the Soviet Union, and other nations. When the Cold War ended, this support diminished, and governments that relied on it often fell apart. Nations such as Yugoslavia, Somalia, Liberia, and Sudan disintegrated as different groups within them fought for wealth, power, and control.

The events in Central Africa, beginning in 1994 and continuing to the present, are a particularly horrifying example. Zaire (current day Democratic Republic of the Congo), Rwanda, and Burundi were nations where repressive regimes received high levels of support from Western nations that viewed them as bulwarks against Soviet advances in Africa. In the early 1990s, as this support began to decline, these nations began to fall apart. The government of Zaire began to teeter in 1990, but the Rwandan genocide of 1994 was the critical event destabilizing the area.

Most Rwandans are either Hutu or Tutsi. Although they all speak the same language, the Hutu majority are primarily farmers, whereas most Tutsi are herders. The rivalry between the Hutu and Tutsi originated well before Rwanda was colonized, first by Germany and then by Belgium. However, colonial policies favored the Tutsi and exacerbated tensions between the two groups. Since 1959, there have been numerous clashes between Hutu and Tutsi, but in 1994, in a matter of weeks, Hutus murdered 800,000 to 850,000 Tutsis and their Hutu friends and supporters. Only about 130,000 Tutsis in Rwanda survived the massacre. Every level of society was involved, and in many cases women led the killings (Fenton 1996; Prunier 1995). Tutsis were massacred by their clergy in churches where they sought sanctuary: 2800 in Kibungo, 6000 in Cyahinda, 4000 in Kibeho, and more in many other places. Although most of the killing was done with machetes, technology played an important part, as the Hutu-controlled Radio Mille Collines—called "the radio that kills" by its opponents—spewed out a daily message of hate and encouragement to slaughter (Destexhe 1995). In the weeks following the genocide, a Tutsi army from neighboring Uganda took over the government, and more than 2 million Hutu refugees fled to neighboring countries. The refugees fueled unrest already seething in these nations. By 1997 the government of Congo had fallen and a succession of military and elected regimes attempted unsuccessfully to establish control of the nation. By the early 2000s, much of Central Africa was engulfed in what was increasingly called Africa's World War. By the late 2000s, this war was believed to have cost over 4 million lives (Prunier 2008) and no end was in sight.

# Migration

Widespread political, economic, and social instability combined with relatively inexpensive air travel and economic opportunity has led to a boom in international migration, particularly of people from poor nations. Today, an estimated 200 million people, 3 percent of the world's population, live outside of the countries of their birth (Martin 2007). These migrants have enormous influence both on the countries they leave and those where they settle.

When migrants leave, they often make their home communities poorer by depriving these areas of their skills and labor. High-skilled workers can earn many times their local wages through migration. It is difficult to convince people to remain in poor, unstable countries when the salaries paid for their skills may be 30 or more times higher in wealthy nations. This has led to a "brain drain" from poor nations to rich nations.

Although home communities lose members, they may gain many other benefits. Migrants provide their communities of origin with connections to the rest of the world, creating a broad network of support for community members. People in seemingly isolated villages often have connections with family and friends throughout the world. These connections bring information, ideas, products, and, perhaps most importantly, money. In 2005, the World Bank estimated that $232 billion was sent by migrants to people in their home countries. Of this sum, $162 billion was sent to poor countries. By comparison, total U.S. humanitarian aid in 2005 was about $27 billion, almost 30 percent of which was spent in Iraq and Afghanistan (Organization for Economic Opportunity and Development 2007; World Bank 2006). In some nations, remittances from migrants constitute a substantial percentage of the national economy. For example, remittances account for 20 percent of the GNI in Honduras, 12.75 percent in the Philippines, and 21.77 percent in Lebanon.

Migrants also affect profound changes in the countries in which they arrive. Some of these effects are cultural. Cities and small towns throughout the wealthy nations are increasingly multiethnic. Immigrants bring their cultural traditions, increasing the complexity and enriching the variety of the places where they settle. Immigrants provide a pool of inexpensive labor that creates large profits for businesses in wealthy countries and low prices for consumers. However, the availability of immigrant labor also suppresses wages in their host countries.

Economic immigrants come to new nations for their own profit, but they face discrimination in the places they settle. They increase their wealth, but often at the price of decreasing their social status (Haines 2007:62). Discrimination resulting in isolation and alienation has led to unrest among immigrant communities in Europe, particularly among African and Muslim immigrants in England and France. This was revealed dramatically by rioting in France in 2005 and by terrorist attacks in London that same year. Illegal immigrants are in a particularly weak position. Their status makes them extremely vulnerable to exploitation. Further, although host countries may create programs to attract migrants in times of economic prosperity, in hard economic times, they frequently turn against migrants. This was apparent as the world economy faltered in 2008 and 2009. In many cases, wealthy nations began offering immigrants incentives to leave. For example, Spain has offered to pay benefits to immigrants who agree to return home for at least 3 years (Fuchs 2008). Japan offered Latin American guest workers $3000 toward a plane ticket to their country of origin to leave Japan on the condition that they never return (Tabuchi 2009). In the Czech Republic, unemployed foreign workers are eligible for free one-way air or rail fare and about $700 in cash if they wish to return home. Although not many take these offers, those who stay face increasing discrimination. For example, Vietnamese workers in the Czech Republic increasingly face taunts and are denied admission to restaurants and clubs. In a recent poll, two-thirds of Czechs said that they would not like to have a Vietnamese person as a neighbor. This represents a substantial setback for a community that had been considered successful. Many Vietnamese immigrants speak Czech, own businesses, and have children who are extremely successful in the Czech public school system (Bilefsky 2009).

Immigrants frequently come to their new nations with an "ideology of return" (Brettell 2003, 2007). They understand their immigration as temporary and hope to return to their home countries. However, they wish to return after having achieved prosperity. Returning home with little or nothing to show is, in many cases, deeply embarrassing and therefore worse than remaining in poverty in a foreign country. Even for those who do achieve prosperity, belief in return has been more common than return itself. Historically, immigrants have remained in their new countries because maintaining communication with those left behind was difficult, because travel was expensive, and because they established social ties in their new country. The first two of these reasons are no longer true, and we do not yet know the effect this will have on return migration.

# Looking to the Future

Although the world is faced with grave problems, we have greater means at our disposal to solve them and to improve people's lives than ever before. Anthropology can play a critical role in this process. The anthropologi-

In the 21st century, contrasts and conflicts, both within and among cultures will increase. Anthropology, with its emphasis on analyzing diversity and complexity, will play an important role in increasing our understanding of these phenomena. In this photograph, Libyan women in modest dress consider the fashions on display in a shop window.

© Charles O. Cecil/Alamy

dressed some of these problems (see Paiement 2007). Perhaps above and beyond solving any particular problem, anthropology has a significant role to play in ensuring that people's stories are told and heard, and not forgotten.

Anthropology particularly offers hope for success in solving problems because it shows us that biology is not destiny. The human capacity for culture rests on biological foundations. We have culture because our brains and bodies have evolved to learn and to be dependent on it. Our biology may predispose us to behave in certain ways, but no aspect of human culture can be firmly tied to a gene. Instead, anthropologists have shown over and over that culture is enormously flexible, fantastically changeable, and almost incredibly varied. This implies that the problems we face are not the result of a fixed and unchanging human nature. War, poverty, pollution, and the other ills that we face do not exist because humans are invariably given to warfare or human nature somehow demands extreme wealth and desperate poverty. These are social facts, aspects of human culture and human society. Because of this, they can be changed. We can continue to invent new cultural forms, new designs for living.

More than a century ago, E. B. Tylor, the man often considered the founder of British anthropology, wrote that anthropology was a reformer's science. By this he meant that if we could first understand that culture was not simply a reflection of human biology, and if we could then analyze and understand culture itself, we could discover ways to improve humanity's lot. Understanding that culture is flexible and variable gives us hope for a better future. Anthropology gives us some of the analytical tools to act on that hope.

cal methodology and perspective emphasizes understanding the meaning and experience of cultural differences. It teaches us about the dynamic elements of social organization and their interrelationships. Anthropology cannot solve all of the problems we have described. But it does have important contributions to make. With our holistic approach and our emphasis on the importance of local cultures, anthropologists can develop frameworks to analyze and understand events and processes. We can help governments, organizations, and other groups find solutions that are sensitive to local cultural traditions and respond to people's needs and aspirations. Applied anthropologists have successfully ad-

# The Global and the Local: How Flat Is Your World?

In 2005 Thomas Friedman published the bestselling book *The World Is Flat*. In it he argues that political changes, free trade, and recent technological innovations have enormously increased productivity and efficiency. The Internet, the fall of the Berlin Wall, outsourcing, the development of collaborative software, and other innovations have enabled individuals and corporations to compete and connect with each other across vast distances. Friedman claims that the result is a world that is "flat" in the sense that economic and social opportunities are increasingly available to all people, regardless of their geo-

graphical location. Friedman cites numerous examples to show how companies and individuals in India, China, and elsewhere use technology to engage effectively with the world and to build prosperity. He interviews Bill Gates, who says that 30 years ago, the life chances of an average American were better than those of a genius born in India or China; but today, it would be better to be a genius in India or China than an average American. Friedman does see problems, including persistent poverty in some places, AIDS, and the use of technology by terrorist organizations. However, he is an optimist, perhaps even a utopian. He believes that pursuing the correct kinds of training and making the right decisions will bring us a world of peace, prosperity, and opportunity, a world in which culture is enriched and preserved as technology allows each person his or her own voice and vehicle of expression.

John Grey is a critic of Friedman. Grey (2005) notes that Friedman ignores or minimizes numerous problems in globalization. For example, Friedman contrasts the road leading to a company in India, "pockmarked" and filled with jostling "sacred cows, horse-drawn carts and motorized rickshaws," and the sedate and luxurious corporate campus at its end. However, he does not consider the relationship between the two. The same forces of technology and globalization that open possibilities for companies and elites may foreclose them for the poor, denying them jobs, affordable food, housing, and education. Friedman believes that complex trade and communication links between nations create peace and stability, but Grey points out that historically these have created friction and warfare as well. Nationalism fueled the growth of capitalism in Europe and the United States and is doing the same in China and India. Countries promote globalization in the hopes of prosperity but also in the pursuit of international power. Finally, Friedman sees a connection between globalization, the free market, and Western-style democracy. But Grey notes that the forces of globalization and technology operate effectively in both democratic and nondemocratic countries such as China. Grey (2005) says that globalization does make the world smaller and may make some parts of it richer, but it does not necessarily make it more peaceful, more democratic, or flat.

## Key Questions

1. Is Bill Gates right that today it is better to be a genius in China or India than an average person in America? Do you think your opportunities would be greater if you were born in India or China? Do you think you will one day live in countries such as India and China?

2. Friedman hopes for a world in which culture is enriched because every individual has the ability to be creative and to reach other people through web technologies. Is his definition of culture the same as one you would find in anthropology? Does creating websites enrich culture?

3. Given Friedman and Grey's positions, do you believe that global culture will be more or less homogeneous 100 years from now?

# Summary

1. **Describe the level of inequality in the world and tell how inequality affects wealthy and poor nations.** We live in a world of extreme inequality. The wealthy and the poor often live very different lives in close proximity to each other. Although all nations suffer problems of inequality and poverty, these problems are particularly acute in poor nations and have a profound effect on many of the people that anthropologists have historically studied.

2. **What is development and what different approaches have been taken to it?** After World War II, economists believed that many nations were poor because they had undeveloped economies. Development was the idea of creating wealth in poor nations. In the 1950s and 1960s, modernization approaches to development were common. In the 1970s, approaches focused on basic human needs. Since the 1980s, structural adjustment programs have focused on enforcing free markets in the hope that these will create more efficient delivery of services.

3. **What are multinational corporations (MNCs) and why is their roll in poverty important?** Multinationals are corporations that own business enterprises in more than one nation. They are able to seek the most profitable venues to produce and market goods regardless of national boundaries. Many MNCs have annual budgets far larger than most countries. This and their mobility give them huge economic and political power. MNCs search for the most profitable places to buy, sell, and manufacture goods. Their effect in poor nations is extremely controversial. However, it is clear that shareholders, located primarily in wealthy nations, are the primary beneficiaries of MNC activities.

4. **What are the major trends in urbanization and why are they problematic?** The world is becoming increasingly urbanized. More than half of the world's population currently lives in cities, and that number is expected to double in the next four decades. In the future, most of the world's largest cities will be in poor countries. Providing services to poor people in these cities is beyond the financial capacity of many nations.

5. **Is overpopulation a critical problem and what critical factors affect our understanding of it?** Overpopulation is an important problem because in many cases the rate of economic growth has failed to keep up with the rising population and in some cases, subsistence strategies have collapsed. However, historically, prosperity and population increase often go together. Further, the ap-

propriate level of human population for any area is a political question involving critical assumptions about distribution of resources and the types of environment people consider desirable.

6. **Are problems of environmental pollution more or less severe in poor nations?** Even though the poor produce only a small percentage of the world's pollution, environments in poor nations frequently are more polluted than those in rich nations. Global warming is anticipated to have more dire effects in poor countries because many of these are located in ecologically fragile zones that have limited financial resources to cope with environmental change.

7. **What role has political instability played in culture change?** Political instability has had horrific consequences for people worldwide. Wars of independence, the Cold War, and ethnic rivalries have led to violence that has destroyed cultures and societies. Although the end of the Cold War led to the resolution of some conflict, it caused others to blossom. Of these, the worst is probably the Central African war that has now claimed more than 4 million lives.

8. **How has migration changed the relationships between cultures and what problems face migrants?** Very high levels of migration have created enormous flows of information and money between nations. Migrants change both the societies they leave and those in which they settle, frequently enriching both. Migrants often face discrimination, alienation, and isolation in the societies where they settle.

9. **What are the prospects for the human future?** Despite the difficulties facing us, the future is not necessarily bleak. Anthropology gives us the tools to deal with a world characterized by diversity. Anthropology instructs us that humans are cultural beings. Cultures can be changed and perhaps improved. For humans, biology is never destiny.

# Key Terms

basic human needs approach
development
gross national income (GNI)

modernization theory
multinational corporation (MNC)
neoliberalism

structural adjustment
sweatshop
World Bank

# Suggested Readings

Bodley, John. 2007. *Anthropology and Contemporary Human Problems* (5th ed.). Lanham, MD: Altamira Press. An anthropological perspective on economic and environmental issues facing the world. Chapters on natural resources, malnutrition, population pressure, conflict, and other critical issues.

Edelman, Marc, and Angelique Haugerud. 2005. *The Anthropology of Development and Globalization.* Malden, MA: Blackwell. This collection of essays traces the history of some of the most important ideas in debates about modernization and development. It pays special attention to issues of gender and possible alternatives to development.

Haenn, Nora, and Richard Wilk. 2006. *The Environment in Anthropology: A Reader in Ecology, Culture, and Sustainable Living.* New York: New York University Press. A collection of 42 essays covering a wide variety of topics including theoretical approaches to ecological anthropology, population pressure, economic development projects, biodiversity, environmental management, indigenous groups, and consumption and globalization.

Hinton, Alexander. 2002. *Genocide: An Anthropological Reader.* Malden, MA: Blackwell. A collection of critical essays on some of the most disturbing and challenging issues of the 20th and 21st centuries. Provides a theoretical framework for analyzing genocide and includes current examples.

# A Brief Historical Guide to Anthropological Theory

People have probably been curious about their neighbors since the emergence of the species *Homo sapiens.* They have investigated these neighbors systematically in many places and at many times. However, for our purposes, we may date the origins of anthropology as an intellectual and academic discipline to the beginning of the 19th century. In fact, the word *anthropologist* was first used in print in 1805 in *The Edinburgh Review* (Kuklick 1991:6). Since that time, numerous different theoretical schools have appeared, each related to its predecessors, but each with its own understanding of the critical issues that surround the analysis of culture. In this Appendix, we provide very brief chronological descriptions of the principal schools of anthropological thought and introduce some of the key thinkers in each school.

## 19th-Century Evolutionism

Various forms of social evolutionary theory held sway throughout most of the 19th century. These theories were loosely based on evolutionary models drawn from biology, particularly the work of **Jean Baptiste Lamarck** (1744–1829) and **Charles Darwin** (1809–1882). Lamarck is best known for his notion of inheritance of acquired characteristics. He argued that organs improve with repeated use and grow weak with disuse and that living things are able to pass these strengths and weaknesses on to their offspring. Lamarck reasoned that over time this would give rise to new species. Darwin, on the other hand, showed that chance endowed certain individuals with traits that allowed them to produce relatively more offspring and that such individuals were able to pass along these successful traits to their offspring. Darwin's theory, examined more fully in Chapter 2, accurately describes biological evolution. However, cultural and social change may hap-

pen in the ways characterized by Lamarck. As interpreted by social thinkers, the key tenet of evolutionary thought was that the history of humanity could be described as progress toward increasingly complex forms of society. This progress followed discoverable natural laws and could be understood by using scientific methodology.

**Herbert Spencer** (1820–1903) was a key early thinker in social evolutionism. He compared societies to biological organisms and proposed that both progressed by increasing in complexity. Although much of Spencer's theoretical position was established before Darwin published his theory of natural selection, Spencer rapidly incorporated elements of Darwin's work into his own.

The Englishman **Sir Edward Burnett Tylor** (1832–1917) and the American **Lewis Henry Morgan** (1818–1881) both proposed that all human societies progressed from a state of savagery, through barbarism, to civilization. Societies progressed at different speeds, however. Western European and European-American societies had achieved the fastest progress. Others, such as the Australian aborigines, had been left far behind in savagery. Although from our perspective this notion is profoundly ethnocentric, it is important to point out that the evolutionary anthropological theorists were deeply critical of their own societies, particularly the entrenched hereditary privilege of the aristocracy and upper classes.

**Karl Marx** (1818–1883), along with **Friedrich Engels** (1820–1895) and **Sigmund Freud** (1856–1939), also proposed evolutionary theories that had profound impacts on anthropology. Marx viewed evolution in terms of conflict between different social groups (see Chapter 12 for more information on Marx). Freud wrote in the 20th century but drew largely on 19th-century sources. He saw evolution as a mental process and believed that the psychological development of the individual repeated that of human society. The children of the "civilized" were thus the emotional equals of adult "savages."

## The Early Sociologists

The key sociological thinker in turn-of-the-century France was **Émile Durkheim** (1858–1917). Durkheim believed that each group of people shared a *collective conscience*. The collective conscience consisted of a shared system of understandings, beliefs, and values that molded and constrained individual behavior. This notion was similar to what many anthropologists today call culture. Durkheim thought that the collective conscience had an existence independent of the people who shared it. It was something that operated by its own laws and could be studied on its own terms. The task of sociologists was to discover the contents of the collective conscience (which Durkheim believed included "social facts" and "collective representations") and the laws by which they functioned. One of the key laws that Durkheim believed he discovered was that the human mind divided things into opposites. The most basic of these divisions was between the sacred and the profane.

Durkheim and his students are often referred to as *L'Année Sociologique,* after a journal they published that reviewed each year's developments in sociology. His students were some of the brightest minds of Europe, including his nephew **Marcel Mauss** (1872–1950) and **Robert Hertz** (1881–1915). Sadly, most of Durkheim's students died in the trenches in World War I.

Whereas Durkheim and his students focused on questions of social cohesion or solidarity, **Max Weber** (1864–1920) was more concerned with conflict. Weber was profoundly influenced by Marx, but he did not believe that social classes necessarily acted in solidarity. Weber is also known for promoting the notion that social scientists must develop empathetic understanding of those they study in order to understand their behavior.

# American Historical Particularism

In the United States, much of anthropology in the late 19th and early 20th centuries had been devoted to the attempt to find scientific justification for institutionalized racism. The German-trained scholar **Franz Boas** (1858–1942) created a new American anthropology that was utterly opposed to this thinking. Boas asserted that all human beings were biological equals and that differences among human societies were the result of culture alone. The form each culture took depended almost entirely on its own specific history (hence *historical particularism,* a term coined long after Boas's death) rather than any panhuman pattern of development as the evolutionists proposed. Boas went on to debunk many 19th-century thinkers, demonstrating that the cultural traits they believed showed general patterning actually arose from quite different histories.

The claim of particular historical development for each culture had important implications. First, it meant that cultures could be evaluated only on their own terms rather than by any universal yardstick of development. Therefore, cultural relativism became a cornerstone of Boasian anthropology. Second, though Boas wrote that controlled cultural comparison was possible and general laws of growth could be found (1896/1988a), his insistence that cultures are unique results of their history and context suggests that this would be virtually impossible. Formulating general laws requires comparing similar elements of different cultures. However, such comparison necessarily removes elements from their historical and social context and thus violates Boasian principles. Boas and his students assiduously avoided making such comparisons or proposing general laws. Instead, Boasians focused on collecting ethnographic data through fieldwork, which became central to American anthropology.

Boas's influence on American anthropology was extraordinary. During his long career at Columbia University, he trained many of the most important American anthropologists of the first half of the 20th century, including **A. L. Kroeber, Robert Lowie, Edward Sapir, Ruth Benedict, Paul Radin,** and **Ashley Montague.**

# Functionalism

In Europe, the trauma of World War I led to the abandonment of social evolutionism. However, many of the ideas of Spencer and Durkheim were retained in British functionalism. Like Spencer, functionalists tended to view societies as analogous to biological organisms. Instead of being interested in their evolution, however, functionalists were concerned with the relations among their parts.

Two critical thinkers in functionalism were **A. R. Radcliffe-Brown** (1881–1955) and **Bronislaw Malinowski** (1884–1942). Radcliffe-Brown is considered a structural functionalist. Profoundly influenced by his reading of Durkheim, he wanted to discern and describe the role of social institutions such as kinship in maintaining the smooth working of society and preserving social solidarity. Malinowski's psychological functionalism focused on human physical and psychological needs. He proposed seven universal human needs: nutrition, reproduction, bodily comfort, safety, relaxation, movement, and growth. He examined cultural institutions in terms of the ways they functioned to meet these needs. Malinowski is also known for his vivid descriptions of Pacific Island culture and his use of empathy as a critical tool in ethnographic description.

Although their theoretical positions were very different, Boas and Malinowski shared some interesting similarities. Like Boas, Malinowski set extremely high standards for fieldwork among his students. Also like Boas, Malinowski trained many important anthropologists, including **E. E. Evans-Pritchard, Meyer Fortes, Audrey Richards,** and **Raymond Firth,** during his long academic career at the London School of Economics.

## Culture and Personality

Boas transmitted to his students his insistence on the historical uniqueness of each culture, but he did not give them any unifying principle around which to organize their work. To remedy this, many of them turned to the notion of personality. **Ruth Benedict** (1887–1948), **Margaret Mead** (1901–1978), and others analyzed culture as "personality writ large." They believed that each culture had a unique configuration that shaped the personality of its members, molding them to fit the culture's dominant type. Benedict, for example, characterized the Zuni as reserved and levelheaded. She argued that they avoided excesses of any kind. She referred to this complex of traits as an Apollonian cultural configuration.

To solve the problem of how cultural configurations were formed and maintained, culture and personality theorists, particularly **Abram Kardiner** (1891–1981) and **Cora DuBois** (1903–1991), turned to Freud. Although they rejected Freud's evolutionary theories, they accepted the notion that early childhood experiences determine later life personality. Thus, they saw child-rearing practices as critical to understanding cultural institutions.

With the coming of World War II, the culture and personality theorists turned to writing national character studies of the United States, its allies, and its opponents. These works, produced by analyzing written data rather than fieldwork, were substantially less successful than their earlier efforts. Although few anthropologists today would consider themselves culture and personality theorists, some of the best-known books in American anthropology are associated with this school of thought. These include Margaret Mead's *Coming of Age in Samoa* (1928) and *Sex and Temperament in Three Primitive Societies* (1935) and Ruth Benedict's *Patterns of Culture* (1934).

## Cultural Ecology and Neo-Evolutionism

By the mid-1930s, a second school of American anthropological thought emerged to compete with the ideas of Boas and his intellectual descendants. Cultural ecology and neo-evolutionism reevaluated the insights of the 19th-century evolutionists and, through new research, attempted to raise their scientific standards. Key thinkers in this enterprise were **Julian Steward** (1902–1972), **Leslie White** (1900–1975), and **George Peter Murdock** (1897–1985). All three searched for general laws of cultural development.

Steward, who coined the term *cultural ecology,* was particularly interested in the relationship between culture and environment. He believed that cultures at similar technological levels, in similar environments, would develop broadly similar institutions. His work thus depended on cross-cultural comparisons.

Leslie White was deeply influenced by his reading of Morgan and Marx. This led him to a concern with cultural evolution and the nature of production. He proposed that cultures evolve as the amount of energy they capture increases, an idea that is known as White's Law. White believed that revolutionary changes in technology were critical to increasing the ability to capture energy.

George Peter Murdock was an intellectual descendant of Spencer. He believed that general principles of culture could be derived from cross-cultural analysis on a massive scale. Thus, he began a project to index and tabulate information on all the world's known cultures. This project, known as the Human Relations Area Files (HRAF), still continues today (see Chapter 3).

## Neomaterialism: Evolutionary, Functionalist, Ecological, and Marxist

Steward, White, Murdock, and others set the stage for many of the anthropological theorists of the 1960s and 1970s. These combined earlier anthropological work with insights from the physical and biological sciences and, sometimes, a deep understanding and appropriation of Marxist thought.

Evolutionary theorists such as **Morton Fried** (1923–1986), **Marshall Sahlins** (born 1930), and **Elman Service** (1915–1996) looked for ways to combine the insights of Steward and White into a single theory of cultural evolution. They developed the band–tribe–chiefdom–state model commonly used in much of modern anthropology (see Chapter 11).

Ecological functionalists took the position that cultures were adaptations that permitted their members to exploit their environments successfully. They examined the ways in which cultural practices were related to physical, technological, and economic aspects of the environment. **Marvin Harris** (1927–2001) is perhaps the best-known functional ecologist. He used the term *cultural materialism* to describe his approach. Harris's analysis of Indian cattle worship (see Chapter 4) is a good example of his approach.

Neo-Marxists were a third group of thinkers within this tradition. Most neo-Marxists were particularly concerned with issues of political economy, particularly colonialism, international economic relations, and, more recently, globalization. Their approaches to these questions varied. In Europe, French scholars such as **Claude Meillassoux** (1925–2005) and **Maurice Godelier** (born 1934) broke with the Soviet scholars who had dominated Marxist anthropology. They proposed new ways of adapting Marx's critical insights to the anthropology of nonindustrial society. In the United States, political economy theorists, led by **Eric Wolf** (1923–1999), focused on the historical development of capitalism and the conflicts it generated. Wolf and others rejected the notion of cultures as bounded wholes that could be studied independently. They urged anthropologists to see issues of conflict, domination of one group by another, and appropriation of wealth as central to understanding culture.

# Structuralism

Structural anthropology is based largely on the work of **Claude Lévi-Strauss** (born 1908). Lévi-Strauss was inspired by Durkheim's work on the nature of human thought as well as advances made in linguistics in the first half of the 20th century. At that time, linguists were concerned with identifying the most fundamental units of language. In a similar fashion, Lévi-Strauss sought to uncover the basic units of culture and the rules by which they operated.

Lévi-Strauss believes that the same basic units and rules of culture found expression in all societies. He reasoned that these could best be discovered through analysis of the folktales and mythologies of primitive people. Like Durkheim, Lévi-Strauss holds that the most fundamental rule of culture is the tendency of human thinking to make binary distinctions. He adds, however, that human thinking is not satisfied with such distinctions and always adds a third category that in some way transcends or reconciles the opposition. The process of structural anthropology involves analyzing cultures to fundamental oppositions as well as the elements that transcend them. Lévi-Strauss's hope is that as this process is completed for more and more cultures, general patterns will emerge, illuminating the fundamental patternings that underlie all human culture.

Although Lévi-Strauss's ideas have always been controversial, structural anthropology has proven a useful source of insight into the interpretation of the symbolic aspects of culture. It has had a profound effect, not only on anthropology but on thinking in literature, political science, and psychology as well. Not surprisingly, this impact was felt first and most strongly in France. Some of the scholars strongly influenced by Lévi-Strauss include **Louis Althusser, Roland Barths, Jacques Lacan,** and **Jacques Derrida,** although many of these were critical of structuralism as well. Scholars such as these were fundamental to the poststructuralist and postmodern anthropology of the United States in the 1980s and 1990s.

# Ethnoscience and Cognitive Anthropology

Ethnoscience and cognitive anthropology were largely American developments. Some of the key scholars associated with these approaches are **Ward Goodenough** (born 1919), **Harold Conklin** (born 1926), **Stephen Tyler** (born 1932), and **James Spradley** (1933–1981). Ethnoscience is based on a critique of anthropological method but draws heavily on Boasian anthropology and structuralism.

Ethnoscientists and cognitive anthropologists claimed that existing anthropological reporting was unreliable because there anthropology lacked consistent methodology. Projects such as Murdock's HRAF were flawed because different ethnographers observed and reported on differing aspects of the societies they studied. Thus, generalizations about cultures could not be made. Ethnoscientists and cognitive anthropologists proposed a way around this dilemma. They asserted that culture was a shared mental model through which people organized their world. Further, they claimed that language was the key means through which this organization was accomplished. Thus, the distinctions that people made in speaking could be used to construct a model for each culture.

Ethnoscientists and cognitive anthropologists developed a fieldwork method designed to discover the linguistic models that members of different cultures used to classify their worlds. They claimed fieldwork done using this method would be consistent and would provide anthropologists the information needed to behave like a member of the culture. Some suggested that a person who fully understood the mental model of another culture could think like a member of that culture as well, though this was hotly disputed.

Ethnoscientists and cognitive anthropologists believed that each culture had a unique mental model. Like Boas, they argued that given enough time and data collection, some universal theory of culture might emerge. However, such a theory was only a long-term possibility.

In the 1980s and 1990s, cognitive anthropologists turned away from the linguistic model. Realizing that many forms of knowledge and behavior did not involve linguistic processing, they began to look at insights from psychology and physiology. The result was the emergence of schema theory and connectivism. Schema theory describes knowledge in terms of generalized representations of experiences, events, and objects that are stored in memory. Connectivists argue that knowledge is structured in "processing units" and examine the ways in which such units might be distributed, linked, and networked. Current cognitive anthropologists attempt to describe the relationship among culture, schema, and behavior (D'Andrade 1995).

# Sociobiology, Evolutionary Psychology, and Behavioral Ecology

Perhaps the most controversial theoretical position in anthropology is sociobiology. It was developed and promoted largely by biologists and anthropologists in the 1960s and 1970s. Some of its key thinkers are biologists **W. D. Hamilton, Robert Trivers,** and **E. O. Wilson,** sociologist **Lionel Tiger,** and anthropologists **Robin Fox, Jerome Barkow, Napoleon Chagnon,** and **Kristen Hawkes.**

Sociobiologists applied the Darwinian idea of natural selection directly to human cultural behavior. They believed that culture reflected an underlying genetic patterning. Further, as in biology, those genetically based culture traits that led to increased reproduction would be selected and transmitted, and thus would appear increasingly in the population. Thus, they viewed much of cultural behavior as a mechanism through which individuals tried to increase their chances of reproduction.

In the 1970s, sociobiologists were particularly concerned with the problem of altruism, defined as an individual's sacrifice of his or her own reproductive chances to benefit those of another, and tried to show how such a trait could evolve. In the 1980s and 1990s, sociobiologists split into three groups: evolutionary psychologists, human behavioral ecologists, and those who study human universals. Evolutionary psychologists theorize that the mind is composed of a collection of specialized suborgans designed for particular tasks. They try to describe these and show what they were designed to accomplish. Human behavioral ecologists emphasize human populations rather than cultures and try to test the hypothesis that culturally patterned traits enhance fitness. Some anthropologists focus on discovering and describing human universals, or characteristics found in all societies.

Sociobiologists have insisted that understanding the connections between biology and culture should be the focus of anthropology. The vast majority of cultural anthropologists, however, believe that culture is almost completely independent of biology. As a result, sociobiology has been strongly criticized by cultural anthropologists, and it has remained a relatively small and isolated theoretical position.

# Anthropology and Gender

The feminist critique of anthropology developed along with the women's movement in the late 1960s and 1970s (see Chapters 3, 4, and 10). Despite the fact that some very prominent anthropologists had been women, anthropology in general had been overwhelmingly concerned with men's activities. Though women constituted half the population, they were often invisible in ethnographic writing. Feminist anthropologists such as **Michelle Zimbalist Rosaldo** (1944–1981), **Louise Lamphere** (born 1940), **Sherry Ortner** (born 1 941), and **Micaela di Leonardo** (born 1949) tried to rectify this situation by focusing attention on women's worlds.

Feminist anthropologists actually took many different theoretical positions, from structuralism to neo-Marxism to postmodernism. However, they all shared an interest in women's position in society. Much of feminist anthropology in the 1970s was concerned with trying to explain female subordination, which some scholars considered to be universal. More recently, feminist anthropologists have focused on the social construction of gender, the relationship of gender to social, economic, and political power, and the cultural variation among different groups of women. They have been joined by others who focus on gay, lesbian, and transsexual populations. Some prominent anthropologists interested in these issues are William Leap, Tom Boellstorff, Ellen Lewin, and Tanya Erzen. The organizing theme that holds these disparate interests together is the idea that gender and relations among genders are a central patterning element of society. Understanding society involves elucidating gender relationships and showing the effect these have on other aspects of culture.

# Symbolic and Interpretive Anthropology

Like ethnoscientists and cognitive anthropologists, symbolic and interpretive anthropologists are fundamentally concerned with the ways in which people formulate their reality. However, unlike the former, who thought of culture in terms of formal linguistic models, symbolic and interpretive anthropologists use models from psychology and the study of literary texts to analyze culture. Some major figures in this group are **Clifford Geertz** (1926–2006), **Mary Douglas** (1921–2007), and **Victor Turner** (1920–1983). Geertz, one of the best-known modern anthropologists, believed that people use symbols to help them understand their own culture. Culture is like a story that people tell themselves about themselves, and in so doing give meaning and poignancy to their lives. Turner, on the other hand, followed the tradition of Durkheim and British functionalist anthropology, viewing symbols in terms of their role in the maintenance of society. He was particularly interested in the study of ritual and outlined the characteristics of symbols. Douglas also drew particular inspiration from her reading of Durkheim. She suggested that shared symbols helped hold societies together. Douglas was particularly interested in beliefs about purity and contamination and held that such notions symbolized beliefs about the social order.

Most anthropologists have argued that their theoretical position rests on scientific principles. Symbolic and interpretive anthropologists make no such claim. Rather, they suggest that anthropology is an art of cultural interpretation, more of a branch of the humanities than a science. Its goal is often to provide people with a deep, empathic understanding of the nature of meaning to members of different cultures rather than to discover general principles or testable laws.

# Postmodernism

Postmodernism grew from the insights of the feminist anthropologists, interpretive and symbolic anthropologists, and neo-Marxists, but its development was critically dependent on the thinking of cultural historian **Michel Foucault** (1926–1984) and literary critic **Jacques Derrida** (1930–2004). Anthropological postmodernists hold that all accounts of culture are partial and conditioned by the observer's personal history and experiences. One result, according to postmodernists, is that anthropological writing tells us a great deal about anthropologists and their society but rather little about the societies that anthropologists observe.

Issues of power and "voice" are critical to postmodern scholars. They assert that a great many different interpretations of history or culture are valid. The interpretations held by the wealthy and powerful are likely to be considered legitimate, while others are discredited. For postmodernists, culture is often viewed as a constant battle between opposing, contesting interpretations. Some, such as **Renato Rosaldo** (born 1941), focus on explanations of culture that highlight conflicting interpretations. Others, such as **Vincent Crapanzano** (born 1939) or **Gananath Obeyesekere** (born 1930), study anthropological writing itself. They analyze ethnographies to show the ways in which they are constructed and explain what they tell us about anthropologists and Western society.

At its most radical, postmodernism asserts that objectivity is impossible, implying that no interpretation or analysis can ever be better or worse than another. If this is the case, fieldwork is irrelevant and anthropology should be understood as a branch of literature, less accurate than fiction because of its pretensions to authority and fact. For these reasons, many anthropologists have been loud in their denunciation of postmodernism. Critics assert that

for anthropology to be useful, it must be based on a scientific model of study rather than a literary one.

However, even postmodernism's detractors would agree that it has made anthropologists more sensitive to the ways that knowledge is generated in anthropology and to issues of whose story they are telling as well as their own motivations and agendas in telling it.

# Anthropology and Globalization

Perhaps the most important new trend within anthropology in the past decade has been a focus on globalization. The fall of the Soviet Union and consequent emergence of new nations in central and eastern Europe, the vast improvements in the technologies of communication, the expansion of global capitalism, the emergence of China as an important capitalist society, the increasing permeability of international borders, and the increasing instability in many areas of the world have led to a new focus on culture contact and change. Anthropologists have turned their attention to the ways in which individuals and societies navigate and negotiate identity, economy, and politics within the context of global connectedness and inequality. One of the foremost spokespeople for this school of thought is Arjun Appadurai (born 1949). Appadurai's influential 1996 book *Modernity at Large* envisioned the cultural world as composed of a series of overlapping "scapes," or understandings of reality, that are at the same time physical, virtual, and cognitive. Appadurai distinguishes five "scapes": ethnoscapes, technoscapes, financescapes, mediascapes, and ideoscapes. Other anthropologists theorizing globalization include **Akhil Gupta, Aihwa Ong, Marc Edelman, Ulf Hannerz, Nancy Scheper-Hughes,** and **June Nash.**

The brief analysis of anthropological theories in this Appendix has been presented in rough order of appearance. This can be deceptive because it seems to imply that one theory simply supersedes another. For example, the fact that postmodernism appears after symbolic anthropology might lead you to believe that anthropologists abandoned symbolic anthropology and took up postmodernism. This is not at all the case. Although very few people today would call themselves historical particularists or psychological functionalists, many schools of anthropological thought are very much alive and well. A healthy debate exists among scholars representing various theoretical positions. New ways of looking at culture emerge from these conflicts.

# Glossary

**acephalous**  Lacking a government head or chief.

**achieved status**  A social position that a person chooses or achieves on his or her own.

**adaptation**  A change in the biological structure or lifeways of an individual or population by which it becomes better fitted to survive and reproduce in its environment.

**affinal**  Relatives by marriage; in-laws.

**African-American Vernacular English (AAVE)**  A form of English spoken by many African Americans, particularly among those of rural or urban working-class backgrounds. Also known as Ebonics.

**age grades**  Specialized associations based on age which stratify a society by seniority.

**age set**  A group of people of similar age and sex who move through some or all of life's stages together.

**agriculture**  A form of food production in which fields are in permanent cultivation using plows, animals, and techniques of soil and water control.

**allophones**  Two or more different phones that can be used to make the same phoneme in a specific language.

**ambilineal descent**  A form of bilateral descent in which an individual may choose to affiliate with either the father's or mother's descent group.

**animatism**  Belief in an impersonal spiritual force that infuses the universe.

**anime**  Animation, as in the popular culture of Japan; usually refers to animation of manga, or comic book graphic art.

**animism**  The notion that all objects, living and nonliving, are imbued with spirits.

**anomie**  A situation where social or moral norms are confused or entirely absent; often caused by rapid social change.

**anthropology**  The comparative study of human societies and cultures.

**antistructure**  The socially sanctioned use of behavior that radically violates social norms. Antistructure is frequently found in religious ritual.

**apartheid**  The South African system of exclusive racial groups—black, white, colored, and Asian—that were formally recognized, segregated, treated differently in law and life, and occupied different and almost exclusive statuses within the society.

**applied anthropology**  The application of anthropology to the solution of human problems.

**arboreal**  Tree-dwelling.

**archaeology**  The subdiscipline of anthropology that focuses on the reconstruction of past cultures based on their material remains.

**arranged marriage**  The process by which senior family members exercise a great degree of control over the choice of their children's spouses.

**artifact**  Any object made or modified by human beings. Generally used to refer to objects made by past cultures.

**arts**  Forms of creative expression that are guided by aesthetic principles and involve imagination, skill, and style.

**ascribed status**  A social position that a person is born into.

**assimilation**  The view that immigrants should abandon their cultural distinctiveness and become mainstream Americans.

**atlatl**  A spear thrower, a device used to increase and extend the power of the human arm when throwing a spear.

**australopithecines**  Members of an early hominid genus found in Africa and characterized by bipedal locomotion and small brain size.

**authority**  The ability to cause others to act based on characteristics such as honor, status, knowledge, ability, respect, or the holding of formal public office.

**avunculocal residence**  System under which a married couple lives with the husband's mother's brother.

**balanced reciprocity**  The giving and receiving of goods of nearly equal value with a clear obligation of a return gift within a specified time limit.

**band**  A small group of people related by blood or marriage, who live together and are loosely associated with a territory in which they forage.

**basic human needs approach**  Projects aimed at providing access to clean water, education, and health care for the poorest of the world's people.

**bhangra**  A musical form originating in the folk music of Punjab in Northern India and Eastern Pakistan that is mixing with British pop music and reggae to become a popular form of world music.

**bifurcation**  A principle of classifying kin under which different kinship terms are used for the mother's side of the family and the father's side of the family.

**bigman**  A self-made leader who gains power through personal achievements rather than through political office.

**bilateral descent**  System of descent under which individuals are equally affiliated with their mothers' and their fathers' descent group.

**bilocal residence**  System under which a married couple has the choice of living with the husband's or the wife's family.

**biological (or physical) anthropology**  The subdiscipline of anthropology that studies people from a biological perspective, focusing primarily on aspects of humankind that are genetically inherited. It includes osteology, nutrition, demography, epidemiology, and primatology.

**biopsychological equality**  The notion that all human groups have the same biological and mental capabilities.

**bipedalism**  Walking on two feet, a distinctive characteristic of humans and our ancestors.

**blended family**  Kinship networks occasioned by divorce and remarriage in the United States which include the previously divorced spouses and their new marriage partners.

**body art**  Marking and adorning the body as an expression of cultural and personal identity, or which serves other functions.

**bound morpheme**  A unit of meaning that must be associated with another.

**bride service**  The cultural rule that a man must work for his bride's family for a variable length of time either before or after the marriage.

**bridewealth**  Goods presented by the groom's kin to the bride's kin to legitimize a marriage (formerly called "bride price").

**call system**  The form of communication among nonhuman primates composed of a limited number of sounds that are tied to specific stimuli in the environment.

**capital**  Productive resources that are used with the primary goal of increasing their owner's financial wealth.

**capitalism**  An economic system in which people work for wages, land and capital goods are privately owned, and capital is invested for profit.

**cargo system**  A ritual system common in Central and South America in which wealthy people are required to hold a series of costly ceremonial offices.

**caste system**  Social stratification based on birth or ascribed status in which social mobility between castes is not possible.

**chiefdom**  A society with social ranking in which political integration is achieved through an office of centralized leadership called the chief.

**chronemics**  The study of the different ways that cultures understand time and use it to communicate.

**citizenship**  Membership in a state.

**civilizing mission**  The notion that colonialism was a duty for Europeans and a benefit for the colonized.

**clan**  A unilineal kinship group whose members believe themselves to be descended from a common ancestor but who cannot trace this link through known relatives.

**class**  A category of persons who all have about the same opportunity to obtain economic resources, power, and prestige and who are ranked relative to other categories.

**class system** A form of social stratification in which the different strata form a continuum and social mobility is possible.

**clinal distribution** The frequency change of a particular trait as you move geographically from one point to another.

**code switching** The ability of individuals who speak multiple languages to move seamlessly between them.

**cognatic descent** Any nonunilineal system of descent.

**cognitive anthropology** A theoretical approach that defines culture in terms of the rules and meanings underlying human behavior, rather than behavior itself.

**collaborative anthropology** Ethnography that gives priority to informants on the topic, methodology, and written results of research.

**collateral kin** Kin descended from a common ancestor but not in a direct ascendent or descendent line, such as siblings and cousins.

**colonialism** The active possession of a foreign territory and the maintenance of political domination over that territory.

**colony** A territory under the immediate political control of a nation state.

**communication** The act of transmitting information.

**communitas** A state of perceived solidarity, equality, and unity among people sharing a religious ritual, often characterized by intense emotion.

**comparative linguistics** The science of documenting the relationships between languages and grouping them into language families.

**complementary opposition** A political structure in which higher-order units form alliances that emerge only when lower-order units come into conflict.

**composite (compound) family** An aggregate of nuclear families linked by a common spouse.

**conflict theory** A perspective on social stratification that focuses on economic inequality as a source of conflict and change.

**conjugal tie** The relationship between a husband and wife formed by marriage.

**consanguineal** Related by blood.

**consanguineal relatives** Relatives by blood.

**consanguinity** Blood ties between people.

**contagious magic** The belief that things once in contact with a person or object retain an invisible connection with that person or object.

**conventionality** The notion that, in human language, words are only arbitrarily or conventionally connected to the things for which they stand.

**corporate descent groups** Permanent kinship groups that have an existence beyond the membership at any given time.

**corvée labor** Unpaid labor required by a governing authority.

**cosmology** A system of beliefs that deals with fundamental questions in the religious and social order.

**crafts** The application of aesthetic principles to the production of utilitarian objects and activities.

**creole** A first language that is composed of elements of two or more different languages. (Compare with *pidgin*.)

**cross cousins** The children of a parent's siblings of the opposite sex (mother's brothers, father's sisters).

**cultural anthropology** The study of human thought, meaning, and behavior that is learned rather than genetically transmitted, and that is typical of groups of people.

**cultural construction of gender** The idea that gender characteristics are the result of historical, economic, and political forces acting within each culture.

**cultural ecology** A theoretical approach that regards cultural patterns as adaptive responses to the basic problems of human survival and reproduction.

**cultural materialism** A theoretical perspective that holds that the primary task of anthropology is to account for the similarities and differences among cultures and that this can best be done by studying the material constraints to which human existence is subject.

**cultural relativism** The notion that cultures should be analyzed with reference to their own histories and values, in terms of the cultural whole, rather than according to the values of another culture.

**cultural resource management (CRM)** The protection and management of archaeological, archival, and architectural resources.

**culture** The learned behaviors and symbols that allow people to live in groups. The primary means by which humans adapt to their environments. The way of life characteristic of a particular human society.

**culture and personality theory** An anthropological perspective that focuses on culture as the principal force in shaping the typical personality of a society as well as on the role of personality in the maintenance of cultural institutions.

**culture shock** Feelings of alienation and helplessness that result from rapid immersion in a new and different culture.

**deep play** Performances (like sports) that are expressive forms of culture with functions similar to the other arts.

**descent** The culturally established affiliation between a child and one or both parents.

**descent group** A group of kin who are descendants of a common ancestor, extending beyond two generations.

**descriptive or structural linguistics** The study and analysis of the structure and content of particular languages.

**development** The notion that some countries are poor because they have small industrial plants and few lines of communication and that they should pursue wealth by acquiring these and other things.

**dialect** Grammatical constructions that deviate from those used by the socially dominant group in a society.

**diffusion** The spread of cultural elements from one culture to another through cultural contact.

**displacement** The capacity of all human languages to describe things not happening in the present.

**divination** A religious ritual performed to find hidden objects or information.

**domestic group (household)** Persons living in the same house, usually, but not always members of a family.

**double descent** The tracing of descent through both matrilineal and patrilineal links, each of which is used for different purposes.

**dowry** Presentation of goods by the bride's kin to the family of the groom or to the couple.

**Dutch East India Company** A joint stock company chartered by the Dutch government to control all Dutch trade in the Indian and Pacific Oceans. Also known by its Dutch initials VOC, for Verenigde Ostendische Compagnie.

**Ebonics** A form of English spoken by many African Americans, particularly among those of rural or urban working-class backgrounds. Also known as African-American Vernacular English.

**ecological functionalism** A theoretical perspective that holds that the ways in which cultural institutions work can best be understood by examining their effects on the environment.

**economic system** The norms governing production, distribution, and consumption of goods and services within a society.

**economics** The study of the ways in which the choices people make combine to determine how their society uses its scarce resources to produce and distribute goods and services.

**economizing behavior** Choosing a course of action to maximize perceived benefit.

**efficiency** Yield per person per hour of labor invested.

**egalitarian society** A society in which no individual or group has more privileged access to resources than any other.

**emic (perspective)** Examining society using concepts, categories, and distinctions that are meaningful to members of that culture.

**enculturation** The process of learning to be a member of a particular cultural group.

**endogamy** A rule prescribing that a person must marry within a particular group.

**engaged anthropology** Anthropology that includes political action as a major goal of fieldwork.

**ethnic boundaries** The perceived cultural attributes by which ethnic groups distinguish themselves from others.

**ethnic groups** Categories of people who see themselves as sharing an ethnic identity that differentiates them from other groups or the larger society.

**ethnicity** Perceived differences in culture, national origin, and historical experience by which groups of people are distinguished from others in the same social environment.

**ethnobotany** A field of anthropological research focused on describing the ways in which different cultures classify and understand plants.

**ethnocentrism** Judging other cultures from the perspective of one's own culture. The notion that one's own culture is more beautiful, rational, and nearer to perfection than any other.

**ethnography** The major research tool of cultural anthropology; includes both fieldwork among people in society and the written results of fieldwork.

**ethnohistory** Description of the cultural past based on written records, interviews, and archaeology.

**ethnology** The attempt to find general principles or laws that govern cultural phenomena.

**ethnomedicine** A field of anthropological research devoted to describing the medical systems and practices of different cultures.

**ethnoscience** A theoretical approach that focuses on the ways in which members of a culture classify their world and holds that anthropology should be the study of cultural systems of classification.

**etic (perspective)** Examining societies using concepts, categories, and rules derived from science; an outsider's perspective, which produces analyses that members of the society being studied may not find meaningful.

**evolution** In its broadest sense, directional change. For biologists, descent with modification from a single common ancestor or ancestral population.

**exogamous group** A group within which one is not permitted to marry.

**exogamy** A rule specifying that a person must marry outside a particular group.

**extended family** Family based on blood relations extending over three or more generations.

**factions** Informal alliances within well-defined political units such as lineages, villages, or organizations.

**feminist anthropology** A theoretical perspective that focuses on describing and explaining the social roles of women.

**fieldwork** The firsthand, systematic exploration of a society. It involves living with a group of people and participating in and observing their behavior.

**firm** An institution composed of kin and/or non-kin that is organized primarily for financial gain.

**foraging (hunting and gathering)** A food-getting strategy that does not involve food production or domestication of animals and that involves no conscious effort to alter the environment.

**forensic anthropology** The application of biological anthropology to the identification of skeletalized or badly decomposed human remains.

**fraternal polyandry** A custom whereby a woman marries a man and his brothers.

**free morpheme** A unit of meaning that may stand alone as a word.

**functionalism** The anthropological theory that specific cultural institutions function to support the structure of society or serve the needs of individuals in society.

**gender** A cultural construction that makes biological and physical differences between male and female into socially meaningful categories.

**gender hierarchy** The ways in which gendered activities and attributes are differentially valued and related to the distribution of resources, prestige, and power in a society.

**gender role** The cultural expectations of men and women in a particular society, including the division of labor.

**gene flow** Mixing of genetic material that results from the movement of individuals and groups from place to place.

**generalized reciprocity** Giving and receiving goods with no immediate or specific return expected.

**genetic drift** Changes in the frequencies of specific traits caused by random factors.

**genitor** A biological father.

**genocide** The deliberate and systematic extermination of a national, racial, political, or cultural (ethnic) group.

**genus** In biological classification, a group of similar species.

**Ghost Dance** A Native American religious movement of the late 19th century.

**globalization** The integration of resources, labor, and capital into a global network.

**glottochronology** A statistical technique that linguists have developed to estimate the date of separation of related languages.

**god** A named spirit who is believed to have created or to control some aspect of the world.

**government** An interrelated set of status roles that become separate from other aspects of social organization, such as kinship, in exercising control over a population.

**gross national income (GNI)** The total value of all goods and services produced in a country.

**haptics** The analysis and study of touch.

**Heeren XVII** The Lords Seventeen, members of the board of directors of the Dutch East India Company.

**hegemony** The dominance of a political elite based on a close identification between their own goals and those of the larger society.

**hijab** A widespread term used for the head covering worn by some Muslim women as part of modest dress.

**hijra** An alternative gender role in India conceptualized as neither man nor woman.

**historical linguists** Study relationships among languages to better understand the histories and migrations of those who speak them.

**holistic/holism** In anthropology an approach that considers culture, history, language, and biology essential to a complete understanding of human society.

***Homo erectus*** A species of early human found in Africa, Asia, and Europe. *Homo erectus* were present between 1.8 million and about 200,000 years ago.

***Homo habilis*** A species of early human found in Africa. *Homo habilis* were present between 2.5 and 1.8 million years ago.

***Homo sapiens*** A species of human found throughout the world. The earliest *Homo sapiens* appeared about 500,000 years ago.

**horticulture** Production of plants using a simple, nonmechanized technology; fields are not used continuously.

**household** A group of people united by kinship or other links who share a residence and organize production, consumption, and distribution among themselves.

**Human Relations Area Files (HRAF)** An ethnographic database that includes descriptions of more than 300 cultures and is used for cross-cultural research.

**human variation** The subdiscipline of anthropology concerned with mapping and explaining physical differences among modern human groups.

**hybridization model** A theory that seeks to explain the transition from archaic to modern *Homo sapiens* by proposing that modern and archaic forms interbred.

**imitative magic** The belief that imitating an action in a religious ritual will cause the action to happen in the material world.

**incest taboos** Prohibitions on sexual relations between relatives.

**indigenous peoples** Societies that have occupied a region for a long time and are recognized by other groups as its original (or very ancient) inhabitants.

**industrialism** The replacement of human and animal energy by machines in the process of production.

**industrialized agriculture** A production technology that adapts mechanized manufacturing processes in production, processing, and distribution of food.

**informant (consultant)** A person from whom an anthropologist gathers data.

**informed consent** The requirement that participants in anthropological studies should understand the ways in which their participation and the release of the research data are likely to affect them.

**inheritance** The transfer of property between generations.

**innovation** A new variation on an existing cultural pattern that is subsequently accepted by other members of the society.

**institutional review board (IRB)** A committee organized by a university or other research institution that approves, monitors, and reviews all research that involves human subjects.

**International Phonetic Alphabet (IPA)** A system of writing designed to represent all the sounds used in the different languages of the world.

**interpretive (symbolic) anthropology** A theoretical approach that emphasizes culture as a system of meaning and proposes that the aim of cultural anthropology is to interpret the meanings that cultural acts have for their participants.

**joint stock company** A firm that is managed by a centralized board of directors but is owned by its shareholders.

**kindred** A unique kin network made up of all the people related to a specific individual in a bilateral kinship system.

**kinesics** The study of body position, movement, facial expressions, and gaze.

**kinship** A culturally defined relationship established on the basis of blood ties or through marriage.

**kinship system** The totality of kin relations, kin groups, and terms for classifying kin in a society.

**kinship terminology** The words used to identify different categories of kin in a particular culture.

**Kula ring** A pattern of exchange among trading partners in the South Pacific islands.

**law** A means of social control and dispute management through the systematic application of force by a politically constituted authority.

**leadership** The ability to direct an enterprise or action.

**ledger drawings** Drawings, in ledger books, made by some Native American peoples to record personal and historical events.

**leveling mechanism** A practice, value, or form of social organization that evens out wealth within a society.

**levirate** The custom whereby a man marries the widow of a deceased brother.

**lexicon** The total stock of words in a language.

**life chances** The opportunities that people have to fulfill their potential in society.

**liminal** Objects, places, people, and statuses that are understood as existing in an indeterminate state, between clear-cut categories.

**lineage** A group of kin whose members trace descent from a known common ancestor.

**lineal kin** Blood relations linked through descent, such as Ego, Ego's mother, Ego's grandmother, and Ego's daughter.

**linguistic anthropology** A branch of linguistics concerned with understanding language and its relation to culture.

**machismo** A cultural construction of hypermasculinity as essential to the male gender role.

**magic** An attempt to mechanistically control supernatural forces. The belief that certain words, actions, and states of mind compel the supernatural to behave in predictable ways.

**mahu** An alternative gender role in Tahiti.

**mana** Religious power or energy that is concentrated in individuals or objects.

**manga** Japanese comic book art.

**manhood puzzle** The question of why in almost all cultures masculinity is viewed not as a natural state but as a problematic status to be won through overcoming obstacles.

**market exchange** An economic system in which goods and services are bought and sold at a money price determined primarily by the forces of supply and demand.

**marriage** The customs, rules, and obligations that establish a socially endorsed relationship between adults and children, and between the kin groups of the married partners.

**matrilineage** A lineage formed by descent in the female line.

**matrilineal descent** A rule that affiliates a person to kin of both sexes through females only.

**matrilocal residence** System under which a husband lives with his wife's family after marriage.

**mediation** A form of managing disputes that uses the offices of a third party to achieve voluntary agreement between the disputing parties.

**medical anthropology** A subfield of cultural anthropology concerned with the ways in which disease is understood and treated in different cultures.

**melanin** A pigment found in the skin, hair, and eyes of human beings, as well as many other species, that is responsible for variations in color.

**menarche** A woman's first menstruation.

**messianic** Focusing on the coming of an individual who will usher in a utopian world.

**millenarian** Focusing on a coming catastrophe will signal the beginning of a new age and the eventual establishment of paradise.

**modernization theory** A model of development that predicts that nonindustrial societies will move in the social and technological direction of industrialized nations.

**monoculture plantation** An agricultural plantation specializing in the large-scale production of a single crop to be sold on the market.

**monogamy** A rule that permits a person to be married to only one spouse at a time.

**monotheism** Belief in a single god.

**morpheme** The smallest unit of language that has a meaning.

**morphology** A system for creating words from sounds.

**multiculturalism** The view that cultural diversity is a positive value that should be incorporated into national identity and public policy.

**multinational corporation (MNC)** A corporation that owns business enterprises or plants in more than one nation.

**multiregional model** A theory that seeks to explain the transition from *Homo erectus* to *Homo sapiens* by arguing that different populations of *Homo sapiens* are descendant from different populations of *Homo erectus*.

**multivalent** Containing many different and sometimes contradictory meanings in a single word, idea, or object.

**mutation** A random change in genetic material; the ultimate source of all biological variation.

**myths** Sacred stories or narratives.

**nation-state** A sovereign, geographically based state that identifies itself as having a distinctive national culture and historical experience.

**Native American Church** A religious revitalization movement among Native Americans, also known as the peyote religion.

**native anthropologist** An anthropologist who does fieldwork in his or her own culture.

**nativism** Focusing on the return of society to an earlier time that believers understand as better, more holy, than the current era.

**natural selection** The mechanism of evolutionary change; changes in traits of living organisms that occur over time as a result of differences in reproductive success among individuals.

**Neanderthal** Members of a population of archaic *Homo sapiens* that lived between 130,000 and 35,000 years ago.

**negative reciprocity** Exchange conducted for the purpose of material advantage and the desire to get something for nothing.

**neo-evolutionism** A theoretical perspective concerned with the historical change of culture from small-scale societies to extremely large scale societies.

**neoliberalism** Political and economic policies that promote free trade, individual initiative, and minimal government regulation of the economy, and oppose state control

or subsidy to industries and all but minimal aid to impoverished individuals.

**neolocal residence** System under which a couple establishes an independent household after marriage.

**neo-Marxism** A theoretical perspective concerned with applying the insights of Marxist thought to anthropology; neo-Marxists modify Marxist analysis to make it appropriate to the investigation of small-scale, non-Western societies.

**nepotism** The granting of privilege or favoritism on the basis of family relationships.

**nomadic pastoralism** A form of pastoralism in which the whole social group (men, women, children) and their animals move in search of pasture.

**nonunilineal descent** Any system of descent in which both father's and mother's lineages have equal claim to the individual.

**norm** An ideal cultural pattern that influences behavior in a society.

**nuclear family** A family organized around the conjugal tie (the relationship between husband and wife) and consisting of a husband, a wife, and their children.

**Oldowan tools** Stone tools made by *Homo habilis*.

**omnivore** An animal that eats both plant and animal foods.

**oricha** An African deity identified with a Catholic saint in Voudou and Santeria.

**Orientalism** Scholarship and art generated by Europeans, representing their views of the Middle East.

**paleoanthropology** The subdiscipline of anthropology concerned with tracing the evolution of humankind in the fossil record.

**parallax** The slight difference in the image of an object seen from two different vantage points.

**parallel cousins** The children of a parent's same-sex siblings (mother's sisters, father's brothers).

**participant observation** The fieldwork technique that involves gathering cultural data by observing people's behavior and participating in their lives.

**pastoralism** A food-getting strategy that depends on the care of domesticated herd animals.

**pater** The socially designated father of a child, who may or may not be the biological father.

**patrilineage** A lineage formed by descent in the male line.

**patrilineal descent** A rule that affiliates a person to kin of both sexes through males only.

**patrilocal residence** System under which a bride lives with her husband's family after marriage.

**peasants** Rural cultivators who produce for the subsistence of their households but are also integrated into larger, complex state societies.

**Peyote Road** The moral principles followed by members of the Native American Church.

**pharmacopoeia** A collection of preparations used as medications.

**phone** A sound made by humans and used in any language.

**phoneme** The smallest significant unit of sound in a language. A phonemic system is the sound system of a language.

**phonology** The sound system of a language.

**phratry** A unilineal descent group composed of a number of clans whose members feel themselves to be closely related.

**pidgin** A language of contact and trade composed of features of the original languages of two or more societies. (Compare with *creole*.)

**pillage** To strip an area of money, goods, or raw materials through the threat or use of physical violence.

**plasticity** The ability of humans to change their behavior in response to a wide range of environmental demands.

**political ideology** The shared beliefs and values that legitimize the distribution and use of power in a particular society.

**political organization** The patterned ways in which power is used in a society.

**political process** The ways in which individuals and groups use power to achieve public goals.

**polyandry** A rule permitting a woman to have more than one husband at a time.

**polygamy** A rule allowing more than one spouse.

**polygyny** A rule permitting a man to have more than one wife at a time.

**polytheism** Belief in many gods.

**population density** The number of people inhabiting a given area of land.

**postmodernism** A theoretical perspective focusing on issues of power and voice. Postmodernists suggest that anthropological accounts are partial truths reflecting the background, training, and social position of their authors.

**potlatch** A form of redistribution involving competitive feasting practiced among Northwest Coast Native Americans.

**power** The ability to compel other individuals to do things that they would not choose to do of their own accord.

**prayer** Any communication between people and spirits or gods in which people praise, plead, or request without assurance of results.

**prehistoric** Societies for which we have no usable written records.

**prestige** Social honor or respect.

**priest** One who is formally elected or appointed to a full-time religious office.

**primate** A member of a biological order of mammals that includes human beings, apes, and monkeys as well as prosimians (lemurs, tarsiers, and others).

**private/public dichotomy** A gender system in which women's status is lowered by their almost exclusive cultural identification with the home and children, whereas men are identified with public, prestigious, economic, and political roles.

**productive resources** Material goods, natural resources, or information used to create other goods or information.

**productivity (linguistics)** The ability of humans to combine words and sounds into new meaningful utterances.

**productivity (subsistence)** Yield per person per unit of land.

**proxemics** The study of the cultural use of interpersonal space.

**race** A culturally constructed category based on *perceived* physical differences.

**racism** The belief that some human populations are superior to others because of inherited, genetically transmitted characteristics.

**rain forest** Tropical woodland characterized by high rainfall and a dense canopy of broad-leaved evergreen trees.

**rank society** A society characterized by institutionalized differences in prestige but no important restrictions on access to basic resources.

**rebellion** The attempt of a group within society to force a redistribution of resources and power.

**reciprocity** A mutual give and take among people of equal status.

**redistribution** Exchange in which goods are collected then redistributed to members of a group.

**refugees** People who have been uprooted from their native lands and forced to cross national boundaries.

**religion** A social institution characterized by sacred stories; symbols and symbolism; the proposed existence of immeasurable beings, powers, states, places, and qualities; rituals and means of addressing the supernatural; specific practitioners; and change.

**replacement model** The theory that modern people evolved first in Africa and then spread out to inhabit virtually all the world, outcompeting or destroying other human populations in the process.

**revolution** An attempt to overthrow an existing form of political organization and put another type of political structure in its place.

**rickets** A childhood disease characterized by the softening and bending of leg and pelvis bones. Rickets is related to insufficiency of vitamin D and/or calcium.

**rite of intensification** A ritual structured to reinforce the values and norms of a community and to strengthen group identity.

**rite of passage** A ritual that moves an individual from one social status to another.

**ritual** A patterned act that involves the manipulation of religious symbols.

**sacred narratives** Stories held to be holy and true by members of a religious tradition.

**sacrifice** An offering made to increase the efficacy of a prayer or the religious purity of an individual.

**Sapir-Whorf hypothesis** The hypothesis that perceptions and understandings of time, space, and matter are conditioned by the structure of a language.

**secret societies** West African societies whose membership and rituals are known only to society members. Their most significant function is the initiation of boys and girls into adulthood.

**sedentary** Settled, living in one place.

**segmentary lineage system** A form of sociopolitical organization in which multiple descent groups (usually patrilineages) form at different levels and function in different contexts.

**semantics** The subsystem of a language that relates words to meaning.

**sex** The biological difference between male and female.

**sexual selection** The theory that the evolution of certain traits can be explained by competition for opportunities to mate.

**shaman** An individual who is socially recognized as having the ability to mediate between the world of humanity and the world of gods or spirits but who is not a recognized official of any religious organization.

**social complexity** The number of groups and their interrelationships in a society.

**social differentiation** The relative access individuals and groups have to basic material resources, wealth, power, and prestige.

**social mobility** Movement from one social strata to another.

**social stratification** A social hierarchy resulting from the relatively permanent unequal distribution of goods and services in a society.

**society** A group of people who depend on one another for survival or well-being as well as the relationships among such people, including their status and roles.

**sociobiology** A theoretical perspective that explores the relationship between human cultural behavior and genetics.

**sociolinguistics** A specialization within anthropological linguistics that focuses on speech performance.

**sorcery** The conscious and intentional use of magic.

**sororal polygyny** A form of polygyny in which a man marries sisters.

**sororate** The custom whereby, when a man's wife dies, her sister is given to him as a wife.

**species** In biological classification, a group of organisms whose members are similar to one another and are able to reproduce with one another but not with members of other species.

**speech community** A group of people who share a set of norms and rules for the use of language.

**Standard Spoken American English (SSAE)** The form of English spoken by most of the American middle class.

**state** A hierarchical, centralized form of political organization in which a central government has a legal monopoly over the use of force.

**stem family** A nuclear family with a dependent adult added on.

**stratified society** A society characterized by formal, permanent social and economic inequality in which some people are denied access to basic resources.

**structural adjustment** A development policy promoted by Western nations, particularly the United States, that requires poor nations to pursue free-market reforms in order to get new loans from the International Monetary Fund and World Bank.

**structural anthropology** A theoretical perspective that holds that all cultures reflect similar deep, underlying patterns and that anthropologists should attempt to decipher these patterns.

**subculture** A system of perceptions, values, beliefs, and customs that are significantly different from those of a larger, dominant culture within the same society.

**subsistence strategy** The way a society transforms environmental resources into food.

**succession** The transfer of office or social position between generations.

**surrogate motherhood** A variety of reproductive technologies in which a woman helps a couple to have a child by acting as a biological surrogate, carrying an embryo to term.

**sweatshop** Generally a pejorative term for a factory with working conditions that may include low wages, long hours, inadequate ventilation, and physical, mental, or sexual abuse.

**swidden (slash and burn) cultivation** A form of cultivation in which a field is cleared by felling the trees and burning the brush. Typical of horticulture.

**symbol** Something that stands for something else.

**syncretism** The merging of elements of two or more religious traditions to produce a new religion.

**syntax** The part of grammar that has to do with the arrangement of words to form phrases and sentences.

**termite fishing** The learned use of twigs or blades of grass to extract termites from their mounds characteristic of some groups of chimpanzees.

**Tirailleurs Sénégalais** Senegalese Riflemen. An army that existed from 1857 to 1960 composed largely of soldiers from French West African colonies led by officers from Metropolitan France.

**totem** An animal, plant, or other aspect of the natural world held to be ancestral or to have other intimate relationships with members of a group.

**totemism** Religious practices centered around animals, plants, or other aspects of the natural world held to be ancestral or to have other intimate relationships with members of a group.

**transculturation** The transformation of adopted cultural traits, resulting in new cultural forms.

**transhumant pastoralism** A form of pastoralism in which herd animals are moved regularly throughout the year to different areas as pasture becomes available.

**transmigrant** Immigrants who maintain close relations with their home countries.

**transnationalism** The pattern of close ties and frequent visits by immigrants to their home countries.

**tribe** A culturally distinct population whose members consider themselves descended from the same ancestor.

**tributary mode of exchange** Primary producers are allowed access to the means of production, and tribute is exacted from them by coercion.

**trickster** A supernatural entity that does not act in the best interests of humans.

**two-spirit role** An alternative gender role in native North America (formerly called berdache).

**unilineal descent** Descent group membership based on links through either the maternal or the paternal line, but not both.

**universal grammar** A basic set of principles, conditions, and rules that underlie all languages.

**urban archaeology** The archaeological investigation of towns and cities as well as the process of urbanization.

**value** A culturally defined idea of what is true, right, and beautiful.

**"Venus" figurines** Small stylized statues of females made in a variety of materials by early modern humans.

**vision quest** A practice common among many Native American groups in which individuals seek to achieve direct contact with the supernatural.

**vitalism** Looking toward the creation of a utopian future that does not resemble a past golden age.

**war** A formally organized and culturally recognized pattern of collective violence directed toward other societies, or between segments within a larger society.

**wealth** The accumulation of material resources or access to the means of producing these resources.

**Wiccan (or neopagan)** A member of a new religion that claims descent from pre-Christian nature worship. A modern-day witch.

**witchcraft** The ability to harm others by harboring malevolent thoughts about them; the practice of sorcery.

**word** The smallest part of a sentence that can be said alone and still retain its meaning.

**world art** The contemporary visual arts and cultural performances of non-Western peoples, as they are increasingly part of a capitalistic global art world that includes international collections, museum exhibits, and tourism.

**World Bank** Officially called the International Bank for Reconstruction and Development, an international agency that provides technical assistance and loans to promote international trade and economic development, especially to poor nations. The World Bank has often been criticized for interfering in the affairs of these nations.

**world music** World music incorporates different musical styles from cultures throughout the world.

**xanith** An alternative gender role in Oman on the Saudi Arabian peninsula.

# References

AARP, Gallup Organization. 2004. Civil Rights and Race Relations. Princeton, NJ: The Gallup Organization. Available at http://assets.aarp.org /rgcenter/general/civil_rights.pdf.

Abdo, Geneive. 2006. *Mecca and Main Street: Muslim Life in America After 9/11.* New York: Oxford University Press.

Aberle, David F., Urie Bronfenbrenner, Eckhard Hess, Daniel Miller, David Schneider, and James Spuhler. 1963. "The Incest Taboo and Mating Patterns of Animals." *American Anthropologist* 65:253–265.

Abesalom, Vekua, David Lordkipanidze, et al. 2002. "A Skull of Early *Homo* from Dmanisi, Georgia," *Science* (July 5, 2002), 85–89.

Abrahams, Roger D. 1970. *Deep Down in the Jungle.* Chicago: Aldine.

Abu-Lughod, Lila D. 1993. *Writing Women's Worlds: Bedouin Stories.* Berkeley, CA: University of California Press.

Acheson, James M. 1989. "Management of Common-Property Resources." In S. Plattner (Ed.), *Economic Anthropology.* (pp. 351–378). Stanford, CA: Stanford University Press.

Adams, Kathleen M. 1990. "Cultural Commoditization in Tana Toraja, Indonesia." *Cultural Survival Quarterly* 40(1):31–34.

Adams, Kathleen M. 1993. "Theologians, Tourists and Thieves: The Torajan Effigy of the Dead in Modernizing Indonesia." *Kyoto Journal* 22:38–45.

Adams, Kathleen M. 1995. "Making-Up the Toraja? The Appropriation of Tourism, Anthropology, and Museums for Politics in Upland Sulawesi, Indonesia." *Ethnology* 34:143–152.

Adams, Kathleen M. 2006. *Art as Politics: Re-Crafting Identities, Tourism, and Power in Tana Toraja, Indonesia.* 2006. Honolulu, HI: University of Hawai'i Press.

Adcock, Gregory J., Elizabeth S. Dennis, Simon Easteal, Gavin A. Huttley, Lars S. Jermiin, W. James Peackock, and Alan Thorne. 2001. "Mitochondrial DNA Sequences in Ancient Australians: Implications for Modern Human Origins." *Proceedings of the National Academy of Sciences USA* 98(2):537–542.

Adetunji, Jimoh I. 2006. "Nigeria: An End to Gas Flaring." *E Magazine* 17(4):38–39.

Aijmer, Goren, and Jon Abbink (Eds.). 2000. *Meanings of Violence: A Cross Cultural Perspective.* New York: New York University Press.

Akom, A. A. 2008. "Toward an Eco-Pedagogy: Urban Youth Use Digital Media to Combat Environmental Racism." *Anthropology Newsletter,* November, p. 51.

Albers, Patricia C. 1989. "From Illusion to Illumination: Anthropological Studies of American Indian Women." In S. Morgen (Ed.), *Gender and Anthropology: Critical Reviews for Research and Teaching* (pp. 132–170). Washington, DC: American Anthropological Association.

Ali, Hirsi Ayaan. 2006. *The Caged Virgin: An Emancipation Proclamation for Women and Islam.* New York: Free Press.

Allen, Charlotte. 2001. "The Scholars and the Goddess." *Atlantic Monthly* 287(1):18–22.

Allen, Theodore W. 1997. *The Invention of the White Race* (Vols. 1 and 2). London: Verso.

Allitt, Patrick. 2002. *Victorian Britain.* (Audio recording.) Chantilly, VA: The Teaching Company.

Allotey, P., and D. Reidpath. 2001. "Establishing the Causes of Childhood Mortality in Ghana: The 'Spirit Child'." *Social Science & Medicine* 52:1007–1012.

Alloula, Malek. 1986. *The Colonial Harem* (Myrna Godzich and Wlad Godzich, Trans.). Minneapolis: University of Minnesota Press.

Almond, Gabriel, Emmanuel Sivan, and R. Scott Appleby. 1995. "Fundamentalism: Genus and Species." In E. Marty and R. Scott Appleby (Eds.), *Fundamentalisms Comprehended* (pp. 399–424). Chicago: University of Chicago Press.

Alonso, Ana Maria. 1994. "The Politics of Space, Time and Substance: State Formation, Nationalism, and Ethnicity." In B. Siegel (Ed.), *Annual Review of Anthropology* (Vol. 23, pp. 379–405). Stanford, CA: Stanford University Press.

Amadiume, Ifi. 1987. *Male Daughters, Female Husbands.* Atlantic Highlands, NJ: Zed Books.

American Anthropological Association (AAA). 1986. "Statements on Ethics: Principles of Professional Responsibility." Available at http://www.aaanet.org/stmts/ethstmnt.htm.

American Anthropological Association. 1998. *Statement on Race.* Available at http:// www.aaanet.org/stmts/racepp.htm.

Ammon, Paul R., and Mary S. Ammon. 1971. "Effects of Training Black Preschool Children in Vocabulary Versus Sentence Construction." *Journal of Educational Psychology* 62(5):421–426.

Amnesty International. 2005. "Iraq: Decades of Suffering, Now Women Deserve Better. Amnesty International." Available at: http://www.amnesty.org/en/library/info/MDE14/001/2005/en.

Anagnost, Ana. 1989. "Transformations of Gender in Modern China." In S. Morgen (Ed.), *Gender in Anthropology: Critical Reviews for Research and Teaching* (pp. 313–342). Washington DC: American Anthropological Association.

Andersen, Margaret L., and Patricia Hill Collins (Eds.). 1995. *Race, Class, and Gender: An Anthology* (2nd ed.). Belmont, CA: Wadsworth.

Anderson, Benedict. 1991. *Imagined Communities: Reflections on the Origin and Spread of Nationalism.* New York: Verso.

Anderson, Elijah. 1999. *Code of the Streets.* New York: Norton.

Andrews, George Reid. 1992. "Racial Inequality in Brazil and the United States: A Statistical Comparison." *Journal of Social History* 26(2):229–263.

Aoki, K. 2002. "Sexual Selection as a Cause of Human Skin Colour Variation: Darwin's Hypothesis Revisited." *Annals of Human Biology* 29:589–608.

Archibold, Randal C. 2006. "Arizona Is Split Over Taking Hard Line on Immigrants." *New York Times,* December 14, p. A 30.

Arens, William. 1975. "The Great American Football Ritual." *Natural History* 84:72–80.

Artz, Georgeanne, Peter F. Orazem, and Daniel M. Otto. 2007. "Measuring the Impact of Meat Packing and Processing Facilities in Nonmetropolitan Counties: A Difference-in-Differences Approach," *American Journal of Agricultural Economics* 89(3):557–570.

Aufderheide, Arthur. 2003. *The Scientific Study of Mummies.* Cambridge, UK: Cambridge University Press.

Australian Institute of Health and Welfare. 2008. "Cancer—Australian Cancer Incidence Statistics Update, December 2008." Available at http://www.aihw.gov.au/cancer/index.cfm.

Babcock, Barbara. 1995. "Marketing Maria: The Tribal Artist in the Age of Mechanical Reproduction." In Brenda Jo Bright and Liza Bakewell (Eds.), *Looking High and Low: Art and Cultural Identity* (pp. 125–150). Tucson: University of Arizona Press.

Baer, Hans A., Merrill Singer, and Ida Susser. 1997. *Medical Anthropology and the World System: A Critical Perspective.* Westport, CT: Bergin & Garvey.

Bailey, Stanley R., and Edwar E. Telles. 2006. "Multiracial Versus Collective Black Categories: Examining Census Classification Debates in Brazil." *Ethnicities* 6(1):74–101.

Bajaj, Vikas, and Ron Nixon. 2006. "Subprime Loans Going from Boon to Housing Bane." *New York Times,* December 6, p. C1.

Balikci, Asen. 1970. *The Netsilik Eskimo.* Prospect Heights, IL: Waveland.

Balter, Michael. 2004. "Skeptics Question Whether Flores Hominid Is a New Species." *Science* 306:1116.

Balter, Michael. 2005. "Are Humans Still Evolving?" *Science* 309:234–237.

Baochang, Gu, Wang Feng, Guo Zhigang, and Zhang Erli. 2007. "China's Local and National Fertility Policies at the End of the Twentieth Century." *Population and Development Review* 33(1):129–147.

Barfield, Thomas J. 1993. *The Nomadic Alternative.* Englewood Cliffs, NJ: Prentice Hall.

Barker, Randolph, Robert W. Herdt, and Beth Rose. 1985. *The Rice Economy of Asia.* Washington DC: Resources for the Future.

Barnes, Virginia Lee, and Janice Boddy. 1994. *Aman: The Story of a Somali Girl as Told to Virginia Lee Barnes and Janice Boddy.* New York: Vintage Books.

Barnes-Dean, Virginia Lee. 1989. "Clitoridectomy and Infibulation." *Cultural Survival Quarterly* 9(2):26–30.

Barnett, Homer. 1953. *Innovation: The Basis of Cultural Change.* New York: McGraw Hill.

Barth, Fredrik. 1964. "Capital Investment and Social Structure of a Pastoral Nomad Group in South Persia." In R. Firth and B.S. Yamey (Eds.). *Capital Savings and Credit in Peasant Societies* (pp 69–81). London: George Allen and Unwin.

Barth, Fredrik. 1998. *Ethnic Groups and Boundaries: The Social Organization of Culture Difference.* Prospect Heights, IL: Waveland. (Originally published 1969.)

Bassani, Ezio, and William Fagg. 1988. *Africa and the Renaissance: Art in Ivory.* New York: Center for African Art.

Basso, Keith. 1979. *Portraits of "The Whitemen."* New York: Cambridge University Press.

Basson, Lauren L. White. 2008. *Enough to Be an American? Race Mixing, Indigenous People, and the Boundaries of State and Nation.* Chapel Hill, NC: University of North Carolina Press.

Bates, Daniel G., and Susan H. Lees (Eds.). 1996. *Case Studies in Human Ecology.* New York: Plenum.

Bates, Marston. 1967. *Gluttons and Libertines: Human Problems of Being Natural.* New York: Random House.

Begun, David R. 2004. "The Earliest Hominids—Is Less More?" *Science* 303:1478–1480.

Behringer, Wolfgang. 2004. *Witches and Witch-Hunts: A Global History.* Malden, MA: Polity Press.

Bell, D. 1981. "Women's Business Is Hard Work: Central Australian Aboriginal Women's Love Rituals." *Signs* 7:318–337.

Benedict, Ruth. 1934. "Anthropology and the Abnormal." *Journal of General Psychology* 10:791–808.

Benedict, Ruth. 1961. *Patterns of Culture.* Boston: Houghton and Mifflin. (Originally published 1934.)

Bennett, Andrew. 1997. "Bhangra in Newcastle: Music, Ethnic Identity and the Role of Local Knowledge." *Innovation: The European Journal of Social Sciences* 10(1):107–117.

Berdan, Frances F. 1982. *The Aztecs of Central Mexico: An Imperial Society.* New York: Holt, Rinehart and Winston.

Berdan, Frances F. 1989. "Trade and Markets in Precapitalist States." In S. Plattner (Ed.), *Economic Anthropology* (pp. 78–107). Stanford, CA: Stanford University Press.

Bereiter, Carl, and Siegfried Engelmann. 1966. *Teaching Disadvantaged Children in Preschool.* Englewood Cliffs, NJ: Prentice Hall.

Berlo, Janet C. (Ed.). 1996. *Plains Indian Drawings, 1865–1935. Pages from a Visual History.* New York: Abrams.

Berreman, Gerald D. 1981. *Social Inequality: Comparative and Developmental Approaches.* New York: Academic Press.

Berreman, Gerald D. 1988. "Race, Caste, and Other Invidious Distinctions in Social Stratification." In J. Cole (Ed.), *Anthropology for the Nineties: Introductory Readings* (pp. 485–518). New York: Free Press.

Besnier, Niko. 1996. "Polynesian Gender Liminality Through Time and Space." In G. Herdt (Ed.), *Third Sex, Third Gender: Beyond Sexual Dimorphism in Culture and History* (pp. 285–328). New York: Zone.

Beteille, Andre. 1998. *Society and Politics in India: Essays in a Comparative Perspective.* New Delhi: Oxford India.

Bettelheim, Bruno. 1996. *Symbolic Wounds* (rev. ed.). New York: Collier. (Originally published 1962.)

Bhagwati, Jagdish. 1996. "The Demand to Reduce Domestic Diversity Among Trading Nations." In Jagdish Bhagwati and R. E. Hudec (Eds.), *Fair Trade and Harmonization.* Cambridge, MA: MIT Press.

Bialostok, Steve. 2009. "Revisiting Class on Campus: Patching the Pipeline." *Anthropology News,* March, p. 43.

Bickerton, Derek. 1998. "Catastrophic Evolution: The Case for a Single Step from Protolanguage to Full Human Language." In James Hurford, M. Studdert-Kennedy, and C. Knight (Eds.), *The Evolutionary Emergence of Language: Social Function and the Origins of Linguistic Form* (pp. 341–358). Cambridge: Cambridge University Press.

Bilefsky, Dan. 2008. "13 Years After Peace Accord, Fear Grows of New Ethnic Conflict in Divided Bosnia." *New York Times,* December 14, p. A6.

Bilefsky, Dan. 2009. "Czechs Cool to Presence of Workers From Asia." *New York Times,* June 6. Available at: http://www.nytimes.com/2009/06/07/world/asia/07viet.html.

Bitterli, Urs. 1986. *Cultures in Conflict: Encounters Between European and Non-European Cultures, 1432–1800.* Stanford, CA: Stanford University Press.

Bittman, Mark. 2008. "The Meat of the Matter." *The Dallas Morning News,* February 10, 2008.

Blackwood, Evelyn. 1984. "Sexuality and Gender in Certain Native American Tribes: The Case of Cross-Gender Females." *Signs: Journal of Women in Culture and Society* 10:27–42.

Blaser, Mario. 2009. "The Threat of the Yrmo: The Political Ontology of a Sustainable Hunting Program." *American Anthropologist* 111(1):10–20.

Blumenfield, Tami. 2004. "Walking Marriages." *Anthropology Newsletter* 45(5).

Boas, Franz. 1988. "The Limitations of the Comparative Method of Anthropology." In P. Bohannan and M. Glazer (Eds.), *High Points in Anthropology* (2nd ed.) (pp. 85–93). New York: McGraw-Hill. (Originally published 1896.)

Boas, Noel T., and Alan J. Almquist. 1999. *Essentials of Biological Anthropology.* Upper Saddle River, NJ: Prentice Hall.

Bodley, John H. 1999. *Victims of Progress* (4th ed.). Mountain View, CA: Mayfield.

Bodley, John H. 2000. *Cultural Anthropology: Tribes, States, and the Global System* (3rd ed.). Mountain View, CA: Mayfield.

Bodley, John. 2007. *Anthropology and Contemporary Human Problems* (5th ed.). Lanham, MD: Rowman and Littlefield.

Bonvillain, Nancy. 1997. *Language, Culture, and Communication* (2nd ed.). Englewood Cliffs, NJ: Prentice Hall.

Bordes, Francois. 1968. *The Old Stone Age.* New York: McGraw-Hill.

Borgerhoff Mulder, Monique. 1995. "Bride-wealth and Its Correlates: Quantifying Changes over Time." *Current Anthropology* 36:573–603.

Borlaug, Norman. 2000. "The Green Revolution and The Road Ahead." Lecture to the Norwegian Nobel Institute. Available at http://www.nobel.se/peace/articles/borlaug/borlaug-lecture.pdf.

Bornstein, Avram S. 2002. *Crossing the Green Line Between the West Bank and Israel.* Philadelphia: University of Pennsylvania Press.

Borofsky, Robert. 1994. "On the Knowledge and Knowing of Cultural Activities." In R. Borofsky (Ed.), *Assessing Cultural Anthropology* (pp. 331–347). New York: McGraw-Hill.

Borofsky, Robert. 2005. *Yanomami: The Fierce Controversy and What We Can Learn from It.* Berkeley, CA: University of California Press.

Bouche, Denise. 1966. "Les Écoles Françaises au Soudanà l'Époque de la Conquête. 1884–1900." *Cahiers d'Etudes Africainnes* 7(2):228–267.

Bourgois, Philippe. 1996. "Confronting Anthropology, Education, and Inner-City Apartheid." *American Anthropologist* 98:249–265.

Bowen, John R. 2007. *Why the French Don't Like Headscarves: Islam, the State, and Public Space.* Princeton, NJ: Princeton University Press.

Bowerman, M. 1996. "Learning How to Structure Space for Language: A Cross-Linguistic Perspective." In P. Bloom, M.A. Pewterson, L. Nadel, and M.F. Garett (Eds.), *Language and Space* (I pp. 385–436). Cambridge, MA: MIT Press.

Bowles, Samuel, et al. (Eds.). 2005. *Unequal Changes: Family Background and Economic Success.* Princeton: Princeton University Press.

Boxer, C. R. 1965. *The Dutch Seaborne Empire 1600–1800.* New York: Knopf.

Boyd-Bowman, Peter. 1975. "A sample of sixteenth century 'Caribbean' Spanish phonology." In W. Milan, J. Staczek, and J. Zamora (Eds.), *1974 Colloquium on Spanish and Portuguese linguistics* (pp. 1–11). Washington, DC: Georgetown University.

Boynton, Robert S. 2006. "The Plot Against Equality" (Book Review of *The Trouble with Diversity: How We Learned to Love Identity and Ignore Inequality,* by Walter Benn Michaels). *The Nation,* December 25, pp. 23 ff.

Bracken, Christopher. 1997. *The Potlatch Papers: A Colonial Case History.* Chicago: University of Chicago Press.

Brady, Emily. 2008. "The Year of Living Nervously." *New York Times,* December 7, p. C1.

Brain, James L. 1989. "An Anthropological Perspective on the Witchcraze." In Jean R. Brink, A. P. Coudert, and M. C. Horowitz (Eds.), *The Politics of Gender in Early Modern Europe* (pp. 15–27). Kirksville, MO: Sixteenth Century Journal Publishers.

Brandes, Stanley. 1981. "Like Wounded Stags: Male Sexual Ideology in an Andalusian Town." In S. B. Ortner and H. Whitehead (Eds.), *Sexual Meanings: The Cultural Construction of Gender and Sexuality* (pp. 216–239). Cambridge: Cambridge University Press.

Brandt, Deborah. 2008. *Tangled Routes: Women, Work, and Globalization on the Tomato Trail* (2nd ed.). Lanham, MD: Rowman and Littlefield.

Brecher, Jeremy. 1972. *Strike.* San Francisco: Straight Arrow Books.

Bremner, Brian. 2006. "What's It Going to Cost to Clean Up China?" *Business Week,* September 27. Available at http://www.businessweek.com/globalbiz/content/sep2006/gb20060927_774622.htm?chan=top1news+top+news+index_global+business.

Brettell, Caroline. 2003. *Anthropology and Migration: Essays on Transnationalism, Ethnicity and Identity.* New York: Altamira Press.

Brettell, Caroline B. 2007. "Adjustment of Status, Remittances, and Return: Some Observations on 21st Century Migration Processes." *City and Society* 19(1):47–59.

Breusers, Mark. 1999. *On the Move: Mobility; Land Use and Livestock Practices on the Central Plateau in Burkina Faso.* Münster, Hamburg, and London: LIT Verlag.

Briggs, Jean L. 1991. "Expecting the Unexpected: Canadian Inuit Training for an Experimental Lifestyle." *Ethos* 19:259–287.

Bright, Brenda Jo, and Liza Bakewell (Eds.). 1995. *Looking High and Low: Art and Cultural Identity.* Tucson: University of Arizona.

Brito, Silvester J. 1989. *The Way of a Peyote Roadman.* New York: Peter Lang.

Broadhead, Robert, Yael Van Hulst, and Douglas Heckathorn. 1999. "Termination of an Established Needle Exchange: A Study of Claims and Their Impact." *Social Problems* 46(1):48–56.

Brosius, Peter J. 1999. "Green Dots, Pink Hearts: Displacing Politics from the Malaysian Rain Forest." *American Anthropologist* 101:36–57.

Brown, Donald. 1991. *Human Universals.* New York: McGraw-Hill.

Brown, Dorothy. 2009. "Two Americas, Two Tax Codes," *New York Times,* March 9, p. A23.

Brown, Drusilla, Alan Deardorff, and Robert Stern. 2003. "The Effects of Multinational Production on Wages and Working Conditions in Developing Countries." *National Bureau of Economic Research, Working Paper 9669.* Cambridge (MA): National Bureau of Economic Research. Available at http://www.nber.org/papers/w9669.

Brown, Judith. 1965. "A Cross Cultural Study of Female Initiation Rites." *American Anthropologist* 65:837–855.

Brown, Judith. 1975. "Iroquois Women: An Ethnohistoric Note." In R. R. Reiter (Ed.), *Toward an Anthropology of Women* (pp. 235–251). New York: Monthly Review Press.

Brown, P., and A. Podelefsky. 1976. "Population Density, Agricultural Intensity, Land Tenure, and Group Size in the New Guinea Highlands." *Ethnology* 15:211–238.

Brown, Peter, T. Sutikna, M. Morwood, R. P. Soejono, Jatmiko, E. W. Saptomo, et al. 2004. "A New Small-Bodied Hominin from the Late Pleistocene of Flores, Indonesia." *Nature* 431:1055–1061.

Brumberg, Joan Jacobs. 1989. *Fasting Girls: The History of Anorexia Nervosa.* New York: Penguin.

Brumfiel, Elizabeth. 1991. "Weaving and Cooking: Women's Production in Aztec Mexico." In J. M. Gero and M. W. Conkey (Eds.), *Engendering Archaeology: Women and Prehistory* (pp. 224–251). Cambridge, MA: Basil Blackwell.

Brumfiel, Elizabeth. 2006 "Cloth, Gender, Continuity and Change: Fabricating Unity in Anthropology." *American Anthropologist* 108(4):862–877.

Brunet, M., et al. 2002. "A New Hominid from the Upper Miocene of Chad, Central Africa." *Nature* 418:145–151.

Bryant, Vaughn M. 2003. "Archaeology: Invisible Clues to New World Plant Domestication." *Science* 299(5609):1029–1030.

Buck, Pem Davidson. 1989. "Cargo-Cult Discourse: Myth and the Rationalization of Labor Relations in Papua New Guinea." *Dialectical Anthropology* 13:157–171.

Burbank, Victoria K. 1989. "Gender and Anthropology Curriculum: Aboriginal Australia." In S. Morgen (Ed.), *Gender and Anthropology: Critical Reviews for Research and Teaching* (pp. 116– 131).Washington DC: American Anthropological Association.

Bureau of Labor Statistics (BLS). 2009. *Economic News Release: Employment Situation Summary.* Available at http://www.bls.gov/news.release/empsit.nro.htm.

Burenhult, Goran (Ed.). 1993. *The First Humans: Human Origins and History to 10,000 BC.* San Francisco: Harper.

Burton, John W. 1992. "Representing Africa: Colonial Anthropology Revisited." *Journal of Asian and African Studies* 27:181–201.

Burton, John W. 2001. *Culture and the Human Body: An Anthropological Perspective.* Prospect Heights: Waveland.

Burton, Thomas G. 1993. *Serpent-handling Believers.* Knoxville: University of Tennessee Press.

Buruma, Ian. 2006. *Murder in Amsterdam: The Death of Theo van Gogh and the Limits of Tolerance.* New York: Penguin.

Cagan, Jonathan, and Craig M. Vogel. 2002. *Creating Breakthrough Products: Innovation from Product Planning to Program Approval.* Upper Saddle River, NJ: Prentice Hall.

Calman, Neil, Charmaine Ruddock, Maxine Golub, and Lan Le. 2005. *Separate and Unequal: Medical Apartheid in New York City.* New York: Institute for Urban Family Health.

The Canadian Broadcasting Company. 1982. Ear Pull Hoopla. Broadcast March 21. Available at http://archives.radio-canada.ca/IDC-1-41-1194-6705/sports/arcticgames/clip4.

Cancian, Frank. 1989. "Economic Behavior in Peasant Communities." In Stuart Plattner (Ed.), *Economic Anthropology* (pp. 127–170). Stanford, CA: Stanford University Press.

Cannon, Walter B. 1942. "The 'Voodoo' Death." *American Anthropologist* 44: 169–180.

Cardillo, Cathy. 1997. "Violence Against Chinese Women: Defining the Culture Role." *Women's Rights Law Reporter* 19(1):85–96.

Carlson, Robert G., Harvey A. Siegal, Jichuan Wang, and Russel S. Flack. 1996. "Attitudes Toward Needle 'Sharing' Among Injection Drug Users: Combining Qualitative and Quantitative Research Methods." *Human Organization* 55:361–369.

Carneiro, Robert. 1970. "A Theory of the Origin of the State." *Science* 169:733–738.

Carneiro, Robert. 1981. "The Chiefdom: Precursor of the State." In Grant Jones and Robert Kautz (Eds.), *The Transition to Statehood in the New World* (pp. 37–79). Cambridge: Cambridge University Press.

Carneiro, Robert. 1988. "Indians of the Amazonian Forest." In J. S. Denslow and C. Padoch (Eds.), *People of the Tropical Rain Forest* (pp. 73–86). Berkeley, CA: University of California Press.

Carod-Artal, Francisco Javier, and Carolina Vázquez-Cabrera. 2007. "An Anthropological Study About Headache and Migraine in Native Cultures From Central and South America." *Headache: The Journal of Head & Face Pain* 47(6):834–841.

Casey, Catherin E. 1999. "'Come, Join Our Family': Discipline and Integration in Corporate Organizational Culture." *Human Relations* 52(2):155–178.

Cashdan, Elizabeth. 1989. "Hunters and Gatherers: Economic Behavior in Bands." In S. Plattner (Ed.), *Economic Anthropology* (pp. 21–48). Stanford, CA: Stanford University Press.

Castle, Sarah. 2001. "'The Tongue Is Venomous': Perception, Verbalisation and the Manipulation of Mortality and Fertility Regimes in Rural Mali." *Social Science and Medicine.* 52: 1827–1841.

Catholic News Agency. 2007. "Pope Calls For Protection of Environment, Says Creation-Evolution Debate is 'Absurdity.'" Available at http://www.catholicnewsagency.com/new.php?=59968.

Center for Muslim-Jewish Engagement. 2008. Available at http://www.usc.edu/dept/MSA/humanrelations/womeninislam/whatishijab.html.

Cerroni-Long, E. L. 1993. "Teaching Ethnicity in the USA: An Anthropological Model." *Journal of Ethno-Development* 2(1):106–112.

Cerroni-Long, E. L. 1995. "Introduction." In E. L. Cerroni-Long (Ed.), *Insider Anthropology* (Napa Bulletin, Vol. 16). Washington, DC: American Anthropological Association.

Chagnon, Napoleon. 1997. *Yanomamo* (5th ed.). Fort Worth: Harcourt Brace Jovanovich.

Chance, Norman. 1990. *The Inupiat and Arctic Alaska: An Ethnography of Development.* Fort Worth, TX: Holt.

Chang, Leslie T. 2008. *Factory Girls: From Village to City in a Changing China.* New York: Spiegel & Grau.

Chapman, C.A., and D.A. Onderdonk. 1998. "Forests Without Primates: Primate/Plant Codependency." *American Journal of Primatology* 45:127–141.

Chapman, Mary M. 2008. "Black Workers in Auto Plants Losing Ground." *New York Times,* December 30, p. A1.

Chavez, Leo R. 1998. *Shadowed Lives: Undocumented Immigrants in American Society*. Belmont, CA: Wadsworth.

Checker, Melissa. 2005. *Polluted Promises: Environmental Racism and the Search for Justice in a Southern Town*. New York: New York University Press.

Checker, Melissa. 2009. "Anthropology in the Public Sphere: 2008: Emerging Trends and Significant Impacts." *American Anthropologist* 111(2):162–169.

Chelala, Cesar. 2006. "Chronically Hungry Children of America." *The Japan Times*, September 18.

Chelala, Cesar. 2007. "Changing Cultures to Value Women." *Philadelphia Inquirer*, April 29, p. D1.

Chelala, Cesar. 2008. "Violence Against Women in the Arab World." *The Middle East Times*, December 15.

Chevannes, Barry. 1994. *Rastafari: Roots and Ideology*. Syracuse, NY: Syracuse University Press.

Chodorow, Nancy. 1974. "Family Structure and Feminine Personality." In M. Rosaldo and L. Lamphere (Eds.), *Women, Culture, and Society* (pp. 43–66). Stanford, CA: Stanford University Press.

Chodorow, Nancy. 1978. *The Reproduction of Mothering*. Berkeley, CA: University of California Press.

Chomsky, Noam. 1965. *Syntactic Structures*. London: Mouton.

Chomsky, Noam. 1975. *The Logical Structure of Linguistic Theory*. New York: Plenum Press.

Cisse, Almahady. 2007. "Mali: Wood—The Gift that Can't Keep On Giving." *Inter Press Service* (Johannesburg), April 13.

Clark, J., C. Yallop, and J. Fletcher. 2007. *An Introduction to Phonetics and Phonology* (3rd ed.). Oxford, UK: Blackwell.

Clark, Kamari Maxine, and Deborah A. Thomas (Eds.). 2006. *Globalization and Race: Transformations in the Cultural Production of Blackness*. Durham, NC: Duke University Press.

Clark, Lauren, and Ann Kingsolver. n.d. "Briefing Paper on Informed Consent." *AAA Committee on Ethics*. Available at http://www.aaanet.org/committees/ethics/bp5.htm.

Clarke, Mari H. 2000. "On the Road Again: International Development Consulting." In Paula Sabloff (Ed.), *Careers in Anthropology: Profiles of Practitioner Anthropologists* (pp. 71–74). Washington, DC: National Association for the Practice of Anthropology.

Cleaveland, A. A., J. Craven, and M. Danfelser. 1979. Universals of Culture. *Intercom* 92/93, 8–10.

Clemetson, Lynette. 2006. "U.S. Muslims Confront Taboo on Nursing Homes." *New York Times*, June 13, p. A1.

Clendinnen, Inga. 1991. *Aztecs: An Interpretation*. Cambridge: Cambridge University Press.

Clifford, James. 1988. *The Predicament of Culture: Twentieth-Century Ethnography, Literature, and Art*. Cambridge, MA: Harvard University Press.

Clifford, James, and George E. Marcus (Eds.). 1986. *Writing Culture: The Poetics and Politics of Ethnography*. Berkeley, CA: University of California Press.

Cohen, Abner. 1969. *Custom and Politics in Urban Africa*. London: Routledge and Kegan Paul.

Cohen, Ronald, and Elman R. Service. 1978. *Origins of the State: The Anthropology of Political Evolution*. Philadelphia: Institute for the Study of Human Issues.

Cohen, Yehudi. 1971. *Man in Adaptation: The Institutional Framework*. Chicago: Aldine.

Cole, Alistair, and Gino Raymond. 2006. *Redefining the French Republic*. Manchester: Manchester University Press.

Cole, David. 2003. *Enemy Aliens: Double Standards and Constitutional Freedoms in the War on Terrorism*. New York: The New Press.

Coleman, Michael C. 1999. "The Responses of American Indian Children and Irish Children to the School, 1850s–1920s: A Comparative Study in Cross-Cultural Education." *American Indian Quarterly* 23(3/4):83–112.

Condon, Richard G., with Julia Ogina and the Holman Elders. 1996. *The Northern Copper Inuit: A History*. Toronto: University of Toronto Press.

Condry, Ian. 2005, January. "Must-Download TV and Cool Japan." *Anthropology Newsletter* 53.

Connolly, Bob, and Robin Anderson. 1983. *First Contact*. [film]. Watertown, MA: Documentary Educational Resources.

Connolly, Bob, and Robin Anderson. 1987. *First Contact: New Guinea's Highlanders Encounter the Outside World*. New York: Penguin.

Conroy, Ronan. 2006. "Editorial: Female Genital Mutilation: Whose Problem, Whose Solution?" *British Medical Journal* 333:106–107.

Constable, Julie L., M. Ashley, J. Goodall, and A. Pusey. 2001. "Noninvasive Paternity Assignment in Gombe Chimpanzees." *Molecular Ecology*. 10:1279–1300.

Conway-Long, Don. 1994. "Ethnographies and Masculinities." In Harry Brod and Michael Kaufman (Eds.), *Theorizing Masculinities* (pp. 61–81). Thousand Oaks, CA: Sage.

Coquery-Vidrovitch, Catherine. 1988. *Africa: Endurance and Change South of the Sahara*. Berkeley, CA: University of California Press.

Corak, Miles. 2004. *Generational Income Mobility in North America and Europe*. Cambridge, UK: Cambridge University Press.

Cosentino, Donald J. 2000. "Hip-Hop Assemblage: The Chris Ofili Affair." *African Arts* 33, 110 l(Spring):40–51, 95–96.

Costa, LeeRay, and Andrew Matzner. 2007. *Male Bodies, Women's Souls: Personal Narratives of Thailand's Transgendered Youth*. Binghamton, NY: Haworth Press.

Cotter, Holland. 2009. "Putting 'Primitive' to Rest." *New York Times*, June 5. p. C1.

Counts, Dorothy Ayers, and David R. Counts. 1985. *Aging and Its Transformations: Moving Toward Death in Pacific Societies*. New York: Lanham/University Press of America.

Covington, Dennis. 1995. *Salvation on Sand Mountain: Snake Handling and Redemption in Southern Appalachia*. Reading, MA: Addison-Wesley.

Crespin, Pamela. 2005. "The Global Transformation of Work." *Anthropology News* 46(3):20–21.

Crush, Jonathan. 1995. *The Power of Development*. New York: Routledge.

Culotta, Elizabeth. 1999. "Neanderthals Were Cannibals, Bones Show." *Science* 286:18b–19b.

Culotta, Elizabeth. 2008. "Hobbit Redux?" *ScienceNow Daily News*, 11 March. Available at http://sciencenow.sciencemag.org/cgi/content/full/2008/311/1.

Cunningham, Lawrence S., John Kelsay, R. Maurice Barineau, and Heather Jo McVoy. 1995. *The Sacred Quest: An Invitation to the Study of Religion* (2nd ed.). Englewood Cliffs, NJ: Prentice Hall.

Curtis, Lewis P. 1968. *Anglo-Saxons and Celts: A Study of Anti-Irish Prejudice in Victorian England*. Bridgeport, CT: University of Bridgeport.

Dalton, George. 1961. "Economic Theory and Primitive Society." *American Anthropologist* 63:1–25.

Damon, Frederick H. 1983. "What Moves the Kula: Opening and Closing Gifts on Woodlark Island." In J.W. Leach and E. Leach (Eds.), *The Kula: New Perspectives on Massim Exchange* (pp. 309–342). Cambridge: Cambridge University Press.

Danaher, Kevin, and Michael Shellenberger (Eds.). 1995. *Fighting for the Soul of Brazil*. New York: Monthly Review Press.

D'Andrade, Roy G. 1995. "What Do You Think You're Doing?" *Anthropology Newsletter* 36(7): 1,4.

D'Andrade, Roy G., Nancy Scheper-Hughes, et al. 1995. "Objectivity and Militancy: A Debate." *Current Anthropology* 36:399–420.

Dalrymple, William. 2007. *The Last Muchal: The Fall of a Dynasty*. New York: Knopf.

Danfulani, Umar Habila Dadem. 1999. "Exorcising Witchcraft: The Return of the Gods in New Religious Movements on the Jos Plateau and the Benue Regions of Nigeria." *African Affairs* 98(391):167–193.

Daniel, G. Reginald. 2006. *Race and Multiraciality in Brazil and the United States: Converging Paths?* University Park: Pennsylvania State University Press.

Darian-Smith, Eve. 2004. *New Capitalists: Law, Politics, and Identity Surrounding Casino Gaming on Native American Land*. Belmont, CA: Wadsworth.

Dart, Raymond Arthur. 1996. "The Discovery of *Australopithecus*." In Brian M. Fagan (Ed.), *Eyewitness to Discovery* (pp. 37–45). New York: Oxford University Press. (Originally published 1959.)

Das, Gurcharan. 2009. "The Next World Order," *New York Times*, January 2, p. A23.

Das, Raju. 1998. "The Green Revolution, Agrarian Productivity and Labor." *International Journal of Urban and Regional Research* 22(1):122–135.

Daugherty, Mary Lee. 1993. "Serpent-Handling as Sacrament." In A. C. Lehmann and J. E. Myers (Eds.), *Magic, Witchcraft, and Religion: An Anthropological Study of the Supernatural* (pp. 343–348). Mountain View, CA: Mayfield. (Originally published 1976.)

Defleur, Alban, Tim White, and Patricia Valensi. 1999. "Neanderthal Cannibalism at Moula-Guercy, Ardeche, France." *Science* 286:128–131.

Dei, Kojo. 2002. *Ties that Bind: Youth and Drugs in a Black Community*. Prospect Heights: Waveland.

Delcore, Henry D. 2007. "The Racial Distribution of Privilege in a Thai National Park." *Journal of Southeast Asian Studies* 38(1):83–105

Demian, Melissa. 2008 "Fictions of Intention in the 'Cultural Defense'." *American Anthropologist* 110:4, December:432–442.

Dentan, Robert K. 1979. *The Semai: A Nonviolent People of Malaya*. New York: Holt, Rinehart and Winston.

Destexhe, Alain. 1995. *Rwanda and Genocide in the Twentieth Century* (Alison Marschner, Trans.). New York: New York University Press.

De Vos, George A., and Hiroshi Wagatsuma. 1966. *Japan's Invisible Race: Case Studies in Culture and Personality*. Berkeley, CA: University of California Press.

De Vos, George, and Lola Romanucci-Ross. 1995. "Ethnic Identity: A Psychocultural Perspective." In Lola Romanucci-Ross and George A. De Vos (Eds.), *Ethnic Identity: Creation, Conflict, and Accommodation* (3rd ed.) (pp. 349–380). London: Sage.

de Waal Malefijt, Annemarie. 1968. *Religion and Culture: An Introduction to the Anthropology of Religion*. Prospect Heights, IL: Waveland Press.

di Leonardo, Micaela. 1984. *The Varieties of Ethnic Experience: Kinship, Class, and Gender among California Italian-Americans*. Ithaca, NY: Cornell University Press.

di Leonardo, Micaela (Ed.). 1991. *Gender at the Crossroads of Knowledge: Feminist Anthropology in the Postmodern Era*. Berkeley, CA: University of California Press.

Diamond, Jared. 1992. "The Arrow of Disease." *Discover* 13(10):64–73.

Diamond, Jared. 1994. "Race Without Color." *Discover* 15(11):82–89.

Divale, William Tulio, and Marvin Harris. 1976. "Population, Warfare and the Male Supremacist Complex." *American Anthropologist* 78:521–538.

Dollard, John. 1937. *Caste and Class in a Southern Town*. New Haven, CT: Yale University Press.

Dominguez, Virginia. 1986. *White by Definition*. New Brunswick, NJ: Rutgers University Press.

Downum, Christian E. and Laurie J. Price. 1999. "Applied Archaeology." *Human Organization* 58(3):226–239

Dozon, Jean-Pierre. 1985. "Les Bété: une creation coloniale." In J. L. Amselle and E. M'bokolo (Eds.), *Au Coeur de l'ethnie* (pp. 49–85). Paris: Editions La Decouverte.

Dreyfuss, Robert. 2009. "Iraq's Resurgent Nationalism." *The Nation*, March 9:13–16.

Duncan, David Ewing. 1995. *Hernando de Soto: A Savage Quest in the Americas*. New York: Crown.

Duncan, David James. 2000, March/April. "Salmon's Second Coming." *Sierra*, pp. 30–41.

Dundes, Alan (Ed.). 1980. *Into the Endzone for a Touchdown: A Psychoanalytic Consideration of American Football*. Bloomington: Indiana University Press.

Duranti, Alessandro. 1997. *Linguistic Anthropology*. Cambridge: Cambridge University Press.

Durkheim, Émile. 1961. *The Elementary Forms of the Religious Life*. New York: Collier. (Originally published 1915.)

Durrenberger, E. Paul. 2001. "Explorations of Class and Consciousness in the U.S." *Journal of Anthropological Research* 57(1): 41–60.

Durrenberger, E. Paul, and Judith Marti (Eds.). 2006. *Labor in Cross-Cultural Perspective*. Lanham, MD: Altamira Press.

Eakin, Hugh. 2009. "The Affair of the Chinese Bronze Heads." *New York Review of Books* 56(8):19.

Earle, Timothy K. 1987. "Chiefdoms in Archaeological and Ethnological Perspective." *Annual Reviews in Anthropology* 16:279–308.

Early, John D., and Thomas N. Headland. 1998. *Population Dynamics of a Philippine Rain Forest People: The San Ildefonso Agata*. Gainesville, FL: University of Florida Press.

Eaton, S. Boyd, and Melvin Konner. 1989. "Ancient Genes and Modern Health." In A. Podolefsky and P. J. Brown (Eds.), *Applying Anthropology* (pp. 43–46). Mountain View, CA: Mayfield.

Echenberg, Myron. 1991. *Colonial Conscripts: The Tirailleurs Sénégalais in French West Africa, 1857–1960*. Portsmouth, NH: Heinemann.

Eck, Diane. 2001. *A New Religious America*. San Francisco: Harper.

Eck, Diane. 2003. *Encountering God: A Spiritual Journey from Bozeman to Banaras*. Boston: Beacon Press.

*Economist, The.* 2005. "Mind the Gap." June 9.

*Economist, The.* 2007. "The Good Consumer." Jan. 17, 2008.

Eggan, Fred. 1950. *The Social Organization of Western Pueblos*. Chicago: University of Chicago Press.

Eldredge, Niles, and Stephen Jay Gould. 1972. "Punctuated Equilibria: An Alternative to Phyletic Gradualism." T. J. M. Schopf (Ed.), *Models in Paleobiology* (pp. 82–115). San Francisco: Freeman, Cooper and Co.

Elkin, A. P. 1967. "The Nature of Australian Totemism." In J. Middleton (Ed.), *Gods and Rituals* (pp. 159–176). Garden City, NY: Natural History Press.

Eller, Jack David. 2006. *Violence and Culture: A Cross-Cultural and Interdisciplinary Approach*. Belmont, CA: Wadsworth.

Ellison, James. 2009. "Governmentality and the Family: Neoliberal Choices and Emergent Kin Relations in Southern Ethiopia." *American Anthropologist* 111(1):81–92.

El Saadāwā, Nawāl. 1980. *The Hidden Face of Eve: Women in the Arab World*. London: Zed Press.

Ember, Carol. 1983. "The Relative Decline in Women's Contribution to Agriculture with Intensification." *American Anthropologist* 85(2):285–304.

Ember, Carol R., and Melvin Ember. 2005. "Explaining Corporal Punishment of Children: A Cross Cultural Study." *American Anthropologist* 85(2):285–304.

Ember, Melvin, and Carol R. Ember. 1971. "The Conditions Favoring Matrilocal vs. Patrilocal Residence." *American Anthropologist* 73:571–594.

Erickson, Jon. 1995. *The Human Volcano: Population Growth as Geologic Force*. New York: Facts on File.

Escobar, Arturo. 1997. "The Making and Unmaking of the Third World Through Development." In M. Rahnema and V. Bawtree (Eds.). *The Post-Development Reader* (pp. 263–273). Atlantic Highlands, NJ: Zed Books.

Estioko-Griffin, Agnes. 1986. "Daughters of the Forest." *Natural History* 5:37–42.

Evans, Peter. 2000. "Fighting Marginalization with Transnational Networks: Counter Hegemonic Globalization." *Contemporary Sociology* 29:230–241.

Evans-Pritchard, E. E. 1958. *Witchcraft, Oracles, and Magic among the Azande*. Oxford: Clarendon Press. (Originally published 1937.)

Evans-Pritchard, E. E. 1968. *The Nuer*. Oxford: Clarendon Press. (Originally published 1940.)

Ewing, Katherine Pratt (Ed.). 2008. *Being and Belonging: Muslims in the United States since 9/11*. New York: Russell Sage Foundation.

Fábrega, Horacio. 1997. *Evolution of Sickness and Healing*. Berkeley, CA: University of California Press.

Fagan, R. 1993. "Primate Juveniles and Primate Play." In Michael E. Pereira and Lynn A. Fairbanks (Eds.), *Juvenile Primates: Life History, Development and Behavior* (pp. 182–196). New York: Oxford University Press.

Fairbanks, Lynn A. 1988. "Vervet Monkey Grandmothers: Interactions with Infant Offspring." *International Journal of Primatology* 9:425–441.

Feinberg, Richard. 1986. "Market Economy and Changing Sex-Roles on a Polynesian Atoll." *Ethnology* 25:271–282.

Feinberg, Richard. 1994. "Contested Worlds: Politics of Culture and the Politics of Anthropology." *Anthropology and Humanism* 19:20–35.

Feldman, Douglas A. (Ed.). 2009. *AIDS, Culture, and Gay Men*. Gainesville, FL: University of Florida Press.

Fenton, James. 1996. "A Short History of Anti-Hamitism." *New York Review of Books* 43(3):7–9.

Ferguson, R. Brian. 2007. "Eight Points on War." *Anthropology News*, February, p. 5.

Ferguson, R. Brian, and Neil L. Whitehead (Eds.). 1992. *War in the Tribal Zone: Expanding States and Indigenous Warfare*. Santa Fe, NM: School of American Research Press.

Ferraro, Gary P. 1994. *The Cultural Dimension of International Business* (2nd ed.). Englewood Cliffs, NJ: Prentice-Hall.

Fix, Michael, and Randy Capps. 2005. "Immigrant Children, Urban Schools, and the No Child Left Behind Act." *Migration Policy Institute*. Available at http://www.migrationinformation.org/USFocus/display.cfm?ID=347.

Fix, Michael, and Jeffrey Passel. 1994. *Immigration and Immigrants: Setting the Record Straight*. Washington, DC: Urban Institute.

Flamm, Bruce L. 2002. "Faith Healing by Prayer: Review of Cha, KY, Wirth, DP, Lobo, RA. Does Prayer Influence the Success of In Vitro Fertilization-Embryo Transfer?" *The Scientific Review of Alternative Medicine* 6(1):47–50.

Flood, Merielle K. 1994. "Changing Gender Relations in Zinacantan, Mexico." *Research in Economic Anthropology* 15:145–173.

Fluehr-Lobban, C. 1998. "Cultural Relativism and Universal Human Rights." *Museum of Natural History AnthroNotes* 20(2). Available at http://anthropology.si.edu/outreach/anthnote/Winter98/anthnote.html.

Fondacaro, Steve, and Montgomery McFate. 2008. "In Memoriam—Michael Bhatia." Available at http://humanterrainsystem.army.mil/bhatia.html.

Foner, Eric. 1988. *Reconstruction: America's Unfinished Revolution 1863–1877.* New York: Harper.

"For Indian Church, A Critical Shortage." 1995. *New York Times,* March 20, p. A8.

For Teachers: *Religion & Culture: Suppression or Liberation: Islam, Hijab, and Modern Society.* Available at http://www.pbs.org/wnet/wideangle/classroom/21p5c.html.

*Forbes.* 2008. "#12 Miami Heat." Available at http://www.forbes.com/lists/2008/32/nba08_Miami-Heat_329036.html.

Forde, Daryll. 1950. "Double Descent among the Yako." In A. R. Radcliffe-Brown and D. Forde (Eds.), *African Systems of Kinship and Marriage* (pp. 285–332). London: Oxford University Press.

Fortune, Reo F. 1932. *Sorcerers of Dobu.* Prospect Heights, IL: Waveland Press.

*Fortune.* 2006. "Global 500." Available at: http://money.cnn.com/magazines/fortune/global500/2005/.

Foster, Robert J. 1991. "Making National Cultures in the Global Ecumene." *Annual Reviews of Anthropology* 20:235–260.

Fouts, Roger, and Deborah Fouts. 1989. "Loulis in Conversation with the Cross-Fostered Chimpanzees." In R. Allen Gardner, Beatrix T. Gardner, and Thomas Van Cantfort (Eds.), *Teaching Sign Language to Chimpanzees* (pp. 293–307). Albany: State University of New York Press.

Frank, Robert, and Phillip J. Cook. 1996. *The Winner-Take-All Society: Why the Few at the Top Get So Much More than the Rest of Us.* New York: Penguin.

Frankenberg, Ruth. 1993. *White Women, Race Matters: The Social Construction of Whiteness.* Minneapolis: University of Minnesota Press.

Frankl, Victor. 1946. *Man's Search for Meaning.* Boston: Beacon Press.

Frankl, Victor E. 1962. *Man's Search for Meaning; An Introduction to Logotherapy.* Boston: Beacon Press.

Fredrickson, George M. 2009. *Diverse Nations: Explorations in the History of Racial and Ethnic Pluralism.* New York: Paradigm.

Freed, Ruth S., and Stanley A. Freed. 1985. "The Psychomedical Case History of a Low-Caste Woman of North India." *Anthropological Papers of the American Museum of Natural History* 60(2):102–228.

Freeman, Carla. 2007. "The 'Reputation' of Neoliberalism." *American Ethnologist* 34(2):252–267.

French, Howard W. 2006. "Rush for Wealth in China's Cities Shatters the Ancient Assurance of Care in Old Age." *New York Times,* November 3, p. A8.

Freyre, Gilberto. 1946. *The Masters and the Slaves: A Study in the Development of Brazilian Civilization.* New York: Knopf.

Fried, Morton. 1967. *The Evolution of Political Society.* New York: Random House.

Friedheim, William, with Ronald Jackson (Eds.). 1996. *Freedom's Unfinished Revolution: An Inquiry into the Civil War and Reconstruction.* New York: New Press.

Friedl, Ernestine. 1975. *Women and Men: An Anthropologist's View.* New York: Holt, Rinehart and Winston.

Friedman, Ariella, and Judith Todd. 1994. "Kenyan Women Tell a Story: Interpersonal Power of Women in Three Subcultures in Kenya." *Sex Roles* 31:533–546.

Friedman, Jonathan. 1992. "The Past in the Future: History and the Politics of Identity." *American Anthropologist* 94:837–859.

Friedman, Jonathan. 2003. *Globalization, the State and Violence.* Walnut Creek, CA: AltaMira.

Friedman, Thomas L. 2005. *The World is Flat: A Brief History of the Twenty-First Century.* New York: Farrar, Straus, and Giroux.

Frost, P. 1994. "Geographic Distribution of Human Skin Colour: A Selective Compromise Between Natural Selection and Sexual Selection?" *Human Evolution* 9:141–153.

Fuchs, Dale. 2008. "Spain to Pay Immigrants to Leave." *The Guardian* July 21. Available at: http://www.guardian.co.uk/world/2008/jul/21/spain.

Fuller, Christopher J. (Ed.). 1995. *Caste Today.* Delhi: Oxford University Press.

Gardner, R. A., and B. T. Gardner. 1969. "Teaching Sign Language to a Chimpanzee. *Science* 165:664–672.

Geertz, Clifford. 1963. *Agricultural Involution: The Process of Ecological Change in Indonesia.* Berkeley, CA: University of California Press.

Geertz, Clifford. 1973a. "Deep Play: Notes on the Balinese Cockfight." In C. Geertz (Ed.), *The Interpretation of Cultures* (pp. 412–453). New York: Basic Books.

Geertz, Clifford (Ed.). 1973b. *The Interpretation of Cultures.* New York: Basic Books.

Geertz, Clifford. 1995. "Culture War." *New York Review of Books* 15(19):4–6.

Geertz, Clifford. 2001. "The Visit." *New York Review of Books* 48(16).

Geertz, Clifford. 2008. "Deep Play: Notes on a Balinese Cockfight." In R. Jon McGee and Richard L. Warms (Eds.), *Anthropological Theory: An Introductory History.* Boston: McGraw Hill.

Ghosh, Anjan. 1991. "The Structure of Structure, or Appropriation of Anthropological Theory." *Review* 14(1):55–77.

Gibbs, James L., Jr. 1988. "The Kpelle Moot: A Therapeutic Model for the Informal Settlement of Disputes." In J. B. Cole (Ed.), *Anthropology of the Nineties* (pp. 347–359). New York: Free Press.

Gibbs, W. Wayt. 2002. "Saving Dying Languages." *Scientific American* 287:78–96.

Gibson, Margaret A. 1997. "Ethnicity and School Performance: Complicating the Immigrant/Involuntary Minority Typology." *Anthropology and Education Quarterly* 28(3):431–454.

Gibson, Margaret A., and John Ogbu. 1991. *Minority Status and Schooling: A Comparative Study of Immigrant and Involuntary Minorities.* New York: Garland.

Gilbert, Matthew. 2007. "Farewell, Sweet Ice." *The Nation* May 7, pp. 26–27.

Gilberthorpe, Emma. 2007. "Fasu Solidarity: A Case Study of Kin Networks, Land Tenure and Extraction in Kutubu, Papua New Guinea." *American Anthropologist* 109(1):101–112.

Gill, Lesley. 2005. "Empire, Ethnography and Engagement." *Anthropology Newsletter.* January, p. 12.

Gilliland, Mary. 1995. "Nationalism and Ethnogenesis in the Former Yugoslavia." In Lola Romanucci-Ross and George A. De Vos (Eds.), *Ethnic Identity: Creation, Conflict, and Accommodation* (3rd ed.) (pp. 197–221). London: Sage.

Gilmore, David D. 1990. *Manhood in the Making: Cultural Concepts of Masculinity.* New Haven, CT: Yale University Press.

Gilmore, David D. 1996. "Above and Below: Toward a Social Geometry of Gender." *American Anthropologist* 98:54–66.

Gimbutas, M. 1989. *The Language of the Goddess.* London: Thames and Hudson.

Glazer, Nathan and Daniel P. Moynihan. 1970. *Beyond the Melting Pot* (2nd ed.). Cambridge, MA: MIT.

Glick-Schiller, Nina, Linda Basch, and Christina Szanton-Blanc (Eds.). 1992. *Towards a Transnational Perspective on Migration: Race, Class, Ethnicity and Nationalism Reconsidered.* New York: New York Academy of Sciences.

Glick-Schiller, Nina. 1992. "Transnationalism: A New Analytic Framework for Understanding Migration." In N. Glick-Schiller, L. Basch, and C. Szanton-Blanc (Eds.), *Towards a Transnational Perspective on Migration: Race, Class, Ethnicity and Nationalism Reconsidered* (pp. 1–24). New York: New York Academy of Sciences.

Glucklich, Ariel. 1997. *The End of Magic.* New York: Oxford University Press.

Gmelch, George. 2000. "Baseball Magic." In James Spradley and David McCurdy (Eds.), *Conformity and Conflict* (pp. 322–331). Boston: Allyn and Bacon.

Godelier, Maurice. 1993. "L'Occident, miroir brisé: une evaluation partielle de l'anthropologie sociale assortie de quelques perspectives." *Annales* 48:1183–1207.

Goldschmidt, Walter. 1986. *The Sebei: A Study in Adaptation.* New York: Holt, Reinhart and Winston.

Goldstein, Donna. 1999. "'Interracial' Sex and Racial Democracy in Brazil: Twin Concepts?" *American Anthropologist* 101:563–578.

Good, Kenneth, and David Chanoff. 1996. *Into the Heart: One Man's Pursuit of Love and Knowledge Among the Yanomamo.* Old Tappan, NJ: Addison-Wesley.

Goodale, J. 1971. *Tiwi Wives.* Seattle: University of Washington Press.

Goodall, Jane. 1971. *In the Shadow of Man.* Boston: Houghton Mifflin.

Goodstein, Laurie. 2009. "Poll Finds U.S. Muslims Thriving, but Not Content." *New York Times,* March 1, p. 11.

Goody, Jack. 1995. *The Expansive Moment: Anthropology in Britain and Africa 1918–1970.* Cambridge: Cambridge University Press.

Gordon, Adam D., L. Nevell, and B. Wood. The Homo floresiensis Cranium (LB1): Size, Scaling, and Early Homo Affinities. *Proceedings of the National Academy of Sciences USA* 105:4650–4655.

Gordon, Peter. 2004. "Numerical Cognition Without Words: Evidence from Amazonia." *Science* 306(5695):496–499.

Gordon, Robert J. 1992. *The Bushman Myth: The Making of a Namibian Underclass.* Boulder, CO: Westview Press.

Gough, Kathleen. 1961. "The Nayar: Central Kerala." In David Schneider and Kathleen Gough (Eds.), *Matrilineal Kinship* (pp. 298–442). Berkeley, CA: University of California.

Graburn, Nelson H. H. (Ed.). 1976. *Ethnic and Tourist Arts: Cultural Expressions from the Fourth World.* Berkeley, CA: University of California Press.

Graham, Laura R. 2006. "Anthropologists Are Obligated to Promote Human Rights and Social Justice: Especially Among Vulnerable Communities." *Anthropology News* 47(7):32–33.

Graham, Laura, Alexandra Jaffe, Bonnie Uriciuoli, and David Valentine. 2007. "Why Anthropologists Should Oppose English Only Legislation in the U.S." *Anthropology News* 48(1):32–33.

Greenberg, James B. 1997. "Á Political Ecology of Structural-Adjustment Policies: The Case of the Dominican Republic." *Culture and Agriculture* 19(3):85–93.

Greene, Candace W. 2001. *Silver Horn: Master Illustrator of the Kiowas.* Norman: University of Oklahoma.

Greenhalgh, Susan. 2005. "Globalization and Population Governance in China." In Ong, Aihwa and Stephen J. Collier (Eds.), *Global Assemblages: Technology, Politics, and Ethics as Anthropological Problems* (pp. 354–372). Malden, MA: Blackwell.

Greenhalgh, Susan. 2007a. *Just One Child: Science and Policy in Deng's China.* Berkeley, CA: University of California Press.

Greenhalgh, Susan. 2007b. "China's Future with Fewer Females." *China From the Inside.* Washington, DC: Public Broadcasting Service. Available at: http://www.pbs.org/kqued/chinainside/women/population.html.

Greenhouse, Carol J. 2005. "Hegemony and Hidden Transcripts." *American Anthropologist* 107(3):356–368.

Greenhouse, Steven. 2008. *The Big Squeeze: Tough Times for the American Worker.* New York: Knopf.

Gregor, Thomas. 1985. *Anxious Pleasures: The Sexual Life of an Amazonian People.* Chicago: University of Chicago Press.

Grey, John. 2005. "The World Is Round." *New York Review of Books* 52(13).

Grindal, Bruce, and Frank Salamone (Eds.). 1995. *Bridges to Humanity: Narratives on Anthropology and Friendship.* Prospect Heights, IL: Waveland.

Groneman, Carol. 2000. *Nymphomania: A History.* New York: Norton.

Grosfoguel, Ramon. 2003. *Colonial Subjects: Puerto Ricans in a Global Perspective.* Berkeley, CA: University of California Press.

Guthrie, R. D. 1984. "Ethnological Observations from Paleolithic Art." In *La contribution de la zoologie et de l'ethnologie `a l'interpretation de l'art des peuples chasseurs prehistoriques: 3ème Colloque de la Société Suisse de Sciences Humaines* (pp. 35–73). Fribourg: Editions Universitaires.

Hackenberg, Robert. 2000. "Advancing Applied Anthropology: Joe Hill in Cyberspace: Steps Toward Creating 'One Big Union.'" *Human Organization* 59(3):365–369.

Hacker, Jacob. 2002. *The Divided Welfare State: The Battle Over Public and Private Social Benefits in the United States.* New York: Cambridge.

Hadden, Jeffrey K., and Anson Shupe. 1989. "Is There Such a Thing as Global Fundamentalism?" In Jeffrey K. Hadden and Anson Shupe (Eds.), *Secularization and Fundamentalism Reconsidered* (pp. 109–122). New York: Paragon House.

Haines, David. 2007. "Labor Migration and Anthropology: Reflections from the Work of Philip. L. Martin." *City and Society* 19(1):60–71.

Hakken, David. 2001. "'Our' Anthropology of Technoscience." *American Anthropologist* 103(2):535–539.

Hale, Charles. 2001. "What Is Activist Research?" *Items and Issues: Social Science Research Council* 2(1–2):13–15.

Hale, Sondra. 1989. "The Politics of Gender in the Middle East." In S. Morgen (Ed.), *Gender and Anthropology: Critical Reviews for Research and Teaching* (pp. 246–267). Washington, DC: American Anthropological Association.

Hall, Edward T. 1959. *The Silent Language.* Greenwich, CT: Fawcett.

Hall, Edward T. 1966. *The Hidden Dimension.* New York: Doubleday.

Hall, Edward T. 1968. "Proxemics." *Current Anthropology* 9:83–109.

Hall, Edward T. 1983. *The Dance of Life: The Other Dimension of Time.* New York: Anchor/Doubleday.

Halperin, Rhoda H. 1990. *The Livelihood of Kin: Making Ends Meet "The Kentucky Way."* Austin: University of Texas Press.

Hamid, Ansley. 1990. "The Political Economy of Crack-Related Violence." *Contemporary Drug Problems* 17:31–73.

Hamid, Ansley. 1992. "The Developmental Cycle of a Drug Epidemic: The Cocaine Smoking Epidemic of 1981–1991." *Journal of Psychoactive Drugs* 24:337–348.

Hamid, Ansley. 1998. *Drugs in America.* Gaithersburg, MD: Aspen.

Hamilton, James W. 1987. "This Old House: A Karen Ideal." In D.W. Ingersoll, Jr., and G. Bronitsky (Eds.), *Mirror and Metaphor: Material and Social Constructions of Reality* (pp. 229–245). Lanham, MD: University Press of America.

Hammar, Lawrence. 1989. "Gender and Class on the Fringe: A Feminist Critique of Ethnographic Theory and Data in Papua New Guinea." Working paper 189, Women and International Development Program, Michigan State University, East Lansing.

Handler, Richard. 1988. *Nationalism and the Politics of Culture in Quebec.* Madison: University of Wisconsin Press.

Handloff, Robert E., and Thomas Duval Roberts. 1991. *Cote d'Ivoire: A Country Study* (3rd ed.). Washington, DC: The Division.

Hansen, Edward C. 1995. "The Great Bambi War: Tocquevillians versus Keynesians in an Upstate New York County." In J. Schneider and R. Rapp (Eds.), *Articulating Hidden Histories: Exploring the Influence of Eric R. Wolf* (pp. 142–155). Berkeley, CA: University of California Press.

Harrell, Steven. 2002. "Book Review of A Society without Fathers or Husbands: The Na of China" by Cai Hua, trans. Asti Hustvedt, *American Anthropologist* 104(3):982–983.

Harries, Patrick. 1987. "The Roots of Ethnicity: Discourse and the Politics of Language Construction in South-East Africa." *African Affairs* 87:25–52.

Harrington, Spencer. 1993. "Bones and Bureaucrats: New York's Great Cemetery Imbroglio." *Archaeology* 46:28–38.

Harris, Marvin. 1966. "The Cultural Ecology of India's Sacred Cattle." *Current Anthropology* 7:51–66.

Harris, Marvin. 1989. *Our Kind: Who We Are, Where We Came From, Where We Are Going.* New York: Harper Perennial.

Harris, Michael S. 1991. "Diversity in a Bangladeshi Village: Landholding Structure, Economic Differentiation, and Occupational Specialization of Moslems and Hindus." *Research in Economic Anthropology* 13:143–160.

Harrison, Faye V. 2009. "The Paradox of Democracy in the New Racial Domain." *Anthropology News,* January, p. 15.

Harrison, Paul, and Fred Pearce. 2000. *AAAS Atlas of Population and Environment.* Berkeley, CA: University of California Press.

Hart, C. W. M. 1967. "Contrasts between Prepubertal and Post-pubertal Education." In R. Endelman (Ed.), *Personality and Social Life* (pp. 275–290). New York: Random House.

Hart, C. W. M., and Arnold R. Pilling. 1960. *The Tiwi of Northern Australia.* New York: Holt, Rinehart and Winston.

Hartigan, John. 1997. "Establishing the Fact of Whiteness." *American Anthropologist* 99:495–505.

Haskins, Ron, Julie Isaacs, and Isabel Sawhill. February 20, 2008. "Getting Ahead or Losing Ground: Economic Mobility in America." Economic Mobility Project. *The Pew Foundation.* Available at http://www.brookings.edu/multimedia/video/2008/0220_mobility_sawhill.aspx.

Hauptman, William. 1985. "Renoir's Master." *EMR* 15:48–66.

Hearn, Maxwell K. 1996. *Splendors of Imperial China: Treasures from the National Palace Museum, Taipei.* New York: Metropolitan Museum of Art.

Hefner, Robert. 2002. "Global Violence and Indonesian Muslim Politics." *American Anthropologist* 104(3): 754–765.

Heimer, Robert, Ricky Bluthenthal, Merill Singer, and Kaveh Khoshnood. 1996. "Structural Impediments to Operational Syringe-Exchange Programs." *AIDS Public Policy Journal* 11:169–184.

Helman, Cecil G. 1998. "Medicine and Culture: Limits of Biomedical Explanation." In G. Ferraro (Ed.), *Applying Cultural Anthro-*

*pology: Readings* (pp. 3–6). Belmont, CA: Wadsworth. (Originally published 1991.)

Henrich, Joseph, et al. 2004. *Foundations of Human Sociality: Economic Experiments and Ethnographic Evidence From 15 Small-Scale Societies*. Oxford: Oxford University Press.

Henry, Jules. 1973. *Pathways to Madness*. New York: Random House/Vintage.

Herdt, Gilbert H. 1981. *Guardians of the Flutes: Idioms of Masculinity*. New York: McGraw-Hill.

Herdt, Gilbert H. 1987. *The Sambia*. New York: Holt, Rinehart and Winston.

Herdt, Gilbert H. (Ed.). 1996. *Third Sex, Third Gender: Beyond Sexual Dimorphism in Culture and History*. New York: Zone.

Herrmann, Gretchen. 2003. "Negotiating Culture: Conflict and Consensus in U.S. Garage Sale Bargaining." *Ethnology* 42:237–252.

Hevia, James. 2007 "Plunder, Markets, and Museums: The Biographies of Chinese Imperial Objects in Europe and North America." In Morgan Pitlka (Ed.), *What's the Use of Art? Asian Visual and Material Culture in Context* (pp. 29–141). Honolulu, HI: University of Hawai'i Press.

Hill, Catherine M. 2002. "Primate Conservation and Local Communities-Ethical Issues and Debates." *American Anthropologist* 104(4):1184–1194.

Hill, Jane H. 1998. "Language, Race, and White Public Space." *American Anthropologist* 100:680–689.

Himmelgreen, David A., and Nancy Romero-Daza. 2008. "Food Security and the Battle against HIV/AIDS." *Anthropology News*, October, p. 13.

Hinton, Devon E., Lim Nguyen, and Mark H. Pollack. 2007. "Orthostatic Panic as a Key Vietnamese Reaction to Traumatic Events: The Case of September 11, 2001." *Medical Anthropology Quarterly* 21(1):81–107.

Hirschfeld, Lawrence A. 1996. *Race in the Making*. Cambridge, MA: MIT Press/Bradford Books.

Hobsbawm, Eric, and Terence Ranger (Eds.). 1983. *The Invention of Tradition*. Cambridge: Cambridge University Press.

Hochschild, Adam. 1998. *King Leopold's Ghost*. New York: Houghton Mifflin.

Hochschild, Adam. 2005. "In the Heart of Darkness." *New York Review of Books*, October 6, pp. 39–42.

Hochschild, Jennifer L. 1995. *Facing Up to the American Dream: Race, Class, and the Soul of the Nation*. Princeton, NJ: Princeton University Press.

Hockett, Charles F. 1973. *Man's Place in Nature*. New York: McGraw-Hill.

Hoebel, E. Adamson. 1960. *The Cheyennes: Indians of the Great Plains*. New York: Holt.

Hoebel, E. Adamson. 1974. *The Law of Primitive Man*. New York: Henry Holt.

Hoffer, Carol P. 1974. "Madam Yoko: Ruler of the Kpa Mende Confederacy." In M. Z. Rosaldo and L. Lamphere (Eds.), *Women, Culture and Society* (pp. 173–188). Stanford, CA: Stanford University Press.

Hoffman, Danny. 2003. "Like Beasts in the Bush: Synonyms of Childhood and Youth in Sierra Leone." *Postcolonial Studies* 6(3):295–308.

Hoijer, Harry. 1964. "Cultural Implications of Some Navajo Linguistic Categories." In D. Hymes (Ed.), *Language in Culture and Society* (pp. 142–160). New York: Harper and Row.

Holmquist, R., M. M. Miyamoto, and M. Goodman. 1988. "Higher Primate Phylogeny: Why Can't We Decide?" *Molecular Biology and Evolution* 5:201–216.

Holthouse, David. 2007. "Minute Mess." *Intelligencer*, Summer:57.

Homiak, John P. 1998. "Dub History: Soundings on Rastafari Livity and Language." In Barry Chevannes (Ed.), *Rastafari and Other African-Caribbean Worldviews* (pp. 127–181). New Brunswick, NJ: Rutgers University Press.

Hooks, Bell. 1989. *Talking Back: Thinking Feminist, Thinking Black*. Boston: South End Press.

Hopkins, Nicholas. 1987. "Mechanized Irrigation in Upper Egypt: The Role of Technology and the State in Agriculture." In B. Turner II and S. B. Brush (Eds.), *Comparative Farming Systems* (pp. 223–247). New York: Guilford.

Horowitz, Irving L. (Ed.). 1967. *The Rise and Fall of Project Camelot*. Cambridge, MA: MIT Press.

Horsley, Richard A. 1979. "Who Were the Witches? The Social Roles of the Accused in the European Witch Trials." *Journal of Interdisciplinary History* 9:689–715.

Horst, Heather A., and Daniel Miller. 2006. *The Cell Phone: An Anthropology of Communication*. Oxford, UK: Berg.

Howell, Nancy. 1990. "Surviving Fieldwork." Washington, DC: American Anthropological Association.

Hua, Cai. 2001. *A Society without Fathers or Husbands: The Na of China*. New York: Zone Books.

Huang, Wanpo, et al. 1995. "Early *Homo* and Associated Artifacts from Asia." *Nature* 378:275–278.

Huffman, Michael A., and Duane Quiatt. 1986. "Stone Handling by Japanese Macaques (*Macaca fuscata*): Implications for Tool Use of Stone." *Primates* 27:413–423.

Hughes, David McDermott. 2006. *From Enslavement to Environmentalism: Politics on a Southern African Frontier*. Seattle, WA: University of Washington Press.

Hutton, Ronald. 1999. *Triumph of the Moon*. Oxford: Oxford University Press.

Igoe, Jim. 2004. *Conservation and Globalization: A Case Study of Maasai Herders and National Parks in East Africa*. Belmont, CA: Wadsworth.

Indonesia. 1997. "Issues and Perspectives: A Solution to Java's Overcrowding." Embassy of the Republic of Indonesia in London—United Kingdom. Available at http://www.indonesianembassy.org.uk/transmigration-7.htm.

Intergovernmental Panel on Climate Change. 2007. "Summary for Policymakers." In Solomon, S., D. Qin, M. Manning, Z. Chen, M. Marquis, K. B. Averyt, M. Tignor, and H. L. Miller (Eds.), *Climate Change 2007: The Physical Science Basis. Contribution of Working Group I to the Fourth Assessment Report of the Intergovernmental Panel on Climate Change*. Cambridge: Cambridge University Press.

International Telecommunications Union (ITU). 2008. "Worldwide Mobile Cellular Subscribers to Reach 4 Billion Mark Late 2008." Available at http://www.itu.int/newsroom/press_releases/2008/29.html.

International Union for the Conservation of Nature (IUCN). 2008. "IUCN Red List: Threatened Primates by Habitat Country." *IUCN*. Available at http://www.primate-sg.org/RL08.countries.htm.

Ireland, Doug. 2005. "Why Is France Burning?" *The Nation*, November 28.

Isaac, Barry L. 1993. "Retrospective on the Formalist-Substantivist Debate." *Research in Economic Anthropology* 14:213–233.

Isaacman, Allen. 1996. *Cotton Is the Mother of Poverty: Peasants, Work, and Rural Struggle in Colonial Mozambique (1938–1961)*. Portsmouth, NH: Heinemann.

Ishemo, Shubi L. 1995. "Cultural Response to Forced Labour and Commody Production in Portugal's African Colonies." *Social Identities* 1(1):95–110.

Jablonski, Nina G., and G. Chaplin. 2000. "The Evolution of Human Skin Coloration." *Journal of Human Evolution* 39:57–106.

Jackson, Michael. 2002. "Familiar and Foreign Bodies: A Phenomenological Exploration of the Human-Technology Interface." *The Journal of the Royal Anthropological Institute* 8(2):333–346.

Jacobs-Huey, Lanita. 2006. "The Arab is the New Nigger: African American Comics Confront The Irony and Tragedy of September 11." *Transforming Anthropology* 14:60–64.

Jain, Vaibhav. 2008. "M.F. Husain—The Wronged One." *Nazar: A South Asian Perspective*, March 5. Available at http://nazaronline.net/arts/2008-03/mf-husain-the-wronged-one.

Jamali, Hafeez. 2007. "Anthropologists Should Shed Light on the Violence in Balochistan Province, Pakistan." *Anthropology News* 48(5):37–38.

Janik, V. M. & Slater, P. J. B. 1998. "Context-Specific Use Suggests That Bottlenose Dolphin Signature Whistles Are Cohesion Calls." *Animal Behaviour* 56:829–838.

Jelly-Schapiro, Joshua. 2009. "The Bob Marley Story." *New York Review of Books*, April, pp. 34–37.

Jennie, Keith, et al. (Eds.). 1994. *The Aging Experience: Diversity and Commonality Across Cultures*. Thousand Oaks, CA: Sage.

Jia, Lan-Po, and Haung Weiwen. 1990. *The Story of Peking Man*. New York: Oxford University Press.

Johnson, Allen. 1989. "Horticulturalists: Economic Behavior in Tribes." In S. Plattner (Ed.), *Economic Anthropology* (pp. 49–77). Stanford, CA: Stanford University Press.

Johnson, Douglas H. 1982. "Evans-Pritchard, the Nuer, and the Sudan Civil Service." *African Affairs* 81:231–246.

Johnson, Kevin R. 2007. *Opening the Floodgates: Why America Needs to Rethink Its Borders and Immigration Laws*. New York: New York University Press.

Johnstone, G. N. 1976. "The Growth of the Sugar Trade and Refining Industry." In Derek J. Oddy and Derek S. Miller (Eds.), *The Mak-*

ing of the Modern British Diet (pp. 58–64). Totowa, NJ: Rowman and Littlefield.

Jolly, Alison. 1985. The Evolution of Primate Behavior (2nd ed.). New York: Macmillan.

Jonaitis, Aldona (Ed.). 1991. Chiefly Feasts: The Enduring Kwakiutl Potlatch. Seattle: University of Washington Press.

Jones, Ann. 2009. "Iraq's Invisible Refugees." The Nation, March 9, pp. 17–21.

Jones, Anna Laura. 1993. "Exploding Canons: The Anthropology of Museums." Annual Reviews of Anthropology 22: 201–220.

Jones, Delmos J. 1995. "Anthropology and the Oppressed: A Reflection on 'Native' Anthropology." In E. L. Cerroni-Long (Ed.), Insider Anthropology (Napa Bulletin, Vol. 16, pp. 58–70).Washington, DC: American Anthropological Association.

Judt, Tony. 2005. Postwar: A History of Europe Since 1945 (p. 35). New York: Penguin.

Kaberry, P. 1939. Aboriginal Woman: Sacred and Profane. New York: Gordon Press.

Kahn, Hilary E. 2006. Seeing and Being Seen: The Q'eqchi' Maya of Livingston, Guatamala and Beyond. Austin, TX: University of Texas.

Kaprow, Miriam Lee. 1991. "Magical Work: Firefighters in New York." Human Organization 50:97–103.

Karlen, Arno. 1995. Man and Microbes: Disease and Plagues in History and Modern Times. New York: G. P. Putnam's Sons.

Katrak, Ketu H. 2002. "Changing Traditions: South Asian Americans and Cultural/ Communal Politics. Massachusetts Review 43(1):75–88.

Kaufman, Sharon R. 2000. "In the Shadow of 'Death with Dignity': Medicine and Cultural Quandaries of the Vegetative State." American Anthropologist 102:69–83.

Keating, Neal B. 2007. "UN General Assembly Adopts Declaration on the Rights of Indigenous Peoples." Anthropology News, November, p. 22.

Kehoe, Alice Beck. 1989. The Ghost Dance: Ethnohistory and Revitalization. Fort Worth, TX: Holt, Rinehart and Winston.

Kelly, Aidan A. 1991. Crafting the Art of Magic. St. Paul, MN: Llewellyn.

Kelly, Gail P. 1986. "Learning to Be Marginal: Schooling in Interwar French West Africa." Journal of Asian and African Studies 21:171–184.

Kenny, Mary. 1997. Hidden Heads of Households: Child Labor in Northeast Brazil. Doctoral Dissertation, Columbia University.

Kenny, Mary. 2007. Hidden Heads of Households: Child Labor in Urban Northeast Brazil. Peterborough, Ontario: Broadview Press.

Kenyatta, Jomo. 1938. Facing Mount Kenya: The Tribal Life of the Gikuyu. London: Secker and Warburg.

Kepel, Gilles. 2005. The Roots of Radical Islam. London: Saqi.

Kiernan, Ben. 2007. Blood and Soil: A World History of Genocide and Extermination from Sparta to Darfur. New Haven, CT: Yale University.

Kilbride, Philip. 1994. Plural Marriage for our Times: A Reinvented Option? Westport, CT: Bergin and Garvey.

Kilbride, Philip L. 2004. "Plural and Same Sex Marriage." Anthropology News 45(5):17.

Kilker, Ernest Evans. 1993. "The Culture and Politics of Racial Classification." International Journal of Politics, Culture, and Society 7:229–258.

Kim, Jim Yong, Joyce V. Millen, Aleck Irwin, and John Gershman. 2000. Dying for Growth: Global Inequality and the Health of the Poor. Monroe, ME: Common Courage Press.

Kimmelman, Michael. 2007. "In Marseille, Rap Helps Keep the Peace." New York Times, December 19, p. C1.

Klass, Morton. 1995. Ordered Universes: Approaches to the Anthropology of Religion. Boulder, CO: Westview Press.

Klein, Laura F. 1976. "'She's One of Us, You Know': The Public Life of Tlingit Women: Traditional, Historical, and Contemporary Perspectives." Western Canadian Journal of Anthropology 6(3):164–183.

Klein, Laura F. 1995. "Mother as Clanswoman: Rank and Gender in Tlingit Society." In L. F. Klein and L. A. Ackerman (Eds.), Women and Power in Native North America (pp. 28–45). Norman: University of Oklahoma Press.

Klein, Laura F., and Lillian A. Ackerman (Eds.). 1995. Woman and Power in Native North America. Norman: University of Oklahoma Press.

Kleinman, Arthur. 1995. Writing at the Margin: Discourse Between Anthropology and Medicine. Berkeley, CA: University of California Press.

Kluckhohn, Clyde. 1959. "The Philosophy of the Navaho Indians." In M. H. Fried (Ed.), Readings in Anthropology (Vol. 2). New York: Crowell.

Knauft, Bruce. 1987. "Reconsidering Violence in Simple Human Societies: Homicide among the Gebusi of New Guinea." Current Anthropology 28: 457–482.

Knight, Alec, P. A. Underhill, H. M. Mortensen, L. A. Zhivtovsky, A. A. Lin, B. M. Henn, D. Louis, M. Ruhlen, and J. L. Mountain. 2003. "African Y Chromosome and mtDNA Divergence Provides Insight into the History of Click Languages." Current Biology. 13(6):464–473.

Kofinas, Gary. 2007. Subsistence Hunting in a Global Economy. Available at http://arctic-circle.uconn.edu/NatResources/subsist-global.html.

Kohn, Hans. 1958. "Reflections on Colonialism." In R. Strausz-Hupe and H. W. Hazard (Eds.), The Idea of Colonialism (pp. 2–16). New York: Praeger.

Kolata, Alan, O. Rivera, J.C. Ramirez, and E. Gemio. 1996. "Rehabilitating Raised-Field Agriculture in the Southern Lake Titicaca Basin of Bolivia: Theory and Practice." In Alan Kolata (Ed.), Tiwanaku and its Hinterlands: Archaelogy and Paleoecology of an Andean Civilization 1, Agroecology (pp. 203–230). Washington, DC: Smithsonian.

Kosmin, Barry A., and Ariela Keysar. 2009. American Religious Identification Survey (ARIS 2008) Summary Report. Hartford, CT: Trinity College. Available at http://www.americanreligionsurvey-aris.org/reports/ARIS_Report_2008.pdf.

Kottak, Conrad P. 1992. Assault on Paradise: Social Change in a Brazilian Village (2nd ed.). New York: McGraw-Hill.

Kovats-Bernat, J. Christopher. 2002. "Negotiating Dangerous Fields: Pragmatic Strategies for Fieldwork amid Violence and Terror." American Anthropologist 104(1):208–222.

Krauss, Michael E. 1992. "The World's Languages in Crisis." Language 68(1):6–10.

Kristoff, Nicholas, and Sheryl WuDunn. 2000. "The Cheers for Sweatshops." New York Times, September 24.

Kuklick, Henrika. 1991. The Savage Within: The Social History of British Anthropology 1885–1945. Cambridge: Cambridge University Press.

Labov, William. 1972. Language in the Inner City. Philadelphia: University of Pennsylvania Press.

Labov, William, Sharon Ash, and Charles Boburg. 2005. Atlas of North American English: Phonetics, Phonology and Sound Change. Berlin: Mouton de Gruyter.

Lacey, Marc. 2006. "The Case of the Stolen Statues: Solving a Kenyan Mystery." New York Times, April 16.

Lacey, Marc. 2008. "A Lifestyle Distinct: The Muxe of Mexico." New York Times, December 7, p. 4.

Ladefoged, Peter. 1982. A Course in Phonetics. New York: Harcourt Brace Jovanovich.

LaFraniere, Sharon. 2009. "Chinese Bias for Baby Boys Creates a Gap of 32 Million." New York Times, April 11, p. 5.

Lamason, Rebecca, et al. 2005. "SLC24A5, a Putative Cation Exchanger, Affects Pigmentation in Zebrafish and Humans." Science 310(5755):1782–1786.

Lamphere, Louise (Ed.). 1992. Structuring Diversity: Ethnographic Perspectives on the New Immigration. Chicago: University of Chicago Press.

Lamphere, Louise. 1997. "The Domestic Sphere of Women and the Public World of Men: The Strengths and Limitations of an Anthropological Dichotomy." In C. B. Brettell and C. F. Sargent (Eds.), Gender in Cross Cultural Perspective (2nd ed.) (pp. 82–91). Upper Saddle River, NJ: Prentice Hall.

Lamphere, Louise. 2001. "Whatever Happened to Kinship Studies? Reflections of a Feminist Anthropologist." In Linda Stone (Ed.), New Directions in Anthropological Kinship (pp. 21–47). Lanham, MD: Rowman and Littlefield.

Lancaster, Jane B. 1989. "Women in Biosocial Perspective." In S. Morgen (Ed.), Gender and Anthropology: Critical Reviews for Research and Teaching (pp. 95–115). Washington, DC: American Anthropological Association.

Lapidus, Ira M. 1988. A History of Islamic Societies. Cambridge: Cambridge University Press.

Lareau, Annette. 2003. Unequal Childhoods: Class, Race, and Family Life. Berkeley, CA: University of California.

Larsen, Clark Spencer. 1995. "Biological Changes in Human Populations with Agriculture." Annual Review of Anthropology 24:185–213.

Larson, Luke. 2004. "The Foreign-Born Population in the United States: 2003." Current Population Reports. Washington, DC: US Census Bureau.

Lassiter, Luke Eric. 2004. "Collaborative Ethnography." AnthroNotes. 25(1):1–9.

Lathrop, Stacy. 2004. "Broadening the Marriage Debate." *Anthropology News* 45(5):23.

Laurence, Jonathan, and Philippa Strum (Eds.). 2008. *Governments and Muslim Communities in the West: United States, United Kingdom, France and Germany.* Washington, DC: Woodrow Wilson International Center for Scholars.

Lawler, Nancy Ellen. 1992. *Soldiers of Misfortune: Ivoirien Tirailleurs of World War II.* Athens, OH: Ohio University Press.

Leacock, Eleanor Burke. 1981. *Myths of Male Dominance.* New York: Monthly Review Press.

Leakey, Mary, and Louis Leakey. 1996. "The Discovery of *Zinjanthropus boisei.*" In Brian M. Fagan (Ed.), *Eyewitness to Discovery* (pp. 46–52). New York: Oxford University Press. (Originally published 1984.)

Leathers, Dale G. 1997. *Successful Nonverbal Communication* (3rd ed.). Boston: Allyn and Bacon.

LeDuff, Charlie. 2006. "Dreams in the Dark at the Drive-Through Window." *New York Times,* November 27, p. A12.

Lee, Anru. 1996. "A Tale of Two Sisters: Gender in Taiwan's Small Scale Industry." In Anthony Marcus (Ed.), *Anthropology for a Small Planet: Culture and Community in a Global Environment* (pp. 67–99). St. James, NY: Brandywine Press.

Lee, Dorothy. 1987. *Freedom and Culture.* Prospect Heights, IL: Waveland.

Lee, Richard B. 1968. "What Hunters Do for a Living, or How to Make Out on Scarce Resources." In R. B. Lee and I. DeVore (Eds.), *Man the Hunter* (pp. 30–48). Chicago: Aldine.

Lee, Richard B. 1979. *The !Kung San: Men, Women, And Work in a Foraging Society.* Cambridge, UK: Cambridge University Press.

Lee, Richard B. 1984. *The Dobe !Kung.* New York: Holt, Rinehart and Winston.

Lee, Richard B. 2000. "Indigenism and Its Discontents: Anthropology and the Small Peoples at the Millennium." Keynote address at the annual meeting of the American Ethnological Society, Tampa, FL, March 2000.

Lee, Richard B. 2003. *The Dobe Ju/'hoansi* (3rd ed.). Belmont, CA: Wadsworth.

Lee, Richard B., and Ida Susser. 2008. "Confounding Conventional Wisdom: The Ju/'hoansi and HIV/AIDS." In Douglas A. Feldman (Ed.), *AIDS, Culture, and Africa* (pp. 18–34). Gainesville, FL: University of Florida Press.

Lee, Trymaine. 2008. "Mukasey Vacates Panel's Decision Denying Asylum to Malian Woman." *New York Times,* September 23, p. A18.

Lefever, Harry G. 1996. "When the Saints Go Riding In: Santeria in Cuba and the United States." *Journal for the Scientific Study of Religion* 35:318–330.

Lemert, Edwin M. 1997. *The Trouble with Evil: Social Control at the Edge of Morality.* Albany: State University of New York Press.

Lesser, Alexander. 1933. *The Pawnee Ghost Dance Hand Game: Ghost Dance Revival and Ethnic Identity.* Lincoln: University of Nebraska.

Lessinger, Hanna. "Love and Marriage in the Shadow of the Sewing Machine: Case Studies from Chennai, India." Paper presented at the conference Marriage in Globalizing Contexts, Exploring Change and Continuity in South Asia, IIT, New Delhi, December 25–27, 2008.

Levine, Mary Ann, and Rita Wright. 1999. "COSWA Corner." *Society for American Archaeology Bulletin* 17(2).

Levine, Morton. 1957. "Prehistoric Art and Ideology." *American Anthropologist* 59:949–962.

Levinson, David. 1989. *Family Violence in Cross Cultural Perspective.* Thousand Oaks, CA: Sage.

Levinson, David. 1996. *Religion: A Cross-cultural Dictionary.* New York: Oxford University Press.

Lévi-Strauss, Claude. 1969. *The Elementary Structures of Kinship.* Boston: Beacon Press. (Originally published 1949.)

Levy, Robert. 1973. *Tahitians: Mind and Experience in the Society Islands.* Chicago: University of Chicago Press.

Lewchuk, Wayne A. 1993. "Men and Monotony: Fraternalism as a Managerial Strategy at the Ford Motor Company." *Journal of Economic History* 53(4):824–856.

Lewin, Ellen. 2009. "How Gay Fathers Dream the Family." In Focus, *Anthropology News,* February, p. 14.

Lewis, Oscar. 1966. *La Vida.* New York: Random House.

Lewis, Richard D. 1996. *When Cultures Collide: Managing Successfully Across Cultures.* London: Nicholas Brealey.

Lewis, Rupert. 1998. "Marcus Garvey and the Early Rastafarians: Continuity and Discontinuity." In Nathaniel Murrell, William Spencer, and Adrian McFarlane (Eds.), *Chanting Down Babylon: The Rastafari Reader* (pp. 145–158). Philadelphia: Temple University Press.

Lewis, Tom. 1991. *Empire of the Air: The Men Who Made Radio.* New York: Harper Perennial.

Lewis, William F. 1993. *Soul Rebels: The Rastafari.* Prospect Heights, IL: Waveland.

Lewis-Williams, J. D., and T. A. Dowson. 1988. "The Signs of All Times." *Current Anthropology* 29:201–217.

Lichtenberg, Judith. 1994. "Population Policy and the Clash of Cultures." In L. A. Mazur (Ed.), *Beyond the Numbers: A Reader on Population, Consumption, and Environment* (pp. 273–280). Washington, DC: Island Press.

Lieberman Daniel E. 2007. "Homing in on Early Homo." *Nature* 449:291–292.

Lieberman, Leonard, and Rodney C. Kirk. 1996. "The Trial of Darwin Is Over: Religious Voices for Evolution and the 'Fairness' Doctrine." *Creation/Evolution* 16(2):1–9.

Lieberman, Phillip. 2003. "Language Evolution and Innateness." In M. T. Banich and M. Mack (Eds.), *Mind, Brain and Language* (pp. 3–22). Mahwah, NJ: Lawrence Erlbaum Associates.

Lindstrom, Lamont. 1993. *Cargo Cult: Strange Stories of Desire from Melanesia and Beyond.* Honolulu: University of Hawaii Press.

Linton, Ralph. 1936. *The Study of Man.* New York: Appleton-Century-Crofts.

Lipsitz, George 1994. *Dangerous Crossroads: Popular Music, Post-modernism, and the Poetics of Place.* London: Verso.

Lockwood, Victoria. 2005. "The Impact of Development on Women: The Interplay of Material Conditions and Gender Ideology." In Caroline B. Brettell and Carolyn F. Sargent (Eds.), *Gender in Cross Cultural Perspective* (4th ed., pp. 500–514). Upper Saddle River, NJ: Prentice Hall.

Loewen, James W. 1988. *The Mississippi Chinese: Between Black and White.* Prospect Heights, IL: Waveland.

Loftin, John D. 1991. *Religion and Hopi Life in the Twentieth Century.* Bloomington, IN: Indiana University Press.

Lopez, Haney. 2006. *White by Law: The Legal Construction of Race* (Revised and updated 10th anniversary ed.). New York: New York University Press.

Lordkipanidze, David, et al. 2007. "Postcranial Evidence from Early Homo from Dmanisi, Georgia." *Nature* 449(6134):305–310.

Lovejoy, Paul E. 1983. *Transformations in Slavery: A History of Slavery in Africa.* Cambridge: Cambridge University Press.

Lowie, Robert H. 1948. *Social Organization.* New York: Holt, Rinehart and Winston.

Lowie, Robert H. 1963. *Indians of the Plains.* Garden City, NY: Natural History Press. (Originally published 1954.)

Lozada, Eriberto P., Jr. 2002. "East Asian Section: Desensationalizing the Mosuo." *Anthropology News* 43(5):47.

Luce, Edward. 2007. *In Spite of the Gods: The Strange Rise of Modern India.* New York: Doubleday.

Luhrmann, Tanya M. 2000. *Of Two Minds: The Growing Disorder in American Psychiatry.* New York: Knopf.

Luker, Kristin. 1996. *Dubious Conceptions: The Politics of Teenage Pregnancy.* Cambridge, MA: Harvard University Press.

Luo, Michael. 2009. "Forced Down the Job Ladder, From Executive Pay to Hourly Wage." *New York Times,* March 1, p. A1.

Lutkehaus, Nancy C., and Paul B. Roscoe (Eds.). 1995. *Gender Rituals: Female Initiation in Melanesia.* New York: Routledge.

Lynch, Owen K. 1969. *The Politics of Untouchability.* New York: Columbia University Press.

MacClancy, Jeremy. 2002. "Introduction: Taking People Seriously." In Jeremy MacClancy (Ed.), *Exotic No More: Anthropology on the Front Lines* (pp. 1–15). Chicago, IL: University of Chicago Press.

Macfarlane, Gwyn. 1985. *Alexander Fleming: The Man and the Myth.* New York: Oxford University Press.

Macintyre, Martha. 1983. "Kune on Tubetube and in the Bwanabwana Region of the Southern Massim." In J. W. Leach and E. Leach (Eds.), *The Kula: New Perspectives on Massim Exchange* (pp. 369–379). Cambridge: Cambridge University Press.

Madrigal, Lorena, and William Kelly. 2007. "Human Skin Color Sexual Dimorphism: A Test of the Sexual Selection Hypothesis." *American Journal of Physical Anthropology* 132:470–482.

Mahdavi, Pardis. 2009. *Passionate Uprisings: Iran's Sexual Revolution.* Stanford, CA: Stanford University Press.

Malinowski, Bronislaw. 1929a. "Practical Anthropology." *Africa* 2:22–38.

Malinowski, Bronislaw. 1929b. *The Sexual Life of Savages.* New York: Harcourt, Brace and World.

Malinowski, Bronislaw. 1935. *Coral Gardens and Their Magic.* New York: American Book Company.

Malinowski, Bronislaw. 1948. *Magic, Science and Religion and Other Essays.* New York: Free Press.

Malinowski, Bronislaw. 1984. *Argonauts of the Western Pacific.* Prospect Heights, IL: Waveland. (Originally published 1922.)

Malinowski, Bronislaw. 1992. *Magic, Science, and Religion.* Prospect Heights, IL: Waveland. (Originally published 1954.)

Malveaux, Julianne. 2005. "Sweatshops Aren't History Just Yet." *USA Today,* March 18.

Manji, Irshad. 2003. *The Trouble with Islam: A Wakeup Call for Honesty and Change.* Toronto, Canada: Random House Canada.

Marcus, George E. (Ed.). 1992. *Rereading Cultural Anthropology.* Durham, NC: Duke University Press.

Marcus, George E., and Michael M. J. Fischer. 1986. *Anthropology as Culture Critique: An Experimental Moment in the Human Sciences.* Chicago: University of Chicago Press.

Marcus, George E., and Fred R. Myers (Eds.). 1995. *The Traffic in Culture: Refiguring Art and Anthropology.* Berkeley, CA: University of California Press.

Marks, J., C. W. Schmidt, and V. M. Sarich. 1988. "DNA Hybridization as a Guide to Phylogeny: Relations of the Hominoidea." *Journal of Human Evolution* 17:769–786.

Marshack, Alexander. 1978. *Ice Age Art: 35,000–10,000.* New York: American Museum of Natural History.

Marshall, Donald. 1971. "Sexual Behavior on Mangaia." In D. S. Marshall and R. C. Suggs (Eds.), *Human Sexual Behavior: Variations in the Ethnographic Spectrum* (pp. 163–172). New York: Basic Books.

Marshall, John. 2002. *A Kalahari Family* (video). Watertown, MA: Documentary Educational Resources.

Marshall, Mac. 1979. *Weekend Warriors.* Palo Alto, CA: Mayfield.

Martin, Emily. 1987. *The Woman in the Body.* New York: Beacon Press.

Martin, M. K., and Barbara Voorhies. 1975. *Female of the Species.* New York: Columbia University Press.

Martin, Philip. 2007. "Managing Labor Migration in the 21st Century." *City and Society* 19(1):5–18.

Marx, Anthony. 1998. *Making Race and Nation: A Comparison of South Africa, the United States and Brazil.* Cambridge: Cambridge University Press.

Maskus, Keith. 1997. "Should Core Labor Standards be Imposed Through International Trade Policy?" *World Bank Working Paper 1817.* Washington, DC: World Bank. Available at http://www.worldbank.org/research/trade/wp1817.html.

Mason, Paul. 2007. "Kenya in Crisis." *BBC News.* Available at http://news.bbc.co.uk/2/hi/technology/6242305.stm.

Mateu-Gelabert, Pedro, and Howard Lune. n.d. "Street Codes in High School: School as an Educational Deterrent." Report for National Development and Research Institutes, Inc. (NDRI). New York.

Mateu-Gelabert, Pedro, and Howard Lune. 2003. "School Violence: The Bidirectional Conflict Flow Between Neighborhood and School." *City & Community* 2(4):353–368.

Mateu-Gelabert, Pedro, and Howard Lune. 2007. "Street Codes in High School: School as an Educational Deterrent." *City & Community* 6(3):173–191.

Mathias, P. 1976. "The British Tea Trade in the 19th Century." In Derek J. Oddy and Derek S. Miller (Eds.), *The Making of the Modern British Diet* (pp. 91–102). Totowa, NJ: Rowman and Littlefield.

Matory, J. Lorand. 1994. *Sex and the Empire That Is No More: Gender and the Politics of Metaphor in Oyo Yoruba Religion.* Minneapolis: University of Minnesota Press.

Matsumoto, David, and Tsutomu Kudoh. 1993. "American-Japanese Cultural Differences in Attributions of Personality Based on Smiles." *Journal of Nonverbal Communication* 17(4):231–243.

Matthews, Richard. 1997. "The Ebonic Plague Will Kill America Yet." *Atlanta Journal and Constitution,* January 23, p. A18.

Matthiessen, Peter. 2007. "Alaska: Big Oil and the Whales." *New York Review of Books,* November 22:57–64.

Mattingly, Cheryl, Mary Lawlor, and Lanita Jacobs-Huey. 2002. "Narrating September 11: Race, Gender, and the Play of Cultural Identities." *American Anthropologist* 104(3):743–753.

Mattison, Siobhan. 2009. Personal communication.

Matzner, Andrew. 2001. *'O Au No Keia: Vocies from Hawai'i's Mahu and Transgender Communities.* Philadelphia, PA: XLibris.

Mauss, Marcel. 1990. *The Gift: Form and Reason of Exchange in Archaic Societies* (W. D. Halls, Trans.). New York: W.W. Norton. (Originally published 1924.)

Maybury-Lewis, David. 1997. *Indigenous Peoples, Ethnic Groups, and the State.* Boston: Allyn and Bacon.

McAllester, David P. 1954. *Enemy Way Music.* Cambridge, MA: Harvard University, Peabody Museum.

McCloud, Aminah Beverly. 2006. *Transnational Muslims in American Society.* Gainesville, FL: University Press of Florida.

McCombie, Susan, and Ariela Eshel. 2008. "Tugende Uganda: Issues in Defining 'Sex' and 'Sexual Partners' in Africa." In Douglas A. Feldman (Ed.), *AIDS, Culture, and Africa* (pp. 201–219). Gainesville, FL: University of Florida Press.

McDermott, LeRoy. 1996. "Self-Representation in Upper Paleolithic Female Figurines." *Current Anthropology* 37:227–275.

McDougall, Ian, F. Brown, and J. Fleagle. 2005. "Stratigraphic Placement and Age of Modern Humans from Kibish, Ethiopia. *Nature* 433:733–736.

McGee, R. Jon. 1990. *Life, Ritual, and Religion Among the Lacandon Maya.* Belmont, CA: Wadsworth.

McGee, R. Jon, and Richard L. Warms. 2008. *Anthropological Theory: An Introductory History.* Boston, MA: McGraw Hill.

McHenry, Henry. 1992. "Body Size and Proportions in Early Hominids." *American Journal of Physical Anthropology* 87:404–431.

McIntosh, Peggy. 1999. "White Privilege: Unpacking the Invisible Knapsack." In A. Podolefsky and P. J. Brown (Eds.), *Applying Cultural Anthropology: An Introductory Reader* (4th ed.) (pp. 134–137). Mountain View, CA: Mayfield.

Mead, Margaret. 1963. *Sex and Temperament in Three Primitive Societies.* New York: Dell. (Originally published 1935.)

Mead, Margaret. 1971. *Coming of Age in Samoa.* New York: Morrow. (Originally published 1928.)

Meier, Matt S., and Feliciano Ribera. 1993. *Mexican Americans/American Mexicans: From Conquistadors to Chicanos.* New York: Hill & Wang.

Melendez, Edwin. 1993. *Colonial Subjects: Critical Perspectives on Contemporary Puerto Ricans.* Boston: South End Press.

Mercader, Julio, M. Panger, and C. Boesch. 2002. "Excavation of a Chimpanzee Stone Tool Site in the African Rainforest." *Science,* 296:1452–1455.

Merlan, F. 1988. "Gender in Aboriginal Social Life." In R. Berndt and R. Tonkinson (Eds.), *Social Anthropology and Australian Aboriginal Studies: A Contemporary Overview* (pp. 15–72). Canberra: Aboriginal Studies Press.

Merrick, Amy. 2004. "Gap Offers Unusual Look at Factory Conditions. . ." *Wall Street Journal,* May 12.

Merrill, Heather. 2006. *An Alliance of Women: Immigration and the Politics of Race.* Minneapolis: University of Minnesota Press.

Merry, Sally E. 1981. *Urban Danger: Life in a Neighborhood of Strangers.* Philadelphia: Temple University Press.

Merry, Sally E. 1991. "Law and Colonialism." *Law and Society Review* 25:891–922.

Merry, Sally E. 2000. *Colonizing Hawai'i: The Cultural Power of Law.* Princeton, NJ: Princeton University Press.

Merwine, Maynard. 1993. "How Africa Understands Female Circumcision." *New York Times,* November 24.

Messenger, John C. 1971. "Sex and Repression in an Irish Folk Community." In D. S. Marshall and R. C. Suggs (Eds.), *Human Sexual Behavior: Variations in the Ethnographic Spectrum* (pp. 3–37). New York: Basic Books.

Messina, Maria. 1988. "Henna Party." *Natural History* 97(9):40.

Mestel, R. 1994, October. "Ascent of the Dog." *Discover,* pp. 90–98.

Meyer, Steven. 2004. "The Degradation of Work Revisited: Workers and Technology in the American Auto Industry, 1900–2000." *Automobile in American Life and Society.* Available at http://www.autolife.umd.umich.edu/Labor/L_Overview/L_Overview3.htm.

Mintz, Sidney W. 1985. *Sweetness and Power: The Place of Sugar in Modern History.* New York: Penguin.

Mishra, Pankaj. 2006. "The Myth of the New India." *New York Times,* July 6.

Molnar, Stephen. 1983. *Human Variation: Races, Types, and Ethnic Groups* (2nd ed.). Englewood Cliffs, NJ: Prentice Hall.

Monaghan, Leila. 1997. "Ebonics Discussion Continues." *Anthropology Newsletter* 38(2):44–45.

Montagu, Ashley. 1978. *Touching: The Human Significance of the Skin* (2nd ed.). New York: Harper and Row.

Mooney, James. 1973. *The Ghost-Dance Religion and the Sioux Outbreak of 1890.* Glorieta, NM: Rio Grande Press. (Originally published 1896.)

Moore, Kathleen. 2002. "'United We Stand:' American Attitudes toward (Muslim) Immigration Post-9/11." *Muslim World* 92(1 and 2) Spring:30–58.

Moore, Molly. 1998. "To Guatemalan Scientist, Dead Men Do Tell Tales." *Washington Post,* July 19, p. A22.

Moore, Omar Khayyam. 1969. "Divination: A New Perspective." In Andrew P. Vayda (Ed.), *Environment and Cultural Behavior* (pp. 121–128). Austin: University of Texas Press.

Morgan, Lynn M. 1996. "When Does Life Begin? A Cross-Cultural Perspective on the Personhood of Fetuses and Young Children." In W. A. Haviland and R. J. Gordon (Eds.), *Talking About People: Readings in Contemporary Cultural Anthropology* (2nd ed.) (pp. 24–34). Mountain View, CA: Mayfield.

Morgan, Marcyliena. 2004. "Speech Community." In Alassandro Duranti (Ed.), *A Companion to Linguistic Anthropology* (pp. 3–33). Malden, MA: Blackwell.

Morin, Richard. 1998. "Keeping the Faith." *The Washington Post,* Jan. 12.

Morison L., C. Scherf, G. Ekpo, K. Paine, B. West, R. Coleman, and G. Walraven. 2001. "The Long-Term Reproductive Health Consequences of Female Genital Cutting in Rural Gambia: A Community-Based Survey." *Tropical Medicine and International Health* 6:643–653.

Moser, Caroline. 1993. *Gender Planning and Development: Theory, Practice, and Training.* New York: Routledge.

Mourant, A. E., A. C. Kopec, and K. Domaniewska-Sobczak. 1976. *The Distribution of the Human Blood Groups and Other Polymorphisms.* London: Oxford University Press.

Muhammad, Dedrick. 2008. "Race and Extreme Inequality." *The Nation,* June 30, p. 26.

Mukerjee, Madhusree. 2003. *The Land of Naked People.* New York: Houghton Mifflin.

Mukhopadhyay, Carol C., and Patricia J. Higgins. 1988. "Anthropological Studies of Women's Status Revisited: 1977–1987." *Annual Review of Anthropology* 17:461–495.

Mullin, Molly H. 1995. "The Patronage of Difference: Making Indian Art, Not Ethnology." In George E. Marcus and Fred R. Myers (Eds.), *The Traffic in Culture: Refiguring Art and Anthropology* (pp. 166–200). Berkeley, CA: University of California Press.

Munn, Nancy D. 1983. "Gawan Kula: Spatiotemporal Control and the Symbolism of Influence." In J.W. Leach and E. Leach (Eds.), *The Kula: New Perspectives on Massim Exchange* (pp. 277–309). Cambridge: Cambridge University Press.

Murdock, George Peter. 1949. *Social Structure.* New York: Free Press.

Murphy, Joseph M. 1989 *Santeria: An African Religion in America.* Boston: Beacon Press.

Murphy, Mary Jo. 2008. "Welcome to the Family Business," *New York Times,* December 21, p. 7.

Murphy, Robert. 1964. "Social Distance and the Veil." *American Anthropologist* 66:1257–1273.

Murphy, Yolanda, and Robert Murphy. 1974. *Women of the Forest.* New York: Columbia University Press.

Murray, Gerald F. 1986. "Seeing the Forest While Planting the Trees: An Anthropological Approach to Agroforestry in Haiti." In D.W. Brinkerhoff and J. C. Garcia-Zamor (Eds.), *Politics, Projects, and Peasants: Institutional Development in Haiti* (pp. 193–226). New York: Praeger.

"Muslim Americans: Middle Class and Mostly Mainstream." *Pew Research Center,* May 22, 2007. Available at www.pewresearch.org.

Mydans, Seth. 2008. "U.S. Deportee Brings Street Dance to Street Boys of Cambodia." *New York Times,* November 30, p. A 6.

Myerhoff, Barbara. 1974. *Peyote Hunt: The Sacred Journey of the Huichol Indians.* Ithaca, NY: Cornell University Press.

Myerhoff, Barbara. 1978. *Number Our Days.* New York: Simon and Schuster.

Myers, Fred. 1986. *Pintupi Country, Pintupi Self: Sentiment, Place, and Politics among Western Desert Aborigines.* Washington, DC: Smithsonian Institution Press.

Myers, Fred R. 2002. *Painting Culture: The Making of an Aboriginal High Art.* Durham, NC: Duke University Press.

Myers, Steven Lee, Andrew C. Revkin, Simon Romero, and Clifford Krauss. 2005. "Old Ways of Life are Fading as the Arctic Thaws." *New York Times,* October 20, p. A1.

Nader, Laura. 2006. "Human Rights and Moral Imperialism: A Double-Edged Story." *Anthropology News* 47(7):6.

Nagashima, Kenji, and James A. Schellenberg. 1997. "Situational Differences in Intentional Smiling: A Cross-cultural Exploration." *Journal of Social Psychology* 137:297–301.

Nagengast, Carole. 1994. "Violence, Terror, and the Crisis of the State." In B. J. Siegel (Ed.), *Annual Review of Anthropology* (Vol. 23) (pp. 109–136). Stanford, CA: Stanford University Press.

Nanda, Serena. 1999. *Neither Man nor Woman: The Hijras of India* (2nd ed.). Belmont, CA: Wadsworth.

Nanda, Serena. 2000. *Gender Diversity: Cross-cultural Variations.* Prospect Heights, IL: Waveland.

Nanda, Serena. 2005. "South African Museums and the Creation of a New National Identity." *American Anthropologist* 106(2, June):379–384.

Nanda, Serena, and Joan Gregg. 2009. *The Gift of a Bride: A Tale of Anthropology, Matrimony and Murder.* New York: Altamira/ Rowman and Littlefield.

Nanda, Serena, and Richard Warms. 2009. *Culture Counts: A Concise Introduction to Cultural Anthropology.* Belmont, CA: Cengage.

Narasimhan, Sakuntala. 1990. *Sati: Widow Burning in India.* New York: Anchor/ Doubleday.

Narayan, Kirin. 1993. "How Native Is a 'Native' Anthropologist?" *American Anthropologist* 95:671–686.

Nash, June. 1986. *Women and Change in Latin America.* South Hadley, MA: Bergin and Garvey.

Nash, June. 1993. "Introduction: Traditional Arts and Changing Markets in Middle America." In June Nash and Helen Safa (Eds.), *Crafts in the World Market* (pp. 1–24). Albany: State University of New York Press.

Nash, June. 1994. "Global Integration and Subsistence Insecurity." *American Anthropologist* 96:7–30.

Nash, June. 2007. Practicing Ethnography in a Globalizing World: An Anthropological Odyssey. Lanham, MD: AltaMira.

Nash, June, and Helen Safa (Eds.). 1986. *Women and Change in Latin America.* South Hadley, MA: Bergin and Garvey.

Nash, Manning. 1967. "The Social Context of Economic Choice in a Small Society." In G. Dalton (Ed.), *Tribal and Peasant Economies* (pp. 524–538). Garden City, NY: Natural History Press.

Neckerman, Kathryn M. (Ed.). 2004. *Social Inequality.* New York: The Russell Sage Foundation.

Nelson, Edward W. 1983. *The Eskimo About Bering Strait.* Washington, DC: The Smithsonian Institution Press.

Nentwig, Wolfgang. 2007. *Biological invasions.* Berlin: Springer.

Netting, Robert. 1977. *Cultural Ecology.* Menlo Park, CA: Cummings.

Newman, Katherine S. 1999a. *Falling from Grace: Downward Mobility in an Age of Affluence* (2nd ed.). Berkeley, CA: University of California Press.

Newman, Katherine S. 1999b. *No Shame in My Game: The Working Poor in the Inner City.* New York: Knopf.

Newman, Katherine S., and Victor Chen. 2007. *The Missing Class: Portraits of the Near Poor in America.* Boston, MA: Beacon.

Newman, Philip L. 1977. "When Technology Fails: Magic and Religion in New Guinea." In James P. Spradley and David W. McCurdy (Eds.), *Conformity and Conflict: Readings in Cultural Anthropology* (3rd ed.). Boston: Little Brown.

Newson, L. 1999. "Disease and Immunity in the Pre-Spanish Philippines." *Social Science and Medicine* 48:1833–1850.

*New York Times.* 2005. *Class Matters.* New York: Times Books.

*New York Times.* 2005. *Graphic: How Class Works.* Available at http://www .nytimes. com/class.

*New York Times.* 2006. "Babies Born to Singles Are at Record: Nearly 4 in 10." November 22, p. A22.

*New York Times.* 2009. "Remade in America: The Newest Immigrants and their Impact." March 15, p. A20.

Nguyen, Tram. 2005. *We Are All Suspects Now: Untold Stories from Immigrant Communities after 9/11.* Boston: Beacon Press.

Nicholson, Oliver. 2000. "Constantine's Vision of the Cross." *Vigiliae Christianae* 51(3):309–323.

Nickerson, Colin. 2006. "Leaders Urge Calm Amid Muslim Fury: US, Europe Make Plea as Protests of Cartoons Spread." *Boston Globe,* February 6, p. A8.

Nicolaisen, Ida. 2006. "Anthropology Should Actively Promote Human Rights." *Anthropology News* 47(7):6.

Nielsen, Joyce McCarl. 1990. *Sex and Gender in Society: Perspectives on Stratification* (2nd ed.). Prospect Heights, IL: Waveland.

Nike. 2005. *Disclosure List.* Available at http://www.nike.com/nikebiz/gc/mp/pdf/disclosure_list_2005-06.pdf.

Nisbett, Richard E. 2009. "Education Is All in Your Mind." *New York Times,* February 8, p. 12.

Nobles, Melissa. 2000. *Shades of Citizenship: Race and the Census in Modern Politics.* Palo Alto, CA: Stanford University Press.

Noonan, James P., et al. 2006. "Sequencing and Analysis of Neanderthal Genomic DNA." *Science* 314(5802):1113–1118.

Norbeck, Edward. 1974. *Religion in Human Life: Anthropological Views.* Prospect Heights, IL: Waveland.

Norgren, Jill. 1996. *The Cherokee Cases: The Confrontation of Law and Politics.* New York: McGraw-Hill.

Norgren, Jill, and Serena Nanda. 1996. *American Cultural Pluralism and Law* (3rd ed.). New York: Praeger.

Norgren, Jill, and Serena Nanda. 2006. *American Cultural Pluralism and Law* (3rd ed.). Westport, CT: Praeger.

Obermeyer, Carla M. 2003. "The Health Consequences of Female Circumcision: Science, Advocacy, and Standards of Evidence." *Medical Anthropology Quarterly* 17(3): 394–412.

O'Brien, Denise. 1977. "Female Husbands in Southern Bantu Societies." In A. Schlegel (Ed.), *Sexual Stratification* (pp. 109–127). New York: Columbia University Press.

Oboler, Regina Smith. 1980. "Is the Female Husband a Man? Woman/Woman Marriage among the Nandi of Kenya." *Ethnology* 19:69–88.

Ochs, Elinor, and Bambi B. Schiefflelin. 1984. "Language Acquisition and Socialization: Three Developmental Stories and Their Implications." In R. Shweder and R. Levine (Eds.), *Culture Theory: Essays on Mind, Self and Emotion* (pp. 276–320). Cambridge: Cambridge University Press.

Offiong, Daniel. 1983. "Witchcraft Among the Ibibio of Nigeria." *African Studies Review* 26:107–124.

Ogbu, John. 1978. "African Bridewealth and Women's Status." *American Ethnologist* 5:241–260.

O'Kelly, Charlotte G., and Larry S. Carney. 1986. *Women and Men in Society: Cross-Cultural Perspectives on Gender Stratification.* Belmont, CA: Wadsworth.

Oliver, Mary Beth. 2003. "Race and Crime in the Media: Research From a Media Effects Tradition." In A. Valdivia (Ed.), *A Companion to Media Studies* (pp. 421–436). London: Blackwell.

Ong, Aihwa. 1989. "Center, Periphery, and Hierarchy: Gender in Southeast Asia." In S. Morgen (Ed.), *Gender and Anthropology: Critical Reviews for Research and Teaching* (pp. 294–303).Washington, DC: American Anthropological Association.

Onishi, Norimitsu. 2009. "Japan's Outcasts Still Wait for Society's Embrace." *New York Times,* January 16, p. A1.

Open Society Initiative for Southern Africa (OSISA). n.d. "Poverty and Cell Phones in Botswana." Available at http://www.osisa.org/node/9876.

Oreskes, Naomi. 2004. "The Scientific Consensus on Climate Change." *Science* 306(5702):1686.

Organization for Economic Opportunity and Development. 2007. *United States Donor Information.* Available at http://www.oecd.org/dataoecd/42/30/41732048.jpg.

Oriard, Michael. 1993. *Reading Football: How the Popular Press Created an American Spectacle.* Chapel Hill: University of North Carolina Press.

Orion, Loretta. 1995. *Never Again the Burning Times.* Prospect Heights, IL: Waveland.

Ortiz, Fernando, 1947. *Cuban Counterpoint: Tobacco and Sugar* (Harriet de Onis, Trans.). New York: Knopf.

Ortner, Sherry B., and Harriet Whitehead. 1981. *Sexual Meanings: The Cultural Construction of Gender and Sexuality.* Cambridge: Cambridge University Press.

Overbey, Mary Margaret. 2007. "RACE Are We So Different? A New Public Education Program." *AnthroNotes* 28(1, Spring.):15–17.

Page, Melvin E. 1987. "Introduction: Black Men in a White Men's War." In M. E. Page (Ed.), *Africa and the First World War* (pp. 1–27). New York: St. Martin's.

Page, Tim. 2007. "Parallel Play: A Life of Restless Isolation Explained." *The New Yorker,* August 20.

Paiement, Jason J. 2007. "Anthropology and Development." *National Association for the Practice of Anthropology Bulletin* 27(1): 196–223.

Paine, Robert. 1994. *Herds of the Tundra: A Portrait of Saami Reindeer Pastoralism.* Washington, DC: Smithsonian Institution.

Palkovich, Anna M. 1994. "Historic Epidemics of the American Pueblos." In C. S. Larsen and G. R. Milner (Eds.), *In the Wake of Contact: Biological Responses to Conquest* (pp. 87–95). New York: Wiley.

Pandya, Vishvajit. 2005. "Deforesting among Andamanese Children: Political Economy and History of Schooling." In Barry S. Hewlett and Michael E. Lamb (Eds.), *Hunter-Gatherer Childhoods* (pp. 385–406). Piscataway, NJ: Aldine.

Paredes, Anthony J. (Ed.). 2006. "Introduction to In Focus: The Impact of the Hurricanes of 2005 on New Orleans and the Gulf Coast of the United States." *American Anthropologist* 108(4):637–642.

Pareles, Jon. 1996. "A Small World After All. But Is That Good?" *New York Times,* March 24, p. B34.

Partridge, Ernest. 1984. "Three Wrong Leads in a Search for an Environmental Ethic: Tom Regan on Animal Rights, Inherent Values, and 'Deep Ecology.'" *Ethics and Animals* (5)3:61–74.

Pascoe, Peggy. 2008. *What Comes Naturally: Miscegenation Law and the Making of Race in America.* New York: Oxford University Press.

Patterson, Orlando. 2006. "A Poverty of the Mind." *New York Times,* March 26, p. 13.

Peacock, James, et al. 2007. *AAA Commission in the Engagement of Anthropology With the US Security and Intelligence Communities Final Report November 4, 2007.* Washington, DC: American Anthropological Association.

Peacock, Nadine R. 1991. "Rethinking the Sexual Division of Labor: Reproduction and Women's Work among the Efe." In M. di Leonardo (Ed.), *Gender and the Crossroads of Knowledge: Feminist Anthropology in the Postmodern Era* (pp. 339–360). Berkeley, CA: University of California Press.

Pearce, Fred. 2009. "Consumption Dwarfs Population as Main Environmental Threat." *Yale Environment 360,* April 13. Available at http://e360.yale.edu/content/feature.msp?id52140.

Peoples, James G. 1990. "The Evolution of Complex Stratification in Eastern Micronesia." *Micronesia Suppl.* 2:291–302.

Pepperberg, Irene Maxine. 2000. *The Alex Studies: Cognitive and Communicative Abilities of Grey Parrots.* Cambridge, MA: Harvard University Press.

Peregrin, Peter N., Carol R. Ember, and Melvin Ember. 2004. "Universal Patterns in Cultural Evolution: An Empirical Analysis Using Guttman Scaling." *American Anthropologist* 106(1):145–149.

Perez, Agnes, and Susan Pollack. 2008. *Fruit and Tree Nuts Outlook.* Washington, DC: USDA Economic Research Service FTS-332. Available at http://www.ers.usda.gov/Publications/fts/2008/05MAY/FTS332.pdf.

Perry, Barbara. 2008. *Silent Victims: Hate Crimes Against Native Americans.* Tucson, AZ: The University of Arizona Press.

Pettitt, George A. 1972. "The Vision Quest and the Guardian Spirit." In J. Jennings and E. A. Hoebel (Eds.), *Readings in Anthropology* (pp. 265–272). New York: McGraw-Hill.

Peyrefitte, Alain. 1992. *The Immobile Empire* (Jon Rothschild, Trans.). New York: Knopf.

Phillips, Wendy. 2005. "Cravings, Marks, and Open Pores: Acculturation and Preservation of Pregnancy-Related Beliefs and Practices among Mothers of African Descent in the United States." *Ethos* 33(2):231–255.

Pigg, Stacy Leigh. 2001. "Languages of Sex and AIDS in Nepal: Notes on the Social Production of Commensurability." *Current Anthropology.* 16(4):481–541.

Pilbeam, David. 1996. "Genetic and Morphological Records of the Hominoidea and Hominid Origins: A Synthesis." *Molecular Phylogenetic Evolution* 5:155–168.

Pinker, Steven. 1994. *The Language Instinct.* New York: William Morrow.

Pitts, Leonard. 2007. "At Large, Replying to Those E-mails about Vick." *Miami Herald,* September 12.

Planty, M., W. Hussar, T. Snyder, S. Provasnik, G. Kena, R. Dinkes, A. KewalRamani, and J. Kemp. 2008. *The Condition of Education 2008 (NCES 2008-031).* Washington, DC: National Center for Education Statistics, Institute of Education Sciences, U.S. Department of Education.

Plattner, Stuart. 1989a. "Economic Behavior in Markets." In S. Plattner (Ed.), *Economic Anthropology* (pp. 209–221). Stanford, CA: Stanford University Press.

Plattner, Stuart. 1989b. "Marxism." In S. Plattner (Ed.), *Economic Anthropology* (pp. 379–396). Stanford, CA: Stanford University Press.

Polyani, Karl. 1944. *The Great Transformation.* New York: Holt, Rinehart and Winston.

Population Reference Bureau. 2005. *2005 World Population Data Sheet.* Washington, DC: Population Reference Bureau. Available at http://www.prb.org/pdf05/05WorldDataSheet_Eng.pdf.

Port, Bob. 2001. "Sweat and Tears Still in Fashion in City." *New York Daily News,* July 8.

Post, Peter, Farrington Daniels, Jr., and Robert T. Binford, Jr. 1975. "Cold Injury and the Evolution of White Skin." *Human Biology* 47:65–80.

Potash, Betty. 1989. "Gender Relations in Sub-Saharan Africa." In S. Morgen (Ed.), *Gender and Anthropology: Critical Reviews for Research and Teaching* (pp. 189–227). Washington, DC: American Anthropological Association.

Powers, Thomas. 2005. The Indians' Own Story." *The New York Review of Books,* April 7, p. 73.

Powledge, Tabitha M. 2006. "What is the Hobbit?" *PLoS Biol* 4(12):e440. Available at http://www.plosbiology.org/article/info:doi/10.1371/journal.pbio.0040440.

Prah, Kwesi K. 1990. "Anthropologists, Colonial Administrators, and the Lotuko of Eastern Equatoria, Sudan: 1952–1953." *African Journal of Sociology* 3(2):70–86.

Press, Eyal. 2007. "The Missing Class." *The Nation,* August 13/20, pp. 22–23.

Preston, Julia. 2009. "A Slippery Place in the U.S. Work Force." *New York Times,* March 22, p. A1.

Price, David. n.d. (in press, 2009). "Soft Power, Hard Power and the Anthropological 'Leveraging' of Cultural 'Assets': Distilling the Politics and Ethics of Anthropological Counterinsurgency." In John Kelly, Sean Mitchell, Bea Jauregui, and Jeremy Walton (Eds.), *Anthropology and Global Counterinsurgency.* Chicago: University of Chicago Press.

Price, Sally. 1989. *Primitive Art in Civilized Places.* Chicago: University of Chicago Press.

Price, Sally. 2007. *Paris Primitive: Jacques Chirac's Museum on the Quai Branly.* Chicago: University of Chicago Press.

Pringle, H. 1998. "The Slow Birth of Agriculture." *Science* 282:1446.

Pruetz, J. D., and P. Bertolani. 2007. "Savanna Chimpanzees, Pan troglodytes verus, Hunt with Tools. *Current Biol* 17: 1–6.

Prunier, Gerard. 1995. *The Rwanda Crisis: History of a Genocide.* New York: Columbia University Press.

Prunier, Gerard. 2008. *Africa's World War: Congo, the Rwandan Genocide, and the Making of a Contintal Catastrophe.* Oxford: Oxford University Press.

Queen, Stuart, and Robert Haberstein. 1974. *The Family in Various Cultures.* New York: J.B. Lippincott Co.

Rabinovitch, Simon. 2009. "China's jobless migrants loath to return to countryside." *Forbes,* February 23. Available at http://www.forbes.com/feeds/afx/2009/02/23/afx6081529.html.

Radcliffe-Brown, A. R. 1956. *Structure and Function in Primitive Society.* Glencoe, IL: Free Press.

Radcliffe-Brown, A. R. 1965. *Structure and Function in Primitive Society.* New York: Free Press. (Originally published 1952.)

Ragoné, Helena. 1994. *Surrogate Motherhood: Conception in the Heart.* Boulder, CO: Westview.

Ramet, Sabrina P. 1996. *Balkan Babel: Politics, Culture, and Religion in Yugoslavia* (2nd ed.). Boulder, CO: Westview.

Rand, Jacki Thompson. 2007. "Why I Can't Visit the National Museum of the American Indian: Reflections of an Accidental Privileged Insider, 1989-1994." *Common-Place* 7(4, July). Available at www.common-place.org.

Rankoana, Agnes. 2001. "Plant Based Medicines of the Dikale of the Northern Province." *South African Journal of Ethnology* 24 (3): 99–104.

*Rasmusen Reports.* 2006. "85% Support English as Official Language of U.S." June 9. Available at: http://www.rasmussenreports.com/public_general_current_events/85_support_english_as_official_language_of_u_s.

Rasmussan, Susan. 2005. "Pastoral Nomadism and Gender: Status, Prestige, Economic Contribution, and Division of Labor among the Tuareg of Niger." In Caroline B. Brettell and Carolyn F. Sargent (Eds.), *Gender in Cross Cultural Perspective* (4th ed., pp. 155–168). Upper Saddle River, NJ: Pearson/Prentice Hall.

Ratliff, Eric A. 1999. "Women as 'Sex-Workers,' Men as 'Boyfriends': Shifting Identities in Philippine Go-Go Bars and Their Significance in STD/AIDS Control." *Anthropology and Medicine* 6(1):79–101.

Reddy, Gayatri. 2005. *With Respect to Sex: Negotiating Hijra Identity in South India.* Chicago: University of Chicago.

Reddy, Gayatri, and Serena Nanda. 2005. "Hijras: An 'Alternative' Sex/Gender." In Caroline B. Brettell and Carolyn F. Sargent (Eds.), *Gender in Cross-Cultural Perspective* (4th ed.) Upper Saddle River, NJ: Prentice Hall.

Reed, Adolph, Jr. 2006. "Undone by Neoliberalism." *The Nation,* September 18, p. 26.

Reeves, Glen. 2006. "Pursuing Opportunities 'Away From Home': Encountering New Challenges and Relationships." *Anthropology News* 47(9):8–9.

Regan, Tom. 1982. *All That Dwell Therein: Animal Rights and Environmental Ethics.* Berkeley, CA: University of California Press.

Reichman, Rebecca. 1995. "Brazil's Denial of Race." *NACLA Report on the Americas* 28 (6):35–43.

Renfrew, Colin, April McMahon, and Larry Trask (Eds.). 2000. *Time Depth in Historical Linguistics* (Vols. 1 and 2). Cambridge, UK: The McDonald Institute for Archaeological Research.

Renteln, Alison D. 2004. *The Cultural Defense.* New York: Oxford.

Revolutionary Association of the Women of Afghanistan. 2009. Available at http://www.rawa.org.

Reynolds, Larry T. 1992. "A Retrospective on 'Race': The Career of a Concept." *Sociological-Focus* 25(1):1–14.

Richards, Audrey I. 1956. *Chisungu: A Girl's Initiation Ceremony among the Bemba of Northern Rhodesia.* New York: Grove Press.

Rickford, John Russell, and Russell John Rickford. 2000. *Spoken Soul: The Story of Black English.* New York: Wiley.

Ricklefs, Merle C. 1990. "Balance and Military Innovation in 17th Century Java." *History Today* 40(11):40–47.

Ricklefs, Merle C. 1993. *A History of Modern Indonesia since c. 1300* (2nd ed.). Stanford, CA: Stanford University Press.

Ringlero, Aleta M. 2008. "Fritz Scholder: The Enigma." *Smithsonian National Museum of the American Indian* Fall: 16–24.

Ritter, M. L. 1980. "The Conditions Favoring Age-Set Organization." *Journal of Anthropological Research* 36:87–104.

Roberton, John. 1827. *Observations on the Mortality and Physical Management of Children.* London: Longman, Rees, Orme, Brown and Green. Available at http://www.neonatology.org/classics/roberton/roberton.html.

Roberts, Alan H., D. G. Kewman, L. Mercier, and M. Hovell. 1993. "The Power of Non-specific Effects in Healing: Implications for Psychosocial and Biological Treatments." *Clinical Psychology Review* 13:375–391.

Roberts, Sam. 2008. "2-Parent Black Families Showing Gains." *New York Times,* December 17, p. A21.

Robins, A. H. 1991. *Biological Perspectives on Human Pigmentation.* Cambridge: Cambridge University Press.

Roland, Edna. 2001. "The Economics of Racism: People of African Descent in Brazil." Paper presented at the International Council on Human Rights Policy Seminar on the Economics of Racism, November 24-25. Geneva, Switzerland.

Romaine, Suzanne. 1994. *Language in Society: An Introduction to Sociolinguistics.* London: Blackwell.

Rosaldo, Michelle Z., and Louise Lamphere. 1974. "Introduction." In M. Z. Rosaldo and L. Lamphere (Eds.), *Women, Culture and Society* (pp. 1–16). Stanford, CA: Stanford University Press.

Rosaldo, Renato. 1993. *Culture and Truth: The Remaking of Social Analysis.* Boston: Beacon Press.

Roscoe, Will. 1991. *The Zuni Man-Woman.* Albuquerque: University of New Mexico Press.

Roscoe, Will. 1995. "Strange Craft, Strange History, Strange Folks: Cultural Amnesia and the Case of Lesbian and Gay Studies." *American Anthropologist* 97:448–452.

Rosenberg, Harriet G. 2003. "Complaint Discourse: Aging and Caregiving among the Ju/'hoansi." In Richard B. Lee, *The Dobe Ju/'hoansi* (3rd ed). Belmont, CA: Wadsworth.

Rosenthal, Elizabeth. 2008. "From Hoof to Dinner Table, A New Bid to Cut Emissions." *New York Times,* December 4, p. A1.

Rosenthal, Elizabeth. 2008. "Rearranging Pantries, Aid Groups Favor Potato." *New York Times,* October 26, p. A6.

Rosman, Abraham, and Paula G. Rubel. 1971. *Feasting with Mine Enemy: Rank and Ex-*

*change among Northwest Coast Societies.* Prospect Heights, IL: Waveland.

Ross, Eric B. 1998. *The Malthus Factor: Poverty, Politics, and Population in Capitalist Development.* New York: St. Martin's.

Rostow, Walt. 1960. The Stages of Growth: *A Non-Communist Manifesto.* New York: Cambridge.

Rothenberg-Aalami, Jessica. 2004. "Coming Full Circle? Forging Missing Links Along Nike's Integrated Production Networks." *Global Networks* 4(4):335–354.

Roth-Gordon, Jennifer. 2009. "The Language That Came Down the Hill: Slang, Crime, and Citizenship in Rio de Janeiro." *American Anthropologist* 111(1):57–68.

Rothstein, Richard. 2005. "Defending Sweatshops: Too Much Logic, Too Little Evidence." *Dissent* 52(2):41–47.

Roybal, Joe. 2007. "Big Beef Buyers." *Beef Magazine.* Available at http://beefmagazine. com/mag/beef_big_beef_buyers/index. html.

Ruhlen, Merritt. 1994. *The Origin of Language: Tracing the Evolution of the Mother Tongue.* New York: John Wiley.

Sacks, Karen Brodkin. 1982. *Sisters and Wives.* Westport, CT: Greenwood.

Sacks, Oliver. 1995. *An Anthropologist on Mars: Seven Paradoxical Tales.* New York: Knopf.

Sage, George H. 1999. "Justice Do It! The Nike Transnational Advocacy Network: Organization, Collective Actions, and Outcomes." *Sociology of Sport Journal* 16:206–235.

Sahlins, Marshall. 1957. "Land Use and the Extended Family in Moala, Fiji." *American Anthropologist* 59: 449–462.

Sahlins, Marshall. 1961. "The Segmentary Lineage: An Organization of Predatory Expansion." *American Anthropologist* 63:332–345.

Sahlins, Marshall. 1971. "Poor Man, Rich Man, Big Man, Chief." In J. P. Spradley and D.W. McCurdy (Eds.), *Conformity and Conflict* (pp. 362–376). Boston: Little, Brown.

Sahlins, Marshall. 1972. *Stone Age Economics.* Chicago: Aldine.

Said, Edward W. 1993. *Culture and Imperialism.* New York: Knopf.

Saitoti, Tepilil Ole. 1986. *The Worlds of a Maasai Warrior: An Autobiography.* Berkeley, CA: University of California Press.

Saleh, Zainab. 2009. *It Is What It Is: Conversations about Iraq.* Interview, A Project by Jeremy Deller. New York: New Museum.

Salzman, Philip. 1999. *The Anthropology of Real Life: Events in Human Experience.* Prospect Heights, IL: Waveland.

Salzman, Philip C. 2000. "Hierarchical Image and Reality: the Construction of a Tribal Chiefship." *Comparative Studies in Society and History* 42(1):49–66.

Salzmann, Zdenek. 1993. *Language, Culture and Society.* Boulder, CO: Westview Press.

Sanchez, Rene. 1997. "Ebonics Debate Comes to Capitol Hill; 'Political Correctness Gone Out of Control,' Sen. Faircloth Says." *Washington Post,* January 24, p. A15.

Sanchez-Eppler, Benigno. 1992. "Telling anthropology: Zora Neale Hurston and Gilberto Freyre Disciplined in Their Field-Home-Work." *American Literary History* 4:464–488.

Sanday, Peggy Reeves. 1981. *Female Power and Male Dominance.* New York: Cambridge University Press.

Sanday, Peggy Reeves. 1992. *Fraternity Gang Rape: Sex, Brotherhood, and Privilege on Campus.* New York: New York University Press.

Sanghavi, Prachi, Kavi Bhatta, and Veena Das. 2009. "Fire-Related Deaths in India in 2001: A Retrospective Analysis of Data." *The Lancet* (Early Online Publication), 2 March: 1–2.

Sapir, Edward. 1949b. "The Status of Linguistics as a Science." In D. Mandelbaum (Ed.), *The Selected Writings of Edward Sapir in Language, Culture and Personality* (pp. 160–166). Berkeley, CA: University of California Press.

SAPRIN. 2004. *Structural Adjustment: The Policy Roots of Economic Crisis, Poverty, and Inequality.* London: Zed Books.

Sarroub, Loukia K. 2005. *All American Yemeni Girls: Being Muslim in a Public School.* Philadelphia, PA: University of Pennsylvania Press.

Savage-Rumbaugh, S. 1987. "Communication, Symbolic Communication, and Language: Reply to Seidenberg and Petitto." *Journal of Experimental Psychology: General* 116(3):288–292.

Savage-Rumbaugh, Sue, Stuart G. Shanker, and Talbot J. Taylor. 1998. *Apes, Language and the Human Mind.* Oxford, UK: Oxford University Press.

Scammell, G. V. 1989. *The First Imperial Age.* London: HarperCollins Academic.

Schele, Linda, and Mary Ellen Miller. 1986. *The Blood of Kings: Dynasty and Ritual in Maya Art.* New York: Braziller.

Schensul, Stephen L. 1997. "The Anthropologist in Medicine: Critical Perspectives on Cancer and Street Addicts." *Reviews in Anthropology* 26(1):57–69.

Schepartz, L. A. 1993. "Language and Modern Human Origins." *Yearbook of Physical Anthropology* 36:91–96.

Scheper-Hughes, Nancy. 1992. *Death Without Weeping: The Violence of Everyday Life in Brazil.* Berkeley, CA: University of California Press.

Scheper-Hughes, Nancy, and Margaret M. Lock. 1987. "The Mindful Body: A Prolegomenon to Future Work in Medical Anthropology." In Peter J. Brown (Ed.), *Understanding and Applying Medical Anthropology* (pp. 208–225). Mountain View, CA: Mayfield Pub. Co.

Schlegel, Alice, and Herbert Barry III. 1991. *Adolescence: An Anthropological Inquiry.* New York: Free Press.

Schneider, Harold K. 1973. "The Subsistence Role of Cattle among the Pokot in East Africa." In E. P. Skinner (Ed.), *Peoples and Cultures of Africa.* Garden City, NY: Natural History Press.

Schneider, Jane. 2002. "World Markets: Anthropological Perspectives." In Jeremy MacClancy, (Ed.), *Exotic No More: Anthropology on the Front Lines.* Chicago: University of Chicago Press.

Schuyler, Phillip. 1995. "The Arts of the Arabic-Speaking Middle East." In *What in the World Is Culture?* (pp. 49–53). 651 World

Series Festival Booklet. New York: King's Majestic Corporation.

Schwartz, Stuart B. 1994. *Implicit Understandings: Observing, Reporting, and Reflecting on the Encounters Between Europeans and Other Peoples of the Early Modern Era.* Cambridge: Cambridge University Press.

Schweitzer, Martin. 2008. Statement of Colonel Martin P. Schweitzer, Commander 4/82 Airborne Brigade Combat Team United States Army, Before the House Armed Services Committee, Terrorism & Unconventional Threats Sub-Committee and the Research & Education Subcommittee of the Science & Technology Committee, United States House of Representatives 110th Congress, 2nd Session Hearings on Role of the Social and Behavioral Sciences in National Security. April 24.

Scoditti, Giancarlo M., with Jerry W. Leach. 1983. "Kula on Kitava." In J. W. Leach and E. Leach (Eds.), *The Kula: New Perspectives on Massim Exchange* (pp. 249–273). Cambridge: Cambridge University Press.

Scott, Elizabeth. 2001. "Food and Social Relationships at Nina Plantation." *American Anthropologist* 103(3): 671–691.

Scott, James. 1992. *Domination and the Arts of Resistance: Hidden Transcripts.* New Haven, CT: Yale University Press.

Scott, Janny. 2005. "Life at the Top in America Isn't Just Better, It's Longer." *New York Times,* May 16.

Seidenberg, Mark S., and Laura A. Petitto. 1987. "Communication, Symbolic Communication, and Language: Comment on Savage-Rumbaugh, McDonald, Sevcik, Hopkins, and Rupert (1986)." *Journal of Experimental Psychology* 116(3):279–287.

Seitlyn, David. 1993. "Spiders In and Out of Court, or 'The Long Legs & the Law': Styles of Spider Divination in Their Sociological Contexts." *Africa* 63:219–240.

Service, Elman. 1962. *Primitive Social Organization.* New York: Random House.

Service, Elman. 1971. *Profiles in Ethnology.* New York: Harper and Row.

Shackel, Paul, and Matthew Palus. 2006. "The Gilded Age and Working Class Industrial Communities." *American Anthropologist* 108(4):828–841.

Shandy, Dianna J. 2007. *Nuer-American Passages: Globalizing Sudanese Migration.* Gainesville, FL: University Press of Florida.

Shanklin, Eugenia. 1994. *Anthropology and Race.* Belmont, CA: Wadsworth.

Sharff, Jagna W. 1997. *King Kong on 4th Street: Families and the Violence of Poverty on the Lower East Side.* Boulder, CO: Westview.

Sheehan, John. 1982. *The Enchanted Ring: The Untold Story of Penicillin.* Cambridge, MA: MIT Press.

Shell-Duncan, Bettina. 2008. "From Health to Human Rights: Female Genital Cutting and the Politics of Intervention." *American Anthropologist* 110(2):225–236.

Sheriff, Robin. 2001. *Dreaming Equality: Color, Race and Racism in Urban Brazil.* East Brunswick, NJ: Rutgers University Press.

Shevoroshkin, Vitaly, and John Woodford. 1991. "Where Linguistics, Archaeology, and Biology Meet." In John Brockman (Ed.), *Ways of Knowing* (pp. 173–197). New York: Prentice Hall.

Shih, Chuan-Kang. 2001. "Genesis of Marriage among the Moso and Empire-Building in Late Imperial China." *The Journal of Asian Studies* 60(2):381–412.

Shostak, Marjorie. 1983. *Nisa: The Life and Words of a !Kung Woman.* New York: Random House.

Shryock, Andrew. 2002. "New Images of Arab Detroit: Seeing Otherness and Identity Through the Lens of September 11." *American Anthropologist* 104(3, September): 917–922.

Sibley, C. G., and J. E. Ahlquist. 1987. "DNA Hybridization Evidence of Hominoid Phylogeny: Results from an Expanded Data Set." *Journal of Molecular Evolution* 26:99–121.

Sibley, C. G., J. A. Comstock, and J. E. Ahlquist. 1990. "DNA Hybridization Evidence of Hominoid Phylogeny: A Reanalysis of the Data." *Journal of Molecular Evolution* 30:202–236.

Simeone, William E. 1995. *Rifles, Blankets, and Beads: Identity, History, and the Northern Athapaskan Potlatch.* Norman, OK: University of Oklahoma Press.

Simmons, Marc. 1991. *The Last Conquistador: Juan de Oñate and the Settling of the Far Southwest.* Norman, OK: University of Oklahoma Press.

Simmons, Marc. 1992. *The Last Conquistador: Juan De Onate and the Settling of the Far Southwest.* Tulsa: University of Oklahoma Press.

Singer, Merrill. 2000. "Update on Projects Recovery and CONNECT." In P. L.W. Sabloff (Ed.), *Careers in Anthropology: Profiles of Practitioner Anthropologists* (NAPA Bulletin, Vol. 20). Washington, DC: National Association of Practicing Anthropologists.

Singer, Merrill. 2008. "The Perfect Epidemiological Storm: Food Insecurity, HIV/AIDS and Poverty in Southern Africa." *Anthropology News*, October, p. 12.

Singer, Merrill, Ray Irizarry, and Jean J. Schensul. 1991. "Needle Access as an AIDS Prevention Strategy for IV Drug Users: A Research Perspective." *Human Organization* 50:142–153.

Singer, Milton. 1968. "The Indian Joint Family in Modern Industry." In M. Singer and B. Cohn (Eds.), *Indian Society: Structure and Change* (pp. 413–423). Chicago: Aldine.

Singer, Peter. 1979. *Practical Ethics.* Cambridge, UK: Cambridge University Press.

Singer, Merrill, Hassan Salaheen, Greg Mirhej, and Claudia Santelice. 2005. "Bridging the Divide: Drinking among Street Drug Users." *American Anthropologist* 108(3):502–506.

Skidmore, Monique. 2003. "Darker than Midnight: Fear, Vulnerability, and Terror Making in Urban Burma (Myanmar)." *American Ethnologist* 30:5–21.

Skin Cancer Foundation Australia. 1998. Available at http://www.scfa.edu.au.

Slackman, Michael. 2007. "In Egypt, a New Battle Begins Over the Veil." *New York Times*, January 28, World Section, p. 3.

Smedley, Audrey. 1998a. "'Race' and the Construction of Human Identity." *American Anthropologist* 100:690–702.

Smedley, Audrey. 1998b. *Race in North America: Origin and Evolution of a Worldview* (2nd ed.). Boulder, CO: Westview.

Smith, David. 2009. "Mobiles Give Africa's Farmers a Chance to Set Out Their Stall." *Mail and Guardian online*, January 4. Available at http://www.guardian.co.uk/katine/2009/jan/04/katine-uganda-africa-mobile-phones.

Smith, Roberta. 2005. "From a Mushroom Cloud, a Burst of Art Reflecting Japan's Psyche." *New York Times*, April 8, p. E33.

Smith, Tom. 2001. "Estimating the Muslim Population in the United States." Report for The American Jewish Committee, New York, NY. Available at http://cloud9.norc.uchicago.edu/dlib/muslm.htm.

Smith, Tom. 2002. "Religious Diversity in America: The Emergence of Muslims, Buddhists, Hindus, and Others." *Journal for the Scientific Study of Religion* 41(3):577–585.

Smith, Tony. 1978. "A comparative study of French and British decolonization." *Comparative Studies in Society and History* 20:70–102.

Sokoloff, Natalie, and Christina Pratt (Eds.). 2005. *Domestic Violence at the Margins: Readings on Race, Class, Gender, and Culture.* New Brunswick, NJ: Rutgers University Press.

Solecki, Ralph. 1975. "Shanidar IV, A Neanderthal Flower Burial in North Iraq." *Science* 190:880–881.

Solomon, Charles. 2005. "The Newest Stars of Japanese Anime, Made in America." *New York Times*, July 24, p. Art 25.

Spector, Janet D., and Mary K. Whelan. 1989. "Incorporating Gender into Archaeology Courses." In S. Morgen (Ed.), *Gender and Anthropology: Critical Reviews for Research and Teaching* (pp. 65–94). Washington, DC: American Anthropological Association.

Speed, Shannon. 2008. "Human Rights and the Border Wall." *Anthropology News*, December, p. 25.

Spencer, Herbert. 1864. *The Principles of Biology* (Vol. 1). London: Williams and Norgate.

Spielmann, Katherine A. 2002. "Feasting, Craft Specialization, and the Ritual Mode of Production in Small-Scale Societies." *American Anthropologist* 104(1):195–207.

Spiro, Melford. 1958. *Children of the Kibbutz.* Cambridge, MA: Harvard.

Sponsel, Leslie E. (Ed.). 1995. *Indigenous Peoples and the Future of Amazonia: An Ecological Anthropology of an Endangered World.* Tucson: University of Arizona Press.

Spradley, James. 1970. *You Owe Yourself a Drunk.* Boston: Little, Brown.

Spuhler, J. N. 1989. "Raymond Pearl Memorial Lecture, 1988: Evolution of Mitochondrial DNA in Human and Other Organisms." *American Journal of Human Biology* 1: 509–528.

Stearns, M. L. 1975. "Life Cycle Rituals of the Modern Haida." In D. B. Carlisle (Ed.), *Contributions to Canadian Ethnology* (pp. 129–169). Ottawa: National Museum of Man.

Steele, James. 1999, May. "Palaeoanthropology: Stone Legacy of Skilled Hands." *Nature*, pp. 24–25.

Steiner, Christopher B. 1994. *African Art in Transit.* Cambridge: Cambridge University Press.

Steiner, Christopher B. 1995. "The Art of the Trade: On the Creation of Value and Authenticity in the African Art Market." In G. E. Marcus and F. R. Myers (Eds.), *The Traffic in Culture: Refiguring Art and Anthropology* (pp. 151–165). Berkeley, CA: University of California Press.

Steiner, Christopher B. 2002. "Art/Anthropology/Museums: Revulsions and Revolutions." In Jeremy MacClancy (Ed.), *Exotic No More: Anthropology on the Front Lines* (pp. 399–417). Chicago, IL: University of Chicago Press.

Stephens, Sharon. 1987, December. "Lapp Life After Chernobyl." *Natural History*, pp. 33–40.

Stepick, Alex. 1998. *Pride Against Prejudice: Haitians in the U.S.* Boston, MA: Allyn and Bacon Publishers.

Stern, Pamela R. 1999. "Learning to Be Smart: An Exploration of the Culture of Intelligence in a Canadian Inuit Community." *American Anthropologist* 101:502–514.

Sternberg, Esther. 2002. "Walter B. Cannon and 'Voodoo' Death: A Perspective from 60 Years On." *American Journal of Public Health* 92:1564–1566.

Stewart, Omer Call. 1987. *Peyote Religion: A History.* Norman, OK: University of Oklahoma Press.

Stolberg, Sheryl Gay. 1999. "Black Mother's Mortality Rate Is Under Scrutiny." In *New York Times*, August 8, p. A1.

Stolcke, Verena. 1995. "Talking Culture: New Boundaries, New Rhetorics of Exclusion in Europe." *Current Anthropology* 36:1–7.

Stoller, Paul. 2002. *Money Has No Smell: The Africanization of New York City.* Chicago: University of Chicago Press.

Stone, Linda, and Caroline James. 2005. "Dowry, Bride-Burning, and Female Power in India." In C. B. Brettell and C. F. Sargent (Eds.), *Gender in Cross-Cultural Perspective* (4th ed.) (pp. 312–320). Upper Saddle River, NJ: Prentice Hall.

Stone, Linda S. 2004. "Gay Marriage and Anthropology." *Anthropology News* 45(5):10.

Stonich, Susan C., Douglas L. Murray, and Peter R. Rossart. 1994. Enduring Crises: The Human and Environmental Consequences of Nontraditional Export Growth in Central America." *Research in Economic Anthropology* 15:239–274.

Strathern, Marilyn. 1995. *Women in Between: Female Roles in a Male World: Mount Hagen, New Guinea.* Latham, MD: Rowman and Littlefield.

Strauss, Lawrence G. 1991. "Southwestern Europe at the Last Glacial Maximum." *Current Anthropology* 32:189–199.

Strier, Karen B. 2000. *Primate Behavioral Ecology.* Boston: Allyn and Bacon.

Strum, Philippa (Ed.). 2005. *Muslims in the United States: Identity, Influence, Innovation.* Washington, DC: Woodrow Wilson International Center for Scholars.

Strum, Philippa (Ed.). 2006. *American Arabs and Political Participation.* Washington, DC: Woodrow Wilson International Center for Scholars.

Strum, Philippa, and Andrew Selee. 2004. *The Hispanic Challenge? What We Know About Latino Immigration.* Washington, DC:

Woodrow Wilson International Center for Scholars.

Strum, Philippa, and Danielle Tarantolo (Eds.). 2003. *Muslims in the United States: Demography, Beliefs, Institutions.* Washington, DC: Woodrow Wilson International Center for Scholars.

Stull, Donald D., and Michael J. Broadway. 2004. *Slaughterhouse Blues: The Meat and Poultry Industry in North America.* Belmont, CA: Wadsworth.

Sturm, Daniel. 2008. "Iraqi Refugees Search for Work in Detroit." *Anthropology Newsletter,* October, p. 59.

Survival International. 2000. *Disinherited: Indians in Brazil.* London: Survival International.

Swisher, Carl, et al. 1994. "Age of the Earliest Known Hominids in Java, Indonesia." *Science* 263:1118–1121.

Tabuchi, Hiroko. 2009. "Japan Pays Foreign Workers To Go Home." *New York Times,* April 22. Available at http://www.nytimes.com/2009/04/23/business/global/23immigrant.html?ref=business.

Talk of the Nation. 2008. "Amazon Tribe Photos Cause Uproar." *National Public Radio.* Available at http://www.npr.org/templates/story/story.php?storyId=91588718.

Tavernise, Sabrina. 2007. "In Turkey, a Step to Allow Head Scarves." *New York Times,* January 29, p. A3.

Tavernise, Sabrina. 2008a. "Bad Times Stall Cash Flow from Tajik Migrants." *New York Times,* Dec. 25, A11.

Tavernise, Sabrina. 2008b. "Tajik Village Shares Fears of Migrants." *New York Times,* December 28, A12.

Tedlock, Barbara. 2005. *The Woman in the Shaman's Body: Reclaiming the Feminine in Religion and Medicine.* New York: Bantam Dell.

Templeton, Alan R. 1985. "The Phylogeny of the Hominoid Primates: A Statistical Analysis of the DNA-DNA Hybridization Data." *Molecular Biology and Evolution* 2:420–433.

Templeton, Alan R. 1986. "Further Comments on Statistical Analysis of DNA-DNA Hybridization Data." *Molecular Biology and Evolution* 3:290–295.

Templeton, Alan R. 1998. "Human Races: A Genetic and Evolutionary Perspective." *American Anthropologist* 100:632–650.

Terrazas, Aaron. 2009. "African Immigrants in the United States." *Migration Information Source.* Available at http://www.migrationinformation.org/USfocus/display.cfm?id=719.

Tessman, Irwin, and Jack Tessman. 2000. "Efficacy of Prayer: A Critical Examination of Claims." *Skeptical Inquirer* 24(2):31–33.

Thompson, A.C. 2009. "Katrina's Hidden Race War." *The Nation,* January 5, pp. 11–18.

Thornton, Lynne. 1994. *Women as Portrayed in Orientalist Painting.* Paris: PocheCouleur.

Thubron, Colin. 2009. "Madame Butterfly's Brothel." *The New York Review of Books,* June 11, p. 24–27.

Tierney, John. 2008. "Sexual Consequences of Female Initiation Rites in Africa." *New York Times,* January 14. Available at http://tierneylab.blogs.nytimes.com/2008/01/14/the-sexual-consequences-of-an-african-initation-rite.

Tishkoff, Sarah A., and K. K. Kidd. 2004. "Implications of Biogeography of Human Populations for 'Race' and Medicine." *Nature Genetics* 36:S21–S27.

Tobin, Joseph J., David Y. H. Wu, and Dana Davidson. 1989. *Preschool in Three Cultures: Japan, China, and the United States.* New Haven, CT: Yale University Press.

Tocqueville, Alexis de. 1956. *Democracy in America.* New York: Penguin. (Originally published 1835–1840.)

Todero, Michael, and Stephen C. Smith. 2003. *Economic Development* (8th ed.). Harlow, UK, Pearson Addison Wesley.

Toensing, Chris. 2008. "Collateral Damage." *The Nation,* November 3, pp. 25–30.

Traphagan, John W. 1998. "Contesting the Transition to Old Age in Japan." *Ethnology* 37:333–350.

Truitt, Allison. 2008. "On the Back of a Motorbike: Middle-Class Mobility in Ho Chi Minh City, Vietnam." *American Ethnologist* 35(1):3–19.

Tsui, Clarence. 2000. "A Hong Kong Anthropologist Spent Months at a Mainland Electronic Plant to Study Lives of Its Female Workers: Hardship, Hope and Dreams in a Factory." *South China Morning Post,* January 9, p. 1.

Tsuruta, Kinua. 1989. *The Walls Within: Images of Westerners in Japan and Images of the Japanese Abroad.* Vancouver: Institute of Asian Research.

Turnbull, Colin. 1961. *The Forest People.* New York: Simon and Schuster.

Turnbull, Colin. 1968. "The Importance of Flux in Two Hunting Societies." In R. B. Lee and I. DeVore (Eds.), *Man the Hunter* (pp. 132–137). Chicago: Aldine.

Turner, Victor. 1967. *The Forest of Symbols: Aspects of Ndembu Ritual.* Ithaca: Cornell University Press.

Turner, Victor. 1969. *The Ritual Process: Structure and Antistructure.* Chicago: Aldine.

*The 2007 Revision Executive Summary.* New York: United Nations.

Tylor, Edward. 1920. *Primitive Culture* (2 vols.). New York: G. P. Putnam's Sons.

Tylor, Edward Burnett. 2004. "The Science of Culture." In R. Jon McGee and Richard L. Warms (Eds.), *Anthropological Theory: An Introductory History* (pp. 41–56). Boston: McGraw Hill. (Originally published 1871.)

UC Atlas of Global Inequality. n.d. *UC Atlas of Global Inequality.* Available at http://ucatlas.ucsc.edu/. Santa Cruz, CA: University of California.

Uchendu, Victor Chikezie. 1965. *The Igbo of Southeastern Nigeria.* New York: Holt, Rinehart and Winston.

Ucko, P., and A. Rosenfeld. 1967. *Paleolithic Cave Art.* New York: McGraw-Hill.

United Nations. 2008. *World Urbanization Prospects.* Available at http://esa.un.org/unup.

United Nations Environmental Programme. 2004. *Childhood Pesticide Poisoning.* Châtelaine, Switzerland: UNEP Chemicals, International Environment House.

United States Census Bureau. 2008. *Statistical Abstract.* Available at http://www.census.gov/compendia/statab/.

United States Environmental Protection Agency. 2007. *Ag 101.* Available at http://www.epa.gov/oecaagct/ag101/index.html.

University of Virginia. 2008. *Choosing and Using Your Major.* University of Virginia University Career Services. Available at http://www.career.virginia.edu/students/resources/handouts/choosing_a_major.pdf.

USDA. 2009. "Briefing Rooms: NAFTA, Canada, and Mexico: Mexico Trade." *United States Department of Agriculture.* Available at http://www.ers.usda.gov/Briefing/NAFTA/.

usenglish.org. 2007. "Misconceptions about Official English." Available at http://www.us-english.org/view/15.

van den Berghe, P.L., and P. Frost. 1986. "Skin Color Preference, Sexual Dimorphism and Sexual Selection: A Case of Gene Culture Coevolution?" *Ethn Racial Stud* 9:87–113.

Walle, Etienne van de. 1992. "Fertility Transition, Conscious Choice, and Numeracy." *Demography* 29(4):487–502.

van Donge, Jan Kees. 1992. "Agricultural Decline in Tanzania: The Case of the Uluguru Mountains." *African Affairs* 91:73–94.

van Gennep, Arnold. 1960. *The Rites of Passage.* Chicago: University of Chicago Press. (Originally published 1909.)

Vayda, Andrew P. 1976. *War in Ecological Perspective.* New York: Plenum.

Venbrux, Eric, Pamela Shefffield Rosi, and Robert L. Welsch (Eds.). 2006. *Exploring World Art.* Long Grove, IL: Waveland Press.

Victor, David A. 1992. *International Business Communication.* New York: Harper Collins.

Vignaud, P., et al. 2002. "Geology and Paleontology of the Upper Miocene Toros-Menalla Hominid Locality, Chad." *Nature* 418:152–155.

Vincent, Susan. 1998. "The Family in the Household: Women, Relationships, and Economic History in Peru." *Research in Economic Anthropology* 19:179–187.

Viswanathan, Gauri. 1988. "Currying Favor: The Politics of British Educational and Cultural Policy in India 1813–1854." *Social Text* 19–20(Fall):85–104.

Vogel, Susan. 1991. *Africa Explores: 20th Century African Art.* New York: Center for African Art.

Vogt, E. Z., and Ray Hyman. 2000. *Water Witching USA.* Chicago, IL: University of Chicago Press.

von Graeve, Bernard. 1989. *The Pacaa Nova: Clash of Cultures on the Brazilian Frontier.* Peterborough, Ontario: Broadview Press.

Walker, Andrew. 2009. "Nigeria's gas profits 'up in smoke.'" *BBC News,* Nigeria, Jan. 13. Available at http://news.bbc.co.uk/2/hi/africa/7820384.stm.

Wallace, Anthony. 1970. *Death and Rebirth of the Seneca.* New York: Knopf.

Wallace, Anthony. 1999. *Jefferson and the Indians: The Tragic Fate of 'The First Americans.'* Cambridge, MA: Harvard University Press.

Wallerstein, Immanuel. 1995. *Historical Capitalism.* London: Verso.

Walley, Christine J. 1997. "Searching for 'Voices': Feminism, Anthropology, and the Global Debate over Female Genital Operations." *Cultural Anthropology* 12:405–438.

Wallman, Joel. 2000. "Common Sense about Violence: Why Research?" In *Year 2000 Report of the Harry Frank Guggenheim Foundation: Research for Understanding and Reducing Violence, Aggression, and Dominance* (pp. 7–25). New York: Harry Frank Guggenheim Foundation.

Walsh, Eileen. 2002. "Book Review of *A Society without Fathers or Husbands: The Na of China*. Cai Hua." *American Ethnologist* 29(4):1043–1045.

Walsh, Eileen Rose. 2004. "Desensationalizing the Mosuo." *Anthropology Newsletter* 45(4).

Wang, Jimmy. 2009. "Now Hip-Hop, Too, Is Made in China." *New York Times,* January 24, p. C1.

Warms, Richard L. 1992. "Merchants, Muslims, and Wahhabiyya: The Elaboration of Islamic Identity in Sikasso, Mali." *Canadian Journal of African Studies* 26(3):485–507.

Warms, Richard L. 1996. "Throwing Away the Bones: The Story of Mory Samake, an African Veteran of the French Colonial Army." In A. Marcus (Ed.), *Anthropology for a Small Planet: Culture and Community in a Global Environment* (pp. 1–18). St. James, NY: Brandywine Press.

Warner, R. Stephen. 2005. *A Church of Our Own: Disestablishment and Diversity in American Religion.* Brunswick, NJ: Rutgers.

Warren, Kay B., and Susan C. Bourque. 1989. "Women, Technology, and Development Ideologies: Frameworks and Findings." In S. Morgen (Ed.), *Gender and Anthropology: Critical Reviews for Research and Teaching* (pp. 382–410). Washington, DC: American Anthropological Association.

Warren, Wilson. 2007. *Tied to the Great Packing Machine: The Midwest and Meatpacking.* Iowa City, IA: University of Iowa.

Webber, Sabra (with Frank Spaulding). 2007. "Efforts to Reject Muslims from the Human Family Prove Ridiculous." *Anthropology News,* September, p. 6.

Weiner, Annette B. 1976. *Women of Value, Men of Renown: New Perspectives on Trobriand Exchange.* Austin: University of Texas Press.

White, Benjamin. 1980. "Rural Household Studies in Anthropological Perspective." In H. Binswanger, R. Evenson, C. Florencio, and B. White (Eds.), *Rural Household Studies in Asia* (pp. 3–25). Singapore: Singapore University Press.

White, Geoffrey M. 1997. "Introduction: Public History and National Narrative." *Museum Anthropology* 21(1):3 6.

White, Jenny B. 1994. *Money Makes Us Relatives.* Austin: University of Texas Press.

White, T. D., G. Suwa, and B. Asfaw. 1995. "*Corrigendum. Australopithecus ramidus,* a New Species of Early Hominid from Aramis, Ethiopia." *Nature* 375:88.

Whitehead, Harriet. 1981. "The Bow and the Burden Strap: A New Look at Institutionalized Homosexuality in Native North America." In S. B. Ortner and H. Whitehead (Eds.), *Sexual Meanings: The Cultural Construction of Gender and Sexuality* (pp. 80–115). Cambridge: Cambridge University Press.

Whiten, A., et al. 1999. "Cultures in Chimpanzees." *Nature* 399:682–685.

Whiting, John, Richard Kluckhohn, and Albert Anthony. 1967. "The Function of Male Initiation Ceremonies at Puberty." In R. Endelman (Ed.), *Personality and Social Life* (pp. 294–308). New York: Random House.

Whorf, Benjamin L. 1941. "The Relation of Habitual Thought and Behavior to Language." In Leslie Spier (Ed.), *Language, Culture, and Personality* (pp. 75–93). Menasha, WI: Sapir Memorial Publication Fund.

Wierzbicka, Anna. 2003. *Cross-Cultural Pragmatics: The Semantics of Human Interaction.* New York: Mouton de Gruyter.

Wikan, Unni. 1977. "Man Becomes Woman: Transsexualism in Oman as a Key to Gender Roles." *Man* (new series) 12:304–319.

Wilk, Richard (Ed.). 2006. *Fast Food/Slow Food: The Cultural Economy of the Global Food System.* Lanham, MD: AltaMira Press.

Wilkie, David S. 1988. "Hunters and Farmers of the African Forest." In J. S. Denslow and C. Padoch (Eds.), *People of the Tropical Rain Forest* (pp. 111–126). Berkeley, CA: University of California Press.

Wilks, Ivor. 1993. *Forests of Gold: Essays on the Akan and the Kingdom of Asante.* Athens, OH: Ohio University Press.

Williams, Trevor. 1984. *Howard Florey: Penicillin and After.* Oxford: Oxford University Press.

Williams, Walter. 1986. *The Spirit and the Flesh* (2nd ed.). Boston: Beacon Press.

Williams, Walter. 1996. "Amazons of America: Female Gender Variance." In Caroline B. Brettell and Carolyn F. Sargent (Eds.), *Gender in Cross-Cultural Perspective* (2nd ed.) (pp. 202–213). Upper Saddle River, NJ: Prentice Hall.

Winkelman, Michael. 1996. "Cultural Factors in Criminal Defense Proceedings." *Human Organization* 55:154.

Winter, Sam. 2009. Available at http://web.hku.hk/~sjwinter/TransgenderASIA/index.htm.

Wise, Steven M. 2002. *Drawing the Line— Science and the Case for Animal Rights.* Cambridge, MA: Perseus Books.

Wolde-Gabriel, Giday, Tim White, and Gen Suwa. 1994. "Ecological and Temporal Placement of Early Pliocene Hominids at Aramis, Ethiopia." *Nature* 371:330–333.

Wolf, Eric R. 1982. *Europe and the People Without History.* Berkeley, CA: University of California Press.

Wong, Bernard. 1988. *Ethnicity and Entrepreneurship: The New Chinese Immigrants in the San Francisco Bay Area.* Needham Heights, MA: Allyn and Bacon.

Wong, Edward. 2006. *The Chinese in Silicon Valley: Globalization, Social Networks, and Ethnic Identity.* Lanham, MD: Rowman and Littlefield.

Wong, Edward. 2008. "Factories Shut, China Workers Are Suffering." *New York Times,* November 14, p. A1.

Woodburn, James. 1968. "An Introduction to Hadza Ecology." In R. B. Lee and I. DeVore (Eds.), *Man the Hunter* (pp. 49–55). Chicago: Aldine.

Woodburn, James. 1998. "Sharing Is Not a Form of Exchange: An Analysis of Property-Sharing in Immediate Return Hunter-Gatherer Societies." In C. M. Hann (Ed.), *Property Relations: Renewing the Anthropological Tradition* (pp. 48–63). Cambridge: Cambridge University Press.

World Bank. 1992. *Development and the Environment: World Development Report 1992.* New York: Oxford University Press.

World Bank. 2005. *African Development Indicators: From the World Bank Africa Database.* Washington, DC: World Bank.

World Bank. 2006a. *Global Economic Prospects. Implications of Remittances and Migration.* Washington, DC: World Bank. Available at http://go.worldbank.org/0ZRERMGA00.

World Bank. 2006b. "Toxic Pollution from Agriculture—An Emerging Story." World Bank Data and Research. Available at http://go.worldbank.org/PTR2NOZUB0.

World Bank. 2008. *World Development Indicators Database.* Washington, DC: World Bank. Available at http://go.worldbank.org/YE0VSHIOZ1.

World Bank Group Archives. 2003. "Pages from World Bank History—Bank Pays Tribute to Robert McNamara." World Bank. Available at http://go.worldbank.org/C5CP4J6JA0.

Worsley, Peter M. 1959. "Cargo Cults." *Scientific American* 200:117–128.

Worthman, Carol M. 1995. "Hormones, Sex, and Gender." In William Durham, E. Valentine Daniel, and Bambi Schieffelin (Eds.), *Annual Review of Anthropology* (Vol. 24) (pp. 593–618). Stanford, CA: Stanford University Press.

Yanagisako, Sylvia, and Jane Collier. 1994. "Gender and Kinship Reconsidered: Toward a Unified Analysis." In R. Borofsky (Ed.), *Assessing Cultural Anthropology* (pp. 190–203). New York: McGraw-Hill.

Yanagisako, Sylvia, and Carol Delaney (Ed.). 1994. *Naturalizing Power: Essays in Feminist Cultural Analysis.* New York: Routledge.

Yardley, Jim. 2004. "Rural Exodus for Work Fractures Chinese Family." *New York Times,* December 21.

Yellen, J. E., A. S. Brooks, E. Cornelissen, M. J. Mehlman, and K. Stewart. 1995. "A Middle Stone Age Worked Bone Industry from Katanda, Upper Semliki Valley, Zaire." *Science* 268:553–556.

Zeegers, Maurice, Frans van Poppel, Robert Vlietinck, Liesbeth Spruijt, and Harry Ostrer. 2004. "Founder mutations among the Dutch." *European Journal of Human Genetics* 12:591–600.

Zihlman, Adrienne L. 1989. "Woman the Gatherer: The Role of Woman in Early Hominid Evolution." In S. Morgen (Ed.), *Gender and Anthropology: Critical Reviews for Research and Teaching* (pp. 21–40). Washington, DC: American Anthropological Association.

Zoepf, Katherine. 2008. "In Booming Gulf, Some Arab Women Find Freedom in the Skies." *New York Times,* December 22, p. A1.

# Photo Credits

This page constitutes an extension of the copyright page. We have made every effort to trace the ownership of all copyrighted material and to secure permission from copyright holders. In the event of any question arising as to the use of any material, we will be pleased to make the necessary corrections in future printings. Thanks are due to the following authors, publishers, and agents for permission to use the material indicated.

## Chapter 1
xxii: © John Warburton-Lee. All Rights Reserved/Danita Delimont 3: © Olivier Asselin/Acclaim Images 6: Courtesy of Ronald Coley 7: © Tomas Bravo/Reuters/Landov 11: © Margaret Bourke-White/Stringer/Time Life Pictures/Getty Images 12 left: © Joan Gregg 12 right: ©Jessie Tarbox/Missouri Historical Society 17: © AP Photo/Steven Senne 19: © Glieson Miranda/FUNAI

## Chapter 2
22: Dan Johanson/Institute of Human Origins/Courtesy of National Museum of Ethiopia 24: © American Museum of Natural History 27: © Taro Yamasaki/Time Life Pictures/Getty Images 28 left: Courtesy of Meredith Small 28 right: © Judith Pearson 32: Institute of Human Origins/Courtesy of National Museum of Ethiopia. 33: © National Museums of Kenya 34: © Patrick Nagel & Harry Thackwray/Bernard Price Institute for Paleontological Research 36: © Kenya Museums of Natural History 37: © William Turnbaugh/The Museum of Primitive Art and Culture 38: © David L. Brill 39: © The Art Archive/Museo Civico Vicanza/Dagli Orti 42: Courtesy of Chandler Prude, Texas State University 45: © Judith Pearson

## Chapter 3
48: © Judith Pearson 51: © Bettmann/Corbis 52: London School of Economics and Political Science Archives, Malinowski/3/18/2 53: © De Zolduondo/Anthro-Photo 55: © Joan Gregg 57: Courtesy of Kojo A. Dei 58: © Joan Gregg 60: © A. T. Willett/Alamy 61: © Bryan & Cherry Alexander 64: © Associated Press 66: © AP Photo/Eraldo Peres

## Chapter 4
72: © Gary Van Wyck/Axis Gallery, Inc. 76: © Marcello Bertinetti/Photo Researchers, Inc. 79: © Dirk Peeters/Peter Arnold, Inc. 80 above: © Joan Gregg 80 below: © Journal Curier/ValZrie Berta/The Image Works 82 left: © Getty Images 82 right: © Pictor/Imagestate 84: © Adam G. Sylvester/Photo Researchers, Inc. 85: © Martha Oppersdorff/Photo Researchers, Inc. 86: © Bryan & Cherry Alexander Photography/Alamy 87: © Barry Kass/Anthro-Photo, Inc. 91: © Peter M. Mattison 92: © Judith Pearson

## Chapter 5
96: Courtesy of Serena Nanda 100 above: Courtesy of Colorado University 100 below: © Myrleen Ferguson Cate/PhotoEdit 104: © Reuters/Corbis 109: Courtesy of Dr. William Labov,

University of Pennsylvania 111: © Mary Evans Picture Library/The Image Works 112: © Jeff Greenberg/PhotoEdit 113: © Frederick Atwood 115: © AP Photo/Katsumi Kasahara

## Chapter 6
120: © Joan Gregg 122: © Judith Pearson 125: © David Austen/Stock, Boston LLC 127: © Bryan and Cherry Alexander Photography/Alamy 129: © Joan Gregg 131: © Jane Hoffer 133: © F. Jack Jackson/Bruce Coleman, Inc. 135: © Robert Caputo/Stock, Boston LLC 139: © Ed Lallo/ZUMA/Corbis

## Chapter 7
144: © Joan Gregg 146: © Jim Kirn/Getty Images 148: © PhotoStock-Israel/Alamy 149: © Doranne Jacobson 150: © Jialiang Gao www.peace-on-earth.org 151 left: © Robert Frereck/Odyssey Productions 151 right: © Jim Olive/Pictor/Imagestate 152: © Doranne Jacobson 156: Alaska State Library Elbridge W. Merrill Photograph Collection No. P57-021 157: © D. Donne Bryant 158: © Photos12/Alamy 159: © Judith Pearson 164 left: © Randa Bishop/Pictor/Imagestate 164 right: © Catherine Li, 2008

## Chapter 8
168: Courtesy of Tom Curtin 170: © SV-Bilderdienst/The Image Works 172: © Soo Ho Choi 174: © Richard Lord/The Image Works 178: © Jeremy Hartley/Panos Pictures 182: © Joan Gregg 186: © Joan Gregg

## Chapter 9
190: Courtesy of Chander Dembla 192: Courtesy of Serena Nanda 193: © Erv Schowengerdt 194: © Sara Gouveia/photographersdirect.com 196: © Judith Pearson 198: © Peter Hvizdak/The Image Works 200: © Evan Hurd/Sygma/Corbis 203: Courtesy of Jean Zorn 205: © Jonathan Nourak/PhotoEdit 208: Courtesy of Soo Ho Choi 209: © Terry Eiler/Stock, Boston LLC 211: © Irven DeVore/Anthro-Photo

## Chapter 10
214: © Judith Pearson 216: © FPG/Getty Images 219: Courtesy of Serena Nanda 222: © Judith Pearson 223: © Welsh/Getty Images 224: © Joan Gregg 226: © Judith Pearson 228: © Judith Pearson 230: Courtesy of waterishope.org 231: © Mike Yamashita/Woodfin Camp & Associates 232: © Joan Gregg 233: © Joan Gregg

## Chapter 11
236: © Mark & Evelyn Bernheim/Woodfin Camp & Associates 239: © Diane Greene Lent 240 left: © Hulton Archive/Getty Images 240 right: © Bettmann/Corbis 243: © Austin MacRae 244: © Irven DeVore/Anthro-Photo 245: © Andrew Arno 246: © Napoleon Chagnon/Anthro-Photo 247: © Caroline Penn/Panos Pictures 249: © Barry D. Kass/ImagesofAnthropology.com 251: © AFP/Corbis 255 left: Courtesy of Serena Nanda 255 right: © Joan Gregg 256: © AFP/Corbis 257: Courtesy of Cultural Survival 258: © Nik Wheeler/Corbis 259: © Jackie Mercandetti Photography

## Chapter 12
264: © AFP/Getty Images 267: © Joan Gregg 269: © Joan Gregg 271: © Nubar Alexanian/Stock, Boston LLC 274: Reproduced by permission of the American Anthropological Association from "RACE: Are We So Different?" <http://www.understandingrace.org/home.html>. Not for sale or further reproduction 276: © MAI/Landov 278: © John Maier/The Image Works 279: © Katsuyoshi Tanaka/Woodfin Camp & Associates 280: © Joan Gregg 281: © Beth Pacheco 283: © AP Images 285: © Jose Fuste Raga/Corbis

## Chapter 13
288: © Judith Pearson 290: © Associated Press 293: © Rosemary Calvert SuperStock 295: © Bob Burch/Bruce Coleman, Inc. 297: © Reuters/Jayanta Shaw/Landov 298: © Bettmann/Corbis 299: © AFP/Corbis 300: © Steve Axford 303: © Chris Lisle/Corbis 304: Courtesy of Serena Nanda 305: © Associated Press 307: © Associated Press 309: © Associated Press 310: © The Granger Collection 312: © Donovan Marks

## Chapter 14
316: © Judith Pearson 319: © Mario Ponderosa/The Brooklyn Museum 320: © Jerry L. Thompson/Courtesy of the Museum for African Art, New York 322: © President and Fellows of Harvard College, Peabody Museum, Alexander Marshack # 2005.16.351.2 324: © AFP/Getty Images 325: © Wendy Bass/Viesti Associates Inc. 326: © Kevin Foy/Alamy 327: Pawnee chased by Cheyenne and a white man killed by Crooked Lance, illustration from the "Black Horse Ledger", 1877–79 (Pencil & crayon on paper), American School, (19th Century)/Newbury Library, Chicago, Illinois, USA/The Bridgeman Art Library 329 left: Courtesy of Serena Nanda 329 right: The Art Archive/Colores Olmedo Mexico/Dagli Orti © 2009 Banco de Mexico Diego Rivera Frida Kahlo Museums Trust, Mexico, D.F./Artists Rights Society (ARS) 331: © Juan Gimenez-Martin/Dahesh Museum of Art 333: © Judith Pearson 334: © George Haling/Photo Researchers, Inc. 335: © Joan Gregg 336: © AFP/Getty Images

## Chapter 15
340: © Richard Warms 343: © Mary Evans Picture Library/Grosvenor Prints/The Image Works 345: © Antman Archives/The Image Works 346: © Corbis 347: © Joan Gregg 349: © Classicstock.com 352: Courtesy of Richard Warms 354: Anti-Slavery International Reg Charity 1039160 356: National Archives Photo No. 306-RNT-57-18116 358: Muséum de Rouen, France

## Chapter 16
360: © Time & Life Pictures/Getty Images 363: © Associated Press 364: © Chris Jackson/Getty Images 368: © Joan Gregg 369: © Ray Dennis/Alamy 372 left: © Bill Bachmann/Stock, Boston LLC 372 right: © David Frazier/Photo Researchers, Inc. 373: © Joan Gregg 376: © Margot Haag/Peter Arnold, Inc. 377: © Associated Press 379: © Charles O. Cecil/Alamy

# Index

*Note:* Glossary words are indicated with an italic *g;* tables with an italic *t;* figures with an italic *f;* maps with an italic *m;* footnotes with an italic *n.*

Relationship
  economic, *145*
  kinship, 169–188. *See also* Kinship
  in patrilineal society, 175–176
Relative. *See also* Kinship
  affinal, 170–171, 170*g*
  consanguineal, 170*g*
  linking, 183
Relative age principle, 182
Relativism
  cultural, 11–12, 11*g*, 51*g*
  moral, 11, 20
Religion, 289–315
  art and, 319, 319*f*
  change and, 306–312
  characteristics of, 291–296, 313
  class and, 271
  defined, 290*g*
  evolution and, 26
  fertility and, 292
  function of, 290–291 290*f*, 313
  fundamentalist, 311–312, 314
  globalization of, 312–313, 312*f*
  Hijra and, 218–219, 219*f*
  Hindu caste system, 282–284, 283*f*
  Muslim. *See* Muslim society
  practitioners of, 301–306
  priest and, 303–304, 314
  prophesy and, 306–307, 314
  Rastafari, 308–309, 308*g*, 309*f*
  rituals of, 296–301. *See also* Ritual
  sacred narrative of, 292–294, 293*f*, 313
  shaman and, 301–303, 303*g*, 314
  supernatural in, 294–296, 295*f*, 313–314
  in Trinidad, 289
  witchcraft and, 304–306, 304*g*, 314
  for women in India, 84
Religious symbol, 313
Renan, Ernest, 342
Repatriation of historical objects, 357–358
Replacement model, 38
Research
  colonization and, 14
  contemporary trends in, 69
  cross-cultural, 57–58
  cultural relativism and, 11–12
  in field, 14, 53–55
Resentment, social stratification and, 266
Residence
  avunculocal, 208, 208*g*
  bilocal, 208, 208*g*
  matrilocal, 176, 208, 208*g*, 210
  in Minangkabau society, 178
  neolocal, 204, 204*g*
  patrilocal, 207, 207*g*, 210
  rules of, 210, 213
Resistance to capitalism, 164–165, 164*f*, 167
Resource
  allocation of, 147–150, 148*f*, 149*f*, 166
  capital, 159
  productive, 147, 147*g*, 166
Resource management, cultural, 6*g*
Respect, 248
Review board, institutional, 53, 53*g*
Revolution, 241, 241*g*
  in China, 284–285
  industrial revolution, 342
Richards, Audrey, 384
Rickets, 43, 43*g*
Rift Valley, 35*g*
Rights, marriage and, 201–204
Ring, Kula, 154–155, 154*g*, 155*g*
Rio de Janeiro, Brazil, 372, 372*f*
Rite of passage, 221–224
  defined, 223*f*, 296*g*
  female, 80–81, 222–223, 223*f*

male, 221–222, 222*f*
  as religious ritual, 296–297, 314
  in Sambia society, 220
  in Spain, 224
Ritual
  art central to, 322
  in Asante society, 251
  defined, 296*g*
  of intensification, 297–298, 297*g*, 298*f*, 314
  liminal objects and, 296
  in Nacirema culture, 4–5
  prayer and, 298
  purification, 5
  of sacrifice, 299
Robust Australopithecine, 33
Role, gender, 225–226, 225*g*
Role reversal, ritual, 296
Romance language, 104
Rosaldo Zimbalist, Michelle, 386
Rostow, W. W., 363–364
Rule
  of behavior, 84
  of caste system, 283
  of endogamy, 198
  of exogamy, 197
  of grammar, 104
  of inheritance, 173
  of kinship and descent, 171
  of language, 116
  language and, 102
  marriage, 200, 212
  residence, 176, 210, 213
Rural migration to cities, 372
Rwanda, genocide in, 377, 377*f*

Saami reindeer herder, 257–259, 258*f*
Sacks, Oliver, 74
Sacred narrative, 292–294, 292*g*, 293*f*, 313
Sahara, Tuareg society of, 229–231
Sahlin, Marshall, 384
Said, Edward, 59
Sambia society, 220
Samburu, 214*f*
Same-sex marriage, 192–193
*Samurai Champloo*, 324
San Antonio, Texas, 375–376
San Blas culture, 224
Sanction, supernatural, 241
Sanday, Peggy, 226–227
Santa Domingo, conquest of, 345*f*
Santeria, 307, 307*f*
Sapir, Edward, 109–111, 383
Sapir-Whorf hypothesis, 109–111, 110*g*, 117
Saudi Arabia, women in, 233
Scapulomancy, 301
Scheper-Hughes, Nancy, 387
Scholder, Fritz, 329–330
Schweitzer, Colonel Martin, 66
Science, magic versus, 52
Scott, Elizabeth, 6
Secrecy, as ethical issue, 63
Secret society, 243, 243*g*
Segmentary lineage system, 175, 175*f*, 175*g*, 243
Selection
  natural, 24–26, 24*g*, 46
  sexual, 44, 44*g*
Semantics, 102*g*, 104–105
Senegalese Riflemen, 352–353, 352*g*, 354
Seniority in Indian society, 180
Serb, 256
Service, Elman, 384
*Sese*, 194–195, 194*f*
Sex. *See also* Gender
  alternative, 217
  defined, 216*g*

gender and, 216–220, 234
  interracial, 275
Sex segregation, 84–85
Sex worker, 80–81
Sexual behavior, 220–221
Sexual relationship in Na society, 194–195, 194*f*
Sexual selection, 44*g*
Sexuality
  cultural construction of gender and, 221
  gender and, 234
Shaman, 301–303, 301*g*, 314
Shanidar Cave, 39
Shantytown, 370
Shared ancestor, 26–27
Sharff, Jagna, 56
Shock, culture, 54*g*
Shundra caste, 282
Sickle cell anemia, 41
Side effect, meanings of, 110
Sierra Leone
  civil war in, 64
  Mende society of, 240
Sign language of chimpanzee, 100–101, 100*f*
Silver, European expansion and, 344
Singer, Merrill, 57
Single language, 117
Sister in Hopi society, 210
Skidmore, Monique, 64–65
Skin cancer, melanin and, 42
Skin color
  biological importance of, 46–47
  clinal distribution of, 41–44
  cold weather and, 44
  race and, 13, 44
  social significance of, 46
  vitamin D and, 43–44
Skull of *Homo sapiens*, 38, 38*g*
Slash and burn horticulture, 132–136, 132*g*, 133*f*
Slave labor, 345–346, 346*f*
Slave market, in art, 331
Slavery
  in Brazil, 275
  European expansion and, 345–346, 346*f*
  in United States, 273
*Slumdog Millionaire*, 370
Small-scale community, 241
Small-scale economics, 147–148
Smiling, culture and, 112
Smith, Adam, 25
Smithsonian Museum of the American Indian, 321
Social birth, 76–77
Social change and religion, 291
Social complexity, 237, 238*g*
Social control
  in band society, 242
  in chiefdom, 248
  law and, 241
  power and, 239–241
  in tribal society, 244–245
Social differentiation, 237, 238, 238*g*, 260
Social institution, 176
Social life of primates, 28–29, 28*f*
Social mobility, 268, 268*g*
  class and, 270
Social obligation, 154
Social order, religion and, 291
Social philosophy, 25
Social rules, 102
Social services, 60–61
Social stratification, 265–287
  in Asante society, 250, 261
  in Brazil, 275–278, 278*f*
  in China, 286
  conflict in, 83
  defined, 265, 266*g*